SOUTHEAST ASIAN AFFAIRS 2005

The **Institute of Southeast Asian Studies (ISEAS)** was established as an autonomous organization in 1968. It is a regional centre dedicated to the study of socio-political, security and economic trends and developments in Southeast Asia and its wider geostrategic and economic environment.

The Institute's research programmes are the Regional Economic Studies (RES, including ASEAN and APEC), Regional Strategic and Political Studies (RSPS), and Regional Social and Cultural Studies (RSCS).

ISEAS Publications, an established academic press, has issued more than 1,000 books and journals. It is the largest scholarly publisher of research about Southeast Asia from within the region. ISEAS Publications works with many other academic and trade publishers and distributors to disseminate important research and analyses from and about Southeast Asia to the rest of the world.

SOUTHEAST ASIAN AFFAIRS 2005

LSEAS

INSTITUTE OF SOUTHEAST ASIAN STUDIES
Singapore

First published in Singapore in 2005 by
ISEAS Publications
Institute of Southeast Asian Studies
30 Heng Mui Keng Terrace
Pasir Panjang
Singapore 119614
E-mail: publish@iseas.edu.sg
Website: http://bookshop.iseas.edu.sg

The responsibility for facts and opinions in this publication rests exclusively with the authors and their interpretations do not necessarily reflect the views or the policy of the publisher or its supporters.

ISEAS Library Cataloguing-in-Publication Data

Southeast Asian Affairs.
1974–
Annual
1. Asia, Southeastern.
I. Institute of Southeast Asian Studies.
DS501 S72A

ISSN 0377-5437
ISBN 981-230-306-5 (soft cover)
ISBN 981-230-307-3 (hard cover)

Typeset by Superskill Graphics Pte Ltd
Printed in Singapore by Utopia Press Pte Ltd

Contents

Foreword

The year 2004 was on the whole a good one for Southeast Asia, though marred towards the end by the tsunami tragedy. There was healthy economic growth, as the region recovered from SARS and benefited from the growth of the American economy as well as strong growth in China. The outcomes of the democratic elections in Indonesia, Malaysia, and the Philippines were positive for regional stability. In Indonesia they ushered in a new political leadership while in Malaysia they provided a resounding vote of confidence in Prime Minister Abdullah Badawi who had succeeded Dr Mahathir Mohamed in late 2003. The tsunami of 26 December 2004 was a terrible tragedy in human terms but is not expected to cause any significant dent in overall economic terms.

Southeast Asian Affairs has established for itself the reputation of being a valuable repository of information on developments in the year under review. ISEAS will continue to bring out this publication in a timely manner.

K Kesavapany
Director
Institute of Southeast Asian Studies

April 2005

Introduction

The year 2004 was a relatively good one for Southeast Asia on both economic and political fronts. The region experienced robust growth of 6.3 per cent, driven by economic rebounds in the United States, Japan, and the European Union and the rapid economic expansion of China. It was also a year in which elections and political transitions took place in a number of countries. They were on the whole positive for the region and in most cases generated hopes for a better future.

Nevertheless, the region continued to have security concerns. Its external security environment was marked by greater uncertainty, in view of concerns that Iraq might become an expanding base for jihad with implications for other regions; as well as concerns relating to the Korean peninsula, the Taiwan Straits and the downturn in Sino-Japanese relations. Within Southeast Asia some countries faced threats from terrorism associated with radical Islamic groups, especially Indonesia and the Philippines. These two countries also had to deal with separatist rebellions and, in the case of the Philippines, a continuing communist insurgency. A troubling new development was the outbreak of violence in the Muslim provinces of South Thailand.

The region was drawing increased attention from the major powers, with signs of keener competition for influence between the United States and China. America's security relations with allies and friends intensified but Southeast Asians felt that America's attention was too narrowly focused on the war on terrorism and that its "soft power" had declined. There were signs towards the end of the year of the United States adopting a broader-based and politically more nuanced policy to the region, in part to meet the competition from China which, through sophisticated diplomacy (some would call, a charm offensive predicated on its message of "peaceful rise of China") and economic leverage (e.g. signing of important agreements on trade and dispute settlement with the Association of Southeast Asian Nations (ASEAN) at the November 2004 summit and targeting an ASEAN-China FTA by 2010), had sought to address Southeast Asian governments' reservations about its emerging role as a major power. Still, these countries were not simply acquiescing in China's rise, but were continuing to hedge their bets, by accepting the need for a continuing US underpinning role in regional security. The interests of Australia, Japan and India in Southeast Asia have provided additional hedging options.

Meanwhile ASEAN seemed unlikely in the near term to develop into a truly coherent vehicle to help members manage more effectively the diverse security problems they faced. Security networking of most Southeast Asian states has largely been bilateral, especially with extra-regional powers. The continuing strong US security interest in the region has enabled Southeast Asian states to view China's rising power with relative equanimity.

ASEAN continued to face formidable challenges. Security cooperation under its auspices remained largely potential rather than actual. On the economic plane, the implementation of the ASEAN Free Trade Area (AFTA) was making good progress, but movement towards fuller economic integration remained essentially slow. The potential building blocks for an ASEAN Economic Community (AEC) based on integration in areas like services and investments were in place, but the will to move forward vigorously to attain it seemed to be lacking. The motivation behind the AEC has been to make the region a more attractive production base for foreign and domestic companies, especially in view of the competition for investments from China and India. Concerns have been voiced that the AEC might be sidetracked or subsumed under ASEAN's trade pacts with China, India and others and the economic agenda of the proposed East Asia Summit. Nevertheless in its dialogue relationships, ASEAN continued to be courted at the highest level by a growing circle of external suitors. ASEAN's 2004 post-summit dialogues (with China, Japan, Korea and India) held in Vientiane in November saw the inclusion of Australia and New Zealand for the first time since 1977 leading to expectations of a regularized ASEAN-ANZ relationship at summit level and an eventual broad economic partnership agreement.

The domestic affairs of Southeast Asian states showed more continuity than change in 2004. The outcome of the democratic elections in Malaysia, Philippines and Indonesia, the expectation that Thai Prime Minister Thaksin Shinawatra's Thai Rak Thai party would be returned to power with an increased majority in general elections scheduled for early 2005, and leadership changes in Indonesia and Singapore were generally positive for regional stability and to outside observers. The elections also demonstrated that in the two largest Muslim majority countries of Southeast Asia, mainstream Muslims voted overwhelmingly for moderate secular parties.

On the whole it can be argued that they advanced the cause of democracy in Southeast Asia, notwithstanding some signs of regression in Thailand and the poor democratic consolidation in the Philippines, which raised questions about political legitimacy of the political leadership. Even tiny Brunei was stirring with the tentative steps in political development when Sultan Hassanal Bolkiah announced the convening of a nominated Legislative Council that would prepare for election to one-third of its seats that was expected before the end of 2005.

In Indonesia, the largest and most populous country of Southeast Asia, Susilo Bambang Yudhoyono, a retired general and a coordinating minister under former President Megawati, won the country's first direct presidential election. Popular at home and with the West, his victory raised such high expectations among the public that he has sought to dampen them because he cannot perform miracles. While he seemed to have his priorities right, the problems of Indonesia are complex and numerous, not amenable to quick or easy solutions. The new president was paying special attention to improving the investment climate and to dealing with the rebellions in Aceh and Papua. Terrorism is another challenge that he has to be seen to be dealing with firmly if he is to convince potential investors that he is serious about improving stability and law and order. By year's end, President Yudhoyono's Vice-President, Jusuf Kalla, was elected chairman of Golkar, the largest parliamentary party, thus providing the government a much-needed parliamentary power base and yet, as others would note, sowing the seeds for future political competition between them.

The general election in Malaysia in March gave the ruling Barisan Nasional (BN) coalition a massive victory that served as a resounding vote of confidence for Prime Minister Abdullah Badawi who had taken over the reins of government from Dr Mahathir Mohamed only in October 2003. The gains that the fundamentalist Islamic party, Parti Islam Se Malaysia (PAS), had made in the 1999 election were more than reversed in the Federal parliament and at the state level where PAS lost control of Terengganu and nearly lost Kelantan, its traditional stronghold.

Abdullah's appointment as Prime Minister and the signals he sent to tackle corruption, improve law and order, curtail mega-projects, improve corporate governance and pay more attention to the rural sector, had raised high expectations. However, by the end of 2004, after more than a year in office, there was some feeling of let down. While remaining personally popular, there was a sense that the problems he had taken on were perhaps too entrenched, some enmeshed with powerful interests, and that Abdullah, unlike his predecessor, did not by nature have the gumption to create too many waves by taking them head on. However, Abdullah's supporters still believed that he would deliver on the reforms but needed more time to do so. Among the fundamental challenges the country faced was how to make the economy more efficient and competitive to meet regional and international challenges while operating in a politically charged domestic context of an affirmative action programme in favour of the ethnic Malay community.

In Thailand, Prime Minister Thaksin Shinawatra was about to complete a full four year term, the first elected government in Thai history to do so, and all signs pointed to another term in office after the general elections scheduled for early 2005.

The economy was booming, with growth during the year expected to be only marginally below the 6.8 per cent achieved in 2003, despite higher oil prices, bird flu and the outbreak of violence in the south. Real output per person exceeded its pre-crisis level of 1996. However, recovery of private investment, both local and foreign direct investment, was slow — by 2003 it had risen to only 16.3 per cent of the GDP compared with over 30 per cent in the years preceding the crisis.

Thailand's recovery from the economic crisis was partly due to the Thaksin government's ability to restore economic confidence by making Thais feel that unlike its immediate predecessors, it was in control and capable of making clear decisions. There was no sign yet of an economic bubble as some critics had feared. However critics also drew attention to the diminished quality of Thai democracy under Thaksin. The main challenges the government will face in the second term include those on which it made little headway in 2004 or during its first term, namely the violence in the south, which was ineptly handled and could worsen, and the need to reform the education system on which the competitiveness of the economy and the efficacy of the poverty reduction programmes depend.

In the Philippine presidential election in May, President Gloria Macapagal Arroyo, the incumbent, was confirmed in the presidency after a narrow win. However, the victory was marred by perceptions of fraud that questioned its legitimacy. Her approval ratings plunged during the year because of public perception that she had done little to combat rampant corruption. There were indications of politicians in general losing legitimacy in the eyes of the public because they were identified with powerful political dynasties out to advance their own interests. Badly needed reforms were not being implemented.

Although it managed a growth rate of about 6 per cent in 2004, the Philippines seemed to be in decline. Unemployment was approaching 11 per cent; about half the people were living below the poverty line (calculated at US$223 per annum at the prevailing exchange rate); the annual population growth rate was estimated to be 2.34 per cent, the highest in Asia; the economy was burdened by large budget deficits and public debt; and the government was fighting two simultaneous insurgencies. Behind the public expressions of solidarity in the war against terrorism, there were signs of exasperation in the United States, the country's principal ally, about the state of affairs in the country and the performance of the government.

The year also witnessed political transition of a kind in Singapore with the smooth handover of prime ministership from Goh Chok Tong to Lee Hsien Loong on 12 August. Goh became Senior Minister in the cabinet replacing Lee Kuan Yew who moved on to be Minister Mentor. Generally, in terms of political parameters and major policy templates, continuity from the Goh regime rather than change was a hallmark in the well-planned transition. Nevertheless the emergence of a more youthful cabinet clearly signalled a generational change in the making. As part of this process continuing efforts were made to reflect a softer approach in terms of further relaxation of social control; a more consultative style of government and greater corporate transparency among government-linked corporations. The pressures of a globalizing economy, the need to remain internationally competitive as well as the changing expectations of a new emerging generation of voters were impacting on governance in the city-state which is expected to go to the polls by 2005 to give a fresh mandate to the new prime minister. In this respect a strong economy (that grew by 8.4 per cent in 2004 as contrasted with 1.4 per cent in the previous year) and is likely to have respectable, though slower, growth in 2005, will provide another underpinning to political legitimacy of the new generation political leadership.

In Myanmar, regardless of its internal problems and the external pressures on it, the military regime remained strong enough to continue in power. The removal of Prime Minister Khin Nyunt from both his government and intelligence positions and the disbanding of his intelligence corps did not affect the stability of the ruling junta. The pro-democracy exile organizations were weaker and could not hope to bring down the regime; the ethnic insurgent groups no longer posed any significant threat to it, and indeed many seemed prepared to go along with its seven-point democracy road map; political activism had declined among the general public, including students and monks, with most people believing that the regime was too strong for the NLD and other opposition groups to bring about any change.

The National Convention to prepare for a new constitution would reconvene in February 2005. The National League for Democracy (NLD) had boycotted the Convention when the junta refused to allow its leaders, Daw Aung San Suu Kyi and U Tin Oo, to be released from detention. Although the boycott weakens the legitimacy of the National Convention, the junta seemed prepared to move ahead to arrive at a constitution that protects its interests. The NLD on its part, totally beholden to Aung San Suu Kyi, showed a singular inability to rethink options and work out a clear strategy to deal with the present situation. The average age of the members of the central executive committee is 80. The changes that the military was planning to introduce through a new constitution would fall well short of what most people desire, but to most people any change that makes their lives easier and hopefully paves the way for larger changes in the future would be acceptable.

Among the three Indochina countries, Vietnam and Laos continued to be run by Leninist parties that felt threatened by the emergence of any organized political opposition. Both faced international criticism for their heavy-handed treatment of minority groups, the Montagnards in Vietnam and the Hmong in Laos.

In terms of economic growth, Vietnam remained among the best performing economies in the region. GDP growth was expected to reach 7.3–7.5 per cent in 2004. Yet it was difficult to avoid the feeling that the country was held back from realizing its true potential by its failure to push ahead more vigorously with reforms. Corruption, slow progress in the equitization of state-owned enterprises, and serious weaknesses in the education and health care systems were drags on efforts to sustain future growth, reduce poverty and integrate successfully into the international economy. Negotiations were taking place with the European Union, the United States and China on accession to the WTO by 2005 — a landmark event for Vietnam. Benefits from accession would depend not only on the good faith of Vietnam's trading partners but also on the ability of Vietnam to make and manage the necessary adjustments.

In Cambodia, the stalemate resulting from the elections of 2003 that prevented any of the parties to achieve a two-thirds majority to govern alone was resolved when in June 2004 Prime Minister Hun Sen and Prince Ranariddh agreed to form a new coalition. The event marked the final overwhelming triumph of Prime Minster Hun Sen in the struggle for the control of the state of Cambodia since the United Nations Transitional Authority (UNTAC) tried in the early 1990s to set it on a path of democracy, free market economics, and human rights. What has emerged is a melding of bureaucratic, military and economic power at the top in an oligopolistic turbo-capitalism that has brought about a socioeconomic transformation marked by extreme polarization. In October the country's constitutional monarch King Sihanouk abdicated and his son Prince Sihamoni was crowned as the new king.

Southeast Asian Affairs 2005 addresses a broad range of issues from a regional perspective in its first five chapters. These are followed by the country surveys and special theme articles on most of the countries covered.

Chin Kin Wah
Daljit Singh
Editors
Southeast Asian Affairs 2005

The Region

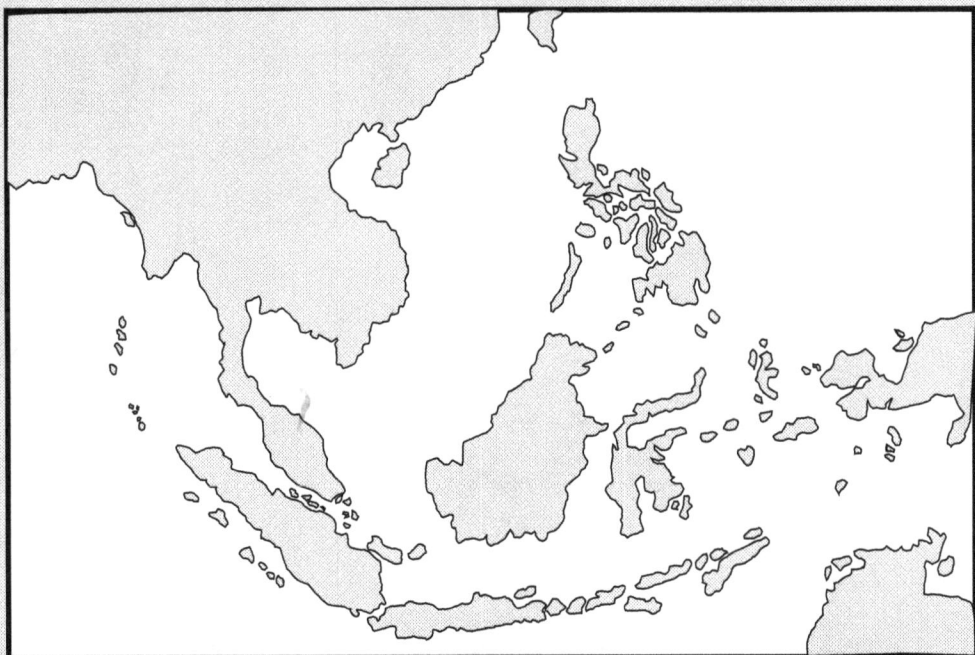

SOUTHEAST ASIA IN 2004
Stable, but Facing Major
Security Challenges

Tim Huxley

During 2004, Southeast Asia's political and security scene featured significant domestic developments in several of its states (notably Indonesia, Malaysia, Myanmar, the Philippines, and Singapore), the continued salience of internal security challenges including a new outbreak of separatist-inspired violence in Thailand's Muslim south as well as the threat from the pan-regional Jemaah Islamiyah (JI) network, the growing interest of extra-regional powers in the sub-region's security, and continuing efforts to make ASEAN (the Association of Southeast Asian Nations) a more useful vehicle for security cooperation. At the year's end, the massive impact of the tsunami generated by the earthquake off Sumatra created humanitarian crises for Indonesia and Thailand, raising the question of whether governments in the region had paid sufficient practical attention to "human security" issues.

Domestic Political Developments

In the three Southeast Asian states where there were national elections during 2004, the popular vote favoured strong leadership and programmatic agendas over charisma, as well as secularism where there was a choice of an Islamist alternative. In Malaysia, the March 2004 general election saw the ruling Barisan Nasional (BN) coalition, dominated by the United Malays National Organization (UMNO), re-elected in a landslide victory bringing it 198 out of 219 parliamentary seats, its greatest ever majority. Crucially, the number of parliamentary seats held by PAS (Parti Islam Se Malaysia, the Malaysian Islamic Party), which had become the

TIM HUXLEY is Senior Fellow for Asia-Pacific Security at the International Institute for Strategic Studies (IISS) in London, and Corresponding Director of IISS-Asia in Singapore.

largest opposition force in parliament following the previous general election in
1999, fell from 27 to 7. In simultaneous state-level elections, the BN regained
control of Terengganu from PAS. The election result resoundingly affirmed the
popularity of new Prime Minister Abdullah Ahmad Badawi, who had succeeded
Dr Mahathir Mohamad in November 2003. However, the redrawing of electoral
boundaries, the use of the Internal Security Act against opposition politicians, the
government's highlighting of apparent links between PAS and terrorist suspects, and
the intolerant image projected by PAS all contributed to the BN's massive win.
Having secured an overwhelming electoral victory, in early September Abdullah
signalled his political confidence by acquiescing in the release of imprisoned
opposition leader, former deputy prime minister Anwar Ibrahim. His damaged
health apparently restored after surgery in Germany, but cold-shouldered by UMNO,
Anwar commenced a struggle to turn the minor Parti Keadilan Rakyat (People's
Justice Party), founded in 1999 primarily to fight for his release from jail, into a
credible political machine in time for the next general election, due in 2008/9.[1]

In the Philippines' national election in May, incumbent President Gloria
Macapagal-Arroyo was re-elected, narrowly defeating her leading challenger,
Fernando Poe Junior, a well-known movie star. Despite his utter lack of political
experience, the charismatic Poe — a friend of Arroyo's presidential predecessor,
Joseph Estrada — was endorsed by a three-party opposition coalition as well as a
clique of 50 retired senior military officers and had great appeal for poorer Filipinos.
Nevertheless, Poe's inexperience, the advantages accruing to Arroyo as incumbent,
the business elite's strong backing for her, and the lustre added to her campaign by
her vice-presidential candidate, former TV news-show host Noli De Castro, were all
factors that contributed to the result. Although in July the kidnapping of a Filipino
worker in Iraq created a political crisis for Arroyo, this was defused (at least
domestically) by the early withdrawal of Philippine forces and the release of the
hostage. Meanwhile, Poe and his supporters contested the election result. The film-
star's death in December initially sparked fears on the government's part that its
opponents, including military officers and Estrada, might exploit the funeral to
incite a revolt aimed at installing a seven-person junta with Poe's wife, Susan Roces,
as figurehead president.[2] However, these concerns soon subsided.

By way of contrast, the second round of Indonesia's first-ever direct presidential
election in September brought significant change when retired three-star general
Susilo Bambang Yudhoyono unseated the incumbent president, Megawati
Sukarnoputri. The disappointing performance of Megawati's PDI-P (Indonesian
Democratic Party for Struggle) in the April legislative elections, and then of Megawati

herself in the presidential election, reflected widespread popular frustration with the government's failure to improve living standards. While Yudhoyono campaigned on a mildly reformist platform, ideology played no significant part in the presidential election; both he and Megawati presented essentially conservative secular-nationalist outlooks. On paper, Yudhoyono's electoral coalition was considerably less impressive than Megawati's, but his campaign mobilized a network of retired military officers and NGOs to work on his behalf, mitigating his lack of formal party machinery. More importantly, Yudhoyono attracted overwhelming backing from supporters of the Golkar party, which had emerged as winner of the earlier legislative elections. Ultimately, Yudhoyono won 61 per cent of the vote against Megawati's 39 per cent. The near-absence of campaign violence represented a triumph for Indonesia's young democracy and Yudhoyono's election highlighted the electorate's increasing sophistication. Moreover, the demonstration of political secularism by most Indonesian voters was reassuring to those worried about the rise of radical Islam. In December Yudhoyono's Vice-President, Jusuf Kalla, was elected chairman of Golkar, the largest parliamentary party, which he then withdrew from the opposition Nationhood Coalition. At least in the short term, this development dramatically strengthened President Yudhoyono's government, which had previously lacked a firm parliamentary power-base.[3]

Elsewhere in Southeast Asia, domestic political change took the form of leadership transition within existing governments. In August a long-anticipated succession occurred at Singapore's political apex when Lee Hsien Loong, deputy prime minister and finance minister, replaced Prime Minister Goh Chok Tong, who became Senior Minister. In turn, Senior Minister Lee Kuan Yew (Lee Hsien Loong's father) was appointed to the new post of Minister Mentor.

In Myanmar in October, the relatively pragmatic prime minister and chief of military intelligence (MI), General Khin Nyunt, was ousted from his position within the country's military regime, the State Peace and Development Council (SPDC), and the MI power structure was dismantled. While the SPDC justified Khin Nyunt's removal on the grounds that he was guilty of insubordination, bribery, corruption, and ultimately of threatening the unity of the armed forces, in reality his dramatic downfall probably resulted from deeper concerns on the part of SPDC Chairman Than Shwe and his deputy, Maung Aye. Most importantly, the growing power of Khin Nyunt, MI and related agencies had begun to threaten the business as well as political interests of other senior regime figures, who also apparently resented the MI chief's relatively favourable international image resulting from his "road map" for political reform and his willingness to leave open the possibility of involving

Aung San Suu Kyi and her National League for Democracy in the political process. The purge within the SPDC regime seemed likely to impede long-awaited political reform. Though a small number of political prisoners was released, the military regime announced that Aung San Suu Kyi would be held under house arrest for a further year.

There were also significant domestic political developments in some of Southeast Asia's smaller states. In Brunei, Sultan Hassanal Bolkiah, absolute ruler since the sultanate gained full independence from Britain in 1984, announced in July that the Legislative Council, which had not sat since 1962, would be reconvened as part of political reforms intended to "engage the citizens". In late September, the unelected Council comprising the Sultan, Foreign Minister Prince Mohamed Bolkiah, government officials, businessmen and community leaders was indeed reconvened. The Council passed constitutional amendments allowing for an expanded council of 45 members, one-third of whom would be elected. The first elections since 1962 are expected by the end of 2005. In Cambodia, where elections in July 2003 had resulted in a stalemate (none of the parties achieving the two-thirds parliamentary majority necessary to govern alone), inter-party bickering had severely undermined the government's effectiveness. However, in June Prime Minister Hun Sen and National Assembly president Prince Ranariddh at last agreed to form a new coalition. In October, the country's constitutional monarch, King Sihanouk, abdicated. By the end of the month, however, Sihanouk's son Prince Norodom Sihamoni had been crowned as the new king. Despite Sihamoni's unlikely background as a French-domiciled ballet dancer and choreographer and lack of political experience, he was widely expected to exert a moderating influence on his country's often tumultuous politics.

Overall, these developments indicated continuity and, in some cases, gradual reform in Southeast Asian states' domestic political structures. The most dramatic change was Yudhoyono's election victory in Indonesia, by far Southeast Asia's largest, most populous and by many measures most important state. But, even in this case, there was a danger of exaggerated expectations. Yudhoyono's record as a senior minister in Megawati's government was not altogether impressive, and critics pointed to his indecisiveness in dealing with security problems, precisely the area where he could have been expected to act authoritatively. Ultimately, the need to satisfy diverse interests may hamper Yudhoyono's policy implementation as much as it did Megawati's. Crucially, it was by no means clear that Jakarta's capacity for handling effectively the serious security challenges that it faced would be substantially increased under the new administration that took office in October.

Internal Security Problems

Although the threat of terrorism continued to loom large for concerned Western governments and other outside observers, governments of the larger Southeast Asian states remained preoccupied with other internal security threats that more obviously threatened the integrity of their countries or their own position. The Indonesian government's main security focus remained its counter-insurgency campaign in Aceh, where Megawati's administration had allowed the TNI (Tentara Nasional Indonesia, Indonesian armed forces) to launch a major military offensive during 2003. This was the largest TNI operation since the invasion of East Timor in 1975. Though a state of "civil emergency" replaced martial law in the province in May 2004, it was far from clear that the military operation had succeeded in crushing separatist sentiment in Aceh, and the government emphasized that troop levels would not necessarily be reduced. The TNI claimed that almost 2,000 Acehnese separatists had been killed, another 2,000 had been arrested and 1,300 had surrendered during the year of martial law. However, it seemed likely that most of these "rebels" were actually just Acehnese civilians caught up in the conflict. Military operations — and widespread human rights abuses perpetrated by not only government forces but also the insurgent GAM (Gerakan Aceh Merdeka, Acehnese Freedom Movement) — continued. A suspiciously high turnout of 94 per cent in the April legislative elections — from which locally-based parties were banned, as they are throughout Indonesia — led to allegations that the authorities had compelled Acehnese voters to participate. After his election, President Yudhoyono expressed his determination to resolve the conflict, and spoke in vague terms of the need for a new agenda in Aceh relating to religion, social issues and the economy. But his record as the Coordinating Minister for Politics and Security who approved the 2003 offensive had hardly marked him out as a conciliator in Aceh, and in November he renewed the province's civil emergency status for a further six months. The prospect of renewed peace talks between Jakarta and GAM, which continued to insist that full independence should be on the agenda, seemed remote.

At the end of the year, the tsunami produced by the earthquake off the coast of Aceh killed an estimated 230,000 people on the western and northern coasts of the province, including whole units comprising hundreds of military and police personnel, and made more than 500,000 people homeless. With the provincial governor already arrested on corruption charges and the provincial capital, Banda Aceh, largely destroyed, the local administration more or less ceased to function. Compounding the disaster was the national government's paralysis in the face of the devastation caused by the tsunami: according to Coordinating Minister for

People's Welfare Alwi Shihab, the administration was in a state of "panic" for the first 48 hours.[4] Though Jakarta allowed foreign journalists into the province, exposing it to the international media for the first time since May 2003, Jakarta was initially apparently reluctant to allow international aid agencies to enter.[5] And while GAM declared a ceasefire and government security forces focused on relief efforts, potential local resentment over Jakarta's tardy and ineffective response, combined with the huge problems of reconstructing the province, could further complicate the Indonesian authorities' efforts to subdue resistance to their rule in the longer term.

At the Indonesian archipelago's other geographical extreme, the OPM (Organisasi Papua Merdeka, Papuan Freedom Organization) continued its struggle. Though OPM's military operations were necessarily considerably more dispersed and less intensive than GAM's and took second place to political activism, the pro-independence campaign necessitated deployment of additional troops to Papua during the legislative and presidential elections. Abuses by the security forces continued, particularly in the highlands where a major military operation began in September.[6] As in the case of Aceh, the "special autonomy" status assigned to Papua in 2001 largely fails to meet local aspirations for self-determination. However, though many Papuans were prepared to accept special autonomy as a step towards independence, a 2003 presidential decree splitting the territory into three provinces — apparently intended by Megawati's administration as a divide-and-rule measure — frustrated efforts to set up a Papuan People's Assembly. Though Indonesia's new president in principle supported the notion of dialogue as a route to solving the Papuan problem, there were no indications that he would preside over any startling initiatives.

Low-level communal clashes erupted again in some parts of Indonesia where there had been serious ethnic conflict earlier in the decade. In Maluku, there was a resurgence of Christian-Muslim fighting in April, resulting in 40 deaths. The clashes prompted Jakarta to deploy additional troops and police and provided a pretext to arrest and prosecute leading figures in the mainly-Christian Front Kedaulatan Maluku (Maluku Sovereignty Front) separatist movement. There was also sporadic violence in Central Sulawesi. However, these incidents did not indicate a return to the conditions that had prevailed in 2000–2001, when it had seemed possible that Muslim-Christian fighting could lead eastern Indonesia into Yugoslav-style civil war and disintegration.

In the southern Philippines, there were considerable grounds for optimism during 2004 that negotiations suspended since 2001 might soon resume, bringing the prospect of an end to the armed rebellion waged by the Moro Islamic Liberation

Front (MILF). Though a key issue — the extent of the Moro people's "ancestral domain" — remained unresolved, both the Manila government and the Muslim insurgents made concessions intended to build confidence. In February, both sides agreed to resume Malaysian-brokered peace talks. March saw an initial visit to Mindanao by a Malaysian army Advance Survey Team, a precursor to the International Monitoring Team intended to supervise the ceasefire once formal talks commence. In July, the MILF agreed to cooperate with government forces against a JI contingent as well as a kidnapping gang that had found sanctuary in rebel-controlled areas. Other confidence-building measures included the government's dropping of criminal charges against MILF personnel over bombings in Davao City in 2003. MILF allegations of ceasefire violation by the government after the Philippine Air Force struck supposed JI and Abu Sayyaf Group terrorist targets inside rebel-controlled territory delayed the resumption of negotiations that had been scheduled for October or November. However, in late December it was announced that formal peace negotiations would re-commence in February.[7]

Meanwhile, the Armed Forces of the Philippines (AFP) viewed the New People's Army (NPA), the armed wing of the Communist Party of the Philippines (CPP), as the country's most serious internal threat. Though there was no sign that the movement's personnel strength was growing, it appeared to be expanding its geographical reach.[8] At the same time, peace negotiations stalled after exploratory talks in Oslo in February and March. At issue was not only the Arroyo government's failure to lobby for the removal of the CPP/NPA from the United States' and European Union's lists of terrorist organizations (which the communists had set as a precondition for further talks), but also what the communists referred to as the "Hacienda Luisita massacre", when police breaking up a violent demonstration at former President Aquino's estate in mid-November killed 14 demonstrators. For its part, Manila pointed to the NPA's killing of ten AFP troops engaged in flood relief, also in November, as evidence of the communists' ill-will. In December, CPP leaders claimed that the NPA had attained a "critical mass" and called on its members to intensify their efforts to overthrow Arroyo's government.[9]

In Thailand, a major eruption of violence in the three Muslim-dominated southernmost provinces, the locus of long-running separatist agitation, revived internal security as a major concern for the government. In January, four soldiers were killed during a raid on an army base during which 380 weapons were stolen. The government led by Prime Minister Thaksin Shinawatra responded by imposing martial law in the three provinces and deploying additional troops including special forces. On 28 April, hundreds of Muslim youths attacked police stations, village defence posts and district offices throughout the south. Government security forces, apparently forewarned, reacted fiercely and killed 108 of the attackers, including many who had sought refuge in a mosque. Throughout the year, there were frequent lethal attacks, apparently by Muslim militants, on police officers, government officials, schoolteachers, and even Buddhist monks and ordinary civilians, as well as arson attacks on government schools. In late October, after troops killed 9 protestors in the town of Tak Bai, almost 80 other demonstrators out of hundreds arrested died from being "stacked like bricks" in army trucks. In all, the southern Thai conflict led to almost 600 deaths during 2004. Despite Thaksin's claim that four "ringleaders" behind the violence had been arrested,[10] at the end of the year lethal bomb attacks and shootings continued.

Given that armed activity mounted by the Pattani United Liberation Organization and other separatist groups had apparently withered a decade previously, the scale of the violence in Thailand's south during 2004 surprised and perplexed the authorities in Bangkok. Though Thailand's government initially blamed "bandits" for the renewed violence, it was soon apparent that it reflected a new wave of separatist activism rooted in socioeconomic and political grievance and orchestrated by new politico-military organizations. It also seemed possible that media coverage of the Palestinian intifada and Iraqi resistance to the U.S.-led occupation of Iraq may have inspired Thai Muslim youths to support this new rebellion against Bangkok's rule. Thaksin acknowledged that discrimination against Thai Muslims had exacerbated militancy, and there was consensus in Bangkok that more responsive governance and the delivery of effective economic and social development were vital if separatist sentiment was to be undermined. Achieving an appropriate balance between a development-oriented hearts-and-minds strategy on the one hand, and tough responses by the security forces on the other was not easy. Bangkok's often heavy-handed policies — seen at their worst in the 28 April and Tak Bai incidents — risked not only expanding local support for the nascent insurgency but also provoking sympathy for the revolt from Muslims elsewhere in Southeast Asia, and possibly stimulating links between local rebels and the pan-regional terrorist network JI, which has used southern Thailand as a sanctuary since 2001. In December, Thaksin's allegations that separatist rebels were using Malaysian territory for training created tensions in bilateral relations between Kuala Lumpur and Bangkok.[11]

In Myanmar, the downfall of Khin Nyunt and MI threatened to imperil ceasefires with ethnic minority rebel groups. As MI chief from 1989, Khin Nyunt had engineered ceasefires with no less than 17 insurgent groups in frontier regions including, most importantly, the United Wa State Army (UWSA), the Kachin Independence Organization, and the New Mon State Army. One ceasefire group, the Democratic

Karen Buddhist Army (DKBA) even agreed to fight alongside Myanmar's Tatmadaw (armed forces). Approximately two dozen other insurgent groups continued their rebellions, though at the time of Khin Nyunt's ouster in October a delegation from the Karen National Union (KNU), Myanmar's oldest and largest ethnic rebel group, was in Yangon for ceasefire talks. After Khin Nyunt's dismissal, the SPDC claimed that there would be no change in policy towards armed groups which had "returned to the legal fold". However, the regime soon presented the ceasefire groups with a 13-point memorandum demanding a formal ceasefire, under which they would be forced to renounce armed struggle, cease recruiting, end military training, and assist Yangon's anti-narcotics campaign. In return, the ethnic minority groups would receive state subsistence funding, and would be given legitimate roles as local armed police forces. Faced with this ultimatum and the loss of their familiar MI contacts, some ceasefire groups began considering resuming their insurgencies. There were particular problems with the Karen and Karenni groups. By early November, clashes were reported between Tatmadaw and DKBA forces, and a re-merger between the DKBA and KNU seemed possible. In December, there were also clashes between Tatmadaw and UWSA forces.[12]

Terrorism and Counter-Terrorism

Jemaah Islamiah, the largest regional terrorist network aligned with Al-Qaeda, remained a key security challenge for several Southeast Asian states during 2004. The Indonesian authorities continued to prioritize counter-terrorism and by March 2004 had convicted more than 30 people (including 3 who were sentenced to death) for their involvement in the October 2002 Bali bombings. Evidence that cleric Abu Bakar Bashir, chairman of the Majelis Mujahidin Indonesia (MMI, Indonesian Mujahidin Council), was JI's "emir" mounted in early 2004, and in April he was immediately rearrested (probably at least in part as the result of pressure from Washington and Canberra) under the 2003 anti-terrorism law on release from serving a prison sentence for immigration offences. Abu Bakar's trial on terrorism charges, most importantly his alleged role in the Bali bombings and the 2003 attack on the Marriott hotel in Jakarta, commenced in late October and continued at the year's end. However, important JI figures, including the bomb-makers Azahari bin Husin and Noordin Mohammad Top, remained at large and the terrorist group's continuing potency was displayed graphically in October when a suicide van-bomber struck outside Australia's Jakarta embassy, killing 9 and injuring 180. At the end of 2004, Indonesia's security forces were on high alert due to concerns over imminent terrorist strikes against hotels, shopping malls and churches. Under

Yudhoyono's administration, a new dimension to the heightened security precautions was the nationwide deployment of multi-agency intelligence teams to provincial police headquarters.[13]

In the Philippines, concern focused on JI's use of sanctuaries in areas controlled by its erstwhile ally, the MILF. In January, six Indonesian JI members were caught trying to infiltrate from the southern Philippines into the Malaysian state of Sabah. The following month, at least 15 new members reportedly graduated from a JI training camp within the MILF stronghold of Camp Abu Bakar. In March, the Philippine authorities despatched intelligence officers to interrogate JI members detained in Indonesia and Malaysia over their links with the MILF. In May, the security forces' Operation Brown Batik uncovered JI's "money trail" in the Philippines and led to the capture of its national financial officer, Jordan Mamso Abdullah.[14]

Worryingly for Manila, there was also evidence that the beleaguered and reportedly factionalized Abu Sayyaf Group (ASG), hitherto oriented towards hostage-taking for ransom and relatively small-scale bombings, was turning to large-scale terrorism and was linked — through people such as Jordan Mamso Abdullah — to JI. In February, the ASG claimed responsibility for the explosion and fire that killed 116 people on board SuperFerry 14 close to Manila. A month later, President Arroyo alleged that the arrest of four ASG members and the seizure of explosives had prevented a "Madrid-level attack" on Manila. Nevertheless, in July the AFP claimed that its operations had reduced the ASG to less than 60 armed personnel, divided amongst several splinter groups. Reports in December that ASG members had entered southern Thailand may have indicated their increasing desperation to evade capture after an AFP air-strike in November reportedly almost killed their leader, Khadafi Janjalani, while he was meeting JI operatives.[15]

Within Southeast Asia, counter-terrorism cooperation remained patchy, and based essentially on bilateral rather than region-wide intelligence links. Nevertheless, in February, delegates from 25 Asia-Pacific nations convened for the Bali Regional Ministerial Meeting on Counter-Terrorism, organized jointly by Australia and Indonesia. Most importantly, the two convening countries announced the impending establishment of the Jakarta Centre for Law Enforcement Cooperation (JCLEC). Intended to be operational by the end of 2004 in both regional capacity-building and operational roles, JCLEC will be led by a senior Indonesian police officer and largely funded by Australia at a cost of almost US$30m over five years. The new centre's operational remit distinguished it from the existing U.S.-financed Southeast Asian Regional Centre for Counter-Terrorism in Kuala Lumpur and the International Law Enforcement Academy in Bangkok, both restricted to training and research roles.

During 2004, the security of shipping against potential terrorist threats as well as piracy in Southeast Asian ports and waters, particularly in the Malacca and Singapore Straits, emerged as a key concern for states in and outside the region. There was no firm evidence of connections between maritime criminals and terrorists in the region. Nevertheless, against a background of rising piracy in the Straits and warnings by Lloyds' List and Singapore ministers in late 2003 over the possibility of terrorists using hijacked vessels as floating bombs to attack ports or maritime chokepoints, in March 2004 Admiral Thomas B. Fargo, commander-in-chief of U.S. Pacific Command, revealed that the Pentagon was formulating a Regional Maritime Security Initiative (RMSI). According to Fargo, RMSI would involve not only closer intelligence-sharing with Southeast Asian states, but also deployment of U.S. Marines and special forces on high-speed vessels to interdict maritime threats. Though Singapore supported RMSI, Indonesia and Malaysia asserted that security in the Straits was the responsibility of littoral states and that the introduction of foreign forces might provoke terrorism. However, the third Asia Security Conference (Shangri-La Dialogue), organized by the International Institute for Strategic Studies in Singapore in early June, facilitated convergence between the positions of the interested parties. In the aftermath of the Shangri-La Dialogue, the ministerial meeting of the Five Power Defence Arrangements (FPDA, involving Australia, Malaysia, New Zealand, Singapore and the United Kingdom) agreed that the scope of the grouping's already maritime-focused military exercises should be widened to include maritime counter-terrorism. Soon afterwards, Indonesia proposed trilateral coordinated naval patrols in the Malacca Strait, involving its own forces and those of Malaysia and Singapore. The first such patrol commenced in late July. Moreover, Admiral Fargo visited Malaysia, and the two sides were reported to have "mended fences", with the United States emphasizing its respect for littoral states' sovereignty and Malaysia welcoming Washington's offer of practical assistance in support of its efforts to combat piracy and to pre-empt maritime terrorism. With its under-funded navy and marine police, poor economic conditions, and inadequate law enforcement, Indonesia, though, crucially remained a weak component of the tentatively emerging regional maritime security architecture.

Extra-Regional Powers and Southeast Asia

The debate over Southeast Asian maritime piracy and terrorism during 2004 highlighted the extent to which the region's security has during the current decade increasingly been of interest to extra-regional powers. The most obvious development has been Washington's view of Southeast Asia as the "second front" in the Global War on Terrorism (GWOT), since late 2001 the most important prism through which the United States sees its security relations with allies and associates. However, as reactions within Southeast Asia to the RMSI proposal demonstrated, the Bush administration's focus on counter-terrorism has accentuated divergences amongst ASEAN members with respect to their security links with the United States.

Washington's security relations with the Philippines, Singapore and Thailand have intensified. During 2003, both Manila and Bangkok were accorded the status of Major Non-NATO Allies and granted substantial security assistance packages, while Singapore announced that it would be negotiating a Framework Agreement on security cooperation with Washington. In 2004, the United States' security and defence cooperation with all three states was far-reaching. Bilateral military exercises with the Philippines included Balikatan 2004 in February, involving 2,500 U.S. troops (mainly Marines) in Central Luzon. Meanwhile, under Operation Enduring Freedom-Philippines, U.S. forces closely supported AFP efforts to destroy the ASG. In Thailand, the annual Exercise Cobra Gold, most recently held in May 2004, remained by far Southeast Asia's largest war-game; over the years it has evolved from a bilateral U.S.-Thai affair into multilateral manoeuvres also involving small contingents from Singapore, the Philippines and Mongolia, with observers from 11 other countries.[16] In 2004, a counter-terrorism element was injected into Cobra Gold for the first time. Thai and U.S. special forces also intensified their joint training. U.S. defence and security cooperation with Singapore remained the closest and most far-reaching in Southeast Asia, reflecting Washington's view that — semantics aside — the city-state was now effectively an ally. All three states provided access to military airfields and, in Singapore's case, Changi Naval Base, facilitating the movement of U.S. forces between their U.S. and Pacific bases and the wars in Iraq and Afghanistan. During 2004, the Philippines, Singapore and Thailand all contributed token forces to the U.S.-led coalition occupying Iraq. The Philippine contingent's premature withdrawal caused temporary irritation in Washington but did not damage the overall bilateral relationship, which remained crucial to U.S. regional objectives in the context of the GWOT.

Indonesia and Malaysia have both, to a degree, cooperated with the United States in the GWOT. While both Washington and Jakarta would like to see the restoration of U.S. military aid to Indonesia, U.S. concern over the TNI's human rights abuses and its role in the 2002 Timika incident in Papua (in which two Americans were killed) continued to prevent defence cooperation beyond the limited provision of training in the United States under the International Military

Education and Training Scheme. Nevertheless, since 2002 Washington has actively supported Jakarta's counter-terrorism efforts, notably by helping to upgrade Indonesia's police force, and has evidently been heartened by President Yudhoyono's election and his emphasis on counter-terrorism.[17] Similarly, in Malaysia's case, Washington quietly welcomed Prime Minister Abdullah Badawi's accession after the tensions in U.S.-Malaysia relations under Dr Mahathir, and gave due credit for Malaysia's efforts against terrorism.[18] Nevertheless, it was clear that the determined U.S. focus on counter-terrorism has increased resentment against the United States in both Indonesia and Malaysia, providing a growing Islamic basis in addition to the established nationalist rationale for unhappiness over the United States' regional role, as the governments of the two states have needed to avoid alienating domestic Muslim constituencies by cooperating too closely or too obviously with Washington.

The U.S. security role in Southeast Asia has become more powerful than at any time since the Cold War, if defined in "hard" military terms. Indeed, as a result of the Pentagon's Global Posture Review, announced in September, its military profile in the region is likely to increase, with more use being made of facilities in Southeast Asia. At the same time, the United States remains Southeast Asia's most important trading partner. However, during 2004 there was a growing sense throughout the region that U.S. influence was nevertheless declining, partly as a result of Washington's counter-terrorism focus. In November 2004, an Asia Foundation report suggested that a more coordinated U.S. strategy for Southeast Asia would involve greater use of "soft power", for example through annual U.S.-ASEAN summit meetings, a U.S.-ASEAN free trade agreement, and a major initiative to engage Southeast Asian Muslims.[19] There were already signs of more nuanced approaches in U.S. policy in the region — for example, Washington's announcement in September that it would provide US$157m to improve basic education provision in Indonesia as part of a US$468m aid package over five years.[20] Moreover, at the end of 2004, all indications were that Washington would seize the opportunity provided by the regional tsunami disaster to display its soft power in terms of leading and funding relief and reconstruction efforts.

While the United States faced challenges in maintaining its regional influence, during 2004 China maintained its drive to become an important strategic player in Southeast Asia. Since the late 1990s, Beijing's more sophisticated diplomacy (epitomized by its New Security Policy and new-found enthusiasm for multilateralism), geo-strategic patience (marked by its less assertive policy in relation to territorial claims in the Spratlys), and its growing economic leverage have substantially undermined Southeast Asian governments' reservations over China's emerging regional role. In November 2004, the two agreements (on trade and dispute settlement) signed at the ASEAN-China summit boosted the institutionalization of economic relations that first found expression in the 2002 Framework Agreement on Economic Cooperation, which established the target of an ASEAN-China Free Trade Area by 2010. Tightening economic relations between China and Southeast Asia have been accompanied by a tentative security entente, encapsulated in the ASEAN-China Strategic Partnership for Peace and Security, agreed in October 2003 and followed by a detailed "Plan of Action" in November 2004.[21] China's intensifying engagement with ASEAN during 2004 was just part of Beijing's broader strategy of multilateralism in Asia as a whole, apparently aimed at leveraging its growing economic and diplomatic clout to heighten the legitimacy of its regional security role while minimizing that of the United States. As well as promoting the ASEAN Plus Three initiative (which will be transformed into the more grandly-titled East Asia Summit in 2005), China has become increasingly enthusiastic with regard to the ASEAN Regional Forum (ARF), taking the lead in establishing the ARF's Security Policy Conference for senior defence officials, which convened for the first time in Beijing in November.[22]

However, the evidence suggests that ASEAN members are not simply acquiescing in China's "peaceful rise", but are continuing to hedge their bets, primarily by accepting the need for the United States to maintain a central role in regional security. In effect, the continuing U.S. security interest, including a substantial military presence in the vicinity of Southeast Asia, relieves Southeast Asian governments of the need for immediate concern over China's increasing security-related activity. At the same time, Southeast Asian states have continued to benefit from the détente between Washington and Beijing that began after 9/11 and which has for the time being deferred the threat of overt competition between them for influence. As long as relations between Washington and Beijing remain on an even keel, Southeast Asian governments — which are keen to enjoy positive relations with both China and the United States — will be spared pressures to choose between taking one side or the other. During 2004, however, one concern for ASEAN members maintaining close security and defence ties with the United States was the potential for Sino-U.S. confrontation over Taiwan, which still held potential to destabilize the major power equilibrium in East Asia, possibly forcing hard choices on Southeast Asian governments.

Compared with the United States' pre-eminence and China's efforts to play a more important part in the region's political and security affairs, the roles played by what might be called the "second-tier" extra-regional powers — Japan, Australia and India — were relatively limited. Since the end of the Cold War, there has been considerable debate in Japan over the widely-perceived need to become a more assertive "normal power". There is every prospect that Japan's emerging capacity for power projection will be integrated into its alliance with the United States and there is little chance of Tokyo becoming an autonomous military actor. Nevertheless, Japan — concerned over the security of its energy supplies — has since the late 1990s suggested joint "Ocean Peacekeeping" (OPK) patrols to Southeast Asian governments as a way to combat piracy.[23] In the face of Southeast Asian governments' ambiguous responses, the speech presented on behalf of Japan Defence Agency Director-General Shigeru Ishiba at the Shangri-La Dialogue in June 2004 reiterated the OPK idea.[24]

Australia, alarmed over what it perceived to be a growing threat to its interests from Islamic terrorism, heightened its security cooperation with several Southeast Asian states. For example, beyond its close counter-terrorism collaboration with Indonesia, Canberra also staged a joint military exercise with Singapore in November focusing on developing responses to potential terrorist use of chemical, biological or radiological weapons and, as part of efforts to expand the Philippines' counter-terrorism capacity, in July deployed special forces to train AFP elements.[25] However, this increasing assertiveness was not always welcomed in the region, and the Indonesian and Malaysian governments maintained their traditional suspicion regarding Canberra's motives. This was particularly clear in December, when Australia provoked the ire of Jakarta and Kuala Lumpur by announcing a planned "maritime identification zone" aimed at pre-empting maritime terrorist threats up to 1,000 nautical miles from the homeland.[26]

While the gradually increasing security roles of Japan and Australia have not been entirely welcome in the region, India's growing role — which may in a small way provide an additional hedge against China's growing assertiveness — has proved less controversial. As in the cases of China and Japan, India's security role in Southeast Asia has grown in tandem with efforts to bolster economic relations. During 2004, India's military links with Singapore intensified in the wake of a bilateral Defence Cooperation Agreement signed in October 2003, and in September the two sides agreed to hold their first naval exercise in the South China Sea during 2005. Indian discussions with Malaysia on enhanced maritime security cooperation in September pointed to the likelihood that New Delhi would soon resume its naval patrols in the Malacca Strait.[27] In the meantime, India continued its series of joint patrols with Indonesia, and in October signed a memorandum with Myanmar on security cooperation, which was soon followed by coordinated bilateral military operations against Manipur and Naga rebels operating on the two countries' borders.

ASEAN Security Cooperation

A plethora of bilateral arrangements, mainly covering intelligence exchange, military training, and joint exercises, remained the most prevalent form of security cooperation between Southeast Asian states. However, the intensity and quality of this cooperation varied widely across the region. For example, while bilateral defence links were particularly strong between Singapore and Thailand (which in November intensified bilateral defence relations with a memorandum of understanding covering air force training), they were virtually non-existent between longer-established ASEAN members on the one hand and Cambodia, Laos, Myanmar and Vietnam on the other. Simultaneously, links between some Southeast Asian states and extra-regional powers, notably the United States and Australia, remained a central feature of the regional security landscape.

Meanwhile, stymied by intra-Southeast Asian rivalry, mistrust and suspicion, security cooperation under the auspices of ASEAN remained largely potential rather than actual. Since the late 1990s, the diversity and seriousness of security challenges confronting Southeast Asia had provoked considerable debate over the Association's security role. Evidence of ASEAN's declining credibility had provoked a radical initiative from Indonesia at the organization's annual heads of government meeting in October 2003. Apparently motivated by a wish to reassert itself as a regional power through ASEAN in the face of perceived challenges from the United States and Australia on the counter-terrorism front, Japan over energy security, and China's and possibly India's potentially wide-ranging regional security roles, Indonesia proposed that the grouping should transform itself into an "ASEAN Security Community" (ASC), as part of a project to establish an ASEAN Community also incorporating economic and social pillars by 2020. The ASC idea focused on using ASEAN's own existing mechanisms for resolving intramural disputes, and much closer collaboration on transnational security challenges including terrorism, narcotics- and people-trafficking, and maritime security issues. As envisaged in the Declaration of ASEAN Concord II agreed at the October 2003 summit, the ASC reflected ASEAN's established collective emphases on comprehensive security and the principle of non-interference, explicitly ruling out an ASEAN defence pact, military alliance or joint foreign policy.

The nature of the ASC was spelled out in more detail in the Vientiane Action Programme (VAP), issued by ASEAN's summit in November 2004, which listed five "strategic thrusts" aimed at achieving results by 2010: political development (including the promotion of human rights and the prevention of corruption), the shaping and sharing of norms (notably efforts to adopt a regional code of conduct in the South China Sea, and various counter-terrorism measures), conflict prevention (including establishment of an ASEAN Arms Register and the promotion of maritime security cooperation), conflict resolution, and post-conflict peace-building.[28]

Though the ASC might help to facilitate cooperation against terrorism and other transnational threats in the long-term, it seemed unlikely to boost Southeast Asian states' collective ability to defuse more conventional threats, whether these were domestic or inter-state in nature. The continued insistence on non-interference, though understandable, seemed likely to impede robust conflict resolution. The VAP spoke rather unconvincingly of "regional arrangements for the maintenance of peace and stability" being established through "national peacekeeping centers" and of building on "existing modes of peaceful settlement of disputes" as the main conflict resolution "innovations" under the ASC; there was no specific mention of how the existing High Council might be transformed into an effective judicial mechanism.

During 2004, ASEAN's apparent irrelevance to worsening internal security problems in Thailand's south and Myanmar's continuing domestic political impasse, despite the acute interest and concern of neighbouring states in both cases, served to highlight again the grouping's shortcomings in the security sphere. At the end of December, despite the nationally-driven efforts of Singapore and, on a smaller scale Malaysia, to help their stricken neighbours, the tsunami-induced humanitarian crisis produced no significant immediate response from ASEAN as an institution, despite the huge amount of discussion in the region of "human security" issues over the previous decade. It was not until the United States proposed a consortium led by itself, Japan, India and Australia to coordinate relief efforts, that Singapore eventually took the initiative in Southeast Asia and called for an ASEAN-organized emergency summit to discuss the crisis.[29] While it remained possible that ASEAN might play a useful role in assisting reconstruction efforts beyond the short term, it was clear that external powers — notably the United States, which had quickly deployed a flotilla with large numbers of helicopters to Sumatra — would dominate the coordination and provision of immediate humanitarian relief.

Conclusion

At the end of 2004, there were grounds for assuming that, following national elections, stability would characterize the domestic politics of Indonesia, Malaysia and perhaps even the Philippines for the next several years. In the cases of Indonesia and the Philippines, which both remained fragile states, the accession of governments with clear democratic mandates could provide firmer bases for ameliorating economic weakness and mitigating serious security problems. Elsewhere in the region, smooth political succession (Singapore), the beginning of gradual reforms (Brunei) and the resolution of inter-party gridlock (Cambodia) also provided reassurance of stability.

Nevertheless, some Southeast Asian states faced serious internal security problems. Though the prospects for ending the MILF rebellion in the southern Philippines seemed fairly rosy, and the ASG was apparently almost neutralized, the NPA appeared to be gaining strength and a negotiated settlement was not in prospect. In southern Thailand, the government and security forces appeared to have little clear idea of how to manage resurgent separatist violence, sometimes responding in a counter-productive fashion. Governments in the region continued to grapple with the problem of JI, which retained the capacity to mount terrorist bombings, and appeared to have found sanctuary in Mindanao as well as in Indonesia. A potential link-up between southern Thai separatists and JI was a worrying possibility, as were connections between pirates and terrorists in the Straits.

Despite the ASC proposal, ASEAN seemed unlikely to develop quickly as a vehicle that could help its members to manage the diverse security problems they faced more effectively. In the absence of effective multilateral security cooperation within the sub-region, Southeast Asian governments' security cooperation policies have increasingly seemed to parallel the fashion for economic bilateralism within ASEAN and between ASEAN members and extra-regional partners. This was seen most clearly in Singapore's bilateral security networking, but every other Southeast Asian government pursued similar arrangements to a greater or lesser degree. The continuing strong U.S. security interest in Southeast Asia has allowed ASEAN governments to view China's rising power and assertiveness with greater equanimity than might otherwise have been the case, while the post-9/11 détente between Washington and Beijing has spared Southeast Asian governments the need to choose between warm relations with one or other of the two main extra-regional powers. The interests of Australia, India and Japan in Southeast Asian security has provided ASEAN governments with additional hedging options.

At the end of 2004, the catastrophic impact of the tsunami on parts of Indonesia and Thailand, and to a lesser extent Malaysia and Myanmar, underlined the inadequacy of existing regional mechanisms for dealing with Southeast Asian crises while reaffirming the continuing importance of external powers, notably the United States, whose ships and helicopters were soon central to relief efforts in Sumatra. The natural disaster also brought Indonesia's conflict zone in Aceh to international attention. However, at the turn of the year, in the midst of the immediate humanitarian crisis, the impact of the tsunami on the prospects for conflict resolution in the province, and on the Thai national election scheduled for February 2005, regional cooperation, and relations between extra-regional powers and Southeast Asian governments and peoples remained uncertain in the extreme.

Notes

1   Reme Ahmad, "Anwar Out to Fashion New Keadilan Platform", *Straits Times*, 20 December 2004.

2   "Philippine Government Calls for National Unity. Military Put on Red Alert", *Philippine Daily Inquirer* website, 24 December 2004, in BBC Monitoring Global Newsline — Asia-Pacific Political, 24 December 2004.

3   "Jusuf Pulling Out of Opposition Coalition", *Straits Times*, 22 December 2004.

4   Interview with "World at One", British Broadcasting Corporation Radio 4, 1 January 2005.

5   "Foreign Aid Agencies Blocked from Entering Indonesia's Aceh", *Jakarta Post* website, 28 December 2004, in BBC Monitoring Global Newsline — Asia-Pacific Political, 28 December 2004.

6   "Highlands Situation in West Papua is Deteriorating", *West Papua News* website, 17 December 2004, http://www.westpapuanews.com/articles/publish/article_ 1642.shtml, accessed 30 December 2004.

7   "Philippine Government, Moro Rebels Agree to Resume Peace Talks", *Philippine Daily Inquirer* website, 24 December 2004, in BBC Monitoring Global Newsline — Asia-Pacific Political, 24 December 2004.

8   Noel M. Morada, "The Philippines: Security Context and Challenges", paper presented at Third Europe-Southeast Asia Forum, Berlin, 13–15 December 2004, p. 6.

9   "Philippine Police on 'Full Alert' for Communist Attacks", *Philippine Star* website, 26 December 2004, in BBC Monitoring Global Newsline — Asia-Pacific Political, 26 December 2004.

10   "Four Suspected Masterminds Arrested", *Straits Times*, 17 December 2004.

11   "Malaysia Denies having Militant Training Base", *Straits Times*, 18 December 2004; "Indonesian Military to Probe Thai Premier's Claims of Links to Militants", *Suara Merdeka* (Semarang) website, 21 December 2004, in BBC Monitoring Global Newsline — Asia-Pacific Political, 21 December 2004.

12   "Wa 'Cease-fire Group', Burmese Troops Clash in Shan State", Democratic Voice of Burma (Oslo) broadcast, 24 December 2004, in BBC Monitoring Global Newsline — Asia-Pacific Political, 24 December 2004.

13   "Indonesia to Deploy Multi-agency Anti-terrorism Teams", *Jakarta Post* website,

21 December 2004, in BBC Monitoring Global Newsline — Asia-Pacific Political, 21 December 2004.

[14] Christina Mendez, "Top JI Leader in RP Arrested", *Philippine Star* (Manila), 6 May 2004.

[15] "Abu Sayyaf Group Reportedly Operating in Southern Thailand", *Puchatkan* (Bangkok), 21 December 2004 in BBC Monitoring Global Newsline — Asia-Pacific Political, 21 December 2004; "Philippine Military Braces for Attacks over Reported Death of Abu Sayyaf Chief", *Philippine Star* website, 23 December 2004 in in BBC Monitoring Global Newsline – Asia-Pacific Political, 23 December 2004.

[16] Cobra Gold 04 Wraps Up', Asia-Pacific Area Network website, http://www.apan-info.net/cobragold/fullstory.asp?id=52, accessed 30 December 2004.

[17] "U.S. Determined to Strengthen Ties with Indonesia, Huhtala Says", U.S. Embassy, Jakarta website, 17 November 2004, http://jakarta.usembassy.gov/press_rel/huhtala.html, accessed 3 January 2005.

[18] "U.S.-Malaysia Relations on 'a Positive Path', LaFleur Says", U.S. Embassy, Malaysia website, 10 September 2004, http://usembassymalaysia.org.my/wf/wf0910_ambLaFleur.htm, accessed 3 January 2005.

[19] "America's Role in Asia. Summary of Findings/recommendations of the Asian Working Group", The Asia Foundation website, http://www.asiafoundation.org/News/ARA/asianviews.html, accessed 1 January 2005.

[20] "U.S. and Indonesian Governments Sign $468 Million Pact to Improve Water, Schools, Health, Nutrition and Environment", U.S. Agency for International Development website, 2 September 2004, http://www.usaid.gov/press/releases/2004/pr040902.html, accessed 3 January 2005.

[21] Chairman's Statement of the 8th ASEAN + China Summit, Vientiane, 29 November 2004, Association of Southeast Asian Nations website, http://www.aseansec.org/16749.htm, accessed 3 January 2005.

[22] "Foreign Ministry Spokeswomen Zhang Qiyue's Remarks on the First ARF Conference on Security Policy", People's Republic of China Ministry of Foreign Affairs website, 26 October 2004, http://www.fmprc.gov.cn/eng/xwfw/s2510/t167107.htm, accessed 31 December 2004.

[23] Christopher W. Hughes, *Japan's Re-emergence as a 'Normal' Military Power*, Adelphi Paper 368–9 (London: International Institute for Strategic Studies, 2004), pp. 119–21.

[24] Speech by Minister of State for Defense Shigeru Ishiba at the IISS Asia Security Conference, Singapore, 5 June 2004, International Institute for Strategic Studies website, http://www.iiss.org/shangri-la.php, accessed 5 January 2005.

[25] "Defence Strengthens Counter-terrorism Cooperation with the Philippines", Australian Government Department of Defence, Defence Media Release, CPA 131/04, 4 July 2004.

[26] "Jakarta Says Plan Breaches its Jurisdiction", *Straits Times*, 17 December 2004; "KL Blasts Canberra's Planned Maritime Anti-Terror Net", *Straits Times*, 21 December 2004.

[27] "India to Resume Patrolling of Malacca Straits", *The Hindu*, 9 September 2004.

[28] "Vientiane Action Programme (VAP), 2004–2010", ASEAN Secretariat website, http://www.aseansec.org/VAP-10th%20ASEAN%20Summit.pdf, pp. 6–8, accessed 30 December 2004.

[29] Chua Mui Hoong, "S'pore Calls for Urgent Asean Talks", *Straits Times*, 31 December 2004.

Political Transitions in Southeast Asia

Mely Caballero-Anthony

Introduction

One could easily be pessimistic about Southeast Asia's prospects given the series of crises that hit the region in 2004. These include the onset of avian flu (coming on the heels of SARS) and the looming pandemic threat, the persistence of terrorist-related incidents, and the devastating earthquake and tsunami that caused massive loss of lives, property and livelihood. Yet, if there is something to be optimistic about it is in the number of general elections that took place in many ASEAN countries within a span of one year. It began in March 2004 with the holding of Malaysia's general elections, followed by elections in Indonesia in April that were spread over six months, and then the elections held in the Philippines in May. This was soon followed by the elections in Thailand in February 2005.

This series of elections is significant for many reasons. First, we see the emergence of new political actors who have taken over the mantle of leadership from long-serving leaders in the region. In Malaysia, Abdullah Badawi replaced long-time Malaysian prime minister Mahathir Mohamed; and while there was no election in Singapore in 2004, there was nevertheless a changing of the guard in August 2004 with the installation of a new prime minister, Lee Hsien Loong, who succeeded Goh Chok Tong. Second, despite having come after three short-lived presidents who had succeeded long-time Indonesian leader Suharto, the country's new president Susilo Bambang Yudhoyono was the first directly elected president of post-New Order Indonesia. The direct presidential elections have capped the six-year process of political transition in the country toward a democratic political system. And third, the two incumbent leaders, Philippines' Gloria Macapagal-Arroyo and Thailand's Thaksin Shinawatra, who could still be considered as relatively new players in the region, are serving their second terms in office after their

MELY CABALLERO-ANTHONY is Assistant Professor, Institute of Defence and Strategic Studies (IDSS), Nanyang Technological University, Singapore.

respective re-elections. Their renewed mandates have however raised some questions on the trajectory of democratic transitions in the region.

Of more significance is the fact that these elections and changes in political leaderships have come in an era characterized by new types of challenges, crises, and forces for change. In the period following the Asian financial crisis in 1997, the impetus for change and push toward democratization have gained more momentum in the region. It is also noteworthy that this impetus for change has taken place within the "old" members of the Association of Southeast Asian Nations (ASEAN) — Indonesia, Malaysia, Philippines, Thailand and even Singapore. Thus, the emergence of new political leaders and the unfolding nature of these new political regimes in these transitions will have important implications on the direction these changes will take in the push for more democratization in the region.

The main objective of this chapter is to examine the nature of the political transitions taking place in the major capitals in Southeast Asia and review the prospects for democratic consolidation in the region. While the mood for change has been upbeat since the recent series of elections, and while hopes for greater democratization may have heightened, this essay argues that expectations for change may have to be tempered against the realities faced by these different states. These realities are reflected in the complex range of socioeconomic, political, and security issues faced by individual states that could hamper efforts at creating a more stable political system at the very least, and a politically liberal regional environment, at the most. This cautious outlook is presented against the caveat that the analyses following this introduction are still exploratory and tentative, and that the observations tend to be more broad than definitive. The various issues that are examined in this chapter would therefore need to be revisited at a more appropriate time when much of the flux that comes with political transitions has begun to settle down.

Understanding Political Transitions in Southeast Asia

While this chapter looks at the nature of political transitions in the region, the processes of the transitions being examined go beyond the analysis of elections and/or changes in governments in these countries. Of greater salience to this analysis are the new actors that have entered the political arena and how they may have altered the power configuration within these states. It is also important to look into the kinds of issues identified in the political agenda of the new regime(s) and examine their impact on state–society relations. With these, one would be able to assess the problems and prospects of promoting a more liberal political environment.

It is therefore important to clarify the concept of political transition that is being analysed here. One could start by drawing a clear distinction between the meaning we attach to change and transition. Transition, for the purpose of this study, refers to some notion of movement from one defined (political) condition or state of being to another, completely different one. Hence, while one often sees changes in governments after general elections, these may not necessarily lead to political transitions. In Southeast Asia, we have already seen the dramatic political transitions of authoritarian regimes to emerging democracies, Indonesia being the latest case in point. Although many Indonesian scholars have argued that the push for change had been building up for some time prior to the 1997 financial crisis, it was essentially that crisis which triggered the fall of Suharto. We have also seen notable movements and/or push within the so-called semi-democratic regimes toward more open and democratic political systems, as in the case of Thailand, and even in Malaysia and Singapore.[1] The Philippines' experience is also often described as one of consolidating its democratic system. These transitions from authoritarianism and semi-democratic regimes to democratizing ones, or from emerging democracies to consolidated democracies, have in fact been the focus of many recent studies on political transitions.[2]

From a broader perspective, one could argue that the continued salience of examining political transitions is explained by the patchy record of "democratic consolidation" among new democracies in the developing world. Since Samuel Huntington's seminal work, *The Third Wave: Democratisation in the 21st Century*,[3] there have been increasing concerns not only about the lack of progress of democratically elected governments in many parts of Asia, but more importantly on the inability of these "democratizing" states to consolidate their democracies. Indeed, although there has been consensus on the non-linear path to democratic regimes, there remains however the underlying assumption that while political transitions were a common phenomenon, the transitions from authoritarianism would lead to the process of democratization and to the consolidation of democracy. The question however is the extent to which this is borne out in Southeast Asia.

Given that Southeast Asia has been through a series of devastating events — starting from the debilitating impact of the Asian financial crisis, the aftermath of the 9/11 terrorist attack in the United States and the increase of terrorist-related incidents in Southeast Asia, the onset of highly infectious diseases like SARS and the avian flu, as well as the increasing list of non-traditional security concerns that cut across national boundaries like transnational crime — an important question to ponder is whether these crises do in fact contribute to democratization, or do they have the reverse effect?[4] Notwithstanding these perennial questions, the recent elections in the region make it all the more timely to analyse the challenges of political transitions and their implications on the project of democratic consolidation. This chapter will therefore examine the dynamics of political transitions taking place in selected states in Southeast Asia against the broader canvas of political change and development in the region. By looking at the 2004 elections as the starting point, this chapter addresses the following questions: How do we describe the nature of political transitions taking place in Southeast Asia? Do these developments lean more toward political pluralism, democratic consolidation, or status quo regimes? Who are the new actors and how have they changed the power configuration in their respective states? The analysis proceeds with a broad survey of the political changes taking place in Malaysia, Indonesia, Thailand and the Philippines. The separate discussion of each state draws out some observations on the emerging political trends during these periods of transition. It concludes with some thoughts on the implications of these trends on the prospects for democratic consolidation in the region.

The Broad Canvas of Political Transitions in Southeast Asia

This section is divided into two parts, starting with a comparison of the nature of transitions taking place in Indonesia and Malaysia — countries that have seen a major transition in political leadership with the arrival of the first elected president in the former and the retirement of a long-serving leader in the latter. In the continuum of political transitions, we can locate these two countries as emerging democracies. In the case of Indonesia, it started with transition from authoritarianism to democracy beginning with the fall of Suharto; while in the case of Malaysia one could argue that, with the departure of Mahathir, the country is going through a process of "re-democratization".

The second part looks at the experiences of Thailand and the Philippines. The respective histories of political transitions in these two countries allow us to place them in the "consolidation" phase of democratization. What is of interest in this study is revisiting where they are on the road to consolidation. This issue is examined in the separate discussion of these two transitions.

From authoritarianism and "half-way" house to democratic systems: Comparing Malaysia and Indonesia

Malaysia

The 11th General Elections in Malaysia held on 21 March 2004 was a significant event for Malaysia's new prime minister, Abdullah Badawi, and his ruling coalition,

Barisan National (National Front). The United Malays National Organization (UMNO)-led Barisan National (BN) won 198 of the 210 parliamentary seats and obtained 65 per cent of the popular vote. This was its most successful victory in Malaysia's electoral history.

This impressive win was even more significant given the fact that in the previous elections in 1999, BN had actually suffered a tremendous setback when UMNO — the core party that forms BN — lost half of its traditional support to the Islamic opposition party, Parti Islam Se Malaysia (PAS), and to the fledgling KeADILan (Justice) party. That was the period when UMNO was in turmoil and Malaysia was reeling from a number of crises. The huge electoral loss however was largely attributed to divisions within UMNO triggered by the impact of the dismissal, arrest, and imprisonment of Anwar Ibrahim, Malaysia's deputy prime minister. The Anwar episode drove a deep wedge within the country's Malay community and unravelled to become one of its worst political crises to the extent that, at the height of the crisis, serious doubts were raised about the survival of UMNO as representing Malay interests. It was also about the only time in Mahathir's leadership of UMNO when he was cast as a liability to the party. Despite the fact that the UMNO crisis was eventually overcome and Mahathir gracefully retired in October 2003, Malaysia's experience during the 1997–98 crisis had generated a strong desire for political change, particularly among the country's younger generation who had clamoured for more political space, more checks and balances, and an end to what has been perceived as a strong collusion between business and politics.[5]

While it can be argued that the 2004 elections have not really altered the political hegemony of the UMNO-backed system, and that not much political transition has really taken place in the sense of having a definitive political transformation, there are however palpable changes in the nature of state–society relations. These can be seen in the new actors who have assumed power, the policies that have been introduced to promote more political openness, and the kinds of institutions that have been established to address the issue of good governance — to respond to public demand for a more liberal political environment.

Leadership change: From a maverick autocrat to Mr Nice Guy

The resounding victory of BN at the 2004 elections has been attributed largely to the country's new prime minister, Abdullah Ahmad Badawi. Although not a new face in Malaysian politics, having served in various capacities as Malaysia's education minister, foreign minister, and as deputy prime minister, Abdullah has brought a breath of fresh air to the country's political climate dominated for more than twenty years by Mahathir, who was often portrayed as an authoritarian leader. Political observers have been quick to point to the contrasts in their leadership styles, with Abdullah projecting a more consensual, less confrontational approach. Fondly addressed as "Pak Lah" by the local Malay community, Abdullah's Islamic credentials have not only burnished his image as a credible Muslim leader,[6] but has also put him in a better position to counter the moral and intellectual high ground of the pro-Islamic opposition PAS.

Badawi's reform agenda and *Islam Hadhari*

Despite some initial reservations about Abdullah's Mr Nice Guy image, the new prime minister immediately set to make an impact by introducing a slew of policies and measures to reflect his administration's reform agenda. Among these were fighting corruption and the shelving of multi-million dollar projects that were perceived as benefiting Mahathir's close associates. He also addressed the issue of governance by taking to task certain state institutions like the police for their inability to address theft and crime, the judiciary for delays in trying corruption cases, and the civil service for their inefficiency. Abdullah's reform-oriented agenda was seen as part of his attempt to distinguish himself from his predecessor and to project the seriousness of his administration's efforts to respond to the demands of establishing transparency and accountability in the government — the issues which happened to also be the clarion call of the Anwar-led *Reformasi* movement. The Malaysian *Reformasi* movement began soon after the detention of Anwar in 1998. The themes outlined by this movement echoed the same themes of the Indonesian *Reformasi* that also emerged soon after the 1997 crisis. These themes were depicted as fighting "corruption, cronyism and nepotism" (KKN).

Abdullah's reform agenda appears to have made some progress. Within one year of Abdullah's leadership, Malaysia has witnessed a number of significant anti-corruption trials such as the arrest of Eric Chia, a close associate of Mahathir and who was also the CEO of the bankrupt Perwaja (National Steel Company), and Kasitah Gaddam, the Minister for Land and Co-operative Development.[7] Several anti-corruption investigations were also carried out against other UMNO officials and in April 2004, the government introduced a code of ethics that required cabinet ministers and elected representatives to disclose their assets. Meanwhile, to improve the tarnished image of the country's police force, Abdullah set up the Police Commission in January 2004 to look into cases of alleged corruption and public complaints about its poor performance amidst the alarming rise in cases of crime, especially murder and rape. The newly created 16-member

Commission brought together a wide range of people from different backgrounds from political, legal, religious, activist, and business communities to propose reforms for the police.[8]

Abdullah has also turned his attention to improving corporate governance by reforming several government-linked companies (GLCs), and in particular the restructuring of Khazanah Nasional, the biggest investment arm of the Malaysian government, which had been tasked to take over many other companies that had been under-performing. Of significance was the appointment of 43-year old Azman Mokhtar, former head of Salomon Smith Barney, as Khazanah's new chief executive, a big departure from the past practice of appointing former high-ranking politicians as senior executives of GLCs.

In a move to counter the challenge from PAS, Abdullah also introduced the policy of *Islam Hadhari*, described as a more progressive approach to Islam that advocates, among other things: religious tolerance, secularism, socioeconomic development in the context of modernization and globalization, as well as the rejection of an "exclusivist and radically oriented Islamic agendas such as establishing an Islamic state".[9] As argued by a Malaysian writer, *Islam Hadhari* encourages a more liberal discourse on Islamic issues to "balance out the obscurantism of Middle East-trained clerics who have sought to preserve their monopoly on the interpretations of the Holy Koran".[10]

Last, but not least among many of the new developments that signal a move to an era of political openness, was the unexpected release of Anwar Ibrahim after six years in prison. Anwar's controversial detention had been a symbol of political oppression and abuse of the judiciary. The Malaysian High Court's decision to uphold Anwar's appeal against a conviction for sodomy has had significant implications on the dynamics of opposition politics in the country and on the voices that had been demanding political reform in Malaysia. It also signals a return to judicial independence that had, during the Mahathir era, been perceived as being compromised.

Indonesia

If there is one country in the region that has made its mark in the way its politics have changed drastically in so short a period, it is Indonesia. The nature of the political transition that has been taking place in the country has been aptly encapsulated in the statement of the newly elected president, Susilo Bambang Yudhoyono, who declared that Indonesia is "… only at the beginning of a long journey … we are running a marathon of five years".[11] While Yudhoyono's comments referred to the challenge he faced in achieving his reform agenda within his term, the analogy of running a marathon could not have been more appropriate.

Indeed, since the fall of Suharto in the aftermath of the Asian financial crisis in 1997–98, the country has come a long way — paradoxically in just a span of six years — towards establishing a democratic political system. The country's general elections of 2004 was therefore extremely important since it capped the sustained efforts to transform the kind of "pre-determined" political order that characterized the Suharto regime to one of a more participatory competition for power. Not only did the 2004 elections allow for the first direct presidential contest, but it also saw distinct changes in the country's political configuration as reflected in the emergence of new political parties and new political actors that vied for votes. The logistical challenge of the exercise was huge. In terms of statistics alone, the 2004 general elections saw 48 political parties with about 450,000 candidates competing for seats from the parliamentary down to the district levels. According to one study, the daunting electoral operations required close to 3.5 million staff to be deployed in about 500,000 polling stations,[12] to handle 148,000,369 registered voters with the newly established election commission — Komisi Pemilihan Umum (KPU).[13] To manage such a massive nation-wide exercise, the elections had to be split into three parts, starting with the holding of the parliamentary elections in April 2004 to vote for members of the House of Representatives, followed by the presidential elections which were conducted in two rounds. The first round was held in July 2004 and the second in September 2004.[14] Overall, the 2004 elections saw 86 per cent of the eligible voters casting their votes in the parliamentary elections and 78.23 per cent in the presidential elections, in what was observed by international monitors as generally "free, fair and safe".[15] Indeed, to the surprise and relief of the international community, the elections were peaceful.

The remarkable success of the 2004 Indonesian elections owes much to the important institutional foundations incrementally established to support the democratic reforms undertaken in the country. At this point, it is important to review some of these institutional reforms and to reflect more on the processes that are unfolding, and appreciate better where Indonesia stands in this transition.

The most important of these democratic foundations were the series of pivotal military reforms introduced starting from the Habibie period which essentially brought the Indonesian military, TNI (Tentera Nasional Indonesia), which had ruled the country for more than 35 years, under civilian control.[16] The restructuring of the TNI's *dwifungsi* (dual function) doctrine and the subsequent adoption of the New Paradigm doctrine paved the way for civilian rule. Under this new doctrine, measures were adopted to remove the military's role and involvement in domestic politics. The incremental reforms began with the reduction of military-appointed seats in the now-defunct People's Consultative Assembly (MPR) and the phasing out of TNI representation in parliament by 2004. The TNI reforms also prohibited active military officers from being elected and/or appointed to government positions, as well as the adoption of the principle of neutrality in politics as reflected in the military severing its formal links with Golkar. These military reforms were further consolidated during Abdulrrahman Wahid's and Megawati Sukarnoputri's presidencies when the military was separated from the police in 1999, and a civilian was appointed as the minister of defence, a post traditionally held by a military general.[17]

The process of military disengagement from politics was reinforced by the development of other institutions to strengthen civilian supremacy and promote democratization in the country. Among salient developments has been constitutional reforms, particularly the election of people's representatives and political leaders. The electoral framework defined by the country's 1945 constitution was revised in 2002, allowing Indonesians to elect their president and their parliamentary representatives directly. The number of political parties in the country was also increased. As a result, Indonesia moved from Suharto's New Order arrangement of having only 3 major political parties comprising the stalwart Golkar, the Indonesian Democratic Party (PDI-P), and the United Development Party (PPP), to having over 40 other parties, which were eventually reduced to 24 political parties that could contest in the 2004 elections. Members of these parties are then voted on a "first past the post system" to form the MPR, the Indonesian legislature. The MPR or People's Consultative Assembly has now been transformed into a bicameral body comprising 550 members of the House of Representatives (DPR) and 128 members of the Regional Representatives Council (DPD). The DPD has four representatives from each of Indonesia's 32 provinces. Members of both houses have a 5-year term. The extent to which the country's political space has been pried open is reflected in the fact that 72 per cent of the current MPR members are newcomers from various backgrounds.[18]

Electoral reforms also included the establishment of an independent KPU comprising non-partisan members, in contrast to the past where the KPU was run by the government or political parties. This is further complemented by the creation of a Constitutional Court composed of three members appointed by the president, three by the parliament, and another three by the Supreme Court, to settle disputes arising from the electoral process, and whose judgments are considered final. International observers have already commended the Court's performance. They cited the Court's ability to rapidly investigate and rule on cases of electoral disputes in the April 2004 elections, and how their rulings were accepted without dissension.[19] Moreover, national sentiments with regard to the conduct of the elections were also captured in a national survey conducted by KOMPAS, which revealed that 83.5 per cent of the respondents were satisfied with the presidential election and that the voters generally felt that "political pressure or money politics were much reduced", while some respondents from the electorates of Banda Aceh, Pangkal Pinang, and Makassar indicated the absence of any pressure.[20] The implications of the degree of independence enjoyed by many voters in their choice of representatives will be discussed more extensively later, but suffice to say at this point that the success of the first direct presidential election is a watershed in Indonesia's political development and moved the country a few steps forward in its democratic consolidation.

Another important institutional development that promotes democratization is the country's decentralization programme introduced in 2002. Although the fledgling decentralization process is currently beset with problems of capacity, clarity in functions and delivery of services, largely due to the perennial problem of poor implementation and lack of resources, this has proven to be one of Indonesia's major tests in its ability to transform the New Order's highly centralized power structure controlled by the military to a more decentralized and democratic system. Specifically, when examined in the context of institutionalizing civilian control of politics, it can be argued that the decentralization programme in effect renders the military's territorial command and power structure irrelevant. Decentralization has therefore become a crucial issue in the implementation of TNI's New Paradigm doctrine, and may require a more calibrated approach to balance the push for democratization by other forces of Indonesian society against the embedded interest of the military in maintaining the country's internal stability in the face of separatist and secession threats while accommodating the military's interest in keeping some of its influence and control.

In summary, the Indonesian story of political transition has seen a significant dispersal of power and as a result there are now multiple layers of political power. As observed by one analyst, "power no longer flows from the centre but now has a local and regional flavour to it".[21]

Political transitions in Thailand and the Philippines: Democracy endangered and elusive democratic consolidation

As noted at the beginning of this section, the earlier democratic transitions in the Philippines and Thailand allow us to ideally locate them in the "consolidation" phase of democratization. But closer analyses of the transitions that are taking place under the re-elected leaders of these two states indicate a more complicated trajectory. This is discussed further below.

Thailand

In contrast to the euphoria that followed the holding of the Indonesian and Malaysian elections, this was visibly absent in the case of Thailand. The 2005 election was the second one held since the adoption of Thailand's 1997 constitution following the 1992 democratic transition, and which was widely hailed as having finally provided a clear, overarching framework for the country's democratic system. One would therefore expect that the holding of the second elections should have been a cause for celebration, not least as an important milestone in Thailand's political development since for the first time in its history, the country's first democratically elected House of Representatives and its prime minister Thaksin Shinawatra were able to complete their four-year term. But while Thaksin's re-election was expected and his party, Thai Rak Thai (TRT) had predicted an easy win, the landslide victory that followed — almost an absolute majority for the TRT — not only took the opposition party by surprise but has raised salient issues with regard to the state of Thailand's democracy. Ironically, rather than regard the second Thai elections as another feather in its democratization process, it appears instead to have caused some concern especially among the critics of the premier about what they see as a backsliding from democratization to authoritarianism.[22]

Revisiting Thailand's democratization

When compared with its neighbours, Thailand's democratization process had a similar trajectory to Indonesia's with military regimes giving way to democratic systems. For several decades following the overthrow of absolute monarchy in 1932, Thailand had largely a history of different military regimes, coming after several military coups. A brief hiatus following massive student-led protests in 1973 saw the country's first attempt at democratization, but was abruptly ended by a bloody coup in 1976. It was not until May 1992 that a major transition to democracy took place, triggered by the unsuccessful coup in May 1992.[23] Since the 1992 upheaval, the road to democratization in Thailand was marked by several institutional developments, most significantly, the promulgation of the 1997 constitution — hailed as the most democratic constitution to date, given that the drafting committee members were from business, academic and legal bodies, as well as leaders of non-governmental organizations. There was also extensive public consultation during the drafting process. The new constitution put in place several measures designed to improve the country's political system, remove the military from politics, and institutionalize democracy. Among the important measures outlined to enhance democracy, and promote transparency and accountability, were the establishment of new independent agencies and courts, namely: the Election Commission, the National Commission on Human Rights, the Constitutional Court, the National Counter Corruption Commission, and the State Audit Commission.

On parliamentary reforms, the new constitution did away with the appointed Senate and transformed the 200-member Upper House into a directly elected body. Members were also prohibited from joining any political party. The 500-member House of Representatives was divided into 400 single constituency members and 100 from the nation-wide party-list. The provision for a party-list has been viewed as an attempt to improve the nature and constitution of political parties in the country, and impose party discipline to prevent instances of "turncoatism".

It was during the first democratic elections of 2001 that Thaksin's TRT party made its first foray into Thai politics. It won the majority in Parliament and has since consolidated its position by negotiating coalitions with other smaller parties. The consolidated position of Thaksin and the TRT in the country's political landscape has raised a lot of concerns about the potential marginalization of opposition parties and the prospect of reduced effective checks and balance in the system.

CEO-style leadership

Thaksin's style of leadership has been portrayed as that of a driven chief executive officer (CEO) who focuses on quick results at the expense of building consensus and allowing for transparency and accountability — themes that the country's drive to democratic consolidation had sought to achieve. Even Thaksin's economic policies, dubbed as "Thaksinomics", have been described as populist, highly-geared, inflationary, and unsustainable.

To Thaksin's supporters, his hands-on, action-oriented leadership was impressive. His declared successes included not only bringing back economic stability to the country,[24] but also raising Thailand's profile as a driver of growth in the region through his policies of promoting Free Trade Agreements (FTAs) both at the bilateral and regional levels and his support for multilateral economic forums like the Asian Cooperation Dialogue (ACD), APEC and ASEAN+3. Although his critics assail his populist policies, he had successfully launched a subsidized health care programme for the poor, issued loans to rural businesses, and a debt moratorium for farmers. Thaksin's high-end infrastructure projects such as the mass-transit system and new airport have generated a certain buzz in the country's economic activities, but these have also raised issues of profligacy and a lack of transparency. Moreover, the rise in readily available credit facilities to boost the consumer demand-driven policies have similarly raised serious concerns about moral hazards that not too long ago were regarded as factors that contributed to the onset of the Asian financial crisis in 1997. Nevertheless, as one analyst astutely observed, it is precisely these types of policies that have "formed the backbone of Thaksin's administration ... explaining [his] resilient popularity ... in the eyes of the voters".[25]

The strong majority held by TRT after the 2005 elections, (winning 376 out of the 400 elected seats in parliament) has drastically altered the complexion of Thai politics. If the smaller parties had been co-opted earlier, the landslide victory of the TRT effectively diminished other smaller parties. Other than the opposition Democrat party, which suffered a stunning defeat having fallen short of its aim to get 200 seats, is now reduced to 96 seats,[26] Thaksin is on his way to forming a one-party administration, a sentiment that he has often articulated. It is indeed ironic that the growing concerns about creeping authoritarianism in Thailand are happening after the country promulgated a democratic constitution and studiously put in place a number of institutions geared to protect and empower its citizens. The twist in this narrative is perhaps aptly captured in Thaksin's statement in December 2003 when he remarked that, " democracy is not the ultimate goal — as long as the country could progress and the people are happy". The Thai case therefore appears to portend more the consolidation of the position of the prime minister in a paradoxically democratic environment, rather than one of counting milestones in a democratic consolidation.

Fears of sliding back into an authoritarian regime have been exacerbated by some worrying trends with regard to Thaksin's lack of regard and disdain for criticisms about his administration. This attitude has been reflected in many ways, for instance, the complaints by civil society organizations about the rising incidence of human rights abuses during Thaksin's term. The August 2004 Report of the National Human Rights Commission assailed the government for failing to address these problems. According to the report, the incidence of human rights abuses was at its worst between 2002–04. Moreover, the report cited the administration's "war on drugs" policy as the main cause in more than 2,500 deaths. As argued in the report, many of the victims were targets of assassinations by the police and none received fair trial or due process of law.[27]

The same report also lamented Thaksin's high-handed approach to the media when it noted that "freedom of expression and rights to monitor the government have been virtually treated as undermining stability and prosperity".[28] It added that there have been attempts to interfere with the media, "... using networks of cronies" to effectively control them. Forms of media coercion have ranged from the subtle form of withdrawing advertising from newspapers that are overly critical of the government, to the police issuing stern warnings.

The government's high-handed approach has also had serious repercussions on the brewing conflict in the country's southern provinces. Since January 2004, violence in southern Thailand has escalated, especially between some Muslim insurgents and the army. The problem has also spilled over into other violent incidents that appeared to target Muslim and other religious groups, thereby complicating the nature of the conflict. The administration's response has been heavily criticized by several sectors — NGOs, academics, the media, and even the King — all expressing concern about the military approach adopted by the government to address the situation. The tragic Tak Bai incident in October 2004 where 84 Muslim protestors died, mostly during detention by the Thai security forces, only aggravated the problem. The tragedy happened during the Muslim holy month of Ramadan and Thaksin's callous remarks that the detainees suffered from exhaustion caused by fasting only served to reinforce the perception that the central government was insensitive to the sentiments of its people in the south. Furthermore, the government's latest zoning plans for the south, which would classify villages into green, yellow, and red zones, have also caused a lot of concern about the inability of the Thaksin administration to consider alternative approaches to addressing the grinding conflict.[29]

Despite these concerns, however, there are still significant indicators that all is not lost in Thailand's democratization. Democratic institutions created earlier to safeguard the system, such as the National Human Rights Commission, remain independent. And, despite reports of a clampdown on the media, there are still independent media organizations like the *Nation* that have refused to be cowed and have persisted in maintaining the country's record of having one of the freest press in the region. Many Thai academics across the country, while critical of Thaksin, have also been campaigning to put politics "back on the right track".[30]

The Philippines

An Unfinished Revolution?

The narrative of democratic transitions in the region becomes less optimistic when one examines the Philippine case. Unlike some of her neighbours that have recently been through significant shifts in their political systems, the Philippines has had a long history of democratization. Moreover, after having experienced a dictatorial regime under former president Marcos, it has had two "People Power" revolutions. While the first People Power in 1986, which toppled the dictatorship of Marcos, was the most salient in its recent democratization story, what is perplexing is that since then the goal of democratic consolidation has remained elusive.

Instead, the Philippines' political transitions since 1986 have been characterized by severe challenges to its political stability and security. A number of examples attest to this perpetual state of crisis: beginning with a series of attempted military coups during the Aquino presidency (1986–92); allegations of corruption and cronyism that led to impeachment proceedings during the short-lived Estrada presidency (1998–2001) that eventually culminated in the 2001 "People Power II"; attempts at "People Power III" and another coup attempt during the first Arroyo presidency (2001 to early 2004); and the potential threat of another "People Power" at the start of the new Arroyo administration in June 2004. So far, it was only during the Ramos presidency (1992–98) that the country had a respite from the types of challenges to regime stability that have characterized the post-1986 political transitions.

The transitions in the Philippines, like the experiences of her neighbours, also involved the different processes of institutional development. After the 1986 People Power, the country amended its constitution in 1987 to guarantee the revival of its liberal democratic system. One of its important constitutional innovations in this regard was to limit the term of the presidency to a single, six-year term, to prevent the abuse of executive power given the country's experience with martial law.[31] Like Thailand, a number of agencies and courts to institute mechanisms for checks and balances, and improve transparency and accountability have been created. These include the Anti-Graft Court (Sandiganbayan), the Philippine Commission on Good Government, and the Commission on Human Rights.

To widen the space for political representation in the country's legislature, the constitution also allocated 20 per cent of the members in the House of Representatives to be elected through a party-list system (PLS) which would come from representatives of NGOs and "disadvantaged" sectors (for example, the elderly and the handicapped).[32] Moreover, to strengthen the country's electoral mechanisms and bring in active participation from NGOs, the National Movement for Free Elections (NAMFREL), one of the largest non-partisan electoral watchdog groups in Southeast Asia, has been sanctioned to assist the country's Commission on Election (COMELEC) to ensure that elections are free and fair.

As in the case of Indonesia, the Philippines also embarked on a decentralization programme. In 1991, the government adopted the Local Government Code to devolve power to the country's provinces and empower local government units once under the central control of the national government. The most significant achievements in this regard were the creation of autonomous regions in Muslim Mindanao and in the Cordilleras.[33] This Local Government Code in fact was a point of reference for Indonesia when it was formulating its own decentralization programme.

Yet, with all these institutions in place and with the added head start from the rest of her neighbours in the experience of political transitions, the Philippines is facing more political instability and security challenges — something that its democratic system is supposed to have mitigated. The country's elections in May 2004 has been described by many as one of the most bitterly contested elections in the country's history.[34] The election for the country's top two posts was very competitive, with five presidential candidates vying for the post including the incumbent, Gloria Macapagal-Arroyo. Among the four candidates, it was Fernando Poe, Jr. a very popular movie star, who posed the most serious challenge to Macapagal-Arroyo.

Contested leadership

After a protracted counting period that lasted almost two months after the elections, Macapagal-Arroyo won by a narrow margin of 1.1 million votes (40 per cent of the total votes) prompting Fernando Poe, who received 36.5 per cent of the votes, to challenge the results and to bring his protest to the country's Supreme Court. Up until his untimely death in December 2004, Poe was still contesting the results. Despite the solid backing that Macapagal-Arroyo received from the country's business elite and (tacitly) from the international community, her slim margin of victory over Poe reflected the electoral sentiments of the Filipinos who were increasingly disillusioned with the country's politicians who were mostly from rich and powerful political dynasties. The narrow difference of 3.5 per cent between Arroyo and Poe was seen by many as indicative of the widening divide within Philippine society. That many people voted for Poe, in spite of his lack of any political experience over the other competent candidates, was perceived even by the Arroyo camp as the people's protest vote against the establishment. To his supporters, Poe was pro-poor — just as deposed president Joseph Estrada had been; both shared similar backgrounds. Estrada and Poe were popular movie stars who played the role of modern-day Robin Hoods who represented the interests of the poor and the marginalized, and who defended the oppressed and the abused.

When one examines the concerns raised about Poe's lack of competence for the presidency against his enduring popularity among the vast majority of Filipinos — not only the poor but even amongst veteran politicians — the aim of consolidating the state's democratic gains appears to have a long road ahead, particularly since issues of social justice and security remain top on the agenda of any incoming president. Thus within the current political context, at least two major issues have to be addressed if the goal of democratic consolidation is to bear the right results: one is weak institutions and the other is the perennial problem of political legitimacy.

With regard to the issue of institutions, the Philippines has often been described as a weak state due to the inability of its institutions to engender a less divisive political climate and provide for an effective regulatory framework. The problems that followed the 2004 elections, for example, reflect much of the weakness of the country's institutions. Two of these stand out. First, the preponderance of money politics: as political families and personalities compete fiercely for votes, money politics becomes almost the order of the day. The cost of a presidential campaign is reported to be around US$53 million — in a country where half of the population lives on less than US$2 a day.[35] Second, the persistence and allegations of electoral fraud: electoral results were often contested on the grounds of massive cheating and vote buying. An informal survey conducted in the Philippine capital, Manila, revealed a widespread popular perception that the May presidential election result was stolen from the popular movie star, Fernando Poe.[36]

The other issue of political legitimacy is equally crucial. In fact, one could argue that the phenomenon of People Power movements in the Philippines is not because of the absence of democracy but rather, the constant challenge faced by political leaders to gain political legitimacy from its people. Thus, one can argue that there will always be the "threat" of People Power or many more permutations of this type of "unconstitutional" means to institute change unless political leaders are able to command the moral authority from its people to lead the Philippines. The issue of political legitimacy dogged Macapagal-Arroyo during her first term in office (2001–2004). The foiled EDSA III revolt, months after she took over from Estrada, and the attempted coup in 2003, were grim reminders to the president that her mandate to rule was questionable given that she was not elected into office.

Although Macapagal-Arroyo was re-elected in the 2004 elections, her narrow victory over Poe has only added more ammunition for her opponents to raise the legitimacy card. To address this, economic recovery has become a pillar of Macapagal-Arroyo's new administration if only to gain much needed mileage of "performance legitimacy" over her critics. Thus, Macapagal-Arroyo's political legitimacy will depend heavily on her ability to steer the country out of its economic malaise and to bring the benefits of a democratic system to her people.

Concluding Remarks

The preceding discussion of several different transitions in the region presents us with an uneven picture of the prospects for democratization in Southeast Asia. Despite the uncertainties caused by the complex problems and issues faced by different transitioning states, there are nevertheless positive trends that point to a more cautiously optimistic scenario.

First, the holding of the recent elections particularly in Indonesia, the biggest state in the region, indicates that democratization has taken root and is becoming an emerging feature in Southeast Asia's political landscape. Even the concerns about backsliding into authoritarianism or lack of progress toward democratization are no longer confined within state borders but are now increasingly shared by societies and states in the region. One only needs to read between the lines of ASEAN communiqués on Myanmar and the exchanges of comments between leaders of Malaysia and Thailand at the height of the problems in the latter's southern provinces to note that democratization is becoming a serious business in the region.

Second, with the current phase of transitions taking place, there have also emerged new leaders who have made democratization an important platform in their political agenda. In the case of Indonesia, for example, despite some concerns about his military background, Yudhoyono has a huge stake within and outside Indonesia in ensuring that democratization in the country is not endangered. With new leaders also came new actors in the political arena such as the proliferation of political personalities and parties in Indonesia, as well as the entry of younger ministers in its government. Similar trends can be discerned elsewhere, whether these new actors are in the government or in the opposition. This indicates a widening constituency in the region which wants to promote greater democratization.

Third, the transitions have also seen an increasingly assertive and less quiescent public in many of these countries. As discussed above, regardless of the concerns about an increasingly autocratic Thai state, this has not stopped the country's civil society, media, and other sectors in the society from speaking out and censuring their government. In the case of Malaysia, the new administration has had to project a more people-oriented image, refraining from micro-managing the country, and returning more power to its citizens. Even the government in Singapore under a new prime minister has introduced more opening up of public discourse in the city-state. These developments reflect efforts taken by new political actors having to confront and calibrate issues of democratization and/or democratic consolidation.

Last, but certainly not least, against the optimism of democratic reforms being put in place, a major challenge for the new leaders in the region is how to respond to the new demands brought about by these transitions, not to mention the need to address the myriad other challenges that come with a globalized international environment. Thus, even a hands-on leader like Thaksin has had to be reminded that the business of being a political leader is more than just managing a huge corporation. To be sure, given the unpredictability of politics, it has become all the more important for political elites in the region to build a network of relations with other political actors, and with the media and civil society, to manage the changes ahead.

Notes

1   Malaysia and Singapore have often been described in existing literature to be "half-way" houses or semi-democratic states. See, for example, William Case, *Politics in Southeast Asia: Democracy or Less* (Richmond, Surrey: Curzon Press, 2001) and the earlier work edited by James W. Morley, *Driven by Growth: Political Change in Asia-Pacific Region* (New York: M.E. Sharpe, 1999).

2   See, for example, *Pathways to Democracy: The Political Economy of Democratic Transitions*, edited by James Hollified and Calvin Jillson (New York: Routledge, 2000); and *Democracy and Political Change in the Third World*, edited by Jeff Hayes, pp. 1–20 (London and New York: Routledge).

3   Samuel P. Huntington, *The Third Wave: Democratization in the Late Twentieth Century* (Norman: University of Oklahoma Press, 1991).

4   See, for example, Garry Rodan, Kevin Hewison and Richard Robison, *The Political Economy of Southeast Asia* (South Melbourne: Oxford University Press, 2001), and Amitav Acharya, B. Michael Frolic and Richard Stubbs, *Democracy, Human Rights and Civil Society in Southeast Asia* (Toronto: Joint Centre for Asia Pacific Studies, 2001).

5   See, for example, Khoo Boo Teik, *Beyond Mahathir: Malaysian Politics and Its Discontents* (London & New York: Zed Books, 2003); Dan Slater, "Iron Cage in an Iron Fist: Authoritarian Institutions and the Personalization of Power in Malaysia", *Comparative Politics* 36, no. 1 (October 2003); and Edmund Terence Gomez and Jomo K.S., *Malaysia's Political Economy: Politics, Patronage and Profits* (Cambridge: Cambridge University Press, 1999).

6   Badawi comes from a family of Muslim historians and religious leaders. He himself holds a degree in Islamic studies.

7   See, for example, "Malaysia's Anti-graft is No Election Ploy, Says PM", *Financial Times*, 19 February 2004, http://web.lexis-nexis.com, accessed 3 February 2005.

8   "Malaysian Police a Force to be Reckoned With", *Asia Times Online*, 2 June 2004, http://www.atimes.com/Southeast_Asia/FF02Ae03.html.

9   As cited in section on "Malaysia", *Regional Outlook Southeast Asia 2005–2006*, edited by Russell Hiang-Khng Heng and Rahul Sen, p. 33 (Singapore: ISEAS, 2005).

10 See Karim Raslan, "Rolling Back the Green Wave", *Philippine Daily Inquirer*, 4 April 2004, http://web.lexis-nexis.com/universe, accessed 3 February 2005.

11 "Indonesia: The Challenge of Change", Speech by Dr. Susilo Bambang Yudhoyono, President of the Republic of Indonesia at the Singapore Lecture, Singapore, 16 February 2005.

12 See Leonard C. Sebastian, "The Paradox of Indonesian Democracy", *Contemporary Southeast Asia* 26, no. 2 (August 2004): 256–79. See also Jusuf Wanandi, "Legislative Elections and Indonesia's Future", *Jakarta Post*, 21 May 2004.

13 See Sebastian, "The Paradox of Indonesian Democracy"; Wanandi, "Legislative Elections and Indonesia's Future", *Jakarta Post*, 21 May 2004.

[14]   The presidential election was held twice. The logic was if in the first round the winner was unable to get a clear majority, i.e. more than 50 per cent of the votes, the second round would allow for a clearer victory.

[15]   Jimmy Carter, "Surprisingly Fair Elections in Indonesia", *International Herald Tribune*, 16 July 2004.

[16]   While it was during Habibie's term when these reforms were adopted, many civil society organizations had already set the process in train by demanding for change in the political system.

[17]   See, for example, International Crisis Group (ICG), "Indonesia: Keeping the Military under Control", ICG Asia Report, no. 9, September 2000; *Coercion and Governance: The Declining Political Role of the Military in Asia*, edited by Muthiah Alagappa (Stanford: Stanford University Press, 2001); and Terence Lee, "The Nature and Future of Civil-Military Relations in Indonesia", *Asian Survey* 40, no. 4 (July/August 2000).

[18]   Kurniawan Hari, "Indonesia to Inaugurate Bicameral Legislature", *Jakarta Post*, 1 October 2004.

[19]   Carter, "Surprisingly Fair Elections in Indonesia".

[20]   See Indonesian Digest, TBSC-Strategic Communications, no. 23.04, 16 July 2004.

[21]   S.P. Seth, "Is Indonesia Loosing its Moorings?", *Jakarta Post*, 20 August 2004.

[22]   See, for example, Thitinan Pongsudhirak, "Thailand: Democratic Authoritarianism", in *Southeast Asian Affairs 2003*, edited by Daljit Singh and Chin Kin Wah, pp. 277–90 (Singapore: ISEAS, 2004).

[23]   See, among others, John Funston, "Thailand: Reform Politics" in *Government and Politics in Southeast Asia*, edited by John Funston; William Case, *Politics in Southeast Asia: Democracy of Less* (Surrey: Curzon Press, 2002, pp. 147–99); and Suchit Bunbongkarn, "Thailand: Democracy Under Siege", in *Driven by Growth*, op. cit.

[24]   The country has been registering economic growth of between 5–6 per cent.

[25]   Pongsudhirak, "Thailand", op. cit., p. 287.

[26]   The Democrats used to hold 132 seats of the Lower House. At the 2005 elections, it was aiming to increase its seats to 200 but instead it lost 32 and now the opposition is reduced to 96 seats.

[27]   See Anucha Charoenpo, "Report Violates State Right to Iron Rule", *Bangkok Post*, 11 August 2004; and "Rights Report is a Mixed Bag", *The Nation*, 6 August 2006.

[28]   Cited in "Thai Panel Criticizes Move to 'Authoritarian' Rule", *International Herald Tribune*, 5 August 2004.

[29]   See "Joint Session Called on South", *The Nation*, 23 February 2005. "Red" zones refer to areas plagued by violence, while "yellow" zones are areas that need to be closely monitored and "green" zones are areas that are considered safe.

[30]   "Rivals Battle to End Thaksin Era", *Bangkok Post*, 22 February 2005.

[31]   With hindsight, this provision has been deemed by some as too restrictive in allowing continuity of policies. For example, toward the end of the Ramos presidency, many of his supporters wanted this provision to be amended on the grounds that it prevented

Ramos from continuing with many of his policies that arguably had steered the country out of its political and economic malaise.

[32] See Joaquin L. Gonzales, "The Philippines: Continuing People Power", in *Government and Politics in Southeast Asia*, edited by John Funston (Singapore: ISEAS, 2002), pp. 252–89.

[33] Ibid.

[34] See, for example, Mely Caballero-Anthony, "Where on the Road to Democracy is the Philippines?", UNISCI Papers no. 7, October 2004.

[35] "The Philippines Special", *The Economist*, 1 July 2004.

[36] *Asia Times Online*, 1 October 2004.

SOUTHEAST ASIAN ECONOMIES
Towards Recovery and
Deeper Integration

Denis Hew

The year 2004 was very good for Southeast Asian economies. The region was well underway towards economic recovery, underpinned by robust growth in the global economy. In 2004, the global economy achieved a growth rate of 5.1 per cent — the highest in three decades — while world trade volume (goods and services) expanded 9.9 per cent.[1] Stronger global growth was driven by economic rebounds in the United States, Japan and the European Union as well as rapid economic expansion in China.

Southeast Asia registered a strong GDP growth rate of 6.3 per cent in 2004 while the whole of East Asia grew by 7.8 per cent.[2] Robust growth in regional economies had been underpinned by strong export performance and continued strengthening of domestic demand.

Singapore, Malaysia and Vietnam were the star performers in 2004. Singapore's economy grew strongly by 8.4 per cent compared to the previous year's lacklustre growth of 1.4 per cent when the city-state was affected by the SARS epidemic. Like Singapore, 2004 was a good year for Malaysia's economy. Although the Malaysian economy showed some signs of easing in the fourth quarter of 2004, strong growth in the first three quarters (averaging 7.6 per cent) delivered a robust GDP growth of 7.1 per cent for the full year. Both countries' economic performance was driven by strong domestic and external demand.

Vietnam's economy grew by a robust 7.5 per cent in 2004 supported by buoyant exports and strong consumer demand. Other Southeast Asian countries such as Thailand and Laos were also expected to report solid GDP growth rates. Table 1 shows real GDP growth rates for the ten member countries of the Association of Southeast Asian Nations (ASEAN) from 2000 to 2004. Figure 1 shows the real

DENIS HEW is a Fellow at the Institute of Southeast Asian Studies, Singapore.

TABLE 1
ASEAN real GDP growth
(percentage, year-on-year)

	2000	2001	2002	2003	2004
Brunei	2.8	3.1	2.8	3.1	1.1^
Indonesia	4.9	3.8	4.3	4.5	5.6
Malaysia	8.9	0.3	4.1	5.3	7.1
Philippines	6.0	1.8	4.3	4.7	6.1
Singapore	10.1	−1.8	3.2	1.4	8.4
Thailand	4.8	2.2	5.3	6.9	6.2#
Cambodia	5.8	5.5	4.0	4.5	5.0*
Laos	5.8	5.8	5.9	5.8	6.7*
Myanmar	5.8	5.5	5.0	4.5	3.2*
Vietnam	6.1	5.8	6.4	7.1	7.5

^ estimates (IMF)
# estimate (Bank of Thailand)
* estimate, *ISEAS Regional Outlook, Southeast Asia 2005–2006*
Sources: Economist Intelligence Unit (EIU); CEIC; Bank Negara Malaysia (BNM); ISEAS
        Regional Outlook, Southeast Asia 2005–2006; Asian Development Bank, Bank of
        Thailand; IMF.

FIGURE 1
ASEAN-5 real GDP growth, 2001–04

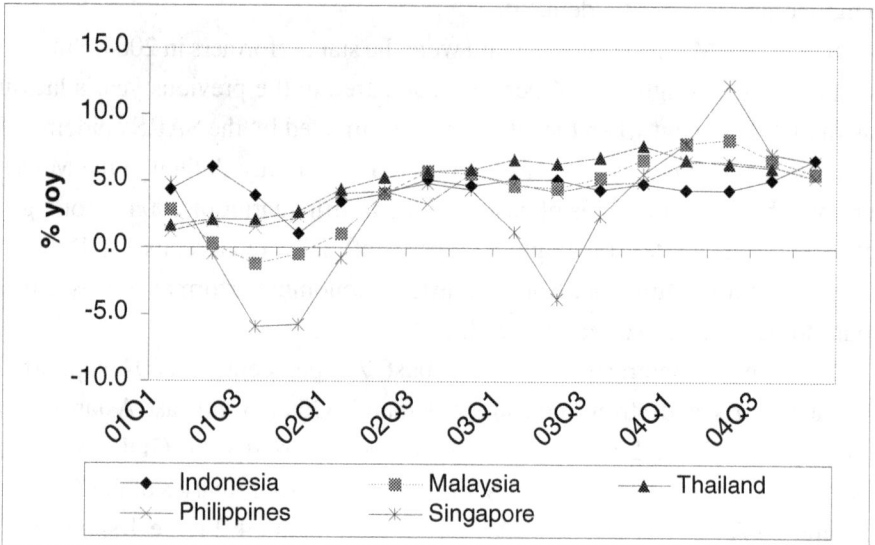

Note: Thailand's GDP growth rates are only up to the third quarter of 2004.
Source: CEIC

GDP quarterly growth for the ASEAN-5 countries (i.e. Indonesia, Malaysia, Philippines, Thailand and Singapore) over the same period.

The favourable external economic environment over the past year led to a rapid expansion of merchandise exports in Southeast Asia with many countries enjoying double-digit growth rates. For the first three quarters of 2004, Southeast Asia's merchandise exports grew by 12.2 per cent, 17.1 per cent and 23 per cent respectively.[3] See also Figure 2, which shows ASEAN-5 countries' quarterly merchandise exports growth from 2002–04.

Consumer spending remained robust in many Southeast Asian countries with private consumption contributing over 50 per cent of 2004 GDP growth in Indonesia, Malaysia, the Philippines and Thailand. (Figure 3 shows the private consumption growth rates of the ASEAN-5 countries.) The continued buoyancy of private consumption in these countries had been supported by lower interest rates, easier access to consumer finance and higher incomes particularly in the rural areas.[4]

Fixed investment was also picking up in Southeast Asia after years of erratic or lacklustre growth. Many of the Asian crisis-affected countries in the region (Indonesia,

FIGURE 2
ASEAN-5 merchandise exports growth, 2001–04

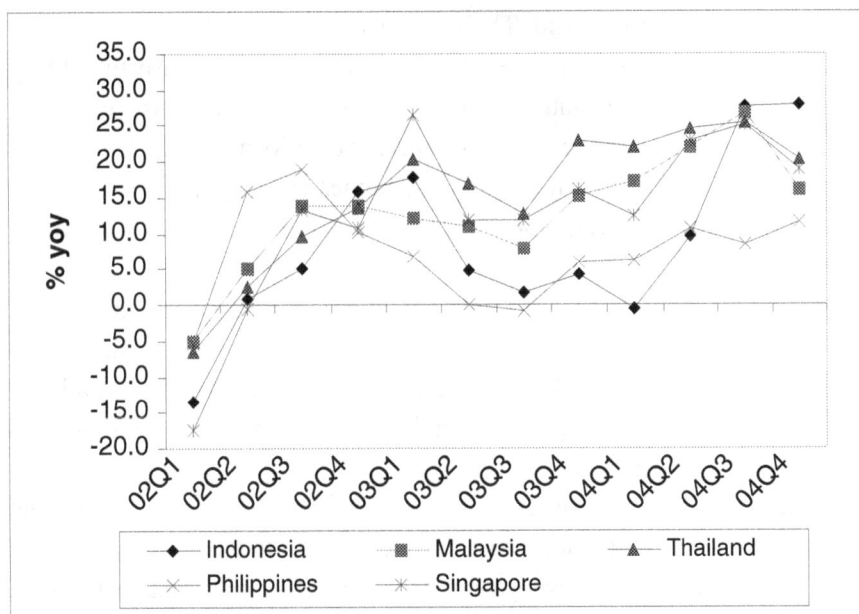

Source: CEIC

FIGURE 3
ASEAN-5 private consumption growth, 2001–04

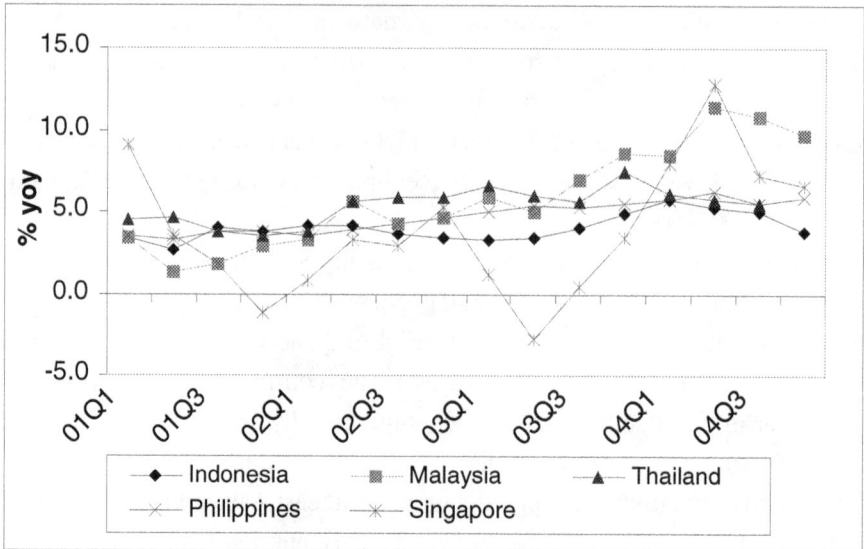

Note: Thailand's private consumption growth rates are only up to third quarter of 2004.
Source: CEIC

Malaysia, the Philippines and Thailand) were largely dependent on private consumption and exports to boost economic growth. But fixed investment began to show a significant positive contribution to GDP growth over the past year or so[5] (see Figure 4). Progress made in reducing non-performing loans, which led to increased bank lending activities, low interest rates, higher capacity utilization, improved business confidence and corporate profitability, all contributing to the revival in investment spending.

Inflation was on the rise in 2004, driven by higher commodity and food prices. This led to tighter monetary policies in countries such as Indonesia, Philippines, Singapore and Thailand over the past year. Looking ahead to 2005, inflation in the region is expected to be manageable with the inflation rate rising slightly to 5.1 per cent from 4.8 per cent in 2004.[6]

Fiscal policies were less expansionary in 2004. However, budget deficits continued to persist in many Southeast Asian countries. In the Philippines, the fiscal situation did not reach a crisis level yet but it remained a serious problem. (Philippines' budget deficit was 4.6 per cent of GDP in 2003 but is estimated to be smaller in 2004 at 3.9 per cent.)[7] New tax measures introduced (e.g., higher taxes on alcohol and

FIGURE 4
Gross fixed investment — contribution to GDP growth in
Indonesia, Malaysia, Philippines and Thailand

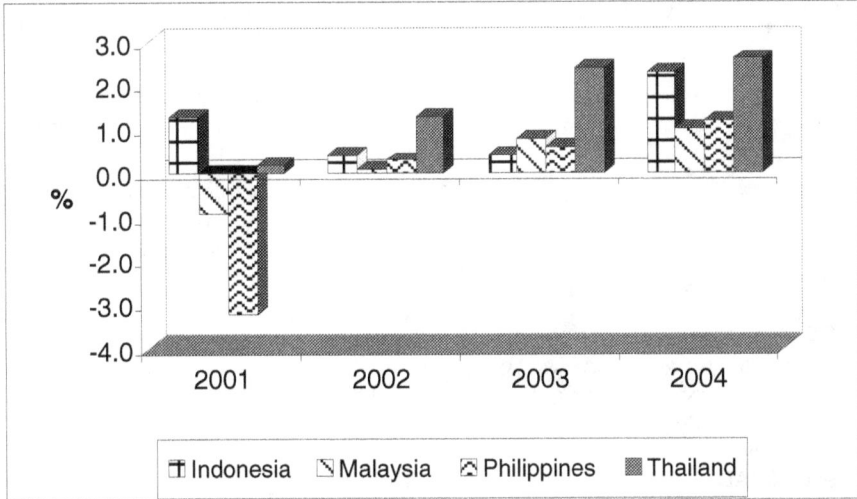

Source: Economist Intelligence Unit.

tobacco) and other revenue-raising legislation bills recently passed (or soon to be passed) as well as efforts to improve the efficiency of tax collection are seen as important steps in fiscal consolidation over the next few years.[8] Malaysia is another country that has been running budget deficits since 1998. Nevertheless, government spending is likely to be moderate in the coming years as the country's new prime minister, Abdullah Badawi, is warier of "mega projects" than his predecessor. The country's budget deficit is expected to reduce from 4.5 per cent of GDP in 2004 to 3.8 per cent in 2005.[9]

China continues to receive the lion's share of the world's foreign direct investments (FDI) — the country received US$53.5 billion worth of FDI in 2003. In the same year, FDI flows to Southeast Asia increased by 27 per cent to US$19 billion.[10] Declining FDI flows to Southeast Asia continued to be a worrying trend (see Figure 5). There continued to be disinvestments in Indonesia although the magnitude was significantly smaller compared to previous years. The remarkably successful general elections in Indonesia in 2004 should improve the investment climate in Southeast Asia's largest and most populous country. According to UNCTAD, there has been a sharp deterioration in Malaysia's FDI performance over the past 10 years. This should be a serious cause for concern as the Malaysian economy is very dependent on FDI to drive its exports.[11] Nevertheless, larger

FIGURE 5
Southeast Asia's FDI inflows compared

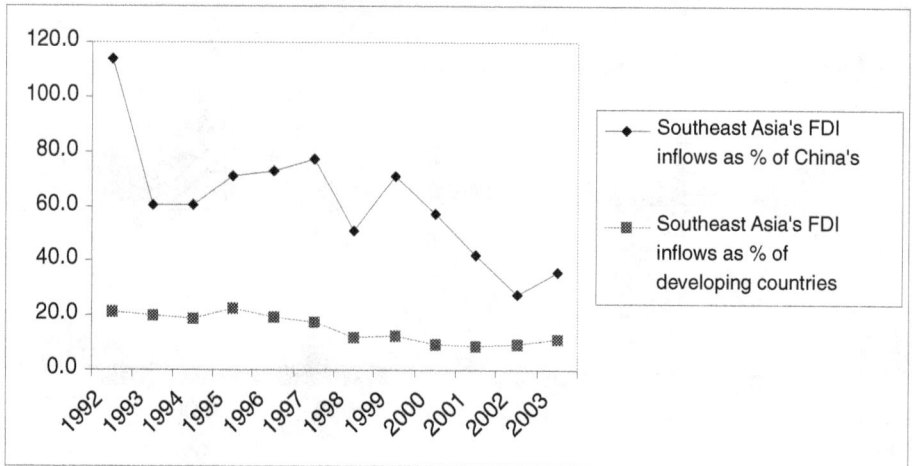

Source: UNCTAD, *World Investment Report 2004.*

investment flows between Asian countries, particularly China, Korea, Malaysia and Singapore, are expected over the next five years, which could benefit Southeast Asia by as much as US$8 billion to US$12 billion.[12]

Risks to Regional Economic Outlook

The main risks that could affect the region's economic outlook in the short term are discussed in some detail below.

•   There are concerns that the United States' persistent and growing fiscal and current account deficits may destabilize the global economy. In particular, the country's current account deficits, which have been increasing since the mid-1990s — rising to an estimated 5.5 per cent of GDP in 2004 — surely cannot be sustainable indefinitely. These deficits are matched or financed by growing surpluses in Japan and a few other countries, creating global imbalances that could disrupt global economic growth.[13] The U.S. dollar's continued weakness against major currencies will also exacerbate the problem of global economic imbalances. (Over the past two years the greenback has depreciated by about 50 per cent against the euro and about 30 per cent against the yen.)

•   Sustained high oil prices could dramatically slow down global economic growth. Oil prices are likely to remain high at least in the short term. Crude oil prices continue to hover over the US$50 per barrel mark, with little sign that prices will fall significantly this year. According to the IMF, a rise of US$5 a barrel could shave 0.3 per cent from global growth.

- Over the past few years, China's booming economy has been an engine of growth not only for Southeast Asia but for the entire global economy. (China's economy grew by 9.1 per cent in 2003 and 9.5 per cent in 2004.[14]) However, China's economy is beginning to show signs of overheating and the Chinese authorities are attempting to facilitate a soft landing through a combination of administrative, monetary and fiscal measures. Nevertheless, there are still concerns that China may face a hard landing (that is, sharp economic slowdown) over the coming year, which would clearly have an impact on the region's growth prospects.

- The terrorist bombing in Jakarta in September 2004, and more recently in Manila in February 2005, underscores the rising threat of terrorism. Indonesia had two other bombing incidents targeting foreigners in Bali in 2002 and Jakarta in 2003. Hence, terrorist hot spots across the region would continue to keep the risk of investing in Southeast Asia high.

- Like the Severe Acute Respiratory Syndrome (SARS) epidemic in 2003, there will undoubtedly be economic costs to the recent outbreak of the H5N1 avian influenza (better known as the bird flu) in several Southeast Asian countries. Since January 2004, 69 cases of H5N1 have been reported in Cambodia, Thailand and Vietnam, of which 46 were fatal.[15] If the bird flu is not monitored and effectively contained, it will surely become a longer-term problem in the region. In fact, the bird flu has re-emerged recently in Vietnam claiming 13 human victims since mid-December 2004. The World Health Organization (WHO) has warned the international community that the bird flu could potentially erupt into a global pandemic.[16]

The Asian tsunami that swamped the coastlines of many countries in South Asia and Southeast Asia on 26 December 2004 was one of the worst catastrophes in over two decades. However, the tsunami disaster will likely have a limited macroeconomic impact on Southeast Asia. The damage caused by the tsunami is largely confined to the rural rather than the industrial areas of affected countries, although the tourism industry will be negatively affected at least in the short term. In fact, the economic costs pale in comparison to the huge loss of human lives (estimated to be over 290,000). To date, US$5 billion of international aid has been pledged while the ADB has set up a US$600 million tsunami emergency fund to support reconstruction and rehabilitation in tsunami-affected countries. It is estimated that a total of US$10 billion would be needed over the next five years for relief aid, reconstruction and rebuilding costs.[17]

Malaysia's diversified economy will only be marginally affected by the Asian tsunami that hit the north-western coast of the peninsula. For example, Malaysia's electronics hub in Penang remains intact as industries there are located in the southeastern part of the island. The province of Aceh, which was the most affected in Indonesia, only accounts for 2 per cent of Indonesia's GDP. Moreover the oil and gas industry in Aceh — which accounts for half of the province's GDP — was not damaged by the tsunami disaster.[18] That said, the loss of human lives (over 100,000 fatalities) and the impact on the local economy in Aceh and North Sumatra have clearly been devastating. The tourism industry in Thailand will certainly be affected as the damage was concentrated in well-known beach resorts in six southern Thai provinces (these provinces account for 1.3 per cent of Thailand's GDP).[19] Heavy industries in Thailand, which are mainly concentrated in the central region, were not damaged by the tsunami. International aid and government spending to facilitate economic recovery in Thailand and Indonesia should begin to take effect from this year.

Peaceful elections in Malaysia, Indonesia, the Philippines in 2004 and in Thailand in February 2005 augur well for the region's short to medium-term economic prospects. Notwithstanding the risks discussed earlier, the global economy should be able to sustain its economic momentum in 2005, albeit at a slower pace. Looking ahead, Southeast Asia's economic growth will be more moderate in 2005.

Recent Developments in ASEAN

The implementation of the ASEAN Free Trade Area (AFTA) has made good progress over the past year. As of September 2004, 98.6 per cent of products in the Common Effective Preferential Tariffs (CEPT) Inclusion List (IL) of the ASEAN-6 countries (ASEAN-5 and Brunei) have been brought down to 0–5 per cent. Meanwhile, 79.1 per cent of products of the newer ASEAN members (i.e. Cambodia, Laos, Myanmar and Vietnam) have been moved into the IL and the tariffs for 69.9 per cent of these products have been brought down to 0–5 per cent.[20] Also, as part of the region's efforts to eliminate non-tariff barriers, a Database on ASEAN Non-Tariff Measures (NTMs) has been established.[21]

During the 10th ASEAN Summit in Vientiane, Laos in November 2004, ASEAN leaders have agreed to eliminate tariffs on 11 priority sectors by 2007 for the ASEAN-6 (ASEAN-5 and Brunei) and by 2012 for the CLMV countries (Cambodia, Laos, Myanmar and Vietnam). This is three years ahead of schedule under the

AFTA.[22] The 11 priority sectors are: electronics, e-ASEAN, health care, wood-based products, automotives, rubber-based products, textiles and apparels, agro-based products, fisheries, air travel and tourism.

Also during the Vientiane Summit, ASEAN signed an agreement with China to remove tariffs on goods, paving the way for an ASEAN-China FTA — potentially the world's largest FTA by 2010 (for the ASEAN-6) and 2015 (for the CLMV countries).[23] ASEAN will also begin FTA negotiations with Japan, Korea, Australia and New Zealand in 2005. Negotiations have also begun for the ASEAN-India FTA, with Malaysia heading the negotiations, and an early harvest programme covering 105 products is expected to be in place by early 2005.

The ASEAN Economic Community

At the Ninth ASEAN Summit in Bali in October 2003, ASEAN leaders have agreed to establish an ASEAN Economic Community (AEC) by 2020. The AEC is one of three pillars (the other two being the ASEAN Security Community and the ASEAN Socio-cultural Community) that make up the ASEAN Community as declared by ASEAN leaders in the Bali Concord II. In line with the ASEAN Vision 2020, it is envisaged that the AEC will be a single market and production base with free flow of goods, services, investments, capital and skilled labour.[24] This bold project would require a greater degree of regional economic integration than exists today in ASEAN.

The ASEAN Economic Ministers' High Level Task Force (HLTF) on Economic Integration unveiled a slew of economic initiatives with clear deadlines to expedite the economic integration process to realize the AEC. These initiatives, which are annexed to the Bali Concord II include:

- Fast-track integration of 11 priority sectors (as highlighted earlier);
- Faster customs clearance and simplified customs procedures;
- Elimination of barriers to trade;
- Accelerated implementation of the Mutual Recognition Arrangements (MRAs) for key sectors (e.g. electrical and electronic equipment and telecommunications equipment); and
- Harmonization of standards and technical regulations.

In the area of trade in goods, the Common Effective Preferential Tariffs (CEPT) Scheme Rules of Origin (ROO) will be improved. This would include making the ROO more transparent, predictable and standardized and taking into account the best practices of other Regional Trading Arrangements (RTAs) including the World Trade Organization (WTO)'s ROO. To ensure transparency on non-tariff measures (NTMs) and eliminate those that are barriers to trade, the following measures will be undertaken over the next two years:

- establish an ASEAN database on NTMs;
- set clear criteria to identify measures that are classified as barriers to trade;
- set a clear and definitive work programme for the removal of such barriers; and
- adopt the WTO agreements on Technical Barriers to Trade; Sanitary and phyto-Sanitary and Import Licensing Procedures and develop implementation guidelines appropriate for ASEAN.

One of the most important recommendations by the HLTF was the creation of a more effective dispute settlement mechanism (DSM) with powers to make legally binding decisions in resolving trade disputes among member states. The number of trade disputes will likely rise significantly as the region moves towards a higher level of economic integration. Hence, a credible DSM would be absolutely critical for the AEC to succeed. The following measures will be undertaken to enhance the DSM:[25]

- establish a legal unit within the ASEAN Secretariat to provide legal advice on trade disputes;
- establish the ASEAN Consultation to Solve Trade and Investment Issues in order to provide quick resolution to operations problems (this would be similar to the EU mechanism); and
- establish the ASEAN Compliance Body.

The complete depoliticization of the DSM process — one of the main aims of the new enhanced DSM — would be a difficult task.[26] Even in the WTO where proceedings are more legalistic, disputes among member countries continue to be politically charged.[27] The other concern is whether there will be sufficient funding to implement the new DSM system. Furthermore, the CLMV countries — and even some of the ASEAN-6 countries — may not have the technical capacity to fully benefit from the ASEAN DSM. Hence, technical assistance and legal training should be incorporated in this new system.

Besides the ASEAN-X formula, ASEAN may also use the "2+X" approach where two member countries that are ready to integrate certain sectors can go ahead first. In fact, the latter approach will particularly benefit Thailand and Singapore since both countries are keen to expedite economic integration and realize the AEC before 2020. Besides having no clear guidelines, this approach could be problematic since it does not require a consensus by all member countries (unlike the ASEAN-X principle). The other concern is that the bilateral nature of this process could lead to a fait accompli where the third "+X" country may be bound to whatever has already been agreed by the first two countries.[28]

Notwithstanding the concerns raised above, the economic initiatives recommended by the HLTF were formulated with the business community in mind. For example, faster customs clearance and the harmonization of product standards and technical regulations are clearly aimed at reducing the transaction costs of doing business in the region to make it attractive to multinational corporations as well as domestic enterprises that want to become regional players.

Why form such an economic community? In this increasingly competitive environment, there are deep concerns that Southeast Asia will be overtaken by the emerging market economies of China and India. In particular, there is a growing perception that FDI inflows are being diverted away from ASEAN towards these two giant economies.

Against this backdrop, economic restructuring and integration of ASEAN economies appear to be the best strategy for moving forward. Economic integration within ASEAN has always been motivated by the need to make the region an attractive production base for domestic and foreign companies. By maximizing the complementarities among member countries to achieve economies of scale, and becoming an efficient manufacturer of products, ASEAN aims to become a single production base that would be a magnet for attracting FDI inflows.

An integrated ASEAN would also be an alternative to China as a regional production base for multinational corporations (MNCs). Some have referred to this as the "China+1" formula as MNCs would prefer to diversify their risk by investing in an alternative regional site rather than "put all their eggs" in one basket and invest solely in China.

Achieving a higher level of economic integration may seem daunting at first glance but ASEAN is not starting from scratch. This is because ASEAN has already put in place potential building blocks towards achieving the AEC. These potential building blocks would include economic integration initiatives such as AFTA, ASEAN Framework Agreement on Services (AFAS) and the ASEAN Investment Area (AIA). Looked at holistically, the formation of an AEC could be seen as a logical step up the economic integration ladder.

The European Experience in Economic Integration

A study by the consulting firm McKinsey provides a good starting point to examine the AEC concept wherein they recommend to start off the AEC with sectoral integration involving the establishment of common external tariff in a few key sectors, such as electronics and consumer goods, in which most ASEAN countries are export-competitive.[29]

This is envisaged to be somewhat similar to the European experience where the first approach in economic integration was sectoral integration along the lines of neo-functionalist theory. It is argued that limited economic integration in a few key sectors will have a positive spillover into other sectors. Thus, the European Coal and Steel Community (ECSC) was set up in 1952 with France, West Germany, Italy and the Benelux countries (Belgium, Netherlands and Luxembourg) as members. It established a customs union in coal and steel, abolishing tariffs and trade restrictions in these goods between member countries. In the Treaty of Rome in 1957, the ECSC was subsumed under the European Economic Community (EEC), which extended the same principles to all manufactured goods.

The ECSC is important as it was the first successful integration exercise and was formed as part of the post-war drive for closer economic and political cooperation in Europe. The ECSC was instrumental in setting up several key institutions (e.g. the Court of Justice) which helped to underpin a unique institutional structure with both supranational and intergovernmental elements.

In some ways, the formation of an AEC could possibly draw valuable lessons from the European experience in economic integration. However, given that the global trading system has changed dramatically since the formation of the EEC, with the advent of the WTO and the rapid proliferation of bilateral and regional FTAs, it is likely that ASEAN should devise its own model of economic integration to suit its needs.

Institutional Development

It is also important to note that deeper economic integration in ASEAN cannot be successfully achieved without establishment of a stronger institutional structure with a better enforcement mechanism. There is thus a need to streamline, strengthen and enhance coordination among the existing institutions, as well as design better enforcement mechanisms in order to facilitate and expedite economic integration. In this regard, the European experience is worth noting as institutional development started at an early stage of economic integration. Creation of new supranational institutions may therefore need to be seriously considered in this context.[30]

ASEAN still maintains a very loose institutional structure although there has been a strengthening of its institutions in recent years. ASEAN does not presently operate on the overriding principle of using a formal, detailed, and binding institutional structure to prepare, enact, coordinate, and execute policies for economic integration. Schwartz and Villinger (2004) argue that ASEAN's weak institutional structure has been a major reason for the relatively low impact of ASEAN's erstwhile initiatives to reduce tariffs and eliminate non-tariff barriers.[31] The ASEAN Secretariat in its present form does not have the resources, the enforcement power and sufficient expertise to carry out many of its economic tasks effectively.

Hadi Soesastro (2003) suggests that a major institutional innovation for ASEAN would be the creation of "regional units" staffed by professionals who are formally independent of governments to expedite the integration process.[32] These regional units should also be given charge of areas where common policy approaches have been adopted such as the management of development programmes (e.g. the Initiative for ASEAN Integration).[33]

What is the Goal of the AEC?

A study by ASEAN-ISIS suggests that the ultimate form of integration for the AEC is the creation of a fully integrated market i.e. a common market by 2020.[34] This would mean that by this time the AEC would be declared a common market but it would take into account areas where member countries could reserve deeper integration for a later stage (beyond 2020). ASEAN-ISIS suggests that ASEAN adopts a "Common Market minus" approach where there is an explicit "negative list" that can be brought under the umbrella of the integration project.

A Common Market is understood to be an arrangement in which there are complete free flows of trade, including internal trade — as in a Customs Union, as well as free mobility of labour and capital. Full mobility of labour involves the right to reside and accept employment in all member countries, and mutual recognition of professional and technical qualifications. Full capital mobility requires lack of exchange controls, and full rights of establishment for firms in all countries. Under a Common Market, credible removal of tariffs may require policy harmonization or common policies on taxes, wages, prices, etc. It may even require common rules governing competition and monopoly, as well as in environmental regulations.

This approach focuses on achieving genuinely and completely free flows of trade and investment as the main vehicle for ASEAN economic integration. In view of the wide tariff differentials as well as varying levels of economic development within the region, it is recommended that the "ASEAN-X" formula be formalized so that ASEAN could proceed on a two-speed mode.

However, as it stands, ASEAN governments are not even prepared to create a customs union let alone a European-style common market. Basically, a customs union is essentially a group of countries where trade barriers among member countries are removed and a common external tariff policy is established with non-member countries. It is one integration level above an FTA where tariffs are harmonized among member countries, but they are allowed to have different tariffs with non-members. Given the different degrees of openness and stages of economic development among ASEAN countries, forming a customs union would be extremely difficult to achieve by the given deadline.

Instead, it would be more realistic to envisage the end-goal of the AEC as an "FTA-plus" arrangement that covers a zero-tariff ASEAN free trade area and some elements of a common market. An "FTA-plus" AEC by 2020 would have the following characteristics:[35]

- Free movement of goods, services, investments and capital. This would include achieving a zero-tariff free trade area and the elimination of all non-tariff barriers;
- An attractive regional production platform that would be a magnet for FDI;
- Free movement of skilled labour and creative talent;
- Free movement of tourists from all ASEAN countries;
- Harmonization of customs procedures and minimization of customs requirements;
- Harmonization of standards that are consistent with international standards; and
- A well-developed institutional and legal infrastructure to facilitate the economic integration of ASEAN.

Concluding Remarks

Regardless of which approach ASEAN eventually adopts, implementation policies to realize the AEC must be credible and effective. This would require clear goals, a realistic blueprint to achieve these goals and strong commitment by all member countries of ASEAN. Also, trade and investment liberalization are key drivers of economic integration and should be expedited.

Although a "two-tier ASEAN" seems inevitable given the different levels of economic development in the region, it is important to ensure that the less developed CLMV countries are not left too far behind as a result of deeper economic integration. Appropriate resources including technical and financial assistance should be allocated to the CLMV countries to ensure their full participation in the integration process. In this regard, there is a need to see how the Initiative for ASEAN Integration could be further improved to narrow the development gap.

The East Asian Summit, which will be held in Kuala Lumpur in December 2005, could pave the way towards institutionalizing the East Asian Economic Community (EAEC). The summit would include ASEAN+3 (China, Korea, Japan) countries and possibly India, Australia and New Zealand. It is too early to tell at this stage whether the Summit would benefit ASEAN's efforts to economically integrate. However, there are some concerns that the AEC could end up being subsumed under the East Asia Summit's economic agenda.[36]

Does ASEAN have the political will to integrate amidst these growing challenges? Certainly one of the most valuable lessons to be learnt from the European experience was a strong political desire and a common vision to integrate their economies to form today's European Union. The big question would therefore be whether ASEAN is able to make the crucial decisions in the long march ahead.

Notes

[1] International Monetary Fund (IMF), *World Economic Outlook: Globalization and External Imbalances* (Washington, D.C.: IMF, April 2005).

[2] Asian Development Bank (ADB), *Asian Development Outlook 2005*, April 2005, http://www.adb.org/Documents/Books/ADO/2005/default.asp.

[3] World Bank, "East Asia Update November 2004: Steering a Steady Course", http://Inweb18.worldbank.org/eap/eap.nsf.

[4] ADB, Asia Regional Information Center, *Asia Economic Monitor* online, December 2004.

[5] World Bank, "East Asia Update November 2004".

[6] Economic Intelligence Unit (EIU), "Asia and Australasia: Regional Overview", January 2005.

[7] EIU, "Country Forecast: Philippines", February 2005.

[8] ADB, *Philippines, Country Economic Review* (Manila: ADB, December 2004).

[9] ISEAS, *Regional Outlook: Southeast Asia 2005–2006*, edited by Russell Hiang-Khng Heng and Rahul Sen (Singapore: ISEAS, 2005).

[10] United Nations Conference on Trade and Development (UNCTAD), *World Investment Report 2004: The Shift Towards Services*, 2004.

[11] Ibid.

[12] DBS Bank, "Asia 2005: Year of the Periphery", *The Edge* (Singapore), 14 February 2005.

[13] "Correcting Global Imbalances — Avoiding the Blame Game", Remarks by Rodrigo de Rato, Managing Director of the IMF Foreign Policy Association Financial Services Dinner, 23 February 2005.

[14] ADB, *Asian Development Outlook 2005*.

[15] World Health Organization (WHO), "Avian Influenza — Situation in Viet Nam — Update 11", World Health Organization, 11 March 2005, http://www.who.int/csr/don/2005_03_11/en/.

[16] WHO, "Avian Influenza: Assessing the Pandemic Threat", 2005.

[17] "Triumph over Tragedy: Calamity Changes Asia's Fortunes as Nations from Around the World Rally in Relief Effort", *The Edge* (Singapore), 10 January 2005.

[18] ADB, "An Initial Assessment of the Impact of the Earthquake and Tsunami of December 26, 2004 on South and Southeast Asia", January 2005.

[19] Ibid.

[20] Eighteenth Meeting of the AFTA Council, 2 September 2004, http://www.aseansec.org/16351.htm.

[21] The database can be assessed from the ASEAN Secretariat website, http://www.aseansec.org.

[22] "ASEAN Accelerates Integration of Priority Sectors", 29 November 2004, http://www.aseansec.org/16620.htm.

[23] First ASEAN Economic Ministers and the Minister for Trade of the Republic of Korea Consultation Joint Media Statement, 4 September 2004, http://www.aseansec.org/16374.htm.

[24] The ASEAN Vision 2020 envisaged "a stable, prosperous and highly competitive ASEAN Economic Region in which there is a free flow of goods, services and investments, a freer flow of capital, equitable economic development and reduced poverty and socio-economic disparities" (p. 12).

[25] For more details regarding the enhanced DSM, please see Recommendations of the High Level Task Force on ASEAN Economic Integration (Annex 1: Mechanism of the Dispute Settlement Mechanism).

[26] To ensure depoliticization of the DSM process, an appellate body comprising of well-qualified, independent and experienced professionals will be established as the appeal body for the panels' decisions. It will also adopt the existing WTO DSM panel selection procedures, including the listing of qualified individuals who can serve as panellists and members of the appellate body.

[27] L. Hsu, "ASEAN Economic Integration — A Fillip for the Future", in Trading Arrangements in the Pacific Rim (New York: Oceana Publications, December 2003).

28 Denis Hew and Rahul Sen, "Towards an ASEAN Economic Community: Challenges and Prospects". ISEAS Working Paper, Singapore, 2004.

29 A. Schwartz and R. Villinger, "Integrating Southeast Asian Economies", *McKinsey Quarterly*, no. 1 (2004).

30 Hew and Sen, "Towards an ASEAN Economic Community", op. cit.

31 Schwarz and Villinger, "Integration Southeast Asian Economies", op. cit.

32 Hadi Soesastro, "Towards an ASEAN Economic Community", in *The 2nd ASEAN Reader*, compiled by Sharon Siddique and Sree Kumar (Singapore: ISEAS, 2003), pp. 503–508.

33 At the Fourth ASEAN Informal Summit in Singapore in November 2000, ASEAN agreed to launch the Initiative for ASEAN Integration (IAI) with the aim of narrowing the development gap within ASEAN and assist the newer members in the process of regional integration.

34 ASEAN-ISIS, *Towards an ASEAN Economic Community — A Track Two Report to ASEAN Policy Makers*, Jakarta, April 2003.

35 ISEAS, Concept Paper on the ASEAN Economic Community, Singapore: ISEAS, 26 February 2003.

36 Denis Hew, "Beware Trade Bloc Losing Momentum", *Straits Times*, 18 April 2005.

The Economic Impact of China and India on Southeast Asia

Manu Bhaskaran

Introduction

China's growing economic clout is increasingly felt in Southeast Asia. Competition has intensified in trade and foreign direct investment (FDI). Many companies in the region are finding it hard to compete against the lower prices offered by Chinese competitors. At the same time, China's voracious appetite for imports and the growing numbers of Chinese tourists have also brought good news. Just as the region is adjusting to China's growing economic presence, it is also now evident that India is also casting a potentially competitive shadow over Southeast Asian economies — it is beginning to attract more FDI and it is clearly highly competitive in several service activities.

This chapter will argue that the emergence of China and India will precipitate substantial policy and micro-level changes to the region. These adjustments will help Southeast Asian economies to respond to the growing competition and so permit them to find their own niches in the emerging new division of labour. In the process, there will be many winners and quite a few losers in the region. Whether the balance is a net positive or a net negative will depend on how effectively each country adjusts to the more competitive world that China and India create. It is argued here that the winners will be those countries that have the political will to reinvent policies and the entrepreneurial capacity to adapt and re-engineer the microeconomy.

This chapter will begin with a review of how China and India have affected the regional economies in trade, investment and other economic areas. It will then review how these countries are adjusting to this new world and conclude with an assessment of what the net impact would be on economic growth and development in the region.

MANU BHASKARAN is Partner, Centennial Group and Adjunct Senior Research Fellow, Institute of Policy Studies, Singapore.

Recent Economic Trends

Goods Trade: China's Increased Share of Exports not at Region's Expense

Recent trends in global exports of merchandise goods and of services are presented in Figures 1 and 2 and Table 1. A number of important features stand out:

- Both China and Southeast Asia increased their share of global merchandise exports in 1990–2002. China's increased share did not come at the expense of Southeast Asia in general. India's share has increased much more slowly in trade. Southeast Asia has seen its share of global merchandise exports slip a little from the peak it reached in the mid-1990s but generally has clung on to its global export position.

Given that India's goods exports have not really posed a challenge to Southeast Asia yet, we will focus on China's impact:

- It is also noteworthy (see Figure 3) that China has increased its share of U.S. imports while many Southeast Asian economies have seen their share of the U.S. market diminish.

FIGURE 1
China, ASEAN, raised share of merchandise exports

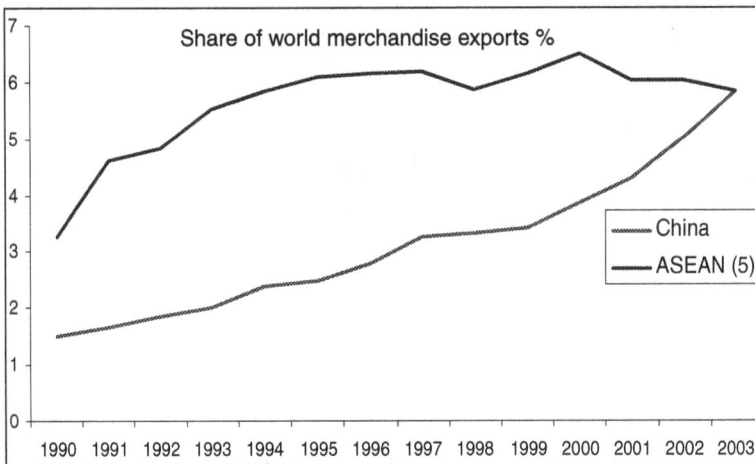

Source: Collated by Centennial Group using CEIC Database and World Trade Organization (WTO) data.

FIGURE 2
Southeast Asian share of U.S. market fell ...

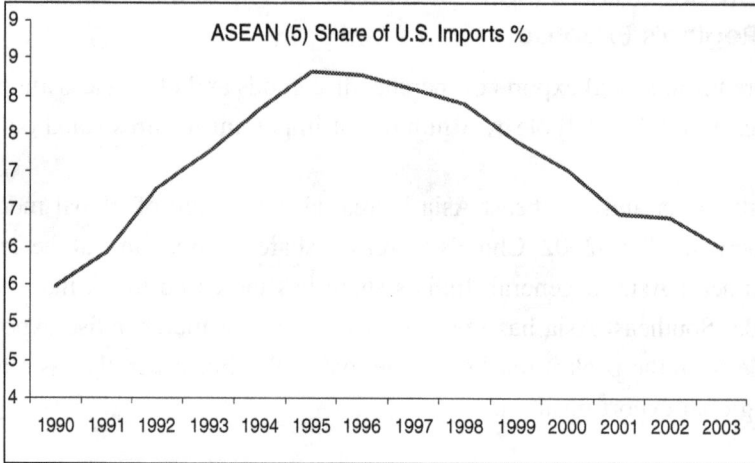

ASEAN (5) Share of U.S. Imports %

Source: Collated by Centennial Group using CEIC Database and WTO data.

TABLE 1
Shares of global merchandise exports by country

	1990	1995	2003
China	1.5	2.5	5.8
India	0.5	0.6	0.8
ASEAN-5	3.3	6.1	5.9
Indonesia	0.8	0.9	0.8
Malaysia	1	1.4	1.4
Philippines	0.2	0.3	0.5
Singapore	1.6	2.4	2.1
Thailand	0.7	1.1	1.0

Source: Collated by Centennial Group using WTO data.

- China's goods imports from Southeast Asia have grown rapidly, in fact with extraordinary strength. As a result, China has seen its trade deficit with Southeast Asia grow rapidly. As Figure 4 shows, the growth of this trade deficit mirrors the expansion of China's trade surplus with the United States.
- At the same time, it is also important to note that Southeast Asian exports to China have grown rapidly (see Figure 5).

FIGURE 3
China's share of U.S. market rose

China - Share of U.S. Imports %

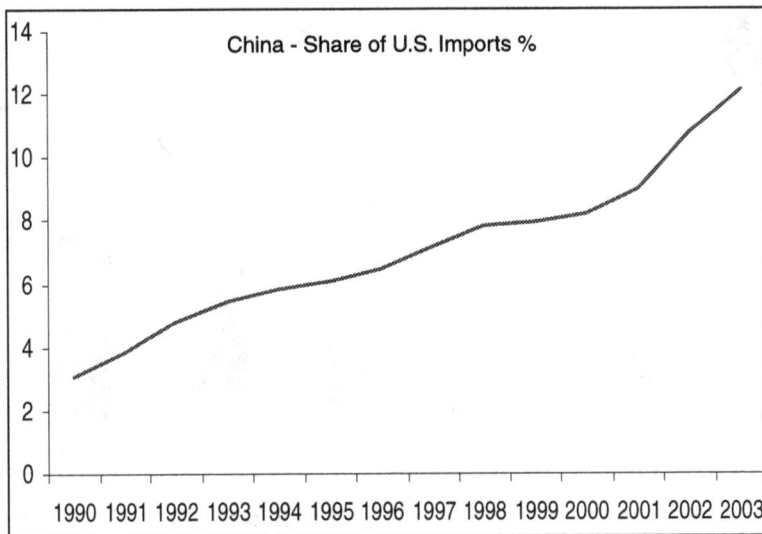

Source: Collated by Centennial Group using CEIC Database and WTO data.

FIGURE 4
China trade surplus with U.S. mirrors deficit with Southeast Asia

China's trade balance with U.S. and Asia, USD bn

■U.S. □ Asia (ex HK)

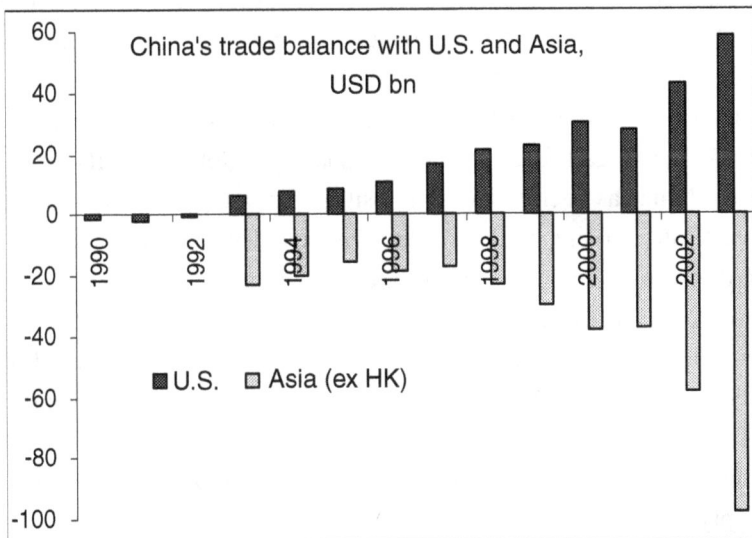

Source: Collated by Centennial Group using CEIC Database and WTO data.

FIGURE 5
Southeast Asian exports to China growing rapidly

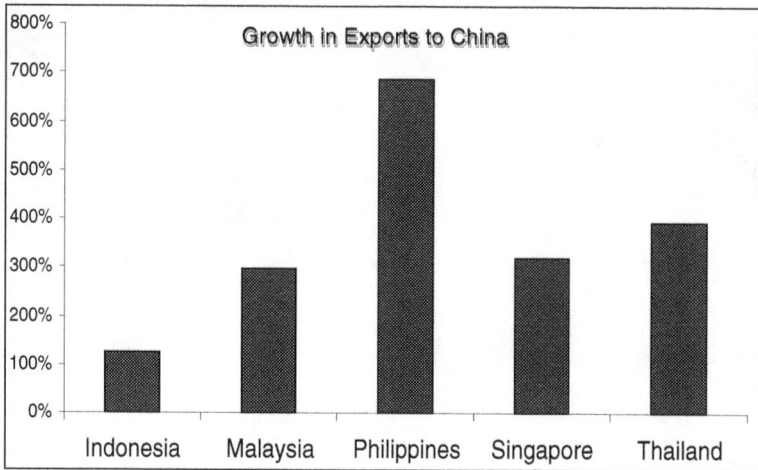

Note: Cumulative percentage growth in exports of each country to China October 1998 to
      October 2004.
Sources: Collated by the Centennial Group using CEIC Database.

This brings out a crucial feature of the new division of labour. China is increasingly
sourcing raw materials and industrial components from Southeast Asia, among
others. Whereas in the past, those industrial components were probably processed
within Southeast Asia into finished goods for export to the U.S. market by a
Southeast Asian economy, these components are now exported to China where the
finished good is assembled and then sent to the U.S. market to be recorded as a
Chinese rather than Southeast Asian export. Since the global data suggest that
Southeast Asia has gained an increasing share of global exports, this changing
division of labour has been a win-win position for both China and Southeast Asia.

Thus, China's rising trade surplus with the United States is a sign of this
changing division of labour — where the latter might have imported these goods
from a range of Asian economies in the past, these imports in final form tend to now
come from China even though much of the intermediate production might have been
undertaken in a Southeast Asian (or other) economy. Similarly, the Southeast Asian
countries' rising trade surplus with China is not indicative of, say, their currencies
being undervalued with respect to the Chinese renminbi (RMB) but of their position
in the supply chain.

Services Exports: ASEAN Share Falling

There is clearer evidence that ASEAN appears to be falling behind in the services arena. Figure 6 shows how:

- Southeast Asia's share of global services exports has fallen (Figure 6). However, if we break down the data by country, this fall is almost entirely due to a sharp fall in the share of the Philippines while the shares of Indonesia, Malaysia, Singapore and Thailand have actually crept up somewhat.
- China's share has grown massively even compared to India's, despite the latter's much-vaunted competitive positioning in offshore services and software development.

FDI Trends — No Respite for Southeast Asia as India Revs Up

China has certainly enjoyed a substantial rise in FDI flows. At the same time, Southeast Asia has seen a material fall in FDI flows, except in Singapore. Many have drawn the conclusion that this means that China is gaining in the FDI stakes at the expense of Southeast Asia. However, the true picture might be somewhat more complex.

FIGURE 6
Chinese share of services exports rose, ASEAN fell

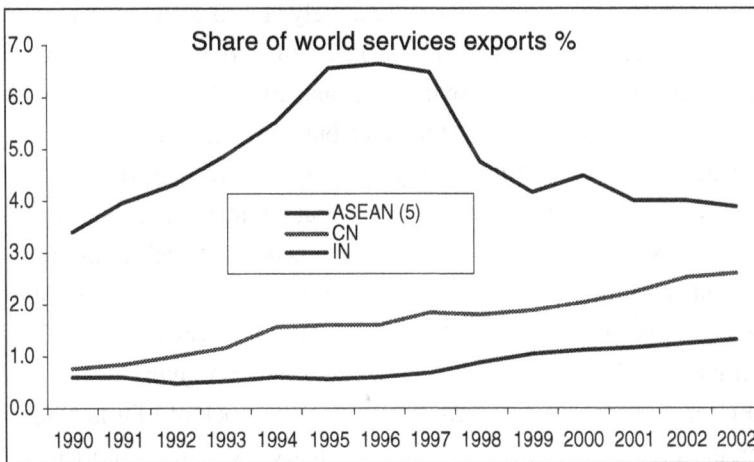

Source: Collated by the Centennial Group using CEIC Database.

As Table 2 shows, while China has seen its share of FDI into developing countries rise sharply in the past two years, on average for the period 1998–2003, its share had actually fallen compared to the 1992–97 period. With the opening of Latin America, the former Soviet Union and India, there are simply more economies that are opening up to foreign investment and making a serious effort to woo FDI. It is not just China that is eating into Southeast Asia's share of global FDI flows: many other countries are involved and China too faces competition.

Note also that year-to-year economic developments and exogenous shocks also play an important role in shaping shares of global FDI flows. Just after the Asian financial crisis (1997–98) it was not just Southeast Asia but also China that seems to have lost out in terms of attracting flows of FDI — to the benefit of Latin America. In 2004, although complete data is not yet available, it is also clear that the euphoria surrounding China's economic prospects has caused China's share of global FDI to rise sharply.

Rising Challenges to Southeast Asia

An analysis of the mechanisms at work in global investing point to more challenges for Southeast Asia in coming years.

China to continue drawing disproportionate share of FDI, India will take more FDI

First, global investors can allocate capital across several countries. Originally, Southeast Asia was open and China and India were relatively closed or investment in these latter countries was difficult for a variety of reasons. Thus, up to the mid-1990s, Southeast Asia received a disproportionate share of global FDI. Then, China opened up and progressively cleaned up its regulatory and business environment thereby making FDI into China feasible and increasingly attractive. Not surprisingly, the optimal allocation of capital to China for any given global company increased sharply — and naturally at the expense of those who had had a head start such as Southeast Asia. It is not clear at what point global investors are comfortable with their allocation to China vis-à-vis Southeast Asia and others — that is at which point FDI flows into China and into Southeast Asia will stabilize at a new optimum level. Currently, the stock of FDI in Southeast Asia is still larger than the stock of FDI in China, which is a substantially larger economy. That suggests that we will still see many more years when China attracts sizeably more FDI than Southeast Asia.

Another reason for believing this is China's huge supply side efficiency gains that have boosted the profitability of investing in China in recent years. In addition,

TABLE 2
Share of FDI flows to developing countries including China, India and Southeast Asia
(per cent)

Regions/Countries	1992–97	1998–2003	1998	1999	2000	2001	2002	2003
Africa	5.0	6.4	4.7	5.0	3.5	8.9	7.5	8.7
Latin America/Caribbean	32.2	38.2	42.5	46.3	38.6	40.1	32.6	28.9
Asia-Pacific	62.8	55.4	52.8	48.7	57.9	51.0	59.9	62.4
China	27.7	23.8	23.4	17.4	16.1	21.3	33.5	31.1
Hong Kong	6.6	11.3	7.6	10.6	24.5	10.8	6.1	7.9
India	1.4	1.6	1.4	0.9	0.9	1.5	2.2	2.5
Indonesia	3.0	–0.7	–0.1	–0.8	–1.8	–1.4	0.1	–0.3
Korea	1.1	2.6	2.6	4.1	3.4	1.7	1.9	2.2
Malaysia	4.9	1.4	1.4	1.7	1.5	0.3	2.0	1.4
Philippines	1.1	0.7	1.1	0.7	0.5	0.4	1.1	0.2
Singapore	7.0	5.8	4.0	6.9	6.8	6.8	3.6	6.6
Taiwan	1.2	1.1	0.1	1.3	2.0	1.9	0.9	0.3
Thailand	1.9	1.9	3.9	2.6	1.3	1.7	0.7	1.0
Vietnam	1.3	0.7	0.9	0.6	0.5	0.6	0.8	0.8

Source: Calculated from UNCTAD, *World Investment Report 2004.*

there is also an added layer of high returns on capital as a result of China being in the upside of its economic cycle. Thus, returns on capital invested in China appear to have caught up and overtaken those available in Southeast Asia (Figure 7) — another reason for FDI to flow into China more than into Southeast Asia.

What is more, India is also more likely to draw investments. As Figure 8 shows, its returns on investment have recovered sharply and as Table 3 shows, its attractiveness to global investors has increased sharply in the past three years, as measured by the A.T. Kearney FDI Confidence Index.

Indian Manufacturing Likely to Become More Competitive

The Indian manufacturing sector is undergoing a significant overhaul, one that is resulting in greater export competitiveness as well as an increased capacity to attract FDI in future.

Efficiency gains from increased competition = greater export competitiveness

Increased external competition as a result of trade liberalization and intensive domestic competition as a result of excess capacity in the 1990s forced Indian manufacturing companies to undergo several years of restructuring. This period has

FIGURE 7
Returns in China up strongly for Southeast Asia

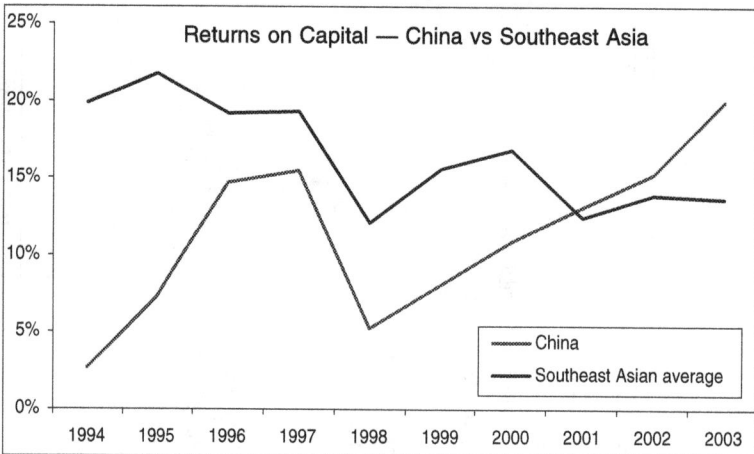

Source: Collated by the Centennial Group using U.S. Bureau of Economic Analysis data.

FIGURE 8
... while Indian returns have recovered

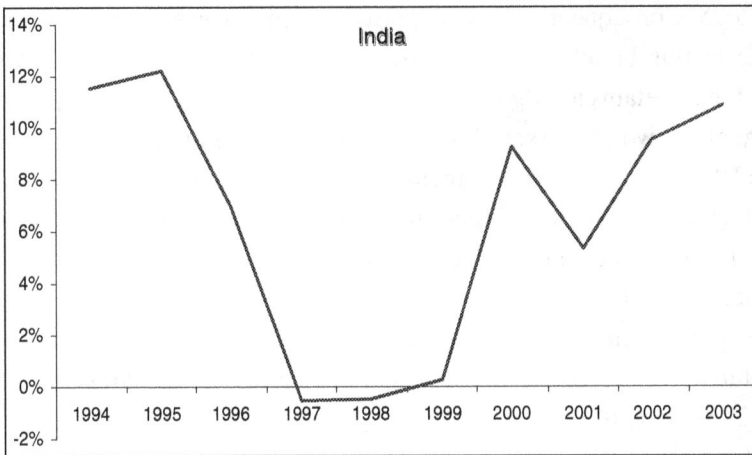

Source: Collated by the Centennial Group using U.S. Bureau of Economic Analysis data.

TABLE 3
India improves in FDI confidence index

A.T. Kearney Survey Ranking	Rank 2004	Rank 2003	Rank 2002
China	1	1	1
India	3	6	15
Hong Kong	8	22	18
Malaysia	15	23	n.a.
Singapore	18	28	22
Thailand	20	16	20
Indonesia	23	25	n.a.
South Korea	21	18	21
Taiwan	25	20	24

Source: Collated by Centennial Group from various issues of the A.T. Kearney FDI Confidence Index.

produced increasing efficiencies. Take Bajaj Auto as an example: exports are expected to be 15 per cent of sales in FY2004/05 compared with less than 5 per cent in FY2002/03. Bajaj used its tie-up with Kawasaki Heavy Industries to re-tool factories, redesign models and expand its product range to include motorcycles. Similarly, Tata Motors used to make 129,000 cars in 1999 with 35,000 workers. Today it makes more than 300,000 with 40 per cent fewer workers.

The textile industry has also been upgrading itself, having invested US$700m in new mills and equipment in the past two years, and US$2.5bn more to be spent through 2005. Consequently, India is poised to exploit several areas of competitive advantage in this broad sector. For example, the consulting firm McKinsey has found that India retains its edge as the world's largest producer of yarn, with a 25 per cent share of the world market plus also being a leading producer of cotton fibre. It also found that Indian skilled labour enables India to be a more competitive producer of terrycloth and denim than China. India also has strong niche positions in upper-market items where customized weaves, colours and embroideries are desired such as bed sheets, towels and rugs.

This process has now also resulted in increasing export competitiveness. Manufactured goods made up 78 per cent of exports in FY2002/03 compared to 56 per cent 20 years ago.

This increased efficiency is now resulting in global producers relocating more production to India: for example, Toyota opened a factory making gear boxes (only the fourth of its kind in the world) for utility vehicles, which will be assembled in other parts of Asia, South Africa and South America. From 2003, Hyundai shifted its entire global production of the Sentro compact car to India. Unilever India was selected by its parent in May 2003 to produce toothpaste for export to Europe after an internal study showed India to be among the cheapest places to manufacture personal care products. LG Electronics of Korea is to spend US$150m by 2007 to make India its second largest overseas production base after China for consumer electrical and electronics products. India is also making headway in information technology (IT) hardware and related manufacturing. IT hardware exports have jumped from around US$300m in 1999–2000 to US$1bn in 2000–2001 and further to US$2.6bn in 2001–2002.

A More Supportive Policy Environment

Policy changes are lending more support to manufacturing sector growth. India has just established its first Chinese-style Special Economic Zone (SEZ) in Chennai. As in China, locating operations in these SEZs frees companies from onerous labour and tax laws. The government is also stepping up infrastructure spending in addition to the US$177bn infrastructure spending already planned. So far in 2004, 12 new private power plants worth US$2.6bn have been approved, which will add 5,000MW to the power grid (see section on construction below). The government has also announced a new trade policy aimed specifically at increasing India's share of exports from 0.7 per cent to 1.5 per cent. Substantial tax and import duty concessions will be offered to exporters.

Surging Investment in Manufacturing

Indian companies are planning US$105bn in capital spending with investment in automobiles, auto parts, machine engineering, textiles and pharmaceuticals estimated to rise 8.2 per cent in 2004 compared to only 3.6 per cent in 2003. For instance, Tata Steel plans to spend US$3.2bn to expand domestic capacity from 3m tonnes to 7.5m tonnes. Foreign investors are also stepping up their investment in Indian manufacturing:

- POSCO is to invest US$8.4bn over 15 years in steel plant with an annual capacity of 10m tonnes. The first phase of 3m tonnes is to be ready by 2009.
- LG Electronics is to invest US$150m in India by 2007 with investments including a second home appliances plant and a GSM handset production plant. Consequently, LG Electronics will double exports of mobile phone sets and other equipment in 2005 to US$140m.

Increased Innovation Capacity

India is also making some headway in developing its capacity to innovate — a key to achieving higher growth rates. Some examples help to substantiate this point: Intel India filed 63 patents in 2003 alone. The clustering of technology firms and schools in Bangalore is providing India's key IT centre with critical mass. Bangalore now has 140,000 IT professionals, 20,000 more than Silicon Valley. Some 50 colleges there produce about 40,000 IT graduates more each year.

India is rapidly expanding its role in global pharmaceutical production and innovation. Eli Lilly is significantly increasing its research & development (R&D) budget from INR85m in 2002 to INR100m in 2003 and INR110m in 2004. The company is mainly focusing on Phase II–IV work in therapeutic areas of diabetes, oncology, infectious diseases, critical care and women's health. Aventis, which had earlier focused more on Phase II and IV studies in India, is now going for Phase III work as well in therapeutic areas of diabetes, cardiovascular diseases and oncology. ABB, the US$23bn global leader in power and automation technologies, plans to double the headcount at its IT R&D centre in Bangalore. The two-year old company will have 100 employees by the end of 2004, with further additions on the cards for the next two years.

But Indonesia Could Well Reverse its Decline

One major reason for ASEAN's underperformance in attracting FDI has been the ongoing political and economic crisis in Indonesia, which meant that Indonesia's

share of global FDI flows has actually been negative. Not only did its decline hurt
the overall figure for all of ASEAN but the travails Indonesia has endured also
served to raise investors' perception of risk for all of Southeast Asia — given that
Indonesia is the giant in Southeast Asia and that its economic and political difficulties
risk spilling over into the rest of ASEAN — especially Singapore, Malaysia and
Brunei to which countries Indonesia is geographically and ethnically close.

However, there are now reasons to be more optimistic about Indonesia. A
revival in political confidence is now underway following Susilo Bambang
Yudhoyuno's election as president. The new administration's policies look likely to
improve governance and reduce the risks that foreign investors had faced as a result
of corruption in the bureaucracy and judiciary. In addition, there are strong signs
that a sustained economic revival is also in process. Data on GDP, capital goods
imports and bank lending are all pointing to the strongest growth since the crisis in
the next one to two years. Higher growth is likely to raise investors' expectations of
returns on capital while improved governance will help reduce the risks associated
with such investment. Flows of net FDI are expected to turn positive in 2005 and rise
thereafter. The tragic effects of the tsunami that hit Indonesia's northern province of
Aceh on 26 December 2004 are not likely to alter this assessment. Aceh as a whole
only contributes about 2.7 per cent of Indonesia's GDP — much of this is from the
natural gas facilities, which being located away from the tsunami-affected areas,
escaped damage. Thus, while the human tragedies should not be underplayed, the
fact of the matter is that the actual economic damage from the tsunami for Indonesia's
economy as a whole was very small.

Nevertheless, FDI is expected to disproportionately favour China and India
with the recovery of FDI into Indonesia only partially mitigating this continuing
trend.

Is Southeast Asia Able to Adjust to These Challenges?

Many observers have felt that Southeast Asia will suffer heavily as a result of
intensified competition from China and India — not only do these two economies
have a significant cost advantage over Southeast Asia but their much larger domestic
market and their impressive pools of scientists and engineers would also provide
them with a competitive edge in higher value activities which Southeast Asia might
attempt to upgrade to.

Such views might be too pessimistic. As Table 4 shows, most companies in
Singapore and Malaysia are reasonably confident of being able to deal with
intensifying competition from the two Asian giants. It is Indonesia and the Philippines

TABLE 4
Southeast Asia confident about competing with China and India

Country	Percentage of respondents agreeing with the view "We can compete with China and India"
Japan	90
Korea	83
Singapore	82
Hong Kong	79
Malaysia	78
Taiwan	77
Indonesia	43
Philippines	38

Source: Survey by Synovate and NFO World Group reported in *Business Times* (Singapore), 10 Dec 2004.
Note: Data for Thai responses not given.

— both countries that have suffered from political crises in recent years — which were less confident.

Adjustments are Underway

The main reason for our confidence that Southeast Asia can cope with the rise of China and India is that there appear to be policy responses at the macroeconomic level as well as companies responding at the microeconomic level to these growing challenges.

Domestic Policy Changes Target Removing Obstacles to Smoother Adjustment

Three sets of countries can be discerned in terms of policy responses to the Asian financial crisis: the relatively better-governed crisis-hit countries of Thailand and Malaysia have moved beyond crisis management to longer-term policy measures targeted at strengthening competitiveness and sustainability. In Thailand, the government of Premier Thaksin Shinawatra has embarked on bold policies to encourage domestic entrepreneurship, achieve greater balance in economic development between urban and rural areas and continue to attract FDI. Similarly, Malaysia is working hard to improve domestic efficiency by forcing the pace of corporate reforms in government-linked companies and by reducing protectionism in some sectors. The government has also introduced policies to grow Malaysia's emerging role as a regional education and health care centre.

Countries less affected by the Asian financial crisis are also responding with increasing resolve. In both Singapore and Vietnam, substantial policy adjustments are underway. Singapore had realized the need for change even before the Asian financial crisis hit it. Since then, it has undertaken sweeping tax reforms and liberalized key sectors such as banking, telecommunications, professional services and the media. The government has also invested heavily in emerging technologies such as biotechnology while successfully attracting global-scale investments in high-end electronics, pharmaceuticals and process chemicals.

But a third group of countries is so saddled with such a heavy burden of political dislocation or such formidable structural weaknesses, that their ability to adjust quickly was impaired, at least until recently. This includes Indonesia and the Philippines. Both Indonesia and the Philippines suffered major political and economic crises in recent years. Indonesia endured the collapse of its currency and banks in 1997, followed by a sharp economic contraction and the ouster of President Soeharto in 1998. The years since have seen a succession of political and economic shocks. It is only in the past two years that the country began to stabilize. With an impressive new administration now in place, Indonesia appears to be now in a position to look beyond the crises and focus on longer-term issues. Thus, its capacity to adjust to the growing competition from China and India is likely to improve.

The Philippines too appears to be coming out of a period of great political uncertainty that included the 2001 ouster of President Estrada in a People's Power coup, which was followed by threats of military and popular unrest. With President Arroyo having won a convincing electoral mandate and the economy performing ahead of expectations, the Philippines too might now be better-placed to undertake longer-term reforms to improve its competitiveness.

Regional Free Trade Agreements

Southeast Asian countries now realize that greater economic integration within the region and stepped up economic ties with other major trading partners will be one means of competing more effectively against China and India. With integration, the Southeast Asian economies can enjoy greater economies of scale and offer investors a larger, more unified, domestic market. Recent months have seen a flurry of new efforts to expand trade and other areas of integration:

- *Regional Initiatives*. ASEAN, the Association of Southeast Asian Nations, is also pursuing greater integration now that the ASEAN Free Trade Area has gained momentum. ASEAN wants to achieve an ASEAN Economic Community by 2020, with 11 industries selected as priority areas for accelerated integration.

- *Bilateral Free Trade Agreements*. Singapore has concluded agreements with New Zealand, Japan, the European Free Trade Area, the United States and Australia. It has also completed negotiations with South Korea and is close to concluding talks with India over similar free trade agreements. As a result of Singapore's success, others are now keen to pursue such bilateral integration initiatives as well — Thailand in particular.

- *ASEAN FTAs with Large Trading Partners*. There are also multilateral trade talks for Southeast Asia to achieve greater economic integration with Northeast and South Asia. China and ASEAN have settled on a framework for a free trade agreement while ASEAN will soon start similar talks with Japan, Korea and India. The United States has also responded with its Enterprise for Asia Initiative under which it has indicated it would favourably consider FTAs with Asian countries.

While ASEAN integration has not been as fast as many have hoped, it has nevertheless made enough progress to produce material economic benefit. For instance, the lowering of tariffs has helped ASEAN-based producers to lower costs by sourcing components from lowest-cost locations. As a result of this improved cost efficiency, there is anecdotal evidence to suggest that, say in motorcycle assembly, ASEAN-based producers have succeeded in mitigating the adverse effect of a surge in Chinese exports. Also, lower barriers to intra-ASEAN trade have enabled producers of consumer goods to consolidate production in one or two locations and thereby enjoy economies of scale they could not enjoy before.

Corporate Restructuring by Domestic Companies Boosts Competitiveness

Corporate restructuring is still a work-in-progress in Southeast Asia. Aggregate data measuring its impact is still unavailable. However, corporate actions in recent years suggests that many companies are working hard to improve their competitiveness. For instance, in Singapore, major companies have been restructuring in order to increase shareholder value. They are focusing on a narrower range of products, relocating lower-value production to cheaper locations, adopting new technologies and extracting more revenue from existing assets. This has been evident, in particular, in the largest companies in Singapore, in particular the government-linked companies. Another response has been mergers and acquisitions to gain economies of scale. This has been evident in the banking sectors in Singapore, Thailand and Malaysia, for instance.

ASEAN Economies Consequently Maintaining Competitive Position

As a result of restructuring and policy changes, ASEAN economies appear to be holding their own in terms of competitiveness. Examples from recent studies on Thailand (Table 5) and Indonesia (Table 6) lend support to this. Thailand has demonstrated a capacity to build competitive advantage in new areas; Table 5 shows new products in which Thailand has developed competitive positioning in recent years. These span a range of processed agricultural as well as manufactured goods as varied as motor vehicles and plastic materials.

Despite all the turmoil it has suffered, it is noteworthy that Indonesia too has managed to maintain some degree of export competitiveness. Note that this applies even in areas such as apparel and clothing where China's competitive advantage is said to be strong.

Chinese and Indian Demand Boosting Southeast Asia

Southeast Asia has benefited in many ways from China's rapid growth and there is increasing evidence that India's resurgent growth is also feeding through to increase demand in Southeast Asia.

TABLE 5
Thailand: Areas of increasing or strong competitive advantage

Improving Competitiveness	New products with strong competitive edge	Declining but still strong competitiveness
Animal feedstuff	Dried fruit	Fresh meat/fish
Food preparations	Natural abrasives	Vegetables
Jute/other fibre	Non-alcoholic beverages	Crude rubber
Leather	Plastic materials	Toys
Rubber articles	Rubber materials	Sound recorders
Textile yarn/thread	Non-electrical wire products	Watches/clocks
Cotton fabrics	Non-metallic mineral	
	manufactures	Footwear
Pottery	Metal tanks	Pearls
Base metal household		
equipment	Road vehicles	Tin
Office machines		Lace
Electrical power machinery		Leather manufactures
Telecommunications equipment		Silk
Domestic electrical equipment		Stone
Other electrical machinery		Spices

Source: Prema-Chandra Athukorala and Suphat Suphachalasai, *ASEAN Economic Bulletin* 21, no. 1 (April 2004): 19–36.

TABLE 6
Indonesia: World Bank assessment of export competitiveness

Product	1995	2001
Coffee, tea, etc	4.3	4.1
Tobacco	0.9	1.5
Crude rubber	15.9	8.9
Pulp/waste paper	2.0	3.2
Metalliferous ores/metal scrap	4.6	4.8
Coal/etc	5.2	7.0
Petroleum/products	3.1	1.9
Gas	15.8	8.0
Fixed vegetable oils/fats	5.6	9.7
Fertilisers	2.0	0.9
Cork/wood manufactures (ex-furniture)	16.7	9.5
Telecommunications/sound recording equipment	1.0	1.3
Furniture	1.9	2.3
Travel goods/handbags	0.9	1.6
Apparel/Clothing	2.4	2.7
Footwear	6.2	4.3
Out of 63 2-digit SITC products		
No. of products with RCA > 1	17	21
% of products with RCA >1	27	33

Source: World Bank Brief for Consultative Group Indonesia Jan 2004, based on UNCOMTRADE data.
Note: RCA = revealed comparative advantage. RCA > 1 implies that country has comparative advantage
in that product.

We have already seen in Figure 5 how Chinese demand has led to a substantial expansion of regional exports to China. Table 7 shows how individual countries have performed — essentially China has increased imports across the board and is set to expand on this when its FTA with ASEAN kicks in and as its demand for commodities and industrial components expands.

Clearly, if China needs to import components from Southeast Asia, that means that Southeast Asians currently possess many areas of competitive advantage; otherwise Chinese demand would have been satisfied by domestic producers.

Tourism — China and India have Rising Impact

Inflows of Chinese and Indian tourists have become progressively more important to Southeast Asia. Table 8 shows how dramatic the impact of Chinese tourism has been in Southeast Asia.

Indian tourism does not appear to have risen as much as Chinese tourism. However, despite their smaller numbers, they have had a disproportionate impact because of their substantially higher spending per head. For instance, in 2003

TABLE 7
Growth of Southeast Asian exports to China

Country	Growth in Exports to China (%) Oct '98 to Oct '04
Indonesia	126.3
Malaysia	297.3
Philippines	686.2
Singapore	319.6
Thailand	393.4

Source: Collated by Centennial Group from CEIC Data.

TABLE 8
**Growing importance of Chinese and Indian tourists
to Southeast Asian countries**

Country	China		India	
% share of Chinese and Indian tourists/total tourists arrivals	1990	2003	1990	2003
Malaysia	0.1	3.3	0.5	1.8
Singapore	negligible	9.3	4.1	5.0
Thailand	1.1	6.2	2.4	2.3

Source: Calculated from CEIC Data.
Note: Data for Indonesia and Philippines not available.

Singapore received 309,423 Indian tourists compared to 568,449 from China but Indian tourists were estimated to have spent S$409.5m compared to S$269.9m by Chinese tourists.

Conclusion

This survey of the impact of the increased economic clout of China and India on Southeast Asia veers towards a more optimistic view of how Southeast Asia will be impacted. Southeast Asia has actually coped quite well in terms of market share of global merchandise exports. Moreover, Southeast Asian economies have expanded their exports to China rapidly while also enjoying the spillovers of growing Chinese and Indian prosperity through, for example, attracting tourists from both the Asian giants. The challenges are real and in some ways will intensify as China continues to draw substantial FDI and as India's manufacturing sector becomes much more competitive in exports as well as in competing with Southeast Asia for FDI. But Southeast Asia will not sit still: Southeast Asian policy-makers are changing policies to cope with the increased competition while Southeast Asian companies are also likely to reinvent themselves so as to be able to find their own niches in which they can prosper.

Note

This chapter focuses mostly on the core Southeast Asian economies of Indonesia, Malaysia, Philippines, Singapore and Thailand due to the lack of data on the other Southeast Asian economies. However, wherever possible every effort has been made to indicate how the other Southeast Asian economies have been impacted.

AUSTRALIA
Contributing to Regional Equilibrium

Robyn Lim

John Howard, Australia's second longest serving prime minister, is now in his "legacy" period. Unlike many, Howard may be smart enough to leave the scene with style, handing over to his successor (presumably the current Treasurer, Peter Costello) with ample time before the next election. From mid-year, Howard will have control of the Senate, which will give him the chance to round off his domestic reform agenda. From unpromising beginnings, Howard may end up being regarded as Australia's most successful prime minister since Sir Robert Menzies.

Howard has also done much to solidify the alliance with the United States, while ensuring that Australia continues to benefit from the booming resource trade with China, which contributed considerably to the 40 per cent rise in the Australian stock market in 2004. Now Howard is intent on improving relations with neighbouring Indonesia.

Having won four successive elections, Howard has also presided over one of the world's strongest economies. Before he retires from the scene, Howard is intent on proving wrong the critics who said that his strong support for the United States in Iraq would undermine Australian interests in Southeast Asia. The success of the Australia-New Zealand-ASEAN summit in Laos in November 2004 provides reason for optimism.

It is a hoary fallacy to claim that Australia's alliance with the United States is at odds with a close relationship with Southeast Asia. Indeed, the opposite has always been the case. Australia's alliance with America has helped underpin strategic stability in East Asia, an area in which great power tensions continue.

Strategic security in Southeast Asia still depends on a maintenance of a balance of power among the East Asian quadrilateral — the United States, China, Japan and

ROBYN LIM is Professor of International Relations at Nanzan University, Japan.

Russia. Unlike in Europe, great power tensions were not resolved with the liquidation of the Cold War. These tensions arise in North Asia, not least in relation to the Korean peninsula. But because East Asia is mostly a maritime theatre, great power tensions manifest themselves around the vital straits that connect the Indian and Pacific Oceans.

Australia can help strengthen security in Indonesia, Malaysia and Singapore by means of bilateral links as well as multilateral arrangements such as the Five Power Defence Arrangements (FPDA). Australia also possesses military strength and related assets that are useful in support of regional security, as well as a growing defence industry and military technology base.

But beyond maritime Southeast Asia, Australia's influence is limited. With a population of only twenty million, its resources are also limited. Further afield, Australia's alliance with America helps tilt the regional balance in ways that suit Australia's interests.

Australia's Choices

Australia is the world's only island continent. Surrounded by water and distant from the main sources of global tension, it is a naturally secure country. Unlike less secure countries such as Singapore, Australia has little instinctive understanding of how strategic interests, military power and threat of force help shape the conduct of international relations. Thus, in the absence of palpable threat, of the kind posed by Japan in 1942, Australia finds it hard to think strategically.

Still, Australia does have strategic choices. One is to remain passive in the face of strategic uncertainty, and concentrate on continental defence. That was the approach which recommended itself to many Australians in the wake of the Vietnam War, widely seen as futile.

Indeed, some politically important elements remain neo-isolationist "little Australians" who say that Australia should defend its coastline, avoiding foreign entanglements. To some, that argument seemed even more cogent in the wake of the 2002 terrorist bombings in Bali, when 89 Australians died. Australia, they said, had made itself more vulnerable to terrorist attack by supporting the United States in the invasion of Iraq.

The Recoil from Vietnam 1972–83: "Other Peoples' Wars"

The neo-isolationist "defence of Australia" approach has its origin in the appalling casualties of the First World War, in which Irish, pacifist and socialist elements were opposed to what they called "other peoples' wars".[1] In the recoil from Vietnam, there was repudiation of the "forward defence" policies under which Australia had previously supported American and British military commitments to Southeast Asia.

The notion of "self-reliance" found expression in the conservative Fraser government's 1976 Defence White Paper. Australia, rather than basing its policy on the expectation of sending forces abroad as part of some other nation's force, would concentrate on continental defence.

Hawke and Keating Governments: Deliberate Ambiguity

In 1986, Kim Beazley, defence minister in the Hawke Labor government (1983–92), commissioned Paul Dibb to review Australia's defence strategy. Dibb concluded that Australia was a defensible continent that, with some important reordering of priorities, could provide for its own defence. That conclusion reflected a desire to assert that Australia's defence would no longer be hostage to the interests of "great and powerful friends".[2]

In Reagan's Washington, the Dibb review caused consternation because it could be read as wishing to take Australia out of the U.S. alliance. The Dibb review also presented difficulties in terms of relations with neighbours. Seeking to present the Cold War as having little to do with Australia, Dibb was forced to find other justifications for defence spending and force structure. Thus the Review gave priorities to "low level contingencies" in the so-called "sea–air gap" to Australia's north which it was said, could arise with little warning. Inevitably, that was seen to be pointing a finger at Indonesia, even though pinprick Indonesian raids in northern Australia were the least likely contingency. Thus the Dibb Review risked making an enemy on the basis of political expediency.

Hawke and Beazley, alive to these risks, modified Dibb's notion of "self-reliance" into the creative ambiguity of "self-reliance within a framework of alliances and regional associations" in the 1987 Defence White Paper.[3] This allowed for possible Australian commitment of forces to situations distant from its immediate region. Such policy flexibility allowed Australia's minimal commitment to the 1990–91 Gulf War, when Hawke sent two frigates and an oiler and called it a "task force". Hawke shrewdly calculated that by committing limited forces at an early stage, Australia would avoid more dangerous options.

Still, this strategy of "shouting early while carrying a small stick" created hostages to fortune. As officially defined in the 1994 Defence White Paper of the Keating government (1992–96), self-reliance required that Australia be capable of defeating any attack that could be credibly mounted against Australia without looking to the United States for combat assistance. That policy seemed prudent, as long as Australia's military means remained sufficient to deter or defeat any threat that it might face. But one problem was that the levels of defence spending envisaged in the Dibb review were never forthcoming.

Moreover, the 1987 White Paper led to a force structure geared towards the least likely contingency — an attack on the continent. That approach, while not as isolationist as during the Whitlam and Fraser years, did little to reassure regional friends and allies. Moreover, the Keating government raised unrealistic expectations, both at home and abroad, about "regional engagement".

"Regional Engagement" under Keating: Old Wine in New Bottles

There was not much that was really new in this approach. That Indonesia was top of the agenda was not surprising, given its proximity and size, as well as the political and economic stabilization under Suharto's New Order. Australia also understood the importance of the moderation of Suharto's foreign policies, which had made possible the formation of ASEAN in 1967. Indeed, in 1995 the Australia-Indonesia security agreement (Agreement to Maintain Security, AMS) sealed a bilateral relationship that had long been evolving.

The agreement provided a basis for general cooperation, and affirmed that their shared security interests outweighed disagreements over such issues as East Timor. It also identified shared interests in regional security that other states were obliged to take into account — including China, which had made vast territorial claims stretching almost to the eastern entrance to the Malacca Straits and seemed to include Indonesia's Natuna gas fields.

The agreement demanded creative diplomacy and bold policy innovation. For Indonesia it was without precedent, while for Australia it was the first agreement concluded with a regional security partner on the basis of reciprocal obligation.

But human rights concerns meant that the AMS, negotiated in secret, was not submitted to the Australian parliament for ratification. That was because the Keating government knew that the East Timor lobby would have been powerful enough to prevent ratification. While the AMS was a remarkable achievement, its long-term viability was always in doubt.

Australia also remained committed to the Five Power Defence Arrangements as a building block of regional security, of which Singapore was the main beneficiary. Singapore armed forces also train, exercise and develop facilities in Australia.[4]

Indeed, among the ASEAN states, tiny Singapore is the strongest reed, as well as the country most willing to say publicly that Australia's alliance with America enhances regional security.[5]

Still, apart from the agreement with Indonesia, FPDA and practical measures of defence cooperation with the Philippines and Singapore, "regional engagement" remained a vague notion. It seemed to refer largely to the pursuit of mutual understanding — and so peace and security — through strategic dialogue, both bilateral and multilateral.

The notion of "regional engagement" had other problems. It implied a congruence of security aims and interests among regional states that simply did not exist. Indeed, ASEAN was to prove itself a weak reed during the 1999 East Timor crisis. There were also some unwelcome surprises in store for the ANZUS alliance.

East Timor: The Limits of Australian "Self-Reliance"

Australians have tended to focus on the risks for them of "entanglement" with the United States. Few seem to realize that alliances are two-way streets. That is, along with security benefits, come risks and costs for both parties. For the United States, for example, alliance with Australia carries the risk of becoming entangled in Australian problems with Indonesia.

During the early stages of the East Timor crisis, the Clinton administration saw risks in supporting Australia. Sandy Berger, the National Security Adviser, believed that the United States did not have a dog in the fight. Yet Howard, despite decades of so-called defence self-reliance, was soon calling for "U.S. muddy boots on the ground". The Dibb Doctrine, concentrating on the so-called air–sea gap, had offered very little to the Army, which was apparently expected to sit on hills in northern Australia. Thus the deficiencies in Army logistics soon became manifest as Australia struggled to convey safely a relatively small number of soldiers a short distance off its shores.

It was not Howard's finest hour, not least because he had ignored warnings about what the Dibb Doctrine had wrought for the Army. Sections of the Australian media were howling "we're on our own". Those Australians usually most hostile to the U.S. alliance were in the forefront of those demanding help from Washington; few appreciated the irony.

As it happened, the Australian military weighed in with their U.S. counterparts, reminding them that Australians and Americans had been fighting together ever since 1918. While the United States did not send combat troops, it played an essential role in the success of the Australian-led intervention. American diplomatic efforts were vital for persuading Indonesia's President Habibie to "request" UN intervention after widespread violence broke out in East Timor after the East Timorese had voted for independence.

A U.S. Navy helicopter carrier, the *Belleau Wood*, carrying 900 U.S. Marines from the Okinawa-based 31st Expeditionary Unit, was sent to deter the Indonesian navy from hindering INTERFET (International Forces East Timor) operations. The U.S. cruiser *Mobile Bay* also helped deter the Indonesian Navy from any thoughts about interdicting coalition ships.

Still, no doubt the experience of the early days of the East Timor intervention was sobering for John Howard. It demonstrated the limits of Australia's vaunted "self-reliance". The Army saw its chance to bury the now discredited Dibb Doctrine.

Thus in a pointed address to the Australian Defence College on 18 June 2002, Senator Robert Hill, the defence minister, rejected the "concentric circles" thinking of the Dibb Doctrine. Hill said that, "threats transcend borders and cannot be met by any one country acting alone. For Australia, it demonstrates again that defence of Australia and its interests does not stop at the edge of the air–sea gap. It probably never made sense to conceptualize our security interests as a series of diminishing concentric circles around our coastline, but it certainly does not do so now".[6] Hugh White, the architect of the 2000 White Paper, continued to preach the Dibb Doctrine from his position as head of the newly formed (government-funded) think-tank, the Australian Strategic Policy Institute (ASPI) until he left in late 2004.[7] But the tide had turned.

That was reflected in the changes in acquisitions policy — especially two large amphibious ships; three air warfare destroyers to be equipped with the *Aegis* battle management system, and airborne early-warning aircraft and air-to-air refuelling aircraft. Opponents in Australia, including those sympathetic to China's interests, complained about a reversion to "forward defence" and fighting "other peoples' wars", to little effect. At last, Australia had moved away from the neo-isolationism induced by its recoil from the Vietnam war.

The "Howard Doctrine": Response to Terrorism

Currently, the terrorist threat has served to remind Australia that it has global interests, including its high dependence on foreign trade, and that threats are best countered at a distance. Howard happened to be in America at the time of the terrorist attacks in New York and the Pentagon. He met President Bush for the first time in Washington on 10th September. Three days after the terrorist attacks,

Australia invoked Article IV of the ANZUS Treaty, on the basis that the United States had been attacked by international terrorists. That was the first time ANZUS had been invoked.

With President Bush determined to attack Afghanistan, which had harbored the Al Qaeda-led terrorists, Australia provided about 1,550 troops to Operation Enduring Freedom. Most of these were members of the Special Air Services (SAS). Especially in light of the UN mandate that the United States sought and received, and the fact that there were few casualties, the Afghan war was relatively uncontroversial in Australia.

Australia's support for the U.S. intervention in Iraq was far more controversial, not least because of the lack of a specific new UN mandate authorizing the use of force. Yet Australia's contribution to the Iraq war consisted, as in Afghanistan, of a "niche commitment". Of the 2,000 forces deployed the main contribution was 150 SAS troops whose tasks included ensuring deployments to the western desert of Iraq to ensure that Iraqi SCUD missiles did not strike Israel.

By the time President Bush announced the end of major combat operations on 1 May 2003, almost all the Australian forces had been withdrawn. There were no casualties. But there were question marks about how long Australia could continue to reap all the benefits of alliance while making only "niche commitments". Many worried that by continuing to pursue defence on the cheap, Australia was creating hostages to fortune.

But in the short term at least, Howard reaped significant rewards at modest cost and risk. When he visited Bush's ranch in Texas in early May 2003, Bush called him a "man of steel".[8] Rewards included an early conclusion of a free trade agreement with the United States that significantly improved Australian access to the huge American market.

Moreover, Howard triumphed over his critics who complained that support for the United States in Iraq would entail serious costs for Australia, especially in its relations with its Asian neighbours. In the lead up to the 9th October 2004 Australian elections, 43 retired diplomats, public servants and senior military officers (the so-called "Gang of 43" whose leading light was Richard Woolcott, former ambassador to Indonesia) signed a petition calling on the electorate to elect Mark Latham, the new Labor leader.

Latham had called for the return to Australia by Christmas of all Australian service personnel still in Iraq. (There were some 850 still there, mostly guarding Australian diplomatic and other military installations.) For the United States of course, that raised the danger that another Western electorate would buckle in the face of terrorist threats, as Spain had done after the Al-Qaeda attacks in Madrid.

Latham also charged that Australia had become more of a terrorist target because of its support for the United States in Iraq. In September 2004, the bombing of the Australian embassy in Jakarta underlined the dangers, even though the improved defences of the building ensured that no Australians died.

But many Australians recalled that Al-Qaeda had threatened Australia because of its intervention in East Timor, an intervention demanded by the anti-American left. Moreover, victims of Al-Qaeda included those in countries such as Tanzania that were not noted for their support for the United States. The "gang of 43"enjoyed much media publicity; whether the electorate was much impressed seems doubtful.

Tactically, Howard showed his usual astuteness, seeing no need to play up national security issues. After all, there had been no casualties in Iraq, and the returning Australian forces had been hailed as "Anzac heroes" — as had the troops sent to East Timor in 1999 and those involved in the mission to stabilize the Solomon Islands in 2003. Yet there was little doubt that security issues played a major role — more so than in any previous election since 1966, fought mainly on the issue of the Vietnam war.

In any event, the Howard government was returned with an enhanced majority. Howard's coalition even unexpectedly gained control of the Senate, which no Australian government had done for more than twenty years.

With the Iraq war now behind it, Australia seems set to resume its traditional bipartisan support for the U.S. alliance. The senior leadership of the Labor party understands that to threaten the alliance is electoral suicide. Indeed, even during the campaign, the long-standing Labor prime minister of New South Wales, Bob Carr, distanced himself from Latham. Not long after the elections Latham stepped down, citing health problems. His successor Kim Beazley is a former leader of the party as well as former defence minister who is a long-standing member of the U.S.-Australia Leadership Dialogue.

Now John Howard, with a fourth election win under his belt and the free trade agreement with the United States in his pocket, is seeking to move towards a similar agreement with China. That is not likely to prove plain sailing. There are divided opinions in Australia, including about the wisdom of granting China "market economy" status and about anti-dumping issues.

"Friend of China?"

Australia's relations with China reached a low point soon after Howard came to office. In the March 1996 Taiwan Strait crisis, when China sought to intimidate Taiwan by firing missiles bracketing its major ports, Australia robustly criticized

China, its then defence minister saying that China's actions would incur consequences. Shortly after, Australia strengthened its alliance with the United States by means of the "Sydney Statement". The U.S.-Japan alliance was strengthened at the same time, leading China to complain about being squeezed between "crab claws". China subsequently challenged Australian warships transiting the Taiwan Strait, an international waterway, and met a robust response from Canberra.

Subsequently, China's efforts to intimidate Australia met with little success. Australia cut aid to China and Howard met the Dalai Lama when he visited Canberra. Yet Howard's visit to Beijing in 1997 proceeded as planned.

Australia also strengthened its alliance with the United States in ways that were not well received in Beijing. For example, in July 2004 Australia signed a Memorandum of Understanding with the United States that foreshadows participation in the development stage of missile defences, despite China's complaints about missile defence.[9]

Moreover, with the re-election of both Bush and Howard, moves are in train for extended training facilities for U.S. forces at three locations in northern Australia.[10] While these will not be permanent bases, the moves are evidence of an expanding U.S. military presence in Australia. Indeed, at any one time most of the military aircraft in the skies over northern Australia are likely to belong to the United States Marine Corps. Australia has also taken a prominent role in the U.S.-led Proliferation Security Initiative, aimed at interdicting North Korean missile exports, contraband and drugs.

With the U.S. alliance beefed up, Howard has sent Beijing a signal that Australia is not easily intimidated, but is keen to benefit from the booming Chinese economy. Thus in October 2003 President Hu Jin-tao was permitted to address a joint sitting of the Australian parliament — previously a privilege reserved for visiting American presidents.

During the visit, Hu signed a letter of intent for a A$25 billion gas deal calling for the China National Offshore Oil Corporation to take an equity stake in an Australian national gas field, and to buy the gas over a 25 year period. It was also widely observed that China's demand for Australian resources meant that China was likely to overtake Japan as Australia's second largest trading partner within five years.

Still, there were more nuances to this visit than met the eye. Australia had not intended that the unelected Hu would be the first Asian leader to address a joint sitting of parliament. After all, Hu, while possessed of considerable personal charm, had been the party secretary of Tibet during a crackdown there, and China remained a Leninist state.

But apple carts were upset when President Bush decided at fairly short notice that he wanted to come to Australia after the APEC summit in Bangkok. He thus addressed a joint sitting of the Australian parliament on 23 October. So because of Bush's late decision, Hu's pre-arranged visit to Canberra had to be put back for a day. He visited Sydney in the interim. Thus the Chinese ambassador was able to leverage this concession by Beijing into a demand that Hu also be allowed to address a joint sitting of parliament. In doing so, Hu upped the ante on Bush by agreeing to a press conference, which Bush unwisely avoided.

Below the surface things were not so smooth. The Australian parliament is noted for robust behaviour. When Bush addressed the joint sitting, he was twice interrupted by members of the Green Party who were strongly opposed to the Iraq war. The U.S. President passed this off with a comment that he valued free speech. But China's ambassador, horrified that Hu would be subject to similar interruptions, successfully demanded that the Greens (as much opposed to China's repression in Tibet as they were to the Iraq war) be silenced when Hu addressed the joint sitting on the following day.

Still, the PRC embassy did not succeed in intimidating the *Australian* newspaper into declining to run a paid advertisement for the Tibetan cause. Howard's own short address in reply to the parliament was also carefully nuanced, using the word "difference" no fewer than four times. It was a considerable test of skill.

Unfortunately, Howard's foreign minister Alexander Downer is not so skilful, not least in relation to the Taiwan problem. But Taiwan is partly to blame for that.

Taiwan Strait Issue

It has long been recognized that differences over the Taiwan Strait issue could present a test of skill for the U.S.-Australia alliance. Australia is a long way from the Taiwan Strait. Moreover, most Australians do not see an issue at stake there that would justify the risk of war with nuclear-armed China — not least because China does not yet have much of a navy. There is no fear of invasion — that is a sharp contrast with how Australians felt about Japan after 1905, when Japan sank the Russian Combined Fleet in the Tsushima Strait. After that, Australians had reason to worry that the British navy might not always be able to protect them.

There is also justified concern in Australia that some in Taiwan seem to think that because Taiwan is a democracy, the United States and its allies are required to support Taiwan whatever it does — including poking China in the eye while expecting the United States to keep it on a leash.

Thus in August 2004, Downer, during a visit to Beijing, said that the ANZUS alliance did not oblige Australia to intervene in a Taiwan Strait contingency. The fact that this statement was technically true did not detract from the furore this statement caused in Australia. Presumably, Downer had fallen victim to the usual Chinese suasion, as well as to concerns that President Chen Shui-bian was pushing the envelope in the lead up to the December legislative elections on Taiwan. Still, it was unwise of Downer to indulge in public hypotheticals.

It was left to the Opposition foreign affairs spokesman Kevin Rudd, a former diplomat who was trained in Taiwan to speak Mandarin, to restate the sensible position that Australia's main interest was the non-use of force, and that Australia was not obliged to say in advance what it would or would not do in a Taiwan Strait crisis.

Indeed, ANZUS does not oblige Australia automatically to offer the United States military support in a Taiwan crisis, or anything else involving attacks on U.S. forces in the Pacific. Alliances simply do not operate that way. But ANZUS does oblige Australia to act, if only diplomatically. Thus the obligation goes a long way towards committing Australia to take sides if it wants to retain U.S. support for its own interests. As noted, such support was expected over East Timor, including by those Australians who normally despise the United States.

Thus the Taiwan issue is shaping up as a test of skill in managing intra-alliances differences. Indeed, in February 2005 press reports suggested that Australia had rebuffed U.S. efforts to persuade it to join in lobbying efforts with Japan and the United States to protest against EU proposals to lift the arms embargo imposed on China in the wake of the 1989 Tienanmen massacre. Indeed, some U.S. officials were even said to have lamented that Australia had been "bullied and bribed" by Beijing.[11]

These reports were overstated. Australia, during Downer's visit to Europe in February, had indicated to the Europeans that he did not think lifting the arms embargo was a good idea. But Howard obviously felt that he had done enough in relation to Iraq to be able to dodge U.S. pressure to engage in a high-profile lobbying effort on this issue. While the United States might have some reason to be concerned about the recent direction of Australia's China policy, the arms embargo issue was not the wisest one on which to hang those concerns.

Rebuilding Relations with Indonesia

As previously noted, Howard is intent on rebuilding relations with Indonesia. In October 2004, he was the only non-ASEAN head of government to attend the inauguration of President Susilo Bambang Yudhoyono. Australia was also quick to support Indonesia after the devastating tsunami that struck Aceh on 26 December 2004. Members of the Australian military were quickly on the ground to help the relief effort. And on a per capita basis, Australia was by far the most generous of all the donors for tsunami relief in the affected regions of the Indian Ocean basin.

Moreover, by the time of the new Indonesian president's inauguration, Alexander Downer was already talking publicly about a new security agreement with Indonesia. While a good idea in principle, this needs to be approached with caution. It should represent the culmination of a process of post-East Timor rapprochement, not the beginning. Otherwise it risks going the way of the 1995 agreement that proved politically unsustainable.[12]

True, for Australia there is considerable appeal in the idea of a new alignment with Southeast Asia's largest country, and the country that has the world's largest population of Muslims. In the wake of the 2002 Bali bombings, cooperation with Indonesia went well. Moreover, good Australian relations with Indonesia, the largest of the Southeast Asian states, enhance Australia's value to the United States as an ally.

For its part, Indonesia might also see value in a security agreement with a U.S. ally, and an agreement that could constrain Australia from actions that challenge Indonesia's integrity in ways that other neighbours cannot. For example, Indonesia is worried about the activities of some Australian human rights advocates, who seek to foster secessionism in West Papua.

Still, many obstacles remain. One large problem is that any new agreement must be ratified by the parliaments of both countries. It is notable that Howard, with his customary canniness, is allowing his foreign minister to run with this idea.

The Vientiane Australia-New Zealand-ASEAN Summit

Australia's presence at the Laos summit on 30 November 2004 was made possible by the departure from the scene of the Malaysian Prime Minister, Mahathir Mohammad, whose anti-Western rhetoric had proved a useful tool for China in its efforts to create a regional grouping that would exclude the United States and Australia. Australia, despite its early support for ASEAN, had been absent from such summits since 1977.[13] Indeed, Abdullah Badawi, the new Malaysian prime minister, seemed willing to resist China's push for an "Asian summit" that would exclude Australia. (Malaysia will be hosting the first meeting of the so-called East Asia Summit in 2005).

With security connections growing between Australia and Japan, Japan was also more willing to resist China's push to exclude U.S. allies such as Australia — not least because it is obvious to most in Tokyo that Japan could not hope to balance

Chinese power on its own in any pan-Asian grouping, especially since South Korea seems more interested in accommodating China than being part of any arrangement that seeks to balance it.

The Laos summit kept on track moves to create an Australia-New Zealand-ASEAN free trade area, building on the free trade agreement that already exists between Australia and New Zealand, as well as between Australia and Singapore, and Australia and Thailand. But all was not plain sailing in relation to pressure on Australia to sign the ASEAN Treaty of Amity and Co-operation (TAC), also known as the Bali Treaty.

The TAC, widely if erroneously referred to as a "non-aggression pact", sets out a code of conduct that binds the parties to settling disputes only by peaceful means. In 1998 the Treaty was amended to allow countries outside the region to accede. China and India did so in October 2003, and Japan and Pakistan followed in mid-2004.

While New Zealand, which in a de facto sense is no longer a U.S. ally, had no qualms about signing up, that was not the case with Australia — even though Japan and South Korea have been willing to sign.

In Canberra, opinion was divided. Some believed that the fact that the United States would not sign the TAC should not prevent Australia from doing so, particularly because they believed that the United States had had no problems with Japan signing the TAC.[14] Indeed, differences between Australia and the United States are not unusual, and Australia is not obliged to follow the United States on every issue. (There are differences for example in relation to the International Criminal Court.) That was the position argued by most of the political class, as well as Kevin Rudd, the shadow foreign minister.

Others, who carried the day at least in the short term, argued that signing the TAC would create too many hostages to fortune. Australia, they believed, had already created too many potential problems for itself by setting up the 1996 Canberra Commission as a means of defusing the public outcry when France resumed nuclear testing in the South Pacific. The Canberra Commission recommended the abolition of nuclear weapons — despite the contradiction created because Australia relies on American nuclear protection, and fervently hopes that Japan will continue to do so. While Howard (who inherited the Canberra Commission from Keating) deftly used it to outflank his Labor opponents from the left, such political expediency always creates hostages to fortune.

For Australia, the problem is that the TAC is linked in spirit to "neutralization" proposals and the 1995 Southeast Asia Nuclear Free Zone (SEANWFZ). While the zone does not inhibit maritime passage, it does encompass the continental shelves and extended Exclusive Economic Zones of the member states. That was presumably a response by ASEAN to fears that China might some day station nuclear-capable missiles on some of the many islands and reefs that it claims in the South China Sea. But given America's strategic needs in relation to maritime mobility and nuclear weapons, even the Clinton administration would not sign onto the SEANWFZ. Moreover, the TAC reminds the United States of a time when it was in strategic paralysis in the mid-1970s, as a product of its withdrawal from Vietnam and the Watergate scandal that destroyed the Nixon presidency.[15]

For these reasons, the Howard government seems unlikely to sign the TAC. But that could change because of the divided opinions in Canberra.

More broadly, whatever the political rhetoric to the contrary, no Australian government is likely to place much faith in so-called non-aggression pacts or the ASEAN Regional Forum (ARF). The tensions among the major actors that determine the East Asian balance of power — and are manifest in Southeast Asia — do not stem from simple misunderstanding. Rather, they are grounded in strategic interest. That is apparent, for example, in rising tension between China and Japan, even as economic interdependence increases.

Dialogue through regional forums such as the ARF is not likely to settle such differences. Only a stable power equilibrium can contain them. Thus Australia's approach to security in Southeast Asia will be to continue to do what it can on the basis of its own resources — while looking to its alliance with the United States as the main means to achieve a balance of power conducive to Australia's own interests. That policy is unlikely to change much whatever government holds power in Canberra.

Notes

Professor Lim is grateful for a Pache A grant from Nanzan University for assistance with this research.

1   60,000 Australians were killed out of a total population of only seven million. Powerful elements of the Australian Labor Party, where the Irish influence was strong, feared that Australian forces would be used to put down Irish rebels.

2   Paul Dibb, *Review of Australia's Defence Capabilities* (Canberra: Australian Government Publishing Service, 1986).

3   Department of Defence, *Defending Australia* (Canberra: Australian Government Publishing Service, 1994).

4   The Singapore army conducts an annual exercise at Shoalwater Bay in Queensland, for example. The Singapore Air Force maintains a permanent training squadron of Supa Puma helicopters at Army Airfield, Oakey, Queensland.

5   Greg Sheridan, "So Much for being Isolated in Asia", *The Australian*, 28 October 2004.

6   "Beyond the White Paper: Strategic Directions for Defence", http://www.stratwise.com/Strategic_Policy_Problems_Ministers_Statement_Fulltext.htm, accessed 1 December 2004.

7   Mr White is now Head of the Strategic and Defence Studies Centre at the Australian National University where Paul Dibb is now Emeritus Professor.

8   Well meant, this remark was utterly inappropriate. Howard remains at heart the suburban solicitor that he always was, even though his middle name is "Winston". Indeed, Tony Blair is supposed to have said that Howard is the most boring man he ever met.

9   See Richard Brabin-Smith, "Australia and Ballistic Missile Defence: Our Policy Choices", *Strategic Insights*, Australian Strategic Policy Institute, April 2004; Rod Lyon and David Dellit, "Ballistic Missile Defence: An Australian Perspective", *Australian Journal of International Affairs* 55, no. 3 (2001): 445–51.

10 These facilities include the Shoalwater Bay Training Area in Queensland, as well as the Bradshaw Training Area and the Delamere Air Weapons Range in the Northern Territory. To be noted in this context is that the railway from Darwin to Alice Springs has finally been completed, linking Darwin by rail with the rest of the country. Shoalwater Bay is to be upgraded to support the first of the *Talisman Sabre* exercises to start in 2007. These exercises will see tens of thousands of Australian and U.S. military personnel undertake land, sea and air training.

11 Greg Sheridan, "PM Defies Bush over China Arms", *The Australian*, 12 February 2005.

12 See Robyn Lim, "Reaching Out: A Security Pact between Canberra and Jakarta has Considerable Appeal but Both Sides should Tread Carefully", *Straits Times*, 26 October 2004.

13 Australia, in 1974, was in fact ASEAN's first dialogue partner. New Zealand followed in 1975.

14 While widely believed, that assertion is not the case. There were considerable differences on this issue in Japan, and the pro-Asia elements in the foreign ministry carried the day in the absence of a powerful defence ministry.

15 The code for this approach is that the TAC is a "relic of the Cold War".

Brunei Darussalam

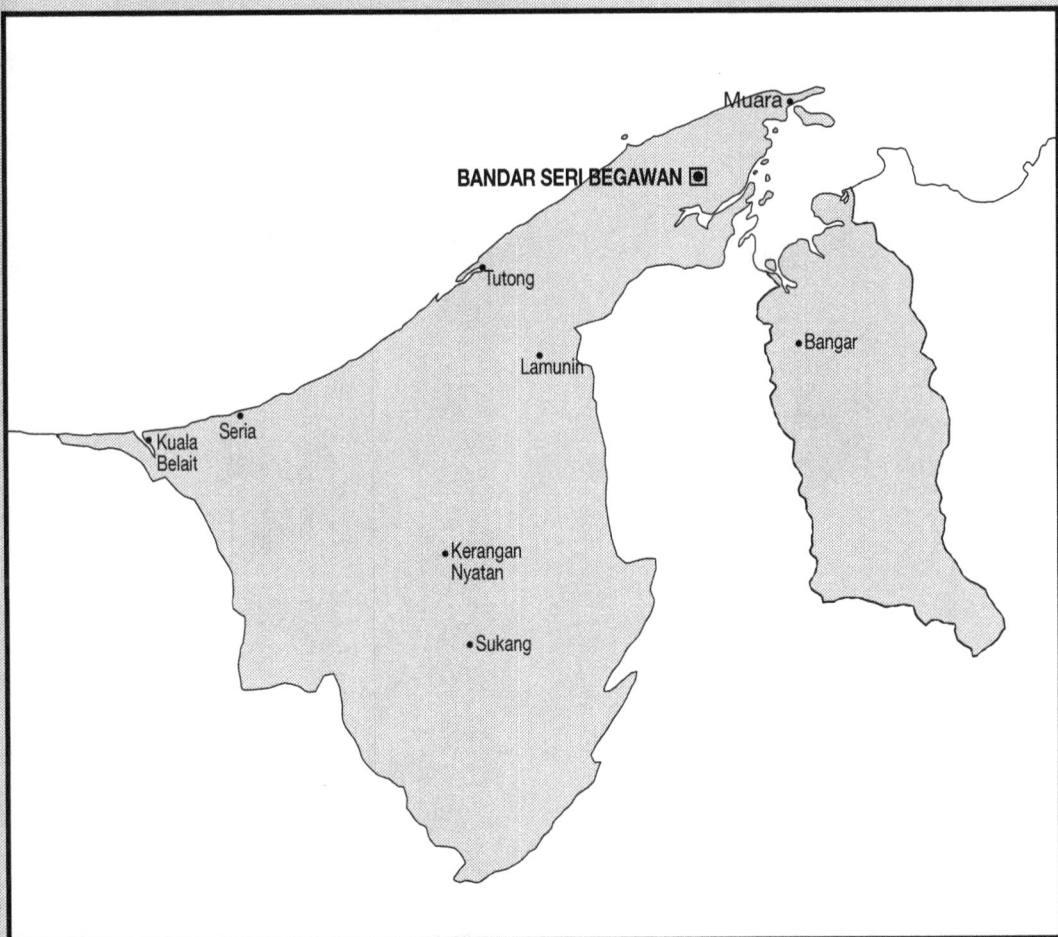

BRUNEI DARUSSALAM
Towards Reform and
Sustainable Progress

Azman Ahmad

Introduction

The year 2004, marking the 20th anniversary of Brunei's independence, signalled unexpected change as the Legislative Council was reinstated after being suspended since 1984. The performance of the economy was lacklustre despite record oil prices. However, the country continued to enjoy peace and stability. The event of the year that most occupied public and media attention was the royal wedding of the Crown Prince.

Human Development

Brunei's quality of life was considered to be on par, if not better, than that attained by some developed countries. The United Nations Development Programme (UNDP) ranked Brunei 33rd among 177 nations on its Human Development Index of 2004 (which took into consideration indices of per capita income, literacy and enrolment in educational institutions, and life expectancy), while in ASEAN, Brunei was ranked 2nd after Singapore.[1]

Education

Brunei scored relatively high in enrolment in educational institutions and literacy rates, surpassing levels attained by some developed countries. Significant efforts have been made to increase resources, broaden access to schools and improve gender parity. Brunei's compulsory education between the ages of 5 and 16 reflected

Azman Ahmad is Dean of the Faculty of Business, Economics and Policy Studies at the Universiti Brunei Darussalam.

the benefits of the learning opportunities in early childhood that promoted subsequent achievement in school and further lifelong learning.

The national schooling structure was in the process of being revamped with the implementation of a pilot scheme of an integrated education system. Since 3 January 2004, a total of 37 government primary schools went for whole day schooling in which pupils in Pre-School, Primaries 1, 2, and 3 were taking either Islamic Education or Extended Civics, and Arabic Language. In this scheme, Arabic Language became a compulsory subject, while Islamic Education was compulsory for all Muslim pupils. Non-Muslim pupils would be provided with the option of studying either Islamic Education or Extended Civics. Previously, children had their secular education in single session government and private schools in the morning, and many then went to religious schools in the afternoon for religious education. However, some 20 to 30 per cent of children either did not go to any school or did not go to religious schools in the afternoon. With the new scheme, parents need to send their children only to one school that would provide both secular and religious education or extended civics.

Universiti Brunei Darussalam (UBD) successfully produced its first PhD graduate, an international student in mathematics, 19 years after its establishment. During the 16th Convocation, His Majesty the Sultan and Yang Di-Pertuan of Brunei, as UBD's Chancellor, hinted at the establishment of another university for the country, while also expressing his delight in the setting up of the Institute for Policy Studies at UBD.

Health

Brunei came in 2nd in ASEAN for achieving and maintaining health standards, right after Singapore, while in the West Pacific region, Brunei was placed 4th, and 40th among 191 countries in the world, according to the World Health Organization (WHO).[2]

The health concerns faced by Brunei authorities were similar to those in developed and affluent societies. Smoking-related diseases, such as cancer, heart disease, diabetes, stroke and emphysema, were listed as the five leading causes of death in the country.[3] The State Mufti issued a *fatwa* or a religious edict that considered cigarettes and smoking as *haram* or forbidden, based on Islamic and scientific findings and views. Cigarettes and smoking adversely affected one's health and with every puff a smoker inhaled 4,000 different chemicals, most of which were deadly. According to the State Mufti, from the Islamic point of view, consuming food and beverage that was toxic was *haram*. This received an endorsement from His Royal Highness the Crown Prince Pengiran Muda Mahkota Haji Al-Muhtadee Billah who stated that the issuance of the *fatwa* on cigarettes and smoking was a step towards achieving a clean and healthy nation free from the adverse effects of smoking. In his opening speech during the National Convention on Health Promotion in July 2004, he further stressed its significance by stating that "the problem and ill effects of cigarettes and smoking habits are not only seen as an individual's problem but as a national and state problem".[4]

Transport

The road accident rate remained high. From January to October 2004, 1,975 accidents were recorded, causing serious injury to 70 people, compared to 52 people in 2003 and 34 people in 2002.[5] A new Road Traffic Act, the Seatbelts For Children Regulations 2004, came into force in January 2004, requiring motorists travelling with children to use appropriate safety gear. Designed to curb the increasing road accidents involving children, those found guilty of violating the regulation would face a stiffer penalty with a maximum fine of B$2,000 and/or imprisonment not exceeding 6 months. In the past 6 years, a total of 1,662 road accidents involving children were recorded in Brunei.

Housing

In the country's efforts towards providing shelter, welfare and comfort to its residents, His Majesty presented land titles and house keys under several housing schemes. In 2004, a total of 605 recipients benefited from such schemes involving grants for houses built on temporary occupied land (TOL) and on land lots under the national housing scheme. However, this number was considered to be inadequate as the demand for housing schemes was far in excess of the ability to meet it. Between 2001 and 2003, the national housing scheme was able to meet less than 2 per cent of the demand.[6] This necessitated a reassessment of both housing and related policies as well as the mechanism for the provision of houses. The national housing scheme faced excessive demand because of a number of factors such as availability of financial loans, provision of land for housing development and infrastructure facilities under the scheme.

A Threatened Natural Environment

Brunei is blessed with natural resources that have been preserved in their pristine condition largely because of the heavy reliance on fossil fuels, small population and strong government support for environmental conservation and sustainable development. Nonetheless, in its pursuit of economic progress, the country has been subjected to ecological degradation and depletion of its natural wealth.

The absence of industries should guarantee an environment with minimal pollution, but Brunei faces a persistent solid waste problem. The country lacks an efficient waste disposal system, particularly noticeable in its well-known Kampong Ayer where domestic rubbish floats along the river as a result of indiscriminate dumping of garbage. It was revealed that Bruneians dumped 490 tonnes of garbage a day, equivalent to 180,000 tones a year, a rate which resembled that of a high-income or developed country.[7] The Sungai Akar landfill is to be closed and a new site, equipped with modern technology, will be designed for the disposal of residual wastes to cope with environmental pollution.[8] Haze made a brief comeback in August 2004, originating from forest fires in Kalimantan and Sumatra. It was not as bad as the haze experienced in 1997/98, but visibility was still affected.

The red tide phenomenon surfaced in Brunei coastal waters stretching from Muara to Seria and lasted for five weeks from mid-February 2004, prompting the Fisheries Department to ban fishing in these areas. Laboratory analysis of water samples taken from the area showed that the concentration of the organism that causes the red tide was more than 30,000 cells per litre of water. This was six times higher than the level that could cause death to those who consumed contaminated fish or shellfish. The Fisheries Department activated the National Red Tide Action Plan and intensified its monitoring activities. The toxic red tide phenomenon resulted in a slowdown of business for fishermen and fishmongers at the local market. A ban was also enforced on the importation of planktivorous fish and shellfish on the basis of reports that red toxins had contaminated several coastal waters in Sabah, Malaysia.

Though Brunei was free from the bird flu virus, which infected several Asian countries, precautionary measures were taken by inspecting nearly all chicken farms in the country to ensure that farmers implemented a farm hygiene programme. Blood samples from chickens were also collected for laboratory testing. The Agriculture Department prohibited the import of birds and chickens and their related species and their products from the affected countries. Brunei health authorities also remained on high alert for any SARS infection by scanning travellers from affected regions.

A Resilient Economy

According to an International Monetary Fund report issued in September 2004, Brunei's economic growth was expected to dip to one per cent in 2004 because of a temporary drop in oil and gas production. Repairs and upgrades of facilities were cited as reasons behind the fall in production.[9] However, the situation was relieved by the hike in world oil prices towards the last quarter of 2004, which was seen as a positive development for the country's economy. Further, in October 2004, Brunei Shell Petroleum (BSP) made a new oil discovery 3 kilometres offshore in the Seria North Flank, in a previously undrilled part of the field. It was estimated that there could be up to 100 million barrels of recoverable oil from the whole of the Seria North Flank.[10]

The Brunei Economic Development Board (BEDB) saw a change at its helm with the appointment of Pehin Orang Kaya Seri Dewa Major General (R) Dato Seri Pahlawan Awg Hj Mohammad bin Hj Daud, a former top military official, as its Chairman. As part of its longer-term efforts to diversify the economy, create jobs and business opportunities, and improve skills of the local workforce, BEDB re-engaged Halcrow Group Ltd, a leading international consultant, to provide advisory services in the marketing and promotion of Pulau Muara Besar as a globally competitive port. Halcrow's experience included planning and implementing successful infrastructure projects at the Jebel Ali Port and Free Trade Zone in Dubai. In view of the high volume and growth in global container shipping and Brunei's strategic position on the main East-West shipping trade route, it was timely to develop Pulau Muara Besar into a world-class port focusing on container trans-shipment.

Halcrow also became the master planner for the investment projects at the Sungai Liang Industrial Park. Halcrow would develop Sungai Liang into a world-class industrial area with shared infrastructure and utilities, including a power plant and a marine terminal to service its manufacturing and downstream projects. The first investment project to start commissioning its plants would be the methanol project in the 4th quarter of 2007. The multi-billion dollar industrial park was estimated to create 6,625 jobs, excluding employment opportunities generated from the spin-offs for small and medium enterprises (SMEs) from related manufacturing and downstream projects.[11]

A B$28 million lens manufacturing plant owned by Unitop Hitech Lens Sdn Bhd, a joint project between a Brunei and Korean company, is to be set up following a groundbreaking ceremony at a 2.4 hectares site in Lambak Kanan (East) Industrial Estate in June 2004. The plant will have the capacity to produce 600,000 lenses of various types for sale in the Asia-Pacific, India, and the Middle East. It will employ 325 personnel for the operation and management of the entire complex.[12]

The two service sectors identified as offering prospects for widening the country's economic base were banking and finance and tourism. Under a newly introduced law, known as the Currency and Monetary Order 2004 (which replaced the Brunei Currency Act 1967), Brunei formed its first Currency and Monetary Board with effect from 1 February 2004. The Board's role was to issue currency notes and coins, maintain external reserves in order to safeguard the international value of Brunei's currency, and promote the monetary policy of Brunei. The new law would streamline the country's banking and monetary laws, bringing them in line with international practice. It was also an indication of Brunei's strong interest in developing a viable offshore banking service. However, the present Currency Interchangeability Agreement between Brunei and Singapore continued to apply, providing for the acceptance of the two countries' currencies at par.

A local Islamic bank, the Islamic Development Bank of Brunei Berhad (IDBB), became the first bank in the country to introduce *syariah*-compliant credit cards, launched by His Royal Highness the Crown Prince. The MasterCards come with zero interest as the bank operation was based on *syariah* principles. They use the M/Chip Select Technology to enhance the security of the card. The cards were also equipped with the MasterCard Merchant Category Code (MCC), which provided enhanced capabilities including protection against transactions not permissible in Islam. Another prominent local Islamic bank, the Islamic Bank of Brunei (IBB) marked a milestone when it became the first Islamic bank in the country to achieve a profit in excess of B$20 million after tax deductions in 2003, an increase of 12 per cent from the previous year, while its assets reached B$2 billion in 2003, a landmark achievement in the bank's history.

In the tourism sector, the Tourism Development Division sought B$13.3 million in 2004 from the B$33.7 million fund allocated under the five-year National Development Plan. The threefold increase in its request (compared to B$4 million in 2003) would be used for events, participation in overseas travel and tourism trade shows, publicity and advertising campaigns. In its bid to lure more tourists, the division focused on ecotourism and adventure as well as golf tourism, targeting tourists from the emerging China market, Hong Kong, and Australia.

Royal Brunei Airlines (RBA), the country's national carrier, contributed considerably to the development of the tourism industry. The airline purchased new Airbus aircraft for its fleet, and opened a new up-to-date First and Business Class passenger lounge at the Brunei International Airport. It introduced "Bluesky Fares" since January 2004, which offered low fares compared to those offered by budget airlines, such as Malaysia's AirAsia, for travel to selected destinations. RBA also unveiled its new Business and Economy Class with state-of-the-art entertainment and seating comfort, which were expected to attract a larger number of passengers in both premium and economy cabins, and introduced Electronic Ticketing (e-Ticketing) to some of its routes as an added convenience.

Restructuring the Political Regime

The year 2004 marked the beginning of a significant transformation of Brunei's political landscape. His Majesty the Sultan and Yang Di-Pertuan of Brunei started off 2004 with his New Year *titah* (royal address) announcing a possible major shake-up of the civil service. After having been suspended since 1984, Brunei reinstated its Legislative Council (LegCo), a move that was widely welcomed when it was announced in His Majesty's 58th birthday *titah*. It implied not only sweeping constitutional changes but exciting political developments.

His Majesty also announced that the committee to review the 1959 Constitution had identified some amendments to be made to the Constitution and other laws. The move was timely, as it would bring the Constitution in line with the special traditions, practices, and customs of Brunei and ensure that it was updated. The amendments also reflected the wish of His Majesty to provide more opportunities to his subjects to contribute constructively to the nation's development through a formal structure of consultation.

Twenty-one members were appointed to the LegCo. They came from the royal family, top civil servants, and community leaders. The six ex-officio members included His Majesty, His Royal Highness Prince Mohamed Bolkiah, Minister of Foreign Affairs, as well as the Ministers for Education, Industry and Primary Resources, and Religious Affairs, and the Attorney General. Five official members were appointed from top civil servants, mainly Permanent Secretaries, while 10 members were drawn from aristocrats and influential members of society.

The LegCo had its first meeting on 25 September 2004 when it discussed key features of the amendments to the 1959 Constitution. The proposed amendments included the reintroduction of elected representatives to the LegCo and increasing its membership to enhance and improve participation and consultation. It was suggested that the number of members in the LegCo be increased from 15 to 45. This would ensure that the composition of the LegCo would be more dynamic and diverse, and facilitate the exchange of views among different interest groups and sectors of society. Another proposal was the introduction of elections in the country, which however would take time as the proper infrastructure needed to be in place to ensure a fair and proper election. Numerous issues were deliberated during the first series of meetings of the LegCo including unemployment, SMEs, housing, bureaucratic immigration and labour procedures.

The milestone announcement understandably ushered exciting response among a cross-section of the community. It was reported that the dying political parties in Brunei, including the Brunei National Solidarity Party (PPKB), were given a new lease of life as they could now become active in the nation-building process.[13] In the wake of the new political climate, PPKB re-elected its party leader Dr Hj Mohd Hatta bin Zainal Abidin, and elected Dr Hj Mohd Shah bin Imam Hj Ahmad as its new Deputy President. The amended constitution of PPKB has now been acknowledged and accepted by the Registrar of Societies (ROS), some three years after the political organization submitted the changes.

While there was no change to the Cabinet set up in 2002, there were several promotions and replacements to top government posts in 2004. The Deputy Finance Minister Dato Awang Haji Yakub bin Abu Bakar was transferred to the Ministry of Culture, Youth and Sports, while Pehin Dato Awang Haji Abdul Rahman bin Ibrahim, the Permanent Secretary at the Ministry of Finance was promoted to the Deputy Finance Minister's post. Several Permanent Secretaries were also appointed at the Prime Minister's Office, and Ministries of Foreign Affairs, Religious Affairs, Finance and Health.

Foreign Affairs and Military Relations

In 2004 Brunei established diplomatic relations with the Republic of Tajikistan and Guatemala. At the same time, it continued to strengthen its existing relations with foreign countries. A number of foreign leaders visited Brunei, including Prime Minister Begum Khaleda Zia of Bangladesh, His Majesty King Carl XVI Gustaf of Sweden, His Majesty King Abdullah II bin Al-Hussein of Jordan, President Leonid Kuchma of Ukraine, and President Sellapan Ramanathan Nathan and Prime Minister Lee Hsien Loong of the Republic of Singapore. These visits generated bilateral agreements encompassing diverse areas including information technology, telecommunications, energy cooperation, education, human resources development, and trade and investment. His Royal Highness Prince Andrew, was in Brunei in late November for a two-day official visit, attending among others the commissioning of the Queen's Gurkha Officers at the British Garrison in Seria.

His Majesty's calendar for the year was occupied with working and informal visits to some friendly nations, including Malaysia, Indonesia, Vietnam, Laos, Egypt and Chile. He attended the 5th Asia-Europe Meeting (ASEM) Summit in

Hanoi, Vietnam, the Asia Pacific Economic Cooperation (APEC) Summit in Santiago, Chile, and the 10th ASEAN Summit in Vientianne, Laos. Some of the issues discussed included trade and investment, human security and counter-terrorism.

His Majesty also travelled to Dalian and Beijing in September 2004, his fifth visit to China. In Dalian, he visited the Dalian Naval Academy, while in Beijing, he met Chinese President Hu Jintao at the Great Hall of the People, and visited China North Industries Corporation, located at Fengtai District, producing mainly defence equipment and products.

Brunei also continued to strengthen its defence ties with its regional and international counterparts through joint manoeuvres. The country's army and navy carried out exercises with Malaysia, Indonesia, Australia and United Kingdom. These military exercises helped promote better understanding and good working relationships through the development of common operational doctrines and procedures.

In October 2004, Brunei joined Malaysia to form a 60-strong international team to monitor a ceasefire between the Philippines and Muslim separatist rebels in Mindanao, where the Moro Islamic Liberation Front (MILF) rebels had been waging a 26-year rebellion for the establishment of an independent Islamic state. Brunei's 10-month participation would mark another milestone in the country's contribution to such overseas operations. The country had been involved in overseas peacekeeping and observing operations in Cambodia in 1993 and 1998. However this time, Brunei's involvement was significant, given that it was invited not only by the Philippine government but also by the MILF itself. The mission suffered an initial hitch when the peacekeepers were denied a base in Zamboanga City by its mayor who feared that their presence could invite violence. Such participation was timely in view of Brunei's renewed commitment to involvement in peacekeeping operations, in line with the Defence White Paper and Defence Strategic Plan Document. The White Paper, launched in 2004, described in detail the roles of the Royal Brunei Armed Forces, their capabilities and the overall contributions from the people that the nation needs for defending Brunei's sovereignty.

A Royal Affair to Remember

Bruneians viewed 2004 as the year of the royal wedding. The opening of the *gendang jaga-jaga* or performance of the royal court musicians, officially marked the beginning of the two-week long ceremonial period of the royal wedding of His Royal Highness the Crown Prince Pengiran Muda Mahkota Haji Al-Muhtadee Billah to Dayangku Sarah binti Pengiran Salleh Ab Rahaman. This was followed by vibrant and elaborate rituals that culminated in the *bersanding* ceremony which was attended by government leaders and blue-blooded guests from around the world, with the likes of Singapore's Prime Minister Lee Hsien Loong and former prime ministers Goh Chok Tong and Lee Kuan Yew, Malaysian Prime Minister Abdullah Ahmad Badawi, Philippine President Gloria Macapagal-Arroyo, Indonesian President Megawati Sukarnoputri, Japan's Prince Naruhito and Prince Richard, the Duke of Gloucester. His Royal Highness the Crown Prince Mahkota Haji Al-Muhtadee Billah would be the 30th Sultan in an unbroken chain of succession of male rulers in Brunei's more than 600 years of history as a Malay Muslim kingdom. The new bride was immediately conferred a royal title after the *bersanding* ceremony as Her Royal Highness Pengiran Anak Isteri Pengiran Anak Sarah.

In a surprise move by His Majesty, the rank of General of the Royal Brunei Armed Forces (RBAF) was conferred to His Royal Highness the Crown Prince shortly before his wedding. It marked a historic chapter for Brunei, particularly for the Royal Brunei Armed Forces. Several top government officials were also bestowed with titles of *Cheterias* and *Pehin Manteris* by His Majesty in preparation for the royal wedding of His Royal Highness the Crown Prince.

The conspicuous absence in 2004 of His Royal Highness Prince Jefri Bolkiah caused as much surprise as had his sudden appearance at several public events in 2003. The Brunei Investment Agency (BIA) had resumed legal proceedings against the former Finance Minister for allegedly reneging on a settlement. The investment arm announced that it was seeking a court order against its former boss to enforce a settlement agreement he signed in May 2000 over the "misappropriation of large amounts of BIA funds". The settlement required the Prince "to give full disclosure of all assets, to explain what had become of funds misappropriated from the BIA and to transfer assets back to the BIA".[14] A younger brother of His Majesty the Sultan, he once headed the Finance Ministry and the Brunei Investment Agency (BIA) before he was relieved of his duties six years ago when his company crashed, leaving billions of dollars in debt. A probe on the billions of dollars missing from BIA took place, but the suit was eventually settled out of court which enabled His Royal Highness Prince Jefri Bolkiah to return to Brunei. He is now believed to have taken up long-term residence in London.

Conclusion

Over the last 20 years, Brunei has achieved development in many areas including infrastructure, the economy and in the social, health and education arenas. The progress and development achieved have enabled the nation to enjoy peace and stability. In 2004, Bruneians continued to benefit from this secure and peaceful environment. The economy still needed diversification from reliance on the oil and gas sector. The resumption of the Legislative Council was seen as a landmark step towards empowering the population in the nation-building process.

Notes

1   *Borneo Bulletin*, 24 October 2004.
2   *Borneo Bulletin*, 30 July 2004.
3   *Borneo Bulletin*, 9 September 2004.
4   *Borneo Bulletin*, 27 July 2004.
5   *Borneo Bulletin*, 9 November 2004.
6   *Borneo Bulletin*, 24 October 2004.
7   *Borneo Bulletin*, 28 July 2004.
8   *Borneo Bulletin*, 1 December 2004.
9   *Borneo Bulletin*, 20 October 2004.
10 *Borneo Bulletin*, 7 October 2004.
11 *Borneo Bulletin*, 2 December 2004.
12 *Borneo Bulletin*, 15 June 2004.
13 *Borneo Bulletin*, 23 Ocotber 2004.
14 *Borneo Bulletin*, 13 October 2004.

Cambodia

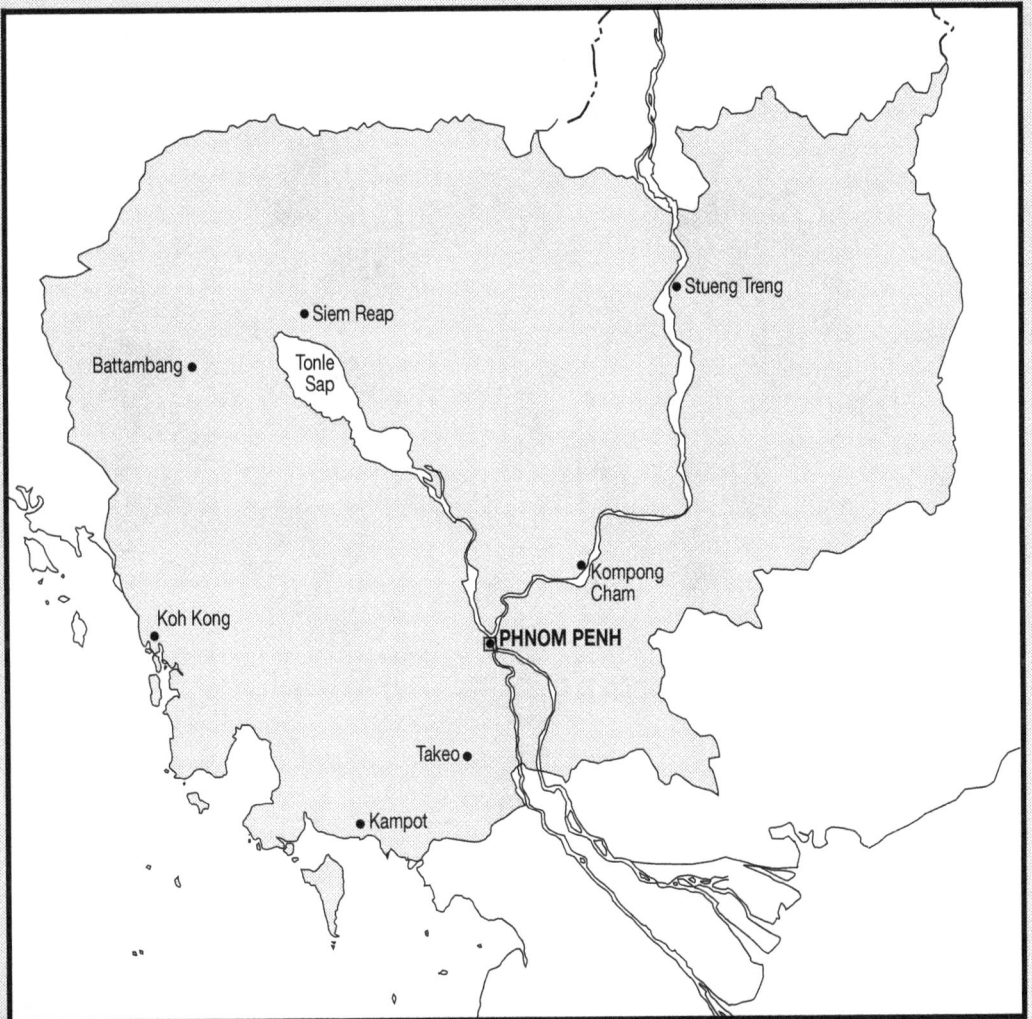

HUN SEN'S CONSOLIDATION
Death or Beginning of Reform?

Steve Heder

Introduction

Events of 2004 were the dénouement not only of the national elections of July 2003 and subsequent political deadlock, but of the decade of political transition since the departure of the United Nations Transitional Authority in Cambodia (UNTAC), and even of the course of Cambodia's political trajectory since the end of French colonialism. The UNTAC elections of 1993 aimed at restoring the country's independence and peace following ten years of communist Vietnamese occupation and insurgency against them and their Cambodian protégées. The elections were intended to launch the country on the path of liberal democracy, free market economics and human rights. None of these had existed in Cambodia since the early 1950s, in the twilight of French colonialism and early years of King Norodom Sihanouk's reign, when nascent liberal democrats and Khmer Issarak insurgents contested his control of the French-constructed administrative state. Democracy, market economics and human rights were suppressed under Sihanouk's post-independence Sangkum regime, murderously expunged during the 1975–78 rule of the Khmer Rouge, and repressed under the Vietnamese who liberated Cambodia from Pol Pot, but imposed their own colonial-like, socialist state-building project.

The UNTAC mandate over Cambodia and the years since have been analogous to the earlier period of contestation for control of a post-colonial state in Cambodia and elsewhere in Southeast Asia. 2004 saw it end with the overwhelming victory of prime minister Hun Sen and his political and economic entourage, self-made

---

STEVE HEDER has researched Cambodian politics since the early 1970s and currently teaches politics at the Faculty of Law and Social Sciences of London University's School of Oriental and African Studies.

men who emerged out of the apparatus created by the Vietnamese and the beginnings of market liberalization in the late 1980s. Their decisive triumph may determine the trajectory of Cambodian politics for many years to come. Their political juggernaut is interknit through marriages among children of key players, including premier Hun Sen, deputy premier Sok An, national police chief Hok Langdy and army procurement czar Moeng Samphan.[1] Family connections and economic interests link them and other members of Hun Sen's political entourage, such as army generals Pol Sareuan and Kun Kim and agriculture minister Chan Sarun, to expanding business conglomerates headed by prominent tycoons, like Cheung Sopheap and Lav Meng Khin of the Pheapimex-Fu Chan company, Kung Triv of the KT Pacific Group, Mong Reuthy of the conglomerate named after him, Keut Meng of the Royal Group, Ly Yong Phat of the Hero King company and Sok Kong of the Sokimex company.[2]

This decisive melding of bureaucratic, military and economic power is rooted in a sea change of socioeconomic transformation driven by this self-regenerating, oligopolistic and predatory entrepreneurial elite,[3] intimately linked with East and Southeast Asian capital. Their revolution is generating unprecedented growth and wealth in a few sectors, while leaving most Cambodians in dire and in some ways deepening poverty,[4] creating unheard of socioeconomic polarization. The losers include perhaps a million landless people, many thrown off their land and out of their forests by the start-up of enormous agro-industrial plantations and rampant land grabbing by the elite.[5] The upheaval has also produced a mostly female proletariat, comprising 265,000 largely unionized employees in garment and other factories[6] and 100,000 sex workers.[7] Runaway urbanization is changing parts of Phnom Penh beyond recognition, amidst the rise of a new generation of semi-educated, under-employed youth, numbering in the tens of thousands.[8] The capital and other towns are also home to the beginnings of a middle class, some with liberal aspirations and connected to the plethora of international financial institutions, foreign embassies and aid auxiliaries, UN agencies and international NGOs that, together, continue to play an indispensable role in financing both the formal state apparatus and a rambunctious domestic civil society and media.[9] Alongside them are the business offices of East and Southeast Asian companies whose activities are creating more conservative strata within the still small middle class.

In this environment, the old Vietnamese-built state is now a vastly elaborated, more western-looking but still substantively empty shell, a vehicle not for good governance, but for serving the interests of Hun Sen and his entourage, a maze of patronage, corruption and repression.[10]

The Alliance of Democrats Challenge

In early 2004, consolidation by Hun Sen did not seem certain. He appeared to face a serious, but non-violent, challenge from a seemingly reunited and supposedly democratic-minded opposition, which railed against the corruption, economic oligopoly, political violence, incompetence, rural poverty, social degradation, environmental destruction and numerous other ills that it attributed to his domination. Ranged against him were Sam Rainsy's eponymous party (SRP), Prince Norodom Ranariddh's FUNCINPEC (National United Front for an Independent, Neutral, Peaceful and Cooperative Cambodia), the octogenarian Sihanouk, parts of Hun Sen's own Cambodian People's Party (CPP) associated with Chea Sim, the elderly CPP chairman and also president of Cambodia's symbolic senate, and urban civil society, including labour unions, students' and teachers' groups, and human rights, environmental, community and development NGOs.[11] Sihanouk's support was implicit in his November 2003 brokering of a deal in which Hun Sen agreed to head a three-party government,[12] and obvious from constant signals of disgust at what was happening under Hun Sen's rule. Royal messages decried political assassinations,[13] other political violence,[14] and clumsy attempts to cover up governmental responsibility for them;[15] popular misery[16] due to poverty in the countryside and unemployment in the cities, corruption, the galloping gap between rich and poor, land seizures, forestry destruction and widespread prostitution;[17] and cultural and moral degradation.[18]

Overtly, the challenge was mounted by the Alliance of Democrats (AD), a coalition between FUNCINPEC and SRP. The AD was formed in the wake of July 2003 national elections, in which the CPP — with 47.3 per cent of the popular vote — won 73 of the 123 seats, FUNCINPEC 26 and SRP 24, but in which the electorate showed signs of hopelessness that voting could change the government or improve their lives,[19] and almost a quarter of the electorate did not cast ballots.[20] Because Cambodia's constitution requires a two-thirds parliamentary vote to confirm a government, the AD was able to create a political paralysis crisis by refusing to attend the assembly. Its strategy was to hold the formation of a government hostage to CPP agreement to basic reforms which, if implemented, would fundamentally undermine Hun Sen's position and create conditions for his eventual downfall by democratic means. It reflected a widespread belief in FUNCINPEC and SRP that unless the two parties permanently joined forces, Hun Sen could never be defeated, the country never be cleansed of residual Vietnamese influence and communist habits, and never be set on a democratic and sustainable development path. It was predicated on a proclaimed recognition by Ranariddh that FUNCINPEC had been hoodwinked, badly discredited and seriously weakened as a result of his decision to join coalitions with CPP after the elections of 1993 and 1998.[21]

The heightened role in FUNCINPEC of party secretary-general Prince Norodom Sirivudh and of veteran FUNCINPEC guerilla commander Nhek Bunchhay, both with histories of strong animosity to Hun Sen, appeared to augur well for a steadfast FUNCINPEC stance. The AD position also opened up possibilities for young, well-educated and liberal figures in FUNCINPEC to link up with like-minded elements who populate SRP, with whom they shared a common concern about both parties' leaders' autocratic leadership practices. It was seemingly encouraged by emissaries of Chea Sim's CPP faction, threatened with eclipse by Hun Sen.[22]

The AD demanded CPP agree to a number of points in political pacts to be signed *before* the convening of the assembly and formation of a tripartite government. The first was to set up a new National Election Commission, replacing a CPP-dominated body that FUNCINPEC and SRP believed had biased the 1998 and 2003 elections against them. The AD proposed that the king appoint the chairman and vice chairman of the new commission, which should include one representative each of CPP, FUNCINPEC and SRP, thus ending CPP control. It also demanded the creation of new village committees with equal representation of all three parties. This reflected AD belief that existing village committees — all controlled by CPP since 1979 — played a key role in skewing election results massively in the CPP's favour. Upon formation, the government would put an amended election law to the assembly to make future elections freer and fairer, thus further levelling the electoral playing field. This was coupled with insistence on a tripartite agreement on reform of the CPP-dominated judicial system, a mainstay of CPP's capacity to use the law against the opposition. Other points the AD wanted agreed in advance were that the assembly would pass an anti-corruption law satisfactory to all three parties, and the government would establish an independent anti-corruption commission acceptable to the AD. This would not only reduce corruption, but also deny the CPP political advantages derived from it.

With regard to the government itself, the AD demanded prior agreement on the abolition of Sok An's post of Minister of the Office of the Council of Ministers, to break this Hun Sen crony's stranglehold on the bureaucracy. At the insistence of Nhek Bunchhay, who had been reduced to position as a vice-president of the powerless senate, CPP was also asked to allocate a number of positions in the army and police to the AD, to neutralize them as anti-AD forces. The clinching AD point was that if any party withdrew from the coalition government, the cabinet must obtain a new parliamentary vote of confidence, and, failing that, new elections would be held.[23] This meant the AD could precipitate the fall of the government and force new elections at any time, elections that would be — if the AD's reforms worked — much freer and fairer than those on 1998 and 2003 and might well sweep a reunited FUNCINPEC-SRP ticket to victory, making it possible to do a deal with Chea Sim to achieve Hun Sen's sidelining, with Sihanouk's blessing.

Hun Sen Fights Back

Hun Sen refused to sign what was intended as his political death warrant, rejecting key AD demands,[24] which Sihanouk, too, thought included unrealistic deal-breakers.[25] Some AD members responded to Hun Sen's recalcitrance by demanding a specific pledge that his next term as premier be his last.[26] He replied by reneging on Sihanouk's tripartite formula and insisting on a return to a CPP-FUNCINPEC coalition,[27] although Chea Sim associates said they still wanted a deal that was "fair for all three parties".[28]

Moreover, appearances of AD unity were deceiving, and behind the scenes, Hun Sen and his entourage were working to exploit rivalries, ambitions, greed, impatience and fear within the AD. With Ranariddh frequently outside of Cambodia, and Sihanouk in China or North Korea for medical treatment and to signal dissatisfaction at the failure of his formula, Hun Sen took particular advantage of conflicts of interest between Nhek Bunchhay and Sam Rainsy. Previous shared animosity to Hun Sen was dissolved by the aging FUNCINPEC ex-guerrilla fighter's fear that a three-party government would leave rustic men like himself with few posts, because these would have to be split three ways and many would be taken by a new generation of whiz-kid politicians, especially from SRP. Nhek Bunchhay also suspected Sam Rainsy was plotting to usurp leadership of the AD from FUNCINPEC.[29] Appealing to the desire of Nhek Bunchhay and other FUNCINPEC members for government posts, Hun Sen promised that if they would join a two-party coalition under his leadership, all would have jobs, because he would create additional posts for them.[30]

Even more fundamental, however, was the issue of money. FUNCINPEC politicians had seen how the enormously growing power of money had helped CPP buy the 2003 election and was giving CPP moguls a lifestyle which FUNCINPEC officials envied. At a deeper level, FUNCINPEC realized that just as CPP had long since chucked the failed ideology of socialism, FUNCINPEC must also become party for which immediate business links were more important than "royalism". Moreover, during the 2003 elections, many FUNCINPEC candidates' campaigns had been bankrolled by Hun Sen crony capitalists, and some were even financed by their CPP competitors. This made FUNCINPEC a partly owned subsidiary of CPP and its tycoons, and left FUNCINPEC parliamentarians-elect with debts they could only repay by obtaining government posts through which they could make money.[31] It also separated FUNCINPEC from SRP, whose candidates were starved for funds by a business community told by CPP that financing SRP was committing economic suicide.[32]

The threat of literal death was a further, crucial factor. In 2003, two prominent FUNCINPEC figures had been killed and a third paralysed from the neck down in contract-style hits, which virtually everyone in AD believed were arranged by Hun Sen or his entourage. Two more such assassinations were carried out during the first half of 2004. The targets were leaders of an SRP-affiliated trade union,[33] but FUNCINPEC members took the murders as deadly warnings to both parties. Additional fear was generated by the spectre of arbitrary arrest and imprisonment by the CPP-controlled police and courts, especially after a FUNCINPEC candidate in the 2003 elections was arrested on charges[34] trumped up by military intelligence dirty trickster Mol Reuap.[35]

This relentless combination of inducements and threats increasingly undermined the AD, separating Ranariddh, Nhek Bunchhay and Norodom Sirivudh from the SRP and reform-minded sectors of FUNCINPEC itself. A crucial juncture was a secret meeting in early March in Bangkok between Ranariddh and Thai defence minister Chaovalit Yongjaiyut, with the latter and the tycoon Ly Yong Phat acting as mediators for Hun Sen. Hun Sen and Ranariddh agreed by telephone that CPP and FUNCINPEC would split "commissions" on government business deals 60–40.[36] This was the basis for a meeting between Hun Sen and Ranariddh on 15 March at which they agreed, without having consulted their own parties, that the future government would be a CPP-FUNCINPEC coalition, but that Ranariddh could include SRP members in slots reserved for FUNCINPEC.[37]

Thereafter, negotiations between CPP and FUNCINPEC took place over the composition of the government and leadership structures of the national assembly, government policy pact and the procedure for approving all three. Ranariddh soon conceded Hun Sen's procedural demand for a "package vote", guaranteeing Hun Sen would be reconfirmed as prime minister at the same time as those occupying all other parliamentary and government posts were named and government policies approved, although this violated the constitution. The quid pro quo, the prince said, was a reformist policy pact agreeable to all three parties.[38] Tedious CPP-FUNCINPEC talks about the pact and power sharing ensued, with CPP tenaciously resisting the substance of the original AD proposals. Some FUNCINPEC negotiators fought back in consultation with SPR and civil society, producing a new sweeping reform proposal on 10 June,[39] while Sirivudh pressed for FUNCINPEC to hold on to key ministerial posts.[40] They also suggested the unconstitutionality of the package vote could be overcome by having Sihanouk agree to a three-party appeal for him to exercise his constitutional authority as a royal arbiter.[41]

However, they increasingly sensed they were operating in a dream world, isolated from the real substance of political developments. One aspect of this was a scramble within FUNCINPEC to take advantage of Hun Sen's promises of a bonanza of government posts.[42] Hopefuls were caught in a bribery contest in which they gave money to Ranariddh or Sirivudh or both.[43] The other was a competition within CPP for posts, in which payments were also made, but to a central party fund, with Chea Sim attempting to replace several Hun Sen loyalists with his own nominees.[44]

Rudely by-passed in all this was Sihanouk, still in piqued exile.[45] The king's offer to host talks to reestablish a serious tripartite deal[46] was deflected by Hun Sen and Ranariddh.[47] Within FUNCINPEC and SRP, many became convinced that Ranariddh had abandoned the whole AD strategy. Rumours spread like wildfire that Ranariddh had been bribed by Hun Sen with money, presents of aircraft and promises that he would be manoeuvred onto the throne when his father died.[48]

Ranariddh's Volte-Face, Hun Sen's Triumph

The worst fears of the reformists and Hun Sen's rivals were realized on 26 June, when he and Ranariddh initialled a protocol on the division of power within the government, to be installed by an unspecified package vote procedure.[49] The size of the government was more than doubled, but, contrary to Sirivudh's demands, important ministries were lost to CPP; contrary to Nhek Bunchhay's hopes, no provision was made for integration of FUNCINPEC military into the security forces or police; and, contrary to the reformists' hopes, there was no sign of their programme. There was general fury and profound disappointment with Ranariddh in both FUNCINPEC and SRP, combined with fear that a tacit part of the deal was exclusion from power of FUNCINPEC liberals and open season for Mol Reuap to go after the most recalcitrant FUNCINPEC and SRP figures.[50] The dropping of Mu Sok Huor, an outspoken FUNCINPEC liberal, for consideration for a ministerial post made an example of her.[51]

Amidst a whirlwind of bidding for FUNCINPEC posts, Ranariddh agreed with Hun Sen to a final protocol from which all reform substance disappeared.[52] Meanwhile, a Hun Sen advisor produced an argument that the package vote procedure was legal if the assembly adopted "a constitution addition law", even without royal approval.[53] Finally, on 1 July, Hun Sen announced that CPP ministers would keep their jobs in the new government, on his say so,[54] contrary to the party's internal regulations.[55] Given the situation in both parties, Ranariddh and Hun Sen agreed that the package vote must be made by a show of hands, to prevent FUNCINPEC and CPP members voting against them in cahoots with SRP.[56]

Suddenly on 6 July, Sihanouk announced that he had decided to abdicate as soon as the new assembly formed and passed legislation activating the Throne Council, a CPP-dominated body constitutionally empowered to select a successor in the event of his death. It was obvious he was expressing his deep exasperation at the whole course of events since November 2003, with the package vote being the final straw. He was ignoring the constitution, which made no provision for abdication, as CPP immediately pointed out.[57]

Two days later, with SRP boycotting, CPP and FUNCINPEC members convened parliament and voted by unanimous show of hands for the constitutional addition authorizing the package vote.[58] It was presumed that the bill would be signed into force by Chea Sim as acting chief of state (in Sihanouk's absence) on 12 July.[59] However, Sihanouk called on Chea Sim to act on his conscience in deciding whether to sign,[60] and, to the consternation of an enraged Hun Sen, he refused to do so.

Suspecting that Rainsy, Chea Sim and Sihanouk were plotting against him, Hun Sen convened a meeting of some CPP senior leaders at which he declared that if Chea Sim continued to obstruct, he must go into exile, so that Nhek Bunchhay, the next available person to be acting chief of state, could sign the legislation, but Chea Sim balked at leaving the country. On 13 July, security forces loyal to Hun Sen surrounded Chea Sim's residence, and he was warned that if he did not go, his life was in danger. He was escorted to the airport and onto a plane for Bangkok, supposedly to undergo medical treatment. He returned politically humiliated to Cambodia a week later.[61] Nhek Bunchhay's signature of the legislation was also a humiliation for him and FUNCINPEC, demonstrating the party's subservience to Hun Sen, and that it could also be used against SRP.[62]

The package vote was carried out by show of hands on 15 July. Hun Sen became premier and Ranariddh president of the national assembly. Among the deputy premiers were Nhek Bunchhay and Sirivudh, who were concurrently co-ministers of defence and interior, respectively. Although Chea Sim's man Sar Kheng retained a position as deputy premier and co-minister of interior, Hun Sen's key crony, Sok An, was promoted to an added deputy premier post, while keeping his position as minister of an undiminished council of ministers' office.[63] Hun Sen triumphantly declared the CPP-FUNCINPEC coalition government formula should last at least another 20 or 30 years.[64] With the later addition of undersecretaries of state, the cabinet expanded even further.[65] The assembly also approved a government political reform programme, which was verbose but vacuous.[66]

FUNCINPEC Self-Destructs; SRP Targeted for Destruction

After the government's formation, the coalition deal of jobs for FUNCINPEC continued to expand. Nhek Bunchhay was empowered to appoint FUNCINPEC officers in certain military units.[67] Hun Sen made even more posts and promotions available to FUNCINPEC, and tycoons began contributing money to the party that it used to distribute gifts to its members.[68] This opened up another round of bidding, with Sirivudh allegedly collecting the envelopes, and resulted in the loss of many posts by FUNCINPEC veterans to upstarts, some with CPP backgrounds and others indebted to CPP-affiliated tycoons. It provoked public protests by FUNCINPEC veterans and widespread commentary that FUNCINPEC was embarking on the path of self-destruction.[69]

One senior FUNCINPEC official explained that the party had made a strategic decision that its relationship vis-à-vis CPP would forever be "subordinate, subservient and lucrative", and that in future elections, it would rely on CPP assistance and follow the CPP model to carry out "organized, paid voting" to get its candidates into the national assembly. In the meantime, FUNCINPEC would also cooperate with CPP to neutralize the SRP opposition and critical civil society organizations by "squeezing their membership at the bottom and scaring their leadership at the top", using the police, the courts and restrictive laws to harass them legally and threatening to use overwhelming force to suppress any demonstrations. Assassinations were not ruled out if other means fail.[70]

FUNCINPEC collusion with Hun Sen to split and intimidate SRP began immediately after government formation. Their attack concentrated on SRP's "shadow government" structures, the function of which was to collect information on corruption and abuse for use in parliamentary debates. While Ranarriddh openly appealed for SRP members to defect so they could be given FUNCINPEC quota government posts,[71] associates of Sirivudh and Nhek Bunchhay covertly did the same with key SRP figures, warning of dire consequences if they did not leave SRP and join FUNCINPEC. The open campaign netted Ou Bun Long, the SRP shadow minister of interior, who became a FUNCINPEC secretary of state. The covert operation focused on SRP MP Cheam Channy, who was the party's shadow minister of defence, and whose active network of informants had made him a constant irritant to Hun Sen. When Cheam Channy rejected all blandishments to join the government,

Mol Reuap fabricated a case that his informants constituted a "secret army" being formed on Sam Rainsy's behalf.[72] This melded into a third prong of the attack, the pursuit of legal cases against SRP. Sirivudh lodged defamation lawsuits against Sam Rainsy and another SRP member of parliament for alleging that Ranariddh had been bribed to betray the AD, and the military court laid charges against Cheam Channy.[73] Meanwhile Ranariddh initiated moves to strip them of their parliamentary immunity, so they could be arrested.[74]

Another quid pro quo has been FUNCINPEC support against Hun Sen's rivals in CPP, such as interior minister Sar Kheng, whose continued differences with the premier were revealed when he expressed skepticism about the existence of an SRP secret army.[75] In retaliation, Ranariddh and Sirivudh supported the notion that Hok Langdy's national police should be removed from the formal control of the interior ministry and placed under Hun Sen's command.[76] Even if this is not achieved, Hun Sen has de jure or de facto control over almost all the combat-ready armed forces and effective police forces in the country, making him virtually immune to the threat of a military coup. FUNCINPEC appointees are kept out of these units.

Sihanouk Retires; Long Live King Sihamoni

While senior CPP and FUNCINPEC officials tried to protray all this as a return to the golden age of political stability under Sihanouk's pre-1970 Sangkum regime, the king made his grave dissatisfaction clear on 18 July, characterizing the government's formation as an "anti-Constitutional, anti-Democratic, anti-Royalty 'Coup d'État' ". He also voiced suspicions of a plot either to replace him upon his death by a "puppet" King — an allusion to the role he feared a Ranariddh enthroned by Hun Sen would play — or to manipulate the succession to make Cambodia "a Republic with a 100 per cent dictatorship regime" under Hun Sen.[77]

Hun Sen at first publicly taunted Sihanouk about his expressed intention to abdicate, asserting that "the Constitution states that the King must stay on the throne until he dies". Sihanouk replied that he wanted implementing legislation to activate the Throne Council so it could select "a male King who is honest, gentle and will try to help the country" as his successor. This was an obvious signal that he wanted his son with Queen Monineath, Norodom Sihamoni, not Sihamoni's half-brother Ranariddh, to be the next monarch.[78] Born in 1953, Sihamoni had spent the first nine years of his life in Cambodia, before going to study in Czechoslovakia and North Korea until 1976, when he returned to Cambodia and lived under Khmer Rouge house arrest with his parents. After the Khmer Rouge regime, he was a personal secretary to his parents, then returned to an academic life in France until he was appointed as the reestablished Kingdom's ambassador to UNESCO in 1993. In a further signal that he was being groomed for the throne, Sihanouk bestowed an elevated royal title upon him in late August, and he joined his parents in Beijing in September.[79]

As SRP proclaimed its support for Sihanouk's desire to abdicate,[80] Hun Sen and Ranarriddh switched to attempting to persuade Sihanouk not to step down.[81] They assuaged him by proclaiming their support for Sihamoni and promising Throne Council implementing legislation that would avoid a succession crisis.[82] However, in late September he announced his Chinese doctors had discovered he was afflicted by yet another illness,[83] and on 6 October he proclaimed he was too weak to be King and asked to "retire". He said he would only return to Cambodia once the Throne Council was operational and named his successor.[84] Although pushed into a corner of desperation, Sihanouk had managed to outfox the CPP strongman and his FUNCINPEC sidekick by forcing them to name Sihamoni.[85] The assembly duly passed a law on the functioning of the council, which declared Sihamoni king on 14 October. Sihanouk and Sihamoni returned to Cambodia six days later,[86] and Sihamoni was enthroned at the end of the month.[87] Public reaction to events was initially muted, but his coronation speech to large crowds indicated that he would follow in the politically critical footsteps of his father, perhaps more cautiously, but also much more actively.[88] A message associated with him promised to criticize "the powerful who only think of themselves" on behalf of "the poor who attempt to survive".[89] He sent a strong signal by giving early and highly sympathetic audiences to victims of human rights violations and to leading Cambodian human rights campaigners. CPP officials soon gave indications that he should not be too ambitious about meeting with the people,[90] while Sihanouk warned that Hun Sen and Ranariddh might still be hoping to replace him with Ranariddh once the retired king finally died.[91]

The International Politics of Reform

At the beginning of the year, AD pleaded for diplomatic and donor support for its challenge to Hun Sen, but these entreaties fell on almost entirely deaf ears. Many western and ASEAN embassies, world and Asian international financial institutions, UN agencies and international NGOs agreed with the AD's critique of Hun Sen's regime as failing to achieve good governance, to establish a genuinely competitive market economy or to reduce rural poverty. However, they described AD demands as unattainable, FUNCINPEC as equally bad if not worse than CPP, and SRP as politically immature and incapable of governing. They also blamed AD obstructionism for the political paralysis, which they in turn saw as blocking their own efforts at promoting good governance and development. They universally welcomed the formation of the new CPP-FUNCINPEC coalition as giving them a viable partner with whom they hoped to be able to constructively engage to pursue — if not political reform — then financial, administrative and other restructuring and policy adjustment. They also steadfastly maintained that unless they did so, the regime would continue to receive unconditional economic and other support from China.[92]

Ironically, the formation of a government snuffing out AD reform proposals was followed by a flurry of highly critical donor and other assessments of Cambodia's performance at good governance, poverty reduction and human rights protection, slamming previous Hun Sen governments' lack of political will to achieve any of these goals. They also predicted that unless at least some of these problems were urgently solved, Cambodia's economy might well go into a serious and prolonged slump, triggered by the opening up of its markets for garment manufacture — the engine of growth over the past several years — to competition from China and other more efficient producers. Some warned of serious socioeconomic unrest among dispossessed peasants, workers let go by closing factories, and angry students, if the economy slowed down and stayed in the doldrums.[93] Worries about this were exacerbated by a severe drought that looked likely to have a significant adverse effect on the 2004 rice crop.[94] The virtually complete ban imposed by the government on demonstrations in Phnom Penh reflected its concern about vulnerability to mass violence in the capital.[95]

Many of the reports were produced in the context of Cambodia's September accession to the World Trade Organization and the run-up to the December meeting of the Consultative Group, which brings together donors and the government to announce aid commitments. Hun Sen saw this coming, and produced his own mountain of paper, accentuating the positive and swearing his new government was dead serious about reform.[96] As the fudged outcome of the Consultative Group gathering showed by promising almost as much aid in the past while making more insistent calls for reform,[97] some diplomats and donors profess a willingness to take Hun Sen at his word. They argue that his consolidation of political and economic power is a positive factor, allowing him to embark on reform. Others believe very much the opposite, at least in private. They fear that Hun Sen's promises are simply another in a long line of lies designed to dupe foreigners into paying to keep him in power and make him richer.

Searching for a post-AD role, Sam Rainsy has begun a new attempt to align himself with international sceptics, believing that Hun Sen will fail to deliver, and a deteriorating socioeconomic and political situation may give SRP new opportunities.[98] In preparation for this possibility, he has embarked upon an attempt to reinvent the SRP to make it a more plausible political force: a party that is more truly democratic, technically capable of governing and politically responsible.[99] The trick for him and SRP will be not only to demonstrate to potential foreign backers that his promises are more sincere, credible and realizable than those of Hun Sen. It will more importantly be to continue to build a coherent coalition of intellectual, student, middle class, and palace liberals; the wretched of Cambodia's towns, countryside and forests; covert dissidents within CPP and FUNCINPEC; and entrepreneurs who want an end to the oligopolies that obstruct their business opportunities, without provoking CPP-FUNCINPEC repression so severe as to destroy the SRP.

Conclusion

Returning to where this chapter began, Hun Sen's consolidation of power over the post (Vietnamese)-colonial state, the melding of administrative, armed and business power over which he has presided, is familiar to Southeast Asians. It is comparable to similar trajectory-defining periods in the Philippines in the late 1940s and 1950s, in Thailand, Malaysia and Singapore in the late 1950s and 1960s and in Indonesia in the late 1960s and 1970s. In each of these cases, powerful individuals, families or institutions presided over profound capitalist transformations that eventually, over periods of two to four decades, produced new socioeconomic and political formations and forces that challenged, more or less successfully and in different ways, their makers. Meanwhile, many in the aging formal CPP party and parliamentary leadership[100] believe that Hun Sen's talk of a 20 to 30-year coalition with FUNCINPEC are indicative of a plan to hold tenaciously on to power for that long, allowing many of them to die off or retire, while the premier and his cronies groom their intermarried children for eventual dynastic successions. Hun Sen's West Point-trained son, Hun Manet, now studying for a PhD in the United Kingdom, is seen as heir apparent.[101]

If the baton is indeed eventually passed to Hun Manet and others like him, the kind of Cambodia they inherit will be determined not only by the relationship between his father's entourage and Cambodian society, but by the immense transformative power — for good and evil — of turbo-capitalism in the era of globalization. If it is not constrained by good governance, the Cambodia of the future may be a socioeconomic and cultural wasteland. If Hun Sen does not make good on his promises, then the best chance of averting catastrophe may also be familiar to Southeast Asians: People's Power uprisings in the capital in alliance with all the political forces that the strongman has alienated on his way to the top and in keeping himself there, combined with intervention by the monarch, the international community or the church. However, even if that happens, whether there will be anyone capable of picking up the pieces remains to be seen.

Notes

1   "Securing Allegiance", *Cambodia Daily*, 17–18 January 2004.
2   Global Witness, *Taking a Cut: Institutionalised Corruption and Illegal Logging in Cambodia's Aural Wildlife Sanctuary*, http://www.globalwitness.org/reports/show.php/en.00066.html.
3   Chamber of Commerce of Cambodia, *CCC Handbook*. Phnom Penh: nd, pp. 18–46.
4   World Bank, "Cambodia at a Crossroad: Strengthening Accountability to Reduce Poverty, A Brief for the Consultative Group for Cambodia, Discussion Draft", 11 October 2004, pp. 7–10.
5   Special Representative of the Secretary-General for Human Rights in Cambodia (SRSGHRC), "Land Concessions for Economic Purposes in Cambodia: A Human Rights Perspective" (Phnom Penh: November 2004), p. 3.
6   "Minister Says Union Strikes Threatening Garment Industry", *Cambodia Daily*, 19 November 2004.
7   UNIFEM, "A Fair Share for Women: Cambodia Gender Assessment", Phnom Penh, April 2004, p. 5.
8   "Road to Nowhere", *Cambodia Daily*, 12 November 2004.
9   Cooperation Committee for Cambodia, *Agency Contact Listing: Contact and Staff Details for over 500 Local and International NGOs, International Organizations and UN Agencies in Cambodia* (Phnom Penh: Cooperation Committee for Cambodia, May 2004).
10 Caroline Hughes and Tim Conway, "Understanding Pro-Poor Political Change: The Policy Process, Cambodia (Second Draft, August 2003)". London: Overseas Development Institute, pp. viii–ix.
11 Author's interviews with civil society leaders, Phnom Penh, March–April 2004.
12 "Communiqué de Norodom Sihanouk, Roi du Cambodge", 5 November 2003.
13 "Thousands of Mourners Take to the Streets" and "Mourners Report No Conflicts with Police", *Cambodia Daily*, 26 January 2004.
14 "Jailed Journalist Released after King Intervenes", *Cambodia Daily*, 17 May 2004; "Prince Ranariddh Defends Policy with CPP", *Cambodia Daily*, 5–6 June 2004.
15 "Villagers: Suspect in Prey Veng Day of Shooting", *Cambodia Daily*, 9 February 2004; "King Says Montagnards Aren't Fleeing Economy", *Cambodia Daily*, 25 May 2004.
16 "FUNCINPEC, CPP Deny They Met", *Cambodia Daily*, 11 March 2004.
17 "King: Cambodia's Social Problems to Worsen", *Cambodia Daily*, 22 June 2004.
18 "King Laments Slayings", *Cambodia Daily*, 24 June 2004.

19 Neutral and Impartial Committee for Free and Fair Election in Cambodia, "Cambodia National Assembly Election Report 2003". Phnom Penh: nd, pp. 7, 25–26.

20 UNDP, *National Assembly Elections in Cambodia, 27 July 2003*. Phnom Penh, September 2003, p. 49.

21 FUNCINPEC interviews, March–October 2004.

22 SRP and FUNCINPEC interviews, March–May 2004.

23 Nhek Bunchhay, *Robaykar Neung Poaramean Sathanakar Nayobay Kraoy Kech Prachum Kampoul Thngai Ti 5 Khae Vichhaka Chhnam 2003* [Report and Information on the Political Situation After the 9 November 2003 Summit]. Phnom Penh: March 2004, pp. 37–40.

24 Nhek Bunchhay, *Robaykar*, pp. 37–40.

25 "King May Leave before Government Forms", *Cambodia Daily*, 13 January 2004.

26 Nhek Bunchhay, *Robaykar*, pp. 42–47.

27 "King goes to Beijing; Leaves Deadlock Behind", *Cambodia Daily*, 20 January 2004; "Hun Sen: Murders couldn't be Prevented", *Cambodia Daily*, 29 January 2004.

28 "US Praises Efforts to Find Killers of Chea Vichea", *Cambodia Daily*, 2 February 2004.

29 "King Supports New Elections to End Deadlock", *Cambodia Daily*, 6 March 2004.

30 "Hun Sen will Trade Jobs for F'pec Vote", *Cambodia Daily*, 26 February 2004.

31 FUNCINPEC interviews, March–November 2004.

32 SRP interviews, May–June 2004.

33 "Union Chief Chea Vichea Gunned down" and "Garment Workers Plan Strike, Demand Justice", *Cambodia Daily*, 23 January 2004; "Union Leader Shot Dead", *Cambodia Daily*, 8–9 May 2004.

34 "FUNCINPEC Candidate Charged with Terrorism", *Cambodia Daily*, 17 February 2004.

35 "Court Finds Accused CFF Rebels Innocent", *Cambodia Daily*, 7 October 2004.

36 FUNCINPEC and diplomat interviews, March–November 2004.

37 Ranariddh-Hun Sen communiqué, 15 March 2004.

38 "Ranariddh to Change F'PEC Leadership", *Cambodia Daily,* 22 March 2004.

39 *Pithisar Ney Kechpromprieng Sahapratebatkar Roveang Kanapak Pracheachun Kampuchea Neung Kanapak FUNCINPEC (Sechkdey Preang Robâs Kanapak FUNCINPEC)* [Protocol to the Cooperation Agreement Between the Cambodian Peoples Party and the FUNCINPEC Party (FUNCINPEC Draft)], 10 June 2004.

40 "Assembly to Convene to Amend Constitution", *Cambodia Daily*, 7 June 2004.

41 *Sechkdey Snaoer âmpi Kar Bâhchhnaot Kânchâp* [Proposal on Package Voting], with handwritten date, 24 June 2004.

42 "Hun Sen Says some are Trying to Buy Positions", *Cambodia Daily*, 18 May 2004; "King Weighs in on Parliamentarians Buying Posts", *Cambodia Daily*, 31 May 2004.

43 FUNCINPEC interviews, May–October 2004.

44 CPP interview, September 2004.

[45] "Lawmaker Appeals for King's Return", *Cambodia Daily*, 10–11 April 2004.

[46] "King Calls for Meeting in N Korea", *Cambodia Daily*, 12 May 2004.

[47] "King Hurt by Rejection of Meeting Offer", *Cambodia Daily*, 17 May 2004.

[48] FUNCINPEC and diplomat interviews, May–June 2004. See also "Prince Gets Helicopter", *Cambodia Daily*, 1 July 2004; "Gov't Returns Plane Once Owned by Ranariddh", *Cambodia Daily*, 12 July 2004; and "Prince Denies being Bribed to join Gov't", *Cambodia Daily*, 16 July 2004.

[49] *Sechkdey Prakas Poaramean Sdei Pi Lataphâl Chumnuop Roveang Sâmdech Krom Preah Norodom Ranarridh Preah Prathean Kanapak FUNCINPEC Neung Sâmdech Hun Sen Anuprathean Kanapak Pracheachun Kampuchea* [Press Communique on the Results of the Meeting Between Samdech Krom Preah Norodom Ranarridh, Royal Chairman of the FUNCINPEC Party, and Samdech Hun Sen, Vice Chairman of the Cambodian Peoples Party].

[50] "Assembly to Convene to Amend Constitution", *Cambodia Daily*, 7 June 2004.

[51] FUNCINPEC and SRP interviews, 26–28 June 2004.

[52] Protocol of the Cooperation Agreement between CPP and FUNCINPEC, 30 June 2004.

[53] Claude Gour, "A *l'attention de S.A.R. le Prince Norodom Ranariddh*", nd.

[54] "All of CPP's Ministers to Keep Jobs", *Cambodia Daily*, 2 July 2004.

[55] "Internal Regulations of the CPP", 28 October 1997, Article 16.

[56] FUNCINPEC interview, 29 June 2004.

[57] "King Says He will Give up the Throne", *Cambodia Daily*, 7 July 2004.

[58] Author's notes on the session.

[59] "New Assembly Paves Way for Package Vote", *Cambodia Daily*, 9 July 2004.

[60] "King: Package Vote Decision is for Chea Sim", *Cambodia Daily*, 12 July 2004.

[61] FUNCINPEC, CPP and diplomat interviews; author's observations at Chea Sim's residence. See also "Flex of Muscle may Signal Split within CPP", *Cambodia Daily*, 14 July 2004; and "CPP President Returns Home from Bangkok", *Cambodia Daily*, 23 July 2004.

[62] FUNCINPEC interviews, 13–14 July 2004.

[63] "Council Opts to Retain All Committees", *Cambodia Daily*, 7 September 2004.

[64] Author's observations at the assembly, 15 July 2004. See also "Deadlock is Over; Government is Formed", *Cambodia Daily*, 16 July 2004.

[65] "Ministry Names 146 Undersecretaries of State", *Cambodia Daily*, 21 July 2004.

[66] *Kamvithi Nayobay robâs Reacharoathaphibal Kampuchea samrap Nitikal Ti 3 nei Roatsaphea* [Political Programme of the Royal Government of Cambodia for the Third Term of the National Assembly)].

[67] "RCAF Makes Room for FUNCINPEC Officers", *Cambodia Daily*, 24 August 2004.

[68] "Coalition Partners Move toward Harmony", *Cambodia Daily*, 10 September 2004.

[69] FUNCINPEC interviews, October–November 2004. See also "CPP Will Hand Future Vacancies to Royalists", *Cambodia Daily*, 1 October 2004; "Outgoing FUNCINPEC

Governors to Skip Ceremony", *Cambodia Daily*, 11 November 2004; and "F'PEC Seeks Land to Relocate Headquarters", *Cambodia Daily*, 15 November 2004

70 FUNCINPEC interview, 6 September 2004.

71 "Hun Sen Says Opposition Plans Revolt", *Cambodia Daily*, 19 July 2004.

72 FUNCINPEC, CPP and SRP interviews, July 2004.

73 "Opposition Member Accused of Arms Gathering", *Cambodia Daily*, 4 August 2004; "Surrender Deadline Passes for Accused Rebels", *Cambodia Daily*, 10 August 2004; Suspected Sam Rainsy Rebels Summoned", *Cambodia Daily*, 13 August 2004; "Opposition Members Miss Second Court Date", *Cambodia Daily*, 1 September 2004.

74 "Push to Try Sam Rainsy over Warning on Hold", *Cambodia Daily*, 21 October 2004; "Opposition Lawmaker could Lose Immunity", *Cambodia Daily*, 26 October 2004; "Vote near on Sam Rainsy's Immunity", *Cambodia Daily*, 1 November 2004.

75 "Gov't Gets RFA to Pull 'Rebel' Story", *Cambodia Daily*, 2 August 2004.

76 "Ranariddh: Hun Sen should Control Police", *Cambodia Daily*, 27 October 2004; "Sirivudh Supports Transferring Police to PM", *Cambodia Daily*, 1 November 2004.

77 "King: Future Kings will only be Puppets", *Cambodia Daily*, 19 July 2004. My interpretation of Sihanouk's remarks reflects conversations with members of the Royal Family and of the king's cabinet, July–August 2004.

78 "Hun Sen Ignores King's Threat to Abdicate", *Cambodia Daily*, 5 August 2004.

79 Ministry of the Royal Palace, *Preah Chivapravoat Sâmdech Preah Baromanat Norodom Sihamoni*, nd.

80 "Hun Sen Ignores King's Threat to Abdicate", *Cambodia Daily*, 5 August 2004.

81 "Top Monk Asks King to Remain on Throne", *Cambodia Daily*, 9 August 2004.

82 Ranariddh-Hun Sen letter to Sihanouk, 2 September 2004.

83 "King's Stomach Ailment to Delay His Return", *Cambodia Daily*, 23 September 2004.

84 Sihanouk letters in author's possession, 6 October 2004.

85 Diplomat interview, November 2004.

86 "City Cheers Arrival of New King", *Cambodia Daily*, 21 October 2004.

87 "Three-Day Coronation Awaits King", *Cambodia Daily*, 26 October 2004.

88 *Cambodia Daily*, Special Supplement, "King Sihamoni's Coronation", nd.

89 "King Sihamoni will also have Critical Pen Pal", *Cambodia Daily*, 8 November 2004.

90 "Gov't is Cool to Idea of King's Forum", *Cambodia Daily*, 25 November 2004; "King Holds Event for Human Rights Day", *Cambodia Daily*, 11–12 December 2004.

91 "Retired King's Pen Pal Stirs more Controversy", *Cambodia Daily*, 27 October 2004.

92 Diplomat and donor interviews, March–July 2004.

93 For examples, see World Bank, "Cambodia at a Crossroad" and SRSGHRC, "Land Concessions".

94 "NGO Donates Rice in Wake of Late Harvest", *Cambodia Daily*, 5 November 2004; "Gov't Drought Efforts Falter, Hunger Looms", *Cambodia Daily*, 16 November 2004.

95 "Marchers Seek Repeal of Peaceful Protest Ban", *Cambodia Daily*, 1 December 2004.

[96] For examples, see "Address by Samdech Hun Sen, Prime Minister of the Royal Government of Cambodia, on 'Rectangular Strategy for Growth, Employment, Equity and Efficiency', First Cabinet Meeting of the Third Legislature of the National Assembly at the Office of the Council of Ministers, Phnom Penh, 16 July 2004"; Royal Government of Cambodia, "Implementing the Rectangular Strategy and the Development Assistance Needs (Prepared for the 2004 Consultative Group Meeting for Cambodia, December 2004, Phnom Penh, Cambodia, Draft as of 15 October 2003 [sic])".

[97] "$504 Million Pledged by Int'l Donors", *Cambodia Daily*, 8 December 2004.

[98] "Sam Rainsy Says Gov't Exploits Poverty for Aid", *Cambodia Daily*, 3 December 2004.

[99] "Sam Rainsy Promises to Reform Opposition", *Cambodia Daily*, 26 November 2004; "Sam Rainsy Blames Gov't for Drought", *Cambodia Daily*, 23 November 2004.

[100] "Age Does Matter", *Cambodia Daily,* 20–21 March 2004.

[101] CPP interviews, September 2004.

Indonesia

INDONESIA
The Year of a Democratic Election

Leo Suryadinata

The 2004 general election in Indonesia began on 5 April with the parliamentary election and ended on 20 September with the second round of the presidential election. This was the longest election that the country had ever witnessed and a marked success in Indonesia's quest for democracy as it was conducted in an orderly and peaceful manner. This chapter examines both parliamentary and presidential elections and their significance for Indonesian politics; the formation of the new cabinet; and the problems faced by the new Yudhoyono administration. It also looks at the tsunami disaster and Indonesia's foreign relations with special reference to military relations between Indonesia and the United States.

The 2004 Election: Another Victory for Democracy[1]

The 2004 election differed from the 1999 election in the sense that this was the first direct presidential election. Unlike the last election at which the president was elected by the MPR (People's Consultative Assembly), this time the people directly elected the president.

In 2003, the Dewan Perwakilan Rakyat (DPR, House of Representatives, the Indonesian parliament) completed the debates on the presidential election bill, concluding the discussion regarding the 2004 election. All laws and regulations regarding the parliamentary and presidential elections were passed. The parliamentary election — for members of DPR, Dewan Pimpinan Daerah (DPD, Regional Representatives Council) and Dewan Perwakilan Rakyat Daerah (DPRD, Regional House of Representatives) — was to be held on 5 April 2004, while the presidential election would be conducted in two phases, the first round would be on 5 July 2004 and the second, on 20 September 2004.

LEO SURYADINATA is Senior Research Fellow, Institute of Southeast Asian Studies, Singapore.

More than 200 political parties registered to take part in the 2004 elections but only 24 parties were qualified to contest, including 6 leading parties which had taken part in the 1999 election: the Partai Demokrasi Indonesia-Perjuangan (PDI-P), Partai Golkar, Partai Kebangkitan Bangsa (PKB), Partai Persatuan Pembangunan (PPP), Partai Amanat Nasional (PAN) and Partai Bulan Bintang (PBB).

The electoral platforms of these six parties were very similar. Economic, educational and social problems were the main concerns of the voters. Unemployment and corruption were highlighted. Every party addressed these issues in general terms. Interestingly, *syariah* law was not raised as a major election issue as most Muslim voters were more concerned with their daily needs rather than this controversial Islamic issue.

Prior to the April 2004 election, many observers had focused on the two major parties: the PDI-P and Golkar. These two parties, despite internal conflicts, still commanded the resources to garner votes. Because of various scandals that rocked the PDI-P and perceptions about Megawati's weak leadership, there was a general expectation that the PDI-P might receive fewer votes in the 2004 election. But Golkar, which was also rocked by scandals, was able to ride on the "nostalgia" of the population. In addition, despite the end of the New Order, Golkar's machinery was intact and the party was reportedly "rich". General elections are an expensive business and a party with considerable wealth is likely to win more votes during a parliamentary election. Many observers predicted that no party would emerge dominant as the vote would be divided among many parties, with Golkar and the PDI-P getting the lion's share.

Many predicted that Islamic parties would not become dominant in the April 2004 election despite the growth of Islam in the last decade. In fact, in 1999 the combined vote for the Islamic parties was about 17 per cent. If the PKB and PAN were added to the category of "Islamic parties", the combined vote was about 37 per cent. In 2004, the combined vote of five Islamic parties were 21 per cent, a bit higher than in 1999.[2] If the PKB and PAN were added to the category, the combined vote was about 39 per cent, indicating that the voters still preferred a secular rather than an Islamic state.

The results of the 2004 parliamentary election were not surprising, except for the rise of two "new" parties: the Partai Keadilan-Sejahtera (PKS, the Prosperous Justice Party, formerly Partai Keadilan or PK) and the Partai Demokrat (PD or the Democrat Party). The former was an "old" Islamic party which gained 1.4 per cent of the vote in the 1999 election, and was forced to change its name as it had failed to gain the minimum electoral threshold of 2 per cent to qualify to contest. The latter was a new party formed by Susilo Bambang Yudhoyono, chief security minister in the Megawati cabinet, until he resigned in March 2004 prior to the presidential election.

In this parliamentary election, Golkar secured 21.6 per cent of the vote, gaining a lower percentage than in 1999 (22.5 per cent) but still emerging as the largest party. The PDI-P only gained 18.5 per cent of the vote and occupied the second position, but compared to 1999, the party lost more than 15 per cent of the vote, implying that many urban poor who supported it during the 1999 election no longer did so in 2004. The PKB (10.6 per cent) and the PPP (8.2 per cent) occupied the third and fourth positions respectively but gained lower percentages of the vote compared to 1999. The PAN, the party of Amien Rais, was in the fifth place in 1999 but was relegated to the seventh position. The fifth and sixth positions were taken by the "new" stars: the PD (7.5 per cent) of Yudhoyono, and the PKS (7.3 per cent) of Hidayat Nur Wahid.

From the results of the parliamentary election of 2004, it is clear that the multi-party system of 1999 remained in place. In fact, the parliament became more fragmented than in 1999 as major parties gained lower percentages in 2004. The new parliament (DPR) consists of 550 members who are elected on party tickets. In addition, in the 2004 election, there was a new institution called the DPD. These representatives, numbering 128 members, do not represent political parties but themselves. Unlike the regional representatives in the past who were nominated and selected either by political parties or the government, these new representatives were elected directly by the voters themselves. This system, when developed, can serve as a senate-type institution in the Indonesian parliamentary system. Both the DPR and DPD constitute the MPR (Majelis Permusyawaratan Rakyat or People's Consultative Assembly) or the People's Consultative Assembly but DPD members are not legislators and do not have the power to propose bills in parliament.

The April parliamentary election also marked the end of the military-nominated seats in the Indonesian legislature. As all representative institutions in 2004 consisted of elected members, there was no room for nominated MPs from the TNI (Indonesian Armed Forces) and Polri (Indonesia Police Force). Although the military's formal involvement in Indonesian politics has ended, the military is still influential as retired military officers joined political parties to contest in the election and got into parliament. In addition, the military-business complex has not been touched as the government is not likely to be able to rule effectively without the military's support.

The 2004 presidential election was more democratic than the previous one as the nomination of presidential candidates was more open and democratic. The president was no longer decided by the MPR but by the people directly. However,

Table 1
Results of the Parliamentary Election (1999 and 2004)

Party	Percentage (2004)	Percentage (1999)	No. of Seats (2004)	No. of Seats (1999)
Golkar	21.58	22.46	128	120
PDI-P	18.53	33.73	109	153
PKB	10.57	12.66	52	51
PPP	8.15	10.72	58	58
PD	7.45	–	57	–
PKS/PK	7.34	1.36	45	7
PAN	6.44	7.12	52	34
PBB	2.62	1.94	11	13
PBR	2.44	–	13	–
PDS	2.13	–	12	–
PKPB	2.11	–	2	–
Others	10.24	10.04	11	26

Note: The PD, PBR, PDS and PKPB are new parties.
Source: Leo Suryadinata, *Elections and Politics in Indonesia* (Singapore: ISEAS 2002), pp.
220–23 and I Made Leo Wiratna, "Perkembangan Politik Triwulan Kedu (April–Juni:
Dari Pemilu Legislatif Menuju Pemilu Presiden", *Analisis CSIS* 33, no. 2 (June 2004):
143.

the laws governing the elections were not entirely new. Major political parties were still favoured and candidates nominated by major political parties had a better chance to be elected as president. There were also traces of collusion between parties regarding the presidential elections. Major parties proposed various bills, meant to block the possible presidential candidates of rival parties. For instance, Golkar proposed that the president should be a university graduate, which was clearly aimed at Megawati Sukarnoputri; the PDI-P proposed that a person with a criminal record would not be qualified to contest the presidency — this was aimed at Akbar Tanjung, the Golkar chairman who was then Speaker of the House. However, the parliament eventually dropped these restrictions, paving the way for Megawati and Akbar to contest.

The direct presidential election law did not allow an independent candidate to contest the presidency unless he or she was nominated by a political party which obtained 3 per cent of the DPR seats or 5 per cent of the valid votes for the DPR.[4] Nevertheless, a party which failed to reach the target could combine forces with other parties to nominate their candidates. Political parties were also allowed to nominate a person who was not originally a party member. This would offer a chance to some well-known non-governmental organization leaders to be presidential candidates.

Before the April 2004 election results were announced, there were a number of presidential hopefuls: apart from Megawati and Akbar Tanjung, General (retired) Susilo Bambang Yudhoyono (then Security Coordinating Minister), General (retired) Wiranto (former Security Co-ortinating Minister), General (retired) Agum Gumelar (then Minister for Communications), Dr Nurcholish Madjid (Leading Islamic Scholar), Sultan Hamengku Buwono X (Sultan of Yogyakarta), Hamzah Haz (then Vice President), Jusuf Kalla (then Coordinating Minister for People's Welfare), Hasyim Muzadi (then General Chairman of NU), Dr Amien Rais (then Speaker of the MPR and leader of PAN) and Surya Paloh (Acehnese business tycoon) were also included on the list. Later, Hadijanti Rukmana alias Tutut, daughter of Suharto, was also proposed by her newly formed party, the Partai Karya Peduli Bangsa (The Party Concerned about the Nation), and Megawati's sisters, Rachmawati and Sukmawati, were all reported to be interested in contesting the highest position in Indonesia.

The First Direct Presidential Election

During the presidential election in July 2004, presidential and vice-presidential candidates were required to be proposed in tandem. The pairing could depend on the results of the parliamentary election, as the official candidates were to be announced after the results of the parliamentary election were known. Observers felt that Megawati still had a chance, but she was unlikely to gain more than 50 per cent of the vote in the first round of the presidential election. A second round would therefore have to be held.

When the results of the parliamentary election were announced, it became clear that only seven parties were qualified to propose their presidential and vice-presidential candidates. Other parties could only do so when they combined their votes. On the closing date of the nomination, only six parties had proposed their candidates: Wiranto-Solehuddin Wahid (proposed by Golkar), Yudhoyono-Jusuf Kalla (proposed by the PD), Amien Rais-Siswono Husodo (proposed by PAN), Megawati-Hasyim Muzadi (proposed by the PDI-P), Hamzah Haz-Agum Gumelar (proposed by the PPP) and Gus Dur-Marwah Daud (proposed by the PKB). The PKS did not propose any presidential candidates. However, the Gus Dur-Marwah Daud pair was declared unqualified to contest as Gus Dur failed the physical fitness test, and when the election campaign started, there were only five pairs of presidential candidates. It is worth noting that Akbar Tandjung, who was expected to represent Golkar, was defeated by General (retired) Wiranto at the Golkar convention.[5]

The five pairs of presidential candidates had different characteristics and these characteristics may have had a bearing on the election results.

Both religion and ethnicity played a role in the choice of Indonesia's leaders. All of the presidents of Indonesia, except Habibie who assumed office by default, were Javanese. They were also Muslim rather than Christian. Among the Indonesian vice-presidents, there were both non-Javanese and Javanese.

Looking at the ethnic and religious backgrounds of the candidates, it is obvious that in terms of religion, all were Muslim, but in terms of ethnicity, all but one (Hamzah Haz) were Javanese. Of the vice-presidential candidates, all were also Muslim; in terms of ethnicity, it was also similar — all but one (Jusuf Kalla) were Javanese.

The first pair, Wiranto-Wahid, consisted of two Javanese, and therefore might not have been too attractive to non-Javanese voters. In addition, Wiranto is a retired general who was accused of being responsible for human rights abuses in East Timor, while Solehuddin Wahid, an NU leader, was deputy chairman for the promotion of human rights. This interesting combination could have helped Wiranto somewhat.

The second pair, Megawati-Hasyim, also comprised two Javanese and therefore could have been less attractive to the non-Javanese voters. However, Mega was considered to be "secular" in her political views while Hasyim was from NU, which was regarded as "more Islamic", therefore, in theory they would be able to attract both secular and Islamic voters. They are also civilians who may have appealed to voters who disliked the military.

The third pair, Amien-Siswono, were both Javanese and thus they were less attractive to the non-Javanese voters. However, as Amien had a reputation of being "Islamic" and "reformist" while Siswono had a reputation of being a "civilian nationalist", they could have appealed to voters who disliked the New Order and the military.

The fourth pair, Yudhoyono-Kalla, was a combination of Javanese and non-Javanese. This pair could have appealed to both Javanese and non-Javanese voters. Moreover, Yudhoyono's ex-military background and Kalla's civilian and "Islamic" background may also have increased these candidates' chances in the election.

The final pair, Hamzah-Agum, was a combination of non-Javanese and Javanese. The pair may have appealed more to the non-Javanese rather than Javanese. However, Agum was also relatively unknown and Hamzah's record as Megawati's vice-president was unimpressive.

It should also be noted that the presidential election was the election of individuals rather than parties. Therefore, personal image and popularity were more important than party affiliation. Although during the first round of the election, candidates with major party support tended to gain some advantage, it was not crucial. The Yudhoyono-Kalla pairing obtained 33.57 per cent of the vote. The pair was followed by Megawati-Hasyim Muzadi (26.61 per cent), Wiranto-Solehuddin Wahid (22.15 per cent), Amien-Siswono (14.66 per cent), and Hamzah-Gumelar (3.01 per cent). This showed that party affiliation was not crucial; otherwise, Yudhoyono would have obtained only about 10 per cent (the PD and PBB votes), while Amien would have only secured about 6.8 per cent (the PAN vote).

Why did Yudhoyono lead in the first round? Perhaps he was seen by many Indonesian voters as a strong candidate likely to "solve" Indonesia's problems. His partner, Jusuf Kalla, might also have helped to get the non-Javanese vote. As expected, none of the pairs gained more than 50 per cent of the vote, and the two highest pairs therefore had to contest in the second round. Wiranto was unhappy with the results and complained about irregularity. However, the Constitutional Court decided that the results were valid and Yudhoyono-Kalla and Megawati-Hasyim were delared the final contestants.

The Australian Embassy Bombing

Prior to the second round of the presidential election, on the morning of 9 September, there was a big bomb blast in front of the Australian embassy in Jakarta, resulting in at least 9 dead and more than 150 people injured. This was the third major bomb blast in Indonesia since the Bali bombing on 12 October 2002 and the Marriott Hotel bombing on 5 August 2003. This signified that terrorist activities in the region, especially in Indonesia, were still a fact of life: there had been a major bombing incident almost every ten months.

Table 2
Results of the First Round

Candidates	Number of vote	Percentage
Yudhoyono-Jusuf Kalla	39,838,184	33.57
Megawati-Hasyim Muzadi	31,569,104	26.61
Wiranto-Solehuddin Wahid	26,286,788	22.15
Amien-Siswono Husodho	17,392,931	14.66
Hamzah-Agum Gumelar	3,569,861	3.01
Total	118,656,868	100.00

Source: Calculated from "Hasil Pemilu Presiden dan Wakil Presiden Putaran I Ditetapkan dalam Keputusan KPU No.79/SK/KPU/2004", http://www.kpu.go.id/penetapanhasil/lihat-dalam.php?ID=5&cat=peneta...12/7/2004.

It was reported that the Jemaah Islamiyah (JI) admitted that it masterminded the Australian embassy bombing, implying that it was still able to strike at will. Since the capture of Hambali, the leader of the Indonesian JI, in Bangkok in August 2003, the JI had been reportedly crippled. However, it appeared that its capability to stage terrorist attacks was not undiminished. The bomb specialist in JI, Dr Azhahari, a Malaysian, remains at large probably in Indonesia. Security experts commented that JI members had enough chemicals to make bombs for sometime to come.

Why did the blast take place on 9 September, two days before the anniversary of the September 2001 attacks? Apart from its symbolic nature, there was no doubt that Australia — a close ally of the United States, the greatest enemy of terrorist organizations — was the target. It served as a warning to Western governments that terrorists would continue to attack the United States and its allies. However, the attack also meant to unsettle the Western community in Indonesia so that Westerners would leave the country. Furthermore, as the blast coincided with the trial of Abu Bakar Bashir, the spiritual leader of JI, it was meant to force the Indonesian government to compromise.

The Jakarta bombing once again showed that Indonesia was still very vulnerable to terrorist attacks for many reasons. But one thing is clear, the new democratic government often found it difficult to deal with terrorist issues, especially when they were connected to Islam. The terrorists were using Islam as their political spear and human rights as their political shield to attack the government and their perceived enemies. Courts were often reluctant to put the guilty in prison because of adherence to democratic principles and due legal process. However in the process, innocent people were killed and wounded, and the country suffered. The Marriott Hotel bombing in 2004 and the subsequent blast in front of the Australian embassy in Jakarta clearly showed that the victims were the ordinary people, especially poor Indonesians.

Anti-terrorist law in Indonesia is weak and has to be revamped to make it more effective. However, Jakarta elites who are concerned with their own political interests are often reluctant to give too much power to the authorities, especially to the police and the army, as they fear that this power would be abused. But without giving more power to them, counter-terrorism cannot be effective. This is a dilemma of the new Indonesian democratic system.

The bombings also showed that the Megawati government was ineffectual in its handling of the terrorist issue. One could argue that they may also have affected the 20 September presidential election, as Yudhoyono and Megawati were competing neck and neck. It was reported that Megawati was catching up in the opinion polls before the attack. In any case, the Jakarta blast on 9 September, 11 days before the election, helped Yudhoyono in the presidential race. Yudhoyono had a stronger image because of his military background and may have gained more support for his candidacy. However, one should not exaggerate this factor, as the majority of voters were more concerned with economic issues and they saw terrorism as a minor issue, unlike foreigners who saw terrorism as a major concern.

The Second Round of the Presidential Election

It should be noted that there was a new alliance of political parties during the second round of the election. As there were only two candidates, major and medium-sized political parties began to form alliances in order to reap post-election benefits. Golkar, under the leadership of Akbar Tanjung, sided with Megawati, hoping that he and Golkar would be able to gain cabinet and other important positions if Megawati won. The PPP under the leadership of Hamzah Haz also joined the Megawati camp. These three major parties and a few smaller parties formed the so-called National Coalition (Koalisi Kebangsaan), to challenge the People's Coalition (Koalasi Kerakyatan), led by Yudhoyono's PD.

On a party coalition basis, Megawati had the upper hand, but the direct presidential election was based on personality, not political parties, and party support was not as crucial as personal image and perceived capability by the voters. The first round of the presidential election showed that party loyalty was not a decisive factor among the voters in the 2004 election. Individual image and personality once again influenced, if not determined, the winner during the second round. Yudhoyono had a better image than Megawati. The former was described as a "thinking general", and one day before the second round of the election, he passed the oral examination for his PhD degree from the Institute of Agriculture in Bogor. During the second round of the presidential candidates' debate, Yudhoyono also showed his superiority over his opponent.

The campaign theme may also have helped Yudhoyono. His team highlighted "change" as its slogan while the Megawati team stressed "continuity" as Megawati felt that she had proven herself in the past three years. She argued that Indonesia under her leadership had achieved relative political and economic stability. However, the voters appeared to disagree with her. They wanted to have a "better" president to lead Indonesia for the next five years, and the Yudhoyono-Kalla team emerged victorious.

Table 3
Results of the Second Round

Candidates	Number of vote	Percentage
Megawati-Hasyim Muzadi	44,990,704	39.38
Yudhoyono-Jusuf Kalla	69,266,350	60.62
Total	114,257,054	100

Source: KPU, 4 October 2004.

The 2004 Cabinet: A Political Compromise

During the presidential campaign, Yudhoyono promised that he would improve Indonesia's economic, social and security situations. To achieve these goals, he said that he needed a cabinet of "professionals" rather than "politicians".

On midnight of 20 October, after a delay of almost four hours, Yudhoyono eventually announced his cabinet line-up.[6] There were last minute negotiations and bargaining. The cabinet is not the "professional cabinet" that he promised. Rather, it is a "compromise cabinet", made up of political appointees and professionals. At least 14 members are from political parties. Apparently he had to accept political realities.

The most surprising was the appointment of Aburizal Bakrie, a Golkar leader who was a friend of Jusuf Kalla (Vice-President) and a foe of Akbar Tanjung, as the Coordinating Minister of Economy. Bakrie is not an economist. He was trained in electrical engineering but became a business tycoon. He was reported to have been US$1 billion in debt during the economic crisis.[7] The appointment of a not-so-successful business tycoon who is a non-economist to lead the economic team is disappointing. There is no guarantee that there is no conflict of interest.

The economic team was "saved" by the inclusion of those who are either well-trained economists or bureaucrats with experience in the Pacific Economic Cooperation Council (PECC): Trade Minister Mari Pangestu, Finance Minister Jusuf Anwar, and Bappenas head Sri Mulyani Indrawati. When the cabinet line-up was announced, the value of the rupiah dropped slightly and the Indonesian stock market was negative.

Both Bakrie and Jusuf Kalla had a reputation for being advocates of "indigenism" or "affirmative action". Even after being elected vice-president, Kalla's continued talk about indigenism and affirmative action was well publicized in the media and caused some concern among domestic and foreign investors.[8]

What about Yudhoyono's promise to combat corruption? His campaign for a clean government started well with the appointment of the new attorney general Abdurrahman Saleh because Abdurrahman has a courageous and clean image in his dealings with the Akbar Tanjung corruption case appeal. Out of the four high court judges, he was the only one who resisted pressure and voted for the guilty verdict against Akbar. His appointment was encouraging but it does not mean that he will be able to do much as the judicial system in Indonesia still needs to be reformed. He has an uphill task in combating corruption and requires the president's support if he wants to act.

With regard to security and anti-terrorism, Yudhoyono brought five retired military generals into his cabinet, including a retired Admiral, Widodo A.S., who was appointed as the Coordinating Minister for Political and Security Affairs. M. Ma'ruf who was appointed as Home Affairs Minister is also a retired general. Although Yudhoyono himself was the chief security minister in the Megawati cabinet when major bombings took place, he was not at the helm and had not been able to do much. The situation is different now as he is the president and he will be fully responsible for the security of the country. Further turbulence will destabilize the political situation and deter foreign investment.

Tsunami, Domestic Politics, and Foreign Policy

Soon after Yudhoyono became President, Indonesia encountered a major natural disaster, which has some implications for both domestic politics and foreign relations.

Indonesia's Aceh province was the area worst hit by the tsunami on 26 December 2004. There were more than 100,000 casualties and another 100,000 are missing.[9] American leaders initially responded a bit slowly, but as events unfolded, Washington realized the seriousness of the disaster and quickly acted. The U.S. military offered to air-drop aid in remote places and rescue the survivors in Aceh. President Yudhoyono permitted international aircraft, "including U.S. helicopters from a battle fleet carrier", to land at the military airport. The *New York Times* reported that, "in normal times, Indonesia's worst nightmare was having American marines arrive on the Banda Aceh tarmac … Yet here we are in the middle of this operation and we have marines here. It's a sign of progress".[10]

Some Indonesians were suspicious of the presence of foreign forces, particularly the Americans, whose government was critical of Indonesia and whose Middle East policy was unpopular among many Indonesian Muslims. The local Indonesian military, which has controlled Aceh since the imposition of martial law on 19 May 2003, was also uneasy about the presence of foreigners. However, the Indonesian central government, especially President Yudhoyono, on 8 January stated that the foreign troops were on a humanitarian mission.[11] They were welcome and Indonesians should be grateful to them. The major daily *Kompas* also echoed the president's view.[12]

Indeed, top U.S. leaders made efforts to show that Washington was a friend in need. Initially the U.S. pledged only US$35 million in aid but within a few days it increased the amount tenfold. President Bush and two former presidents came together to urge the American people to donate generously to help the countries affected by the disaster; they particularly highlighted Indonesia. On 3 January 2005, President Bush and his wife, accompanied by two former presidents, George Bush Sr. and Bill Clinton, visited the Indonesian embassy in Washington D.C., expressing their deepest sympathies to the Indonesian government and people.[13]

The outgoing Secretary of State Colin Powell together with Jeb Bush, brother of President Bush and governor of Florida, visited Indonesia to see the devastation at first hand, and subsequently attended the ASEAN summit convened to discuss rescue and rebuilding efforts. The American delegates reiterated their pledge to help.

All of these signs show that American-Indonesian relations are improving, but has it improved significantly? Earlier, during the meeting held on the sidelines of the APEC summit in Santiago on 21 November 2004, Bush had offered Yudhoyono, the newly elected president, the opportunity of resuming U.S. military cooperation with Indonesia, which has been withheld for the last few years. However, the U.S. imposed six conditions, which included human rights demands. Washington wanted Jakarta to seriously punish the human rights violators in East Timor (1999) and Timika (2002). The next day, Indonesia's Minister for Defence, Juwono Sudarsono commented that, "we don't accept calls from outside parties to try the cases involving Indonesia based on their regulations".[14] He also noted that, "The U.S. often made worse violations than those that took place in Indonesia".

In fact, Washington-Jakarta relations had deteriorated towards the end of Suharto's rule over the issue of Indonesia's poor human rights record. After the fall of Suharto, relations did not improve either, mainly due to events in East Timor, Papua, and Aceh. On the eve of East Timor's independence, the Jakarta authorities were alleged to have supported the militia to terrorize the East Timorese population and commit atrocities. In August 2002, two Americans and one Indonesian were killed when a group of armed men opened fire on two buses carrying staff of the giant mining company, Freeport Indonesia, in Timika.[15] Non-governmental organizations in Papua accused the military of launching the attack, but with no strong evidence.[16] The U.S. Congress imposed an arms embargo on Indonesia. In addition, Indonesian military operations in Aceh had also drawn criticism in the United States.

The Indonesian government, seemingly annoyed with the United States, looked for an alternative. During the Megawati presidency, Jakarta even tried to purchase arms from Russia and China to counterbalance the reliance on America. In addition, U.S. policy towards the Middle East did not have Jakarta's support. The rise of political Islam in Indonesian politics and the presence of many Islamists in past and current governments also hindered the improvement of bilateral relations.

Although the tsunami disaster appeared to offer a golden opportunity for better relations between Jakarta and Washington, it also reflected internal divisions within Jakarta. The presence of foreign, especially U.S., troops, in Aceh after the tsunami became an issue. Hidayat Nur Wahid, the chairman of the People's Consultative Assembly (who was leader of the PKS), wanted the troops to leave in one month and Jusuf Kalla, the vice-president, would give them only 3 months.[17] Strong suspicion of American power lingered. However, Yudhoyono stressed the contribution of the foreign troops in helping the Acehnese. Juwono Sudarsono also defended the foreign presence. Many observers pointed out the differences and even a possible power struggle between Yudhoyono and Kalla.

Washington under Bush has been eager to normalize military relations with the largest Muslim country in the world and his administration was able to convince Congress that Indonesia, under Yudhoyono, has improved its human rights record. A suspended military training operation programme was eventually resumed but military relations have not been fully restored.

The tsunami has also helped improve Indonesia's relations with other ASEAN states. Soon after the disaster, upon the suggestion of Singapore, there was an ASEAN summit to discuss post-tsunami reconstruction, and both ASEAN and non-ASEAN countries pledged to assist Thailand and Indonesia.

The tsunami has been used by Indonesia's neighbours to improve bilateral relations with Jakarta. Singapore was one of the first countries to send aid to the disaster-affected areas and received special mention and thanks from both the president and vice-president of Indonesia. Malaysia also sent a special rescue mission to help the Acehnese, showing neighbourly friendship. In February 2005, Yudhoyono visited Malaysia and Singapore to further cultivate cordial relations.

While Indonesia's relations with Singapore continued to improve, with the exception of a small demonstration at the Singapore embassy in Jakarta over alleged toxic waste dumping in Batam, Indonesia's relations with Malaysia were far less cordial, due to the presence of two major problems: the lingering illegal immigrant issue and the dispute over the sovereignty of the Laut Ambalat (Ambalat Sea near Sulawesi). Soon after the tsunami, Malaysia decided to set a final deadline for Indonesian illegal workers to leave the country and penalize those who continued to stay. This led to protests from Jakarta. Besides, Malaysia had also given a permit to a Dutch oil company to undertake exploration in the Ambalat Sea, which Indonesia claims as being within its territory. Indonesian naval ships moved into the area to stop the exploration. Tension arose and unfriendly exchanges took place between these two neighbours. Nevertheless, they eventually cooled down but the problems remain largely unresolved.

Admittedly, prior to the tsunami, Jakarta had already been seeking to improve foreign relations generally. Following the results of the presidential election, foreign dignitaries for the first time were invited to witness Yudhoyono's swearing-in ceremony. Present were not only ASEAN leaders, but also John Howard, the Australian Prime Minister. There was discussion of a new security agreement between the two countries.

Concluding Remarks

2004 was the year of elections; it marked another successful milestone for Indonesia's young democracy as the events took place in an orderly and peaceful manner. It also indicated the continuing triumph of secular rather than Islamic ideology in Indonesia as represented by the victories of Golkar, the PDI-P and the PD. However, the number of Islamic party votes has increased, and the challenge to Indonesia of becoming a Muslim, if not an Islamic state, remains.

Yudhoyono not only faces the challenge of Islamists, he also has to resolve major economic, security, and political problems in the foreseeable future.

The Indonesian economy has not deteriorated since Yudhoyono assumed the presidency. The "new" economic policy is more a continuation of the past and "indigenism" has not been reflected in the policy so far. This is intended to stabilize the domestic political economy and encourage foreign investment.

The Indonesian government has been in deficit and aware of the danger of continuing to subsidize fuel prices since Megawati's presidency. However, due to widespread opposition, the subsidies were not reduced. Nevertheless, the government has difficulty in maintaining the subsidies; and eventually decided to reduce the oil subsidies.[18] This measure will be unpopular among the voters but the Yudhoyono administration will have to face it.

Furthermore, the 26 December 2004 tsunami in Aceh and north Sumatra which killed more than 200,000 people, tended to divert government attention from other areas to Aceh. However, the tsunami ironically has also provided an economic opportunity for Indonesia as international donations poured in and are likely to provide capital for the reconstruction of the affected places and hence stimulate local economic growth.

It is also important to resolve the problem of terrorism if Indonesia is to encourage foreign investment. It is not surprising that the Yudhoyono government decided to reissue arrest warrants on the two leading terrorist fugitives, Azahari Husin and Noordin Mohammad Top, the JI bomb-makers. Although the president has allied with some Islamic "fundamentalist" parties, he has not stopped the new trial of Abu Bakar Bashir. It shows that the president has been able to convince his Islamic allies that the campaign against terror should be taken seriously if Indonesia is to improve its economy and be respected in the international community. People believe that a president with a military background will somehow be more successful in handling terrorism.

Yudhoyono also has strategies to deal with the rebellions in Aceh and Papua (formerly Irian Jaya). He is willing to talk to the rebels provided that their goal is not independence from the Republic of Indonesia. Nevertheless, he has a difficult task winning the hearts and minds of the rebels if he is unable to combat corruption, since the problem is partly connected with corruption on the part of both the civilian administrators and armed forces.

Being a leader of a medium-sized party, which allied with small and other medium-sized parties such as the PBB and PKS, he may have difficulties in getting parliamentary bills passed. Nevertheless, the alliance of opposition parties, known as the National Coalition, is no longer united. The PPP left the coalition and the major parties, especially Golkar, have suffered internal splits. Akbar Tanjung was ousted at the Golkar National Congress in Bali in December 2004 and Jusuf Kalla became the new general chairman of the party.[19] This may make the passing of bills in parliament easier for the Yudhoyono government. Moreover, he is the first directly elected president and may use his popularity to impress parliament that he is backed by 61 per cent of the Indonesian people. It may make opposition to him more difficult, at least initially.

Nevertheless, the rise of Kalla also poses a problem for Yudhoyono. The vice-president, who is supposed to have a largely ceremonial role, is too eager to participate in the government. He has even issued decrees, which are supposed to come from the presidential office. In fact, there have been reports of a split between the president and vice-president, which could result in political instability.

Yudhoyono is aware of the myriad problems that Indonesia faces and that the promises that he made during the campaign are difficult to achieve. People who were disappointed with Megawati and voted for Yudhoyono want to see change, if not miracles, under the new president. He knows that people have very high expectations of him. Not surprisingly, during his swearing-in as the sixth president of Indonesia, he told the people that they should not have too high expectations.

Yudhoyono has been able to maintain the present economic performance and economic stability in the early days of his administration, but the terrorist leaders are still at large. Nevertheless, in his first 100 days, there were no major terrorist attacks. But the problem of terrorism is not resolved. His record on combating corruption has also been modest: so far no big fish has been prosecuted. Some analysts noted that not many things could be done within such a brief period. Capital investment, for instance, will take at least a year before it starts flowing back. As stated by two observers in the *Jakarta Post*, "For sure it will take 1,000 days, or even more, to rid the country of its terrorists, put more people back to work and bring about a cleaner government".[20]

Notes

[1] For a detailed analysis of the 2004 election in Indonesia, see Aris Ananta, Evi Nurvidya Arifin and Leo Suryadinata, *Emerging Democracy in Indonesia* (Singapore: Institute of Southeast Asian Studies, forthcoming).

[2] These Islamic parties were Partai Persatuan Pembangunan or PPP (8.31 per cent), Partai Keadilan Sejahtera or PKS (7.19 per cent), Partai Bulan Bintang or PBB (2.57 per cent), Partai Bintang Reformasi or PBR (2.31 per cent) and Partai Persatuan Nahdlatul Ulama Indonesia or PPNU (0.78 per cent).

[3] The PD stands for Partai Demokrat (Democrat Party), the PBR stands for Partai Bintang Reformasi (a splinter group of the PPP), the PDS stands for Partai Damai Sejahtera, a Christian-based party, and the PKPB stands for Partai Karya Peduli Bangsa (led by a retired army general, Hartono and Tutut, Suharto's eldest daughter).

[4] See "Undang-Undang Republik Indonesia No. 23 Tahun 2003 tentang Pemilihan Umum Presiden dan Wakil Presiden", Bab XIV, pasal 101, issued on 31 July 2003.

[5] Five leaders competed for the Golkar presidential candidates (Wiranto, Akbar Tandjung, Aburizal Bakrie, Surya Paloh and Prabowo Subianto). Akbar Tandjung who was the favourite of National Leadership Board was unable to gain enough votes and was eventually defeated by Wiranto. "Setelah Suara Akbar Roboh", *Tempo*, 2 May 2004, p. 30.

[6] For the new cabinet line up, see "United Indonesia Cabinet line up", *Jakarta Post online*. http://www.thejakartapost.com/detaillatestnews.asp?fileid=20041021...

[7] The *Straits Times* commented that "The US$1 billion (S$1.68 billion) in debts his conglomerate racked up during the Asian financial crisis had raised concerns for markets

even before his appointment." See, "Who's Who in New Government," *Straits Times*, 21 October 2004.

8   "Jusuf Kalla: Perlakuan ke Kelompok Pengusaha Akan Dibedakan", *Sinar Harapan*, 12 October 2004.

9   "The Toll so Far", *Straits Times*, 26 February 2005.

10   Jane Perlez, "In Crisis, Jakarta was Slow to Respond", *New York Times*, 4 January 2005.

11   "Foreign Troops Help: SBY," *Jakarta Post*, 9 January 2005.

12   "Tajuk Rencana: Jangan Curiga, justru Berterima Kasih," *Kompas*, 19 January 2005.

13   "Bush dan Dua Mantan Presiden AS ke KBRI," *Sinar Harapan*, 4 January 2005.

14   "Indonesia Refuses to have Timika and East Timor Cases as a Condition of Resuming Indonesia-US Military Cooperation," *Tempo Interactive*, 23 November 2004, 00:28.

15   "No TNI chief-FBI Team Meeting Scheduled: TNI", *Jakartapost.com* (Latest News), 21 January 2003, 8:33 PM.

16   Ibid.

17   "Yinni xiwang wuaiguo junren, zuihao jinkuai cheli Yaqi" [Indonesia hopes that foreign troops leave Aceh quickly], *Lianhe Zaobao*, 13 January 2005.

18   "Govt Asked to Time Oil Price Hike", *Jakarta Post*, 4 December 2004.

19   "Pagi yang Pahit di Nusa Dua", *Tempo*, 2 January 2005, pp. 158–60.

20   James Van Zorge and Dennis Heffernan, "The Myth of the First 100 Days and Susilo's Real Challenges", *Jakarta Post*, 1 October 2004.

INDONESIAN FOREIGN POLICY
A Wounded Phoenix

Donald E Weatherbee

Introduction: Heightened Expectations

On 16th August 2004, Indonesian President Megawati Sukarnoputri gave the annual presidential state address to Indonesia's Dewan Perwakilan Rakyat, its House of Representatives. As it was, this turned out to be her final appearance in that role since five weeks later she was decisively defeated in the run-off presidential election by Susilo Bambang Yudhoyono. In her speech documenting the achievements of her stewardship of the republic, little reference was made to foreign policy. This was understandable given the critical political and economic domestic crises facing the Indonesian leadership. The event that was singled out in her brief allusion to foreign affairs was telling, however, signalling as it did the assertion of a re-emergent regional leadership role for Indonesia. The touchstone for the claim was the 9th ASEAN Summit held in Bali in October 2003, where she said,

> In ASEAN, which constitutes a priority in the conduct of our foreign policy, Indonesia was once again able to show its leadership. The success of Indonesia, during the 9th Summit, in preparing the Bali Concord II has strengthened the role, commitment, and the leadership of Indonesia within ASEAN.[1]

This was not just posturing by Megawati. More neutral Indonesia-watchers picked up the theme. Anthony Smith wrote: "The Bali Summit witnessed Indonesia's re-emergence to the role of group leader, or at least demonstrated Jakarta's desire to begin to steer the direction of the grouping again."[2]

Megawati's celebration of Indonesia's important role in formulating the heralded Bali Concord II (ASEAN Concord II) evoked memories of the 1976 Bali Summit

DONALD E. WEATHERBEE is the Donald S. Russell Distinguished Professor Emeritus at the University of South Carolina, Columbia, USA.

hosted by President Suharto. That summit was the collective response of the five non-communist states of ASEAN to the change in the regional geostrategic environment following the 1975 communist victories in Vietnam, Cambodia, and Laos. At this first ASEAN Summit, the leaders of the ASEAN-five proclaimed the politically path-breaking "Declaration of ASEAN Concord". This reflected then, as the ASEAN Concord II reflects now, the felt urgent need for greater political and economic cooperation among the ASEAN members faced by common external challenges. The first Bali Concord in its political programme called for the "strengthening of political solidarity by promoting the harmonization of views, coordinating positions and, where possible or desirable, taking common action".[3] That Bali summit cemented Indonesia's position as the key local player in Southeast Asia's international relations.

In a sense, at the ASEAN level, the 2003 Bali Summit and its formal documents signified a rededication to the goals expressed more than a quarter of a century earlier at Bali. The challenges for an ASEAN-ten, however, are different from those that faced the core five. Today's security agenda is topped by terrorism and transnational crime to be addressed through an ASEAN characterized by intramural political divergence and diminishing international relevance. The Bali Concord II's objective is the creation of "a dynamic, cohesive, resilient and integrated ASEAN Community" by the year 2020.[4] The rubric "ASEAN Community" is an umbrella vision sheltering three separate but, conceptually at least, integrative initiatives: an ASEAN Security Community (ASC), an ASEAN Economic Community (AEC), and an ASEAN Social and Cultural Community (ASCC). It fell to Indonesia, whose turn it was to chair ASEAN, to give content to the previous 8th ASEAN Summit's "Phnom Penh Agenda Towards A Community of Southeast Asian Nations".[5] The outline of "community" that was developed by the "ASEAN-ocrats" between the 8th and 9th summits went well beyond the limited call at Phnom Penh.

At the Indonesian national level, the Bali Summit was the first opportunity for a post-Suharto leadership to lay claim to an important role in shaping the region's future — a reassertion of Indonesian primacy in Southeast Asia. The Indonesian government, backstopped by Track II intellectual inputs, most vigorously promoted the idea of an ASEAN Security Community. The ASC was deemed Indonesia's "opportunity to reclaim its 'strategic centrality' within ASEAN, which in turn would enable the Association to reclaim its 'diplomatic centrality' within the international community".[6] As one Indonesian commentator put it, the focused foreign policy of the Megawati government had repositioned Indonesian foreign policy, in particular re-establishing its cardinal position in ASEAN.[7]

At the ASEAN level, the ASC is supposed to give the regional grouping a political and security coherence it has lacked since the ending of the Third Indochina War — before the membership expansion from six to ten. Since the dissolution in 1991 of the political cement of external challenge offered by Vietnam in Cambodia, ASEAN leaders have sought to find new frameworks for collective efforts. The 1992 ASEAN Summit's "Singapore Declaration" was a call for action for ASEAN "to move towards a higher plane of political and economic cooperation to secure regional peace and security".[8] On the economic side, the "higher plane" is represented by the ASEAN Free Trade Arrangement (AFTA), which, spurred on by Thailand and Singapore — not Indonesia, provides a foundation for the mooted ASEAN Economic Community. Now, with the Bali Concord II on record and the ASC under construction, one might think that ASEAN finally is poised to reach a higher political plane with Indonesia its putative steward.

Patterns of Indonesian Foreign Policy

Indonesia's national emblem is the mythical *garuda*, the man-bird on whom the god Vishnu is mounted. In terms of Indonesia's international capabilities the *garuda* can be metaphorically paired with the phoenix, the fabulous bird that arises from the ashes of the fire that consumed the body of its predecessor. Under Sukarno, Indonesia's "possible dream" became a nightmare in a self-isolating foreign policy of confrontation with the West and undeclared war with Malaysia.[9] The politically polarizing domestic consequences of "guided democracy" ultimately led to the 1965 communist-backed attempted coup and the transfer of power to Gen. Suharto. Out of the ashes of Sukarno's "old order", Suharto's "new order" government engaged with the West and, in the creation of ASEAN, with its neighbours in a foreign policy "designed to undo the damage" that Sukarno's policy had done to the country.[10] By the mid-1980s Indonesia was secure in a heightened regional profile underpinned by economic growth and political stability. It had become the implicit leader of ASEAN, mediator of regional disputes, and a respected spokesman for the interests of the so-called South, or Third World, in regional and global forums.[11] By the mid-1990s, Indonesia had been classified as a *pivotal* state in an analytical scheme that saw the country poised at a critical point whose choices would strongly affect regional and even global security.[12]

Indonesia's dominance in ASEAN and its growing regional high visibility, perhaps best illustrated by the 1994 Bogor APEC Summit, dissolved in the financial meltdown of the "crash of '97". The economic abyss was deepened by the political collapse of the Suharto regime and the domestic turmoil of a problematic transition to democracy. The vaunted political stability underpinning Indonesia's regional leadership gave way to the competition of conflicting political agendas, the erosion of social cohesion, and a serious degradation of the institutional capabilities of the republic. The sorry state of Indonesia's international affairs was compounded by the violent aftermath of the August 1999 East Timorese overwhelming vote for independence after nearly a quarter of a century of Indonesian occupation. This was followed by the internationally condemned horrific assault on the pro-independence East Timorese population by military-backed pro-Indonesian militias.

The East Timor tragedy could also be seen as ASEAN's shame. In its commitment to the fundamental principles of sovereignty and non-interference, ASEAN had tacitly ignored what was happening in East Timor from the Dili massacre in 1991 onwards, until an outraged international community demanded action. This was the "ASEAN way" at work. Jakarta's unwillingness or incapacity to control the violent rampage in its former province led to international intervention, first by the International Force for East Timor (INTERFET), succeeded by a UN peacekeeping force and transitional administration (UNTAET). To the chagrin of Indonesia's ultranationalists, several ASEAN countries ultimately participated in the intervention, with Thailand and the Philippines making battalion-sized military contributions. The uniformed troops in the international force from ASEAN countries were not part of an ASEAN force. They were national contingents dedicated to the Australian-led multinational force fielded in the ASEAN region. Then, as they met in 2002, the ASEAN foreign ministers, with straight faces, "commended Indonesia for all its efforts in resolving the East Timor issue".[13] The East Timor case diminished ASEAN's international credibility as contributor to regional stability and peaceful order. To examine ASEAN's inaction in the East Timor case is to better understand its inaction today in the Myanmar case.

Both ASEAN's every-country-for-itself response to the "crash of '97" and the East Timor case raised serious questions with respect to the relevance of ASEAN to the post-Cold War issues confronting the region. To this was added the loss of Indonesian regional leadership. The future of a downward spiralling Indonesia itself had become a matter of great concern for even the survival of ASEAN.[14] Recrudescent separatist sentiment and low-level insurgency in Aceh and Papua, emboldened by East Timor's independence, menaced the territorial integrity of the state that was wracked by increasing sectarian and ethnic conflict. Being a pivotal state did not necessarily only have positive outcomes in terms of contributions to regional development and security. Indonesia, if its problems remained unresolved, rather than being the core of regional stability, threatened to destabilize the region. Singapore's Prime Minister Goh Chok Tong expressed the view held by most

ASEAN leaders that if Indonesia unravelled "the consequence for the entire region will be horrendous".

It is from the ashes of the Suharto regime that an Indonesian phoenix struggles to find wing. The brief B.J. Habibie presidency only stirred the ashes and got burned again in East Timor. Foreign policy in the foreshortened Abdurrahman Wahid presidency was characterized by erratic eccentricity. The groundwork laid in the Megawati government for an interest-based policy centred on the region was nearly undone by a fumbling reaction to the new security demands of the war on terrorism, the spreading war in Aceh, corruption, and economic nationalism. A sympathetic review of her legacy concluded that she should feel content that she "helped resuscitate foreign policy, which at one point in time, during the Wahid government, lost its soul".[15] At the least, she left a platform on which the Yudhoyono government can build "in order to capitalize", in the words of a *Jakarta Post* analyst, "on the gains the country has achieved from its international relations to build a stronger and more respected Indonesia".[16]

A symbolic expression of Indonesia's new-found international self-confidence was the planning for a golden jubilee commemoration of the 1955 Asian-African Conference to be capped by an Asian-African Summit, 21–23 April 2005. The original Bandung Conference marked Indonesia's formal debut under President Sukarno as a regional power to be reckoned with. Looking back, current Indonesian Foreign Minister Hassan Wirajuda has identified the Bandung Conference as "a defining moment" in the histories of the Afro-Asian countries.[17] The decision for a 2005 commemoration of the Bandung Conference echoes the April 1985 convening by Indonesia of an 80-nation thirtieth anniversary celebration, giving the Suharto government its first significant extra-regional platform from which to project Indonesia's leadership. Although initially planned for Megawati to be front and centre, Yudhoyono will hold the stage for Indonesia.

The election of Yudhoyono has led to even greater expectations about Indonesia's new role. A respected former editor of the *Far Eastern Economic Review* wrote that with Yudhoyono's presidency "it's time for the country to revive its role in regional and world affairs. This is important, because without Indonesia's presence and responsible leadership, Southeast Asia's chemistry is thrown out of balance and it becomes a region diminished in the eyes of the world".[18] In the domestic discussions of Indonesia's reassertion of an ASEAN leadership role there is a whiff of what Michael Leifer famously described as Indonesia's "sense of regional entitlement".[19] Few Indonesians would disagree with the proposition that "as single largest member of the group, Indonesia is expected to assume the leadership position within ASEAN" since "the future of more than 500 million people, to a large extent, depends on Indonesia's leadership".[20]

In his inaugural address Yudhoyono staked out his own vision of foreign policy in terms of continuity: "My administration will continue to uphold the free and active principle of foreign policy and Indonesia is determined to become a voice that promotes peace, increases prosperity, and defends justice."[21] In his first venture in a major multilateral forum, the November 2004 APEC meeting in Santiago, Chile, Yudhoyono was in command of an Indonesian agenda little different from that of his immediate predecessor — the search for investment, cooperation in the fight against terrorism, support of Indonesian territorial integrity, normalizing defence relations with the United States, and, failing that, the search for alternative arms sources.[22]

His appeal to the "free and active" principle, of course, reiterates a constant element in the rhetorical underpinning of Indonesian foreign policy. First articulated in 1948 by Mohammad Hatta, Indonesia's founding vice president, in the Cold War context it referred to Indonesia's nonaligned posture. Radicalized by Sukarno, it called for an ultimately self-destructive revisionist overthrow of the "imperialist" world order. Suharto's twinning of domestic stability and economic progress with advocacy of the South's agenda in a cooperative dialogue with the developed world gave a different nuance to the principle. Operationally, "free and active" defines a foreign policy in pursuit of national interests as determined by the incumbent regime. Success or failure in promoting those interests is not a function of rhetorical appeal to principle but the mobilization and deployment of real capabilities.

Despite the hopes and expectations that with the election of Yudhoyono a critical corner has been turned in Indonesia, it is much too early to speculate on whether or not a new Indonesian foreign policy phoenix can launch itself into the ASEAN and East Asian international political atmosphere. The assertions of a resurrected leadership role for Indonesia are balanced by sober appraisals of Indonesian capabilities to lead in fact, pointing out resistance in ASEAN to Indonesian pretensions.[23] The argument to be made here is that if Indonesia actively seeks to recapture the regional predominance attributed to Indonesia as the ASEAN *primus inter pares* in the Suharto era, it would be a wounded phoenix, lacking the capabilities of its Suharto predecessor, competing with other possible claimants to leadership,[24] and in an international environment in which structures and institutions based on Southeast Asian political and economic exclusivity have an air of anachronistic irrelevance.

Indonesian regional leadership would have to be expressed through an increasingly inchoate ASEAN whose integral sense of common purpose has been dissipated through expansion, economic and political tiering, deepening cultural gulfs, and multiple bilateral irritations. Proposed future "community" structures remain embedded in the fundamentals of sovereignty and non-interference, the historical stumbling blocks to truly integrated ASEAN initiatives. Furthermore, Jakarta would be seeking to influence the behaviour of Southeast Asian states that in critical issue areas tend to look outside the region, especially to China, for direction. The question is, unlike the case of pre-1997 Indonesia, would Jakarta's putative lead have any followers? Part of the answer can be found in the ASEAN responses to Indonesia's chosen leadership vehicle, the ASEAN Security Community.

The ASEAN Security Community (ASC)

In platitudinous manner, the authors of the Bali Concord II announced that the ASEAN Security Community:

> is envisaged to bring ASEAN's political and security cooperation to a higher plane to ensure that the countries in the region live at peace with one another and the world at large in a just, democratic and harmonious environment. The ASEAN Security Community members shall rely exclusively on peaceful processes in the settlement of intra-regional differences and regard their security as fundamentally linked to one another and bound by geographic location, common vision and objectives.

The notion of an ASEAN security community is not new. It has been a matter of theoretical and analytical discourse for at least two decades.[25] A general definition of a security community is a group of states "which have developed a long-term habit of peaceful interaction and ruled out the use of force in settling disputes with other members of the group".[26] In its usual formulation, the empirical evidence for such a community has been the absence of war. The intellectual roots of this approach reach back to the elaboration of the framework established nearly half a century ago by Karl Deutsch and his collaborators for the analysis of Western European political integration.[27] A security community is a condition of peaceful interstate relations among a defined set of states. A more limited framework utilizes regime theory to describe patterns of security relations within ASEAN in which the common interests of the ASEAN states converge to reduce substantially the possibility of armed conflict among them. Emmers described ASEAN as a "regime for cooperative security" concentrating on conflict avoidance and management.[28] Buzan coined the term "security complex" to describe the "durable and relatively self-contained patterns of security relations generated by the local states themselves".[29]

In discussions of a security community or security regime, an underlying theoretical thread is that of norm building through which a values-based shared regional identity can be created. Beyond norms and values, the policy emphasis has been on institutional and informal mechanisms to mediate and limit intra-ASEAN conflict. The tools the member states have employed have been largely the traditional methods of statecraft — suasion, diplomacy, mediation, and even coercion — usually utilized in bilateral settings in which traditional measures of capabilities and interest are at play.[30] Although an ASEAN multilateral structure for regional security exists on paper in the Treaty of Amity and Cooperation in Southeast Asia (TAC), national self-interests have prevented the institutionalization and application of its conflict resolution provisions.[31] It is commonly agreed that ASEAN "does not have strong mechanisms to enforce norms on its member governments, nor institutionalized means of conflict resolution".[32]

What does the ASC offer in terms of intra-ASEAN security relations that is new? In a programmatic sense, the ideal foundations of the ASC already exist in one form or another in ASEAN's lengthy documentary and rhetorical record. As noted by one commentator, "The ASC appears to be an extension of existing ASEAN arrangements".[33] As such, the fundamental obstacle to integrative regionalism in Southeast Asia that has for nearly forty years prevented ASEAN from turning high flights of rhetoric to policy reality persists. This is the working of the "ASEAN way" in which the principles of consensus, sovereignty, and non-interference are central to the association's operational code. This means that state compliance with norms, rules, and practices will remain voluntary and issue-selective, so that rather than a community, the organization can still be more accurately described as an association. As in all other ASEAN injunctions for collective action, these principles are enshrined again in the Bali Concord II, which explicitly states: "Member countries shall exercise their rights to lead their national existence free from outside interference in their internal affairs".

As planning moved from the declaratory Bali Concord II to an action document at the November 2004 Vientiane 10th ASEAN Summit, divergent official perceptions of what an ASEAN Security Community would be became evident. It was easier to define what it is not to be: not a defence alliance, not a common foreign policy. The tricky question had to do with the political permeability of sovereign state boundaries to the requirements of an ASEAN security community. The discourse took place usually behind the scenes, but occasionally the issues were publicly vented. Two back-to-back speeches in August 2004 by two ASEAN heads of government are informative. On 7 August, Malaysia's Prime Minister Abdullah Badawi asserted at a Kuala Lumpur conference that, "there should be universal acceptance that community interests should prevail over national interests on issues affecting the community".[34] He went on to argue that a "rules based" as opposed to "policy based" community should have the capacity to enforce its decisions. Finally, he insisted that community members should adhere to a common set of community values. He sidestepped the problem of reconciling his vision of establishing a community with clear rules and structure but at the same time fully respecting the sovereignty of its member states. He captured the dilemma by stating that the ASEAN community "will not require member states to forfeit their sovereign rights or competencies". The "individuality of the member states will be allowed to flourish", but at the same time the member states will share common principles, practices and values.

A day later, Vietnam Prime Minister Phan Van Khai gave a speech celebrating ASEAN Culture Week in Hanoi.[35] The Vietnamese Prime Minister praised the wise and flexible application of ASEAN's fundamental principles including consensus, non-interference and sovereignty as mechanisms for balancing regional cooperation and national interests. In addressing the issues of constructing an ASEAN community, he insisted that national participation in the regional integration process was on a voluntary and non-binding basis. He emphasized that in terms of fundamental organizational principles, alterations in ASEAN should "neither be used as a pretext to intervene in the internal affairs of a nation nor be harmful to what has made up the strength of ASEAN".

The issue of intervention has bedevilled ASEAN political integration from its inception. ASEAN's timidity with respect to the regional embarrassment of the East Timor crisis was justified in term of non-intervention. The continuing ASEAN inaction over Myanmar is testimony to the principle of non-interference. While ASEAN's Western dialogue partners tighten their sanctions on the Yangon junta, ASEAN pursues its Thai-led policy of business-as-usual "constructive engagement". Although some Southeast Asian leaders have expressed frustration with Yangon's stonewalling, ASEAN remains united in maintaining ranks with Yangon's military regime, seeing no political contradiction between Bali Concord II's commitment to a just and democratic regional environment and their tacit acceptance of the status quo in Myanmar. On 17 October 2004, Lt. Gen. Khin Nyunt, the Myanmar prime minister and presumed champion of a vague "road map" for constitutional development, was dismissed and arrested by junta hardliners. ASEAN's reaction was epitomized in a text crawl across the top of the ASEAN Secretariat website:

"ASEAN to Pursue Constructive Engagement with Myanmar After Power Struggle".[36]

The Indonesian foreign minister was the first ASEAN senior official to meet Lt. Gen. Soe Win, the newly installed Myanmar prime minister. Hassan Wirajuda flew to Yangon in early November, two weeks before the Vientiane meet, for a "mutual sharing of information".[37] Hassan said of the regime's assurances of change, "this is something which many would accept with skepticism".[38] Speaking in advance of the summit, Malaysian Foreign Minister Syed Hamid said that Myanmar must prove that it is moving toward democracy since "the credibility and integrity of ASEAN as a whole is going to be affected".[39] Yangon's indifference was demonstrated on the eve of the summit when ASEAN leaders were caught off guard by the junta's extension of the house arrest of democratic icon Aung San Suu Kyi. In encounters with his counterparts on the sidelines of the summit, Prime Minister Soe Win offered no details or explanations. Given the "ASEAN way", it is not surprising that the situation in Myanmar was not mentioned in the documentation of the gathering; this despite growing misgivings about an ASEAN calendar that has Myanmar chairing the 12th ASEAN Summit.

The Myanmar case does not mean that the fact that political and security events in one ASEAN state can negatively impact bordering states or the region as a whole is ignored. As noted above, in the ASC, the Bali Concord II regards the member states' security as fundamentally linked to one another. The practical problem is how ASEAN as an organization can bring its collective influence to bear upon, let alone discipline, a member whose sovereign domestic problems spill over to threaten regional order and stability or ASEAN's international image. In the existing pattern of intra-ASEAN relations, there is no structure for collective decision-making to determine what issues are of regional concern and what are internal matters. The practice of decision by consensus is really avoiding difficult decisions. Leadership in ASEAN is essentially defensive of national interests.

More activist ASEAN members have floated initiatives such as "constructive intervention", "flexible engagement", and "enhanced interaction". These ideas have been coolly received by the membership in general and scorned by would-be targets, so that "in the final analysis non-interference is still sacrosanct to the grouping".[40] But, non-interference does have limits.

In the months leading up to the 10th ASEAN Summit in Vientiane, the deteriorating security situation in Thailand's Muslim-populated southern provinces and the Thai government's harsh repression caused great concern in Malaysia and Indonesia. The killing of 85 Muslims at Tak Bai on 25 October 2004 particularly inflamed Muslim opinion. As angry voices were raised in the Islamic world, Thai

Prime Minister Thaksin Shinawatra warned his ASEAN partners not to interfere in Thailand's domestic affairs, denying that the situation in the south had regional implications. Bangkok angrily rejected the prospect of the issue being put on the table at the summit by Malaysia and Indonesia. In this, Thailand was supported by the Lao hosts whose summit spokesman said at a briefing, "I think we have a golden rule, that is non-interference in the internal affairs of each other."[41]

Malaysian Foreign Minister Syed Hamid insisted that what was happening in south Thailand was in fact a potential security threat requiring regional attention. He added an implicit corollary to the so-called "golden rule": "There is no such thing as absolute non-interference".[42] The tension over the issue came to a head as Malaysia and Indonesia seemed ready to put the issue on the Vientiane agenda. Prime Minister Thaksin threatened to walk out of the ASEAN summit if this matter of Thai internal affairs was raised. This was an unprecedented threat to ASEAN's solidarity. Rather than see the summit fail, Prime Minister Abdullah Badawi and President Yudhoyono agreed to Thaksin's demand that the problem of violence in Thailand's south not be mentioned in the ASEAN official setting.[43] To be sure, the unrest in south Thailand and Tak Bai has been discussed by Thailand outside of the ASEAN context with concerned neighbouring states in informal bilateral and sub-regional meetings. In these settings, Thaksin's effort to place part of the blame for Islamic violence on Muslim militants in Malaysia and Indonesia has led to diplomatic tension with Jakarta and Kuala Lumpur.

The ironic spin to the Vientiane summit's silence on both Myanmar and Tak Bai is the fact that it was this summit that adopted the "Vientiane Action Programme" (VAP) with its theme: "Towards shared prosperity and destiny in an integrated, peaceful and caring ASEAN community".[44] In the language of the accompanying "ASEAN Security Community Plan of Action" the community would be democratic, tolerant, participatory, and transparent.[45] The action plan's "annex" of political development activities includes items such as strengthening of democratic institutions and popular participation, strengthening of the rule of law, and promotion of human rights and obligations. The political programme of the ASC stands in sharp contrast to the absence of commitment by some member states to the norms supposedly giving a democratic values base to the embryonic community. In a scathing editorial following the November summit, Thailand's *The Nation* newspaper claimed that "by ignoring Tak Bai and Burma, the grouping has damaged its moral authority".[46] "In dealing with sensitive issues", the editorialist continued, "the ten leaders failed miserably to show that ASEAN has the maturity to handle controversy". With respect to the VAP, he counselled not to hold one's breath for implementation.

From Bali to Vientiane

Indonesia, the chief proponent of an ASEAN Security Community, was tasked with fleshing out the Bali Concord II's generalizations about the ASC. As already discussed in the introduction, this was seized upon in Jakarta as an opportunity to take centre stage again in ASEAN. The ASEAN foreign ministers at their June 2004 annual ASEAN Ministerial meeting commended Indonesia for "developing and elaborating the ASEAN Security Community".[47] In the next sentence, they stated that the "action plan" text they approved for the ASEAN summit was that developed from the "substantive work" of the ASEAN senior officials. This was ASEAN-speak for "massaged to the lowest common denominator". While Indonesia may have wanted to lead, ASEAN was not ready to be led. The final version for the ASC agreed to at Vientiane represented not so much Indonesian leadership but significant retreat from earlier proposals. In its present form, the ASC has been ASEANized, recycling old programmes into new programme boxes. Its strategies for greater political cooperation call for studies, workshops, stock-taking, harmonization, and strengthening other existing modes of promoting cooperation — but not the creation of integrative community structures. As a document, it reminds one of its many ASEAN bureaucratic predecessors such as "Vision 2020", the "Hanoi Plan of Action", the "Initiative for ASEAN Integration", etc. Its tone was one of reaffirming old ideal aspirations but not rocking the boat of ASEAN solidarity.

In a 24 February 2004 keynote address to the fourth UN-ASEAN Conference, Foreign Minister Hassan Wirajuda spelled out the security threats that had to be addressed in the ASC: terrorism, transnational crime, the inability of regional countries to effectively address their own security problems, and the spill-over of internal strife in an embattled country to the region.[48] In the ASC, he said, ASEAN must be "enabled to discuss with candour sensitive issues and to resolve them amicably instead of relegating them to a back burner". Most extraordinary is the fact the pall of terrorism that has hung over ASEAN since 2001 was only referenced with respect to norm building and working towards an ASEAN convention on counter-terrorism. Rather than an ASEAN centre for counter-terrorism, the organization has not really moved beyond its 2001 "ASEAN Declaration on Joint Action to Counter Terrorism",[49] and the hodge-podge of subsequent statements of cooperation.[50] What Rizal Sukma called the "Age of Terror" was the stimulus for Indonesia's opportunity to regain "strategic centrality" in ASEAN.[51] However, in the absence of real policy content, it is difficult to see, despite Indonesian hopes, how the ASC contributes to this goal.

The architects of the original Indonesian draft for the ASC laid out more than 70 specific proposals that if adopted would have set ASEAN on a new course for comprehensive security cooperation including areas of political and human rights.

The action plan set out the practical steps needed to realize the future "condition" of a security community. A centrepiece of the Indonesian conception, and for the realists an obvious non-starter, was the attention-getting proposal to create a regional peacekeeping capacity. This had been specifically mentioned by Foreign Minister Hassan in his UN-ASEAN Conference speech. It was seen as part of the institutionalization of an expanded ASEAN conflict resolution role. At the minimum, an ASEAN peacekeeping role would have provided a framework for ASEANizing military-to-military links, something ASEAN has studiously avoided in the past. Military cooperation among ASEAN states has always been viewed as extra-ASEAN and a function of bilateral or multilateral agreement. The Indonesian initiative went well beyond simply enhancing defence cooperation among the ASEAN countries. An underlying Indonesian interest may have been to give the region its own security capacity so as to minimize the necessity for extra-regional security influence and interventions. Although Indonesia's lingering bitterness over East Timor may have lurked in the psychological background, a more proximate stimulus would have been Australian blustering about pre-emptive attacks in neighbouring countries harbouring terrorists.

Jakarta's conviction that an arrangement for ASEAN peacekeeping should be the backbone of a security community was not shared. In part, as one Track II contributor put it, "All too often, regional states are part of the problem and not part of the solution".[52] There were a number of issues: command and control, conditions of deployment, differing military capabilities, ASEAN helmets or national contingents, standby status, and, importantly, the use of force in peacemaking or post-conflict peacekeeping. A critical political issue was whether consensus was necessary, including that of the affected state. No other ASEAN country embraced the plan and by the March 2004 Senior Officials Meeting, Singapore and Vietnam publicly rejected it.[53] Indonesia's most creative innovation was a dead letter by the June Ministerial Meeting and there is not a trace of it in the VAP's strategies for the ASC or the ASC action plan.

The Indonesian draft ASC provided that the community would be committed to the promotion and protection of human rights in the ASEAN region. It called for the establishment of an ASEAN human rights structure. As far back as the 1993 26th Ministerial Meeting, shortly after the Vienna World Conference on Human Rights, the ASEAN foreign ministers agreed that ASEAN should consider the establishment of a regional mechanism. There the matter has rested. The democratization of Indonesia, and its eagerness to burnish its own badly tarnished human rights record, have newly prompted Indonesia to project internationally its interest in human rights and democracy. Indonesia has indicated it will accede to the international covenants on Economic, Social, and Cultural Rights and on Civil and Political Rights.[54] In June 2004, Foreign Minister Hassan promised at the Fourth Workshop on the ASEAN Regional Mechanism on Human Rights, hosted by the Ministry of Foreign Affairs, that such a mechanism would be an important feature of the ASEAN Security Community concept in which democracy and respect for human rights would be nurtured.[55] There is no endorsement of a human rights mechanism in either the VAP's strategies or the ASC action plan. The only nod to institutional promotion of human rights mechanisms is to encourage networking among existing human rights mechanisms. Only four ASEAN countries have their own human rights mechanisms: Indonesia, Malaysia, the Philippines, and Thailand.

An a priori guideline for the ASC and the other elements of community building in ASEAN was that the organization would move at a pace acceptable to all of its members. In ASEAN activities that pace is simply to reaffirm existing commitments. For example, the ASC action plan will work for the establishment of an ASEAN extradition treaty. This was already on the table in Bali Concord I. If the slow progress in simply negotiating bilateral extradition treaties is an indicator, a standard inclusive ASEAN extradition treaty will be almost impossible to achieve, especially given the question of political refugees and different perceptions of political and civil rights. The Indonesian proposal for an ASEAN non-aggression treaty would have only reaffirmed what is already stated in the TAC. This did not survive the scrutiny of Jakarta's colleagues. A proposal for an ASEAN Charter was accepted. This would be a normative statement; nowhere in the founding documents of the ASC is compliance to norms touched upon.

At this early point in the evolution of the ASC, leaving aside the issues of functional relevance, it does not seem a real perch from which the wounded Indonesian foreign policy phoenix could soar again. As the Indonesian-drafted plan of action made its way upwards through the layers of ASEAN decision-making, from senior officials to foreign ministers to heads of government, it became clear that, despite Indonesian prodding, the ASC would not spur any substantial change in the way that ASEAN does business. One long-time observer of ASEAN affairs opined that Indonesia's partners "appear to regard its energetic promotion of an ASEAN Security Community as a blatant and unacceptable bid to reassert itself over the rest of the region".[56] The gutting of Indonesia's draft with its specific proposals led the *Jakarta Post* editorialists to the conclusion that "it was so heavily watered down that the document had virtually been turned into a worthless scrap of paper".[57] There was the suggestion that this raised questions about Indonesia's capabilities to provide "necessary and effective" leadership to ASEAN. The Indonesian Foreign Ministry's senior official for ASEAN affairs responded to what he called the *Post*'s "hasty judgment" by stating that Indonesia's "bold and visionary ideas" were designed to stimulate responses from other ASEAN countries.[58] Looking to the need to meet the challenges of 2020, he argued that "we should not be straight-jacketed to think in terms of what are 'doable' in 2004". He averred that, "on its part, Indonesia will consistently pursue this matter". This begs the question of how, given the controlling political culture of ASEAN and its structuring, Indonesia can lead ASEAN from the visionary to the "doable".

Where do Indonesia's Interests Lie?

One interpretation of the fate of Indonesia's vision of the ASC is that its rejection by its ASEAN partners made it clear that "they don't regard Indonesia as first among equals within ASEAN".[59] Whether or not one agrees with that conclusion, it does raise the question of how much significance Indonesia should assign to its relative power position in the workings of the grouping. Indonesia's quest for "leadership" in ASEAN may reflect more a nostalgia and bruised *amour propre* than a calculated foreign policy in pursuit of real self-interest. The distribution of political and economic power in contemporary Southeast Asia means that the role that Indonesia played in post-1977 Southeast Asia cannot be recaptured. The "diplomatic centrality" that ASEAN had, with Indonesia at its centre, was not a function of ASEAN's strengths but of the contending policies of external powers. The political cohesion of Suharto's ASEAN stage has been shredded by membership expansion and political change. To suggest that the ten member states now or by 2020 will act collectively on the basis of common norms and shared values flies in the face of reality. Furthermore, ASEAN itself has less international credibility and relevance than it did as part of a Southeast Asian balance of power.

In the long run, a perhaps more significant regional dynamic than the evolution of the three ASEAN communities is underway, incorporating the ASEAN countries in a broader East Asian regionalism. The ASEAN-China "Strategic Partnership for Peace and Prosperity" is but the most notable of the broader frameworks for relations already developed between ASEAN and its major Asian dialogue partners including Japan, South Korea, and India. The ASEAN+3 format already overshadows exclusively ASEAN dealings. According to Malaysia's Prime Minister Abdullah, the East Asian Summit to be held in Malaysia in December 2005 "should carry and drive the process of East Asia Community building".[60]

The building process is underway with first on the prospective agenda the establishment of an East Asian Free Trade Area. Beyond that, Abdullah has promoted an East Asian Community Charter and an East Asian Zone of Amity and Cooperation.

His concept is more grandiose than Prime Minister Mahathir's earlier, failed East Asia Economic Grouping scheme that was doomed by Suharto's de facto veto. The extent of the proposed community's geographic footprint remains to be settled — India, Australia, and New Zealand — but the idea that ASEAN states would be the hub of such an integrative process ignores the fact of the inherent asymmetries already so visible in the ASEAN-China relationship. An officially unstated political motive of ASEAN endorsement of multilateralism is to balance China's growing ascendancy. In fact, an ASEAN Secretariat senior officer has ascribed the organization's zeal for regional free trade agreements to the fact that "ASEAN does not wish to be in a tributary relationship with China".[61] Malaysia's championing of the process, backed by Thailand, stems in part from the economic tiering in ASEAN. They have more to gain economically than Indonesia. In this wider regionalist urge, Indonesia is not in the vanguard. Indonesia has misgivings about the structuring of wider regionalism. Looking to the December East Asian Summit, the Indonesian senior official responsible for ASEAN affairs wrote: "The challenge, essentially, is how to ensure that present and future attention on the Summit does not detract from what must remain the priority effort to build an ASEAN Community".[62]

At the same time that ASEAN as a community is threatened by functional irrelevance as the East Asia-wide integrative processes accelerate, the minimum internal political cohesion the grouping has is being lost to deepening divisions. A two (or three)-tiered ASEAN economy is paralleled by a multi-tiered political culture in which generally democracy is subordinated to authoritarianism because of the ground rules of intra-mural relations. The external defence and security links of the member states also set them apart. Myanmar has become a Chinese military client. The Philippines and Thailand are "major non-NATO allies" of the United States. Singapore is an important facilitator for the U.S. Pacific Command. Malaysia and Singapore are part of the Five Power Defence Arrangement with Australia, New Zealand, and Great Britain. The ASC, in the words of the Bali Concord II, recognizes "the sovereign right of the member countries to pursue their individual foreign policies and defence arrangements". Even though Indonesia would like to restore normal defence relations with the United States, until the U.S. Congress is satisfied that its human rights conditions are satisfied, the barriers to normalization will stay in place.

Ethnic and religious differences in ASEAN have become important. This is evident in both bilateral relations — the Tak Bai incident — and wider security perceptions. The three Muslim-majority countries have viewed the war on terror and the Iraq war differently than their non-Muslim partners. The Malaysian and Indonesian governments condemned the U.S. war in Iraq. Thailand, the Philippines, and

Singapore supported it. ASEAN was unable to reach a collective position on Iraq. Explaining the failure of the ASEAN states to forge a common security position on U.S. policy, ASEAN Secretary-General Ong Keng Yong said: "Each of the members has every right to formulate its own national position based on circumstances that will best serve its own national interests."[63]

The continental–maritime geostrategic zones of Southeast Asia have been given political/economic definition within ASEAN. Thailand's historic "continentalism" has new expression in the sub-regional framework of the ACMECS (Ayeyawady-Chao Phraya-Mekong Economic Cooperation Strategy). The CLMV (Cambodia-Laos-Myanmar-Vietnam) countries, ASEAN's "second tier", have their own sub-ASEAN agreement on economic cooperation and integration. The Greater Mekong Sub-region Economic Cooperation Program (GMS) held its 13th ministerial meeting in Vientiane in December 2004. The GMS's first summit was in 2002. In addition to Thailand and the CLMV countries, the ADB-backed GMS includes China. Meanwhile, sub-regional arrangements in the maritime zone are moribund.

Indonesian insistence that ASEAN is its primary foreign policy focus seems increasingly backward-looking. Southeast Asia certainly is the first circle of Indonesia's geostrategic interests, but a realist perspective would suggest that priority in that circle is not a major political and prestige investment in the amorphism of the ASC or ASEAN itself. A greater priority is its relationships with its immediate neighbours. The Yudhoyono government has moved to improve relations with Malaysia, Singapore, East Timor, and Australia, dealing with disputes and irritations, some of which date back to the Suharto era. But even in this more limited foreign policy venue, the Indonesian phoenix is wounded. For a truly "free and active" foreign policy that can secure national interests, the Yudhoyono government will have to restore its capabilities so severely depleted in the wreckage of the downfall of Suharto, weak and *immobiliste* succeeding governments, separatist conflict, terrorist violence, and the other signifiers of what some saw through Megawati's presidency as a failing state. The phoenix will fly only once its domestic perch is secure.

Notes

[1]   The full text of the State Address is as given at http://www.thejakartapost.com/mega_speech_2004.asp.

[2]   Anthony L. Smith, "ASEAN's Ninth Summit: Solidifying Regional Cohesion, Advancing External Linkages", *Contemporary Southeast Asia* 26, no. 3 (December 2004): 423.

3   The "Declaration of ASEAN Concord", http://www.aseansec.org/1217.htm.
4   The "Declaration of ASEAN Concord II (Bali Concord II)", http://www.aseansec.org/15160.htm.
5   "Press Statement of the Chairman of the 8th ASEAN Summit, the 6th ASEAN+3 Summit and the ASEAN-China Summit", Phnom Penh, 4 November 2003, http://www.aseansec.org/13188.htm.
6   Rizal Sukma, "The Future of ASEAN: Towards a Security Community", paper presented at a seminar on "ASEAN Cooperation: Challenges and Prospects in the Current International Situation", New York, 3 June 2003.
7   Teuku Faizasyah, "Megawati's Foreign Policy Legacy", *Jakarta Post* online, 24 October 2004, http://thejakartapost.com.
8   The "Singapore Declaration of 1992", http://www.aseansewc.org/5125.htm.
9   Howard P. Jones, *Indonesia: The Possible Dream* (New York: Harcourt Brace Jovanavich, 1971).
10 Dewi Fortuna Anwar, *Indonesia in ASEAN: Foreign Policy and Regionalism* (New York: St. Martin's Press, 1995), p. 57.
11 For overviews of Suharto's foreign policy see Leo Suryadinata, *Indonesia's Foreign Policy under Suharto: Aspiring to International Leadership* (Singapore: Times Academic Press, 1996); also Donald E. Weatherbee, "Indonesia: From Pivot to Problem", in *Comparative Foreign Policy: Adaptation Strategies of the Great and Emerging Powers*, edited by Steven W. Hook, pp. 194–218 (Upper Saddle River, NJ: Prentice Hall, 2002).
12 John Bresnan, "Indonesia", in *The Pivotal States: A New Framework for U.S. Policy*, edited by Robert Chase, Emily Hill, and Paul Kennedy (New York: W.W. Norton, 1999), pp. 15–39.
13 "Joint Communiqué of the 33rd ASEAN Foreign Ministers Meeting, Bangkok, Thailand, 24–25 July 2002", http://www.aseansec.org/3659.htm.
14 James Clad, "Fin de Siècle, Fin de l'ASEAN?" *PacNet Newsletter* 9 (3 March 2000).
15 Faizasyah, "Megawati's Foreign Policy Legacy", op. cit.
16 Bantarto Bandoro, "Foreign-policy Agenda for the New President", *Jakarta Post* online, 24 October 2004.
17 "Remarks at the Launching of the Theme and Logo for the Asian-African Summit 2005 and the Golden Jubilee Commemoration of the Asian African Conference 1955", Department of Foreign Affairs Republic of Indonesia, http://www.deplu.go.id/2003/detail.php?=5597ffbb4f81e7057627af48b08f8ed2.
18 Michael Vatikiotis, "Susilo, Regional Affairs and Lessons from Sukarno", *Jakarta Post* online, 3 November 2004.
19 Michael Leifer, *Indonesia's Foreign Policy* (London: Allen & Unwin, 1983), p. 173.
20 Opinion and Editorial, "Leading ASEAN", *Jakarta Post* online, 12 August 2004.
21 President Yudhoyono's Inauguration Speech, 21 October 2004, text as given at http://www.thejakartapost.com/sby_speech.asp.

22 "Diplomacy keeps Yudhoyono busy in Chile", *Straits Times Interactive*, 24 November 2004, http://straitstimes.asia1.com.sg.

23 See, for example, the remarks of Soedjati Djwandono and Bantarto Bando as reported in "RI far from leading ASEAN: Analysts", *Jakarta Post* online, 19 August 2004.

24 See, for example, Thai Prime Minister Thaksin's claim to have revived ASEAN in the Foreign Ministry's 2005 "blue book", *New-Age Diplomacy: People are at the Heart,* as cited in Anuraj Manibhandu, "New-Age Diplomacy, Old-Style Blundering", *Bangkok Post*, 1 February 2005.

25 The most comprehensive discussion is Amitav Acharya, *Constructing a Security Community in Southeast Asia* (London: Routledge, 2001). See also Mely Cabellero-Anthony, *Regional Security in Asia: Beyond the ASEAN Way* (Singapore: ISEAS, 2005).

26 Acharya, p. 2.

27 Karl Detusch, et al., *Political Community in the North Atlantic Area: International Organization in the Light of Historical Experience* (Princeton: Princeton University Press, 1957).

28 Ralf Emmers, *Cooperative Security and the Balance of Power in ASEAN and the ARF* (London: RoutledgeCurzon, 2003), p. 10.

29 Barry Buzan, "The Southeast Asian Security Complex", *Contemporary Southeast Asia* 10, no. 1 (June 1992), p. 2.

30 This is the case made in chapter 5, "Conflict and Conflict Resolution in Southeast Asia", in Donald E. Weatherbee, *International Relations in Southeast Asia: The Struggle for Autonomy* (Lanham, MD: Rowman & Littlefield, 2005), pp. 120–55.

31 This point was made specifically by Malaysian Foreign Minister Syed Hamid with respect to the Indonesia-Malaysia dispute over Sipidan and Ligitan (as reported by Malaysia's national news agency Bernama, 20 December 2002).

32 R. James Ferguson, "ASEAN Concord II: Policy Prospects for Participant Regional 'Development' ", *Contemporary Southeast Asia* 26, no. 3 (December 2004): 399.

33 Smith, "ASEAN's Ninth Summit", p. 432.

34 Prime Minister Abullah Badawi's address, "Towards an ASEAN Community" at the National Colloquium on ASEAN", 7 August 2004, http://domino.kln.my/english/Fr-speeches.html.

35 "ASEAN Lecture by H.E. Mr. Prime Minister Phan Van Khai", 8 August 2004, http://www.aseansec.org/16299.htm.

36 http://aseansec.org/afp/78p.htm, accessed 26 October 2004.

37 "Indonesian Foreign Minister Visits Myanmar after Regime Shake-up", *Jakarta Post* online, 12 November 2006.

38 "Indonesia Says Myanmar Promised to Press Reforms", *Jakarta Post* online, 22 November 2004.

39 "Myanmar 'Must Reassure Asean' ", *Straits Times Interactive*, 23 November 2004.

40 Robin Ramcharan, "ASEAN and Non-interference: A Principle Maintained", *Contemporary Southeast Asia* 22, no. 1 (April 2000): 60–88.

41 As reported in "ASEAN Summit: KL Rebuffs Thaksin over Walkout Vow", *The Nation*, 27 November 2004.

42 As reported in "Okay for Asean to Query Bangkok, Says KL", *Straits Times Interactive*, 27 November 2004.

43 Achara Ashayagachat, "PM's 'Gag Order' Respected", *Bangkok Post,* 30 November 2004.

44 "Vientiane Action Programme (VAP) 2004–2010", http://www.aseansec.org/VAP-10th%20ASEAN%20Summit.pdf.

45 "ASEAN Security Community Plan of Action", http://www.aseansec.org/16826.htm.

46 "Editorial: A Ringing Silence at the Asean Summit", *The Nation,* 6 December 2004.

47 "Joint Communiqué of the 37th ASEAN Ministerial Meeting", Jakarta, 29–30 June 2004, http://www.asean sec.org/16193.htm.

48 "Keynote Address by H.E. Dr. Hassan Wirajuda Minister of Foreign Affairs Republic of Indonesia at the Opening Session of the Fourth ASEAN-UN Conference", 24 February 2004, Department of Foreign Affairs website http://www.deplu.go.id.

49 http://www.aseansec.org/5620.htm

50 "ASEAN Effort to Counter Terrorism", http://aseansec.org/14396.htm.

51 Sukma, "The Future of ASEAN: Towards a Security Community".

52 Bantarto Bandoro, "Undesirable Consequences of an ASEAN Peacekeeping Force", *Jakarta Post,* 2 March 2004.

53 "Asean Makes Good Progress on Security Community Proposals: Indonesia", http://www.aseansec.org/afp/39.htm.

54 This will bring to three the number of ASEAN states that have acceded to both of these key elements of the UNCHR's treaty body basis.

55 "Keynote Speech by H.E. Dr N. Hassan Wirajuda Minister for Foreign Affairs Republic of Indonesia at the Fourth Workshop on the ASEAN Regional Mechanism on Human Rights", Jakarta, 17 June 2004, Department of Foreign Affairs website, http://www.deplu.go.id.

56 Barry Wain, "Jakarta Jilted", *Far Eastern Economic Review*, 10 June 2004, p. 20.

57 Opinion and Editorial, "Leading ASEAN", *Jakarta Post* online, 12 August 2004.

58 Marty Natalegawa, Director General for ASEAN Cooperation, Ministry of Foreign Affairs, "Leading ASEAN", *Jakarta Post* online, 13 August 2004.

59 Wain, "Jakarta Jilted".

60 "Towards an Integrated East Asia Community", keynote address by YAB Dato'Seri Abdullah HJ Ahmad Badawi, Prime Minister of Malaysia, at the Second East Asia Forum, 6 December 2004, Prime Minister's Office website, http://www.pmp/gov.my.

61 Lee Yoong Yoong, "FTAs with dialogue partners: Compatible with ASEAN integration?", *ASEANone*, 2 (January 2005), http://www.aseansec.org/aseanone/article213.pdf.

62   R.M. Marty M. Natalegawa, "ASEAN+3 versus the East Asia Summit", Department of Foreign Affairs website, http://www.deplu.gov.id.

63   As quoted in "ASEAN Split over Iraq to be Expected", *Straits Times Interactive*, 27 May 2003.

Laos

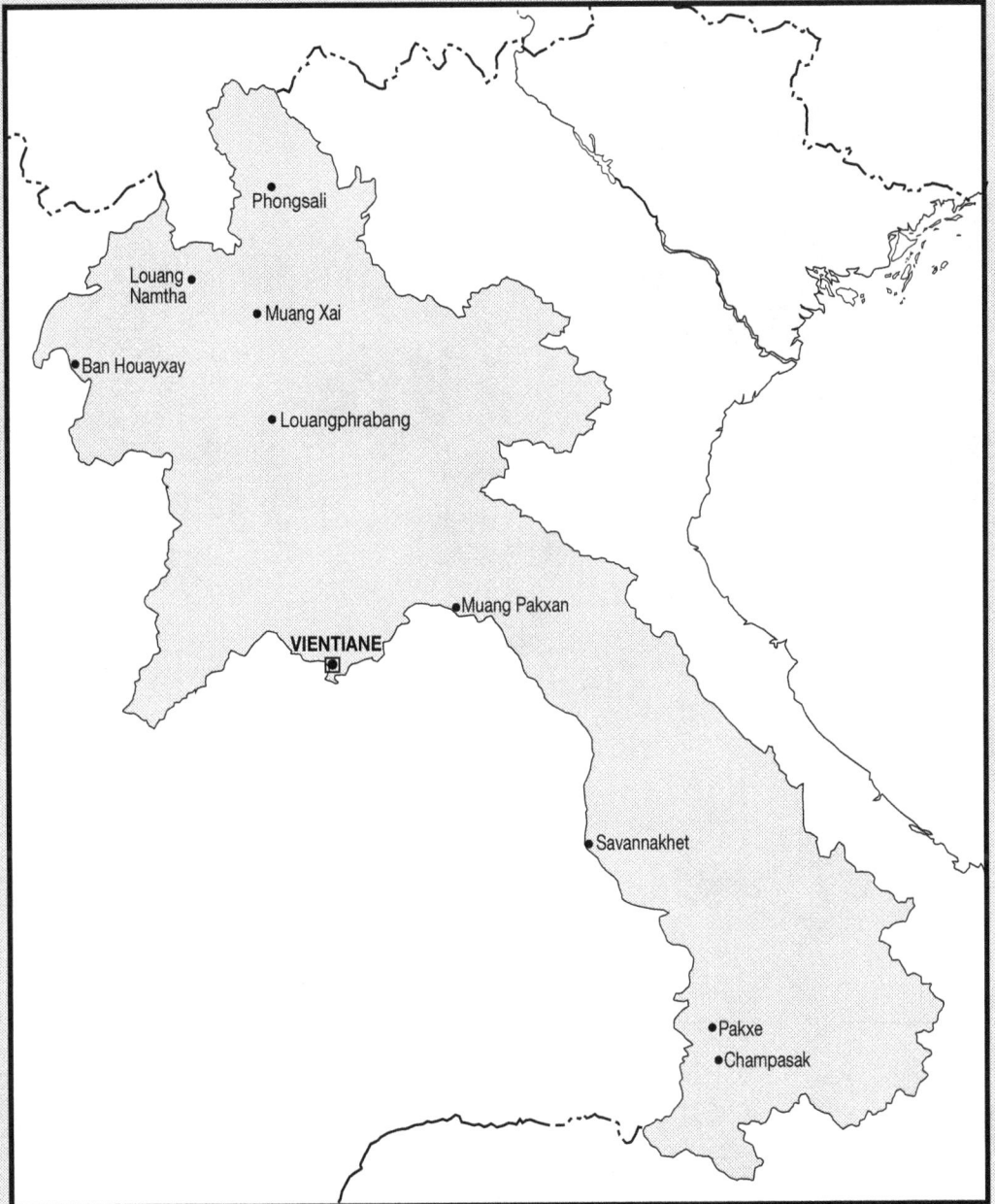

Phongsali

Louang
Namtha

Muang Xai

Ban Houayxay

Louangphrabang

Muang Pakxan

VIENTIANE

Savannakhet

Pakxe

Champasak

LAOS IN 2004
Towards Subregional Integration:
10 Years on

Vatthana Pholsena

Introduction

The year 2004 marked the tenth anniversary of the opening of the first Lao-Thai Friendship Bridge that permits travel by road between Vientiane and Nongkhai. The completion of the bridge seemed to signal the beginning of a new era. Wars in the region had frozen the project for almost three decades. As recently as 1987–88, Thailand and Laos were involved in a border dispute that escalated into a military conflict. The bridge therefore appeared to highlight a significant shift in the relationship between the two countries, with cooperation being privileged over confrontation. Yet, Martin Stuart-Fox sounded a note of caution when he wrote in 1995 that "the Friendship Bridge [serves] as a symbol of threat or hope, depending on perspective".[1] His article in this annual was among the rare analyses of Laos' post-Cold War challenges regarding regional integration. The historian furthermore observed: "whether the bridge exists or not, Laos will still find it impossible to isolate itself from the changes now occurring in mainland Southeast Asia".[2] His comment was accurate, albeit somewhat premature. The 1997 Asian financial crisis brutally hit all the Southeast Asian countries' economies and Laos began to have second thoughts over the direction of her own economic development;[3] her rapprochement with China thus reached a new level during that period. Nevertheless, despite the general slowdown of regional projects in the aftermath of the Asian crisis, Laos' economic subregional integration was always to be an irreversible movement, favoured by all sides, i.e., the country itself, its neighbours (first and

VATTHANA PHOLSENA is Assistant Professor, Southeast Asian Studies Programme, National University of Singapore.

foremost, Thailand and Vietnam) and international lending organizations, as well as China. As Stuart-Fox explained in 1995: "Transport routes and other communications between the principal member states — Thailand, China, Vietnam — cannot help but pass through Laos if long and costly detours are to be avoided."[4] The road to development for Laos has to some extent become embodied in one expression, namely "land-linked", in the hope that the realization of this goal will conjure away the nation–state's fate as the only country in Southeast Asia with no direct access to the sea, thereby overcoming its remoteness from world markets.[5]

Bridges possibly best represent this vision, linking emblematically, if not economically, countries and symbolically transcending national boundaries. Perhaps to celebrate the tenth anniversary of the opening of the first Friendship Bridge, a second bridge opened in October 2004 that connects the province of Loei in northeastern Thailand to the province of Sayaboury in northwestern Laos. The opening of the small bridge — 110-metres long — saw the presence of the Thai and Lao foreign ministers, Surakiart Sathirathai and Somsavat Lengsavath. A few months earlier (in March), the first Thai-Lao joint cabinet retreat took place in Pakse (southern Laos), led by the two countries' prime ministers, Thaksin Shinawatra and Bounyang Vorachit. A series of agreements were signed but most significantly, the two-day meeting marked the official start of the construction of the second Lao-Thai Friendship Bridge between the towns of Savannakhet (southern Laos) and Mukdahan (northeastern Thailand). It is scheduled to be completed in 2006. During the same month, the Thai government approved partial funding (amounting to 1.5 billion baht) for the construction of another Lao-Thai bridge, linking Huay Xai (northwestern Laos) and Chiang Rai (northern Thailand). China is expected to be the other investor.[6] In the light of the accelerating development of the country's cross-border transport infrastructure, will Laos become the "heart of the region, the crossroads where trade routes intersect" in the twenty-first century?[7] Ten years after the opening of the first Lao-Thai friendship bridge, the answer still cannot be but tentative.

Towards a Land-linked Laos?

The Greater Mekong Subregion (GMS) Program plays an essential role in the process of moving towards the realization of this objective. Launched in 1992, this initiative involves the participation of six countries — Cambodia, China (Yunnan Province), Laos, Myanmar, Thailand and Vietnam — as well as the strategic support of the Asian Development Bank (ADB). The multilateral lending institution has provided loans to GMS governments amounting to some US$1.2 billion and mobilized about US$30.9 billion in co-financing for 17 priority GMS projects.[8] The GMS

Program entered its final phase in 2000, entailing the full implementation of all its projects. In November 2001, the 10th GMS Ministerial Conference adopted the Strategic Framework for the Greater Mekong subregion. The document addresses the GMS "Flagship" programmes, which focus on 9 key areas: transportation ("economic corridors"), telecommunications, energy interconnection and trade, cross-border trade and investment, private sector involvement, development of human resources, environment and natural resources management, and tourism. Of particular and immediate concern among these GMS priority programmes as far as Laos is concerned are the transportation, energy and environment sectors.

The GMS transport programme primarily consists of the building and development of three "economic corridors", namely the North-South, the East-West and the Southern Corridors. The first two of these "corridors" will cross Laos. The North-South Economic Corridor (NSEC) will link northern Thailand, northwestern Laos and southwestern China; and the East-West Economic Corridor will connect central Vietnam in the east with Myanmar in the west, cutting across southern Laos and north and northeastern Thailand. These roads, composed of highways and feeder roads (the latter serving to link rural communities with the highways) are presented by the ADB and its partner countries with the goal of developing an efficient transport system, which will allow goods and people to move around the subregion without excessive cost or delay. The logic that underlies the construction and conception of these "economic" or "growth corridors" posits a causal connection between free — or as free as possible — cross-border movements and poverty reduction via economic growth. At the country level, three highways, two of which are sections of those Economic Corridors, form the backbone of Laos' national road network. The longest and most important of these all-weather highways is Road N.13, partly financed by Swedish and Japanese aid agencies, which connects the north and the south of the country, from Luang Prabang via Vientiane, Savannakhet and Pakse, to the Lao-Cambodian border. It is approximately 1,500-km long. A second national highway is Road N.9 (209 km) that crosses the southern province of Savannakhet from the provincial capital in the west to Lao Bao on the Lao-Vietnamese border. Its upgrading was co-funded by the ADB and Japan, and completed in February this year. Road N.9 is the Lao section of the East-West Economic Corridor. Other east-west road links connecting Thailand and Laos to the border with Vietnam have also been completed (Roads N.6 and N.7). A third national road which is also a component of an economic corridor (the "North-South Economic Corridor") is Road N.3. It is 228-km long and crosses northwestern Laos (from Houayxay to Boten). Most importantly, it will link Thailand to China. In December 2002, the ADB approved a loan (with flexible reimbursement conditions) amounting to US$30 million to the Lao government for the reconstruction of Road N.3. The financing of Road N.3's upgrading is a rare, if not unique, example in which two GMS member countries, Thailand and China, co-invest (a third of the total amount each) with the financial help of the ADB in a third GMS country.[9] The road is expected to be completed by 2007.

In addition to the construction of a second Lao-Thai Friendship Bridge between Savannakhet and Mukdahan, there are plans to expand Savannakhet airport into a regional hub. The Thai and Lao governments are expected to sign a memorandum of understanding on the development of Savannakhet airport by the end of next year, in the hope that the volume of air traffic will be sufficient to justify the functioning of a subregional airport serving as a travellers hub in that geographical zone.[10] Economic corridors are not merely highways; they can combine roads, bridges, seaports and airports. Their raison d'être is to be more than a transportation system, however: the objective is to attract investment and build up economic centres along these corridors. The expectations are high. In an ADB-GMS Program document one reads: "When completed, the growth corridors will transform Northern Lao PDR and Yunnan Province into vital gateways between the People's Republic of China (PRC) and Southeast Asia ..."[11] During a press conference on business opportunities in the East-West Economic Corridor, the Lao vice-minister for Communication, Post, Transport and Construction expressed his optimism that the eastern part of the corridor would turn the western provinces of Laos and northeastern Thailand into a centre for economic growth.[12] To this end, an industrial base, the Savan-Seno Special Economic Zone ("SASEZ"), was established in Savannakhet province in late 2003. The initiative aims "to create the prerequisites for gradual industrialization and modernization by using its vantage ground as a transit place within the sub-region, for developing the Lao PDR market economy so as to integrate it into the Regional and Global economies ..."[13] Special incentive policies have been devised to attract local and foreign enterprises, including overseas Laotian investors, such as periods of tax exemption or special tax rates on imported products and custom duties exemption on exported merchandise. The initiative has not (yet?) attracted a significant number of private investors. As a matter of fact, prospects for the East-West Economic Corridor's contributions to economic development in Laos appear rather limited at present. Due to the lack of short and medium-term alternatives, investment opportunities are frequently narrowed down to the development of "services" — such as small restaurants, hotels or guest houses, and petrol stations — along the road.[14] As far as Laos is concerned, the East-West Economic Corridor is still closer to a transportation than an economic axis. There are also concerns regarding the potential negative impacts of the corridors, notably with regard to the accelerated spread of HIV/AIDS.

Another challenge is the improvement and maintenance of the country's national road network. The latter may appear limited or extensive, depending upon which perspective one adopts: the size of the territory (equivalent to that of the United Kingdom) or the density of population and the volume of traffic (both very low). The transport network in Laos covers 32,600 km, including approximately 7,100 km of national roads, 8,950 km of provincial roads and 9,800 km of rural roads. During the 1990s, huge amounts of money (mainly from foreign aid sources) were invested in the construction and renovation of roads — adding more than 3,000 km to the road network by the end of the decade.[15] Only just over 50 per cent (4,590 km) of the national road network, however, is paved, and only 70 per cent of the national road network is passable throughout the year. The maintenance of the road transport network remains an issue. A Road Maintenance Fund was established in 2001, but it aims firstly at financing the maintenance of the national roads.[16] The implementation of a system of toll highways may help to solve the problem but, although it has been considered, there is no sign at present that it will be adopted in the near future. Yet, despite the relatively low level of traffic, the roads are deteriorating rapidly and at a higher rate than one would expect considering their normal economic life expectancy. The insufficient level of funding for road maintenance is surely one factor, to which must be added poor construction in some cases and the damage caused by overloaded trucks.

In spite of this great effort to develop transport infrastructure over the last 15 years, around 40 per cent of the population still live 6 km or more from the nearest road.[17] The development of a rural road network — linking provinces and districts, and giving villages access to the roads — is nonetheless gaining a more prominent place in the government's and donors' agendas. The ADB approved in June a US$17.7 million loan for the Lao government to rehabilitate 292 km of roads in three provinces, focusing on areas that are amongst the 47 poorest districts in the country. The Roads for Rural Development Project aims at connecting district and provincial centres and will also provide funding for road maintenance. The government is expected to contribute the equivalent of US$8.2 million to the estimated US$39.2 million total project costs.[18]

Nam Theun II and the Politics of Dams

In 2004, the World Bank hosted an unprecedented series of public consultations between August and September in five capitals (Bangkok, Tokyo, Paris, Washington and Vientiane) over Laos' largest and highly controversial hydropower project, Nam Theun 2 (NT2). The World Bank has yet to decide on whether it will provide a risk guarantee to the international investors who would fund most of the project costs. A final decision is expected from the Bank by May 2005. The proponents and opponents of the dam project unsurprisingly turned the highly-publicized international workshops into an exercise in public relations for the former and a platform for criticism for the latter.

The dam project is located on the Nam Theun River in Nakai district, Khammouane province, in the centre of the country. It is expected to produce 1,070 megawatts, 93 per cent of which will be exported to Thailand while the rest will supply domestic demand.[19] The estimated total project costs have reached a colossal US$1.2 billion — more than half of the country's GDP (which amounted to approximately US$2 billion in 2003). The hydroelectric project is expected to be financed by loan facilities of US$855 million and shareholders' equity of US$330 million.[20] Net revenue estimates for the government have varied over the years, although the trend has been for them to be downgraded. Net revenue is now estimated to be around US$13 million in the first year of production.[21] The Lao government has in effect made the NT2 hydroelectric project the vital vector of its long-term poverty reduction strategy.[22] However, the dam, if built, will have significant environmental and socioeconomic impacts. The dam reservoir will flood an area of approximately 450 km — a large part of which is situated on the Nakai plateau renowned for its rich biodiversity.[23] Several thousand people (between 5,000 and 6,000 from 17 villages) will furthermore need to relocate to another area. These villagers, many of whom belong to ethnic minority groups, have social and cultural systems intertwined with their present environment; hence, they are likely to find the adjustment to a different livelihood unsettling. In addition, it is now estimated by the Nam Theun 2 Power Company — the project sponsor[24] — that some 40,000 people[25] who live along the Xe Bang Fai River (into which will flow large amounts of water from the Nam Theun River after passage through the turbines) will be affected by NT2. The projected negative impacts on biodiversity and local people's livelihoods of the dam construction and power production have consequently raised serious concerns among foreign NGOs (working inside and outside the country), academics and development analysts. At the start of the project preparation phase, the World Bank informed the project developers that they would need to comply with Bank policies on public consultation in order for the Bank to provide a loan guarantee. Thus, in 1996–97, the project sponsor (initially the Nam Theun 2 Electricity Consortium [NTEC], subsequently incorporated in the Nam Theun 2 Power Company [NTPC]) launched the NTEC/NTPC's Public Participation Process. But after almost 10 years of preparation and in spite of over 200 consultations and workshops, it is a troubling fact that villagers who would be most affected by the hydroelectric project have not always been adequately informed about the project and its consequences on their livelihood.[26] Many believe, nonetheless, that the "point of no return" has been crossed and the long-delayed project will in all likelihood go ahead.[27]

ASEAN Summit in Vientiane

Laos hosted the 10th ASEAN Summit in Vientiane on 29 to 30 November 2004. It was the first ASEAN summit and the largest regional event ever hosted by the country. Over 3,000 delegates, including 800 foreign journalists, were invited. In addition to the existing accommodation, a five-star hotel and a set of 28 luxury houses were speedily built to accommodate the participants. The authorities left no room for improvisation in their preparations: the issuance of tourists visas was stopped a week before the event; severe restrictions were placed on entry into the capital from 22 November to 1 December; government offices and schools were closed from 29 November to 1 December, *tuk-tuk* vehicles were forbidden to circulate in town and a 10 pm curfew was imposed. Logistics and security imperatives were behind these drastic measures. Two small explosions were reported at the Friendship Bridge checkpoint on the Lao side in early November; and another two blasts caused damage to an unused government facility outside Vientiane just three days before the start of the meetings. A series of bomb blasts have hit the capital and the main southern cities in recent years. Their perpetrators remain unidentified, although groups of exiled opponents to the regime have claimed responsibility for some of these bombings.[28] Bomb threats in the run-up to the summit appeared to be credible enough for the U.S. embassy in Vientiane to send a warning to U.S. embassies in other countries and representative offices of international organizations in Laos a month before the summit.[29] By focusing almost exclusively on security issues and on the authorities' apparent struggle to cope with the challenges, many foreign news reports neglected to cover the symbolic importance of an ASEAN summit held by a country that joined the organization less than ten years ago after decades of war followed by several years of diplomatic and economic ostracism from the international community.[30] It was no small achievement. And in spite of bomb threats and doubts cast over the country's capacity to organize such an event, there were no disruptions during the series of bilateral and multilateral meetings.

Among the impressive volume of agreements (over 30 documents) signed during these meetings, those that most directly concern Laos are arguably the Vientiane Action Programme (VAP) and the ASEAN Framework Agreement for the Integration of Priority Sectors, to which must be added the creation of an ASEAN Development Fund to support the implementation of the VAP and other future action programmes. The adoption of the ASEAN Framework Agreement for the Integration of Priority Sectors aims at accelerating the integration of 11 sectors in order to achieve the creation of the ASEAN Economic Community (AEC), a free trade zone, by 2020. The 11 priority sectors are wood-based products, automotives, rubber-based products, fisheries, textiles and apparel, electronics, agro-based products, e-ASEAN, health care, air travel and tourism. The ASEAN-Six members (Brunei, Indonesia, Malaysia, Philippines, Singapore and Thailand) will eliminate tariffs and remove trade barriers in these 11 sectors by 2007; Cambodia, Laos, Myanmar and Vietnam will follow in 2012.[31] Since the latter joined the organization during the 1990s, one of their top priorities has been to "narrow the (socioeconomic) gap" between the ASEAN-Six and the CLMV (Cambodia-Laos-Myanmar-Vietnam) group. Bounyang Vorachit, the Lao Prime Minister, in his opening remarks again addressed this issue: "Apart from those challenges [unprecedented rise in oil prices, bird flu and other impacts of globalization] the development gap between the old and new members of ASEAN is still large".[32] The CLMV summit was held for the first time one day prior the official opening of the larger ASEAN meeting. The gathering was to promote further economic cooperation and mutual assistance among the four countries, as well as to send a message to the ASEAN-Six: while affirming their commitment to "substantiate their contribution to the ASEAN integration", their leaders also called upon "the ASEAN members to renew more effective assistance and support to the CLMV countries in accelerating implementation of the initiatives of ASEAN integration to ensure sustainable benefits to all ASEAN members". At the conclusion of this summit, the leaders of the four countries signed the Vientiane Declaration on Enhancing Cooperation and Integration among Cambodia, Laos, Myanmar and Vietnam. It was also decided that a CLMV summit would be held annually, starting with Cambodia in 2005, followed by Myanmar in 2006, Vietnam in 2007 and Laos in 2008.[33]

The risk of a two-tiered organization prompted the adoption of the Hanoi Plan of Action during the ASEAN summit in the Vietnamese capital in 2000, although the need to narrow the gap between the ASEAN-Six and the CLMV group was not officially recognized and prioritized until 2001 in the Hanoi Declaration on Narrowing Development Gap for Closer ASEAN Integration. The Vientiane Action Programme succeeds the HAP and will end in 2010. Perhaps the most innovative measure announced in the VAP is the creation of a common pool of financial resources, an ASEAN Development Fund, to be made up of contributions of member countries. This Fund will have a restricted funding mission, however: it will only fully support "small scale projects of a confidential or strategic nature"; as for "complex projects of relatively large scale", it will limit the funding to "initial activities … leading towards obtaining major funding to implement the full project, from a Dialogue Partner or donor institution". In other words, external funding (from Dialogue Partners, donor institutions and private sector) will remain an essential funding source for ASEAN projects.[34]

Human Rights, Foreign Relations, and Political Stability

In early March, there were reports of apparent mass surrenders (their exact number and composition were not confirmed) in Luang Prabang and Xieng Khouang of Hmong fighters and their relatives, occurring allegedly in return for amnesty and land allocation.[35] The Lao authorities denied any surrender, however.[36] Some hundreds of Hmong have clashed with the Lao army over many years in the northern provinces for reasons that are linked to both the government's development projects (particularly its policies of relocation and opium reduction) and a lingering past — part of the Hmong population was entangled in a proxy alliance with the United States and fought during the Vietnam War against the Lao communists.[37] The Hmong issue made the headlines again in September when Amnesty International accused the Lao government of "war crimes". Allegations by the London-based human rights organization, apparently supported by a videotape smuggled out of the country, regarding the brutal killing of Hmong teenagers in the Special Zone of Saysomboune (north of Vientiane) by a group of Lao soldiers in May, reignited serious concerns within the international community on the issue of human rights violations in Laos.[38] The Lao authorities swiftly rejected the accusations and dismissed the video footage as a "fabrication".[39] The reactions were particularly strong in the United States. A Hmong and Lao-American lobby, led by the Lao Veterans of America (LVA), has been opposing the communist regime for years (thousands of members of the Hmong minority group fled the country after the end of the war; many of them took refuge in the United States). Distance is not a problem. Via satellite phones they are kept informed by their Hmong relatives of events in remote areas of Laos.

In part due to the Hmong issue, the relationship between Laos and the United States blew hot and cold in 2004. Accusations by some U.S. Congressmen and Lao exile groups over purported violations of human rights and religious freedom continued to dog the relationship between the two countries.[40] In May, the U.S. House of Representatives passed a strongly worded resolution (Resolution 402), which urged the Lao government to allow human rights monitors into the country, to release all political and religious prisoners and to establish a multi-party democracy. As expected, the resolution was condemned a few days later as "interference in another country's internal affairs" by Vientiane.[41] Yet despite appearances, the U.S.

administration is divided, like the Hmong-American community, over the attitude to adopt to Laos. After years of equivocation and despite strong opposition from members of the Congress and anti-Lao government lobbyists, the U.S. Senate passed legislation reinstating Laos' normal trade relations (NTR) status on 19 November 2004. The bill was signed by President George W. Bush on 3 December.[42] The relationship between Laos and the United States does not revolve only around the Hmong or human rights issues, however. Continued cooperation with Lao authorities over opium reduction programmes in the north of the country and the search programme for American military and civilian MIAs in the eastern regions remain top U.S. priorities in Laos.[43]

No such tensions are to be expected between Laos and her two closest political allies, Vietnam and China. The latter is confidently building up a more prominent presence in the country's economy. During his visit to Laos in March, Wu Yi, the vice-premier of the State Council of China, met with Khamtay Siphandone, president of the Lao PDR, and expressed China's determination to increase bilateral trade between the two countries to $200 million by 2005.[44] China is among the main investors (US$28 million of foreign direct investment approved in 2003/4) in Laos and Chinese companies already account for a third of the Lao construction market.[45] The trade-off seems to be well established: "Laos is endowed with rich natural resources and China has funds, technology and a market".[46] For instance, the Chinese government has pledged financial aid of US$3.6 million this year to develop Laos' rubber sector. The country currently produces little rubber, but demand for the commodity in China is high. Chinese firms are increasing their investments in the sector in the northern provinces of Oudomxay and Phongsaly.[47]

As a consequence of warmer relations between Laos and Thailand this year, the 16 Lao dissidents who participated in the attack against a customs checkpoint in southern Laos in 2000 were extradited from Thailand to Laos in July, after four years of legal and diplomatic disputes between Laos, Thailand and the United Nations High Commissioner for Refugees (UNHCR), and despite the rejection in December 2003 by a Bangkok Appeals court of Vientiane's previous extradition request.[48] Their extradition was agreed between the Thai and Lao Prime Ministers during their meeting in March.[49] The sixteen prisoners, who have been constantly referred to as "bandits" by the Lao authorities, were sentenced to a jail term in October by the Champassak People's Court. The court in southern Laos handed out twelve-year jail sentences to eight dissidents and sentences ranging from two to seven years were passed on the eight other members of the group.[50]

The ASEAN Summit gave the opportunity to Laos to renew or strengthen her bilateral ties with ASEAN member countries, as well as with non-Southeast Asian countries. Malaysia further increased her volume of investment in the country: the Malaysian construction company Gamuda Bhd signed an agreement on 28 November to invest US$550 million in the Nam Theun 1 hydroelectric power project in central Laos. Under the agreement, Gamuda will hold a 50 per cent share, Laos 20 per cent and the rest will be held by other stakeholders. The dam construction is expected to start in early 2006 and to be completed by 2010.[51] The Russian Foreign Minister, Sergei Lavrov, was invited to Laos and met with his Lao counterpart, Somsavath Lengsavad, during his visit on 29–30 November. Russia has recently agreed to write off Laos' debts.[52] The Lao National Chamber of Commerce and Industry and the Confederation of Indian Industry signed a Memorandum of Understanding on 29th November. The Indian Prime Minister Manmohan Singh visited Laos for the Third India-ASEAN Summit organized in parallel with the 10th ASEAN Summit. Despite international condemnations of the continued detention of the Myanmar opposition leader, Aung San Suu Kyi, Laos continues to quietly deepen her ties with Myanmar. The Prime Minister Bounyang Vorachit visited the country from 7–10 December in response to an invitation from the Myanmar Prime Minister, Lt Gen Soe Win, with whom he held talks "to strengthen cooperation between the two countries".[53]

The ASEAN countries' leaders stopped short of delivering any strong statement against the Myanmar regime at the closure of the summit. The principle of "flexible engagement", once supported by Thailand and the Philippines, seems to have faded away. Economic priorities were far more prominent than political issues on the agenda of the 10th ASEAN Summit. Threats to Laos' political stability are thus highly unlikely to come from ASEAN; the regime, on the contrary, must feel comforted by the Association's political inertia. Nonetheless, the government is acutely aware of the damaging effects that such high-profile cases as those concerning the Hmong rebels have on their image abroad, especially among international institutions such as the United Nations, Western governments and the international media. In a rather unusual fashion, Lao officials informed foreign journalists on the last day of the summit[54] of the release in October of two former senior officials, Latsami Khamphoui (former Deputy Minister of the Economy and Planning) and Pheng Sakchittaphong (former official in the Ministry of Justice), who were sentenced to 14 years in jail for criticizing Laos' one-party political system in 1990.[55] The two men have since gone to France for medical treatment.

Conclusion

During their political rule over Indochina (1887–1945), the French tried to link their colonies, Laos and Vietnam, in the hope of opening a commercial route that would rival the trade between their western Lao territories and the Kingdom of Siam. They even planned and started to build a railway from Laos to Vietnam. But their ambitions came to naught, except for a seven-km railway track that lies long-abandoned near the Khon Falls in southern Laos. The situation is different today, though: the integration of Laos into a subregional transport network is a regional collaborative project, supported (financially and politically) by multiple national and international actors: ADB, World Bank, Southeast Asian neighbours (Thailand, Vietnam, Cambodia, Myanmar), and China. The issue, therefore, is not so much whether Laos will become "land-linked" but rather, how the country will negotiate the new socioeconomic opportunities and risks that a greater opening of her frontiers will inevitably create. In any case, the success of the organization of the 10th ASEAN Summit in Vientiane showed Laos' commitment to regional affairs and her determination not to be "left behind". But the country still faced international criticism in 2004. In particular, the lack of transparency on the part of the Lao authorities in their handling of the Hmong issue seriously hampers any process of settlement, while diasporic anti-Lao government lobbying (especially in the United States) that posits no alternative other than the demise of the regime, further aggravates the conflict. This lingering past will not go away until the government is prepared to deal with it. It may do so if the pressure from donors becomes too strong; yet, Laos will still find support from Vietnam and China (and Myanmar) in the face of Western accusations of human rights abuses. Meanwhile, the country steadily continues her regional integration within an Association less than interested in interfering in her internal affairs.

Notes

[1]   Martin Stuart-Fox, "Laos: Towards Subregional Integration", *Southeast Asian Affairs 1994* (Singapore: ISEAS, 1995), p. 178.

[2]   Ibid., p. 178.

[3]   Vatthana Pholsena and Ruth Banomyong, *Le Laos au XXI° siècle. Les Défis de l'intégration régionale* (Bangkok: Irasec, 2004) p. 66.

[4]   Stuart-Fox, op. cit., p. 179.

[5]   During a lecture at the Institute of Foreign Affairs, Ministry of Foreign Affairs, Alounkeo Kittikhoun, Lao Ambassador to the United Nations, pointed out that "landlocked countries remain in remote isolation from the world market. Their sea-borne trade unavoidably depends on transit through another country, which increases the total cost of transport service", "Geography still Hampering Development", *Vientiane Times*, 7 December 2004. Laos chairs the Landlocked Developing Countries in the United Nations.

During the ASEAN summit held in Vientiane in late November, Bounyang Vorachit, the Lao Prime Minister, reiterated his call for his ASEAN counterparts' support to turn "Laos from a land-locked country to a land-linked one, by helping Laos to have rail-road link with a Singapore-Kunming ASEAN rail network". Bernama (Malaysia), 29 November 2004.

6   "Thai Government Approves Budget for Third Bridge on Lao Border", *The Nation* (Bangkok), 9 March 2004.

7   Stuart-Fox, op. cit., p. 179.

8   Asian Development Bank (ADB), "The GMS Program — Progress and Achievements", http://www.adb.org, accessed on 7 November 2004.

9   Pholsena and Banomyong, *Le Laos au XXI° sièle* ..., p. 135.

10   Jeerawat Na Thalang, "Help to Upgrade Savannakhet Airport", *The Nation*, 27 July 2004.

11   ADB, "Building on Success. GMS Flagship Programs and Development Matrix", p. 3, http://www.adb.org, accessed on 7 November 3004.

12   Jeerawat Na Thalang, "Help to Upgrade Savannakhet Airport", op. cit.

13   Savan-Seno Special Economic Zone Authority, *Compilation of Decrees of the Prime Minister Concerning the Savan-Seno Economic Zone* (Savannakhet Province, 2004).

14   Interview with James Nugent, ADB Country Director in the Lao PDR, 12 November 2004.

15   Pholsena and Banomyong, op. cit., pp. 113–14; Ministry of Communication, Transport, Post and Construction, *Summary of Road Statistics for 2002* (Vientiane: Government of the Lao PDR, 2003).

16   The Road Maintenance Fund (RMF) was established in 2001 by Prime Minister's Decree. Under the decree, 10 per cent of the RMF annual revenue is allocated to the local road network (provincial, district and community roads), 0.5 per cent to road safety programmes, and up to 90 per cent to national roads. The RMF is partially financed by the World Bank, Swedish International Development Institute and ADB, *Lao PDR — National Growth and Poverty Eradication Strategy* (NGPES), (Vientiane: Government of the Lao PDR, 2003), p. 99.

17   Pholsena and Banomyong, op. cit., p. 113.

18   Xinhua News Agency, "ADB Approves Loan for Laos to Improve Road Transport Network", 28 June 2004.

19   Electricity Generating Authority of Thailand (EGAT) and the Nam Theun 2 Power Company (NTPC) signed the 25-year Power Purchase Agreement (PPA) on 8 November 2003. NTPC has 18 months (by May 2005) from the date of signing to secure the project financing.

20   World Bank, *Nam Theun 2 Hydroelectric Project Update* (Updated September 2004), http://web.worldbank.org/WBSITE/EXTERNAL/COUNTRIES/EAST ASIAPACIFICEXT/LAOPDREXTN/0,,contentMDK:20172670~page

PK:141137~piPK:217854~thesitePK:293684,00.html, accessed 26 October 2004; World Bank Vientiane Office, *Lao PDR Economic Monitor*, http://siteresources. worldbank.org/INTLAOPRD/Resources/293582-1096519010070/lao_ econ_monitor_nov2004.pdf, November 2004.

21   World Bank, *Nam Theun 2 Hydroelectric Project Update*, ibid.

22   Somdy Douangdy, the Lao Vice-Minister of Finance, thus declared during the NT2 public consultation in Tokyo on 31 August: "We don't have much choice, we don't have many alternatives to promote the kind of growth we need to reduce poverty", "World Bank: Tokyo Workshop for Nam Theun 2 Concludes.", M2 Presswire, 9 September 2004.

23   A National Protected Area (NPA) has been established in this zone: it encompasses the Nakai-Nam Theun Protected Area (NNTPA); the Southern Corridor that links NNTPA with the Hin Nam No Protected Area in the south; and the Corridor which links NNTPA to the Khammouane Limestone Protected Area.

24   NTPC shareholders are: Electricité de France International (EDFI), 35 per cent; Electricité du Laos (EDL), 25 per cent; Ital-Thai Development, 15 per cent; and Electricity Generating Company of Thailand (EGCO), 25 per cent.

25   Independent studies have given a much high number: between 100,000 to 150,000 people, "NGO Visit to the Proposed Nam Theun 2 Hydroelectric Project in Laos. December 2003. Trip Report", February 2004, p. 6.

26   A 2004 study quotes a World Bank review of the consultations carried out on NT2 hydroelectric project (World Bank, *Public Consultation in Nam Theun 2 Project*, 2003) concluding that "the previous process [the over 200 public consultations carried out between 1996 and 2001; mostly between 1996–1997] was biased towards promoting the positive benefits of the project while the negative impacts were largely ignored. Thus, it was often concluded that affected peoples were not reported a *balanced* view of the project", James R. Chamberlain, "Proposed Nam Theun 2 Hydroelectric Project. Assessing Quality of the Local Consultations. Interim Draft Report", 2004, p. 2 (original emphasis) http://siteresources.worldbank.org/INTLAOPRD/491761-1094074854903/20251512/ local%20consultations.pdf.

27   "Lao Nam Theun Dam Project on Global Tour to Convince Opponents", Agence France Presse (AFP), 29 August 2004; "World Bank Consults on Big Laos Dam Project", *The Guardian*, 1 September 2004.

28   "Groups Claims Responsibility for String of Laos Bombings", AFP, 9 February 2004.

29   The U.S. Ambassador apologized later on for this report, however, which the Lao government saw as a violation of Lao sovereignty and interference in the country's internal affairs, "Laos Protests against U.S. Embassy's Report", 28 October 2004, Vietnam New Agency.

30   See, for example, Didier Lauras, "Security Concerns Threaten to Disrupt ASEAN Summit in Laos", AFP, 11 November 2004; Peter Llyod, "U.S. Warns ASEAN Summit

Targeted by Hmong Rebels", *ABC Online*, 27 November 2004; Nopporn Wong-Anan, "Communist Laos Bans Fun for Asian Summit", Reuters, 26 November 2004.

31 "ASEAN Accelerates Integration of Priority Sectors", http://www.aseansec.org/ 16621.htm, accessed on 15 December 2004; "ASEAN Speeds up Free Trade Move", *BBC News*, 29 November 2004.

32 R. Ravichandran, "ASEAN Faces Many Challenges Despite Remarkable Progress, Says Lao PM", Bernama, 29 November 2004.

33 KPL (Kaosan Pathet Lao) News, 29 November 2004.

34 "Vientiane Action Programme (VAP)", 2004–2010, p. 23, ASEAN Secretariat, http://www.aseansec.org/, accessed 15 December 2004.

35 "Up to 700 Hmong Rebels Reportedly Surrender to Lao Authorities", *The Nation*, 5 March 2004; "Hundreds of Hmong Rebels Surrender in Laos: Report", AFP, 4 March 2004.

36 "No one surrendered, there are no rebels and there is no war in Laos. Lots of people are coming out of the forests to take advantage of our poverty eradication programmes", Lao Foreign Ministry spokesman Yong Chanthalangsy told the foreign media, Ben Rowse, "Amnesty Urges Laos to Treat Surrendered Rebels Humanely", AFP, 5 March 2004.

37 Grant Evans, *Laos: Situation Analysis and Trend Assessment*, A WriteNet Report, United Nations High Commissioner for Refugees, Protection Information Section, May 2004, pp. 18–19, http://www.unhcr.ch/cgi-bin/texis/vtx/publ/opendoc.pdf? tbl=RSDCOI&id=40c723992&page=publ.

38 "New Video Shows Murdered, Starved Children in Laos", *The Nation*, 14 September 2004; "Five Children Tortured and Killed by Military in Laos: Amnesty", AFP, 14 September 2004.

39 "Hmong Slaughter Tape: Video a 'Fabrication', says Laos", *The Nation*, 15 September 2004; "Laos tells US Embassy Ethnic Cleansing Report False", Deutsche Presse-Agentur, 18 September 2004; "Lao Army says Massacre of Hmong Children was Fabricated", AFP, 4 October 2004.

40 The U.S. State Department in its 2004 annual report on international religious freedom released in September maintains that the Lao government "restricts" the right of freedom of religion, U.S. Department of State, "Laos. International Religious Freedom Report 2004", Bureau of Democracy, Human Rights, and Labor, 2004, http://www.state.gov/g/ drl/rls/irf/2004/35404.htm, accessed 26 October 2004. There were reports and accusations from Lao-exiled groups of arrests of ethnic minority Christians between January and August: "11 Detained over Christmas Prayer Meetings in Laos: Rights Group", AFP, 2 January 2004; "Exile Group says Laos Targeting Christians to Renounce Faith", AFP, 9 March 2004; "Laos Arrests 12 Christians for Refusing to Renounce Faith: Exile Group", AFP, 20 May 2004; "Exile Group Accuses Laos of Anti-Christian Repression", AFP, 4 September 2004.

[41] "Laos Condemns U.S. Congress Rights Resolution", AFP, 11 May 2004.

[42] "Bush Signs Bill Extending Normal Trade Relations to Laos", AFP, 8 December 2004.

[43] See, for example, "U.S. Southeast Asia Pledge Cooperation on American MIAs", AFP, 30 July 2004.

[44] "Wu Yi Meets with Laotian State President Khamtai Siphandon", Xinhua News Agency, 18 March 2004.

[45] The World Bank Vientiane Office, *Lao PDR Economic Monitor*, November 2004, p. 19; "China, Laos to Strengthen Ties: Chinese Ambassador", *Xinhuanet*, 26 November 2004.

[46] "Wu Yi Meets with Laotian State President Khamtai Siphandon", Xinhua News Agency, 18 March 2004.

[47] The World Bank Vientiane Office, *Lao PDR Economic Monitor*, November 2004, p. 2.

[48] "Vientiane Dissidents: Thailand Deports 16 to Laos", *The Nation*, 8 July 2004; "Thailand Hands 16 Rebels to Laos Despite Court Ruling", AFP, 6 July 2004; "Thai Court Rejects Laos' Request for Extradition of 16 Lao Dissidents", *The Nation*, 31 December 2003.

[49] According to the Thai Foreign Minister, Surakiart Sathirathai, "Laos Says it won't Execute 'Bandits' Handed over by Thailand", Deutsche Presse-Agentur, 8 July 2004.

[50] AFP, "Laos Jails 16 Rebels Recently Extradited from Thailand", 23 October 2004.

[51] "Gamuda Clinches US$550 Million Laos Hydro Power Project", *The Star Online*, http://www.thestar.com.my/, 29 November 2004.

[52] "Joint Declaration of Laos and Russian Federation", KPL News, 29 November 2004;

[53] "PM to Attend World Religion Meeting", *Vientiane Times*, 7 December 2004; "Visite du Premier ministre lao au Myanmar", *Le Rénovateur*, 14 December 2004.

[54] Apparently in response to a question raised during the press conference.

[55] "Laos Frees Two Communist Party Critics Jailed 14 Years Ago", AFP, 30 November 2004.

Malaysia

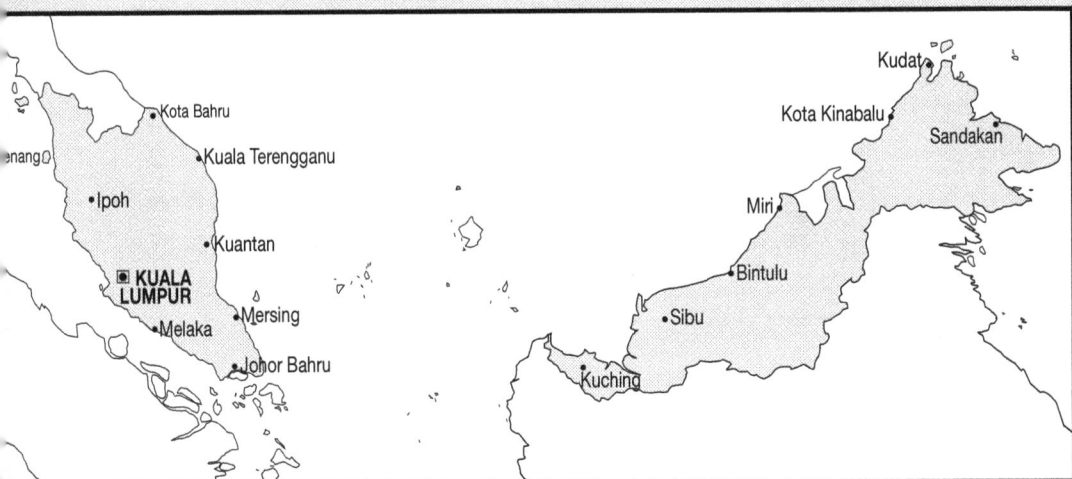

MALAYSIA IN 2004
Abdullah Badawi Defines his Leadership

Patricia A Martinez

Politics and National Issues

2004 was very much Abdullah Ahmad Badawi's year. In defining his leadership, he experienced the whole gamut from the triumph of being the reason for one of the most sweeping election wins in history for the ruling coalition … to heeding the rumblings that had him say publicly at the end of the year that his honeymoon was over.

Abdullah quickly forged his own course for the nation, but kept some fundamental dynamics in consonance with his predecessor, the man who steered Malaysia for 22 years. One fundamental he shared with Mahathir Mohamed was a deep sense that it was the government, but more specifically the leader and "the role of leadership", which made the difference in the success or failure of a nation. Abdullah said, "Why is it that some Islamic countries are poor and weak? Why is it that some [Islamic] countries are not poor and weak? There is a difference, and the difference is in terms of the government, the role played by the government and the role of the leadership.[1]

Such a sense of leadership — whether Abdullah's or Mahathir's — is a heavy mantle to assume. It is even more burdensome when the medium and the messenger change. Mahathir's style of leadership was about deciding, demanding, and if necessary, deriding. However, Abdullah is courteous and consensual, not wont to showing — and thus giving notice — that he wants his way. But Abdullah Badawi knew the enormous task he faced as a leader, because of his huge mandate from the people. Amidst celebrations over their electoral victory in March, he constantly reminded his political party that much was now expected of them.

PATRICIA A MARTINEZ is Associate Professor, Senior Research Fellow and Head of Intercultural Studies, Asia-Europe Institute, University of Malaya.

With that overwhelming electoral mandate from Malaysians came expectations which he seemed to have not fulfilled sufficiently by the end of just one year. Abdullah has undertaken the enormity of reforming governance and politics, but at the helm of the same crew who are used to a far stronger style of leadership and the ensuing conformity it demanded.

The 11th General Elections

After assuming the office of prime minister in October 2003, much of Abdullah's focus was on the 11th general elections that were described as a test of his acceptance by Malaysians and specifically his party's constituency of ethnic Malays. This was a widespread perception because even in his own party, he ascended by appointment instead of being voted into leadership. Abdullah's premiership was less than five months old when he dissolved parliament and called for a general election. Therefore the elections were too early to be interpreted as a referendum on his government. Instead, as the huge voter turnout indicated, the 11th general election was about a postcolonial electorate who felt empowered by the right to vote and who turned out in large numbers to do so. The positive and upbeat outlook of such an electorate resonated with the constructive optimism of the Abdullah campaign which offered Malaysians the slogan "Excellence, Glory and Distinction".

But most of all, the election results were about hope — the hopes of an electorate with a feudal focus on personalities, and who were ready for a change of leadership even though they gave Mahathir a fond farwell. The vote for the Barisan Nasional (BN, the coalition of 14 multi-ethnic parties that is led by the United Malays National Organization or UMNO, Abdullah's party) was also the particularly developing-nation penchant of staying with the security of a government that delivers a better life, which is measured largely in material terms.

In the 1999 general elections, held in the aftermath of the sacking of deputy prime minister Anwar Ibrahim and various financial scandals and bail-outs, voters handed a rebuke to the Barisan Nasional by giving 41 parliamentary seats and a whole state to the opposition. The BN lost the northern state of Terenggannu to the Islamic opposition party, Parti Islam SeMalaysia (PAS), which also won 26 parliamentary and 98 state seats. The Democratic Action Party (DAP) won 10 parliamentary and 11 state seats throughout the country. Parti KeADILan Nasional (the National Justice Party led by Anwar Ibrahim's wife and which is now known as Parti Keadilan Rakyat or PKR after its merger with Parti Rakyat) won 5 parliamentary and 5 state seats in its first outing.

In a reversal of fortunes in 2004, the opposition only won a total of 20 parliamentary seats. The BN swept 199 parliamentary and 453 state seats, PAS was reduced to just 6 parliamentary seats with virtually its entire leadership including president Hadi Awang losing their seats. The DAP increased its share to 12 seats so it took over the leadership of the opposition in parliament, and PKR lost all but one of its seats. The BN wrested back Terenggannu from PAS, and almost won the state of Kelantan, taking 21 out of 45 state seats. The BN now has 90.8 per cent of the seats in parliament and 62.37 per cent of the popular vote.[2]

In the BN's favour was the shortest campaign period in the electoral history of Malaysia, the ruling coalitions' control of all the main media, a re-delineation of electoral boundaries, and the serious shortcomings of an Elections Commission that some deem not sufficiently independent. In addition, Abdullah insisted on a clean campaign, which worked in his favour beyond the approval of his sense of fair-play. When the opposition received more media coverage than normal, the mainstream media was perceived as more objective than usual during an election period. This resulted in more credibility for the media's blitz, and ultimately, for the ruling coalition.[3]

The Abdullah team's strategy for the elections gives interesting insights into the way Malaysians are evolving. The strategy was based on a good sense of who the electorate said they were, rather than the usual paternal paradigm of political leaders only offering what they thought was best for the electorate.

Some aspects of the strategy were obvious: even the online polls of PAS conceded that Abdullah's persona after Mahathir's abrasiveness was a winning factor. The leading Malay language newspaper, *Utusan Malaysia* conducted a readership poll, eliciting 6,919 responses of which 51.5 per cent thought the new Prime Minister was a good reason for voting in the BN, and 25 per cent indicating that the opposition had no issues since Abdullah's five months in office.[4]

But Abdullah's team also commissioned surveys and polls which showed that Malaysians are young — 76 per cent were under 40 years old. Respondents selected "the economy" as the most important national issue, with religion only coming in sixth after transition of power, education, social problems, domestic political stability and national security and peace (in that order). Over 60 per cent of respondents agreed with the statement that political parties that champion the interests of specific races are no longer relevant, an evolution which politics still does not reflect. However, from the inception of his premiership, Abdullah's inclusive style and frequent statements that he was "the leader of all Malaysians" showed he was far more in tune with his people.[5] His statement for National Day in August was not just visionary but bold, given the discourse of Malay privilege. He wrote, "Let all citizens of Malaysia, without feeling inferior, without feeling sidelined, irrespective of race or religion, rise to become statesmen in our own land. We are equal, we are all Malaysians. No individual in this country is more Malaysian than another."[6] These and other similar sentiments expressed throughout the year were deemed indicative of a different mode of politics in Malaysia, and a new phase of the nation's growth.

Thus, Abdullah seemed to have found a resonance with the way ordinary Malaysians have evolved. This resonance included Abdullah abandoning the overwhelming and often uncivil one-upmanship between UMNO and PAS over who deserved the credentials of being more Islamic. Nevertheless, he too used the Islamic medium and metaphor. As he has described it, Islam continues to have a strategic utility. He said "… for Malays, Islamic teachings hold strength. For the Malays, if the religion says that this is a good way, they will do it. Islam becomes an imperative, an inspiration, a call that the Malays will readily accept…"[7] and like Mahathir, Abdullah too is banking a great deal on this conformity to push through his radical reforms.[8]

In addition, the resounding mandate at the 11th general elections was because Abdullah promised and initiated a slew of reforms that co-opted the *reformasi* agenda of the opposition, and which Malaysians felt set the nation back on track.

Among the initiatives Abdullah delineated were: combating corruption, ensuring a better public delivery system, reforming the police force, improving the quality of education, prudent fiscal policies, re-emphasizing the rule of law, transparency and disciplining corporate governance, and making agriculture a major component of his new economic thrust so as to alleviate poverty.

Abdullah had articulated clearly where he would take Malaysia, and asked the people for a mandate. Malaysians then voted for hope in a better future, expressing their expectation that the new prime minister would deliver.

Other Key Political Developments

Key political developments included the release of Anwar Ibrahim from prison, and the UMNO General Assembly.

In September, the UMNO general assembly confirmed Abdullah unopposed as the president, and Najib Tun Razak — whom he had finally appointed in January — as deputy. The top leadership of the women's wing, Wanita UMNO, and the UMNO Youth wing were also confirmed unopposed. This included the meteoric ascendancy of Khairy Jamaluddin, the prime minister's son-in-law, to the no. 2 position in the Youth wing. All this lack of contest belied the intense politicking for the seats below the top few. This politicking included the bane that UMNO speaks a great deal about

— "money politics" or the use of gifts in cash and kind, despite Abdullah's exhortations to stop as well as a few public inquiries and suspensions by the UMNO disciplinary committee.

As great an impact on the UMNO proceedings was the spectre of Anwar Ibrahim who was denounced early in the Assembly, mostly by those who fear for their political future if he returns to UMNO. This culminated in Abdullah declaring that Anwar would not be allowed back. The other issue was the prime minister's oft-stated objective of taking Malays to the next phase of the affirmative action programme (or NEP, the New Economic Policy as it is still referred to by the public although it has evolved under a variety of names including NDP or New Development Policy). The NEP was instituted after the race riots of May 1969. Like Mahathir before him, Abdullah had been giving notice that the government could no longer afford to subsidize the programme after over 30 years of doing so. With the establishment of a solid well-educated Malay middle class as one successful outcome of the NEP, Abdullah's focus was trained on establishing the principle of meritocracy in education and competing instead of quotas and preferences in business so as to enable Malays to excel and succeed. This was a pragmatic move, given that the entire country has to hone its skills in competing internationally because of a domestic market of just 23 million people. Some Malays — both prominent personalities but also the younger generation — were comfortable with this next phase, or at least accept its logic. However, the ensuing insecurity by some who are used to over 30 years of shelter became an issue that was exploited by elements in UMNO, including the Malay press. The media seemed to bait Abdullah over "the Malay agenda" — conflating Malay ethnic dominance with the government's affirmative action responsibilities, describing this agenda for "the future of the race" and that the success of the NEP had peaked in 1990 and Malay gains had been eroding since then. Nonetheless, the disparity between the Malays and non-Malays continues and needs to be addressed. For example, in terms of corporate share ownership (an important vehicle for Malay participation in the economy), the Malay proportion had increased from 2.0 per cent to 19.3 per cent from 1970–90, but went down to 18.7 per cent in 2002. However, this focus on inter-ethnic issues did not reflect the other real issues including the intra-ethnic class schism among the Malays: growing disparities between rural and urban Malays, and not just the Malays and non-Malays, continues, despite all the government's efforts.

Apart from Anwar, money politics and NEP insecurities, the UMNO general assembly also had to deal with a leader who wanted to exemplify the clean and fair campaign he exhorted and who refused to endorse or legitimate his preferred candidates (unlike his strong predecessor). The persons who emerged as the three vice-presidents of UMNO and the twenty-five members of the Supreme Council were a hodge-podge of politicians. These included some who had had their heyday in the earlier period of the Mahathir administration, such as former Malacca chief minister Rahim Thamby Chik, and some who had been perceived as on the wane, such as Mohamed Isa, the former chief minister of Negeri Sembilan. Some candidates reputed to be closer to Abdullah and his preference for a high-integrity image either lost their seats or barely squeaked in. Finally, in the debate over Abdullah's policy speech, the newly elected deputy speaker Badaruddin Amiruldin — whether for political mileage or as a reflection of sentiments on the ground — issued a tirade threatening that "questioning" Malay rights and Islam was tantamount to stirring a hornet's nest. He referred to non-Malay citizens as people whom the Malays had allowed to *menumpang* (temporarily reside) in their land, and is reported to have received thunderous applause.[9] The response was silence from Abdullah and the UMNO leadership. This silence seemed to extend till the end of the year, with Abdullah significantly muted about enhancing racial and religious interaction and his leadership of "all Malaysians".

PAS' leader Hadi Awang also seemed muted, beleaguered after their election debacle. The PAS annual convention or *muktamar* reaffirmed his leadership uncontested. It installed the charismatic preacher Haron Din as the deputy *Mursyidul Am* (Spiritual Leader) and his meteoric ascendancy may have Haron Din in line for even the no. 2 position in the 2005 *muktamar*. Otherwise, the *muktamar* gave notice of the growing tension between the *ulama* (loosely defined as clergy) and the younger generation of PAS members. It is less of a schism between the *ulama* and professionals, or the secular and theocratic, as younger *ulama* are part of those who want to see reform in PAS. The reform that is described euphemistically as "a change in strategy" is largely about the next generation of leaders creating their momentum and support base, as much as it is to enable PAS to reinvent itself for the next elections.

Anwar Ibrahim hovered over the political scenario after his release from prison in September, when the courts would not uphold the sodomy conviction. He was operated on in Germany and the PAS leadership's visit to his hospital bed gave rise to the Malaysian rumour mill's incredible but short-lived belief that he had been offered the leadership of PAS. Back home in Malaysia, Anwar positioned himself as low key and uncontroversial, not provoking the mass demonstrations that rocked the country in 1998 but which Malaysians would have less sympathies with under Abdullah. He was conciliatory, or at least making statements about thanking Abdullah for his release and saying that he forgave Mahathir. Anwar travelled a great deal all over the world and reinvigorated his image abroad as a potential leader of the nation. KeADILAN, meanwhile, continued to maintain the perception that it was floundering as it cast around for a clear sense of who its constituency was.

The bitter two-year leadership clash of Sarawak's main Dayak party, Parti Bansa Dayak Sarawak or PBDS resulted in its deregistration in October for a second and final time. James Masing moved onto the newly-registered Parti Rakyat Sarawak (PRS), which immediately registered to join the BN coalition at state level.

Other Key Issues

There was the usual slew of issues that crop up with regularity and that are invariably analysed or championed in terms of the constant negotiation for power and space in a nation defined and divided by ethnic (and religious) difference. These included the National Service (NS) programme that targets enabling better racial integration, mobilizing over 85,000 youth in 2004 and which is indicative of the government's serious concern about diminishing ethnic integration. The new cabinet also came up with a compulsory course in ethnic studies that will be offered in all Malaysian universities as one antidote to widespread perceptions of ethnic polarization, to join other compulsory courses such as Islam and Asian Civilizations. These top down, heavy-handed approaches came in for considerable critique from all segments of society, including the political opposition that describes the NS as brainwashing for BN legitimacy. In addition, among the issues that cropped up in 2004 was the uproar over top students — mostly non-Malays — whose multiples of A grades did not get them university places in their first choice of fields of study, which are invariably medicine and engineering.

In an interesting development, Malaysia's sultans (the nine traditional Malay rulers who are part of the constitutional monarchy that defines the nation) took a higher profile in 2004. This was as much about whether they were bestowing too many awards and their much-coveted honorary titles, as it was about redefining their relevance in the balance of power that configures the nation: the executive, the legislative, the judiciary, and in what is unique to Malaysia, the sultans. Despite diminished power after two constitutional crises in the past twenty years, the rulers still have power — for example, legislation over Islam can only be enacted at the level of individual states, as the sultans are the heads of Islam in each state. In July, the Sultan of Perak and former Lord President of the Judiciary in the 1980s, spoke out about returning independence to the judiciary. His son Raja Nazrin Shah, who is the Crown Prince of Perak, gave a number of high-profile interviews and lectures describing why the sultans are relevant, in the context of new generations of Malaysians who perceive them as an anachronism.

Islam continued to be prominent, but with a less strident tenor. There was a great deal about *Islam Hadhari* or Progressive Islam, which is Abdullah's bold attempt to offer Malaysian Muslims an articulation of principles from Islam as a model to follow. UMNO's past practice was simply criticizing the PAS model but not offering an alternative to Malaysian Muslims. The 10 principles of *Islam Hadhari* include a principle protecting the rights of minority groups and women and another on safeguarding the environment, both of which are in tandem with Abdullah's more inclusive vision of Islam. On a less positive note, the lacunae and overlaps between Islamic law or the Shari'a and the common-law system enshrined in the constitution became even more evident in high-profile cases before the courts. Also to be decided by the courts of law was the issue of whether Muslims had full rights under Article 11 of the Malaysian Constitution that guarantees freedom of religion. However, convictions under Shari'a law that criminalize apostasy were upheld.

The issue of the conversion of two children who were minors, without the knowledge of the non-Muslim parent who had been given custody of the children upon her divorce from their father, received considerable publicity. This was reflective of growing non-Muslim concern about the way Islam impacts on them. The common law courts ultimately decided that Shamala Sathiayaseelan would retain custody of the children but that she was responsible for raising them as Muslims, rather than decide on the legality of the conversions. In another case that is representative of many similar cases which are outstanding in the courts of law, was the petition of Azalina Jelani or Lina Joy who had renounced Islam many years earlier. She wanted the National Registration Department, which issues Malaysians the mandatory identity card, to drop the word "Islam" from hers. The case will be decided on in 2005.

The issue of illegal migrant workers also received a great deal of publicity, including confusion about precisely when the announced amnesty for illegal immigrants to return home would end, which precipitated significant numbers thinking that the government was not serious. Estimates were provided of over 800,000 migrant workers without valid documentation,[10] but by the year's end, Abdullah conceded yet again to Indonesia's request for another delay in ending the amnesty. At issue was not just security, health, crime and the need to regulate and legalize who is in the country and on what terms. What is at stake is also the enormous economic impact for both Malaysia and Indonesia of shifting a labour force from a country which depends on it to a nation which depends on the income they repatriate.

The Economy

In tandem with some of the fastest-paced growth of the world economy in 30 years, 2004 was a good year for the Malaysian economy. The positive year would strengthen the new administration's resolve to continue with its focus on prudence and fiscal consolidation, reforming business practices, public service delivery, and addressing the cronyism of political patronage, all of which will be imperatives for years to come and which Abdullah has acknowledged from the start. The new administration's focus on raising the quality of life for Malaysians and especially on alleviating poverty through a variety of measures, was also clearly established during 2004.

Malaysia's gross domestic product (GDP) grew by 7.1 per cent in 2004, the fastest pace since 2000. In consonance with the Abdullah administration's intent and the measures subsequently instituted, this growth was propelled by the private sector which contributed 6.2 percentage points to overall economic expansion. This is a healthy development: that growth was based not so much on public expenditure but on the back of strong export performance and robust consumer spending. Despite a considerable slowdown to 5.6 per cent growth in the fourth quarter, the final figures for 2004 were buoyed by strong growth in the first two quarters of the year, including first quarter growth of 7.6 per cent, amongst the highest in the region.[11] Private consumption increased significantly, supported by higher disposable incomes, a rebound in consumer confidence following the Severe Acute Respiratory Syndrome (SARS) outbreak, various tax rebates and low interest rates. Private investment also accelerated during 2004, and all sectors except for construction registered positive growth.

Rescinding contracts for mega-projects such as the cancellation of the railway double-tracking project in 2003 gave the government more fiscal leeway and also sent the signal that cronyism had been put on notice — because a significant percentage of registered contractors are linked or claim links to UMNO. However, with the construction industry in severe doldrums, by July the government relented somewhat and decided to implement RM8.5 billion (US$2.24 billion, the Malaysian ringgit fixed peg at US$1=RM3.8) worth of construction, housing and infrastructure projects and the building of schools. In terms of the administration's stated objectives of raising the quality of life and alleviating poverty, priority was given to developing and upgrading infrastructure, low and medium cost-housing, and flood mitigation.

In the manufacturing sector, both export and domestic-oriented industries expanded strongly due to the upturn in global electronics as well as stronger domestic demand. The services sector experienced strong expansion to contribute 57.4 per cent of the GDP in 2004, driven mainly by higher consumer spending amidst rising disposable incomes, increased trade-related activities as well as higher tourist arrivals. Out of a total of 15.7 million tourists, there was an all-time record of tourists from Singapore who spent the highest amount ever — over 9 million visits from Singapore residents brought more than RM17.5 billion (US$4.61 billion) in foreign exchange. Malaysia experienced a 50 per cent plus jump in tourist arrivals compared with 2003. This increase was also attributed to growing numbers of Arabs who no longer go to Europe and the United States. The SARS scare seemed to be over although the tsunami at the year's end had a significant effect on both foreign and domestic tourism during one of the peak tourist seasons.

The sustained strong expansion of the agriculture sector to 8.5 per cent of GDP in 2004 was driven by higher production of crude palm oil and rubber as well as food-related crops, and good prices for agricultural products. Focus on the agricultural sector was not only because it is a priority with the new administration due to persistent rural poverty, and the fact that the rural population are mostly Malays who are UMNO's main constituency. The new focus on agriculture is also because of deindustrialization, with factories choosing to relocate elsewhere, especially China. Finally, the emphasis on the agricultural sector was also because of Malaysia's food import bill, which was almost RM20 billion (US$5.3 billion) in 2004, up from RM11.4 billion in 2000, the cumulative result of the single-minded focus on manufacturing as the vehicle for import-substitution from the mid-1970s.

Net international reserves registered an increase of RM83.1 billion or US21.9 billion to RM253.5 or US66.7 billion by the end of 2004. This indicated stronger export performance as well as substantial inflows of foreign direct investment (FDI). Notably, the increase in reserves occurred amidst higher outflows during the year. There was a record net inflow of RM15.4 billion compared to RM12.1 billion in 2003, and this was attributed by the central bank to higher FDI inflows and portfolio funds. However, when foreign reserves rose by 19 per cent or RM40.7 billion (US$10.7 billion) in the fourth quarter of 2004 alone, it became obvious that it was because from November onwards there was considerable interest expressed publicly in having the government review the ringgit peg. High-profile institutions and individuals weighed in, led by no less than former prime minister Mahathir who had instituted the peg but who now called for the review "because the weak U.S. dollar has caused us to lose a lot".[12] However, the government remained adamant that the peg would stay.

Among the most decisive measures taken by the new administration in 2004 was when Abdullah Badawi addressed the remaking of "Malaysia Inc." or the previous administration's policy of a close partnership between the government and business (that ultimately became too cosy). He shifted focus from partnership to achievement and performance on the part of the private sector, and enhanced public service delivery on the part of the government. His advisors trained their sights on GLCs or government-linked companies, which account for a substantial component of the Malaysian economy. Since GLCs constitute over 30 per cent of the total market capitalization of the Malaysian stock exchange, or over RM200 billion

(US$52.6 billion) or more than half of the nation's GDP, Abdullah and his advisors were cognizant that any improvement after years of dismal performance would bring massive benefits to the nation. In a hard-hitting speech to GLCs gathered at the Ministry of Finance in May, Abdullah disclosed that GLCs fell short in numerous ways, including that "the total return to shareholders [which would be largely the government and its political parties] of public-listed GLCs' actually trails behind overall market performance by 21 per cent over the last five years". He asked that "we move away from the culture of the iron rice-bowl and of promotion by seniority, towards a culture which recognizes and promotes performance".[13] He reiterated the scheme of key performance indices or KPIs and specified the 13 identified. He also announced the expansion beyond the original two GLCs (Malaysian Airline Systems or MAS and Malaysia Airports which is running the KLIA) in the pilot for KPIs that started in 2003.

Instituting measures that were needed some years ago, Abdullah also announced that government regulators could no longer be directors of GLCs, that senior management would be employed on a contract basis, and that the government would restructure and reduce the board of one of the government's premier investment vehicles, Khazanah. He also announced the setting up of a high-level corporate governance committee headed by the chairman of the Securities Commission, with the director of the Commercial Crimes Division of the Police among its members and that the committee would submit regular reports to the prime minister. This corporate governance committee would complement the corporate law reform committee that had also been recently established. The DRB-Hicom fiasco over ownership which played out very publicly in October, with the prime minister's name and "government approval" inevitably claimed and counter-claimed, was just one reminder about the problematic condition of the GLCs.

The banking sector continued to be consolidated under the guidance of the central bank or Bank Negara Malaysia. Of particular interest was Malaysia positioning itself as an international Islamic financial centre, with the central bank fast-tracking the liberalization of the Islamic banking sector. The total capital base of Islamic banks rose to RM7.8 billion (US$2 billion) in 2004, and the central bank announced its pursuit of the development of an Islamic reference rate as a benchmark for the pricing of Islamic banking products. In further liberalizing this banking sector, foreigners are now allowed to acquire up to a 49 per cent stake in Islamic bank subsidiaries of local banking groups.

Yet another mark of a good year was that the benchmark Kuala Lumpur Composite Index rose 2.5 per cent, making it the world's 10th best-performing primary index.[14] Institutional investors began streaming back into the bourse with the Kuala Lumpur Stock Exchange breaching the 900 index barrier in November, the highest level in four and a half years. Of the 18 sovereigns rated by Standard & Poor's (S&P) in the region, Malaysia's were among the 5 upgraded in 2003. In May 2004, S&P affirmed Malaysia's foreign currency rating of A–/A–2 and local currency rating of A+/A–1. Such solid sovereign rating means both the Malaysian government and its private sector can borrow from foreign banks, especially European banks in London, at relatively low interest rates.

Among measures announced during 2004 was that the current sales and service tax would be replaced with a single consumption tax generally known as the Goods and Services Tax (GST), effective 1 January 2007, in line with many other ASEAN countries. Then smuggling was targeted because of the huge loss of about 30 per cent of income from cigarette duties. Security inking and tax stamps on cigarettes as well as a customs crackdown which began in June, yielded a significant drop in smuggling and higher duty collection of RM800 million (US$210.5) for just the period from June to September, compared with RM600 (US$157.9) million collected for the first three months of the year. However, industry sources say that there is still much more to be done.

As indicated earlier, the nation's strong dependence on migrant labour continued to be cause for concern. The four year old government programme to entice home skilled Malaysian citizens who choose to work and live abroad was largely ineffective. Since 2001, there have been only 665 applications, of which a mere 279 were accepted, indicating perhaps too-stringent requirements or what some attribute to a bureaucratic apathy about actually bringing home ethnic minority citizens.

Abdullah Badawi's early focus on fiscal consolidation as soon as he assumed power — not just deferring mega-projects but shifting direction to consolidation and prudence after the Mahathir administrations' big-spending focus — was apparent in Malaysia's share of external debt to GNP improving to 46.6 per cent from 50.2 per cent in 2003. The debt service ratio improved to 4.3 per cent in 2004 (6.2 per cent in 2003). After eight straight years of growing deficits, the decline of the Federal Government's deficit to 4.3 per cent of the GDP from 5.3 per cent in 2003 reflected prudent measures demanded of the administration and its related institutions.

The message was mostly heeded. For example, the Employees Provident Fund (EPF) whose declining dividends have been a sore point with citizens, declared a 4.75 per cent dividend for 2004. However, this fell far short from former highs of up to 8.5 per cent. This and the EPF's statement of accounts listing deductions for "unrealized losses" came in for criticism and were indicative of the general sense that while consolidation and prudent management of the nation's economy, resources and finances were happening, there was still much to be done. Also adding to the urgency of the reform agenda was Malaysia's descent from 37th to 39th place in Transparency International's Corruption Perceptions Index.

Although the poverty rate was reduced to 5 per cent compared with 49.3 per cent in 1970 (but there is controversy about what constitutes the threshold poverty line income), Malaysia was given the dubious distinction of being the country with the worst income disparity in Southeast Asia. According to the United Nations Human Development Report for 2004, the richest 10 per cent in Malaysia control 38.4 per cent of the country's economic income as compared to the poorest 10 per cent controlling 1.7 per cent. Malaysia's top 10 per cent of the population is 22.1 per cent times richer than the poorest 10 per cent, an income gap higher than those of Singapore (17.7), the Philippines (16.5), Thailand (13.4), Vietnam (8.4) and Indonesia (7.8)

Abdullah's economic performance has been credible, and this has been important in configuring his leadership after his first full year in office.

Projections for Malaysia in 2005 are more modest. Nevertheless, GDP growth of 5–6 per cent would still make it the fastest growing economy in Asia behind China and India. It will be driven again by the private sector despite uncertainties arising from slowing global expansion, the U.S. economy heading towards a possible crisis, rising oil prices and external interest rates and a worldwide downturn in the world-wide electronics sector. The central bank predicts rising inflation although it will remain among the lowest in Asia. Foreign exchange (forex) administration rules are expected to be further liberalized, undoing the host of forex rules introduced in 1998 when the ringgit was pegged to the U.S. dollar during the Asian financial crisis. Although there were small increases to consumers in the price of petrol and diesel, the government may have to review its hefty subsidy of approximately RM9 billion annually to maintain petrol and diesel prices, and which have thus far kept domestic pump prices among the lowest in the region.

Foreign Affairs and Security

In a consistency of style, the defining characteristics that were established in 2004 of the foreign policy of the Abdullah Badawi administration were engagement, quiet diplomacy, constructive solutions (as in bilateral relations with Singapore) and perhaps a few wasted opportunities. This shift from the blunt, critical, sometimes adversarial champion of the Third World — Mahathir Mohamed — remained about style, because the pillars of foreign policy established during the previous administration were rearticulated and reaffirmed. However, Abdullah did not shy away from levelling critique, although it was aimed more at organizations he headed such as the Non-Aligned Movement or NAM. He referred to NAM as a "debating society" instead of being "an indispensable forum for developing countries", in an address to a gathering of NAM leaders in October.

Apart from the routine requisite visits of a new leader to key countries — twice to the United States and Britain, to most of the nations of the Middle East, Singapore, Indonesia, Thailand, China, Japan, India, Pakistan, France, and Cuba — it was ASEAN, China, and the Muslim world especially the Organization of Islamic Countries (OIC), that continued to be the focus. There were significant Malaysian initiatives, especially in terms of the OIC and ASEAN, and this confidence to move on issues was perhaps the result of Abdullah's tenure as Malaysia's Foreign Minister for almost nine years from 1991–99.

Cognizant of the OIC's reputation as a "talk shop" with a track record of over 3,000 resolutions and not much else in various meetings since the first summit meeting in 1974 (although the OIC was established in 1969), Abdullah set to work galvanizing the OIC during the last segment of Malaysia's chairmanship of the body. Using the Malaysian experience in successful development, during much of 2004, a programme of capacity-building for Islamic nations that would also involve the Islamic Development Bank was worked on, and will be launched in 2005.

During his visits to the Middle East and at meetings of Muslim nations elsewhere, Abdullah constantly described the Muslim world as being in deep crisis because it is mired in violence. He spoke boldly about the need for reinterpreting text and law to enable Muslims to embrace modernity, exhorted good governance and the alleviation of poverty and illiteracy, and negated the growing insularity of Islamic nations. He said

> We must actively seek out and engage the Other, for there is much that we
> can learn and benefit from them ... War must cease to be an option among
> Muslim nations, and between Muslim nations and others. So must terrorism
> ... the peace and stability we seek cannot be imposed by the barrel of
> a gun.[15]

Most remarkable of all for its uniqueness for any Muslim leader, Abdullah spoke powerfully in the Middle East and Pakistan about women, stating that much of the Muslim world is guilty of neglecting "one of our most precious resources: the women in our societies". He elaborated about how Muslims have failed to provide women adequate access to education and employment, and "failed to accord women the dignity and the equal respect that they fully deserve. In doing so we have only impoverished ourselves and marginalized one full half of Muslim humanity..."[16]

Abdullah continued Mahathir's call for the creation of a global Islamic network, urging the potential and power of greater cooperation among Muslim nations because Muslims account for one-fifth of the world's population, but only have 8.6 per cent of the world's gross domestic product (GDP) and 10 per cent of its global trade despite the massive natural resources at their command. Specifically, he pointed to *halal* foods where the market is approximately US$150 billion annually, and Islamic financial services — confirming that Malaysia is pioneering Islamic treasury bills.

To Western nations, in particular the United States, Abdullah gave a consistent message: about addressing "the root causes of terrorism", with the need to resolve the issue of Palestinian nationhood as a burning issue. He articulated the clearest enunciation since September 2001 of Malaysia's position/solutions on addressing militancy in the Muslim world: the imperative of multilateralism in addressing problems, the inadequacy of military action alone, the need to battle for the minds of potential perpetrators, that the methods used to hunt down or end terrorism must not lead to the breeding of new recruits and sympathizers, that root causes such as Palestine and poverty be addressed, and that it was an oversimplification to see the solution as only the introduction of democracy and good governance.[17]

In July Abdullah offered Malaysia as a mediator of conflicts involving Islamic nations. There was a need, he said, for acceptable mediators beyond the Camp David paradigm, in the context of Muslims viewing the West with suspicion. Nevertheless, it is unfortunate that this offer from a moderate, modern Muslim nation that is deeply committed to peaceful resolutions has been largely unnoticed both abroad but also at home, where the idea has evolved into a Centre for Conflict Resolution that is still at the brainstorming stage.

Abdullah fared better in mediating good relations with Singapore, and new Prime Minister Lee Hsien Loong's own determination to improve relations helped things along. Since 1965 and the acrimonious split between the two nations, 2004 was perhaps one of the most cordial years on record, with both leaders and their top officials agreeing quickly to resolve some outstanding issues. Negotiators agreed on settling a dispute over reclamation works by Singapore in the shared straits; Singapore offered to release Malaysians' pension contributions in exchange for access to Malaysian airspace; and Abdullah approved the sale of stakes in a local bank and the state-owned telecoms company to Temasek, the Singapore government's main investment arm. Both nations made statements about the additional possibility of their governments planning joint investments overseas and their stock exchanges trading one another's shares.

Abdullah also worked on better relations with Australia — describing the nation as "a friend" in the middle of the year with the first visit in over 20 years being planned for 2005. But Malaysia's absence was conspicuous in December in Indonesia, at an Australian-initiated Asia-Pacific meeting of 124 religious leaders to encourage moderate forms of religiosity. The reason was Australia's plan to create a maritime surveillance zone around it, although Abdullah's response was typically non-abrasive. However, that he responded at all to what is essentially a problem for Indonesia, although he only described the potential threat to Indonesia's sovereignty as an example of Australia's insensitivity to its neighbours, was indicative of a larger issue. Implicit in this statement was annoyance over Australia choosing to identify ASEAN as a collective security arrangement and the Treaty of Amity and Cooperation in Southeast Asia (TAC) as a non-aggression pact only. This was in comparison to China's accession to the TAC, which induced Japan and South Korea (both allies of the United States) and India, Russia and South Korea to follow suit, with New Zealand describing itself as "considering the step positively".

In terms of ASEAN, Malaysia pushed through a number of initiatives, the most important among them the East Asia summit that will be held in Kuala Lumpur in 2005. After 37 years of existence, ASEAN agreed to move beyond the traditional formula of ASEAN summit meetings plus separate meetings with the leaders of China, Japan and Korea. At the ASEAN summit in Vientiane in December, for the first time all the leaders from East Asia as well as those from India, Australia and New Zealand met back to back at both group and individual meetings. The meeting with all present was a first, and the percursor to the East Asia Community (EAC), which if it materializes, will be formidable. However, the agreement to have the East Asian Summit is not without rumbles and their potential for scuttling a cohesive meeting: Japan wants to see the United States, Australia and New Zealand at the meeting, and Indonesia has floated the idea that perhaps they qualify for seats at the table.

In the East Asian Summit remains the hope of an East Asian Economic Grouping (EAEG), first floated by Mahathir in 1990. At the East Asia Forum held in December, seven milestones were demarcated by Abdullah Badawi for the creation of an East Asian Community: holding of the East Asia Summit, drawing up a charter of the East Asia Community, establishing an East Asia Free Trade area, having an agreement on an East Asia zone of amity and cooperation, setting up an East Asia transportation and communications network, and drawing up an East Asia declaration of Human Rights and obligations.

There is impressive empirical evidence that the region is getting more interlinked. Apart from very significant trade, there are more than 500 meetings at senior official level generated by ASEAN and its counterparts in Northeast Asia each year, with another 200 meetings in the various Track 2 fora. All this points towards one of the main reasons for pushing for greater cooperation with China beyond the obvious reason of economic benefits: it has to do with ASEAN wanting to engage and induct its neighbouring giant into the ASEAN way of resolving conflicts through diplomatic solutions and thus contain future problems. It is the ASEAN priority of not just prosperity but also stability and the pragmatism of enjoining both.

In another initiative by Malaysia, in November Malaysian parliamentarians, in a non-partisan caucus, brought together legislators from neighbouring ASEAN countries and issued a strong statement calling for the release of Nobel Peace Laureate and opposition leader Aung San Suu Kyi. Over the past few years there has been mounting impatience with ASEAN's rigid adherence to the convention of non-interference which has made it difficult for neighbouring countries to propose measures or even help to resolve, for example, the burgeoning conflict in southern Thailand. A regional parliamentary caucus of the kind that is crystallizing around the Myanmar issue could help regional governments overcome their resistance to dialogue and cooperation on sensitive domestic issues. First of all, because it moves this kind of dialogue and action out of the realm of officialdom, and more importantly, because it is some of ASEAN's august parliamentarians, not activists, who are quite happily airing their problems and making proposals to each other. The level of resonance with the Malaysian leadership was apparent when in November, foreign minister Syed Hamid Albar is reported to have said "there is no such thing as absolute non-interference" when asked about the violence in southern Thailand.[18]

Malaysia's relations with Thailand were already sliding downwards when in July the Thai prime minister Thaksin Shinawatra, told the media that Malaysia was not really cooperating over the arrests of leaders blamed for separatist violence. Nor did the situation improve later when Malaysia asked for its deputy prime minister and foreign minister to visit Thailand over the Tak Bai incident and the Thai response was a postponement "to avoid misinterpretation by certain quarters".[19] Nevertheless pragmatism won the day, and in August, Thailand and Malaysia agreed to promote cross-border transport links, trade, investment and other initiatives to foster economic progress in the southern provinces of Thailand.

In what was intended to be transparency exemplified, the Malaysian media featured an accusation by an UMNO politician that PERKIM or the Malaysian Islamic Welfare Organization had contributed significant funding to the outlawed Pattani United Liberation Organization or PULO.[20] The accusation was later clarified as unfounded, in what was generally deemed a less-than satisfactory manner by the foreign minister, with a statement that the Malaysian government does not support movements or groups that use violence and if such funds were provided "it would have been done without the knowledge of the government".[21] But Malaysian–Thai relations really took a dive later in December, when the Thai prime minister is reported to have alleged that the northern Malaysian states were a safe haven and training ground for militants in southern Thailand. Abdullah expressed his "shock and disappointment" and chided Thailand in what are strong words for him, saying "It is not right to make a statement in the media and then wait for us to reply to court sensational publicity."[22]

Perceptions of Thai insensitivity and public belligerence about Thai concern regarding links and empathy between Muslims across the border are not conducive to having both countries work closely to contain a serious problem, nor is Malaysia's defensive prickliness about Muslims and Islam being described as terrorists. The real imperatives need to be given priority — cooperating and coordinating to curb militancy and terrorism because the Malaysian government has a track record of seriously pursuing genuine leads and taking firm action against militant activity, and collaborating to combat terrorism together with other nations.

Borders and boundaries continued to be a source of unease. In April two Malaysians and the Indonesian skipper of a tugboat were kidnapped by Abu Sayyaf-linked Filipino gunmen in the Sulu Sea. Nevertheless in Mindanao, Malaysia continued to monitor a ceasefire and also attempt to broker a peace agreement between the Philippine government and the Moro Islamic Liberation Front. There have been snags and postponements and dispatching Najib Tun Razak, the Malaysian deputy prime minister, did not seem to make much headway with entrenched positions and deep suspicions.

The state oil company Petronas issued at least one statement during the year about possibly granting concessions for oil exploration around the Ambalat Island off north Kalimantan, with little response from its neighbours. This was perhaps because the dispute with Indonesia over the Sipidan and Ligitan islands in the same Sulawesi Sea was settled in Malaysia's favour by the International Court of Justice in 2002, and Malaysia's claim over Ambalat and the Unarang Reef is based on that judgment. Indonesia claims to use the rules of the Convention of the Law of the Sea to draw a straight line 12 nautical miles from Indonesia's Sebatik border to also claim Ambalat, thus having its own formula for ownership. Herein lies potential for dispute especially with oil as the prize.

Nevertheless, with an eye on higher priorities, in July, Malaysia, Indonesia and Singapore began coordinated 24-hour patrols of the congested Straits of Malacca, which carries more than a quarter of world trade and almost all oil imports from the

Middle East to Japan and China. However, perhaps deputy prime minister Najib was giving notice of what was to come when he stated that user nations should start considering contributing to the safety and security of the sea lane, because "there should be no more free rides" and that only Japan had contributed substantially to the escalating costs.[23]

It has been argued that Malaysia has wasted opportunities to be more assertive with the United States and its allies, or developed nations/First World, given its limited tenure heading the OIC and NAM. However, it is Abdullah's style to work quietly but constructively and to focus on "putting the house in order" first, whether at home in Malaysia, in the OIC or in NAM.

Conclusion

Abdullah had a mixed year that started with a bang and then seemed to taper off. Long-term elements of his agenda for the structural reforms needed and which he had both the foresight and courage to articulate, were put in place. For example, understanding that it would be a process of not just uncovering and criminalizing corruption but changing mind-sets from a culture of patronage and entitlement, he instituted the National Integrity Plan (NIP) in April and launched a National Integrity Institute that would conduct courses and set standards and evaluations for the civil service, among others. Some of these institutional capacity-building measures let him down: the Royal Commission on the Police which he had the King appoint in 2003 did not materialize the report it was tasked to produce by the end of 2004.

The reforms he has promised would, by any logic, take time. But for a citizenry used to the high-profile edicts and ensuing grand gestures of 22 years, Abdullah's quiet, measured governance appeared less effective. But there are still Malaysians who gave him a mandate for change, who are willing to give him a little more time.

Notes

[1]   Transcript of Bernama news agency interview with Prime Minister Abdullah Ahmad Badawi, Thursday, 10 February 2005.

[2]   For a full breakdown of the election results, see the Prime Minister's Office website, specifically, http://eppublic2.pmo.gov.my/onepage/servlet/FWControllerServlet? mvcapp=FWMyOnePage&command=myonepage&rid=1&b=i&sid=240246D85021Y0312188& b=i&tabset=1&temp=3&p=1&taborder=1&fp=1.

[3]   Conversation with Professor Syed Arabi Idid of the International Islamic University;

regarding his findings/results of the survey on media credibility and the BN during the past four general elections, 14 February 2005; also article about the survey findings on http://www.malaysiakini.com/news33540, 14 February 2005.

[4]   http://www.utusanmalaysia.com.my, Banci, accessed 19 March 2004.

[5]   National Poll III, "How Malaysian Voters Perceive Voting Preferences, Leadership and Politics, The Economy, Issues and Political Islam", Merdeka Centre, November 2003, unpublished document.

[6]   Abdullah Ahmad Badawi "Unleash Your Potential", *New Straits Times*, 31 August 2004, p. 1.

[7]   Transcript of Bernama news agency interview with Prime Minister Abdullah Ahmad Badawi, 10 February 2005.

[8]   I have analysed Islam in the Mahathir administration and how the former prime minister harnessed Islam for his nation-building agendas in two articles: "Mahathir, Islam and the New Malay Dilemma", in *Mahathir's Administration: Performance and Crisis in Governance*, edited by Ho Khai Leong and James Chin (Singapore: Times Books International, 2001); and "Perhaps He Deserved Better: The Disjuncture between Vision and Reality in Mahathir's Islam", in *Reflections: The Mahathir Years*, edited by Bridget Welsh (Washington D.C: Southeast Asian Studies Program, SAIS, Johns Hopkins University, 2004).

[9]   "Don't Stir the Hornet's Nest Called Malay Rights", http://www3.malaysiakini.com/news/30305.

[10] "Leave or Face Whipping, Illegal Immigrants Warned", *New Straits Times*, 30 November 2004.

[11] Statistics on the economy's performance from the Bank Negara *2004 Annual Report* (Kuala Lumpur: Bank Negara Malaysia, 2004).

[12] "Dr M: Time to Review Ringgit Peg", *New Straits Times*, 20 January 2004, p. 2.

[13] Keynote address at the seminar on "Culture of High Performance for GLCs", delivered by the Prime Minister Abdullah Ahmad Badawi, 14 May 2004, Kuala Lumpur.

[14] Bloomberg News, 21 January 2005.

[15] Speech entitled "Muslims and Islam in the 21st Century: Image and Reality", delivered by PM Abdullah Ahmad Badawi, Kuala Lumpur, 4 August 2004.

[16] Speech at the Arab Strategy Forum, Dubai, by PM Abdullah Ahmad Badawi on 15 December 2004.

[17] Speech to the Malaysian Heads of Mission, by PM Abdullah Ahmad Badawi, Kuala Lumpur, 6 July 2004.

[18] "Rethinking Principle on Non-Interference", *New Straits Times*, 1 February 2005, p. 18.

[19] "Thailand Requests to Defer Visit by DPM", *The Star*, 24 November 2004, p. 22.

[20] "Perkim Funds Sent to Pattani Movement, Says Annuar", *New Straits Times*, 9 December 2004, p. 1.

[21] "We Don't Support Such Groups", *New Straits Times*, 10 December 2004, p. 4.

[22] "Pak Lah Refutes Thaksin's Claim", *New Straits Times*, 19 December 2004, p. 1.

[23] "Najib: Free Rides in Straits Must End", *New Straits Times*, 12 October 2004, p. 8.

Affirmative Action in Malaysia

Lee Hock Guan

Introduction

The prevailing practice of affirmative action typically involves introducing measures to raise the participation of members of an economically disadvantaged group in the areas of education, employment and business, where they had been historically excluded or underrepresented. Measures taken are generally in the form of preferential policies toward members of a designated group, based on criteria such as a particular ethnicity, gender, or religion. Precisely because affirmative action measures entail bestowing preferential treatment on members of a designated group, they invariably will generate controversy; in particular preferential treatment on the basis of ethnicity and gender has generated intense, passionate debate.

While affirmative action policies vary substantially across countries in terms of the beneficiary groups, nevertheless, in nearly all countries the beneficiaries are groups which are economically and socially disadvantaged and politically subordinate.[1] Malaysia's affirmative action policy differs from those of other countries in one crucial respect — it is "the politically dominant majority group which introduces preferential policies to raise its economic status as against that of an economically more advanced minorities".[2] The majority ethnic group that has the power to legislate the affirmative action policies and receive the benefits from those policies in Malaysia are the Malays.[3] Conversely, it is the Chinese and Indian ethnic minorities, the most advanced economic groups, who have felt most victimized by the affirmative action policies.

Another unique feature of Malaysian affirmative action is that preferential treatment for the Malays and other indigenous groups was written into the Malaysian Constitution, under Article 153. In other words, affirmative action in Malaysia is a consitutionally sanctioned and exclusively ethnic-based policy where only the Malays and other native groups are entitled to receive preferential treatment. Besides being written into the Constitution, the wording of Article 153 links the ethnic preferential

---

Lee Hock Guan is a Fellow at the Institute of Southeast Asian Studies, Singapore.

treatment to the safeguarding of the "special position" of the Malay community. This has given rise to the prevalent and prevailing Malay popular opinion that views preferential treatment as part of their "special rights" and thus not open to negotiation.[4]

It would be incorrect to think that affirmative action was implemented in Malaysia only after 1971. During the colonial period, the British had already put into practice preferential treatment of sorts in the selection and training of Malays for the elite administrative service. In 1948, an article in the Federation of Malaya Agreement stipulated the Malay Ruler to

> safeguard the special position of the Malays and to ensure the reservation for Malays of such proportion as he may deem reasonable of positions in the public service and of scholarships, exhibitions and other similar educational or training privileges ... and, ... of [business] permits and licenses.

This later became part of Article 153 of the Malaysian Constitution. What changed after 1971 was that a Malay-dominated state formulated and systematically implemented a comprehensive ethnic preferential policy to benefit the Malay community.

The ethnic preferential policy has invariably generated intense controversy in Malaysian society, with the majority of Malays, Chinese, and Indians, taking diametrically opposing views. This inflammatory public issue and the emotionally charged debate it has generated, however, has not deteriorated into outright ethnic violence as had happened earlier in 1969. A combination of punitive laws (such as Internal Security Act [ISA] and the Sedition Act) and coercive actions were used throughout the 1970s and 1980s to stifle debate. However, because the state was suppressing the discussion, the quality of reasoned arguments for and against affirmative action also stagnated.

Since the late 1990s, however, a number of factors and developments have contributed to opening up the public space for Malaysian citizens to debate the country's ethnic preferential policy. Perhaps the single most important development is that of the emergence from within the Malay community of voices that are sceptical and critical of the policy. Even from within the United Malay National Organization (UMNO), doubts and anxieties have plagued certain leaders regarding the negative impacts of affirmative action on the Malays, individually and as a community.

This article will first examine the extent to which affirmative action has assisted in expanding Malay participation in the economy and higher education. The next section considers how affirmative action has impacted on ethnic integration.

The third section will argue that while the ethnic preferential policy has helped to narrow ethnic inequality, it, however, was inadequate as an instrument to narrow growing intra-ethnic inequality. The fourth section looks at how the policy has affected economic competitiveness and the national aim to achieve a knowledge-based economy.

Expansion of Malay Economic and Higher Education Participation

Public debates over the economic backwardness of the Malay community and the segmentation of the economy along ethnic lines were already widespread in the 1960s. Affirmative action measures introduced in the sixties were largely ineffective and inadequate. Consequently, increasing numbers of Malays, especially those residing in the urban areas, grew impatient with the glacial pace of their economic progress. The official White Paper on the 13 May 1969 race riots unsurprisingly singled out Malay economic grievances as one of the key factors that brought about the rioting. Economic restructuring along ethnic lines was one of the two objectives of the New Economic Policy (NEP) which was implemented from 1971–90. A comprehensive system of ethnic preferential policies, programmes and instruments that benefited the Malay community were formulated and implemented.[5]

Prior to the implementation of the NEP, in 1970 the mean monthly incomes for Malay and Chinese households in Peninsular Malaysia were RM172 and RM394 respectively. By 1990 the *bumiputera* mean household income had reached RM940, and then it grew speedily to RM1,984 in 1999. Chinese mean household income also grew but at a slower pace; RM1,631 in 1990 and RM3,456 in 1999. Consequently, the gap between the Malay and Chinese household mean income disparity ratio had narrowed from 2.29 in 1970 to 1.74 in 1999.

Segmentation of the economy along ethnic lines was omnipresent before the implementation of the NEP. The overwhelming majority of Malays were employed in the agricultural sector and resided in the rural areas. In 1970, Malays employed in the agricultural sector made up 67.8 per cent of the total Malays employed compared to 31.4 per cent of Chinese, and 48.6 per cent of Indians. Indeed, the only other sector where Malays were found in significant numbers was in government services. By 1995, however, Malays employed in the agricultural sector had decreased to 22.2 per cent and in fact manufacturing had taken over as the sector that employed the most Malays with 24.9 per cent, followed closely by the services sector (including government services) with 24 per cent. Unsurprisingly, the high proportion of 62.3 per cent of Malay workers engaged in agricultural and related occupations in 1970 decreased to 25.3 per cent in 1995, while the share of Malay manufacturing workers increased from 18 per cent to 27.5 per cent during this period.

In 1970, the tertiary enrolment of Malays was 54.1 per cent of the total enrolment, constituting 82.9 per cent and 39.7 per cent at certificate and diploma and degree levels respectively.[6] Of the total number of graduates from 1959–70, Malays and Chinese comprised about 26 per cent and 60 per cent respectively. More importantly, 60 per cent of Malays graduated in the arts faculty while Chinese made up from 80 to 90 per cent of the graduates in science, engineering and medicine. To redress this imbalance an ethnic-based admission policy that made it mandatory for all local public universities to reserve 55 per cent of their places for Malay students was implemented in 1971.

In practice, however, Malay admission into local universities exceeded the 55 per cent figure because policy-makers included in the total university ethnic enrolment figures Malaysians enrolled in overseas universities, the majority of whom were non-Malays. With the inclusion of non-Malay students studying overseas, invariably Malay enrolment in local public universities would be higher than the 55 per cent in order for the Malay enrolment figure to account for 55 per cent of the total university enrolment.

For enrolment of students in public and private (including overseas) tertiary institutions, in 1980 Malays made up 46 per cent of the total, constituting 46.3 per cent and 45.7 per cent in the certificate and diploma and degree courses respectively. By 1999, Malay enrolment made up 53.9 per cent and 58.7 per cent at the certificate and diploma and degree levels respectively, totalling 56 per cent of the total tertiary enrolment. However, since the ethnic quotas were applicable only with regard to admission into public higher institutions, Malay students were hence mostly enrolled in these. For example, in 1980 they made up 72.8 per cent of the total enrolment in local public tertiary institutions, constituting 87.7 per cent and 62.7 per cent in the certificate and diploma and degree programmes respectively.[7]

The success of the ethnic preferential policies in education and employment has led to the growth of a noticeable Malay professional class. While in 1970 and 1980 there were few Malay architects, accountants, engineers, dentists, doctors and lawyers, since 1990 their numbers in these professions have increased significantly except for accountants and less so for architects and engineers. In 2000, for instance, about one out of three dentists, doctors and lawyers and one out of four architects and engineers were Malays. And unlike in the past, Malay professionals today are found in both the public and private sectors.

In terms of ownership of share capital of limited companies, Malay and Chinese shares were 4.3 per cent and 38.3 per cent respectively in 1971 — with foreign ownership taking up the lion's share of 61.7 per cent. By 1995, the Malay share had increased to 20.6 per cent (this figure was disputed because the official figure excluded the nominee share) while the Chinese share had reached 40.9 per cent. Perhaps, more importantly, state privatization programmes have helped to develop a growing Malay corporate and business community. The significance of the Malay corporate and business community is clearly shown by the fact that individual Malay ownership of share capital has surpassed the Malay trustees ownership; in 1995, individual Malay ownership made up nearly 90.3 per cent of the total Malay share. The growth of the Malay corporate and business community, however, suffered a setback after the 1997 Asian financial crisis.

Ethnic preferential policies have greatly enhanced Malay participation in the economy and higher education. The economic disparities between the Malay and non-Malay communities have narrowed significantly. Malay horizontal and vertical participation in the economy has expanded substantially, especially in the modern sector. Malay enrolment in higher education, including university, has exceeded the 55 per cent quota reserved for them. Thus, the ethnic preferential policies have created a more broad-based differential Malay employment structure and successfully fostered a growing Malay middle-class and corporate and business community.

Ethnic Integration in Society

The government has frequently argued that the preferential policy of raising Malay participation in the economy and higher education would help to ensure stability and foster national integration. Prior to their introduction, ethnic segregation along geographical location, residential neighbourhoods, economic activities and occupations, and education institutions was prevalent. For example, while the majority of Malays resided in the rural areas and worked in the agricultural sector, the majority of Chinese, in contrast, resided in the urban areas and worked in the non-agricultural sectors. Ethnic preferential policies have dramatically altered the ethnic segregation pattern in Malaysian society.

In all the major urban areas, push and pull factors, assisted by ethnic preferential policies, have led to a significant influx of Malay emigrants such that all urban areas are today ethnically heterogeneous. To promote ethnic integration, a national housing policy decreed that new residential neighbourhoods must be ethnically diverse. Thus while the old neighbourhoods in the urban landscape remain racially homogenous, new ones are invariably ethnically pluralistic. As discussed, preferential policies too had clearly raised the representation of Malays in nearly all occupations and economic sectors and higher education by the 1990s.

Ideally, the increasingly multiethnic workplaces and campuses should have facilitated face-to-face ethnic interaction and thus have helped to generate better intra-ethnic group tolerance and understanding.[8]

On closer inspection, however, ethnic preferential policies have contributed to the formation of ethnic enclaves in the society. Preferential treatment of Malays in employment, business and education necessarily meant the foregoing of the principles of meritocracy and equal opportunity. State establishment of ethnicized programmes and institutions as means to expand Malay representation in employment, business, and education has formed ethnic enclaves in the economy and education. Conversely, the Chinese and Indians, confronted with systemic discrimination against them, have also formed their ethnic enclaves as survival strategies.

The public service sector is an excellent example of how preferential hiring has transformed a previously ethnically diverse sector into one that is almost ethnically homogenous. Prior to the implementation of NEP in 1971, although Malays dominated the public service sector, it had nevertheless quite a sizable representation of Chinese and Indians. Systematic preferential hiring of Malays at the expense of recruiting non-Malays had by the 1990s transformed the civil service into a wholly Malay enclave. Concern that an overwhelmingly Malay-dominated public service sector might have a negative impact on ethnic integration has periodically led to calls and half-hearted efforts to recruit more non-Malays. However, for various reasons, recruitment drives to employ more non-Malays into the public sector have largely yielded miserable results.[9]

Anecdotal evidence would suggest that ethnic enclaves in the business sector are quite pervasive at the company level. On the one hand, corporatized and privatized public services and enterprises, such as Petronas, Proton, Telekom, Tenaga and so on, have remained largely Malay entities. Malay-owned companies generally also tended to have a predominantly Malay workforce. On the other hand, the majority of Chinese-owned companies, especially the small and medium enterprises, employ a largely Chinese (in fact Mandarin-speaking) workforce. Interestingly, it is the multinational companies that are likely to have an ethnically diverse workforce.

The presence of ethnic enclaves is evident in the education sector as well. The Ratnam Committee investigating the alleged practice of ethnic segregation by race streaming in national primary schools found that of the 2.2 million students enrolled in the national primary school in 2002, only 2.1 per cent and 4.3 per cent were Chinese and Indians respectively. In other words, the investigation revealed the prevalence of ethnic segregation along national and national-type primary schools.

At the university level, while the 55:30:10 (*bumiputera*:Chinese:Indian) ethnic quotas ensured an ethnically diverse university population, nevertheless, the distribution of students by university showed that the majority of the non-Malay students are found in University Malaya (UM) and Science University Malaysia (USM). In contrast, the percentage of Malay students in Putra University Malaysia (UPM, formerly Agricultural University of Malaysia), Technology University Malaysia (UTM), National University of Malaysia (UKM), and Northern University Malaysia (UUM) far exceeds 70 per cent. Moreover, in the rush to raise the proportion of Malay enrolment in the local public universities, ethnic enclaves were formed when the state established several *bumiputera*-only programmes and institutions.

The Majlis Amanah Rakyat (MARA), or Council of Trust for the Indigenous Peoples, was designated as a key vehicle to train and assist the indigenous peoples to participate actively and progressively in both commercial and industrial enterprises. MARA implemented a number of programmes, especially establishing educational institutions, to enhance the knowledge and skills levels of the Malay labour force. The MARA College of Business and Professional Studies was upgraded in October 1967 to the MARA Institute of Technology (MIT) and then to university status in 1999. By 1986, MARA had established a branch in every state and offered a wide variety of programmes with the bulk of courses offered being at the certificate and diploma levels.[10] It enrolled a total of 6,900 students in 1975 and by 1996 the enrolment figure was nearly 45,000.

MARA also established the MARA Junior Science Colleges (MJSC) with the objective to increase the enrolment of Malay students in the science and science-related in the universities. Essentially residential-type schools, they received generous funds from the state as well as the best teachers, and thus were highly sought after by Malay parents. In 1984, there were 10 MJSC schools with 6,311 students, and in 2000, the number of schools had increased to 25, enrolling a total of 15,424 students.

Another educational system established in 1971 to help increase the number of science and science-related subjects students was the Residential Secondary School (RSS). In 1984, there were 27 residential schools in Peninsular Malaysia with an enrolment of 12,115, and by 2000, the total number of students had doubled to about 24,000. Finally, the two-year Matriculation Program was initiated in 1970 to expedite the intake of Malay students into the local universities. Initially, both the RSS and Matriculation were opened to non-*bumiputera* students, albeit in limited numbers, but by the 1980s they became largely the preserve of *bumiputera* students.

On the other side, the Malaysian Chinese Association (MCA) was authorized to establish a government-assisted college for non-Malays to pursue certificate and diploma education, the Tunku Abdul Rahman (TAR) College. Compared to MIT, however, TAR College was a much smaller institute and over the years funding for its development and expansion was rather limited. Not surprisingly, TAR College's enrolment growth has been unimpressive: from 4,036 students in 1975 to about 6,000 in 1980 and to about 9,000 in 1996.[11]

The establishment of MARA, MJSC, RSS, and Matriculation Program created largely Malay-only education enclaves within the national education system. Only TAR College was established to cater for the non-Malay students to receive certificate and diploma education; even then limited resources were channelled to develop and expand the college. Moreover, ethnic quota admission policies made it much more difficult for the Chinese and Indian students to get a place in the local public universities. Chinese and Indian students thus had to look for other avenues to pursue their higher education ambitions. In the 1970s and 1980s, the scarcity of local higher educational opportunities for the Chinese and Indian students induced growing frustrations and thus tense ethnic relations.[12] Needless to say, the majority of non-Malay parents could not afford to send their children to study overseas.

In the 1990s, the privatization and internationalization of higher education provided Chinese and Indian students with more opportunities to realize their higher education goals. Pent-up demand for higher education among the non-Malays led to a proliferation of private colleges in Malaysia.[13] As expected, the enrolment in private higher education institutions was overwhelmingly non-Malay; in 1980, for diploma and certificate courses Malays, Chinese, and Indians made up 15.7 per cent, 71.2 per cent and 12.8 per cent respectively, and for university courses the figures were 26.8 per cent, 59.4 per cent, and 13.8 per cent respectively.

The underrepresentation of Malay students in the private higher education sector worried state planners. By the late 1990s, steps were taken to partly address this problem. Thus in 1999, the ethnic breakdown had evened out especially for the certificate and diploma courses where Malays and non-Malays constituted 44.5 per cent and 55.5 per cent. On closer inspection, however, the increase in Malay enrolment in the private higher education did not lead to the creation of a more ethnically integrated private education sector. This was because ethnic enclaves continued to persist as the majority of Malays were enrolled in the Malay-owned colleges. The ethnic segmentation of private higher education continued to be most glaring in 1999 in the enrolment of students in the degree programmes where the Malay and non-Malay student breakdown was 16.3 per cent and 83.7 per cent respectively.

Class Inequality in an Ethnicized Polity

The ethnic-based affirmative action policy has contributed to creating a more class-differentiated Malay community and, indeed, successfully fostered a growing Malay middle-class and corporate and business group. More generally, the policy was reasonably successful in achieving what it was set up to do, that is, to narrow the intra-ethnic inequality gap, especially between Malays and Chinese. The rural–urban inequality gap also narrowed from the middle of 1970 to 1990. However, a number of salient developments in the inequality landscape in Malaysia have led to calls to rethink and reformulate the ethnic basis of the existing affirmative action policy.

In 1970, half the population of Malaysia lived in poverty,[14] and the incidence of poverty among the *bumiputera*, Chinese and Indians was 66 per cent, 27 per cent and 40 per cent respectively. Needless to say, the incidence of poverty in rural areas, where the bulk of Malays lived, was much higher than that of urban areas. Thus, besides restructuring ethnic inequalities the NEP also had another objective, which was the eradication of poverty, regardless of ethnicity. By any measure the implementation of the NEP has significantly reduced poverty, particularly poverty amongst the Malays.

The overall incidence of poverty has been reduced from 52.4 per cent in 1970 to 16.5 per cent in 1990 and to 5.5 per cent in 1999. Rural poverty has declined to 21.8 per cent in 1990 and to 10 per cent in 1999, and Malay poverty, much of which is in the rural sector, has declined to 20.8 per cent in 1990 and to 10.2 per cent in 1999. The incidence of poverty among the Chinese and Indian communities has also declined significantly. However, questions have been raised regarding the government's refusal to redefine the poverty line in Malaysia; the argument is that urban poverty is distinctly different from rural poverty and the existing single definition of the poverty line would underestimate the extent of the problem in the urban areas.

Incidence of Poverty in Malaysia (per cent)

	1970	1990	1999
Rural	58.7	21.8	10.0
Urban	21.3	7.5	1.9
Overall	52.4	16.5	5.5
Bumiputera	65.9	20.8	10.2
Chinese	27.5	5.7	2.6
Indians	40.2	8.0	1.9

Sources: Malaysian Plans 1991, 1996, 2001.

Nevertheless, while poverty has continued to decline since 1990, income inequality, measured in terms of the "gini coefficient" factor, has worsened. The late Malaysian economist Ishak Shari suggested that government policy reversal towards liberalization, deregulation and privatization since the late 1980s has contributed to this trend of increasing inequality.[15] In particular, it is the emergence of a new dimension of income inequality — that of intra-ethnic inequality, particularly of the high intra-Malay — that has raised queries about the existing formulation and implementation of the ethnic preferential policy.[16]

The increasing class differentiation of the Malay community has inadvertently played a role in accentuating the inequality within the community. The success of the ethnic preferential policy in making social classes more multiethnic meant that there now exists a significant Malay middle class. Children of the growing Malay middle class families in the urban areas would naturally be in a more advantageous position to benefit from the ethnic preferential policies and programmes. The rationale of the ethnic-based preferential policy was to close the intra-ethnic inequality gap between groups and not between individuals. The former prime minister Mahathir puts it this way:

> The NEP ... was not concerned with making all the bumiputeras earn equally, or share equally, the wealth distributed amongst them ... The intention of the NEP was to create in the bumiputera community the same division of labour and rewards as was found in the non-bumiputera communities, particularly the Chinese. ... The equitableness was not to be between individuals, but between communities.[17]

Thus the ethnic-based preferential policy had disproportionately benefited the better off members of the Malay community, and contributed to growing frictions within the community. The frictions within the Malay community over the use and abuse of the ethnic preferential policy were greatly accentuated in the aftermath of the 1997 Asian financial crisis. The Mahathir government channelled considerable resources to bail out several prominent Malay businesses and businessmen, but was perceived to have not done much, or enough, to help the other segments of the community. This generated much resentment among the working and middle class Malays, particularly among the small and medium Malay businessmen who were severely affected by the economic downturn. The growing class inequality within the community contributed to weakening Malay solidarity, especially support for UMNO. This factor partly contributed to the poor UMNO electoral showing in the 1999 general election. There has hence emerged growing support among the Malays for the state to revise the existing ethnic-based preferential policy, including making income a criterion as well.[18]

In theory, the ethnic preferential policy was supposed to assist all *bumiputera* groups including the Kadazans, Ibans, Orang Asli, and other indigenous groups. In practice, however, it appeared that the ethnic preferential policy has disproportionately benefited the Malay community. The majority of the non-Malay *bumiputeras* are found in Sabah and Sarawak, and together they made up about 10 per cent of the total population of Malaysia. Findings indicate that the non-Malay *bumiputeras* have lagged behind the Malays economically.[19] For example, in terms of participation in the modern economy, equity ownership, and enrolment in higher education, non-Malay *bumiputeras* from Sabah and Sarawak remained underrepresented. More importantly, the incidence of poverty among the non-Malay *bumiputeras* remained noticeably higher than among the Malay *bumiputera* community.

Perhaps, the experience of the indigenous Orang Asli (aboriginal group) best indicates how the existing ethnic preferential policy has benefited the *bumiputera* groups unevenly. The Orang Asli, comprising 0.5 per cent of the total population, has the highest incidence of poverty; in 1997, 81 per cent of the community lived below the poverty line while the overall poverty rate was 7.5 per cent. Several studies have indicated that the Orang Asli groups' overall condition had worsened considerably over the years despite their status as a *bumiputera* group.[20]

Among the non-*bumiputera* groups, there is growing evidence of rising poverty among the Indian community. Large numbers of Indians working in the plantation sector are condemned to a life of poverty precisely because socioeconomic conditions in the sector neither help to promote education nor enable the acquisition of critical skills. Moreover, since 1990, the rapid economic growth resulted in many plantations making way for industrial and residential development, which in turn caused the plantation Indian labour force to be displaced and forced to migrate to the urban areas. By and large, because of their low skills and educational levels, they ended up living in squatter areas and joining the ranks of the urban poor.[21] The marginalization of the Indian community has led to concern that unless the ethnic preferential policy is revised in such a way as to assist the community, the Indian poverty situation would only worsen.

Economic Competitiveness and the Knowledge Economy

There is a growing concern among certain Malay individuals that prolonging the ethnic preferential policy might have deleterious effects on Malay individual and collective competitiveness.[22] More generally, the ethnic preferential policy might weaken the economic competitiveness of the country as well as hinder the national goal to upgrade to a knowledge-based economy.

Some Malays have pointed out that prolonging the ethnic preferential policy could create a culture of dependency.[23] A culture of dependency would not merely be a psychological problem, but would also have an important economic consequence

— it could hinder the development of an economically competitive Malay community. This is because the ethnic preferential policy meant that Malay individuals, and as a collective, would not have to strive as hard as the Chinese or Indians in order to get admitted into local higher education institutions, receive scholarships, succeed in business, and so on.

For example, critics have pointed out that the manner in which the ethnic preferential policy was implemented in Malaysia has not created a highly competitive Malay corporate and business community, but, instead, a largely rentier Malay capitalist group.[24] This group's lack of competitiveness was painfully exposed by the 1997 Asian financial crisis such that many of them had to beseech support from the government. In an era of economic globalization dictated by neo-liberal thinking, where free market competition rules the day, for the Malay community to perform it must be able to compete without any crutches — indeed, in the global world economy there are no ethnic quotas.[25]

Indeed, it is not only the Malay individual or community that has to become more competitive — but the Malaysian nation as a whole that has to become more competitive in the new neo-liberal dominated world economy. Given the economic juncture that Malaysia is in, the understanding is that for the country to stay competitive it must upgrade from a production to a knowledge-based economy. This transformation would necessarily entail upgrading the skills and knowledge of the Malaysian labour force — since knowledge has become a key competitive advantage in the new economy. While the Malaysian state has introduced a number of measures to enable the economy to move from a capital investment to a productivity-driven one, prolonging the ethnic preferential policy, critics claim, would impede and slow down the transition to a knowledge-driven economy.

The lack of skilled manpower and technology innovation and advancement has been identified as a key factor that has slowed down the development of a knowledge-based economy in Malaysia. The percentage of its labour force with tertiary education, which is critical to the drive to create a knowledge-based economy, is still small, about 13.9 per cent (1990–2000). Some of the world's top technology firms were reluctant to invest in Malaysia precisely because they felt that there are too few skilled knowledge workers. While the state has expanded the tertiary education sector in order to increase the percentage of graduates in the labour force, it has also turned to looking into ways to attract experienced Malaysian knowledge workers living abroad to return home. Needless to say, the existing ethnic preferential policy was one of the push factors that resulted in the brain drain of non-Malay Malaysian skilled workers to live and work abroad.[26]

In 1995, to encourage more Malaysian talent to come home, the government launched a programme called "Brain Gain" to reverse the brain drain losses incurred over the years. This was an ambitious policy to attract 5,000 talented expatriate Malaysians (in particular) annually to work in Malaysia. The programme fared poorly and managed to attract only 23 Malaysians before it was suspended following the 1997 Asian financial crisis. In total, between 1995 and 2000, the "brain gain" scheme attracted 94 scientists, including 24 Malaysians, in the fields of pharmacology, medicine, semi-conductor technology and engineering.[27] However, 23 of the Malaysians who returned eventually gave up because, among other things, of the discriminatory policies that they felt sacrifice meritocracy and reward mediocrity. When the Brain Gain Scheme was reintroduced in 1 January 2001, it received a total of nearly 600 applications by 2003, with slightly more than 200 approved, but only about 130 Malaysians returned.

Despite the various incentive schemes that the government has introduced to attract skilled Malaysian knowledge workers to return, they were obviously not sufficiently attractive. There is no doubt at all that the remuneration packages offered by the Malaysian government would still be below what expatriate Malaysians could earn abroad, since most of them are working in the advanced economies. Besides the less than attractive remuneration packages, one factor that would discourage Malaysians abroad — but which the government has not publicly acknowledged — from returning would be the ethnic preferential policy. For example, many Malaysian Chinese and Indians who ended up working abroad are there because they could not get admission into the local public universities due to the ethnic quotas and had to study overseas. Hence, based on their personal experience, expatriate Malaysian Chinese or Indians would hesitate to return because they would assume that they and their children would not have equality of employment and educational opportunities as long as the ethnic preferential policy is in place.

Conclusion

Without any doubt, the implementation of ethnic preferential programmes and policies has helped to redress the underrepresentation of Malay participation in the economy, especially in the modern economic sector, and in tertiary education. The inequality gap between the Malays and Chinese has narrowed considerably and Malay equity ownership had reached more than 20 per cent by 1990. A growing Malay professional middle class and corporate and business community have emerged.

However, it is clear that the existing ethnic preferential policy has been found inadequate in addressing the rising new phenomenon of intra-ethnic inequality for all ethnic groups, especially in the Malay community. Moreover, the other non-

Malay *bumiputera* groups have not benefited equally from the existing ethnic preferential policy. Conversely, a preferential policy based on ethnicity would continue to disproportionately benefit the better-off members of the designated group — in this case the Malays — thus further accentuating intra-ethnic inequality. As such, there is a growing support — including within the Malay community — to modify the bases of the preferential policy such as including an income selection criterion as well.

The implementation of ethnic preferential programmes and policies has led to the development of ethnic enclaves in the economy and education system. In particular, the public sector has become essentially a Malay enclave where very few non-Malays are employed. In the corporate world, Malay- and Chinese-owned businesses continued to employ members of their own ethnic groups with only the multinational companies having a more diverse workforce. In education, ethnic enclaves have existed because the state established a number of Malay-only programmes and institutions as a means to advance and raise Malay enrolment in the universities, and the existence of ethnic admission quota resulted in non-Malay students enrolling in the largely non-Malay dominated private tertiary education sector.

Also, prolonging the ethnic preferential policy might create a culture of dependency that would weaken the economic and educational competitiveness of the Malay community. The national objective to upgrade to a knowledge-based economy has been partly hindered by the failure to attract skilled Malaysian knowledge workers abroad to return. Because the majority of the overseas Malaysian workers are non-Malays, one major disincentive for them to return to Malaysia is the ethnic preferential policy that denied them of equality of employment and educational opportunities.

In recent years, the government has introduced various steps to modify the ethnic preferential policy. In part to address the ethnic polarization of the education system and in part to raise the competitiveness of Malay students,[28] in 2001 the government decided to "re-open" MRSM colleges, residential schools and matriculation programmes to non-*bumiputera* students; the goal was to reserve 10 per cent of the enrolment for non-Malay students. However, the response from the non-Malays was less than enthusiastic, with MARA reporting a take-up rate of about 70 per cent.[29]

Also in 2001, the ethnic admission quota system was dropped and in its place a merit-based system is being used for admission to the local public universities. The implementation of this merit-based admission policy yielded surprising results: Chinese and Indian student intakes fell sharply from the previous quota of 35 per cent to 26.4 per cent and 10 per cent to 4.7 per cent respectively. *Bumiputera* intake, in contrast, was about 68 per cent — significantly exceeding the previous quota of 55 per cent. Thus the admission figures appeared to indicate that the Malays are doing much better than the Chinese and Indian students.[30]

The government has also announced its intention to look into ways to increase the number of non-Malays in the civil service. While these tentative measures are commendable, perhaps more radical modifications are needed to rethink and reformulate the affirmative action policy. The existing ethnic-based preferential policy was established at a time when ethnic inequality was the most glaring form of inequality in the society and when the majority of Malays lived in the rural sector and in poverty. Also, it was implemented at a time when the Malaysian economy was making the transition from agriculture to manufacturing. Today, new problems, situations and challenges have arisen which the existing ethnic preferential policy would not be able to effectively address. While historically the criticisms of the ethnic preferential policy had largely came from the aggrieved ethnic groups, especially the Chinese and Indians, in recent years the criticisms are also coming from members of the Malay community. Most critics of the ethnic preferential policy would not advocate doing away with it, but, rather, that it needs to be modified.

Notes

[1] For a comparative analysis of affirmative action policies, see Daniel Sabbagh, "Affirmative Action Policies: An International Perspective", United Nations Development Program (Geneva: Human Development Report Office, Occasional Paper, 2004).

[2] Ibid., p. 1.

[3] In theory, the affirmative action policies also benefit the non-Malay *bumiputera* groups, such as the indigenous Ibans, Kadazans, and others, as well. In practice, however, the politically dominant Malays have benefited disproportionately from these policies.

[4] The Malay special rights were, the Malays claim, part of the social contract agreed to by the non-Malays in exchange for their receiving citizenship status during the constitutional negotiations. The 1956 Reid Commission, however, explicitly called for the removal of Article 153 ten years after independence as it regarded this article an anomaly and in conflict with the principle of equality of all citizens, regardless of ethnicity. But in the haste to achieve independence, the leaders of the Malay(si)an Chinese Association and Malay(si)an Indian Congress chose to support the Tunku's suggestion to stop quibbling and reject this recommendation, and that they could re-evaluate it after independence.

[5] Although the NEP was supposed to be for 20 years from 1971 to 1991, based on the argument that the targets were not met, it continues to be enforced.

[6] These figures are only for local public institutions, and given that the majority of private

and overseas students are non-Malays, the total Malay percentage would be lower than 54.1 per cent.

7   Undoubtedly, the effectiveness of the ethnic quota policy in enhancing Malay participation in higher education was most evident in their enrolment gains in the science and technical subjects at the university level. Historically, the number of Malays enrolled in higher education, especially university level, was disproportionately in the humanities and arts such that their numbers were much lower than the non-Malays in the sciences and engineering. For example, between 1959 and 1970, the Malay to Chinese graduates ratio for engineering, science, and medicine were 1:100, 1:20, and 1:9 respectively. The proportion of Malay graduates in the sciences and engineering has, however, increased significantly since the implementation of the ethnic preferential policies.

8   However, several studies have shown that intra-ethnic interaction outside of the classrooms or workplaces remained minimal. Similarly, in the new neighborhoods that are largely multiracial, intra-ethnic interaction remained limited — ethnic groups live in close proximity but lead separate social lives. A 1999 survey study of student interaction at the University of Malaya revealed that the interaction between students of different races outside the classroom was almost non-existent. A October 12, 1999 *New Straits Times* survey found that 98 per cent of Malay students, 99 per cent of Chinese students, and 97 per cent of Indian students did not mix socially with students of other races. In 2003, to address the problem of ethnic polarization among Malaysian youths, the government introduced a national service program which it hopes will foster ethnic interaction and thus promote national integration.

9   Besides the preferential treatment hurdle, low wages, poor promotion prospects, and other factors have made civil service employment unattractive to most non-Malays. The problem of non-Malay representation in the uniformed services, such as the police and armed forces, is especially acute. In 1992, out of the 115,000 officers in the armed forces, non-Malays made up less than 10 per cent. In 2002, the latest naval recruitment of 645 recruits had only 50 non-Malays.

10 Besides MIT, MARA also established and operated educational institutes such as the MARA Professional College and MARA Infotech Academy. Also in 1985, a College for Preparatory Studies, or MARA College, was established to provide pre-university studies for government-sponsored students to enable them to join American, Canadian and Australian universities at junior year. MARA operated a number of MARA Skills Institutes with 13 campuses.

11 The Malaysian Chinese Association was given permission to establish University TAR in 2001.

12 An additional frustration among the Chinese was the refusal by the state to recognize the qualifications of Chinese students who graduated from the Independent Chinese Secondary Schools, which enrolled a total of about 50,000 students though the number has been decreasing since the 1990s.

13   In the late 1990s, the government permitted the establishment of private universities in Malaysia. Among the foreign universities which established Malaysian branches were Monash University and Curtin University from Australia, and University of Nottingham, United Kingdom.

14   Poverty assessment is based on the official definition of poverty incomes. For example, in 1995 the poverty line incomes were RM425 per month for a family of 4.6 in Peninsular Malaysia, RM601 per month for a household of size 4.9 in Sabah and RM576 per month for a household of 4.8 in Sarawak.

15   Ishak Shari, "Economic Growth and Income Inequality in Malaysia, 1971–95", *Journal of the Asia Pacific Economy* 5, no. 1 (1 February 2000): 112–24.

16   A.H. Roslan, "Income Inequality, Poverty and Development Policy in Malaysia", http://poverty.worldbank.org/library/view/13714/.

17   As quoted in Roslan 2001.

18   This was clearly articulated in the KeADILan Party's manifesto. One of the first things the Abdullah Badawi government did was to channel more resources to the small and medium Malay businessmen and middle and working class Malays in order to win back their support. Also, his administration started to channel more resources to develop the rural sector, which was largely neglected during Mahathir's rule.

19   Madeline Berma's speech delivered at the inaugural Bumiputera Minorities Economic Congress, 6–7 February 2005.

20   See, for example, Colin Nicholas, *The Orang Asli and the Contest for Resources: Indigenous Politics, Development and Identity in Peninsular Malaysia* (Subang Jaya: Center for Orang Asli Concerns, 2000).

21   "These displaced people with low levels of education and skills are largely unemployable and find themselves competing with foreign workers for low paying dead end type of jobs thus perpetuating their poverty. The majority find themselves alienated and excluded from markets institutions that define legitimate career path and work function. Escapes from poverty take on the easiest but not necessarily the most legitimate form. The incidence of involvement of Indians in organized and serious crime, drug racketeering and gambling has been on the increase. Recent statistics show alarming crime statistics involving the Indian community with numbers disproportionate to their population composition. This results in the community being marginalized and socially stigmatized. The failure of effective community leadership and poor performance of community based organizations have contributed to immiserization of segments of Indian community which have neither economic nor political clout. Solutions for the problems of the community should transcend narrow ethnic boundaries and be conceived as a comprehensive part of overall development effort." Sulochana Nair, *Poverty in the New Millennium — Challenges for Malaysia* http://www.devnet.org.nz/conf/Papers/nair.pdf.

22   For example, see then DPM Abdullah Badawi's speech at the UMNO 2002 general assembly.

[23]   In his speech given at the Harvard Club of Malaysia dinner on 29 July 2002 Mahathir asked "whether they should or should not do away with the crutches that they have got used to, which in fact they have become proud of". He also added that "There is a minority of Malays who are confident enough to think of doing away with the crutches, albeit gradually. But they are a very small minority. Their numbers are not going to increase any time soon. They are generally regarded as traitors to the Malay race".

[24]   E.T. Gomez and Jomo K.S. *Malaysia's Political Economy: Politics, Patronage and Profits* (Cambridge University Press, Cambridge, 1997; revised edition, 1999).

[25]   In his deputy presidential speech to UMNO 2002, Prime Minister Abdullah Badawi reiterated "a mental revolution is crucial in facing an increasingly competitive world. The national economy now faces external pressures such as WTO and AFTA; our products and services face competition from other countries. If we are slow in changing attitudes, if we do not raise our competitiveness, we will lose investments, lose jobs and lose business opportunities to nations that are more cost efficient and more competitive".

[26]   Lim Kit Siang estimated that "There may be over 100,000 Malaysian professionals who have moved to the U.S., Canada, Australia and New Zealand since the 1970s, and this figure does not include ... Malaysians who intended only to study abroad, but then chose to stay on". Also, there is a sizable community of Malaysian professionals working in Singapore as well.

[27]   Speech by Dr Jamaluddin Jarjis, Minister for Science, Technology and Innovation, in Parliament on 20 September 2004.

[28]   "Malay students should view this as an opportunity to enhance their competitiveness and resoluteness so that they are seen as not only being able to succeed when competing amongst their own but also succeeding among all students regardless of race". Abdullah Badawi, Speech at UMNO 2002.

[29]   Many factors could help to explain this lukewarm response and a major factor was the perceived or real discrimination that the non-Malays believed existed in the MRSM and matriculation programmes.

[30]   However, the majority of Chinese and Indians remain highly sceptical of the merit basis of the new university admission selection policy. Their views were probably close to Lim Kit Siang, the opposition leader: "... whether the merit-based selection system is honest, impartial, professional and can bear public scrutiny or whether the government has a lot of things to hide about the system. A particular concern has to do with the special formula used to match the matriculation results and the STPM grades — the crux of the matter was whether the formula was objective and fair. Under this new system, entrance to public universities are by way of two examinations — matriculation and Sijil Tinggi Pelajaran Malaysia (STPM). Only 10 per cent of Mara matriculation courses are open to non-bumiputeras. Many have decried this system as being unfair as the one-year matriculation program is deemed to be not on par with the more trying two-year STPM examination", http://www.malaysia.net/dap/lks1561.htm.

Myanmar

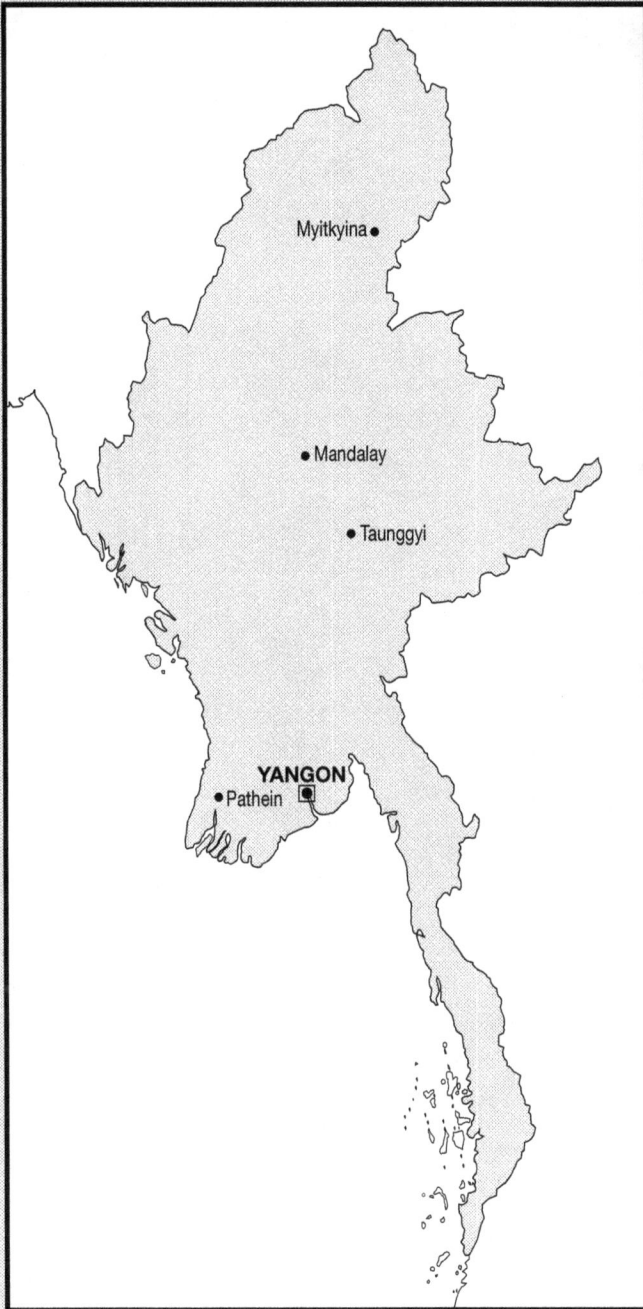

MYANMAR IN 2004
Why Military Rule Continues

Kyaw Yin Hlaing

Since it took power, the current military government of Myanmar has been beleaguered by several opposition forces. Its legitimacy has been questioned by a majority of the people, the international community, several political parties formed by the participants of the Four Eights democracy movement,[1] and veteran politicians who have been involved in Myanmar politics since colonial days. The military's hold on the country has also been challenged by several insurgent groups. At the same time, the junta is believed to be riddled with internal power struggles, a view seemingly confirmed by the abrupt dismissal in October 2004 of the powerful intelligence chief and then Prime Minister Khin Nyunt and the discharge of his entire intelligence corps. Because Khin Nyunt was the architect of the 7-point road map[2] for democratic transition in Myanmar and ceasefire agreements with insurgent groups, his dismissal was accompanied by rumours that the first step of the road map, the National Convention[3] (resumed in May 2004 and adjourned in July 2004), would not convene again and that the ceasefire agreements would break down, with rebels returning to the jungles to resume their armed struggle against the government. Therefore, several observers read Khin Nyunt's dismissal as a signal of instability in the junta.

Yet, although the incident did highlight internal tensions between senior officials in the government, the junta did not appear to be a government that was on the verge of collapse. Apart from detaining some senior intelligence officials, the junta was found to be conducting its business as usual in the remaining two-and-a-half months of the year. It announced that the National Convention would be resumed in mid-February 2005 and that it would abide by all ceasefire agreements. As 2004 came to an end, senior government officials publicly noted with confidence that the

KYAW YIN HLAING is Assistant Professor in the Department of Political Science, National University of Singapore.

government would continue to rule the country without Khin Nyunt and his powerful intelligence apparatus.

Why is the junta still in power? Why did the tension between the intelligence and army units not lead to the break-up of the regime? Both questions will be addressed in this paper by an examination of the internal structure of the Myanmar Tatmadaw (armed forces), and the junta's interaction with opposition parties, insurgent groups and other major societal actors. In order to fully understand the complex nature of the junta's continued rule in Myanmar, one should consider the internal dynamics of the opposition parties, exiled pro-democracy organizations, ethnic insurgent groups, and other societal forces that affect the junta.

The Impact of the Intelligence-Army Factional Struggle on Military Rule

While it has always been the most organized institution in the country, the Tatmadaw has never been considered monolithic. It has always been perceived as fraught with internal factional and power rivalries. The dismissal of Khin Nyunt and the entire intelligence corps was doubtlessly a major political event in Myanmar. Despite the uncertain political climate of the country, however, the military does not seem to be on the verge of collapse. In this section, I will explain why the recent factional struggle in the junta did not lead to its break-up.

In fact, the power struggle between the army and intelligence corps was of a long-standing nature. A local analyst noted that this struggle broke out whenever the intelligence chief was appointed to an important position in the government, bypassing army officers who were senior to him.[4] When the military took power in 1988, Khin Nyunt was made Secretary-I of the State Law and Order Restoration Council (SLORC) which was renamed in 1997 as the State Peace and Development Council (SPDC). He was the most junior member of the SLORC. However, his control of the intelligence corps meant that he was privy to all manner of information, which he could control and use to his benefit. Using both his positions as Secretary-I of the SLORC and the head of the intelligence corps, he was able to successfully consolidate his position in the government. Accordingly, some senior military officers were disgruntled with the growing power of Khin Nyunt. Although they emphasized collective leadership, senior officials were not prepared to set aside the hierarchical nature of their organization. Most senior officials tried to publicly show that they were as powerful, if not more so, than Khin Nyunt. They objected to any of Khin Nyunt's proposals that countered theirs because they interpreted his actions to be presumptuous and out of order. In many cases, senior ministers and regional commanders attempted to prove that they were no less powerful than Khin Nyunt. For example, the Northern Military Command Commander, Lt. General Kyaw Ba (later minister of Hotels and Tourism), tried to restrict the power of Khin Nyunt and his intelligence officers by demanding that military intelligence agents inform him before launching regional operations.[5]

Many senior ministers and regional commanders also attempted to ensure sufficient coverage of their activities on television news programmes. When receiving foreign guests, the placement of their seats could not be less important than that of Khin Nyunt. They castigated the responsible officials from the television station if they felt that their activities were not sufficiently covered. In some cases, senior officials also bribed television crew and newscasters with gifts. Similarly, some senior officials were said to have asked their subordinates to rearrange seating whenever they felt that Khin Nyunt was assigned to a seat for more senior officials.

Khin Nyunt, however, kept himself out of direct confrontation with senior military officers by confining his activities to policy spheres related to ethnic affairs, international relations, health and education. He did not encroach into the other officers' areas of interest. Khin Nyunt was thus able to maintain cordial relationships with some army officers and keep problems with others under control. As argued elsewhere, the power structure of the SLORC/SPDC between from 1988 to the mid-1990s was more like a multi-polar world.[6] While regional commanders enjoyed a lot of leeway in administering their respective regions, many ministers ran their ministries as their own business corporations. Since the forced retirement of the first Chairman of the governing council, Senior General Saw Muang, after a nervous breakdown, no senior officers were powerful enough to fire the others. However, the situation had changed by late 1997 when several senior military officers were removed. As corruption among senior military officers increased, SLORC Chairman Senior General Than Shwe, Vice-Chairman General Maung Aye, Secretary-I General Khin Nyunt, and Secretary-II General Tin Oo, moved against the remainder of the SLORC and removed a number of highly corrupt members. From 1997 to 2004, there were only four top members of the government, Than Shwe, Maung Aye, Khin Nyunt and Tin Oo. This number decreased to three when Tin Oo died in a helicopter crash in 1999. From then on, Maung Aye and Khin Nyunt reportedly considered one another as rivals.

There were reportedly disagreements between Khin Nyunt and Maung Aye from 1997 through to 2004 and they often went to Than Shwe for mediation. In so doing, they were able to stay out of direct confrontation with each other. As discussed elsewhere, Than Shwe took advantage of his position as a middle man to become the most powerful official in the Military Council.[7] Maung Aye and Khin

Nyunt did not have any outright clashes, as they limited their activities to their separate domains. They apparently also tried to maintain a cordial relationship. Khin Nyunt, for example, performed Maung Aye's daughter's wedding. In asking Khin Nyunt to do so, Maung Aye implied that Khin Nyunt was an influential member of his circle of family and friends.

If all other intelligence officers had followed Khin Nyunt's lead in discreetly exercising their powers in their own areas of responsibility, things could have been different in 2004. Intelligence officers, especially those in local areas, did not conduct themselves appropriately and became very unpopular. Intelligence officers were often described as bullying, overbearing, arrogant and corrupt. Indeed, the degree of corruption among the intelligence corps was significant. This was especially so among those assigned to local and border areas, as they would often use the information they controlled to solicit bribes from illegitimate businesses. For instance, there are many bookmakers running underground lotteries or illegal betting on soccer matches. In order to continue their activities, they bribed the local intelligence officers. The bribes offered to intelligence officers were at least three to four times greater than those offered to regular police officers or other local authorities. The friends and families of intelligence officers, on the other hand, could circumvent rules and regulations quite easily. For instance, they could operate illegally imported cars by obtaining letters from local intelligence officers that permitted them to do so.[8] When these people were stopped by traffic police, they would show these letters, in the face of which the traffic police were unable to enforce the law. Policemen who wanted to take action would get into trouble, as the intelligence officer concerned would demand an explanation for the revocation of his order. Furthermore, the intelligence officers were aware of the illegal business dealings or other corrupt activities of other local authorities. Little wonder then that most people were wary of intelligence officers and sought to give them a wide berth. There were cases of some local civilian officials who were penalized for undertaking actions which ran counter to the interests of local intelligence officers.

Many intelligence officers were themselves involved in illegal business activities. A jade merchant revealed that he could smuggle big jade stones out of the country because he had local intelligence officers as business partners. On the whole, intelligence officers tended to be very prosperous. Businesspeople often said that because the intelligence officers collected so many bribes, they had amassed enough wealth for their next three or four lives. Local intelligence officers were also malicious toward those who were unable to bribe them. In an incident in northeastern Myanmar, an intelligence sergeant refused to allow an old woman to bring 10 apples from China into Myanmar. However, truckloads of Chinese apples enter Myanmar daily without any such impediment.

The commanders of intelligence battalion units often acted as if they were as powerful as regional commanders. Similarly, lower-ranking intelligence officers often did not pay proper respect to higher-ranking military officers. It was rumoured that intelligence officers did not give intelligence clearance to those officers they disliked.[9] Naturally, many army officers were disgruntled with this state of affairs. To be sure, not all intelligence officers were corrupt. For example, those who were in charge of ethnic issues and international relations were known to be well educated and generally clean. Many of them spoke English quite fluently and frequently liaised with foreign diplomats, non-governmental organization personnel, journalists and academics. However, they were known to think highly of themselves and to look down upon regular army officers. A local analyst noted that army officers frequently considered English-speaking intelligence officers "arrogant and pompous bastards".

It is quite clear that many intelligence officers did not act like their boss, Khin Nyunt. That is, they did not abstain from doing things that brought them into direct confrontation with army officers. As a result, tensions between intelligence units and army units existed throughout the SLORC/SPDC period. The question one might ask here is, "why did senior army officers not get rid of Khin Nyunt and his disciples before 2004?" While senior army officers viewed intelligence officers with antipathy, they appeared to realize that they needed Khin Nyunt and an experienced intelligence corps to deal with the outside world, minority groups, and the political opposition. What they did not want was Khin Nyunt and his intelligence officers to wield real power. Thus, for the sake of stability, Khin Nyunt was made prime minister in the aftermath of the 30 May 2002, Dipeyin incident when alleged government supporters assaulted Aung San Suu Kyi and her National League for Democracy (NLD) supporters. It is also believed that the powerful head of the military council, Than Shwe, wanted to keep Khin Nyunt in the government (as distinct from his position as intelligence chief) as late as October 2004, but this has not yet been confirmed.

However, the repeated contention by the diplomatic community, including the UN Special Envoy, Ambassador Razali Ismail, the foreign media, and perhaps even some intelligence officers, that Khin Nyunt was a liberal reformer may have undermined his position within the SPDC. Some foreign diplomats and journalists reported on a few occasions that Khin Nyunt sought political change, but he could not do so effectively because Than Shwe blocked his alleged attempts to reach accommodation with opposition groups such as the NLD or some of the ceasefire groups. While the veracity of these reports cannot be confirmed, a local analyst surmised that the senior army officers were offended by this portrayal of Khin Nyunt as a liberal and Than Shwe and the others as hardliners.

When a clash between intelligence and army units occurred in the northeastern Myanmar city of Muse on the Chinese border in September 2004, senior army officers came to the conclusion that the intelligence corps was getting out of hand. It was common knowledge that the local intelligence officers solicited bribes from people engaged in illegal activities. When the regional commander received a letter of complaint from a civilian officer about corruption along the Sino-Myanmar border, he sent the tactical commander and a military unit to investigate the matter. The intelligence officers from the border checkpoint refused to allow the tactical commander and his team into the district to conduct their investigation. It was rumoured that there was an exchange of fire between intelligence officers and the tactical commander and his soldiers. The regional commander, in this case, happened to be a former personal assistant to Maung Aye, the second most powerful man in the government. Senior military officers, especially Than Shwe and Maung Aye, were reportedly infuriated by this turn of events. Than Shwe asked Khin Nyunt to take action against the intelligence officers responsible for the incident.

Even prior to the incident at Muse, Khin Nyunt was asked by Than Shwe to relinquish his position as intelligence chief. While he did not seem to be pleased with the idea, he agreed to give up his post at the end of 2004. When Than Shwe ordered him to dismiss the intelligence officers who were involved in the Muse incident, Khin Nyunt reportedly refused to do so. Khin Nyunt's desire to ensure that his men would continue to dominate the intelligence corps after he relinquished his position as intelligence chief was his likely motivation for taking this position. In an attempt to preserve the authority of military intelligence, Khin Nyunt reportedly had a secret meeting with his close aides and ordered them to uncover information on the corrupt activities of regional commanders, which he planned to submit to Than Shwe at a cabinet meeting. Khin Nyunt was aware that he could not compete with senior army officers openly without Than Shwe's backing. His behaviour did not amount to an attempt to take over the government; rather, he was trying to convince the chairman that his men were not the only corrupt people. A local analyst noted that Than Shwe must have been angry over Khin Nyunt's refusal to take disciplinary action against his corrupt subordinates while his attempt to investigate senior army officers was seen as threatening the unity of the armed forces.

A meeting among a small number of military officers without the permission of a higher authority is considered tantamount to mutiny in the Tatmadaw. Some local observers believed that had Khin Nyunt obeyed Than Shwe's order to discipline his subordinates, he might not have been removed. As noted by an old politician, the leader of a military regime would not want to keep a powerful fellow officer who not only disobeyed his orders but whose actions had also caused instability in the government. In October 2004, Than Shwe replaced Khin Nyunt with Lt General Soe Win, a man known to be his loyalist, as the new prime minister. Although the government initially announced that Khin Nyunt retired on grounds of health, General Shwe Mann, the third highest ranking official in the SPDC, charged Khin Nyunt with corruption, insubordination and an attempt to break up the Tatmadaw in a speech given to top government and military officials as well as some local business people. The corruption charge apparently was the result of Khin Nyunt's decision to allocate a large amount of the financial assistance provided by the Thai government to Bagan Cyber Tech, a firm jointly run by military intelligence and a company owned by his son, Ye Naing Win.

The junta immediately detained Khin Nyunt and other senior intelligence officers. In mid-December 2004, the junta also dismissed most other members of the intelligence corps and also many former intelligence officers who had been transferred to other government agencies after 1988. Subsequently, there were rumours circulating that Khin Nyunt and members of his intelligence corps were given long prison terms. What is known for certain, however, is that the junta disbanded the national intelligence bureau which Khin Nyunt had led. The government also disbanded the military intelligence corps as a separate unit. Intelligence units are now under the control of regional commanders. They no longer fall under a separate directorate within the military.

In general, many army officers were said to have had respect for Khin Nyunt as a political leader. However, they could not accept him as their commander-in-chief because he did not have sufficient combat experience. There was also no indication that any army officer was disappointed at the dismissal of the arrogant and overbearing intelligence officers. An old politician noted, "No one in the right mind would expect that some army officers might try to stop the downfall of intelligence officers. Intelligence officers were very unpopular in the Tatmadaw. Worse still, they went after regional military commanders who controlled several combat units. Most soldiers must be happy to see arrogant, corrupt and mean intelligence officers go". Similarly, the public was also antipathetic towards the intelligence officers. In a survey on recent changes in the country,[10] 15 per cent of the 300 respondents replied that they felt unhappy that Khin Nyunt had to go. However, none of them said that they felt unhappy that the intelligence officers were fired. They further added that those intelligence officers ought to have been fired as they were corrupt. Given that the public did not take to the streets to protest against

Daw Aung San Suu Kyi's house arrest, it was not surprising that they did not protest Khin Nyunt's dismissal. Although it expressed concern for the political future of Myanmar, the international community too did not do anything to ensure Khin Nyunt's continued survival in the top ranks of the leadership.

The dismissal of the entire intelligence corps brought an end to a long-standing factional struggle between the intelligence and army units. The events of the last fifteen years have demonstrated that the Tatmadaw became more unified whenever powerful senior officials were forced to retire or were dismissed. After many senior military officers were purged in 1997, the government became more coordinated and more unified. Now that Khin Nyunt is no longer in power, the power structure of the military government stands thus: Than Shwe, Maung Aye, Shwe Min, Soe Win and Soe Win's successor as Secretary-I, Lt General Thein Sein. They also appear to be friendly and loyal to each other. At this point in time, there is only one potential problem, namely the apparently limited avenues for the elevation of many junior military officers who are awaiting promotion. However, this is not a major issue, as the top five members of the military council can easily expand the number of ministries or force some ministers to retire. At least for the near future, the promotion issue is not likely to generate conflict within the armed forces. Regardless of the events that have happened, the army is still the most organized institution in Myanmar and it seems more unified now than before. It does not look like an organization that is teetering on the verge of collapse due to internal power struggles. However, if a factional struggle emerged between the remaining senior army officers, it could create more problems than the one between army and intelligence officers. All are now army officers with combat experience and many of them have combat units under their command. Therefore, a power struggle amongst them is more likely to contribute to the break-up of the government than the one between intelligence and army officers.

The Regime and the Political Parties

Although more than 90 political parties contested the 1990 elections, only the NLD, the National Unity Party[11] (NUP) and the Shan National League for Democracy (SNLD) remain active. Among them, the NUP,[12] which has been mistakenly labelled as the government-backed party, acted neither as an opposition party, nor as a ruling party. It merely functioned within the framework of the rules and regulations adopted by the junta and rarely criticized the government. The NLD and the SNLD, on the other hand, functioned in some ways like major political parties. Because the

SNLD was a small ethnic-based party, it could not oppose the government as much as the NLD. In most cases, it acted more like an associate party of the NLD, as its positions are more or less in line with those of the NLD. The regime primarily concerned itself with its relationship with the NLD, for the NLD was the only party that could pose a credible threat to its rule. The relationship between the NLD and the army has always been fraught with hostility. When the military came to power, its first priority was to impose order by forcefully halting the popular pro-democracy movement, whereas the NLD emerged out of that same movement. Thus, the military and the NLD did not trust each other, especially after the party's leader, Daw Aung San Suu Kyi, became publicly critical of the army and its former leader, General Ne Win. As a result, they sought to undermine each other's position. The military government often used the state-controlled media to openly attack the NLD and its leaders. It also restricted campaigning and other political activities. When opposition party members broke the rules, severe action was taken against them and they were detained for long periods without trial. On its part, the NLD also tried to delegitimize the government domestically and internationally. They tried to expose all the anti-democratic actions taken by the military by distributing anti-government propaganda throughout the country. They also informed the international media and foreign governments of their version of the latest developments within the country. In response, the military government took severe action against the NLD. Confrontation between the army and the NLD reached a climax when Daw Aung San Suu Kyi was placed under house arrest in July 1989. Aung San Suu Kyi has since been detained two additional times. At the time of writing, she was once more under detention following the Dipeyin incident in May 2003.

Unsurprisingly, when the NLD won the election in 1990, the military government refused to concede power to it. The NLD responded by stepping up measures intended to delegitimize the government by undermining the junta's reputation both inside and outside the country. However, the military government resisted these attempts and in turn took steps to undermine the NLD's position within the country. It not only arrested party leaders; it tried to neutralize these individuals upon their release from prison. Before their release, they had to sign an agreement in which they vouched that they would refrain from politics. While it was not mandatory for some individuals to sign such agreements, all were warned against participating in opposition movements. The many writers among the arrested NLD leaders were reportedly told that they could write freely on any non-political topic so long as they remained out of politics. When these individuals joined opposition parties, the government's censorship board banned the publication of their articles, thereby depriving them of an income. As a result, many people stopped participating in opposition activities. A prominent writer who was also a leading NLD member told the author,

> My family suffered a lot when I was in prison. My children had to support me. I am a writer. I make a living by publishing news articles and short stories in local magazines and journals. If I continued to be involved in politics, I would not be able to publish my articles and short stories. In such case, I would not be able to support myself or my family. I, therefore, had to stay away from politics. I stopped working for the NLD since my release from prison.

Intelligence officers, for their part, did not always resort to repression. They also tried to persuade former NLD members to retire from politics by offering them assistance. A former central executive committee member who has since retired from politics told the author,

> When I was released from prison, the intelligence officer instructed me to turn to him for help should I require assistance. He hinted that the government was willing to help people like me as long as we were no longer involved in the activities of the opposition groups. Not long after that, I wrote an article. However, the censorship board refused to issue clearance to my article. Perplexed by this, I called up the intelligence officer I knew. He apologized and told me that he would solve the problem. A few hours later, I learned that my article would be published. The censorship board instructed the magazine that my article must be published. The instruction sounded that the magazine editor would be penalized if he did not publish my article. The intelligence officer called me up to apologize and assure me that I would not encounter any such problems in the future.

Not every former NLD member tried to solicit help from intelligence officers. Five ex-political prisoners told the author that their credentials as political activists were seriously undermined by their resignation from the NLD. They then said they did not want to further undermine their credentials by associating with intelligence officers. However, they admitted that some of their former comrades did try to get assistance from intelligence officers. The junta's repression, neutralization and cooptation strategies seriously weakened the NLD as a leading opposition party. An NLD local leader confirmed that while they still supported the party, a large number of members left the party for they could no longer bear the constraints imposed on NLD members by the government. While acknowledging the impact of the actions taken by the junta on the NLD, some retired politicians have also noted that the weakening position of the NLD also had something to do with the internal problems of the party itself.

The NLD was a political front made up of two major groups, a group of intellectuals comprising lawyers and writers led by Daw Aung San Suu Kyi, and a group of former military commanders.[13] Although the former military commanders had more political experience, the intellectual group was more influential. In 1989 and in the early 1990s, the intellectuals in the NLD were more confrontational and wanted to resort to civil disobedience. The former military commanders, on the other hand, wanted to take the non-confrontational approach. There has always been this tension within the NLD. In fact, Daw Aung San Suu Kyi once clashed with these former military commanders who cautioned her against taking too bellicose a stance against the government. Many NLD leaders at that time appeared to think that with the backing of the international community and the public, they were stronger than the military government. However, "the government was prepared to take all necessary measures to keep the NLD at bay", noted an old politician, "the NLD did not appear to have any backup plan as to how it should deal with the government".

That the NLD lacked contingency plans is also discernible in the way its leaders approached the army after the 1990 elections. Ignoring the advice given by some old politicians that the NLD should try to find a way to work with the regime, the NLD, led by the intellectual group, sent an ultimatum to the military government. The ultimatum which was known as the Gandhi declaration stated that the government should hand over power to the NLD by the end of September 1990. A member of the former military commander group, Major Chit Khine, reportedly disapproved of this ultimatum because the party did not have a contingency plan in the event of its failure. The intellectuals ignored this warning, leading some old politicians to conclude that after winning the election, NLD leaders were too conceited to see the reality of the situation. A former NLD leader noted in remorseful manner,

> We initially thought that U Chit Khine was very cowardly. But in retrospect, I think that he was more farsighted than most of us. When we could not do anything in response to the government's refusal to comply with our demand, our enemy would just conclude that it did not have to heed our future demands. We just kept making demands without having a backup plan as to what we should do when the government did not comply with our demands. Many of us at that time considered that we were staging a revolution. We should have understood that we were also playing power politics. Perhaps, we were prepared for a revolution but we were not very prepared for the political tussle.

The failure of the NLD caretaker leaders — the ones that are in control of the party when Daw Aung San Suu Kyi is under house arrest — to manage the party as effectively as she had done also has had something to do with the weakening position of the organization. When General Khin Nyunt reiterated the army's pre-election announcement that the winning party of the election would have to convene the national convention and draw up a constitution prior to its ratification in a referendum and a further election in order to form a new government, the NLD's caretaker leadership accepted these terms. The central executive committee then declared that the party would try to finish drafting the constitution within a year. During that period, the military would govern the country. Once the constitution was ready, the NLD would call for the constituent assembly to be instituted so that it could form a new government. However, many NLD members from local areas were disgruntled with this decision, as they wanted to adhere to the ultimatum. Due to this, the NLD was spilt by an internal disagreement. The more radical proponents attempted to form an alternative parliament, but were arrested before they could put their plan into action.

At about the same time, some old politicians whose parties did not win any seats in the 1990 election advised the NLD's caretaker leadership that the NLD should organize a national convention by inviting representatives of the Tatmadaw, ethnic minority groups and old politicians. The NLD leadership, at that time, reportedly reasoned that these old politicians called for such a national convention because they wanted to continue to play a role in politics. A former NLD central executive committee member said, "In retrospect, those old politicians were politically shrewder and more farsighted than us. If we had done that, it would be more in line with what Khin Nyunt had said at the press conference. It would be hard for the government to reject such an attempt by the NLD".

Some old politicians appeared to believe that the NLD squandered a possible opportunity to lead in organizing a national convention. They believe that things might have been different had the NLD managed to organize a national convention as the old politicians had suggested. Instead, the NLD issued an ultimatum to the military without a viable contingency plan. After all these things fell through, the NLD was unable to do anything further as its intellectual members were arrested. "Seen in this light", said a former NLD central executive committee member, "we should have more perspicacious. They [i.e., the military government] were stronger than us. We should have been a better strategy to deal with stronger enemies". There is no way of knowing if things would have been different if NLD leaders had managed to organize the national convention as the old politicians had suggested.

However, it is quite clear that NLD leaders failed to exploit this possible opportunity for peaceful political change.

When most of the NLD intelligentsia were arrested in the 1990s, the party was left in the hands of the former military commanders. Although these former military commanders had more political experience, they were not sure whether they had the mandate of the public. In general, they were somewhat indecisive. Rather than giving Daw Aung San Suu Kyi sound political advice, they followed her instructions. It seems that influential societal actors do not have much trust in some members of the current executive committee of the NLD. Many of these former military commanders, especially the current spokesperson, U Lwin, had links to the previous regime. A prominent writer was quoted as saying that U Lwin, who was once a deputy prime minister, might have been planted in the NLD by Ne Win, the former military dictator, so as to sabotage the NLD's activities. In the late 1990s, the military government invited the chairman of the NLD, Aung Shwe, to discuss the country's political situation. He declined because he did not want to engage in any talks without Daw Aung San Suu Kyi. Some NLD members felt that the NLD leadership should have taken up the government's offer. Others go so far as to say that they should continue to fight for Daw Aung San Suu Kyi's release from house arrest while negotiating with the military for political change. They would not gain anything from refusing the offer to enter into discussions with the military.

One might also make a similar argument for the NLD's decision to boycott the National Convention which resumed in May 2004. The NLD caretaker leadership announced, after the junta allowed it to meet Daw Aung San Suu Kyi who was under house arrest, that it would attend the National Convention. However, the NLD decided to boycott it when the junta refused to release its leaders, Daw Aung San Suu Kyi and U Tin Oo, and abandoned the 104 principles which were "adopted before the national convention was suspended in 1996".[14] The SNLD later joined the NLD and boycotted the Convention — when it was held in May 2004, "representatives of some societal groups which were mainly hand-picked by the government, some selected members of ceasefire groups and the National Unity Party attended" it.[15] Although the NLD's boycott undermines the legitimacy of the National Convention, the junta seems quite prepared to proceed so as to move forward with a constitution which protects its interests. After General Khin Nyunt was removed in October 2004, the government released more than 14,000 prisoners including some prominent politicians. However, Daw Aung San Suu Kyi and some NLD leading members remain in detention. Some senior government officials have hinted that the NLD would not be invited to attend the next round of the National Convention.

All in all, many NLD members appear to think that the future of the party is uncertain given the tutelage of the current NLD leaders. The average age of the central executive committee is 80. It appears that these old NLD leaders do not really want to do much for the party beyond striving to keep it alive. They do not take initiatives or formulate bold policy positions. However, bold initiatives are needed if the party is to reform and rearm itself with a clearer strategy. Whenever local party members request the NLD leadership to do something for them, the leadership only say that the matter would be considered. This means that they will only institute reforms after consulting with Daw Aung San Suu Kyi. The party defers to her decision in everything and needs to ascertain her views prior to any decision. These former military commanders are like incapable caretakers, as they are unable to do much without Daw Aung San Suu Kyi.

The Regime and Pro-democracy Exile Organizations

Several pro-democracy exile organizations emerged in the wake of the military crackdown on the 1988 democracy movement and subsequent repression of the activities of the opposition groups. Many student leaders and political activists who fled to border areas formed various pro-democracy organizations in neighbouring countries, especially Thailand. Among these organizations are the National Coalition Government of the Union of Burma (NCGUB), the National Council of Union of Burma (NCUB), the All Burma Students' Democratic Front (ABSDF), the Free Burma Coalition (FBC), the Burma Strategic Group, the NLD (Liberated Area or NLD-LA), the All Burma Federation of Students Unions (ABFSU), the Association to Assist Political Prisoners (AAPP), the Forum for Democracy in Burma (FDB), Federation of Trade Unions of Burma (FTUB), and the Vigorous Student Warriors. All these organizations actively engaged in various anti-government activities in several foreign countries such as Thailand, EU member states and the United States.

Whereas the ABSDF and the Vigorous Student Warriors engaged in armed struggle, other organizations sought to draw international attention to incidents in Myanmar. Members of these organizations travel and give talks on Myanmar politics as well as human rights violations within the country. They also provide information about political developments in the country to international media. The pro-democracy organizations in exile have successfully managed to draw international attention to events in Myanmar. The FTUB, for instance, drew the attention of the ILO to the state of forced labour in Myanmar. The FBC also successfully pressured foreign governments to discourage, if not ban, foreign investment by multinational corporations in Myanmar. Due to the FBC's activities, over 50 international corporations withdrew from Myanmar and many others stayed away from the country. Likewise, the efforts of these organizations led to the establishment of U.S. and EU economic sanctions on Myanmar. These economic sanctions did impact negatively on the military government as the government had no foreign assistance to devote to legitimating activities such as infrastructural development, the restoration of historical sites and so on. However, these sanctions have yet to undermine the military government to the point where it will step down in favour of the NLD or an interim government. Regardless of the financial and economic problems generated by the imposition of western economic sanctions, the junta does not appear to be on the verge of bankruptcy. The financial and political support from China, India, Thailand and other ASEAN countries and the availability of abundant natural resources in the country have alleviated the impact of the Western economic sanctions on the junta as regional trade has grown.

On the other hand, the current condition of the pro-democracy movement is quite bleak. According to a former leading activist, the movement has been in decline since the late 1990s. This was in part because of the long tenure of the movement itself. After engaging in pro-democracy activism in exile for several years, many people decided to retire from it because they simply lost steam. Others decided to leave so that they could take care of their families. The peace negotiations between the regime and the Karen National Union (KNU) and the shortage of funding also made it hard for many exile groups to maintain the momentum of their respective activities. A former ABSDF member disappointingly noted,

> Many of us operated in the Karen controlled areas. Now, the KNU is thinking seriously about making ceasefire with the government. If this happened, we wouldn't be able to remain in the Karen controlled areas. The worse thing is that we are not getting funding from foreign donors as much as we used to. The living condition of our comrades is not very good. Other exile organizations also have funding problems. As a result, many of us had to think more about what we should do to get funding than what we should do to promote democracy in our country.

Eight other former leading members of exiled pro-democracy groups also acknowledged the serious negative impact of the peace negotiations between the KNU and the government and the shortage of funding. Another reason for the weakening of the exile movement has been the internal power struggles within and between individual organizations. Despite their claims of cooperation, these pro-democracy organizations are disunited. Members of some organizations have gone so far as to say that there was no democracy in their organizations and that some leaders were no different from the Myanmar military leaders. Leaders of various exile organizations have also sought to assassinate each other's characters. For instance, Naing Aung, the former chairman of the ABSDF, was originally admitted to the John F. Kennedy School in Harvard. However, he was unable to study there because he was blackmailed by some rival ABSDF members. When he was the chairman of the organization, the ABSDF was accused of involvement in a massacre in northern Myanmar. Despite the fact that he was at the Thai-Myanmar border at that time, several hundred miles away from the area where the massacre happened, Harvard cancelled his admission on receipt of a poison-pen letter from some former members of his organization. In another case, an exiled activist sought revenge against his former leader who had expelled him from an organization by siding with his opponent in an ethics-related court case. The activist lied to the court under oath that his former leader was mentally ill.

To add insult to injury, Zar Ni, the founder of the FBC, secretly went to Myanmar on 31 May 2004. Prior to his secret trip, he was a strong proponent of economic sanctions on Myanmar. After his trip, he changed his mind and expounded the view that sanctions would not result in any significant political changes in the country. In short, his views were now more in line with the anti-sanctions advocates who claim that economic sanctions undermine civil society and penalize the poor more than they harm the government. While in Myanmar, he and the then Prime Minister Khin Nyunt's aides discussed the matter of working with the government for political reforms. He later noted in an interview with an international radio station that the NLD was unable to do much for Myanmar because it has been seriously undermined. The country could not wait for Daw Aung San Suu Kyi's release if it was truly desirous of moving forward. While criticizing Daw Aung San Suu Kyi, whom he regarded as somewhat authoritarian, he stated that he would welcome political changes without the NLD leader. As most exile pro-democracy organizations were unable to accept such a position, they accused Zar Ni of being an opportunist. Zar Ni's detractors claimed that he did not qualify as a pro-democracy leader because he had left for America before the outbreak of the Four Eights democratic movement. While he was involved in the movement, he differed from the rest of them in that he was never at the Thai-Myanmar border, fighting against the government.

Many members of the FBC were also disgruntled that Zar Ni did not consult them about his trip to Myanmar. They were also chagrined that he had been critical of the NLD and Daw Aung San Suu Kyi in his interviews with the media. They felt that he should have consulted them on the nature of the interviews and his replies. As a result, some FBC members tried to expel him from the organization. While he narrowly escaped expulsion, Zar Ni had no choice but to distance himself from other pro-democracy organizations. As a result, the FBC lost contact with the networks it has established in various parts of the United States and Zar Ni became a single voice in the exile pro-democracy movement there. It was also rumoured that some political activists had informed the U.S. State Department that Zar Ni went to Myanmar on a U.S. refugee card. They argued that he no longer qualified as a refugee, as he could return to Myanmar. Although the U.S. State Department did not publicly acknowledge it, a former state department official stated at the Burma Studies conference in Dekalb, Illinois, in November 2004 that the State Department was aware of Zar Ni's trip to Myanmar. While this official did not reveal whether the U.S. State Department had granted Zar Ni permission, he did reveal that the U.S. had always supported dialogue between the Myanmar political opposition and the military government. Thus, this indicates that the exile pro-democracy movement is rather disorganized and fragmented. The disjuncture led a political analyst who is very close to many exiled Myanmar pro-democracy groups to note,

> The government did not have to do anything to get rid of these groups. It only had to let the groups undermine each other's position and make them fight over petty things. If these groups persisted in their squabbles, they would not have a role to play in the political future of the country.

Some exiled political activists, however, were aware that they had better chances of effecting political change if they banded together. Accordingly, a group of activists brought the different political groups which had participated in the 1988 pro-democracy movement in Myanmar together in 2004 to form the FDB. The group is also part of the NCUB. While made up of many organizations, the FDB explicitly stated that it did not wish to be a rival pro-democracy group. The FDB was formed to facilitate coordination between the different political groups. In an interview with the author, Naing Aung, the general secretary of the FDB said, "The military government will not take these groups seriously unless they are united".

However, some misunderstandings within and between exile organizations remain unresolved. An ABSDF member bitterly noted that the organization was suffering from the mistakes of the previous leaders.[16] More than twenty activists from five different exiled organizations said to the author that they did not trust many of their fellow pro-democracy activists both from their own and other organizations.

Regardless of the significant impact on the military government by the actions taken by exile pro-democracy groups, it is quite evident that these actions have failed to undermine the government sufficiently to force it to step down. Given the fragmented nature of all these organizations, it seems unlikely that they will be able to enact effective change in the near future. A leading political activist pointed out,

> Even if the military government were to invite these groups to a dialogue session, none of them are ready to talk. They are currently in the process of forming a front that is capable of unifying all exile political groups. However, there is still a long way to go in this respect. We are doing all that we can to bring political change to the country and we are doing whatever we can to undermine the government. But, we haven't been able to do that.

The Regime and the Ceasefire Groups

Ethnic insurgent groups in Myanmar have been fighting the central government since before independence in 1948. Although all past governments have tried to make peace with the insurgent groups, it was not until late 1989 that a central government actually succeeded in the task. The present military government managed to establish ceasefires with the Kokang and Wa, which were, during the 1980s, a part of the Burma Communist Party (BCP). Both Wa and Kokang groups foresaw the imminent collapse of the BCP and were therefore anxious to expedite a ceasefire agreement. Unlike previous governments, the present government could be prevailed upon to make concessions to the insurgent groups in order to consolidate its position vis-à-vis the NLD.

Seventeen major armed groups have entered into ceasefire agreements with the government. Once the ceasefires were in place, the insurgent groups were supposed to function as politically conscious civil society organizations representing the interests of their own peoples. However, the ability of the ceasefire groups to effect political change in the country is quite limited. Although most of them claim to represent the entire ethnic minority groups whose names they bear, most function more like patriarchal organizations. The bulk of the economic benefits granted by the government were enjoyed by the leading members. Most ceasefire groups dared not criticize the government in a hostile manner. They have always had to try to present their problems and grievances to government officials in a friendly and subtle manner.

Although its ceasefire agreements with the 17 insurgent groups allowed the government to better administer the country, for all its outward display of military might, it has been unable to establish a civil administration in the Wa area. The government, ironically, proved powerless to stop the continued Wa production of opium and amphetamines. On its part, the Wa group has never tried to openly challenge the government. However, recent United Nations Office on Drugs and Crime reports have noted a decline in drug production in the Wa-controlled area.

It remains to be seen whether these ceasefire groups will indeed bring about positive political change to the country in the long run. Their wariness about rocking the placid yet potentially volatile boat could be attributed to their belief that the current state of peace is better than fighting wars against the state and each other; as such, they are unwilling to overtly pressure the government. At present, the New Mon State Party (NMSP) is the only group which is extremely critical of the government. As punishment for their recalcitrance, the Mons are marginalized and given fewer government economic concessions.[17]

A recent trip by this author to the minority areas and meetings with minority leaders revealed that a lot of minority ceasefire groups were prepared to go along with the government's 7-point democracy road map. While they are largely supportive of Daw Aung San Suu Kyi and the NLD, they are willing to move forward without her and her party. When the government invited them for the National Convention, some ceasefire groups initially asked the government to release Daw Aung San Suu Kyi and to allow the NLD to be involved in the National Convention. Nonetheless, they did not boycott the National Convention when their demands were not met. A minority leader explained to the author that it was immaterial whether they negotiated with the military or the NLD, as they would still be discussing the future of their peoples with majority Burmans. He acknowledged, moreover, that the military government was willing to make a number of compromises.

The ceasefire talks between the KNU and the governments in Thailand and Yangon led to the KNU vice-chairman, General Mya, to express his admiration for the government and his willingness to collaborate with it. According to some reliable sources, General Mya was extremely encouraged by the government and its peace plans upon his return from Yangon in January 2004. His enthusiasm for the government's peace plans, in turn, led the leaders of the KNU to criticize Daw Aung San Suu Kyi. The KNU leadership accused her of being nothing more than a power-hungry politician. Likewise, the KNU faction that did not want to reach a ceasefire with the government was accused of undermining the unity of the union. According to the one source, KNU leaders have stopped criticizing the government and have turned, instead, to criticizing each other. In mid-2004, however, peace negotiations between KNU and the government reached a stalemate because the pro-peace Karen leader, Bo Mya, fell ill. During this time Karen leaders opposed to the peace process tried to take control of the organization. As a result, small skirmishes broke out between government forces and the KNU troops. At the end of 2004, the government and Karen leaders were reportedly trying to revive their negotiations.

While insurgent groups posed a significant threat to the government at the time the military took control of the government, most had ceased to be a threat by the middle of the 1990s. It is, of course, hard to know how long the army will manage to maintain the ceasefire agreements with the ethnic insurgent groups. However, a veteran political activist who has dealt with various insurgent groups in the last fifteen years noted that "unless they all rose up collectively, insurgent groups no longer pose any major threat to military rule".

The Regime and the General Public

The 1988 pro-democracy movement proved that Myanmar people were capable of bringing down an authoritarian government. However, it is widely believed that political activism among the general public in Myanmar is no longer strong. For instance, although student organizations have played a crucial role in the political movements of the country since the colonial days, interviews with 45 students revealed that student activism has declined since the late 1990s. When asked whether they knew of any underground student organizations, commonly known as reading groups, only 5 answered in the affirmative. However, all 45 respondents believed that reading groups should exist so as to facilitate students' understanding of politics. Despite their support for reading groups, only 2 respondents would join these groups, 7 would not and the rest were uncertain. While 40 students made it quite clear that they would not join political parties, 5 revealed that they would give the matter some thought when the opportunity arose. It is interesting to note that no student answered this question in the affirmative. When asked whether they were aware of the Four Eights movement, 2 said yes and the rest revealed that they did not know much about it. When asked whether they would participate in a movement like the Four Eights democratic movement, 23 answered in the negative, 10 declined to answer and the rest would consider it if their lives would not be in danger. Forty-three respondents said that they were not very interested in politics, while 3 answered in the positive. Ten of the students were aware of the 7 July incident[18] but only one knew of the Hmaine centenary movement.[19] In Myanmar, it is widely accepted that students who are interested in activism would know of these student movements. Most were not ignorant of politics. All of them claimed that although they had never had a serious discussion about the NLD's role in politics or its platform, they were worried about political instability in the country. They all said that they always discussed rumours about political developments in the country with friends and families. However, all the students expressed anxiety for the safety and welfare of their families and their future; they had no desire to involve themselves in politics because it was synonymous with trouble. All 45 students told me that no one had tried to recruit them into political parties on campus.

Many political activists also noted that university students were no longer politically very active. Most students who wanted to bring about political change did not remain in Myanmar. Instead, they fled to the border areas and joined organizations there. Only a handful of students have tried to organize protests since the late 1990s and most of them were arrested before they could really do much. A student activist who fled to Thailand in 2000 noted that he left the country because he could not convince any of his friends to help organize student protests. Government repression may not be the main reason for the decline of student activism — student activism survived the harsh repression of the previous socialist regime. However, since the collapse of the BCP, no new organization has made an attempt to help set up informal student groups. It appears that the NLD and other pro-democracy organizations spent more time attracting international attention than on strengthening civil society or underground political movements. Due to political constraints, the NLD did not approach students; it only worked with the students who came and joined the party. Likewise, exiled organizations including the ABFSU did not try to mobilize the students in the way the BCP had.

There has also been a decline in political activism among the Buddhist monkhood or Sangha. Although the Sangha played a prominent role in the opposition movement in the first five years of military rule, a number of monks abandoned political activities due to severe government repression. The government banned all Sangha organizations except the nine official sects that have existed since pre-colonial days. The government has also seriously curtailed the activities of the Sangha since the outbreak of anti-Muslim riots in 2003. Since then, large monasteries have not been allowed to accommodate more than 300 monks. Senior Buddhist monks no longer participate openly in politics as they do not want their monks and monasteries to be in disorder while they would be serving detention. Some senior Buddhist monks said that when they were arrested in the early 1990s, their monasteries and the monks under their supervision experienced many difficulties.

The withdrawal of several monks from the political arena did not imply that the Sangha community is now politically apathetic. Many Buddhist monks listen to political news on the BBC, VOA and RFA Burmese language programmes. When the former Prime Minister, General Khin Nyunt, visited a monastery in mid-2004, a group of Buddhist monks shouted anti-government slogans at him and were duly arrested. They were later sentenced to five to six-year prison terms. However, this seems to be the exception rather than the norm. The ten Buddhist monks that this author interviewed in late 2004 said that they were doing all they could to stay out of trouble. They added that they tried to ensure that the monks under their supervision stayed out of politics. If they failed to do so, the situation could get out of control and they would not be able to do much for the promotion of Buddhism. Though seven of these ten monks had been actively involved in the 1988 pro-democracy movement, they felt that a large scale Sangha-led anti-government movement would remain almost impossible for some time.

Most ordinary people did not seem prepared for involvement in any open political protests. When 300 survey respondents were asked whether they would join a movement like the one in 1988, only 10 per cent said yes, 68 per cent said no, and the rest said they did not know. Currently, the public seems unwilling to be involved in any political movement that seeks to bring down the regime. When asked whether they would join the NLD, 80 per cent of the 300 survey respondents said they would not, 15 per cent said they would, and the rest expressed no opinion. When asked why they did not want to join a political movement, 75 per cent said they were afraid of government reprisals, 21 per cent cited economic difficulties and a shortage of time for political activities, and the remainder answered "don't know". When asked what they spent most of their time, energy and resources on, 78 per cent answered "economic survival", 12 per cent said "on their academic studies", 5 per cent said "religious practices", and the rest expressed no opinion.

The reluctance of the majority to participate in political activities might also have something to do with the absence of a vanguard organization. A former student leader and politician said, "The people are politically conscious, but in the absence of any form of leadership, they are drawn into non-political things". In fact, people are not completely politically apathetic. Eighty-five per cent of the 300 survey participants said that they discussed politics with their friends and families. Evidence abounds of the importance of vanguard organizations in keeping political activism alive. As noted above, the BCP's underground activities kept political activism alive in the midst of the harsh repression of the previous socialist government. Since the collapse of the BCP, no other legal or illegal organization has tried to systematically mobilize the public into underground political activities. In order words, no pro-democracy organization has invested significant resources into promoting a politically conscious civil society inside the country.

As a rule, the general public seems supportive of the NLD. Among its 300 respondents, 54 per cent said they supported NLD, 12 per cent said they did not, and the rest said they were uncertain. Many people, however, did not appear to have trust in the NLD's ability to effect political change. When asked whether they believed that the NLD would bring change to the country, 65 per cent said no, 20 per cent said yes, and the remainder had no opinion. It is also worth noting that regardless of the general unhappiness with the prevailing social, political and economic situation, not all people hold a negative attitude towards the government. The author discovered that 38 per cent of 300 survey participants conceded that some senior officials were helpful to the public. The author's interviews with people from various parts of the country, revealed that General Shwe Mann was popular in the Delta area. More than ten farmers in that area said that General Shwe Mann was very helpful. They only had to approach him with their problems during his inspection tours and he would do all he could to assist them. Major General Thar Aye from the Northwestern military command was, similarly, said to be obliging to the rural community. Major General Maung Maung Swe from the Northern military command was quite popular with people in northern Myanmar. More than 20 people in the area told the author that he was not only very helpful to the people, but also that he never gave the public a hard time.

These attitudes towards the government might be attributable to different ways of understanding legitimacy. When 50 people were asked how they would define legitimacy, the author received three different answers: (1) a democratically elected government, (2) a government that helps the people to resolve their problems, and (3) a government that leaves them alone. It is clear that the democratic criterion of judging a government's legitimacy is not universal in Myanmar. Those who answered that a democratically elected government was a legitimate one were mostly educated people. They accounted for only 25 per cent of the 50 respondents. This does not mean that most people did not care about democracy: 89 per cent of survey participants thought that democracy would bring peace and prosperity to the country.

However, many people appeared to believe that the military was much stronger than any of the opposition groups and that the country would not become a democracy in the near future. When asked which organization would be able to match the strength of the military government, 79 per cent said none, 9 per cent said the NLD, one per cent said the United States and the rest answered "don't know". When asked if they thought that Myanmar would become a democracy in the near future, 49 per cent said no, 4 per cent said yes, and the rest said "don't know". When asked how Myanmar could become a democratic country, 11 per cent answered if "Daw Suu Kyi were released", 12 per cent said, "if the entire country rose up against the regime", 25 per cent said, "if all political groups found a way to work with the junta", 30 per cent answered "if the U.S. invaded the country", and the rest answered "don't know".

All in all, the people of Myanmar do not appear to be politically apathetic. However, it is evident that they lack confidence in the ability of the opposition groups to change the current political situation. Despite their frustration with their present position, most people devote more time and energy to their struggle for survival than thinking about what they can do to effect political change in the country.

Looking to the Future

Regardless of the internal problems and the pressure imposed on it by the opposition groups and the international community, the junta has remained strong enough to keep itself in power. There is no indication that the Tatmadaw will return to the barracks any time soon. This does not mean that the government is insensitive to public opinion. In order to raise the profile of the National Convention, the government invited former NLD members and old politicians to participate in it. The junta also invited some old politicians to evaluate the Convention once it is over. Although most former NLD members and veteran politicians declined the invitation to the National Convention, many of the latter reportedly submitted reports on their positions on the ongoing Convention to the government. In spite of the fact that the Convention delegates were subject to several constraints, they did not simply have to act as a rubber stamp to the draft constitution prepared by the government. Delegates representing ethnic groups managed to obtain the government's compliance on some of their demands. However, there is no group negotiating with the government on broader political issues. Thus, some people viewed the NLD's boycott of the National Convention as a mistake because there is no group that is strong enough to act as a check against what the regime wants to achieve.

Despite the current political impasse, the possibility for political change in Myanmar still exists. The constitution that could emerge from the National Convention will set new rules for the governance of the nation. While many ardent proponents of the NLD, especially Daw Aung San Suu Kyi, will not accept the constitution, it must be acknowledged that they appear unable to take any countermeasures beyond asking the international community to reject the National Convention. However, some local activists, frustrated with the inability of the pro-democracy groups to bring about any tangible change in the country, have expressed their willingness to work with the military and accept the constitution if it guarantees a role for opposition parties in policy-making and implementation. Although they did not rule out a role for Daw Aung San Suu Kyi in a transition, these politicians and activists seem prepared to grasp any space which might open for the opposition. A former leading member of the NLD noted, "Although I love and respect Ma Suu, I don't worship her. I will accept any changes that are genuinely good for the country". Given the way the National Convention is headed, one can assume that the changes the army is prepared to introduce will be well short of the changes the majority of people are yearning to see. On the other hand, while wishing for the day when the country becomes a full-fledged democracy, most people are not likely to reject any moves that would make their lives easier and open the way to larger change in the future.

Notes

The author wishes to thank Professor Robert Taylor for his valuable comments and editorial assistance.

[1]   The Four Eights democracy movement, which was initially launched by university students on 8 August (the eighth month of the year) 1988, was the first nation-wide anti-government protest that brought down the military-dominated Socialist government that had ruled the country between 1962 and 1988.

[2]   The 7-point road map "included reconvening the National Convention (NC), drafting a new constitution according the principles adopted at the NC, holding a national referendum for the new constitution, holding free and fair elections according to the new constitution, convening the Hluttaw (parliament) and the formation of a new democratic government". See Kyaw Yin Hlaing, "Myanmar in 2003: Frustration and Despair?", *Asian Survey* 44, no. 1 (January/February 2004): 87–92.

[3]   The National Convention was first held by the junta in 1993 as part of the attempt to draft a new constitution. More than 60 per cent of the delegates to the Convention were handpicked by the military government. The Convention met two to three times a year. With the help of its chosen delegates, the military government successfully pressured the Convention "to adopt the 104 principles that would guarantee the military's continued role in politics. The junta, however, had to suspend the Convention in 1996 when the NLD boycotted it after the junta refused to allow Daw Aung San Suu Kyi, who was released from house arrest in 1995, to attend it". See Kyaw Yin Hlaing, "Myanmar in 2004: Another Year of Uncertainty", *Asian Survey* 45, no. 1 (January/February 2005): 174–79.

[4]   Most of my interviewees did not want to be cited by name. Some of them asked me not to mention their job titles and the exact interview dates in my work. Therefore, I have provided only such vague references as "a local analyst", "an old politician", "a former NLD member", "a jade merchant", "a journalist", etc.

[5]   *Far Eastern Economic Review*, 24 October 1991; interviews, 1998, 1999.

6   For details on factional struggles in the junta, see Kyaw Yin Hlaing, "Factional and
    Power Struggles in Post-Colonial Myanmar", paper presented at the 2002 Burma
    Studies Conference, Gothenberg, Sweden, 2002.
7   Ibid.
8   After the military intelligence was disbanded, the government announced that the
    owners of illegally imported cars would be penalized severely if they did not surrender
    them to the government.
9   Military officers needed intelligence clearance before they could be promoted.
10 This survey was conducted by the author with the help of some friends and family
    between October and December 2004.
11 The National Unity Party is the new name of the Burma Socialist Program party, which
    was the only legal party under the previous socialist regime.
12 In the last 16 years, the NUP has been referred to as the military-backed party. A senior
    NUP member told the author that the first Chairman of the SLORC General Saw Maung
    and some leading members of the NUP did not get along. It was rumoured that General
    Saw Maung was angry at some NUP officers who had given negative reports on a
    military operation headed by Saw Maung when he was a unit commander. It was also
    rumoured that some NUP leaders and General Saw Maung had a heated argument when
    the latter ordered serving military officers not to play golf with NUP members. More
    than 20 NUP local leaders told the author that many members of the regime were quite
    hostile toward them when they sought assistance. Several regional commanders noted
    publicly that they did not have anything to do with the NUP. Although the military
    would have preferred the NUP to the NLD, there was no evidence that the NUP received
    any assistance before or after the 1990 election.
13 The NLD was initially made up of three groups. The group led by former Brigadier
    Aung Gyi left the party after Aung San Suu Kyi refused to expel so-called communists
    who were members of the intellectual group.
14 Kyaw Yin Hlaing, "Myanmar in 2004: Another Year of Uncertainty", p. 174.
15 Ibid., p. 175.
16 The ABSDF was seriously weakened after the departure of the two previous leaders.
    Although it currently has only a few hundred active members (down from more than
    10,000), the ABSDF has re-emerged as an organization free of internal power struggles
    under the leadership of Than Khe. Like other organizations, the ABSDF, however, has
    to struggle hard to get resources.
17 The fact that the MNSP-controlled areas were dispersed, small, and isolated, further
    undermined its position vis-à-vis the government.
18 The Seven July incident of 1962 is an important event in Myanmar political history
    because the Revolutionary Council dynamited the historic student union building in an
    attempt to quell a student demonstration.
19 The Hmaine centenary movement was organized by leftist students to honour the
    hundredth birthday of a prominent and well-respected nationalist leader, Thakin Kodaw
    Hmaine.

MYANMAR'S ENERGY SECTOR
Banking on Natural Gas

Tin Maung Maung Than

Introduction

Commercial energy use in Myanmar was constrained by both supply and demand factors in the second half of the twentieth century and the associated industries such as coal, oil and electricity played a relatively minor role in the nation's economic growth since independence in 1948. In fact, the two oil shocks (in the early 1970s and 1980s) that followed the action by the OPEC (Organization of the Petroleum Exporting Countries) to raise oil prices barely affected Myanmar's autarkic economy under one-party Socialist rule in which energy independence was maintained through fuel rationing, load shedding and administrative measures. Nevertheless, realizing the importance of energy in modernization and economic development, the Socialist regime formed the Ministry of Energy (MOE) in 1985. The MOE was tasked to oversee offshore oil and gas exploration and development (on a production-sharing basis with foreign oil companies) that apparently held some promise of a major gas find.[1]

When the military regime that assumed power in September 1988 decided to liberalize the state-controlled command economy by introducing market-oriented reforms and allowing foreign direct investment (FDI) in many economic sectors, the pent-up demand for commercial energy rapidly increased. Meanwhile the issue of energy security became an important concern for many developing and developed countries in recent years. These probably led the Myanmar government to undertake institutional reforms in the production and regulation of energy. The MOE was reconstituted in 1989 with one department (Energy Planning Department) and three state-owned enterprises, viz., Myanma Oil and Gas Enterprise (MOGE), Myanma Petrochemical Enterprise (MPE) and Myanma Petroleum Products

Tin Maung Maung Than is a Senior Fellow at the Institute of Southeast Asian Studies, Singapore.

Enterprise (MPPE). A new Ministry of Electric Power (MEP) was instituted in November 1997 to promote and effectively operate the power sector. The MEP comprises the Myanma Electric Power Enterprise (MEPE, Myanmar's only electricity utility) and a planning and support department called the Department of Electric Power.

The government's current energy policy has the following objectives:

- To maintain energy independence
- To employ hydroelectric power as one of the vital sources of energy sufficiency
- To increase the generation and distribution of electricity for economic development
- To conserve non-renewable energy for the nation's future energy sufficiency
- To promote efficient utilization of energy and emphasize energy conservation
- To prevent deforestation caused by excessive use of firewood and charcoal.[2]

Together with the ministries of mines (responsible for coal mining), forestry (development of biomass fuels), education (basic and applied research) and science and technology (development of renewable power sources and measures to increase energy efficiency), the MOE and MEP are the main government agencies that control and influence the supply of commercial and household energy in Myanmar.

In the following sections the current status of energy stocks and trends in the supply, management and consumption of Myanmar's energy resources are delineated — though the study has to contend with the paucity of information on Myanmar's energy sector.

Energy Resources

In line with the international convention on classification of energy resources, Myanmar's energy resources may be categorized as non-renewable and renewable sources depending on their nature and characteristics. The former constitutes oil and gas, coal, and fissile material while the latter, for all practical purposes, include hydropower, wind, solar, geothermal and biomass energy sources.

Oil and gas

Many of Myanmar's onshore oil fields, after yielding over 300 million barrels, are now severely depleted and only three of the six new fields discovered since 1991 are currently producing crude oil regularly.[3] Nevertheless, MOGE claimed to have discovered some 3.15 billion recoverable reserves of crude oil (onshore and offshore) by the end of 2002.[4]

The official estimate of (ultimately) recoverable natural gas reserves, according to data released by MOGE in April 2002, was nearly 51 tcf (trillion cubic feet) or 1.4 billion cubic metres (ibid.) owing to the discovery of two large offshore fields in the southeastern coast (opposite Thailand) and a potentially larger one further west (opposite Bangladesh).[5]

Coal

Myanmar's coal deposits are of lower quality than the standard anthracite with the majority classified as sub-bituminous. A small amount of lignite deposits are also present. Myanmar's mines ministry claimed to have discovered a total of some 258 million tons of coal deposits by 2001.[6]

Fissile ore for nuclear energy

Myanmar government's website for the MOE described nuclear energy as an option for "producing power in high volume and densities" that needed to be studied as "an ongoing programme on alternative energy sources" and identified five locations with known deposits of uranium oxide without giving any details on the recoverable amount of ore.[7]

Hydroelectric potential

Water power obtained through damming Myanmar's many rivers is regarded to be the most abundant source of electricity production in the country. A theoretical potential of 100,000 megawatts has often been mentioned but a more realistic estimate of feasible potential is closer to 40,000 megawatts (Xinhua News, 1 April 2004).

Wind

Small, locally constructed windmills have long been utilized in rural Myanmar, mainly for drawing water but large-scale commercial exploitation has yet to be initiated. Theoretical potential for wind energy was estimated at around 365 terrawatt-hours/year.[8]

Solar

Myanmar, being a tropical country near the equator, receives a fair amount of sunshine, especially in the central dry zone. Like wind power, solar heat has been traditionally applied in rural areas for drying purposes but it has not been utilized as a commercially viable source of electricity or thermal energy. Data collection on geographical and temporal aspects of solar radiation as well as research and development work on solar electricity generation and solar-powered appliances is being encouraged by the government. Several government agencies (under the ministries of energy, electric power, education, agriculture, and science and technology) are involved in studying the application of solar energy for households (cookers, water heaters, driers, distillers and ovens) as well as communities (village/ward electrification, stand-alone solar cells). Thus far, no overall estimate of Myanmar's solar potential has been available in the public domain.

Geothermal

Up to 2002, a total of 93 hot springs had been identified in Myanmar and MOE had done some preliminary investigations on 43 of them. However, no reliable figure for Myanmar's geothermal potential has been estimated yet.

Biomass

The most common use of biomass energy resources in Myanmar is in the form of solid fuels (firewood and charcoal), that have also traditionally served as the mainstay of household energy use. Byproducts of the timber industry such as lops and tops (around 20 per cent of processed timber), sawdust and wood chips are also utilized on a much smaller scale. Crop residues and waste such as rice husks, straw, bagasse and stalks are also used to produce thermal energy locally albeit in small-scale operations. Excrement from farm animals has rarely been used as fuel until recently when biogas production technology was introduced by the government.

Myanmar's forests have been the primary source of firewood and charcoal. The actual amount of forest cover (as a basis for computing a sustainable annual yield) is difficult to ascertain with the government claiming (c. 2002) that 50.7 per cent of land area was forested.[9] Based on that optimistic figure, the total annual increment could be of the order of 30–50 million cubic metres (around 20–35 million cubic tons) of wood at best, of which the recoverable yield from natural growth depends upon the efficiency of extraction and net yield could be as small as 20 per cent.[10] Milling waste from some 0.2 million tons of timber (2001/02) is usually used within the industry itself while the tops and lops from felled timber may be used as firewood.

Agricultural residues from some 15 million hectares of crops could be up to 50 million metric tons annually but its use as fuel has to compete with other utilizations such as compost, animal feed, insulation, building material and raw material for handicrafts. As such, the amount left over for combustion may range only from 10–20 per cent of the gross output. Rice husk from milling (21.6 million tons in 2001/02) could yield up to 4 million metric tons of solid fuel. Sugar cane residue (based on 2001/02 figures) may yield about 1–1.5 million metric tons of solid fuels, while bagasse from sugar production (7 million tons in 2001/02) is traditionally utilized as fuel for the mills.[11]

Myanmar's cattle could produce up to 6 million metric tons of excrement but the amount available for biogas production could be much less given that most of that would be recycled in the field as a natural fertilizer. Droppings from pigs (4.3 million in 2001/02) and poultry (55 million in 2001/02) could yield up to 1.5 million cubic metres of biogas daily.[12]

Exploitation of Commercial Energy Sources

The government has monopolized exploitation of commercial energy resources since the nationalization of the oil industry in 1963. It has been part and parcel of the government's strategy to maintain energy independence. Nevertheless, faced with rapidly increasing demand, depleting reserves, human resources shortfalls, technological and financial (especially foreign exchange) constraints and rising energy prices, the government has relaxed its hold on the energy industry since the early 1990s by allowing FDI in the oil and gas sub-sector as well as private participation in fuel supply (coal) and electricity production.

Oil, natural gas and refined products

Myanmar used to be a net oil exporter before World War II but the war-ravaged oil industry could not regain pre-war level of production until 1975. However, after peaking at over 11 million barrels (mb) in fiscal year 1979/80 the combined output of Myanmar's onshore fields stagnated then declined steadily in the late 1980s.[13] This downward trend continued throughout the decade of the nineties and was not reversed until the turn of the century (see Table 1). This happened despite the discovery of eight new onshore oil and gas fields since 1980.[14]

To compensate for the shortfalls in domestic production crude oil had been imported irregularly from regional suppliers since 1988. This inevitably led to huge expenditures of scarce foreign exchange on imports of fuel and crude oil to satisfy the rising demand from industry and transport (see Tables 2 and 3).[15]

Since 1989, the government has been soliciting FDI and foreign technical inputs to rehabilitate the existing onshore oil fields and to explore and develop new

TABLE 1
Crude oil production in Myanmar

Fiscal Year	1985/ 86	1991/ 92	1992/ 93	1993/ 94	1994/ 95	1995/ 96	1996/ 97	1997/ 98	1998/ 99	1999/ 2000	2000/ 01	2001/ 02	2002/ 03	2003/ 04
Million barrels	10.25	5.48	5.36	5.23	5.04	4.28	3.79	3.63	3.38	3.48	4.14	4.84	6.39	7.17
Index	100	53.1	52.3	51.0	49.2	41.8	37.0	35.4	33.0	34.0	40.4	47.2	62.3	70.0

Note: Fiscal year beginning 1 April.
Sources: Selected Monthly Economic Indicators (Yangon: CSO); and Statistical Yearbook (Yangon: CSO), various issues.

TABLE 2
Value of crude oil imports by Myanmar

Fiscal Year	1990/ 91	1991/ 92	1992/ 93	1993/ 94	1994/ 95	1995/ 96	1996/ 97	1997/ 98	1998/ 99	1999/ 2000	2000/ 01	2001/ 02	2002/ 03	2003/ 04
Million kyats	54.8	n.a.	n.a.	n.a.	51.3	–	–	–	225.3	554.6	95.7	1,555.5	872.8	79.1

Note: Fiscal year beginning 1 April. n.a. denotes not available; – denotes negligible. The exchange rate averaged about kyats 6 per US dollar.
Sources: Selected Monthly Economic Indicators (Yangon: CSO); and Statistical Yearbook (Yangon: CSO), various issues.

TABLE 3
Value of crude oil imports from Malaysia

Calendar Year	1992	1993	1994	1995	1996	1997	1998	1999	2000	2001
Million ringgits	32.7	51.9	69.4	101.4	148.2	256.5	269.8	369.6	543.6	327.9

Sources: *Malaysia External Trade Statistics* (Kuala Lumpur/Putrajaya: Department of Statistics), various
issues.

onshore and offshore oil deposits. Altogether 46 onshore blocks and 24 offshore
blocks have been apportioned in this respect.

Three type of contracts are offered for onshore blocks:

* exploration (EP);
* improved oil recovery (IOR); performance compensation contract (PCC); and
* reactivation of suspended fields (RSF).

By November 2001, 21 foreign companies had signed 33 contracts with
MOGE to work on onshore fields. In early 2002, 9 companies working in 14 areas
were still operating, while 21 EP, four RSF and two IOR blocks remained open for
bidding.[16] Their operations seem to have reversed the downward trend in recent
years (see Table 1). A recent foreign joint venture in onshore oil development is
between China's Dian-Qian-Gui Petroleum Exploration Bureau of SINPOEC and
MOGE who signed a production-sharing contract (PSC) to exploit onshore Block D
in central Myanmar in early September 2004.[17] Energy officials expected that the
aforementioned efforts would increase onshore oil production from around 12,000
barrels/day to 20,000 barrels/day in the near future and eventually to meet the
estimated demand of some 40,000 barrels/day with the help of offshore condensate
oil and discovery of new fields.[18]

Natural gas was first produced commercially as feedstock for the nation's first
fertilizer factory in 1971 and its production was rapidly expanded for both industrial
use and power generation by gas turbines. The output quadrupled within a decade
after 1973, then stagnated in the second half of the 1980s and early 1990s, failing to
keep up with rising demand for its use as fuel and feedstock, thereby retarding
industrial production and power generation.[19] Thereafter the output rapidly increased
(see Table 4) as new onshore deposits came on stream together with substantial
production (mainly for export) from two new offshore gas fields.

Of the fifteen PSCs signed with seven international oil companies/consortia
between 1990 and 2001, two (Moattama and Tanintharyi blocks) yielded substantial
gas deposits and the third reportedly found an even larger deposit in the Rakhine
block while the rest lapsed or were relinquished.

TABLE 4
Natural gas production in Myanmar

Fiscal Year	1985/ 86	1991/ 92	1992/ 93	1993/ 94	1994/ 95	1995/ 96	1996/ 97	1997/ 98	1998/ 99	1999/ 2000	2000/ 01	2001/ 02	2002/ 03	2003/ 04
Piped gas														
(billion cu.ft.)	35.5	31.7	31.2	38.7	48.3	54.0	58.5	63.4	119.9	219.3	299.3	310.3	330.3	349.8
Index	100	89.3	87.9	109.0	136.1	152.1	164.8	178.6	337.7	617.7	843.1	874.1	930.4	985.4
CNG														
(million cu.ft.)	–	76.0	78.5	76.3	78.5	80.1	101.0	80.9	70.0	67.7	73.6	73.1	64.6	74.5

Notes: Fiscal year beginning 1 April; CNG denotes compressed natural gas.
Sources: *Selected Monthly Economic Indicators* (Yangon: Central Statistical Organization); and *Statistical Yearbook* (Yangon: CSO), various issues.

The first offshore gas project to be developed in Myanmar named Yadana (jewel) encompassing M-5 and M-6 blocks off Moattama cost US$1.2 billion, with reserves of the order of 6.5 tcf. It began exporting gas to Thailand in 1988 via a 255-mile (36-inch diameter) pipeline to the tune of 525 mmcfd (million cubic feet per day). Myanmar also receives 125 mmcfd of its output.[20]

The second offshore project to come on stream at a cost of about US$700 million is the Yetagun (Valiant Banner) off the Tanintharyi coast in southeastern Myanmar. The project constitutes blocks M-12, M-13, and M-14 with reserves estimated at 3.2 tcf. Exports to Thailand started in 2000 through a 169-mile (24-inch diameter) pipeline at the rate of 200 mmcfd eventually rising to 300 mmcfd if there is demand. It could produces 8–9,000 barrels per day of gas condensate as well.[21]

The third PSC with Daewoo International of Korea for exploration in Block A-1 off the Rakhine coast opposite Bangladesh made news when MOGE announced on 15 January 2004 that a "world class commercial gas deposit" was discovered. It was also revealed that a consortium formed with Daewoo (60 per cent), Korea Gas Corporation (10 per cent), and two Indian firms ONGC Videsh (a subsidiary of Oil and Natural Gas Corporation, 20 per cent) and Gail (India) (Gas Authority of India, 10 per cent), would develop the gas field with a potential yield of 4.2 tcf to 5.8 tcf.[22] In February, Daewoo upped the ante by holding a news conference in Seoul in which it was predicted that the project now named "Shwe" (gold) could yield, for the company, annual net profits of some US$86 million for 20 years beginning 2010. It was also speculated that Myanmar's takings could rise from US$800 million to several billion annually.[23] In the following months excited Indian industrial circles mooted several schemes for utilizing that giant gas field to satisfy India's huge appetite for energy and this further fuelled speculation. Liquefied Natural Gas (LNG) plants, Liquefied Petroleum Gas (LPG) plants, new onshore infrastructures, pipelines across Bangladesh or other routes were some of the projects discussed publicly and privately, despite the fact that up to the end of 2004 only one test well had yielded substantial output of 32 mmcfd.[24] On 13 January 2005, after a two-day tri-nation meeting of energy ministers from Myanmar, India and Bangladesh in Myanmar's capital Yangon, a memorandum of understanding (MoU) was signed with all parties pledging to cooperate in a project to pipe M-1's natural gas output to India across Bangladesh.[25] While, by January 2005, two test wells had been drilled and a planned series of six test wells had begun on the third one, it remains to be seen whether the speculation that the field's potential yield could go up to double digits of tcf with future extension of drilling area would actualize. Meanwhile, in October 2004, Daewoo sold 30 per cent of its stake in A-3, which is adjacent to A-1, to its two Indian partners of the A-1 project.

Probably encouraged by the successful projects, new players had also entered into the offshore stakes in which six blocks in Rakhine (Arakan), nine blocks in Moattama (Martaban) and four blocks in Tanintharyi had been open for new PSCs.[26] In November 2003, Thailand's PTTEP (PTT Exploration and Production Plc, an exploration subsidiary of PTT Plc) took up PSCs for Blocks M-7 and M-9 situated between Yadana and Yetagun, promising to spend up to US$16 million in the next four years.[27] Again, in August 2004, PTTEP raised its investment in Myanmar by taking up Blocks M-3 and M-4 next to Yadana.[28] In February 2004, it was announced that Daewoo had also secured the rights to explore Block A-3 adjacent to its Shwe field in the Bay of Bengal.[29] The latest offshore joint venture, thus far, is the PSC between MOGE and a China-Singapore consortium (CNOOC or China National Offshore Oil Company [Myanmar]; China Huanqiu Contracting and Engineering Corporation; and Golden Aaron of Singapore) which succeeded in a bid to explore Rakhine Block A-4 and Moattama Block M-10.[30]

The successful implementation of the Yadana and Yetagun projects enabled Myanmar to become an energy exporter in the form of natural gas exports to Thailand, thereby garnering scarce foreign exchange for the country (Table 5). In fact, natural gas exports accounted for some 40 per cent of the export income in fiscal year 2002/03 and recently helped reverse the perennial trade deficit that had plagued Myanmar's economy for decades.

As part of "downstream" activities in the energy sector, MPE operates three refineries with a combined capacity of 57,000 bbl (thousand barrels) a day, three urea fertilizer plants with a total capacity of 1,270 tons/day, one LPG extraction plant with a capacity of 24 mmcfd (natural gas), two skid mounted LPG plants (10 & 15 mmcfd), one methanol plant with a capacity of 450 metric tons/day and a bitumen plant.[31]

Plans to build a LPG plant of 150,000 metric tons/year capacity to process natural gas from the Yetagun field during the first five year plan cycle (of the 30-year perspective plan) beginning 2001/02 seemed to have been delayed. A Polyethylene plant utilizing Yetagun gas was also envisaged. In the second five-year plan cycle another LPG plant of similar capacity was envisaged to come on stream in 2008/09, while a 100,000 barrels/day refinery and a 1000 metric tons/day urea fertilizer factory were planned to be commissioned by 2006/07.[32]

Commercial fuels

The major commercial fuels currently in use in Myanmar are liquid fuels derived from petroleum and natural gas (for electric power generation, transport and household

TABLE 5
Natural gas exports to Thailand from Myanmar

Fiscal Year	1998/99	1999/00	2000/01	2001/02	2002/03	2003/04
Volume Million cu.ft.	954.1	6,527.1	65,359.4	237,080.7	350,900.5	200,155.6
Value Million kyats	4.9	31.2	1,110.5	4,247.1	5,919.0	3,478.3

Note: Fiscal year beginning 1 April.
Sources: Selected Monthly Economic Indicators (Yangon: Central Statistical Organization), various issues.

use) and solid fuels such as coal (for power generation and industrial use), firewood and charcoal (for household and industrial use). One consistent feature of the last decade has been the escalating demand for all kinds of liquid fuels due to fuel substitution in household use, urbanization pressures, substantial increases in motorized vehicles and expansion of private industries.

Liquid fuels

Myanmar's refineries have been running much below capacity since the mid-1980s as oil output stagnated and declined. Though augmented by oil imports, even if constrained by the shortage of foreign exchange and inadequate infrastructure in the supply chain, combined output of those refineries was not enough to fully satisfy the demand for refined products such as gasoline, diesel and fuel oil. As evident from Table 6 the production of gasoline (mainly a motor fuel) barely rose above the 1985 level until the turn of the century despite the fact that the number of passenger cars (overwhelmingly gasoline driven) tripled and the number of motorcycles increased by 530 per cent between 1985/86 and 1999/2000.[33] Similarly, production of diesel, whose demand has been larger in volume with the proliferation of private river craft, increasing reliance on generators (due to brownouts and blackouts in electric power supply in the last decade) and doubling of the number of (mainly diesel-powered) buses as well as the introduction of heavy long-haul trucks since the early 1990s, fell short of the demand of some 330 million gallons annually.[34] The overall demand for gasoline and diesel is further aggravated by the existence of hundreds of thousands of unregistered and off-road vehicles used on farms and in various industries.[35] The output of fuel oil (mainly used for producing heat and steam) had worsened following a downward trend throughout.

TABLE 6
Production of major liquid fuels in Myanmar
(million gallons)

Fiscal Year	1985/86	1991/92	1992/93	1993/94	1994/95	1995/96	1996/97	1997/98	1998/99	1999/2000	2000/01	2001/02	2002/03	2003/04
Gasoline	69.4	41.9	47.4	51.5	58.3	65.1	53.2	77.7	81.8	82.0	80.6	70.8	84.3	109.3
Index	100	60.3	68.3	74.2	84.0	93.8	76.6	111.9	117.8	118.1	116.1	102.0	121.5	157.5
Diesel	100.3	92.4	85.5	87.7	107.1	116.6	91.5	123.1	119.1	116.1	112.6	97.1	113.9	78.9
Index	100	92.2	85.2	87.5	106.8	116.2	91.2	122.7	118.8	115.8	112.3	96.8	113.6	78.7
Furnace oil	45.0	33.9	36.1	34.8	24.0	27.4	24.5	28.1	28.6	30.5	33.7	28.6	28.7	18.7
Index	100	75.4	80.1	77.3	53.2	60.9	54.3	62.4	63.5	67.7	74.9	63.4	63.6	41.6

Notes: Fiscal year beginning 1 April.
Sources: Selected Monthly Economic Indicators (Yangon: CSO); and Statistical Yearbook (Yangon: CSO), various issues.

On the other hand, products such as LPG (increasingly used as household fuel) and aviation turbine followed an upward trend over the last dozen years as depicted in Table 7. Kerosene (a popular household fuel for cooking and lighting) never recovered from the downward trend that started in the 1980s and though it increased in recent years, the volume has become very small in relation to diesel and gasoline.[36]

To help ameliorate the supply shortfall, the government has been importing diesel fuel from abroad since 1987 (see Table 8 for selected data). Nevertheless, fuel rationing, imposed some two decades ago, has become a permanent fixture of the motoring scene in Myanmar (ibid.).[37] Meanwhile, the government took administrative measures to reduce fuel consumption such as forming a high-level committee to supervise the use of electricity and fuel headed by a junta member and imposing, in September 2002, a "dry day" that prohibits the use of government vehicles in the capital on the second and fourth Sundays of the month.

The government agencies running the sugar mills have experimented with producing gasohol from ethanol (which is derived from molasses) and a pilot plant had been operating since March 2004.[38] However, it is unlikely that gasohol as a low-octane substitute fuel will become viable in the near future.

Coal

Until recently the demand for coal had been mainly for industrial use in steam boilers and small-scale thermal power plants as coal-fired locomotives were phased out decades ago. Local coal production increased from 43,000 metric tons in 1984/85 to over 170,000 metric tons in 2003/04, while imports (in tons) declined from around six figures in the early seventies to a mere fraction of that in the last decade.[39]

A major project to utilize coal from a deposit at Tigyit in Southern Shan State for producing electricity was undertaken by MEPE in mid-2001. The China National Heavy Machinery Corporation (CHMC) won the tender for supplying the 120-megawatt (twin turbine) power plant with nearly US$43 million worth of equipment. A consortium, formed in July 2002 of four local companies led by the Shan Yoma Nagar Company, secured the 20-year contract to exploit the Tigyit deposit (estimated at 20.7 million tons). It will supply 750,000 tons of coal annually as fuel for the power plant with technical expertise and equipment (equipment US$4.3 million) provided by CHNC. The project, reportedly more than half completed in late 2003, was slated to feed power into the national grid.

Gas

The major use of natural gas in Myanmar as fuel is for power generation in gas turbines (see section on electric power and Table 10, below). However, the government

TABLE 7
Other liquid fuel products in Myanmar
(million gallons)

Fiscal Year	1985/ 86	1991/ 92	1992/ 93	1993/ 94	1994/ 95	1995/ 96	1996/ 97	1997/ 98	1998/ 99	1999/ 2000	2000/ 01	2001/ 02	2002/ 03	2003/ 04
Kerosene	1.88	0.47	0.33	0.28	0.22	0.23	0.28	0.24	0.04	0.04	0.19	0.36	0.39	0.39
Index	100	24.9	17.7	14.9	11.5	12.5	15.0	12.5	2.2	2.0	9.9	19.4	20.6	21.0
LPG	1.3	3.6	4.4	4.8	4.6	4.3	3.3	4.3	4.6	5.6	6.1	6.3	6.2	5.1
Index	100	283.9	349.6	374.7	363.9	334.4	260.3	338.5	364.8	441.6	481.4	492.2	485.5	402.1
Aviation turbine	6.0	10.6	10.3	11.7	14.2	17.5	14.4	15.7	14.1	16.2	17.9	18.6	19.7	21.5
Index	100	175.8	171.0	194.4	235.5	290.5	238.4	260.6	233.0	267.9	296.9	308.0	326.5	356.6

Notes: Fiscal year beginning 1 April; LPG denotes liquefied petroleum gas (also known as gas oil).
Sources: Selected Monthly Economic Indicators (Yangon: CSO); and Statistical Yearbook (Yangon: CSO), various issues.

TABLE 8
Value of liquid fuel products imported by Myanmar

Calendar Year	1989	1990	1991	1992	1993	1994	1995	1996	1997	1998	1999	2000	2001	2002
Diesel
(Malaysia)	n.a.	1.1	3.1	13.1	2.1	0.9	–	n.a.	n.a.	n.a.	n.a.	n.a.	n.a.	n.a.
(Singapore)	1.5	16.2	10.4	15.9	46.1	29.3	21.4	45.6	n.a.	57.9	73.2	72.4	114.7	273.4
Fuel oil for ships
(Singapore)	5.2	14.5	10.0	6.3	7.1	5.9	4.7	5.6	n.a.	6.0	7.1	10.0	12.1	12.9

Notes: Values in millions of Malaysian ringgits and millions of Singapore dollars respectively. n.a. denotes not available; – denotes negligible.
Sources: Malaysia External Trade Statistics (Kuala Lumpur/Putrajaya: Department of Statistics), various issues; *Singapore Trade Statistics* (Singapore: Trade Development Board and International Enterprise), various issues.

has recently begun promoting the use of compressed natural gas (CNG) as a clean and cheap source of motor power. Noting that CNG, available locally in abundance from surplus natural gas, as a substitute for gasoline and diesel in motor vehicles would conserve scarce foreign exchange currently being spent on imports, the government has launched a pilot project to convert 5,200 motor veheicles in the capital to run on CNG during the year 2005, saving over 2 million gallons of fuel a month. State-owned industrial enterprises have developed conversion kits, dedicated engines and supply infrastructure (such as gas tanks and filling stations). The aim is to eventually convert most state-owned vehicles and persuade the privately-owned vehicles to follow suit. In this case, the government is trying to foster demand for CNG through supply-side initiatives backed by administrative measures.[40]

Widespread use of LPG (a government monopoly) as household fuel has been constrained by the lack of supply and poor infrastructure despite government efforts to expand its usage. It was reported that out of some 16,000 metric tons of LPG produced in 2000/01 less than 50 per cent was consumed as household fuel.[41] The usage is mainly confined to registered clients in the capital the majority of whom are civil servants and the urban elite.[42]

Electric power

Electric power is a necessary but insufficient requirement for industrial development and it also contributes to industrial growth by itself. Electricity production and supply has also been the prerogative of state agencies. The government's policy and objectives regarding electric power are:[43]

- To employ gas turbine generation only in the short term and to rely on hydroelectric power generation in the long term as the one vital source of energy sufficiency and export.
- To generate and distribute more electricity for economic development.
- To reduce losses and conserve electric energy for future energy sufficiency of the nation.
- To promote electricity production from new and renewable sources of energy.

To fulfill these objectives, the following strategies have been adopted:

- Exploring all available sources of electricity including new and renewable energy sources for power development.
- Promoting the production level of present electric power resources.
- Updating the demand forecast continuously and looking into the means for fulfilling the country's requirement.

As such, the government claimed that it had substantially increased the generating capacity (see Table 9) of power plants as well as electricity production (see Table 10) by adding extensions to existing gas turbines, introducing combined cycle technology in thermal power plants, and constructing large-scale and mini-hydro plants in the countryside. Meanwhile, the provision of electricity by the state-owned MEPE had extended to 323 towns and 1,101 villages by fiscal year 2001/02; up from 279 towns and 722 villages in 1985/86.

Table 11 shows the trends in the provision of electricity by MEPE. The dip in installed capacity in 2003/04 was probably due to the decommissioning of ageing and inefficient power stations and suspension of some older generating units due to breakdowns. The more substantial reduction in generation in 1998/99 was probably caused by severe drought that led the major hydroelectric plant at Lawpita to cut

TABLE 9
Electric power generation capacity by type
(megawatts)

Fiscal Year	Thermal	Diesel	Hydroelectric	Natural Gas	Total*
1985/86	80	79	226	300	685
	(11.7%)	(11.5%)	(33.0%)	(43.9%)	(100%)
2001/02	216	66	360	523	1,165
	(18.5%)	(5.7%)	(30.9%)	(44.9%)	(100%)

Notes: * Figures may not add up due to rounding; figures in parentheses are shares; only units under MEPE are included.
Sources: Statistical Yearbook (Yangon: CSO), various issues.

TABLE 10
Electric power generation by type
(million kilowatt-hours)

Fiscal Year	Thermal	Diesel	Hydroelectric	Natural Gas	Total*
1985/86	55.0	64.5	1,003.5	996.4	2,119.4
	(2.6%)	(3.0%)	(47.3%)	(47.0%)	(100%)
2003/04	634.2	30.9	1,978.1	2,748.2	5,391.5
	(11.8%)	(0.6%)	(36.7%)	(51.0%)	(100%)

Notes: * Figures may not add up due to rounding; figures in parentheses are shares; only units under MEPE are included.
Sources: Selected Monthly Economic Indicators (Yangon: CSO); and Statistical Yearbook (Yangon: CSO), various issues.

TABLE 11
Electric power installed, generated and sold by MEPE

Fiscal Year	1985/86	1991/92	1992/93	1993/94	1994/95	1995/96	1996/97	1997/98	1998/99	1999/2000	2000/01	2001/02	2002/03	2003/04
Installed (megawatts)	684	837	807	809	845	982	1,033	1,036	1,031	1,171	1,171	1,160	1,570	1,339
Index	100	122.3	117.9	118.2	123.5	143.5	151.0	151.4	150.7	171.7	171.7	169.5	229.4	195.7
Generated (million kwh)	2,119.4	2,650.1	3,006.6	3,385.3	3,594.1	3,762.3	4,130.3	4,550.5	4,139.4	4,639.1	5,117.6	5,674.0	6,614.0	5,391.5
Index	100	125.0	141.9	159.7	169.6	177.5	194.9	214.7	195.3	218.9	241.5	267.7	312.1	254.4
Sold (million kwh)	1,459.5	1,734.2	1,831.5	2,059.2	2,218.0	2,262.4	2,433.8	2,676.1	2,716.4	2,909.9	3,267.9	4,261.7	5,272.0	3,282.0
Index	100	118.8	125.5	141.1	152.0	155.0	166.8	183.4	186.1	199.4	223.9	292.0	361.2	224.9
Sold amount as percentage of generated amount	71%	65%	61%	61%	62%	60%	59%	59%	56%	53%	54%	75.1%	80%	61%
Revenues (billion kyats)	0.4	0.8	0.9	1.0	2.0	2.8	3.1	3.5	4.1	14.1	16.6	24.2	30.0	17.2

Notes: Fiscal year beginning 1 April; kwh denotes kilowatt-hour.
Sources: *Selected Monthly Economic Indicators* (Yangon: CSO); and *Statistical Yearbook* (Yangon: CSO), various issues.

back output, while a more significant drop in 2003/04 could be due to lower capacity utilization. Inefficiency in electricity supply since the early 1990s is reflected in the figures in Table 11, for the ratio of the amount sold to the amount generated remained below 65 per cent except for fiscal years 2001/02 and 2002/03.[44] On the other hand, the price of electricity had been heavily subsidized for decades since the 1960s and only in 1999 did the government raise the price to be more in line with escalating costs.[45] This price hike is reflected in the sudden jump in revenues in fiscal year 1999/00. Nevertheless, there were still irregularities, such as improper and illegal use of electricity that deprived the government of revenues and distorted load distribution.[46]

Although the national grid was supplied by the MEPE under the Ministry of Energy, state agencies under 23 other ministries also produce electricity for their own use. In fiscal year 1997/98, the last year of published data, the combined generating capacity installed by those agencies was equivalent to 35 per cent of MEPE's total capacity and the corresponding electricity production was equivalent to some 14 per cent of that produced by MEPE. As such, the figures depicting industrial and bulk consumption in Table 12 are underrepresented, as public sector own-use generation is not captured. Similarly, the general (mainly private household) consumption is also underrepresented in Table 12 as a substantial number (perhaps running into six figures) of households employ small diesel generators as substitutes or supplements to MEPE's supply shortfalls.

Despite the aforementioned impressive growth trends in capacity build-up and power generation, blackouts and brownouts have been recurrent problems since the early 1990s. These were mainly due to technological obsolescence in both generation and distribution infrastructure, shortage of foreign exchange, and constrained attempts to repair, upgrade and expand deteriorating networks, modernize ageing power plants, and build new plants. To overcome such resource constraints the government relaxed its rules and allowed cooperatives and some private consortia to set up local generating plants (mini- and micro-hydro and small thermal plants), while building major multi-purpose dams that are integrated with hydropower schemes.[47] The government also launched a "thrift" campaign on the electricity usage by forming the (ministerial level) Supervisory Committee for Utilization of Power and Fuel in 2002 to cut down electricity consumption by the public sector and minimize wastage in both the private and public sectors.[48]

Future plans for capacity additions as outlined in the two consecutive five-years plans beginning in 2001/02 were aimed at achieving electricity self-sufficiency by 2010, based on a baseline growth rate of 8.5 per cent per annum. The national target for generating capacity in 2020 was some 15,000 megawatts with virtually all

TABLE 12
MEPE's electricity supply to consumers by type
(million kilowatt-hours)

Fiscal Year	1985/86	1991/92	1992/93	1993/94	1994/95	1995/96	1996/97	1997/98	1998/99	1999/2000	2000/01	2001/02	2002/03	2003/04
Total	1,459.5	1,734.2	1,831.5	2,059.2	2,218.0	2,262.4	2,433.8	2,676.1	2,716.4	2909.9	3,267.9	4,261.7	5,272.0	3,282.0
General	408.7	640.2	770.6	887.9	982.8	972.3	1,089.2	1,206.3	1,132.3	1,157.5	1,361.0	1,789.3	2,214.0	1,308.8
Index	100	156.6	188.8	208.2	240.5	237.9	266.5	295.2	277.0	283.2	333.0	437.8	541.7	320.2
Industrial	882.3	836.6	768.9	850.9	862.9	875.7	875.7	914.0	956.1	1,105.8	1,295.4	1,615.2	1,999.6	1,263.9
Index	100	94.8	87.1	96.4	97.8	99.3	99.3	103.6	108.4	125.3	146.8	183.1	226.6	143.3
Bulk	128.5	213.6	238.4	263.0	302.4	340.2	392.5	472.9	537.5	560.5	626.5	748.0	926.9	614.6
Index	100	166.2	185.5	204.7	235.3	264.7	305.4	368.0	418.3	436.2	487.5	582.1	721.3	478.3
Others	40.5	43.5	53.6	57.4	69.9	74.2	76.4	82.7	90.7	86.1	85.0	109.2	131.5	94.8
Index	100	107.4	132.3	141.7	172.6	183.2	188.6	204.2	224.0	212.6	209.9	269.6	324.7	234.1

Notes: Fiscal year beginning 1 April; MEPE is Myanma Electric Power Enterprise (a state-owned enterprise).
Sources: Selected Monthly Economic Indicators (Yangon: CSO); and *Statistical Yearbook* (Yangon: CSO), various issues.

the additions coming from hydroelectric power plants.[49] These were to be coordinated by the Work Committee for National Electricity Development chaired by the junta's Secretary-1 under the supervision of the Leading Committee for National Electricity Development chaired by the junta Chairman himself.

Probably the most ambitious and controversial plan (because of potential negative environmental consequences) is the Myanmar-Thai cooperative project, announced by Thailand in August 2004, to dam the Thanlwin (Salween) river along the Myanmar-Thai border and construct a series of five hydroelectric power plants to export electricity to Thailand and beyond. The first of that series is going to be the Tasang dam project with a capacity of generating over 7,000 megawatts, which is currently at the stage of advanced surveying and soliciting of investment funds.[50]

Renewable Fuels

Traditionally, renewable energy supplies in Myanmar are in the main derived from forest, plantation and agricultural products. Broadly classified as biomass energy, the most common fuels in this genre are firewood, charcoal, and to a lesser extent bamboo and agriculture residues (such as cotton stalks, pea stalks, sesamum stalks, coconut or palm leaves, rice husks and sawdust) as well as biogas. Although the proportion of biomass fuels in Myanmar's total energy consumption had been falling (from 87 per cent in 1990 to 77 per cent in 1996), biomass still constitutes a very significant source of fuel and energy in Myanmar.

Firewood and charcoal and wood substitutes

Firewood and charcoal together constitutes the most heavily used biomass fuel for Myanmar's household and cottage industries. Firewood and charcoal production is subject to regulation by local authorities as well as agencies under the Ministry of Forestry and the Ministry of Agriculture and Irrigation. However, natural forests, which serve as sources for these traditional fuels, have been under threat of depletion for some time due to increasing demand for their products as household fuels and their exploitation for non-energy uses. Successive Myanmar governments during the last two decades have recognized that firewood and charcoal production are aggravating the problem of the overexploitation, mainly through commercial logging, of forest resources beyond their natural capacity to replenish themselves, and have taken some measures to limit the demand as well as increase the supply through firewood plantations.[51]

As can be seen from Table 13, the volume of firewood consumption (including feedstock for charcoal) had increased steadily since 1970/71 (10.4 million cubic

TABLE 13
Firewood and charcoal production in Myanmar

Fiscal Year	1985/ 86	1991/ 92	1992/ 93	1993/ 94	1994/ 95	1995/ 96	1996/ 97	1997/ 98	1998/ 99	1999/ 2000	2000/ 01	2001/ 02
Firewood												
(million cu.tons)	36.7	17.9	18.0	18.0	18.0	17.8	17.7	17.3	17.6	18.4	18.6	19.0
Index	100	106.8	107.5	107.4	107.8	106.1	106.0	103.2	105.2	109.8	111.0	113.3
Charcoal												
(thousand cu.tons)	866	649	801	418	296	213	150	84	145	201	182	223
Index	100	74.9	92.5	48.3	34.2	24.6	17.3	9.7	16.7	23.2	21.0	25.8

Notes: Fiscal year beginning 1 April.
Sources: Statistical Yearbook (Yangon: CSO), various issues.

tons) peaking at 1989/90 (20.4 million cubic tons) and then fluctuated around 19–20 million cubic tons for the rest of the decade.[52] Estimates based on standing stock of forest cover in the early 1990s gave an annual sustainable yield of around 13 million cubic tons and even with a supplement of around 2 million cubic tons from other sources (plantations, roadside and perimeter trees, lops and tops) there was a shortfall of over 4 million cubic tons given that the consumption was some 20 million cubic tons.[53] This deficit must be borne by the natural forests already besieged by escalated commercial logging resulting from the boom in border trade that began in 1989. Hence, in the early years of the 21st century, when the consumption of firewood remained steady around 19 million cubic tons and with less standing stock (due to further depletion during the decade since the last estimate) — the difference between the sustainable yield and actual exploitation could be as large as the deficit of the early 1990s, if not larger. Since each million cubic tons extracted from natural forests could result in the destruction of some 55,000 acres, it seems that over 2 million acres had been denuded to make up for the firewood shortfall during the last decade. In fact, seven out of fourteen states/divisions in Myanmar suffered from deficits in firewood by the end of the 1990s.[54] While strictly enforcing controls on commercial firewood exploitation, since the mid-1990s the government has also been introducing new, more efficient stoves to the populace, developed by the Ministry of Forestry. They provide for 40 per cent savings over traditional design. By the turn of the century, more than one million improved A-1 stoves had been distributed at below cost and its technology was disseminated to private entrepreneurs. Potential savings from these stoves could be equal to firewood from 150,000 acres of firewood plantations.[55]

Dedicated firewood plantations, on 5-year rotation cycles, for village supply were planted annually by the government since the late 1970s and by 1998 the total area had reached 465,000 acres with annual increment rising to over 30,000 acres in the fiscal year 1996/97. However, the annual planting rate dropped below 15,000 acres in the following year and further down to less than 10,000 acres in 2001/02.[56] An optimistic estimate (based on planned targets for planting) of the total output from these plantations for 1999/2000 was around 0.1 million cubic tons.[57]

Potential yield from trees in and around villages and roadside stands was estimated at around 2 million cubic tons in 1991 and was expected to double by the turn of the century, thereby assuming a significant role in relieving the pressure on the natural forests.[58]

Tops and lops from commercial timber extraction at around 20 per cent of the throughput are rather insignificant and with the cutback in teak and other hardwood production in recent years its potential contribution could be less than 0.05 million cubic tons annually.

The establishment of self-managed community forests in rural areas was a relatively new project in Myanmar and the output from these fast-growing species, on 3-year rotation cycles, was expected to have been only about 0.03 million cubic tons in 1999/2000.

Charcoal, the preferred fuel for urban household use after the supply of kerosene was reduced drastically from the mid-1970s (see Table 13 above), was produced in inefficient locally-designed kilns that require up to eight times by weight of firewood as feedstock. Most of the firewood for charcoal production came from mangrove forests in lower Myanmar and this (together with population pressure) had seriously damaged the mangrove ecosystem vital for agriculture and fisheries. In fact, the annual depletion rate of mangroves in the most abundant region (Ayeyawady Division) over the 1974–90 period was estimated to be 1.63 per cent which was 2.5 times that of the overall depletion rate for natural forests. In response, as a conservation measure, the government has been trying to encourage the use of more efficient charcoal kiln designs that would reduce the firewood requirement to three times the output volume and also control local output since the mid-1990s.[59] As a result, the charcoal output in 2001/02 at 0.22 million cubic tons was only 26 per cent of the volume produced in 1985/86 (see Table 13).

The high demand for firewood and charcoal under the aforementioned supply constraints has led to escalating prices for these fuels in urban centres of Myanmar. The annual average retail price of firewood in the capital octupled between 1988/89 and 1996/97. It further quadrupled between 1997/98 and 2003/04. Similarly, charcoal's retail price sextupled and more than tripled in the corresponding periods.[60]

Briquettes and fuel sticks (made from paddy husk, sawdust, charcoal dust or petroleum coke with a suitable binding agent) were also introduced as wood substitutes by the government on a pilot scale to cottage industries and bulk users (such as food stalls) and some 30 modern briquette-making machines with an combined annual capacity of 0.1 million tons (by weight) were operating by the year 2000. However, due to constraints on raw materials and technology, annual savings are not expected to exceed 0.03 million cubic tons of firewood.

Biogas

Biogas for thermal energy and as fuel for generating electricity has been promoted as an integrated approach (as fuel, fertilizer, for pollution control, to improve health and sanitation) by the government since the early 1980s but failed to catch on in a big way due to technical constraints and probably sociocultural reasons. Starting from a very low base, the number of biogas digesters increased to only 867 in 124 townships (out of 324) by the turn of the century from around 200 in 1985.[61] Its contribution has negligible impact on the energy balance of Myanmar.

FDI and ODA in the Energy Sector

The oil and gas sub-sector and the electric power sub-sector, which together form the bulk of Myanmar's energy sector, suffered from lack of technology, human resources development and capital (primarily because of scarce foreign exchange) since the 1960s. Even when the moribund socialist command economy was opened up rapidly after late 1988, the Japanese and Western states' denial of official development assistance (ODA) that has extended to multilateral financial institutions, such as the World Bank, Asian Development Bank and International Monetary Fund, has deprived Myanmar of potential funds for upgrading and developing its energy sector. Hence, FDI and ODA from friendly regional states such as China and India have become important sources of capital and technology for modernizing and expanding Myanmar's energy sector.

Myanmar's terms for PSCs may be summarized as:

- duty exemption on industrial equipment/materials;
- automatic 3-year tax holidays;
- 30 per cent corporate tax on taxable income;
- no export duty on petroleum exports;
- accelerated depreciation (25 per cent annually);
- pricing for domestic supply is "not too far" below the "fair" market price; and
- renegotiations clause that allows for "necessary adjustments/amendments in the event of situations arising not envisaged in the original contract".[62]

The FDI in Myanmar's energy sector constitutes a substantial portion of the overall value of foreign capital attracted by Myanmar since the military government that assumed power in September 1988 promulgated a law in November 1988 to allow foreign investments after a ban for some three decades. Myanmar's Foreign Investment Commission (FIC) does not provide public information on the actual inflow of FDI but usually releases figures representing approved sums based on commitments by investing companies. As such, not only has there been a time lag between approvals and actual inflow that usually spreads out over the project's duration but the data also do not reflect suspension of projects (especially after the Asian financial crisis of 1998) as such. Nevertheless, the data do indicate trends and give a sense of proportion on the FDI involvement in different sectors of the economy.

TABLE 14
Annual approved foreign investment in the oil & gas sector
(million US dollars)

Fiscal Year	1990/ 91	1991/ 92	1992/ 93	1993/ 94	1994/ 95	1995/ 96	1996/ 97	1997/ 98	1998/ 99	1999/ 00	2000/ 01	2001/ 02	2002/ 03	2003/ 04
Amount	317.0	–	44.5	19.5	1,039.5	14.8	695.6	172.1	–	5.3	47.6	3.3	44.0	54.3

Note: Approved amount is usually less than the actual investment accrued and may not be invested within the same fiscal year.
Sources: Selected Monthly Economic Indicators (Yangon: CSO); and Statistical Yearbook (Yangon: CSO), various issues.

It can be seen from Table 14 that the first wave of major investments was approved in 1990/91 when many foreign oil companies rushed in to sign PSCs for offshore and onshore exploration. The substantial sums approved in 1994/95 and 1996/97 were related to development projects for the setting up of production facilities for the Yadana and Yetagun offshore gas fields (see above) and the associated infrastructure for piping it to Thailand and Myanmar. Smaller amounts approved after the millennium year were for exploration and boosting production of onshore fields and the Rakhine offshore gas project (Shwe) mentioned above.

As of 31 March 2004 (end of financial year 2003/04), the cumulative amount of approved FDI in Myanmar added up to some US$7.59 billion, of which US$2.46 billion belonged to the oil and gas sector. The share of the oil and gas sector at 32.4 per cent, though significant, was a decrease from the 48.4 per cent share registered in the end of the fiscal year 1990/91.

On the other hand, the energy sector — especially the electric power sub-sector — also appeared to be the major beneficiary of ODA from the People's Republic of China (PRC), which has contributed the most in terms of value in the absence of ODA from the West and multilateral financial institutions. Apart from the US$120 million loan approved by the Bank of China in September 2000 to pay for Chinese equipment contracted by the 280 megawatt hydroelectric project completed in late 2004 (after six years of construction), equipment and technical expertise provided by the PRC for many mini-hydroelectric projects and transmission projects are believed to be funded by Chinese ODA.[63]

Conclusions: A Gas Bonanza to Fuel Economic Growth?

Twenty years after the Ministry of Energy was established, Myanmar's energy officials and the local media appear to be have embraced the notion that the gas bonanza is out there in Myanmar's offshore waters to be discovered and exploited to the country's advantage.[64] Optimism abounds that ample foreign exchange earnings from exporting offshore natural gas could be put to good use in financing Myanmar's industrialization. On the other hand, a series of ongoing and planned hydroelectric projects would ensure that the country's electricity needs are more than satisfied, adding further impetus to its drive for industrialization and a higher standard of living for millions of households throughout the country. Participation in the proposed Trans-ASEAN gas pipeline network and an oil pipeline from a western Myanmar port to the capital of Yunnan province in China were also mooted recently as future boosters for the growth of Myanmar's energy sector.[65]

However, in terms of value-added output, Myanmar's energy sector is still a small part of the overall economy. In 1990/91, the earliest financial year for which separate sectoral data is available, the energy (oil & gas plus electricity) sector's contribution to the country's GDP was only 0.99 per cent, whereas the electricity sub-sector alone accounted for 0.68 per cent. A decade later, in 2000/01, the energy sector's share rose to 1.6 per cent, while electricity's share came to 1.09 per cent.

There are also long-standing problems associated with supply shortfalls of fuels for industrial use, transportation and household consumption where substitutes for gasoline, diesel, fuel oil, firewood and charcoal are yet to be adequately provided due to financial, technological and infrastructure constraints that remain formidable despite the government's best efforts. Fuel prices and electricity tariffs need to be rationalized and must reflect capital and recurring expenditures but the social consequences of such pricing policies need to be considered as well.[66] Financing could be a major constraint. It would require around a billion US dollars over the next five years to achieve the electricity-generating target set for 2010 with substantial additional outlays to overhaul the dilapidated distribution networks. An annual outlay of several hundred million dollars would be required to import at least ten million barrels of crude oil if the government were to satisfy the demand in the same period.[67] Moreover, current annual gross income of several hundred million US dollars from gas sales has to be discounted for equity repayments, foreign oil companies' share and operating costs resulting in a net income probably nearer to half that amount.[68] It is more likely that net income from the export of natural gas from the currently operating offshore fields could be better utilized in achieving energy security by spending within the energy sector itself. This leaves little foreign exchange surplus at the national level for, at least, the first half of the 30-year plan.

As for the likelihood of further discoveries in the offshore areas, it remains to be seen whether current PSCs dominated by Asian players would yield significant new finds. The giant U.S. companies which are major players in offshore oil and gas development are deterred from entering the Myanmar offshore market by the U.S. President's executive order of May 1997 that barred new investments in Myanmar because of alleged suppression of democracy and human rights violations by the Yangon regime. Mega projects, involving huge dams and long pipelines, are also opposed by anti-regime lobbies and environmental advocacy groups, who also have been advocating an investment boycott against Myanmar.[69] Whether Asian powers, especially India and PRC with their huge appetite for energy, could take up the slack and fulfil Myanmar's aspirations to become a major regional player in gas exports remains unclear at present.[70]

Notes

[1] See, for example, Tin Maung Maung Than, "Burma's Energy Use: Perils and Promises", in *Southeast Asian Affairs 1986* (Singapore: Institute of Southeast Asian Studies, 1986), p. 75. The venture failed to yield any economically viable results.

[2] See Energy Planning Department of the Ministry of Energy (EPD), http://www.energy.gov.mm.

[3] U Kyaw Nyein, "The Union of Myanmar Ministry of Energy", *Petromin* (January–February 2002), p. 9.

[4] *Myanmar Times*, 23–29 December 2002, p. 14. This estimate probably includes potential reserves in the onshore sedimentary basins (only three out of fourteen have been extensively explored) as well as the three offshore sedimentary basins. The amount of proven reserves (estimated at around 100 million barrels in the mid-1990s; see *Myanview* [April 1996], p. 8) may be much less.

[5] Industry sources, however, place recoverable offshore gas reserves at around 9–10 tcf (John Mueller, "Country File Myanmar", *Asian Oil & Gas* [November/December 2003], p. 11). The recoverable onshore gas reserves stood at around 1.1 tcf in the mid-1990s (*Myanview*, op. cit.) and there has been no evidence of new substantial onshore gas fields being discovered since then.

[6] The total constituted "possible" (142.9 million tons), "probable" (20.7 million tons), "potential" (9.9 million tons) and "proven" (4.6 million tons) categories, EPD, http://www.energy.gov.mm/MOM_1_2.htm.

[7] See EPD, http://www.energy.gov.mm/Nuclear_1_2.htm.

[8] See EPD, http://www.energy.gov.mm/Wind_1_2.htm.

[9] Government statistics maintained this figure as constant since the 1997/98 fiscal year though environmental NGOs (non-governmental organizations) claimed that continued illegal logging had further depleted the forests; see for example, Global Witness, "A Conflict of Interest — The Uncertain Future of Burma's Forests", October 2003.

[10] For computational assumptions, see Tin, op. cit., p. 71.

[11] For the basis of derivations, see ibid.

[12] See ibid.

[13] For details, see *Myanview*, op. cit., figure 1; and Tin, op. cit., pp. 72–73.

[14] They were: two in the 1980s, five in the nineties and one in 2001. See U Kyaw Nyein, op. cit., p. 9.

[15] For example, Myanmar reportedly imported 1.3 million metric tons of crude oil in 1999. See *EIU Country Report, Myanmar (Burma)*, February 2001, p. 22. The apparent discrepancy between the Myanmar and Malaysian data could be due to different classification regarding valuation of probable barter trade or some form of offsetting in some of the transactions.

[16] See U Kyaw Nyein, op. cit., pp. 10–11; and Kyaw Kyaw Aung, "International Companies and Myanmar: Oil and Natural Gas Drilling Projects", [in Myanmar language] *Living Color* (May 2002), p. 55.

[17] *New Light of Myanmar* [hereafter *NLM*], 5 September 2004.

[18] See, for example, Kyaw Thu, "Myanmar to Increase Oil Production", *Myanmar Times* (5–11 July 2004), p. 7. The 40,000 barrels/day figure is believed to be based on suppressed demand. Given that the supply of over 27,000 barrels/day in 1980 was barely enough and the real gross domestic product (GDP) has more than doubled while the number of motor vehicles has more than quadrupled in the following 25 years, the actual demand could be nearer to 60,000 barrels/day.

[19] For details, see *Myanview*, op. cit., figure 2; and Tin, op. cit., p. 73. The domestic pipeline network for natural gas stood at around 1,100 miles in early 2002 (see Kyaw Kyaw Aung, op. cit., p. 56).

[20] This was despite opposition by environmentalists and human rights activists who objected to the alleged ecological damage and human rights violations in laying the pipeline and constructing the associated infrastructure. In fact, UNOCAL recently settled out of court a lawsuit filed by 14 anonymous Myanmar villagers (citing the firm's alleged complicity in human rights abuses associated with the Yadana Project) after eight years of protracted litigation; Agence France-Presse (AFP), "Unocal Strikes Deal with Myanmar Villagers over Alleged Slave Labour Use", 13 December 2004. The project is operated by a consortium comprising TotalFinaElf (France; 31.24 per cent share); UNOCAL (United States; 28.2 per cent); PTTEP (Thailand; 25.5 per cent); and MOGE (Myanmar; 15 per cent). See, U Kyaw Nyein, op. cit., p. 12.

[21] After the leading partner Premier Oil of Britain relinquished its 26.66 per cent share of the Yetagun Project in September 2003, the state-owned Malaysian oil and gas company Petronas increased its share to 40.9 per cent, with both PTTEP and Nippon Oil (Japan) at 19.3 per cent, and MOGE at 20.5 per cent (*Living Color* [November 2003], p. 11).

[22] *NLM*, 16 January 2004.

[23] S. Mukherjee, "Myanmar: Cheers, Jeers over Giant Gas Find", *Asia Times Online*, 13 February 2004, http://www.atimes.com.

[24] *NLM*, 11 November 2004.

[25] Bangladesh, after playing hardball for months, agreed to cooperate after garnering promises from India to settle bilateral issues regarding hydroelectricity supply, trade imbalance and land transit. See, for example, S. Ramachandran, "India Finds Gas and Friends to the East", *Asia Times Online*, 20 January 2005.

[26] For details, see U Kyaw Nyein, op. cit., p. 11.

[27] *Financial Times*, 10 November 2003.

[28] *Kyodo News*, 8 August 2004.

[29] *Korea Herald*, 19 February 2004.

[30] Xinhua, 14 December 2004. Interestingly, Golden Aaron is a small nine-year old trading company with a paid-up capital of S$5 million and revenues of some S$40.7 million in the year 2000. One of the two shareholders is believed to be the son of one-time Golden Triangle drug kingpin Law Hsit Han, who was pardoned by the Myanmar government. See, for example, Bryan Lee, "Tiny S'pore Trading Firm Wins Myanmar Oil Deal", *Straits Times*, 8 December 2004.

31 For details, see Soe Myint, "Oil and Gas Supply, Processing and Refining in Myanmar", *ASEAN Energy Bulletin* (1st quarter 2002), p. 10.

32 Ibid.

33 These numbers do not include tens of thousands of unregistered passenger cars, light trucks and motorcycles smuggled across the Thai and Chinese borders over the last decade. See, for example, Zin Min and Myo Lwin, "Registration Begins for All Illegal Motorbikes", *Myanmar Times*, 12–18 April 2004, p. 5; and Kyaw Zwa Moe, "Dozens of Used Cars Smuggled into Burma Everyday", *Irrawaddy* (online), http://www.irrawaddy.org, 18 March 2004.

34 "Fuel Ration for Motor Vehicles", *Myanmar Times*, 16–22 February 2004, p. 10.

35 Although there were over 476,000 officially registered motor vehicles in 2004, the government claimed that there were over 940,000 vehicles running on gasoline and diesel fuel in Myanmar, *NLM* (online), 14 January 2005, http://www.myanmar.com.nlm.

36 See, for example, Tin, op. cit., Kerosene was the mainstay of urban household fuel and used extensively in rural areas for both light and heat. For example the consumption in 1977 was twice the production of some 48 million gallons ("Woodfuel Production and Marketing in Myanmar, National Workshop", Food and Agriculture Organization (FAO), Regional Wood Energy Development Programme in Asia (RWEDP) Report no. 56 (Bangkok: FAO, March 2001), p. 46.

37 As the free market prices of the subsidized gasoline fluctuated between five to eight times in recent years, a black market for those fuels (which has existed for decades) has become widespread in Myanmar despite frequent crackdown by the authorities.

38 "Myanmar to Produce Fuel Oil Substitute Gasohol", *Business Tank*, online, August 2004.

39 Coal imports in the last two decades were characterized by spurts of substantial volume in certain years with very low volumes in between. For example, the volume of imports throughout the 1980s stood at less than 1,000 tons while it stood at 62,000 and 71,000 tons respectively in fiscal years 1997/98 and 1998/99 followed by another peak of 51,000 tons in 2001/02 (Central Statistical Organization [CSO], Statistical *Yearbook* [Yangon: CSO], various issues).

40 See, for example, May Thandar Win, "Gas Cars Will Save 2.25 Million Gallons of Fuel, Says MOGE", *Myanmar Times*, 15–21 November 2004, p. 7. The first commercial CNG filling station in the capital was opened on 14 January 2005 and by the end of January 2005, five such stations had been commissioned throughout Myanmar. The price for 165 cubic feet of CNG (equivalent to one gallon of gasoline) was set at kyats 100, which was only 56 per cent of the corresponding price for gasoline (*NLM*, 30 January 2005). However, the capital cost could be relatively expensive varying from kyats 700,000 for a conversion kit to kyats tens of millions (up to 25 per cent of the car's market price) for a dedicated CNG engine.

41 See http://www.energy.com.gov.mm/Env_CDM.htm.

42 There is a de facto market for LPG supply for non-registered users as some registered clients sell off their quota at a premium over government rates.

43   See http://www.myanmar.com/Ministry/Electric-Power/moep/policy.html.

44   No plausible explanation could be found for those two outliers in the trend.

45   The price hike was ten times for high-end users in homes and industries. Government departments and public employees still enjoy substantial subsidies on meter rates. Though it was long overdue, the sudden hike caused consternation among consumers and the business community who had been used to getting cheap electricity. Affected SMEs' business costs suddenly escalated as well. See, for example, "Myanmar Reels under Huge Electricity Price Hike", AFP, 3 August 1999, http://www.afp.com/english/home/.

46   See, for example, Win Kyaw Oo, "More Inputs are Needed to Power a Hydro Future", *Myanmar Times*, 4–10 June 2001.

47   See, for example, Win Kyaw Oo, "Promising Power Sector Attracts Private Investment", in Review 2002, *Myanmar Times*, 23–29 December 2002, p. 14. Some enterprising businessmen and industrialists had also been selling electricity to the local community in the capital city's outskirts and in nearby outlying townships. See Yin Min Tun, "Media Roundup: Power Supply" in *Myanmar Times*, 2–8 February 2004, p. 6.

48   *NLM* online, 21 December 2002, and ibid., 23 August 2004.

49   Thein Lwin, "Myanmar Energy Plan up to 2020", *ASEAN Energy Bulletin* (First Quarter 2003), p. 12.

50   *Bangkok Post*, 26 August 2004.

51   See, for example, Tin, op. cit., pp. 86–87. Myanmar's forest cover which stood at around 57 per cent in 1960 (ibid.) was reduced to 50.9 per cent in 1989 (FAO-RWEDP Report no. 56, op. cit., p. 48) but given estimated depletion rates in the 1.4–1.8 per cent range during the 1986–95 period (Jake Brunner, et al. "Logging Burma's Frontier Forests: Resources and the Regime" [Washington, D.C., World Resource Institute, 1998], Table 2) it could have been down to a little over 40 per cent at the turn of the century, when widespread commercial logging concessions were officially curtailed.

52   See FAO-RWEDP Report no. 56, op. cit., p. 55. These estimates reportedly did not include the amount consumed by cottage industries such as brick kilns, potteries, tobacco, jaggery (solidified palm sugar syrup), and condensed milk, whose consumption remains largely unrecorded (see ibid., p. 42).

53   See ibid., p. 182.

54   See, for example, Kyi Maung and Khin Maung Nyunt, "Status and Prospects of Wood Energy in Myanmar", *Myanmar Forestry Journal* (July 2000), pp. 32, 33.

55   Ibid., p. 35; and RWEDP Report no. 56, op. cit., p. 190.

56   CSO, *Statistical Yearbook 2002*.

57   Kyi Maung and Khin Maung Nyunt, op. cit., p. 33.

58   Ibid., p. 34; and RWEDP Report no. 56, op. cit., p. 51.

59   Ibid., pp. 42, 49.

60   See CSO, *Selected Monthly Economic Indicators*, various issues from 1990 to 2004.

[61] See Tin, op. cit., p. 87; and the website at www.energy.gov.mm/MOF_1_2.htm.

[62] U Kyaw Nyein, op. cit., p. 13.

[63] In January 2003, China offered a US$200 million soft loan. See, for example, for details of the US$34.7 million project in "China, Myanmar Sign Contract on Power Transmission", *People's Daily* online, 10 October 2003, at http://english.peopledaily.com.cn/. All nine megawatt-scale hydropower projects completed before 2000 used Chinese equipment, together with another five plants with capacities ranging from 150 to 600 kilowatts, http://www.myanmar.com/build/electricity/0.htm.

[64] See, for example, Nyi Nyi Aung, "Golden Export Outlook for Natural Gas", *Myanmar Times*, 22–28 March 2004, p. 1; and Kyaw Thu, "Myanmar Biggest Gas Exporter in Asia, Says Minister", *Asia Times Online*, 29 November–5 December 2004, p. 7.

[65] See, for example, *Living Color* (in Myanmar language) (May 2004), p. 14; and Phar Kim Beng, "China Mulls Oil Pipeline in Myanmar, Thailand", *Asia Times* online, 23 September 2004.

[66] ESCAP/UNDP, "Sectoral Energy Demand in Myanmar" (New York: United Nations, 1992), pp. 19, 37.

[67] The ambitious CNG scheme with a potential of converting some 250,000 motor vehicles faces many challenges entailing substantial foreign exchange outlays for components of the conversion kits and supply infrastructure as well as lack of qualified workshops to service them. See, for example, May Thandar Win, "Challenges Ahead as Myanmar Aims for Gas-Powered Future", *Myanmar Times*, 27 September – 3 October 2004, p. 7.

[68] See, for example, Bruce Hawke, "How Much Does Rangoon Get from the Gas?", *Irrawaddy*, November 2004, p. 11.

[69] See, for example, Yuki Akimoto, "Hydro-powering the Regime", *Irrawaddy*, June 2004, pp. 8–12; and "Doing Business with Burma", International Confederation of Free Trade Unions (ICFTU) Report (Brussels: ICFTU, January 2005).

[70] See, for example,, "Myanmar's Upstream Sector hobbled by Pipeline Controversy and Poor R&D Results", *Oil & Gas Journal*, 26 June 2000, posted on the Internet newsgroup, soc.culture.burma, on 20 August 2000; and Mueller, op. cit., p. 13.

Philippines

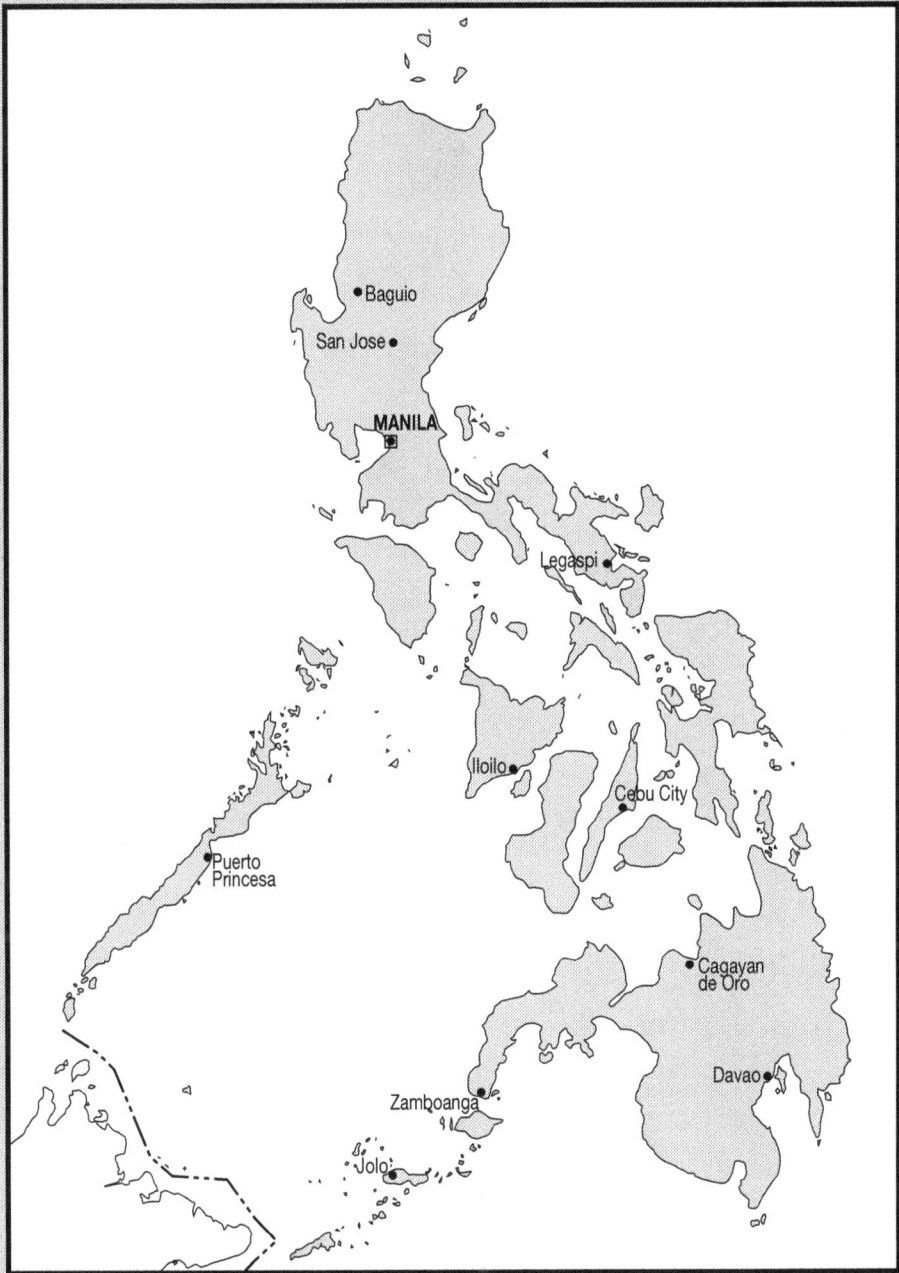

THE PHILIPPINES IN 2004
A Gathering Storm

Benjamin N Muego

For some 85 million Filipinos much of 2004 was spent either gearing up for the country's third presidential election in the post-martial law period or dealing with the election's aftermath amidst charges and counter-charges of "massive election fraud and irregularities", "widespread and systematic cheating", "blatant vote-buying", etc., and a "rigged" and highly controversial congressional vote count for president and vice-president,[1] reminiscent of the *dagdag/bawas* ("vote-padding/vote-shaving") scandal in the 1992 general elections narrowly won by General Fidel V. Ramos over Miriam Defensor-Santiago, who subsequently filed a formal protest with the presidential electoral tribunal, but to no avail.[2] Ironically, two *dagdag/bawas* victims of the 1992 general elections, Aquilino "Nene" Q. Pimentel, Jr., (LDP), and former Armed Forces of the Philippines (AFP) chief-of-staff Rodolfo G. Biazon (Lakas-KMP), both current members of the Philippine Senate, were among the principal players — although this time on opposite sides — in the highly controversial vote canvass.[3] In spite of a determined and valiant effort waged by a handful of opposition lawmakers in both legislative chambers (in the House of Representatives, the effort was spearheaded by rising opposition star Francis "Chiz" G. Escudero [NPC-Sorsogon] while Pimentel led the opposition to the "underhanded tactics" of the numerically dominant pro-administration lawmakers under the leadership of Francis "Kiko" N. Pangilinan, majority floor leader (Pangilinan replaced Loren Legarda-Leviste who left the Senate to join the slate of the Koalisyon ng Nagkakaisang Pilipino (KNP) as its vice-presidential candidate) and Senate president Franklin M. Drilon (LP). On 23 June 2004, Drilon and Jose De Venecia (Lakas), Speaker of the House of Representatives officially proclaimed Gloria Macapagal-

BENJAMIN N MUEGO is Professor of Political Science and Asian Studies, Bowling Green State University, Ohio, USA.

Arroyo and her running-mate, Noli L. De Castro as the "duly elected president and vice-president", of the Republic of the Philippines.

In spite of a formal election protest filed by Macapagal-Arroyo's principal rival, the late Fernando Poe, Jr., (or just plain "FPJ" to his legion of admirers and supporters) with the Presidential Electoral Tribunal and persistent rumours of an imminent EDSA-type uprising[4] by millions of loyal Poe supporters including a number of high-profile retired flag-level officers and active-duty military personnel, Macapagal-Arroyo was inaugurated as the country's fourth post-martial law era chief executive on 30 June 2004. Interestingly enough, Macapagal-Arroyo chose to take her oath of office in Cebu City, in the central Visayas, instead of in Manila, the nation's political and cultural capital. She was only the second post-martial law chief executive to do so.[5] Of course it was widely believed that Macapagal-Arroyo chose to have her swearing-in and inauguration in the Philippines' "Queen City", as a gesture of gratitude to Cebuano voters who gave her an incredible 90 per cent of the city's and province's votes, more than enough to catapult her past Poe who had held his own in strife-torn Mindanao (in spite of alleged widespread poll irregularities) and won handsomely in all of the main island of Luzon, except in Macapagal-Arroyo's home province of Pampanga and Las Pinas in Metro Manila, the bailiwick and political stronghold of congressional spouses Senator Manuel B. Villar, Jr. and Representative Cynthia Aguilar-Villar, both staunch Macapagal-Arroyo supporters.

As with the presidential elections of 1992 and 1998, respectively, when Ramos won the presidency with a measly 21 per cent of the total number of votes cast;[6] and conversely, in the 1998 general elections, when Estrada totally overwhelmed his principal opponent, Lakas standard bearer Jose de Venecia by over five million votes, pre-election skirmishing between and among the so-called "presidentiables"[7] and jockeying for front-runner status began — albeit on the sly and behind the scenes because of a constitutional provision which limits the duration of the election campaign to two months. It began on 30 December 2003, when Macapagal-Arroyo ostensibly took herself out of the running, by declaring that she wanted to "unite and heal the nation" (in the wake of Estrada's forced ouster on 21 January 2001and the deep divisions the latter event provoked) and focus her entire attention on "solving the country's economic problems".

Predictably, Macapagal-Arroyo's surprise and "statesman-like" declaration was greeted with scepticism by most Filipinos who had heard it all before and unlike Lyndon Johnson's Shermanesque declaration of ("… if nominated, I will not run and if elected I will not serve…") in 1968, Macapagal-Arroyo's pious pronouncement was viewed by most Filipinos as yet another ploy to divert public attention away from the Philippines' worsening economic and social problems. Of course, and as predicted by most knowledgeable political observers, Macapagal-Arroyo did later renege on her "I will not run" stance and pursued re-election with a vengeance.

Clearly, an unintended upshot of Macapagal-Arroyo's 30 December[8] surprise announcement was to trigger a spate of declarations of interest in the presidency by a motley assortment of presidentiables, including former senator and education secretary Raul S. Roco (Aksyon/Reporma), incumbent senator and former PNP (Philippine National Police) chief Panfilo M. Lacson (LDP), televangelist Eduardo "Brother Eddie" C. Villanueva of the Bangon Pilipinas Movement (Arise Philippines Movement). In the interim, opposition leaders like senator Edgardo J. Angara (LDP) and Vicente C. Sotto III (LDP) worked frenetically behind the scenes to persuade the late Fernando Poe, Jr., the king of Philippine movies, bosom friend of deposed president Estrada and like the latter, immensely popular with the *masa* (also called the *bakya* crowd in the literature),[9] to lead the "united" opposition as its standard bearer.

After vacillating for what must have seemed like an eternity, Angara, Sotto and other influential opposition leaders like former president Estrada, finally succeeded in persuading Poe to throw his proverbial hat into the ring and run for president. The late entry of Poe into the presidential race in what seemed to most observers tantamount to a draft may have, however, come at a heavy price, i.e., it cost the LDP and the coalition (Koalisyon ng Nagkakaisang Pilipino) the presidency[10] and led to the virtual breakup of the Laban ng Demokratikong Pilipino (LDP) itself, one of the first political parties to be established after the ouster of Ferdinand E. Marcos in 1986. The LDP faction associated with Angara and Sotto had Poe as its titular leader, until the latter's untimely death on 14 December 2004. The other LDP wing (also known as the Lacson wing) is nominally headed by senator Panfilo M. Lacson and two former opposition stalwarts in the House of Representatives, namely Carlos M. Padilla (LDP-Nueva Vizcaya) and Agapito "Butz" A. Aquino (LDP-Makati). In the end all attempts to bring Lacson and Poe together as running-mates in a truly united opposition failed. In a moving eulogy during Poe's funeral, Estrada — on a one-day furlough from his prison quarters in Tanay, Rizal, courtesy of the Macapagal-Arroyo government — openly lamented his "failure" to unite the opposition behind one candidate; that perhaps because he (Estrada) did "not try hard enough", Macapagal-Arroyo and most of her congressional candidates won and as a result, retained control of the executive and legislative branches of the government.

Political Dynasties and Term-Limits

Section 26 of Article II (Declaration of Principles and State Policies), of the 1987 Philippine Constitution provides, inter alia: "The State shall guarantee equal access to opportunities for public service and prohibit political dynasties as may be defined by law." Despite the foregoing prohibition against "political dynasties", however, the latter have not only been in full blossom since the ratification of the 1987 Constitution on 2 February 1987; new political dynasties have emerged all over the political landscape to replace old ones, and there is nothing in the horizon to suggest that this "anti-democratic" institution will disappear (for instance, self-serving calls by some politicians and their allies in the mass media for the break up of these institutions) any time soon. Perhaps a glimmer of hope that public tolerance for political dynasties that have often been linked to graft and corruption may be on the downslide was a highly publicized speech by former president Ramos three years ago in which he put the blame squarely on Congress for its reluctance or inability to enact the necessary enabling legislation to implement the Constitutional ban on political dynasties.

If the results of the last general elections are to serve as a gauge to the supposed decline of political dynasties, however, then the general public is in for a rude awakening. Not only are the old and established political dynasties, e.g., the Ortegas of La Union,[11] the Marcoses of Ilocos Norte,[12] the Josons of Nueva Ecija,[13] the Cuencos and Osmenas of Cebu,[14] the Aquinos/Cojuangcos of Tarlac and Metro Manila,[15] etc., still in business; they seem to have consolidated their power and influence even in certain areas where they did not have any kind of strong presence. By far, however, the most disturbing part of the trend is the emergence of new dynasties such as the Angaras of Aurora and Quezon,[16] the Barberses of Surigao del Norte,[17] the Garcias of Cebu,[18] the Macapagals of Pampanga.[19] Moreover, new political dynasties are emerging in Metro Manila and the suburbs as well, e.g., the Binays of Makati,[20] the Asistios of Caloocan,[21] and as mentioned earlier, the Villars/ Aguilars in Las Pinas.[22]

There are two basic and underlying reasons for the proliferation of political dynasties in the Philippines, e.g.: (1) the country's particularistic or parochial (cf. universalistic) political culture; and (2) the institution of term limits for all elected public officials from the president of the Philippines all the way down to the lowly *barangay* captain.[23] In a particularistic political culture such as that of the Philippines, nearly all political decisions are influenced, shaped, defined and driven by kinship ties, friendship and informal associations, etc., instead of by universal rules of fairness and fair-play, statutory law and where applicable, a written or unwritten constitution, as is usually the case in most Western and highly developed countries. If the people keep voting for political dynasts and their allies, it is usually because the people see their own destinies as intertwined and linked with that of the particular political dynasty in a dyadic, maybe even symbiotic, type of relationship.

There is little doubt that the institution of term-limits for all elected officials in the 1987 Philippine Constitution[24] has helped to promote the emergence, consolidation and proliferation of political dynasties throughout the country. A classic case study of how two members of the House of Representatives — where members are limited to three consecutive three-year terms for a maximum length of service of nine years — circumvented the term-limit rule with apparent impunity are those of Raul V. Del Mar of the 1st District of Cebu City and Eduardo R. Gullas of the 1st District of Cebu province. Because both were ineligible for a fourth consecutive term, Del Mar's son Raulito Del Mar and Gullas' younger brother Jose R. Gullas, ran in their place. The fact that neither relative had ever before run for, let alone held elective public office, did not seem to bother their constituents at all. Today, both Raul V. Del Mar and Eduardo R. Gullas are back in the 13th Congress and in all likelihood will remain in the House of Representatives until 2011, unless of course they choose to seek a seat in the Philippine Senate where the term-limit is two consecutive six-year terms (for a maximum of 12 years), before or after the completion of their current terms. There were several other former members of Congress who passed their congressional seats on to their children as if these were private property, e.g., Socorro Acosta of Bukidnon (to son Nereus); the late Maria Clara Lobregat of Zamboanga City (to son Celso); Thelma Almario of Davao Oriental (to son Mayo); and the list goes on.

The Philippine Senate is similarly dominated by members of old or new and emerging political dynasties. For example, twelve of the twenty-three current members of the Philippine Senate belong to or are parts of old or emerging political dynasties. Four incumbent senators who are second or third-generation dynasts are: Mar Roxas, Sergio R. Osmena III, Ramon B. Magsaysay, Jr., Ralph G. Recto and newcomer Ma. Ana Consuelo "Jamby" Abad Santos Madrigal. Senator Roxas, who received the highest number of popular votes in the 10 May 2004 election is the grandson of Manuel A. Roxas, first president of the Second Philippine Republic (1946–73) and son of one-time Senate president Gerardo Roxas while Sergio R. Osmena III, is the grandson of Sergio Osmena, Sr., former president of the Philippine Commonwealth and son of Sergio Osmena, Jr., who served multiple terms as mayor of Cebu City and in 1969, ran against and lost, to Ferdinand E. Marcos.

Ramon Magsaysay, Jr., is the only son of the late president Ramon F. Magsaysay and nephew of Genaro F. Magsaysay who served in the Philippine Senate before martial law and was Sergio Osmena, Jr.'s running mate in the 1969 presidential election; Recto is the grandson of the great nationalist, Senator Claro M. Recto and the husband of former movie star Vilma Santos, mayor of Lipa City in Batangas, the Rectos' home province. Finally, the freshman senator and surprise winner in the May 10 election, "Jamby" Madrigal is the granddaughter of the national hero and martyr Jose Abad Santos, former chief justice of the Supreme Court and Vicente Madrigal who served in the Philippine Senate in the 1950s as did her aunt, Pacita Madrigal-Gonzales, who also headed the now-defunct Social Welfare Administration during Magsaysay's presidency.

Among the new and emerging dynasts are: Jose "Jinggoy" Estrada, Luisa "Loi" Estrada (Jinggoy's mother and wife of deposed president Joseph Estrada), the first mother and son tandem ever, to serve in Congress simultaneously, even as another brother, "JV" is mayor of San Juan, Jinggoy's and patriarch Joseph's old job. Juan Ponce Enrile's son Jack is a member of the House of Representatives from Cagayan; so too is Rodolfo G. Biazon's son Rossano. Edgardo J. Angara's younger sister Bellaflor Angara-Castillo served three terms in the House but because of term limits, had to step aside in favour of Angara's son who now represents his aunt's old congressional district in Aurora (Bellaflor is Aurora's new governor).

Senator Pia Cayetano, the eldest daughter of the late senator Rene Cayetano who died in office before the end of his term, has a younger brother, Peter Alan, who is a member of the House; and so too does senator Richard Gordon, whose brother James, Jr., and spouse Katherine, represented the 2nd District of Zambales in the 11th and 12th Congress, respectively. Even newly-elected senators Jess Lapid and Ramon "Bong" Revilla, Jr., both former movie actors, are parts of emerging dynasties as well. (Lapid's son Lito is the new governor of Pampanga, the home province of Macapagal-Arroyo, while Revilla's father and namesake served in the Senate in the 11th and 12th Congress until rendered ineligible for reelection, by term-limits). Finally, there is Manuel A. Villar, a potential presidentiable, whose spouse Cynthia, as mentioned earlier, is a member of the House of Representatives (she took over her husband's old seat after the latter was elevated to the Senate) while another Aguilar sibling is mayor of Las Pinas, the only city in Metro Manila carried by Macapagal-Arroyo.

The House of Representatives is similarly structured, i.e., with more than half of its current membership descended from the old political elite; former members of Congress whose political lineage and pedigree go all the way back to the Philippine Commonwealth (1935–45) and the early years of the Second Philippine Republic.

While some political dynasties have virtually disappeared from the political landscape by attrition, e.g., the Laurel family of Batangas, which dominated Philippine politics for nearly four decades beginning in the 1950s (indeed, the patriarch of the Laurel clan, Jose P. Laurel, Sr., was war-time president and former Supreme Court justice). The elder Laurel also served in the Philippine Senate as did two of his sons, e.g., Sotero and Salvador (in addition, the latter served as Corazon Cojuangco-Aquino's vice-president from 1986 through 1992). Another Laurel son, Jose B. Laurel, Jr., was Speaker of the House of Representatives in the 1950s and 1960s, but withdrew from the political scene after losing to Diosdado P. Macapagal (Gloria Macapagal-Arroyo's father) in a bid for the vice-presidency. The death of Salvador H. Laurel in the United States two years ago has all but ended the Laurel political dynasty since no third- or fourth-generation Laurels have yet indicated an inclination to follow in their great grandfather's footsteps.

Graft and Corruption

Ironically, there is little, if any, disagreement even between and among sworn political enemies about the extent of corruption in the Philippines and how this is sapping the country's scarce resources; and how pervasive "graft and corruption" has become and how the latter has impeded and continues to be an obstacle to modernization and economic development. Separate reports by two anti-corruption watchdog groups, one (i.e., Transparency International) based in Germany and the other (i.e., Political and Economic Risk Consultancy, Ltd., PERC) based in Hong Kong identified the Philippines as one of the most corrupt countries in Asia.[25] If there is any disagreement, it usually centres on who is responsible for what some commentators — foreign and Filipino — refer to variously as the country's "culture of corruption", "corrupt way of life", or "corrupt mindset" that appears to permeate every level of activity in both the private and public domains.

Some historians blame Spain and the heritage she left behind after being forced to cede her colony of more than 355 years to the United States in December 1898. Indeed, those who hold this point of view like to call attention to uncanny similarities between the Philippine "way of doing things" and those of former Spanish colonies in the western hemisphere, e.g., Mexico, the Antilles (Cuba, Puerto Rico and the Dominican Republic), Central America (El Salvador, Guatemala, Honduras, Nicaragua and Panama) and South America (all countries in the continent except Brazil, Suriname and Guyana). Like the Philippines, these former colonies are also underdeveloped and mired in poverty; wealth is so unevenly distributed that, while a very small number of people live in the lap of luxury, the overwhelming majority of the population — as much as 85–95 per cent according to some sources — must struggle daily in search of basic necessities. On the other hand, there are those who suggest that Filipinos only have themselves to blame; that graft and corruption is such a vicious cycle, it poisons both the bribe-giver as well as the bribe-taker and when corruption becomes endemic, it truly becomes "a way of life", "an integral part of doing business".

From the beginning of 2004 to the present, the Philippine print and broadcast media have headlined story after story of various public officials who were under investigation by legislative bodies like the Senate Blue Ribbon Committee or some other watchdog group, for "unexplained wealth", usually after a lifestyle-check or some such way of monitoring the conduct of public officials suspected of living beyond their means. Some of the more spectacular exposés involved officials at graft-prone governmental agencies such as the Bureau of Internal Review, Bureau of Customs and the Department of Public Works and Highways, to name just three. There were even inquiries by legislative committees like the Senate Banking Committee into alleged corrupt practices such as money-laundering, extortion, bribery, etc., involving Macapagal-Arroyo's spouse — the "First Gentleman", as the latter is often referred to in the press — after a series of exposes by Senator Lacson, former chief of the Philippine National Police and an old Arroyo nemesis. Then there was the equally spectacular investigation of Code-NGO, a non-governmental organization administered by the sister of former Finance Secretary Isidro Camacho. According to the original exposé, which led to the protracted investigation referred to earlier, Code-NGO allegedly stood to make billions of pesos in profits, without investing a single centavo of their own funds in the venture.

However, like other high-profile investigations in the past, e.g., the highly controversial PEA-Amari land deal, the south Luzon Coastal highway scandal, the scandal surrounding the commemoration of the nation's centenary, the IMPSA payoff scandal (most of which transpired during the presidency of Fidel V. Ramos), recent Senate investigations tend to fade away from the public's collective consciousness. Perhaps this is one of the principal reasons why graft and corruption persists, i.e., that perpetrators — those who have *abilidad* or gall — somehow get away with it; the general perception is that after the initial excitement surrounding a particular investigation has waned the highly-touted resolve to end graft and corruption seems to dissipate as well. Perhaps the maverick pro-administration senator Miriam Defensor-Santiago captured the essence of what is wrong with the Philippines in a recent speech at Trinity College in Quezon City, when she intoned in her rather tortured syntax: "We Filipinos have known for a long time that this country is one of the most corrupt in Asia, possibly the world. It is one of the reasons every year, millions of our people, mostly fresh college graduates, leave for abroad to become overseas Filipino workers (OFWs)".[26]

Even the armed forces have not been spared from allegations of graft and corruption. Perhaps one of the most egregious accusations against ranking AFP officers so far was the one levelled by Gracia Burnham, the widow of Martin Burnham, in a recent book entitled *In the Presence of My Enemies*, a poignant and riveting account of the missionary couple's nearly two-year ordeal in the hands of the Abu Sayaff Group (unfortunately, Martin was killed during the rescue attempt; Gracia, although injured, survived). In a session with Philippine government investigators who travelled to Kansas to obtain her sworn testimony, Gracia accused AFP officers — including certain field-grade and flag-level commissioned officers — tasked with the Burnhams' recovery, skimmed some US$3 million off the US$5 million raised from donors (supposedly including the U.S. government) by the Burnhams' church in Topeka, Kansas, to secure their freedom.

The AFP was also the focal point of various legislative inquiries in late 2004 and early 2005 after certain AFP top brass were implicated in corrupt practices such as frequent overseas trips at the government's expense; demanding kickbacks from prospective vendors before the actual contracts were signed and awarded; rigging bids to favour certain suppliers and vendors; and embezzlement of funds ear-marked for retirement and dependent benefits. The prevalence of graft and corruption within the AFP is reportedly so widespread that the mid-level officers who called themselves the Magdalo and staged an abortive coup on 26 July 2003, cited specific examples of alleged corruption, involving top echelon AFP leaders in some cases, as justification for their failed mutiny. So far, however, only one flag-level officer, recently-retired Major General Carlos Garcia, former AFP Comptroller-General, has been formally charged under the Uniform Code of Military Justice and applicable criminal laws, and is currently undergoing court martial proceedings at Camp Emilio F. Aguinaldo, the AFP headquarters (Garcia also faces similar charges before the Sandiganbayan, a legislative court specifically created to hear cases filed by the Ombudsman against erring public officials). General Garcia is accused of, among other things, salting away huge sums of money in both dollar and peso accounts in various local and overseas banks as well as for acquiring millions of pesos worth of assets in the form of expensive cars, jewellery and choice property.

The Economy and Regime Change

The Philippine economy has been in the doldrums for the last several years, with unemployment hitting 10.9 per cent in 2004 and more than 50 per cent of the population living below the "poverty line", currently calculated at 12,267 pesos (approximately US$223 at prevailing exchange rates).[27] Add the skyrocketing cost of fuel and basic necessities and a population growth rate estimated at 2.34 per cent annually — the highest in Asia — spiralling out of control and one is confronted with all the usual indicators of trouble ahead; a gathering storm, as it were. So far, the Macapagal-Arroyo government has proposed two possible remedies to the country's severe economic and social problems: to enact legislation raising the value-added tax[28] (VAT) from 10 to 12 per cent predicted to yield at least 174 billion pesos in new revenues; and increase foreign borrowings. Some experts suggest that in order to stay afloat, the Philippines would have to borrow at least US$3 billion in 2005 alone, to help cushion the impact of the expected revenue shortfall, service the country's massive local and foreign debt, fund the deficit and support the operations of moribund government-owned corporations like the National Power Corporation.

It may not be as easy to borrow more money from the IMF/World Bank or other major private lending institutions in G-7 countries. For one thing, the Philippines' credit rating has been downgraded by Standard & Poor from BB+ to BB (this would make the cost of borrowing money a lot more expensive than it is now). Reacting to the downgrade, Malacanang Palace spokesman Ignacio Bunye suggested that the public should not give too much credence on credit reports, such as that of Standard & Poor's, vis-à-vis the credibility of the Philippines as a borrower, especially reports that emanate from overseas and prepared by research analysts who have "never set foot in the Philippines and are probably working with old and unreliable" data. Even highly developed and wealthy countries like the United States, Bunye pointed out, are reeling from the high cost of fuel; it is, therefore, not surprising to see that the negative impact of the current oil crunch on the economies of small and poor countries like the Philippines, is far greater especially in sectors or industries that require large quantities of fuel (gasoline or diesel) such as agriculture, transportation, manufacturing and the conventional generation of electrical power.

Another major problem facing the Philippines is the sensitive and volatile population issue (the Philippines leads all of Asia in population growth). Indeed, according to the Philippine National Statistical Coordination Board (NSCB), the country's aggregate population count currently estimated at 85 million, is expected to reach more than 93 million in 2010, less than five years away.[29] The economic, political and social implications of such a projected population increase is simply staggering, especially if put in the context of actuarial, demographic and scientific projections done in the 1960s, which concluded that given its resource base, the "carrying capacity" of the Philippines is around 80 million people. If the latter estimate of the country's carrying capacity is on target, the Philippines has already exceeded it by at least five million. Undoubtedly, the unchanging position of the Catholic Church on the issue of artificial contraception and family planning — 84 per cent of Filipinos identify themselves as Roman Catholic — is the single most important factor behind the Philippines' runaway population growth. The local clergy and the Catholic Bishops Conference of the Philippines (CBCP) — the principal governing body of the Catholic clergy and laity — have opted to adhere closely to the Vatican position on artificial contraception and family planning, two important and related questions, and there are no indications to suggest that this is about to change soon. Quite the contrary, the ascendancy of Ricardo Cardinal Vidal, an arch-conservative vis-à-vis the role of the church and clergy on secular matters, as the new leader of the country's 75 million Catholic faithful is more likely to move the church farther to the right.

Predictably perhaps, the Philippines' severe economic problems and as pointed out earlier, rampant "graft and corruption" at all levels of government has fuelled new speculations on the possibility of another EDSA-type uprising in the near future. In order for these speculations to materialize, the anti-regime forces must win the support of the AFP and the PNP. The defection of one or both of these organizations from the Macapagal-Arroyo camp to the anti-regime side could — as it did in the case of Marcos and Estrada — seal Macapagal-Arroyo's fate and that of her regime. Perhaps this is one of the reasons why Macapagal-Arroyo has been extra cautious in appointing individuals to leadership positions in the AFP and PNP, making sure that her appointees, e.g., AFP Chief of Staff General Efren Abu and PNP Chief Arturo Lomibao, are Macapagal-Arroyo loyalists; men she could count on. According to Macapagal-Arroyo's critics, the same rationale underlies the appointment of recently-retired high-ranking AFP officers to key positions in government, e.g., General Angelo Reyes, former AFP chief of staff and defence chief, whose defection to the Macapagal-Arroyo camp in January 2001 proved to be the coup d'grace that toppled Estrada (Interior and Local Government); General Leandro Mendoza (Transportation and later, Public Works); and General Eduardo Ermita (Executive Secretary).

While Macapagal-Arroyo and her official spokesmen publicly downplay persistent coup d'etat rumours, her private behaviour seems to suggest the contrary, as evidenced by, among other things, her ordering the revival — supposedly on the recommendation of General Abu — of a special anti-coup unit within the AFP high command charged with the collection of actionable intelligence on the activities of recently retired and active-duty officers suspected of harbouring anti-regime sentiments. Speculation about the probability of a possible EDSA-type political event were recently fuelled by two separate and well-publicized speeches[30] by retired general Jose Almonte, a known Ramos alter-ego and confidante, in which he (Almonte) railed against what he described as the "revolving door policy" of rewarding recently-retired high ranking military men (e.g., former AFP chiefs General Narciso Abaya, General Roy Cimatu, General Benjamin Defensor and General Diomedio Villanueva), most of whom served as AFP chief of staff for a year or less, with high-paying jobs. This revolving door policy, according to Almonte, leads to corruption and a "corrupt and mismanaged society" and could lead to another popular uprising similar to EDSA Uno and EDSA Dos.

Foreign Relations

Philippine foreign policy is anchored on two basic tenets: (1) respect for international law and the law of nations; and (2) the renunciation of war as an instrument of national policy. As one of 50 UN charter members, the Philippines considers its membership in the world body as its most important international affiliation. Parenthetically, as one of the founding members of the Association of Southeast Asian Nations (ASEAN), the Philippines is understandably proud of her leadership role in the latter organization. Indeed, some commentators who write about political and security issues in Southeast Asia point to the membership of both Malaysia and the Philippines in ASEAN as one of the factors that has kept the two nations from actually coming to blows over the 41-year old Sabah dispute. In other words, both the Philippines and Malaysia believe that putting ASEAN unity and solidarity in jeopardy is too high a price to pay for the resolution of their territorial dispute.

Despite the fact that she has been independent from the United States for nearly 60 years, the United States remains as the Philippines' closest military and political ally as well her principal trading partner. Not surprisingly, therefore, the issue of Filipino-American relations invariably intrudes into the political arena and has been a staple of Philippine electoral politics for several decades. Of late, however, some minor strains in the relationship have come to the fore, two of which are related to the ongoing war in Iraq and the other, about whether or not American troops who have been helping train Filipino soldiers to fight the Abu Sayaff Group and Jemaah Islamiyah, two "terrorist" groups with supposed ties to Osama bin Laden and Al-Qaeda could get involved in direct combat if attacked by the enemy. The rift grew out of a disagreement between Washington and Manila over whether or not to negotiate with "terrorists" in connection with efforts to secure the freedom of Angelo de la Cruz, a Filipino truck driver employed by a subsidiary of Haliburton, taken hostage by Iraqi insurgents and threatened with decapitation unless the Philippine government acceded to the hostage-takers' demands. In spite of strong U.S. pressure on the Philippine government not to negotiate with "terrorists", the Macapagal-Arroyo government did not only negotiate with the former to secure de la Cruz' release (by supposedly paying an undetermined amount of cash to the hostage-takers); she also complied with the key Iraqi insurgent demand that all Filipino troops in the war-torn country be withdrawn.

The controversy on whether or not the U.S.-Philippine Visiting Forces Agreement (VFA) authorized American soldiers to engage in direct combat while helping train Filipino soldiers in the field, in conjunction with Balikatan, the joint U.S.-Philippine military exercise, became a non-issue after the United States backed off its original stance, and acceded to the Philippine position. The Macapagal-Arroyo government also took exception to the findings and conclusions of the most recent State Department's "Country Economic Review Report",[31] which scored the Macapagal-Arroyo government for its "failure to reform high-level corruption in her administration and the judiciary".[32] The same report noted that in "recent successive surveys ... Filipinos have judged [the 10 May 2004 elections] as having been riddled with massive fraud ... which has cast doubts on Mrs. Arroyo's legitimacy as a contributory factor in foreign investors' lack of interest in doing business in the Philippines."[33] Comments made by departing U.S. Ambassador Francis J. Ricciardone and fresh State Department traveller's advisories warning American citizens about the supposed dangers and hazards of travelling to the Philippines has exacerbated the situation.

Observations and Prognosis

The Philippines in the coming year faces major problems that could spell trouble for the country in general and for the Macapagal-Arroyo government in particular. Some of these problems — rampant graft and corruption, abject poverty, double-digit unemployment, political instability, huge budgetary deficits, heavy domestic and foreign borrowings and two parallel insurgencies — are endogenous or internal to the Philippines. The other problems, on the other hand, such as the spiralling cost of oil (like most developing countries and highly industrialized nations like Japan, the Philippines is almost totally dependent on foreign oil for its fuel needs), the devaluation of the peso by over 100 per cent during the last 15 years alone and capital flight, etc., are exogenous factors beyond the Philippines' control. And as if all that was not enough, there were natural calamities such as the disastrous floods that ravaged the southern Tagalog region — especially in the twin provinces of Aurora and Quezon — which exacted a heavy toll on human life, and wiped out entire rice crops and other precious agricultural and fishery resources, the lifeblood of the region's economy.

Most experts agree that Gloria Macapagal-Arroyo and her administration — whose legitimacy is questionable — currently stands on rather precarious and shaky ground, as evidenced by, among other things, poll numbers that appear to be on a free fall, especially during the last six months. According to the latest internal poll (March 2005), ironically commissioned by Malacanang Palace itself, Macapagal-Arroyo's approval ratings even in supposed Macapagal-Arroyo bailiwicks such as Central Luzon (Region 3), Western Visayas (Region 6) and Central Visayas (Region 7) have plunged.[34] For example, Macapagal-Arroyo's poll numbers in Region 3 (Bataan, Pampanga, Nueva Ecija, Tarlac and Zambales), her "home region", plunged from 38 per cent in May-June 2004 to just 22 per cent in January 2005. For Region 6 (Aklan, Antique, Capiz, Guimaras, Iloilo and Negros Occidental), the drop in Macapagal-Arroyo's approval ratings has been just as precipitous, i.e., from 59 per cent in May–June 2004 to only 24 per cent in January 2005. Finally, in Region 7 (Bohol, Cebu, Negros Oriental and Siquijor) the geographical region that arguably delivered the presidency to Macapagal-Arroyo, her poll numbers in January 2005 had slipped down to 49 per cent, as compared to an impressive 72 per cent in May–June 2004.

By far, however, the Macapagal-Arroyo administration's apparent Achilles heel is the public perception that she has not done anything of substance to put an end to graft and corruption. Even worse, for Macapagal-Arroyo from a personal standpoint, is the public perception that her own family members are either themselves involved in illegal activities or are the "brains" behind a wide range of corrupt and illegal activities. Astute observers of Philippine politics suggest that a regime is in potential trouble when even the so-called "untouchables", i.e., presidential kin and "cronies" become the subject of tasteless coffee-shop jokes and text messages (the Philippines has the dubious distinction of being the "texting capital" of Asia). In a recent opinion piece for the *Philippines Daily Inquirer*, Conrado de Quiros, one of the country's most perceptive social commentators, wrote about a text message left on his cell-phone lamenting the fact that the Philippines came in second in the latest PERC report on corruption in Asia (Indonesia was tagged as "most corrupt"). According to de Quiros, the caller suggested that the Philippines should have been identified as the "most corrupt" nation in Asia because the Philippines ought to be "second to none". The text message was signed by "Jose Pidal", the alias supposedly used by the "First Gentleman" in local and overseas bank accounts where large sums of laundered or ill-gotten money were allegedly deposited.

The survival or demise of the Macapagal-Arroyo government hinges on three factors: (1) continued support of the officer corps and rank and file of the AFP and the PNP; (2) continued support of the United States; and (3) continued support of the Catholic Bishops Conference of the Philippines, the de facto ruling body of the Philippine Catholic Church. Through carefully-rationed and selective appointments in the AFP's and PNP's senior leadership, i.e., of the six AFP chiefs (including the current AFP chief of staff, General Efren Abu) appointed by Macapagal-Arroyo so far, only General Narciso Abaya and General Diomedio Villanueva served for a year or more; the other three former AFP chiefs of staff — General Dionisio Santiago, General Benjamin Defensor and General Roy Cimatu — all served for less than a year. Not surprisingly, all recently retired chiefs of staff have been appointed to high-paying civilian jobs, presumably in an effort to gain their loyalty. If Macapagal-Arroyo has any "problems" with the AFP it might well come from the ranks of junior and mid-level officers (such as the Magdalo group undergoing court martial proceedings in Camp Emilio F. Aguinaldo) and the AFP rank and file. It is not certain whether or not the service chiefs or field-grade commanders could rein in their troops if and when the latter decides to intervene and take matters into their own hands.

While George W. Bush and Gloria Macapagal-Arroyo both claim that their "personal friendship" (the two leaders met briefly in Santiago, Chile, during a break in the last APEC summit held there) remains strong and that Philippine-American relations in general, remains "as close as ever", there are tell-tale signs that seems to suggest the opposite. It is no secret, for example, that official Washington took a dim view of the Macapagal-Arroyo government's decision to negotiate with "terrorists" and even worse, pay an undetermined amount of ransom money to secure the release of Angelo de la Cruz. On the flip side, Gloria Macapagal-Arroyo took umbrage at the U.S. State Department finding of serious human rights violations by the Philippine military and police vis-à-vis the treatment of suspected communist and jihadist cadres and sympathizers. The Macapagal-Arroyo government has also expressed its displeasure with recent travellers' advisories issued by the consular section of the U.S. State Department warning Americans travelling to the Philippines that because of widespread and rampant corruption, law enforcement and the Philippine judicial system are unreliable.

While arguably the Philippine Catholic Church may have lost some of its lustre and political clout, as evidenced by, among other things, the back-to-back election victories of Senator Juan Flavier, in spite of an all-out effort by the Catholic clergy and laity to ensure the latter's defeat,[35] the Catholic Church is still a powerful force to reckon with. After all, it was the hierarchy of the Catholic Church and hundreds of thousands of Catholic faithful — summoned to the EDSA Shrine by the now "retired" Jaime Cardinal Sin — who were primarily responsible for causing the ouster of two popularly-elected presidents (Ferdinand E. Marcos and Joseph E. Estrada) and installing in their stead two devout *colegialas* (i.e., "convent girls"), Corazon Cojuangco-Aquino and Gloria Macapagal-Arroyo, in that order. Should the new spiritual leader of the Philippines' 75 million Catholics, his Eminence Ricardo Cardinal Vidal, withdraw his support for the Macapagal-Arroyo government and other influential religious groups like the Iglesia ni Kristo, a politically-monolithic organization and El Shaddai, a large charismatic religious group follow suit, the Macapagal-Arroyo government might very well find itself in serious jeopardy. In case there are any doubts about the ability of the Catholic Church to influence political outcomes, one needs only to look at the reluctance of Filipino politicians — regardless of party affiliation — to introduce or support legislation on subjects such as absolute divorce or divorce *matrimonii advinculi* ("limited divorce" or divorce *mensa et thoro*), abortion, artificial birth control or contraception and government-sponsored family planning, defined and designated by the church hierarchy as taboo.

Notes

[1]   The 12th Congress voted overwhelmingly to delegate the authority for the actual canvassing of votes for president and vice-president to an administration-dominated bicameral and "bipartisan" committee, over and above the objections of the minority, who argued among other things, that the 1987 Constitution specifically vests the power to canvass votes and proclaim a winner on the entire Congress convened in joint session, not to a committee thereof. The question was rendered academic by a Supreme Court ruling which held that Congress has the power and authority to adopt and enforce its own rules of procedure.

[2]   Miriam Defensor-Santiago's electoral protest against General Fidel V. Ramos was dismissed on a "technicality", after she ran for and won a seat in the Philippine Senate.

[3]   Rodolfo G. Biazon abandoned his former party, the Laban ng Demokratikong Pilipino (LDP) and ran with Macapagal-Arroyo (Lakas-KMP), supposedly as a quid pro quo for Lakas giving way to Biazon's son Rossano, who ran for and won Muntinlupa's congressional seat.

⁴   The first "People Power" uprising that sent Ferdinand E. Marcos into exile in February 1986 is called EDSA Uno; the second "People Power" event that toppled Joseph E. Estrada in January 2001 is called EDSA Dos.

⁵   Joseph "Erap" Ejercito Estrada, the third president of the Republic of the Philippines in the post-martial law period, had his inauguration and oath-taking at the Barasoin Church in Malolos, Bulacan, where Emilio Aguinaldo y Famy, the first president of the republic, proclaimed independence from Spain on 12 June 1898.

⁶   Current Philippine election law provides that in a plural field (i.e., where there are several "serious" candidates) the candidate who polls the highest number of votes (plurality), e.g., in the 1992 general elections, "winner" Fidel V. Ramos polled only 21 per cent of the votes. There is no provision for any kind of run-off election to determine the winner if no candidate polls a majority of the votes cast.

⁷   An apparently unique neologism coined by the print media to refer to anyone who has presidential ambitions.

⁸   Rizal Day is a national holiday in honour of the Philippines' foremost national hero, Jose P. Rizal.

⁹   The *masa* or *bakya* crowd are the poor and unshod, reminiscent of Juan and Evita Peron's *descamisados* and *campesinos*, who constitute the bulk of the Philippine population.

¹⁰ In fact if one adds Poe's vote total of 11,782,232 to that of Lacson's 3,510,000 — assuming of course that the majority of those who voted for the latter would have voted for Poe instead – the Koalisyon ng Nagkakaisang Pilipino (KNP) standard bearer would have out-polled Macapagal-Arroyo by as much as 2,386,424 votes. Be that as it all may, Poe's camp was absolutely convinced that but for the "massive cheating", etc., by Macapagal-Arroyo, their candidate would have won the election by as much as 600,000 votes.

¹¹ The Ortega family of San Fernando, La Union (in the northern Luzon region), is a classic study in what a "political dynasty" is all about. In nearly 60 years, no one other than an Ortega has been elected to represent La Union's first district (a congressional district that stretches northwards from San Fernando, the provincial capital, all the way to the border with Ilocos Sur).

¹² In Ilocos Norte, meanwhile, the children of the late Ferdinand Marcos, e.g., Imelda "Imee" Marcos and Ferdinand "Bong-Bong" Marcos, Jr., have entrenched themselves as their late father's successors and are keeping the Marcos dynasty alive. Because of term-limits, Bong-Bong is now serving his final term as the province's governor even as Imee is also on her final term as one of Ilocos Norte's two congresspersons in the Philippine House of Representatives.

¹³ The Joson family of Nueva Ecija has controlled the politics of that province for nearly 40 years. The current governor of the province, Tomas Joson, is a third generation Joson. In the 1998 and 2004 presidential elections, the Joson political clan was primarily

responsible for giving Joseph E. Estrada and Fernando Poe, Jr., respectively, decisive and resounding victories in Nueva Ecija.

[14] The Osmena family of Cebu City has dominated Cebu City and Cebu provincial politics for well over three generations. The late Don Sergio Osmena, Sr., served as vice-president of the Philippine Commonwealth and then succeeded to the presidency after the death of president Manuel Luis Quezon before the end of World War II. In recent times, all key positions in Cebu — that of provincial governor, mayor of Cebu City and senator, were all held simultaneously by Don Sergio's grandchildren. The Cuenco family, also of Cebu City is just as prominent and legendary. The family patriarch, Don Mariano Jesus L. Cuenco served in the Philippine Senate before martial law and was president of the upper chamber from 1949–51; today Antonio V. Cuenco, represents the 2nd District of Cebu City in the Philippine Congress.

[15] The Cojuangcos trace their political roots to the first decade of American rule; Corazon Cojuangco-Aquino's maternal grandfather was Juan Sumulong, leader of the opposition Partido Democrata Nacional during the Commonwealth period while her father served in the Commonwealth legislature. President Aquino's older brother Jose "Peping" Cojuangco served several terms in the House of Representatives before martial law as well as after martial law. The other half of the Cojuangco clan, led by Eduardo Cojuangco, former governor of Tarlac and presidential contender is just as politically well entrenched. Now, third generation Aquinos and Cojuangcos serve in the House of Representatives.

[16] The Angaras of Aurora and Quezon (the former province of Tayabas in the southern Tagalog region) is a fast-rising dynasty; Edgardo Angara, has served in the Senate for nearly 18 years now, including a stint as Senate president.

[17] The Barbers family of Surigao del Norte is a new and emerging political dynasty. Until his narrow defeat by Rodolfo G. Biazon in the last election, patriarch Robert "Bobby" Z. Barbers of the fledgeling dynasty served one term in the House of Representatives and one term in the Philippine Senate. In between, the elder Barbers served in Fidel V. Ramos' cabinet as Secretary of the Department of Interior and Local Government (DILG). Barbers' son "Ace" is now on his second term in the House of Representatives — representing his father's old congressional district — even as another son, Lyndon, is governor of Surigao Del Norte. A third Barbers offspring was until recently a member of the Makati city council (he currently holds a sub-cabinet position in the Macapagal-Arroyo administration).

[18] Former representative and provincial governor Pablo Garcia, Sr., was succeeded by his daughter Gwendolyn Garcia, Cebu's current governor; while son Winston is head of the giant Government Service Insurance System (GSIS). Another Garcia kin — Alvin Garcia — is former vice-mayor and mayor of Cebu City (he lost to Tommy Osmena in the May 10, 2004, elections).

[19] Gloria Macapagal-Arroyo is the daughter of President Diosdado P. Macapagal (1961–

65). Now Macapagal-Arroyo's son Mickey is a first-term member of the House of Representatives after serving a stint as lieutenant governor of the Macapagals' home-province of Pampanga.

20   The Binays of Makati are an emerging political dynasty. The head of this new political dynasty is Jejomar "Jojo" Binay, a former civil rights lawyer with strong ties to the Aquinos. After sitting out one term — because of term limits — Binay is once again mayor of Makati, the country's business and financial centre.

21   The Asistio family has dominated Caloocan politics — except for an 8–10 year hiatus when a rival family, the Malonzos, took over — for the last 35–40 years or more. Today, the Asistios are back in power, in the person of Luis "Baby" Asistio, who represents Caloocan in the House of Representatives.

22   Manuel A. Villar, former speaker of the House of Representatives, real estate magnate and a putative "presidentiable" married into the powerful Aguilar family of Las Pinas, that has run the city for the last decade and a half.

23   *Barangay* is the lowest-level administrative unit in the Philippines' scheme of provincial and local government (replaced the old "barrio").

24   See Article VI and XVIII of the 1987 Constitution.

25   According to an editorial in the *Philippines Daily Inquirer*, "the Philippines have suffered greatly because of corruption". Citing a 2000 World Bank study, the same editorial pointed out that "the Philippines lost about $48 billion because of corruption over a 20-year period", while another study, Morgan-Stanley Research "estimated that losses from corruption totaled $204 billion from 1965 through 2001. See "Philippines No. 2 on Asia graft list–survey covers 900 foreigners in the region", *Philippines Daily Inquirer*, 9 March 2005; see also "Corruption", in the *Philippines Daily Inquirer*, 14 October 2003.

26   See *Daily Tribune*, 9 March 2005.

27   "Unemployment Rate Higher at 10.9% in October 2004"; see Labor Force Survey (LFS) as released by the National Statistics Office (NSO), 20 December 2004.

28   In an apparent split with Malacanang Palace, the administration-dominated Philippine Senate adjourned without passing the VAT (value added tax) legislation that Macapagal-Arroyo has heavily lobbied for; see *Philippines Daily Inquirer*, 18 March 2005.

29   National Statistical Coordination Board.

30   See "FVR Aide Warns of Military Coup d'Etat: A Mismanaged Society Forces an AFP Takeover", a speech before the Foundation for Economic Freedom; and three days later, General Jose Almonte (ret), Ramos' National Security Adviser, ramped up his criticism of the Macapagal-Arroyo government in "Gloria's EDSA II Payback Cause of AFP Graft: Revolving Door Policy Led to Corruption"; see *Daily Tribune*, 12 March 2005 and 15 March 2005, respectively.

31   See Michaela P. Del Callar, "U.S. State Department gives GMA Government Failing Mark", *Daily Tribune*, 18 February 2005.

32   Ibid.

33   Ibid.

34   See "Malacanang Survey Shows Nosedive in Gloria Ratings", *Daily Tribune*,
      17 March 2005.

35   Senator Juan Flavier (Lakas), a medical doctor, incurred the wrath of the Catholic
      Church when as Fidel V. Ramos' Secretary of Health from 1992 to 1996 he was point-
      person for a relatively successful family-planning programme that the Church opposed.
      Flavier cleverly defined the population problem in medical terms instead of as a social
      or religious issue. After Flavier left the cabinet and announced his intention to run for a
      Senate seat, the Catholic Church urged the Catholic faithful through pastoral letters,
      homilies from the pulpit, personal appeals, etc., to "junk" Flavier. To the credit of much-
      maligned Filipino voters, however, they voted for Flavier in large numbers in 1996 and
      re-elected him to a second term in May 2002.

THE PHILIPPINES
The Continuing Story of a
Crisis-Prone Economy

Cielito F Habito

Being an election year, it was commonly expected that the Philippine economy would grow faster in 2004 compared to the year before. In fact, the expectation was more than realized. Not only did actual economic growth as measured by growth in gross domestic production (GDP) exceed that of 2003, it also went beyond the targets set by the government for the year. Moreover, the economy's growth compared favourably with that of most of its neighbours in the region.

But GDP growth was only one yardstick for the economy. The quality of the growth achieved was put to question by a significant acceleration in prices and increased joblessness within the year. Meanwhile, the government's precarious financial position owing to heavy indebtedness continued to be the weakest link in the economy, prompting economists from the University of the Philippines (UP) to sound the alarm by the third quarter that the country was in the midst of a fiscal crisis threatening to turn into an Argentina-style collapse, unless the government took prompt corrective actions.[1] The alarm resonated and dominated discussions and debates for the rest of the year. But the government response was far from adequate by most assessments, including and especially by the international credit rating agencies.

By year-end, Fitch Ratings and Standard and Poor's had announced widely expected one-notch downgrades on the country's credit rating, telling the world, in effect, that the country's ability to pay for its debts was getting more and more

CIELITO F HABITO is Professor in the Department of Economics and Director of the Ateneo Center for Economic Research and Development (ACERD), Ateneo de Manila University, The Philippines.

questionable. These moves were seen as formal expressions of the external audience's dissatisfaction with the way the Philippine government was addressing current threats to the stability of its economy. But contrary to most analysts' prognoses of dire effects arising from such downgrades, the opening weeks of 2005 saw a surging stock market and a fast appreciating peso, seemingly reflecting improved, not worsened, confidence in the domestic economy. In a moment of jubilation, President Gloria Macapagal-Arroyo declared that the economy was "on a roll". But the euphoria was promptly dampened by a severe two-notch credit downgrade by Moody's in February, further confusing the already mixed signals on the economy. What was the real state of the Philippine economy, as it ended 2004 and entered 2005?

A Half-full Glass: The Good News

In spite of the negativity that has tended to dominate most discussions on the Philippine economy of late, the full year 2004 report on economic performance based on the government's official statistics actually brought much good news. The surging stock market and the improving peso that greeted the opening weeks of 2005 are part of this, but there are more fundamental positive indicators that could partially explain these favourable market trends.

Faster production

Economic growth in 2004 actually exceeded targets set for the year, as well as actual performance in the previous year. The 6.1 per cent growth in both GNP and GDP overshot the 5.0–5.7 per cent targeted by the government, and improved on the 5.5 per cent growth achieved in 2003. A breakdown of growth performance by major sectors reveals the same situation. Services, which grew fastest at 7.3 per cent, went beyond the target range of 5.7–6.6 per cent, and improved from its 5.9 per cent growth in 2003. Industry, with its 5.3 per cent growth, likewise went over its 4.4–5.2 per cent target and bested its 3.0 per cent performance in 2003 (which at the time fell short of the targeted 3.2–3.7 per cent). Even agriculture with its 4.9 per cent growth was near the upper end of the targeted 4.0–5.0 per cent range, and had accelerated from its 3.9 per cent performance.

Particularly noteworthy was industry's substantial pick-up in growth, having improved by a hefty 2.3 percentage points. Manufacturing, a prominent part of the industry sector, performed solidly in 2004, ending the year with a solid fourth quarter growth of 6.9 per cent. Capacity utilization had also improved to 80 per cent from just over 78 per cent the year before. This was a departure from the sector's relatively sluggish performance in recent years, widely blamed on strong competition from imports, especially from nearby China.

All this happened at a time when all regions of the country had been contributing to the economy's growth without exception, i.e. all regions posted positive growth in gross regional domestic product (GRDP) in 2003. This was again a departure from past years' experience wherein one or two regions, i.e. the Autonomous Region of Muslim Mindanao and Region 13 (also in Mindanao), had tended to lag behind with negative growth.

Stronger demand

The improved performance of the productive sectors was likewise reflected on the demand side, with personal consumption and investment expenditures showing strong and faster growth. Personal consumption grew by 5.8 per cent, better than its 5.3 per cent growth in 2003, still supported by the purchasing power provided by brisk growth in overseas Filipino workers' (OFW) remittances. But more noteworthy was growth in real investment, which showed vast improvement from its stagnant 0.1 per cent performance in 2003, to a double-digit 12.7 per cent growth in 2004. In particular, construction recovered from its negative performance in 2003 (–2.9 per cent) to a healthy 6.2 per cent growth in 2004, with both public and private construction growing positively. Election-induced construction was the obvious reason for this, as the first two quarters accounted for most of the growth in public construction in 2004. By the fourth quarter, however, public construction was back into negative growth, clear evidence of how government construction projects were front-loaded in the election year.

Private investments in durable equipment actually slowed down to 4.4 per cent from 8.5 per cent in 2003, consistent with the actual drop in foreign direct investment inflows reported by the Bangko Sentral ng Pilipinas (BSP). Still, the positive albeit slower growth rate indicates that domestic investors continued to place stronger bets on the growing economy.

Poverty improvement

Recent reports from the National Statistical Coordination Board (NSCB) of declining poverty and narrowing income gaps give further reason to be encouraged. NSCB reports that the proportion of Filipino families that are poor has steadily declined from 28.1 per cent in 1997, to 27.5 per cent in 2000, and on to 24.7 per cent in 2003. Furthermore, the ratio of incomes of the richest one-fifth to the poorest one-fifth of the Filipino population has also reportedly declined from 12.6 in 1997, down to 12.4 in 2000, and further down to 11.4 in 2003. While these data have not gone unquestioned,[2] they appear at face value to indicate some improvement in the quality of the country's economic growth in recent years.

Notwithstanding these seemingly positive indicators, the proverbial glass is merely half full. Accelerating inflation and rising unemployment reveal fundamental weaknesses that continue to plague the Philippine economy. The growth in the economy can be described as narrow, shallow and hollow. Furthermore, the precarious state of government finances is a constant threat to the stability of the overall economy. Looking beyond economic indicators, human development and environmental indicators provide similar cause for concern, demanding a more holistic and integrative approach towards pursuing the economy's sustained growth and a sustainable improvement in the people's welfare.

Continuing Challenges

Rising inflation and unemployment

Price increases accelerated in 2004, ending the year with a 7.9 per cent inflation over 2003 year-end price levels. This brought average inflation throughout the year to 5.5 per cent, a significant increase over the 3.1 per cent average inflation rate of the previous two years.[3] The higher inflation was induced primarily by the dramatic rise in oil prices, with international crude oil prices climbing above US$55 per barrel, almost twice the level of the year before.

Meanwhile, the "jobless growth" phenomenon has persisted, with the 6.1 per cent GDP growth accompanied by a perverse movement in employment rate. Unemployment worsened to 10.9 per cent in October 2004, from 10.2 per cent in the same month of 2003, with close to 5 million Filipino workers unable to find jobs. As of October, only 180,000 new jobs had been generated by the economy over the past year, with a net loss of 66,000 jobs in the industry sector. Agriculture contributed 28,000 new jobs, while services produced the most new jobs, numbering 218,000.[4] Still, all this falls far short of the minimum of one million new jobs targeted by the government per year over the next six years, to bring the unemployment rate down to levels closer to those of its immediate neighbours.

Narrow, shallow and hollow growth

The growth of the Philippine domestic economy over recent years is propelled primarily by a narrow set of economic sectors, especially information and communication technology (ICT), particularly telecommunications, which continues to ride on the rapid growth in the cellular phone business, particularly the popularity of text messaging. This sub-sector grew by a rapid 20 per cent in the 4th quarter and 16.7 per cent for the full year, fastest among all sub-sectors in the economy and far outpacing the rest of the economy. At the same time, more than half (56 per cent) of domestic output and incomes are generated in the National Capital Region, and Regions III (Central Luzon) and IV (Southern Tagalog) alone. Growth in the economy is clearly proceeding from a narrow sectoral and geographical base.

Meanwhile, the bulk of the country's exports are accounted for by two industries heavily dependent on imported raw materials and intermediate inputs, namely electronics (64.9 per cent of export revenues) and garments (6.4 per cent). The thin slice of domestic value added on these products is almost entirely accounted for by labour. As such, there is hardly any linkage between these industries and the rest of the productive sectors of the economy. Thus, the benefits from growth in production particularly in these sectors are rather shallow.

Moreover, and as discussed earlier, the seemingly favourable rate of growth of the economy has actually been accompanied by an increase in the unemployment rate. Growth of the economy has not been translating into commensurate growth in jobs for Filipino workers (thereby manifesting a "hollow" growth). Among the consequences of this is the large numbers of Filipino workers who seek employment overseas yearly. This is yet another indication that recent economic growth has led to limited benefits for a limited segment of the Filipino population. Through the years, a more broad-based economic growth and development remained elusive for the Philippines.

The Pressing Threat: Weak Government Finances

An unprecedented fiscal bind

The total public sector debt of the Philippines recently reached 6 trillion pesos (about US$109 billion), after ending 2003 at about 5.4 trillion pesos (US$98 billion). In 2004, the government spent the equivalent of 81 per cent of its revenues to pay for both interest and principal amortization of its total debt, or more than 4 out of every 5 pesos it collected in both tax and non-tax revenues. The situation is projected to get worse in 2005. In data submitted to Congress, the government is allocating the equivalent of over 90 per cent (i.e. more than 9 out of every 10 pesos) of projected revenues to interest and principal payments for outstanding debt.[5] Never in the country's history has the government found itself in such a tight fiscal bind, forcing it to borrow massively to keep operating. The dramatic deterioration in the public finances suggests serious structural and operational flaws in the revenue system. Corruption and tax evasion have been recognized to be rampant, aggravated further by traditional failures in tax administration.

This deterioration in government finances is a revenue problem, and has not been due to any sudden upsurge in budgetary spending. Total spending has in fact averaged only 19 per cent of the GDP, largely by cutting back some of the major infrastructure projects like irrigation. Net of interest payments, primary spending of the national government has actually declined significantly since 1999, and is now at its lowest level in a decade. The bulk of the national budget that remains after interest payments are already committed beforehand to salaries, maintenance and operating expenses, and the internal revenue allotment to local governments, leaving very little for infrastructure spending and other development needs.

This unprecedented situation spells crisis, whichever way one looks at it. President Arroyo was being truthful when she affirmed the presence of a fiscal crisis soon after the UP economists sounded the alarm. But her subsequent declaration in November that the fiscal crisis was over, in the heels of Congressional approval of a watered-down version of the bill raising excise taxes on tobacco products and alcoholic beverages ("sin" taxes), invited widespread disbelief and criticism. That declaration and the current euphoria over the surging peso and stock market can be outright dangerous if they have the effect of removing the sense of urgency and fostering complacency especially among lawmakers and other policy-makers whose actions in the near future are critical to the economy's stability. What is needed to prevent the fiscal crisis from expanding into a financial crisis (i.e. affecting the stability of the entire financial sector) and turning into a full-blown economic crisis (i.e. similar to what Argentina went through in 2002) is far more than what has been forthcoming so far from the executive and legislative branches of government, and from the private sector. While recent developments may seem to have dissipated the danger somewhat, the recent (February 2005) two-notch credit downgrade from Moody's is a stark reminder that the economy is by no means "out of the woods".

Shades of Argentina?

Depending on which data are examined, comparisons with Argentina can either be comforting or alarming. If one considers the size of the overall public debt, the position of the Philippines is worse than Argentina. From 1995–2001, Argentina's public debt/GDP ratio rose from 35 per cent to 65 per cent. From 1997 to 2004, the Philippines ratio has risen from 56 per cent to 80 per cent. This is much higher than that of Argentina and should be cause for concern.

Furthermore, the Philippines' indebtedness to foreigners has risen much faster than that in Argentina. From 1990 to 2000, Argentina's external debt/GDP ratio rose from 44 per cent to 51 per cent, a 7-percentage point increase over 10 years. In the case of the Philippines, external debt from 1997 to 2004 has risen from 32 per cent to 49 per cent, a 17-percentage point rise over just 7 years.[6] This makes the Philippines strongly vulnerable to world interest rate increases, as that would further hike its debt service requirements.

On the other hand, the Philippines fares very well when comparing levels of debt service (i.e. annual payments for interest and amortization of principal) to that of Argentina. From 1997 to 2001, debt service as a proportion of export earnings rose from close to 50 per cent to near 100 per cent in Argentina. In the Philippines, these same ratios from 1997 to 2004 are a mere 11.6 per cent rising to 16.6 per cent. This is explained by the Philippines' far stronger export position compared to Argentina. Since it had pegged its peso to the U.S. dollar, Argentina was unable to devalue and remain competitive with its neighbours, notably Brazil, which had undergone steep currency depreciations. This is simply not the case in the Philippines, where the country remains competitive in terms of exports and has seen its current account move from a deficit of 5.3 per cent in 1997 to a surplus in 2004 of 4.2 per cent. This has largely come from OFW remittances, which continue to appear robust.

The above analysis suggests that the fiscal crisis, while definitely needing urgent response, is not yet an overriding factor hindering growth in the economy. Indeed, overall economic growth in 2004 remained at respectable levels. But there is one important caveat in this seemingly positive assessment. In Argentina, the currency board gave credibility to the exchange rate peg and allowed Argentina's public sector to continue borrowing excessively in international capital markets, and this eventually raised the cost of the collapse even more. For the Philippines, OFW remittances have provided a similar form of credibility in international capital markets in terms of adequate external liquidity. Thus, capital markets have remained open to the Philippines, albeit at higher cost, and allowed the public debt to rise. Late in 2004, the government issued an additional US$1.5 billion worth of new debt, thereby further raising the size of the total public debt and external debt, and effectively leading the country to even greater vulnerability.

Fundamental Weaknesses

The persistent tightness in government finances has had long-term consequences that have led to fundamental weaknesses in the Philippine economy. For decades, the Philippines has lagged behind its Southeast Asian neighbours in key social and economic indicators. This had not always been the case; in the 1960s, the country had been widely considered second only to Japan in its level of economic development in the region. In the 1960s and up to 1970, the country was a virtual identical twin to Thailand, with both having exactly the same population levels, average incomes, saving and investment rates, international trade ratios, and more striking similarities. The divergence between the two erstwhile "identical twins" through the next three decades was rather stark, with the Philippines having 18 million more people and managing only about half the average income of Thailand by the turn of the 21st century.[7]

In particular, the country stands out as having had the lowest growth in labour productivity (output per worker) and total factor productivity since the 1960s. Whereas Thailand, Malaysia, Singapore, Indonesia, Taiwan and Korea all experienced accelerating growth in labour and total factor productivity since the 1960s, the Philippines was the only country among the group that even slid into negative productivity growth in the 1980s, and remained stagnant up to the early 1990s. The average annual labour productivity growth in the seven countries was 4.6 per cent by the early 1990s, up from 3.2 per cent in the 1960s. On the other hand, Philippine labour productivity growth was 2.3 per cent in the 1960s, slipped into negative annual growth rate of –3.0 in the 1980s, and barely recovered at 0.7 per cent in the early 1990s. The annual growth rate of total factor productivity averaged a mere 0.2 per cent in the 1960s, dipped to –4.6 per cent in the 1980s, and was stagnant at 0.0 per cent in the early 1990s.[8]

Another glaring contrast is in how government capital expenditures in the Philippines account for the lowest share of total capital expenditures among the seven countries named. In 2000–02, the share averaged less than 9 per cent for the Philippines, against 16.2 per cent for Thailand, 36 per cent for Malaysia, and 43 per cent for Indonesia.[9] The result has been inferior infrastructure facilities relative to its neighbouring competitor countries. Social expenditures in the Philippines likewise pale in comparison to what its neighbours have invested in this crucial budget item. Thailand and Malaysia spend about two-fifths of their budgets for the social sector, the Philippines only one-fourth. Clearly, those two countries have been investing much more than the Philippines in two critical areas of productivity and competitiveness: infrastructure and human resources. Unless it is able to close this public investment gap, the Philippines is bound to remain uncompetitive in the international economy, and continue to lag behind indefinitely into the future.

Beyond Economics: Human Development and Environment

The weakness of the Philippine economy has directly translated into weak human development and environmental indicators. Among the more disturbing trends is the worsening of nutritional status among Filipino children between 1990 and 2000, evidenced by worsening of indicators on infant birth weight, stunting, protein-energy malnutrition, iron deficiency anaemia, and micronutrient deficiencies. Nearly 30 per cent of children who enter first grade drop out before Grade 4. The quality of education leaves much to be desired, with achievement rates (at 53 per cent in 2001) far short of the target 75 per cent for 2000. Performance was particularly poor in science, mathematics and English.[10]

Meanwhile, the country's forest cover has dramatically declined over the years, coastal areas have deteriorated, and rivers and lakes have become heavily polluted. From about 20 million hectares in the early 1900s, forest cover had declined to about 5.5 million hectares in 2000. Mangrove areas shrank from 450,000 hectares in 1918 to less than a third (120,000 hectares) by 1985. Fish catch in the country's major coastal fisheries had significantly declined, indicative of over-fishing due to strong population pressure in the coastal areas. Coral reefs have likewise deteriorated, with the proportion of those in excellent condition having declined from 5.3 per cent in the 1970s to 2.4 per cent in 1997. Air pollution in Metro Manila is twice above what is considered safe levels by the World Health Organization. The Philippines is classified as one of the biodiversity hotspots in the world, with threatened and endangered species estimated to be increasing by 9.7 per cent annually.[11]

Strengths and Opportunities

In spite of its fundamental weaknesses and short-term difficulties, the Philippine economy can bank on its inherent strengths with which it can seize on emerging opportunities in the world economy and look beyond its current difficulties and challenges.

Human and natural resources

Its abundance of human resources has been both a challenge, in the face of the "jobless growth" discussed earlier, and a boon, in light of the millions of overseas Filipino workers who provide a critical component in the purchasing power that sustains the domestic economy. It is also commonly cited as an asset in attracting foreign direct investment, given the large English-speaking labour force that is highly trainable in various skills needed for a wide range of enterprises.

Abundance of natural resources spanning fisheries to agricultural resources to minerals is likewise considered a key advantage whose potentials have yet to be fully harnessed within a framework of sustainable development. The recent Supreme

Court decision that has opened the way for foreign investments in the mining industry is being banked upon by the government to unlock large amounts of the country's richly endowed natural wealth. While continuing opposition from environmental advocates is likely to moderate the pace of investments in the sector, the government is determined to make the mining industry a key element in the solution to its current fiscal difficulties.

Vigorous local economies

A key element neglected in most discussions about the Philippine economy is the important and growing role that local economies are playing in overall economic growth and development. Since the enactment of the Local Government Code of 1991, which institutionalized strong devolution and decentralization of government functions, responsibilities and budgetary resources, local governments at the provincial, city and municipal levels have taken an increasingly prominent role as drivers of economic activity and social development in different parts of the country.

While experience across local areas varies widely, numerous recognized "islands of good governance" and "best practice" can be found all over the country, exemplifying the new-found dynamism brought about by devolution and decentralization.[12] Certain local economies have grown at rates far outpacing the national average, due either to proactive and professional governance by visionary local executives, or to inherent strategic advantages enjoyed by particular localities, or both.[13] The challenge has been in replicating such local success stories nationwide through active learning exchanges among local government units.

External opportunities

Meanwhile, emerging global trends hold much promise for the Philippine economy, providing opportunities for which the country is well positioned. Three such trends are services outsourcing by developed countries, China's and India's growing demands for resource-based products, and the declining and aging populations in industrialized countries.

The first refers to the way rich countries are now projected to export millions of jobs to developing countries, particularly in the form of jobs in backroom and technology services. High value services such as stock research, project management, underwriting and forecasting are the next level in the chain of jobs that are being exported from high cost structure countries to low cost structure emerging markets. The Philippines is witnessing phenomenal growth in levels of business processes outsourced to its shores, such as call centres, medical transcription services, and similar enterprises.

The opening up of the two formerly closed economies of China and India has spurred an immense demand for resource-based products. As China shapes up to be the "factory of the world" and India as the "backroom of the world", their current growth levels have caused a major realignment in global trade. Most of the rest of Asia's exports to the United States are shifting to feed China's manufacturing and consumer demands, causing a rapid growth in commodity prices, such as gold, silver, copper, platinum, nickel and other precious metals, apart from soybeans, cotton, lumber, cattle, and fruits like pineapples and bananas. The Philippines is actually benefiting from China's dynamic economic growth, and has been enjoying a trade surplus with that country in recent years. Based on records from the Chinese government, total trade between the Philippines and China amounted to US$9.4 billion in 2003, with the Philippines enjoying a trade surplus of US$3.1 billion. In 2004, the counties' bilateral trade amounted to US$13.328 billion, with the Philippines enjoying a trade surplus of US$4.79 billion.[14]

The third trend is seen in the way Europe and Japan project declines in their population, which, while posing a long-term threat to their economies, holds great promise for labour-surplus economies like the Philippines. The government would do well to identify niches in these population-declining countries and gear human resources development programmes to meet these demands, particularly in aging-related services, including retirement estates and care-giving services. With its superior medical practitioners, the country is also positioning to develop a world-class medical tourism industry to attract patients from rich countries where costs of health and medical services have been skyrocketing.

Short-Term Outlook

Market fever and the weak dollar

Current market trends, especially in the stock market and the foreign exchange market, project a certain degree of optimism on the economy's near-term outlook, notwithstanding the many challenges described above. These market trends are to a large extent externally driven, tracing ultimately to the weakness of the U.S. dollar, which has provoked an exodus from U.S. dollar-denominated investments and corresponding inflows into emerging markets, including the Philippines. Analysts project the current dollar weakness to be a protracted trend, in contrast to previous episodes of transitory dollar weakening, due to unprecedented trade and fiscal deficits now prevailing in the United States, each now well in excess of 5 per cent of GDP.

There is clear evidence that the local stock market has indeed been attracting substantial foreign funds since the beginning of 2005. Whereas the amount of money changing hands in the Philippine Stock Exchange averaged only 500 million pesos a day in 2004, current daily market turnover amounts to 2–3 times that level, the bulk of which is foreign money. Foreign funds entering the stock market in the first 28 days of the year amounted to 11.39 billion pesos net, boosted by the 8.79 billion pesos buy-in by Japanese beverage giant Kirin into the San Miguel Corporation. Foreign portfolio investors are also being attracted into equity issues of local telecommunications companies, which reaped substantial profits in 2004 (with PLDT-Smart netting 24 billion pesos or about US$436 million, while Globe Telecoms made 11 billion pesos or about US$200 million). The stock market infusions made up about half of the total net inflow of "hot money" reported by the BSP for the same period of US$427.2 million, or about 23.5 billion pesos. The rest of the inflows went into purchases of government bonds and treasury bills, as well as other IOUs issued by the private sector.

In the same period in 2004, only US$12.9 million came into the country, a mere 3 per cent of what entered in January 2005. These inflows for the first month alone already approach the total value of inflows for the whole year of 2004, which was US$486.8 million. With the supply of dollars in the country surging, it is no surprise that the Philippine peso has become one of the fastest appreciating currencies in the region at the beginning of 2005.

Fiscal fixes: Make or break

All eyes are on the various revenue enhancement measures pending in the Philippine Congress, as the country's ability to avert a looming fiscal collapse depends critically on the government's ability to raise at least an additional 100 billion pesos within the coming year.[15] Seven months after the first declaration of a fiscal crisis, Congress has managed to pass only one (the "watered-down" law raising excise taxes on "sin" products) out of eight revenue measures proposed by the government. Protracted debates continue to delay the proposed increase of the value added tax (VAT) from 10 per cent to 12 per cent and expansion of its coverage by eliminating various exemptions. Meanwhile, tax collection agencies (Bureau of Internal Revenue and Bureau of Customs) are redoubling efforts to improve collection efficiency and curb massive tax evasion.

Without the added spending leeway that such revenue enhancement measures should bring, the government would be severely constrained from playing a more direct role in stimulating more growth and employment, e.g. via increased investments in infrastructure and spending on vital social services. The brunt of sustaining economic growth would then have to fall on the private sector.

Slower private sector growth

Unfortunately, there already are indications that growth from private sector production cannot be sustained in 2005. A closer look at the fourth quarter economic data clearly shows that the economy is on a slowing trend. Agriculture, in particular, had grown by a mere 1.2 per cent in the fourth quarter, a dramatic departure from the previous quarter's performance, and caused by extensive crop damage due to weather disturbances. With the return of the El Niño phenomenon[16] expected in 2005, weather is likely to exert continued pressure on crop production within the year.

Furthermore, overall growth in the economy measured on a quarter-to-quarter basis and adjusted for seasonality was only 0.6 per cent, the slowest quarterly growth since 2001. This seems to presage what most analysts have been predicting for some time, i.e. slower growth in 2005, reflecting a similar outlook of slower growth for the global economy as forecast by the World Bank, IMF, OECD and other multilateral institutions. Higher petroleum prices and imbalances in the world currency and financial markets are among the factors shaping these projections, factors to which the Philippines will be as vulnerable as the rest.

Conclusion

The current economic picture for the Philippines is a mixed, even confused one. On one hand, there is good news in the behaviour of the equity and currency markets, inviting the tempting interpretation that these are precursors of better times ahead. But an understanding of the underlying weaknesses still plaguing the Philippine economy dictates a more prudent outlook. There is a great deal of uncertainty as to how long the bullish sentiment will last. Seasoned observers of the Philippine economy know well enough to understand that the tides can shift very quickly in this vibrant and highly politicized society. "Event risk" is a factor that perhaps figures a bit more prominently in this country than elsewhere, whether in business planning or in overall economic management. But those same seasoned observers know that the country and its people have much going for them in the longer term, given their inherent strengths taken in the face of vast emerging opportunities.

What is clear is that the current fiscal difficulties of the Philippine government call for urgent corrective action. Improvements in tax administration and tax collection efficiency need to be pursued relentlessly, even as the government seeks to enact new revenue measures to raise about 100 billion pesos in additional revenues in 2005. It is also clear that given the magnitude and proportion of the country's debt service burden, efforts to reduce the debt service burden must be seriously pursued through various schemes for negotiated debt reduction that have been employed successfully before.

For the country's leaders, this is not the time for self-serving machinations and political compromises. A country at the crossroads demands statesmanship, magnanimity and political will — the genuine desire to put aside personal interest in favour of the common good — from its political and business leaders, on whose actions hinge the welfare of over 80 million Filipinos.

Notes

[1]   Emmanuel De Dios et al., "The Deepening Crisis: The Real Score on Deficits and the public Debt". UP School of Economics Discussion Paper, 2004.

[2]   A number of analysts have pointed out inconsistencies between the recently released poverty and income distribution statistics, and the Family Income and Expenditures Survey. See, for example, Solita Monsod, "Careful with those Statistics", Get Real column, *Philippine Daily Inquirer*, 5 February 2005.

[3]   NEDA Weekly Economic Indicators, NEDA website, http://www.neda.gov.ph.

[4]   Ibid.

[5]   Department of Finance working tables submitted to the Philippine Congress.

[6]   Bangko Sentral ng Pilipinas website, http://www.bsp.gov.ph.

[7]   Cielito F. Habito, "RP and Thailand: Estranged Twins", No Free Lunch Column, *Philippine Daily Inquirer*, 2 August 2004.

[8]   Ponciano S. Intal Jr., Gerardo Largoza and Associates, "Society, Economy and Philippine Development: Towards a Social Market Economy Framework for Philippine Development", De La Salle University, 2004.

[9]   Data cited in Intal, Largoza and Associates, 2004, ibid.

[10] Government of the Philippines and UNICEF, *Situation of Women and Children in the Philippines, 1997* (Manila: 1997).

[11] Data from briefing materials of the Department of Environment and Natural Resources.

[12] These are publicly highlighted in well-known and respected local governance awards such as the annual Gawad Galing Pook (http://www.galingpook.org) and the League of Cities Best Practices Awards (http://www.cdsea.org/CDSKnowledge/best%20practices/lcp_best_practices.htm).

[13] Examples are given in the author's articles on the city of Vigan and on the municipality of Infanta before it was hit by devastating floods in the third quarter of 2004 (" 'Viganizing' the Philippines" and "The Infanta that was to be", No Free Lunch column, *Philippine Daily Inquirer,* 18 October 2004 and 20 December 2004 respectively).

[14] "RP, China Chart Stronger Ties in 2005", Department of Foreign Affairs Press Release, 26 January 2005.

[15] This is the figure estimated by the UP professors in their analysis as necessary to achieve a sustained improvement in the government's financial standing in the years ahead, and avert, in effect, the fiscal collapse that their celebrated paper warned about.

[16] El Niño is the periodic weather phenomenon marked by a slight but discernible rise in water temperature of the Pacific Ocean, which has had profound effects on rainfall patterns on the Pacific Rim. In the Philippines, the effects are manifested in prolonged droughts, severely affecting crop production in agricultural areas.

Singapore

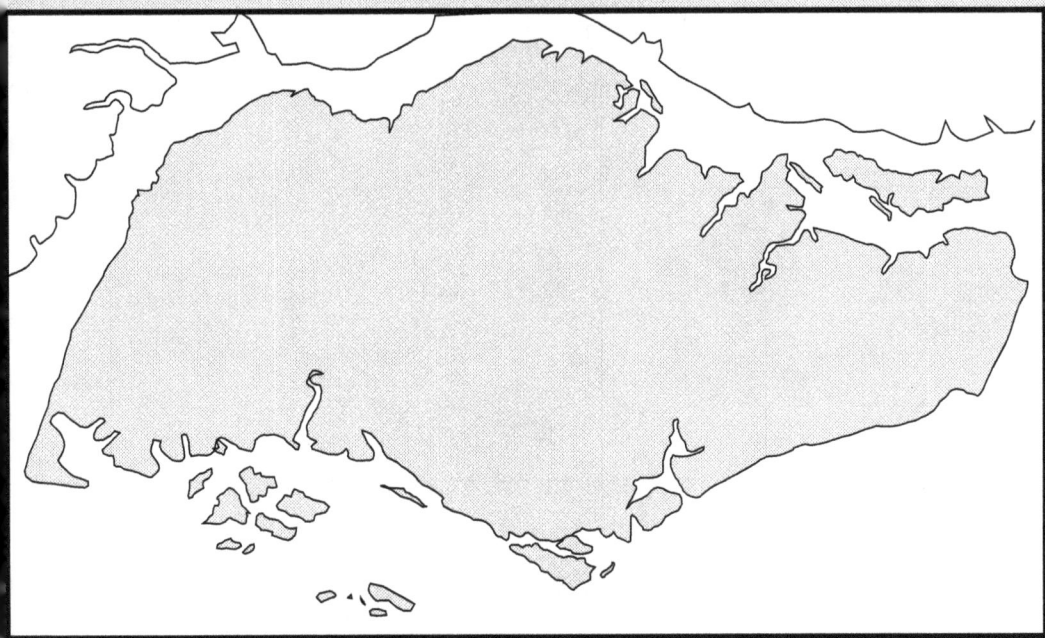

SINGAPORE IN 2004
Vigilance amid Growing Uncertainty

Teo Kah Beng

Singapore has thrived for 32 years since independence. Its traumatic birth spurred a hardworking and resilient population, led by honest and competent political leaders ... Our challenge now is to sustain this performance beyond the founding generation ... Our competition is becoming fiercer. So far, our policies have succeeded beyond expectations. But they need creative rethinking... In a rapidly changing world, we either adapt or become irrelevant.[1]

Lee Hsien Loong, "Singapore of the Future", 1998.

Introduction

Vigilance has been the hallmark of the pragmatic, realist-oriented Singapore government since an unanticipated independence 40 years ago. It is likely to remain so. Singapore simply has no other option. Although Singapore has prospered to become one of the richest states in the world, and its defence capability has improved considerably, the basic mindset of Singapore's leaders has not changed. International politics is seen as being dictated by the law of the jungle. As a small state, Singapore is faced with unique constraints. Singapore has to be able to signal potential aggressors that it has the capability and the will to deter them and defend itself.[2] The first generation of Singapore leaders, led by its first Prime Minister (PM) Lee Kuan Yew, fought to get the island's "internal house" in order to ensure national survival. The opposition was crushed, and the nation set out to carve for itself its place in the world. Forced out of Malaysia in 1965, Singapore decided that it had to become a "Global City", by making the world its hinterland. Its ambition is to

---

Teo Kah Beng is a doctoral candidate in political science at the National University of Singapore and an Associate Lecturer at the Singapore Institute of Management. He is also an Intern at the Institute of Southeast Asian Studies.

become a global hub for international trade, investment, transportation, medical services, and tourism. The result of that sense of vigilance, against great odds, has been an exceptional and unique governmental performance which transformed Singapore's economy from Third World to First World status within a generation.

Singapore had a good 2004. The economy grew by an impressive 8.4 per cent on the back of a strong global economic revival, compared with 1.4 per cent in 2003. The official forecast is for a growth rate of 3–5 per cent in 2005. Given its "strategic positioning", Singapore anticipates problems before they materialize. Its strategic goal is to remain competitive and attractive to foreign investors. Politically, the ruling People's Action Party (PAP) retains hegemonic control in Singapore. Its leadership remains cohesive. In August 2004, Singapore witnessed its second smooth leadership succession. The PAP is recruiting a new generation of younger leaders to contest the next parliamentary election, likely to be held in 2005, ahead of the expiry of its mandate in early 2007. In foreign policy, Singapore enhanced its economic and political space and influence. Strong ties were restored with its close neighbours, especially Malaysia, after two years of uncertainty. Within ASEAN, Singapore took a proactive, leadership role. In particular, Singapore took the lead in forging closer ties between ASEAN and Northeast Asia. When the Asian tsunami struck on Boxing Day 2004, Singapore took decisive action in organizing an ASEAN-led international conference to aid the victims of the disaster. The UN also accepted Singapore's generous offer to act as a regional relief centre for Indonesia, the country worst hit by the disaster.

Political Succession

On 12 August 2004, Lee Hsien Loong, 52, became Singapore's third prime minister in a smooth succession, from Mr Goh Chok Tong. It was Singapore's second leadership change in 40 years. Lee Hsien Loong is the eldest son of Lee Kuan Yew, Singapore's patriarch, who ruled Singapore as its first prime minister from self-independence in 1959 to November 1990. The younger Lee entered politics in 1984. His political ascendancy received the full endorsement of the PAP leadership as well of those of the party's parliamentarians. This served to enhance Lee's political legitimacy, in reference to earlier allegations that his rise was due to his father's influence.[3]

The PAP was concerned with Lee Hsien Loong's public image. He was alleged to be an authoritarian, like his father. Under Goh Chok Tong, Singapore became noticeably more relaxed, and open to alternative views. In his National Day Rally speech in 2003, Goh said that Lee had to learn "to let his softer side show". It was followed by a concerted effort by the local media to soften Lee's public image. The government realizes the need to relax Singapore's social control if it is to foster the culture of innovation it believes is necessary for economic growth.[4] Times have changed and so has Singapore's society. Lee Kuan Yew's authoritarian style was necessary as Singapore was faced with the "politics of survival" in the 1960s and early-1970s.[5] Lee Hsien Loong, in his inauguration speech in August 2004, promised to continue with a more open and consultative approach to government. The government has no choice but to steadily open up Singapore politically: to do otherwise would be counter-productive and detrimental to the island-state's long-term interests.

However, radical shifts in policy are unlikely from the new Lee administration. His priorities are to ensure that Singapore is nimble, flexible, and adaptable. Lee has been innovative in reforming and improving outdated policies. Singapore's guiding principles were spelt out at its independence on 9 August 1965: to make as many friends in the world as possible; and to make Singapore useful to its neighbours. Singapore's current priorities were spelt out on 12 August 2004 by Lee in his National Day Rally speech, when he pledged to a "fresh, bold approach" to governance, and to build an "open and inclusive" society, building on the achievements of his predecessor. In his landmark speech, Lee spelt out his vision and a roadmap to advance Singapore's future. It is likely to set the overall tone and agenda for his administration. Domestically, Lee appealed to all Singaporeans, especially the less successful ones, to join him in a total national effort to build a more cohesive and caring nation. Internationally, Lee highlighted the urgent need to constantly push Singapore forward to greater heights of excellence, and to stay ahead in a world of rapid globalization. The assumption being that for Singapore to stay still is to stagnate and fall behind an ever-growing number of competitors, like China and India. Lee also pledged that he would adopt an action-oriented foreign policy, to forge closer, win-win intra-ASEAN ties, and further enhance regional cooperation with its neighbours. His overall message was one of single-minded devotion to Singapore's national interest, and his determination not to take Singapore's success and prosperity for granted. The Lee administration can be expected to fulfil its pledges, which will affect its credibility and legitimacy.[6]

The new Cabinet announced on 10 August 2004 had few surprises. It emphasized continuity and experience: the heavyweight ministers remained in the Cabinet. Prime Minister Lee retained the finance portfolio, but handed the chairmanship of the Monetary Authority of Singapore (MAS) to his predecessor, Goh Chok Tong, who also took over the post of senior minister (SM), previously held by Lee Kuan Yew. S Jayakumar became a deputy prime minister (DPM). He previously held the posts of both law and foreign affairs minister. He remained as law minister, but gave up the foreign affairs portfolio to the former trade and industry minister George Yeo. Lim Hng Kiang became Trade and Industry Minister. Jayakumar would still chair a cabinet committee on foreign policy matters that cut across different ministries. He also remained in charge of foreign policy issues that involve legal negotiation or international adjudication. The other DPM, Tony Tan holds the post of Coordinating Minister for Security and Defence but he will retire at the end of June 2005; there is speculation that Tony Tan could be a candidate for president if President Nathan steps down at the end of his term in September 2005. Wong Kan Seng, who retained his post as home affairs minister, will replace Tony Tan as DPM in June 2005. Tharman Shanmugaratnam, widely seen as a rising political star, was confirmed as Minister of Education. Another rising political star is the new defence minister Teo Chee Hean. Lee Kuan Yew became "Minister Mentor in the Prime Minister's Office" (MM). As the father of modern Singapore, MM Lee is seen as a valuable resource that the Cabinet can tap on to safeguard Singapore's national interests in a more uncertain, post 9/11 world.

At the PAP's 50th anniversary celebrations in June 2004, outgoing prime minister Goh highlighted the strengths of Singapore's system of political renewal, by comparing it with that of South Asia. He described politics in South Asia as the "politics of divergence" where politicians with zero-sum mentalities pulled their countries in different directions. Goh said that politics in Singapore should be of a positive type: "My example will be set by future prime ministers that the PM will govern for as long as he is making a good contribution but at the right time he would pass on to somebody ... whom he has nurtured ... and if he can carry this on for a few more rounds, Singapore can keep going for the next 30, 40, 50 years, and this will be a system which can perpetuate the prosperity of Singapore."[7] The PAP believes in "consensus politics", with government in the leading role. The PAP's prowess in delivering the economic goods is the basis for its political dominance.[8] In late-December 2004, Goh said publicly that he expected the new Lee administration to lead Singapore for at least the next 10 to 15 years. Lee is expected to call a general election in 2005 to secure a strong personal mandate. The results would appear to be a foregone conclusion as the main opposition parties remain fragmented. Nevertheless the next parliamentary elections will be important. The proportion of votes that the PAP wins will be a sign of the new prime minister's personal popularity.

China Aviation Oil (CAO) Scandal

Singapore takes its reputation as a world-class international financial hub seriously. The CAO financial scandal broke out in November 2004. At a public forum with the

Foreign Correspondents' Association of Singapore in December 2004, Lee Kuan Yew welcomed Beijing's cooperation in the investigations involving CAO, which is controlled by the Chinese government. CAO is the main supplier of jet fuel to China. Civil Aviation Oil's CEO Mr Chen Juilin left Singapore just hours after the company disclosed on 30 November 2004 that it had lost US$500 million (equal to the company's market capitalization) on speculative trading in oil derivatives. Chen came back to Singapore on 8 December 2004. MM Lee stated: "What I consider significant is that the Chinese authorities ... have decided that the CEO should come here and help in the investigations ... To me that signals that they understand the damage that it will do them internationally, not just in Singapore, if the chief executive just absconds. That reduces them to a Third World standard of behaviour".[9] Lee Hsien Loong stated that Singapore should not rush to tighten corporate regulations in the wake of the huge trading losses at CAO. He said that any decision should wait until regulators finish their investigations.[10]

The *Economist*'s Apology

Singapore leaders continued with their long-standing policy, since the 1980s, of suing critics, foreigners and local opposition politicians, who try to defame them. PAP leaders argue that rumours of wrong-doing, unless stopped immediately, would have the long-term effect of undermining their reputation, credibility, and authority to rule effectively. Potential critics are warned that they can expect to be robustly challenged to back up their allegations. This consistent policy has the effect of making potential critics more cautious. Generally, the Western media continued to castigate Singapore as an authoritarian, undemocratic, "nanny state". But the issue here is whether the allegations of nepotism are true. The critics are expected to be prepared to defend their allegations, in court if necessary. If they are not prepared to do so, then their criticisms are considered without merit. In August 2004, the London-based *Economist* magazine decided to publish an apology to MM Lee and PM Lee for making unsubstantiated allegations about political nepotism in Singapore. In its 14–20 August 2004 edition, the *Economist* published an article entitled "Temasek, First Singapore, Next the World". In its apology, the *Economist* admitted that its article meant or was meant to mean that (a) Lee Hsien Loong had appointed, or was instrumental in appointing, his wife, Ho Ching, to Temasek Holdings Ltd, not on merit, but for corrupt nepotist motives for the advancement of the Lee family's interests; and (b) Lee Kuan Yew supported or condoned Ho Ching's appointment for like motives. In its apology, the *Economist* stated: "We admit and acknowledge that these allegations are false and completely without foundation. We unreservedly apologise to PM Lee Hsien Loong and MM Lee Kuan Yew for the distress and embarrassment caused to them by these allegations. We undertake not to make further allegations to the same or same effect." The *Economist* magazine also "agreed to pay PM Lee Hsien Loong and MM Lee Kuan Yew damages by way of compensation, and to indemnify them for all the costs and expenses incurred by them in connection with this matter".[11]

GLCs, Corporate Transparency, and Reforms

Since the mid-1990s, critics have stepped up their scrutiny of the corporate transparency of Singapore companies, especially the two state investment agencies, the Government of Singapore Investment Corporation (GIC) and Temasek Holdings. This issue of the GLCs' economic dominance is likely to become more prominent. In October 2004, PERC reported that expatriates working in Singapore have become more critical of transparency issues involving local companies. The U.S.-based Standard and Poor's (S&P's) also argued that GIC and Temasek had been too guarded in their approach to the release and interpretation of financial data. Singapore's Ministry of Finance disputed S&P's findings. Temasek published its annual report for the first time in 2004, on its 30th anniversary. Established in 1974 with a portfolio of S$350 million, Temasek is today an Asian financial powerhouse with S$90 billion of assets. Temasek-linked companies (TLCs) contribute about a tenth of Singapore's economy and complement the economic roles played by multinational companies (MNCs), as well as small and medium-sized enterprises.[12]

Temasek has global ambitions. In June 2004, CEO Ho Ching announced that Temasek intended "to become a formidable Asian equity-house, operating in Asia, as well as the world". Since June 2003, Temasek has rapidly bought into a growing number of well-managed Asian companies: a 9.1 per cent stake in Korea's Hana Bank; 5 per cent of India's ICICI Bank; a similar stake in Malaysia's largest phone company, Telekom Malaysia; and equity stakes in PT Bank Danamon Indonesia and PT Bank Internasional Indonesia. Temasek owns controlling stakes in 7 of Singapore's 10 biggest companies by market value.[13]

The government is forging ahead with Singapore's internationalization. Goh's 1999 National Day Rally speech highlighted that Singapore had to be transformed from a regional economy to a "first-world economy": "We should now go global by forming strategic alliances or mergers with other major players. Indeed, we have no choice — where the industries are consolidating worldwide, we either become major players, or we are nothing".[14] Australian academic and critic, Garry Rodan, has argued that Singapore's ambition to become an international business and financial hub is being hampered by the government's anti-democratic policies. In his view, the meaning the Singapore government attaches to the concept of transparency did not envisage a generalized loosening of information controls, and it does not extend to a relaxation of constraints on social and political reporting by the media. Singapore has been very sensitive to criticism that the GLCs' alleged lack of transparency concealed poor rates of shareholder return.[15] S&P contended in 2004 that the Singapore government's investment strategy had produced "markedly inferior" returns (between 1.7 per cent and 4 per cent) in the last five years, as compared to those achieved by comparable institutions in Hong Kong. In its 2004 report, Temasek pointed to various adverse factors over the past 10 years that held returns down, including the Asian financial crisis and the impact of SARS and the 9/11 terrorist attacks in the United States. But Temasek declared that over the past 30 years, it had delivered a "robust" total shareholder return of 18 per cent. Temasek's greater transparency has led to favourable ratings from S&P and Moody's for financial stability.

Terrorism and National Security

Singapore remains vigilant against the potential threat of international terrorism, given the island-republic's close ties to the United States. Its leaders highlighted the global nature of the threat posed by militant Islamic terrorists. Addressing the 3rd International Institute of Strategic Studies Asia Security Conference in Singapore in June 2004, PM Goh argued that the most important post-Cold War geopolitical struggle is the war against militant Islamic terrorists. He pointed out that global terrorism is a very dangerous enemy because it is fuelled by an extremist religious belief that brooks no compromise with non-believers (infidels). Global terrorism is seen as a long-term global problem because it has to do with winning the hearts and minds of men. The war against terrorism is both an ideological and geopolitical struggle, with Al-Qaeda trying to split the United States from its European and Asian allies.[16] Investigations by Singapore authorities of detained Jemaah Islamiyah (JI) suspects showed that they had planned to attack United States, Western, and Singaporean targets. The October 2002 Bali bombings and subsequent attacks in Jakarta and the Muslim-majority provinces in southern Thailand highlighted that Southeast Asia had become a battleground in the counter-terrorism war. Indonesian cleric Abu Bakar Bashir's JI is seen to have the ultimate goal of setting up a pan-Southeast Asian Caliphate (*ummah* of believers) comprising Indonesia, Malaysia, southern Philippines, southern Thailand, and Singapore.

Goh also raised the possibility of terrorist attacks on East Asian waterways, which would have catastrophic consequences. The vital oil and shipping lifelines of

Japan, China, and Korea pass through Southeast Asia. If the terrorists were to successfully carry out their attacks, it would disrupt international trade and energy supplies on which the East Asian economies are dependent upon. The fear of maritime terrorism in the Straits of Malacca and Singapore was also raised by defence minister Teo Chee Hean in April 2004. During his speech at the opening of the 2nd Western Pacific Mine Countermeasure and Diving Exercises Exhibition, Teo pointed out that "the primary responsibility for the safety and security of the Malacca Straits lies with the three littoral states (Indonesia, Malaysia, Singapore). But he added that "no single state has the resources to deal effectively with the threat of maritime terrorism".[17] Singapore's position is that the advanced trading nations of the United States, Western Europe and Japan have vested economic and security interest in ensuring that the Malacca Straits is kept open and safe, for the benefit of all states. Singapore takes the terrorism threat very seriously.

In August 2004, the government launched a 68-page book "The Fight Against Terror — Singapore's National Security Strategy", which explained the links between various local terror organizations and gave advice to the public on what they could do in terms of vigilance to minimize the risk of a successful terrorist attack against the city-state. In his preface, Tony Tan warned Singaporeans that they "have to prepare for a long-drawn campaign against terrorism, and we need to learn to live with the real prospect that a terrorist attack could occur in this country".[18] Singapore sees the threat of transnational terrorism as a protracted, strategic problem. The transnational terrorists are also assumed to be very ideologically motivated. The government raised its counter-terrorism profile by upgrading the National Security Secretariat, set up in 1999, into the National Security Coordination Centre (NSCC). The main aim of the NSCC is to strengthen coordination among Singapore's existing security agencies. These are the Ministry of Defence, the Singapore Armed Forces, the Singapore Police Force, the Security and Intelligence Division, the Singapore Civil Defence Force, and the Ministry of Information, Communications and the Arts.[19]

The Economy

The challenge for Singapore is to sustain its economic recovery and remain competitive. PM Lee has signalled that his priority is to continue with policies that can sustain Singapore's competitiveness and economic vitality. The general expectation is for a slowdown in the world economy in 2005. There is concern over the economic slowdown in the United States, the world's main economic growth engine, including worries about the burgeoning U.S. current account and budget deficits. World oil prices are expected to remain high. Geopolitical tensions persist in Iraq, and the Palestinian-Israeli conflict in the Middle East continues. Singapore's leaders have also repeatedly highlighted the serious challenges to the republic's economy posed by the rise of low-cost manufacturers in China, India, and other developing countries in Asia. The Asian states are increasingly feeling the strong gravitational pull of China's growing economy, creating greater mutual interdependence. The rise of China is forcing a rethink on Singapore's part.[20] East Asian nations do not all see a rising China as a threat. At the moment, Beijing's energies are focused on promoting internal economic development, so as to deal with the country's serious systemic deficiencies. Many Asian countries have come around to viewing China more as an opportunity to promote win-win economic and political ties, including an ASEAN-China Free Trade Area. Closer ASEAN-China ties have also made it easier for Singapore to adopt a strategy of promoting higher levels of economic, trade and commercial links between Singapore and China.

Staying Competitive

Economic competitiveness is Singapore's lifeblood. Some industries in Singapore are encountering much tougher foreign competition. The Port of Singapore Authority (PSA) has lost business to Johor's Tanjung Pelepas. Singapore Airlines (SIA) is threatened by the growth of regional budget airlines. Electronics, Singapore's leading export industry, has seen a big shift in business to China. A number of MNCs in other countries that have regional operations in Singapore are shifting at least some of these functions to Shanghai and other major Chinese cities in order to be closer to the China market itself. Singapore's competitiveness appears to be fading in some industries but improving in others, as the island-state readjusts to a changing external economic landscape.[21] Although Singapore cannot match its neighbours in terms of lower labour costs, it compensates by offering a very efficient logistics system, excellent physical infrastructure, a well educated and productive labour force, and tax/other incentives to attract high value-added foreign investments.

Singapore adopts a pragmatic, multi-pronged strategy to stay competitive. First, it is upgrading some industries in order to prevent them from being eclipsed. For example, in response to the Disney Theme Park in Hong Kong, Singapore has unveiled its own plans for an integrated gambling and entertainment complex. Second, Singapore is pushing its GLCs to step up their foreign investments. Temasek is heading this reform drive, which could be helped considerably by a concurrent policy change by the Malaysian government. The GLCs are also lowering their charges so they do not get out of line with rates elsewhere. The government upheld a decision by its telecommunications regulator to force SingTel to lower the access cost to data cables linking office buildings to global data networks. Third, Singapore is targeting to attract more foreign direct investment in cutting-edge industries. So far, the results have been encouraging. The biomedical sector, including research and development facilities, pharmaceuticals, medical devices, biotechnology and health care are the top priorities.[22]

Singapore's strategy to cope with the rise of low-cost manufacturers in other Asian nations is to go for higher value-added exports and services. The island-state is seeking to develop a new business development model, with an emphasis on cutting costs, and providing more efficient services. Singapore's services-dominated economy is trying to make itself useful, focusing on supporting business with China, be it in the form of providing logistics, helping Chinese state-owned companies raise foreign capital, promoting the growth of tourism from China, or advising both Chinese companies and foreign investors in China. For example, Singapore's major port operator, PSA, announced a basic change of policy in September 2003 when it sold a stake in two berths to Cosco, one of China's main shipping companies. This deal should be able to help secure Singapore's position as an entrepôt for trade between Southeast Asia and China. It is also aimed at defending Singapore's position against an erosion of business to the Malaysian port of Tanjung Pelepas.[23]

Singapore's status as a regional aviation hub is also coming under great pressure because of a rising China. Changi Airport and SIA were able to prosper in the past because of the superior way they catered to the tourists, business travellers and freight traffic that passed through the region. Increasingly, China itself is becoming a regional aviation hub, in terms of passenger and freight growth. As a result, Malaysia and Thailand are setting up budget airlines. Short-haul flights are likely to become more important, and they are likely to involve destinations that were not historically serviced from Singapore. Travellers flying between China and Southeast Asia could decide to bypass hubs like Singapore if they have cheaper, more direct alternatives. At the same time, the introduction of new long-haul aircraft, such as the Airbus A340-500, means some airlines can bypass Changi Airport and fly direct to distant destinations.[24]

Global economic competition is intensifying. The "premium gap" between Singapore and her neighbours is narrowing, as the latter are putting their internal houses in order. At the moment, Singapore remains attractive to foreign investors. Despite tougher competition in 2004, Singapore's Economic Development Board (EDB) still managed to attract S$8.3 billion of investments, a strong increase of 11 per cent compared with 2003. EDB's target was S$8 billion. Total investment for the services sector increased to S$2.3 billion in 2004, compared with EDB's target of S$2 billion. The strong investments are expected to generate a total of 21,800 new jobs, an increase of 30 per cent compared to 2003: 70 per cent of the new jobs created are in the professional/skilled sectors. EDB chairman Teo Ming Kian disclosed that EDB had to "compete very hard" in ploughing the new markets in China, India, Indonesia, and Australasia.[25] Singapore aggressively markets itself to investors and has been very successful in attracting MNCs in a range of industries, like foreign banks. Increasingly, one of Singapore's key assets is its potential as a base to support regional economic expansion for MNCs.

The Singapore government offers attractive tax incentives to get foreign companies to locate their HQs in Singapore. The Economic Development Board (EDB) estimated that by end-2003, over 4,000 of the 7,000 MNCs that had invested in Singapore had some form of regional mandate. In addition to banking, fund management, consumer electronics, and precision engineering, Singapore has also been very successful in attracting foreign investment with regional functions in biomedical sciences, international media, logistics, chemicals, hospitality services and education. Compared to Hong Kong, Singapore's competitive edge lies in terms of the range of industries that it has been able to attract MNCs. The development of closer ASEAN-China ties will also benefit Singapore.[26]

Casino Resort Project

In late December 2004, Singapore asked potential investors to submit proposals for a casino resort aimed at boosting the city-state's tourist appeal.[27] The proposed casino, which is to be part of an "iconic lifestyle" resort complex, triggered a strong reaction from religious and civic groups concerned about the negative social effects posed by legalized gambling. To allay such concerns, the government came up with a list of proposed restrictions that would make it tougher for locals to visit the casino. In early 2004, Senior Minister of State (Trade & Industry) Vivian Balakrishnan led a government delegation to study casino operations in Las Vegas. If such a casino is allowed, there will be restrictions in place to prevent Singaporeans, especially those who can ill-afford to gamble away their incomes, from becoming gambling addicts. Proposed restrictions include a S$100 levy for a one-day entry into the casino, and S$2,000 for an annual membership. The government wanted to send out a signal that "if you choose to go to a casino, this is not a means to make a living".

The proposed project drew strong interest from casino giants such as the U.S.-based Caesars Entertainment and Harrah's Entertainment. Industry observers estimated that the proposed project could cost between US$300 million and US$2 billion. Two sites have been identified for the project: the resort island of Sentosa and Marina South, a reclaimed area bordering the financial district. Singaporeans, who enjoy an annual per capita income of about US$23,000, bet billions of dollars annually, and are regular customers at Asian, Australian, and U.S. casinos. The Singapore government also takes in an estimated US$800 million annually in tax duties from regulated horse racing, lotteries and sports betting.[28]

Foreign Policy

Foreign economic diplomacy (FTAs)

In 2004, the government intensified its quest for more bilateral Free Trade Arrangements (FTAs) as part of its strategy to enhance the city-state's economic space. This strategy emerged in the early 1990s due to the formation of trade blocs in North America (NAFTA), the outbreak of the Asian financial crisis 1997/98, the rise of economic/trade protectionism from within the region. The FTA strategy gained greater urgency following the collapse of global multilateral trade talks in Cancun, Mexico, in September 2003. Since 2000, Singapore has signed a number of bilateral FTAs with New Zealand, Japan, the European Free Trade Area, Australia, and the United States. Singapore is in negotiations for bilateral FTAs with Canada, Mexico, Chile, the EU, India, Jordan, and Sri Lanka. Singapore, New Zealand, and Chile are also examining a Pacific Three FTA as a bridge between Latin America, the Pacific, and Asia.[29]

2004 was, despite some minor hiccups, a generally successful year for Singapore's foreign policy. Relations with neighbouring Malaysia and Indonesia improved considerably. Singapore participated actively in ASEAN's diplomacy, especially in enhancing economic and political ties with China, Japan, and South Korea.

Singapore-Malaysia Relations

As next-door neighbours, Singapore's relations with Malaysia are of strategic importance. Under former Malaysian prime minister Mahathir Mohamed, bilateral relations went through a rough patch in 2002–03. In 2004, the bilateral Singapore-Malaysia relationship was restored to a firmer footing after Abdullah Badawi became prime minister in Malaysia in November 2003. Badawi reflected a more pragmatic approach on a whole range of bilateral issues: the price of water supply from Malaysia to Singapore; the building of a new bridge to replace the old Causeway; use of Malaysian airspace by RSAF fighter jets; the release of CPF funds of Malaysian workers; the territorial dispute over Pedra Branca (Pulau Batu Putih); and the dispute over Singapore's reclamation works at Tuas and Tekong island. In mid-January 2005, both countries reached an amicable breakthrough to settle their dispute over reclamation works at Tuas and Tekong, after two years of legal wrangling. Both countries can be expected to reach more win-win agreements on other bilateral issues.[30]

In January 2004, Badawi visited Singapore, signalling his intention for a political reconciliation. He said that outstanding bilateral problems should be solved on an issue-by-issue basis. The previous approach, based on search for a grand package to resolve everything at once, had proved fruitless.[31] In July 2004, Malaysian Trade Minister Rafidah Aziz announced that Malaysian companies, including government-linked companies, should be open to investments from Singapore companies, including Temasek. In talks between then PM Goh Chok Tong and PM Abdullah Badawi in early 2004, both leaders made it clear that they wanted to transcend past differences. Both sides agreed to tackle each bilateral issue on its merits, and to abandon the previous counterproductive "package" approach. Another key factor in the improved bilateral relationship was that both nations wisely realized that they faced far greater external challenges, including the political and economic implications of a rising China and India. Both countries stood to benefit through mutual cooperation.

Lee Hsien Loong made his first overseas trip as prime minister to Malaysia in October 2004, highlighting the importance that the government attached to good and cordial relations with its closest neighbour. During the visit, Lee announced that he had appointed Goh Chok Tong to be Singapore's special envoy on efforts to resolve the bilateral issues. In mid-December 2004, Goh visited Malaysia for direct talks with PM Abdullah. It resulted in some breakthroughs. Both leaders agreed that, "solutions must lead to mutual benefits and not disadvantage the other party". They also agreed that ministers and officials would resume talks ahead of their next meeting scheduled for February 2005. The improvement in bilateral relations is a reflection of their economic pragmatism. Faced with the more serious threat of competition from China and India, both countries have decided to put aside their differences, and focused on fostering closer win-win political and economic cooperation. In November 2003, the Government Investment Corporation (GIC), which manages more than US$100 billion of Singapore's foreign exchange reserves, bought a 5 per cent stake in Malaysia's national carmaker, Proton. In March 2004, Temasek made its first major direct investment in Malaysia, by acquiring a 5 per cent stake in Telekom Malaysia for US$421 million. In November 2004, Temasek also announced a partnership with Malaysian investment bank CIMB to form a Malaysian private investment real estate fund with initial capital of M$500 million.[32]

Singapore-China Ties

Singapore's foreign policy aims at developing mutually beneficial ties, especially with the Great Powers. Singapore has adopted a two-pronged pragmatic response to the rise of China. First, it continues to seek "deep engagement" with China through bilateral diplomacy, exchanges, economic cooperation, and multilateral regional institutions. Second, in a careful balancing act, Singapore seeks to further strengthen its economic-military relationship with the United States, the world's sole superpower. This strategy is necessitated by the evolving strategic environment in East Asia, especially growing support for independence in Taiwan.[33]

In mid-July, then deputy prime minister Lee Hsien Loong's visit to Taiwan caused a major controversy with China. During his visit, Lee met senior Taiwanese politicians, including the president, Chen Sui-bian. Despite Lee's visit being cast in a personal capacity, and the Ministry of Foreign Affairs (MFA) reaffirming its commitment to the "One-China" policy, the PRC strongly criticized the trip. There was fear of a strong negative fallout. A planned trip to China by the Minister for National Development, Mah Bow Tan, was indefinitely postponed. As part of its damage-control strategy, Lee used his first national day rally speech on 22 August 2004 to explain that he had wanted to see for himself the latest trends in the thinking of Taiwanese leaders on developments in cross-strait relations. Singapore has extensive ties with both China and Taiwan. Singapore had made it clear from the beginning of the establishment of diplomatic ties with the PRC in the early 1990s that it would continue to maintain its ties with Taiwan, so as to protect the Republic's national interests. Lee stressed Singapore's "One-China" policy, and that Singapore would not support Taiwanese independence. He also expressed his view that other countries, including the West European states, would not support Taiwan independence. At the UN General Assembly session in New York in September 2004, Foreign Minister George Yeo reiterated Singapore's position on the Taiwan issue. Yeo expressed that the international community should not allow tensions between Taiwan and the mainland to get out of control, and drag other countries into the conflict. He added that other countries would also not support Taiwan independence. Taiwan's foreign minister Mark Chen accused Singapore of trying to curry favour with China. He scathingly attacked Singapore's audacity, as a small state, to prescribe advice to Taiwan on cross-strait relations. Using an offensive Hokkien expletive, Mark Chen described Singapore as a "tiny piece of dried mucus".

Singapore's MFA responded by noting out that "Many other countries have pointed out that Taiwan is pursuing a dangerous policy". Mark Chen later apologized for using crude and intemperate language against Singapore.

Singapore-India Ties

The pragmatic nature of Singapore's foreign policy can be seen in its burgeoning ties with and high-level visits to India and the South Asian region. There are two key considerations. One, as Singapore intensifies its economic links with China, growing economic ties with India would serve to highlight Singapore's even-handed approach to external powers, adding to Singapore's advantage. In terms of domestic politics, the PAP and Singapore cannot afford to be cast as a "Third China". Second, it is part of Singapore's strategy of building a "second wing" for its economy. As in the case of China, Singapore's aim is to leverage on India's opening up to the outside world. Singapore sees itself as a bridge to South Asia, the Persian Gulf and beyond. India is an increasingly important economic partner for Singapore. Today, India has become Singapore's 14th largest trading partner, with total bilateral trade reaching nearly S$8 billion. Singapore was India's 11th largest investor with cumulative investments worth about US$1.45 billion by 2003. In 2004, both countries boosted the momentum of bilateral ties through more high-level official visits. Lee Hsien Loong in his then capacities as deputy prime minister and finance minister visited India in January 2004 at the invitation of his Indian counterpart, Lal Krishna Advani. Minister for Trade & Industry George Yeo visited India in February 2004. Goh himself visited India from 8–11 July 2004. It was his fifth visit to India, where he held talks with the new Indian prime minister, Manmohan Singh and other senior Indian leaders. During the visit, both sides agreed to further widen bilateral economic cooperation. Singapore and India are continuing negotiations on a Comprehensive Economic Cooperation Agreement. During the visit, Goh also launched the Singapore-India Partnership Foundation, a private sector led initiative by the Singapore Business Federation and the Confederation of Indian Industry. The aim of the Foundation is to strengthen bilateral Singapore-India ties, including economic linkages, government relations, academic interaction, and cultural understanding. To take advantage of India's economic reforms, Singapore agencies have made study visits to India to seek out economic and business opportunities in various Indian states.

Singapore-U.S. Relations

In 2004, bilateral Singapore-U.S. ties further strengthened. From the early days of its independence, Singapore sees a strong U.S. economic and military presence as making a vital contribution to ensuring peace and stability in the Southeast Asian region. From Singapore's realist viewpoint, the United States is a benign superpower, helping to maintain a viable regional balance of power, which serves to maximize Singapore's room to manoeuvre. Singapore enjoys excellent relations with the Bush administration. The landmark U.S.-Singapore Free Trade Agreement (USSFTA) came into force in January 2004. It was the first FTA to be concluded between the United States and an Asian country. The USSFTA is expected to cement the already strong economic linkages between the two countries. 2004 was marked by a number of high-level bilateral visits. In April 2004, Tony Tan led a multi-agency delegation to the United States for discussions on higher education and national security. He was accompanied by Education Minister Tharman Shanmugaratnam. In May 2004, PM Goh made an official visit to the United States. Delivering a keynote speech at the Council on Foreign Relations, PM Goh highlighted the priority that Singapore placed on concerted international cooperation in the war against terrorism. The U.S. Congress also approved a resolution thanking Singapore for its steadfast support of the United States during the Iraq War and the war against global terrorism.[34] Both Singapore and the United States are engaged in talks to develop a strategic framework agreement on security and defence expected to expand cooperation in areas such as counter-terrorism, counter-proliferation of weapons of mass destruction, joint military exercises, training, policy dialogues and defence technology.

Conclusion

Singapore's response to the events of 2004 highlighted some important trends for the future. First, we can expect the continued entrenchment of the PAP's political hegemony in Singapore. The political opposition is likely to remain marginalized, unless in the unlikely possibility of a split within the ruling party or a prolonged economic recession. Through a systematic process of political renewal, the PAP continually brings in new talent to rejuvenate its ranks. It continues to scout the island to co-opt the best and the brightest. Its consistent political message to Singaporeans is that the talented do not join the opposition. Second, early signs indicate that Lee Hsien Loong's administration will seek to fulfill its promise to bring about a "more open and inclusive" government. But this process will be carefully managed and controlled, at a suitable pace that would ensure the protection of the interests of the PAP's ruling elite and that of Singapore. A likely pressing issue is the growing sentiment for genuine acceptance of grassroots feedback, amid the steady growth of civil society and a better-educated citizenry. Third, in line with Singapore's ambitions to become a global banking and financial hub, there will be greater scrutiny, especially by foreigners, that the republic is keeping up with international best practices. Finally, Singapore will use its foreign policy to expand its economic and political space, and to strategically position itself so that it can shape a conducive regional environment to the republic's advantage.

Notes

[1] Lee Hsien Loong, "Singapore of the Future", in *Singapore: Re-engineering Success*, edited by Arun Mahizhnan and Lee Tsao Yuan (Singapore: Oxford University Press, 1998).

[2] Evelyn Goh, "Singapore's Reaction to Rising China: Deep Engagement and Strategic Adjustment", Institute for Defence and Strategic Studies (IDSS), Working Paper no. 67, May 2004; Michael Leifer, *Singapore's Foreign Policy: Coping with Vulnerability*, (London: Routledge, 2000).

[3] PRS Group, Country Report on Singapore, "International Country Risk Guide", October 2004, http://www.prsonline.com.

[4] *Economist*, 12 August 2004.

[5] Chan Heng Chee, *Singapore: The Politics of Survival, 1965–1967* (Singapore: Oxford University Press, 1971).

[6] Text of President SR Nathan's speech, *Straits Times*, 13 January 2005, p. 1.

[7] *Channel NewsAsia*, 28 June 2004.

[8] Hussin Mutalib, *Parties and Politics: A Study of Opposition Parties and the PAP in Singapore* (Eastern Universities Press, 2004).

[9] Agence France-Presse, 21 December 2004.

[10] *Straits Times*, 20 December 2004.

[11] *Economist*, 1 September 2004.

[12] *Straits Times*, 3 November 2004, page H23.

[13] Andy Mukerjee, *Bloomberg News*, 6 August 2004.

[14] Garry Rodan, *Transparency and Authoritarian Rule in Southeast Asia: Singapore and Malaysia* (London: RoutledgeCurzon, 2004), p. 57.

[15] Rodan, op. cit., p. 81.

[16] Singapore Government Press Release, Ministry of Information, Communications & the Arts, http://app.sprinter.gov.sg/data/pr/2004060402.htm.

[17] Keynote Address by Minister for Defence, RADM (NS) Teo Chee Hean, at the Opening of the 2nd Western Pacific MCMEX & DIVEX, 26 April 2004, http://www.mindef.gov.sg.

[18] *The Fight against Terror: Singapore's National Security Strategy*, Singapore National Security Coordination Centre, 2004, http://www.pmo.gov.sg/NSCS/FightAgainstTerror.pdf.

[19] Country Risk Report on Singapore, *International Country Risk Guide*, October 2004.

[20] *Asian Intelligence*, 7 January 2005, p. 11.

21   *Asian Intelligence*, 21 July 2004, p. 13.

22   *Asian Intelligence*, 21 July 2004, p. 14.

23   *Asian Intelligence*, 7 January 2004.

24   *Asian Intelligence*, 7 January 2004, p. 11.

25   *Straits Times*, "EDB Exceeds Target for Investment", 11 January 2005.

26   *Asian Intelligence*, 8 December 2004.

27   AFP, 28 December 2004.

28   AFP, 29 December 2004.

29   Linda Low, "A Comparative Evaluation & Prognosis of Asia Pacific Bilateral and
     Regional Trade Arrangements", *Asia-Pacific Economic Literature* 18, no. 1 (May 2004):
     3. Barry Desker, "Why East Asia is Negotiating FTAs", IDSS Commentaries, 3 December
     2004. Chia Siow Yue, "Economic Cooperation and Integration in East Asia", *Asia-
     Pacific Review* 11, no. 1 (May 2004): 2–3.

30   *Straits Times*, 4 January 2005, p. 1.

31   EIU Country Report, September 2004.

32   AFP, 13 December 2004.

33   Evelyn Goh, "Singapore's Reaction to Rising China: Deep Engagement and Strategic
     Adjustment", IDSS Working Paper no. 67, May 2004.

34   *Straits Times*, 6 May 2004. Singapore Ministry of Foreign Affairs' website, http://
     www.mfa.gov.sg.

Singapore's Approach to Homeland Security

Andrew T H Tan

The Threat of Terrorism to Singapore

Following the terrorist attacks in New York and Washington on 11 September 2001, Southeast Asia, especially the Malay archipelago, has come into focus as the so-called "second front" in the war against international terrorism. Subsequent events brought home the fact that the events of 11 September 2001 had great resonance within the region. The existence of an Al-Qaeda-affiliated network in the region was highlighted by the arrests in Singapore since January 2002 of 37 members of the regional extremist network, the Jemaah Islamiyah (JI). The radical Islamist group planned to attack American military personnel at a local subway station, U.S. naval vessels at Singapore's Changi Naval Base, U.S. commercial interests, Western and Israeli embassies, and Singaporean military facilities. Had the planned attacks succeeded, they would collectively have constituted the largest terrorist attack since 11 September 2001. They would have caused many casualties as well as made an immense political, psychological and economic impact on Singapore that would have reverberated throughout the region and internationally. Because Singapore is closely identified with the United States on political, security and economic issues, hosts a naval logistics facility that has supported U.S. naval and military operations in the Indian Ocean, Persian Gulf and Afghanistan, and is home to many U.S. multinationals operating in the region, Singapore is a prime target of radical Islamists. As a consequence, Singapore's response to the war on international terrorism has been the most vigorous of the Southeast Asian states. Like the United States, it has taken homeland security very seriously, and has instituted as a top national priority, the implementation of a new homeland security architecture that would better protect Singapore against terrorism. In August 2004, the government formally

Andrew T H Tan is Assistant Professor at the Institute of Defence and Strategic Studies, Nanyang Technological University, Singapore.

outlined Singapore's National Security Strategy primarily aimed at countering the terrorist threat.

Total Defence

Despite the highly publicized post-11 September 2001 homeland security responses, however, Singapore's policy on homeland defence predated those seminal events. Accompanying the rapid development of the Singapore Armed Forces since independence in 1965 has been an abiding concern over some serious vulnerabilities emanating from its geography. The small island-state lacks strategic depth with its defences and other strategic targets vulnerable to an external attack, making it necessary to be able to detect and pre-empt any such attack, and also to invest heavily in multiple redundancies and the hardening of critical facilities. The heavily built-up, urbanized and densely populated island is also vulnerable to air and artillery bombardment which would cause devastating casualties unless it also invests heavily in a strong civil defence capability. Finally, the heavy dependence on maritime trade means that it can be blockaded by mines or other means of interdicting its seaborne trade, unless it has a strong maritime defence capability. The circumstances of its independence, namely, expulsion from the Malaysian Federation amidst political and racial tensions; the historical experience of Confrontation with a nationalistic Indonesia under Sukarno; and its uncomfortable strategic location in the middle of the Malay archipelago, have also contributed to a strong sense of insecurity.

Acute awareness of its small size, limited resources and geopolitical circumstances has resulted in Singapore developing what amounts to outsiders as a siege mentality. Singapore has adopted an "all citizens to the ramparts" approach, embodied in its doctrine of Total Defence, which not only maximizes the resources for defence but also emphasizes the importance of military deterrence, economic strength, and internal cohesion and stability as the foundations of its security. Through Total Defence, every sector of society is mobilized and has a part to play in ensuring Singapore's security. Under this concept, citizens are organized to defend the country against all forms of attack, both military and non-military.

Total Defence consists of Economic Defence, Psychological Defence, Social Defence, Civil Defence and Military Defence. Under Economic Defence, there is close coordination amongst the various government departments providing essential services to ensure that the economy is organized in such a way that it will not break down in the face of external attack. Psychological Defence consists of the will to defend the nation. Social Defence is aimed at preventing any exploitation of ethnic unrest by stressing the mutual coexistence of the various races. Military Defence consists of strong deterrent forces centred around the Singapore Armed Forces.[1]

Civil Defence measures, coordinated by a corps of professionals and national servicemen in the Singapore Civil Defence Force (SCDF), have been very extensive, rivalled only by Switzerland and Israel. In operational terms, there have been frequent mobilization exercises of civilian vehicles, vessels and aircraft for military use.[2] Stretches of roads in Singapore have been strengthened as emergency runways for the air force.[3] Passive civil defence measures such as an air raid siren system have also been installed. Food and strategic stockpiles are maintained and a huge civilian bomb-shelter programme has been put in place. All new housing estates are now equipped with bomb shelters and underground subway stations have been strengthened against blast so that they can serve as bomb shelters in a war.[4] Air raid siren, fuel, water and food rationing exercises have been held. To better coordinate defence of civilians against attack, the fire service was absorbed into the SCDF, which also operates rescue teams to save victims trapped in destroyed buildings.

After much ongoing investment in resources and publicity, both total and civil defence have been well accepted by the general populace; after all, this was a city that had suffered much from the Japanese attack in 1942.

The Threat of Terrorism

Singapore's recognition of the threat of global terrorism predated the events of 11 September 2001. Singapore's security perceptions are clearly expressed in Singapore's Defence White Paper published in 2000, entitled Defending Singapore in the 21st Century. Significantly, whilst it reiterated the importance of traditional realist tools of military deterrence and diplomacy, it also acknowledged the emergence of non-traditional security threats such as terrorism, cyber-warfare and the proliferation of weapons of mass destruction. It envisaged that the Singapore Armed Forces would have to develop a broader range of capabilities and work with others to meet some of the new security challenges that have arisen in the globalized era.[5] The setting up of the National Security Secretariat to better coordinate Singapore's response to the changed security environment was thus an indication of the high degree of awareness of the authorities of the growing menace from new, asymmetric forms of security threats such as those emanating from international terrorism. This was in tandem with its ongoing interest in enhancing Singapore's conventional military capabilities through the adoption of some of the doctrinal and technological innovations emanating from the so-called Revolution in Military Affairs (RMA) debate and process in the United States.

The terrorist attacks on the World Trade Center in New York, and the Pentagon in Washington, on 11 September 2001 demonstrated that even the world's sole superpower was not safe from asymmetric forms of waging warfare, such as through mass casualty terrorist acts, despite its much vaunted conventional military superiority stemming from the emerging RMA. With casualties running into thousands, it is the first true mass casualty terrorist act in modern times.[6] What security analysts had been predicting for years, that is, the perpetuation of a terrorist act causing massive casualties running into thousands or tens of thousands, had finally come true.[7]

Singapore was quick to recognize the global significance and implications of these events, given its growing concern over the emergence of the so-called "new" or "postmodern" terrorism motivated by apocalyptic religious ideology. Singapore thus came out strongly to support the United States in its declaration of war against international terrorism. As Kishore Mahbuhani, Singapore's then Ambassador to the United Nations, stated on 1 October 2001: "Americans are not alone in this fight against terrorism. Singapore stands with the United States and the international community in this struggle. This is a fight between people who stand for civilized society, and those out to destroy it."[8]

Subsequent events, however, brought home the fact that the international war against terrorism, indeed, the very events of 11 September 2001, had great resonance within the region. Singapore was directly involved in that it was a prime Al-Qaeda target. In Singapore, the smashing of the JI stemmed from ongoing investigations into local militant activity and also the recovery of a videotape from an Al-Qaeda house destroyed by U.S. bombing in Afghanistan in December 2001. The tape revealed that the group planned to attack American military personnel at a local subway station, U.S. naval vessels at Singapore's Changi Naval Base, U.S. commercial interests, Western (specifically, U.S., Britain and Australia) and Israeli embassies, and Singaporean military facilities. Twenty-one tonnes of ammonium nitrate were to be used for several massive truck bombs to carry out the attacks. The planned attacks were to be coordinated by two senior Al-Qaeda operatives, Fathur Rohman al-Ghozi, and Jabarah Mohammed Mansour, both of whom were subsequently arrested.[9] Had the extensive and audacious attacks been successful, they would have caused many American and local casualties, and seriously affected business confidence in Singapore, home to several thousand foreign multinational corporations. Worse, they would have damaged communal relations, given the fact that 15 per cent of the population consists of Malay Muslims.

The JI terrorist threat was also serious. As revealed in the Singapore Government's White Paper entitled "The Jemaah Islamiyah Arrests and the Threat of Terrorism" issued in January 2003, the JI is an extensive regional terrorist network with well-trained operatives in Malaysia, Philippines, Indonesia, Singapore and Australia. As spelt out in its key training manual, the *Pedoman Umum Perjuangan Jemaah Islamiyah* (PUPJI), its objective is the creation of a *Daulah Islamiyah* or Islamic state in the region through the use of violence. Members of the group have been implicated in various subsequent terrorist attacks in the region, for instance, the bomb attack at the popular Kuta Beach in Bali, Indonesia on 12 October 2002 that killed 202 people, including many Australians.[10] This was followed by the Marriott Hotel bombing in Jakarta on 5 August 2003 that killed 12 people.[11] Despite the arrests of over 200 alleged operatives throughout the region, the JI remains dangerous, given its estimated number of 3,000, including several hundred that had been trained in Afghanistan as well as in regional camps.[12] In addition, subsequent investigations also revealed that apart from the JI network, there are also radical Islamists within Southeast Asia with varying levels of linkages both with other radicals in the region and also with Al-Qaeda. Many were ex-*mujahideen* who had fought in Afghanistan against the Soviets in the 1980s and others had attended Al-Qaeda/Taleban training camps there in the 1990s, after the Soviets had left.

Evolution of Singapore's Homeland Security Structure

Given these events, Singapore's response has been the most vigorous of the states in the region. Singapore already had a fairly robust Civil Defence capability as well as a Total Defence approach that was aimed at improving its defence against asymmetric security threats. It thus had a strong foundation upon which to build a new counter-terrorism security structure. Indeed, there was already a well-established National Emergency System (NEST), including a National Emergency Council chaired by the Minister for Home Affairs, and an Executive Group of top civil servants from key ministries that would lead the management of civil security or any civil emergency, such as hijacking, a bomb attack, terrorist sabotage or civil disaster.[13]

Two months after the events of 11 September 2001, Singapore promulgated the doctrine of "Homefront Security", which, according to Defence Minister Tony Tan, would be implemented over the next few years to protect Singapore from the new terrorism. Tan stated that the events of 11 September 2001 demonstrated that the traditional division between external and internal threats no longer held, and revealed that a Security Policy Review Committee would coordinate the building of a new security architecture, which would entail much closer cooperation between the armed forces, police and the Ministry of Home Affairs.[14] Indeed, Tan was also later to speak of the development of "an overarching framework and integrated system to meet the challenges of the new security environment", stating the need for "a new approach and a coordinated multi-agency effort".[15]

To operationalize the new doctrine, Singapore opted for a network approach, consisting of a few inter-ministerial agencies to coordinate various aspects of policy, intelligence and operations. This was deemed to be more effective and practical, in contrast to the U.S. approach, which was to establish a super agency, the Department of Homeland Security, consolidating a number of existing agencies with some 170,000 staff. The government thus established a National Security Task Force to improve operational capability, with a Homefront Security Center designated the principal organization for coordinating operational matters. This agency supervised joint exercises as well as counter-terrorist security operations, and aimed to improve inter-ministry coordination, closely working with the Defence Ministry in counter-terrorism. A second organization that was set up was the Joint Counter-Terrorism Centre, to better coordinate intelligence on terrorism. A third organization, the National Security Secretariat, had as its ambit the coordination of counter-terrorism at the strategic policy level.

The organizational restructuring continued with the establishment in April 2003 of a new agency, the Immigration and Checkpoints Authority (ICA), which merged the immigration and customs departments, in order to strengthen Singapore's first line of defence against terrorism, namely, border control.[16] Indeed, all motorists entering Singapore from Malaysia, at both land border checkpoints at Tuas and Woodlands, are now inspected, with biometric technology being introduced to scan the passports of all travellers to Singapore.[17]

Concern over terrorist attacks involving the use of CBRN (chemical, biological, radiological and nuclear) material also prompted measures to contain the threat. Once again, Singapore was able to build on its civil defence efforts since 1991. On 25 November 2002, the Strategic Goods (Control) Bill was passed. The Act lists 600 controlled items that will require special permits for export or transshipment. The items include chemicals, viruses, computer software and other items that could be used to make nuclear, biological or chemical weapons.[18] In January 2003, the government revealed that it had established a Chemical, Biological, Radiological and Explosives (CBRE) Defence Group the previous year. Although raised primarily to deal with incidents in military installations, this capability is readily available to reinforce the existing resources within the SCDF. In February 2003, it was revealed that 13 of the 16 subway stations on the new Northeast Line had underground chemical decontamination chambers to contain the impact of any chemical attack.

To further improve bio-terror defences, a Regional Emerging Diseases Intervention (REDI) Centre, a joint U.S.-Singapore initiative, was established in 2003.[19] Singapore also joined the U.S.-led Proliferation Security Initiative (PSI) designed to counter the proliferation of weapons of mass destruction and related materials by interdicting the illegal trafficking of such materials. This includes intercepting and searching suspect vessels on the high seas.[20] In the aftermath of 11 September 2001, Total Defence began to take on a more overt anti-terrorism focus, with the SCDF conducting exercises and public awareness programmes to better prepare for any terrorist attack on, for instance, trains, or the use of chemical weapons.[21] Reminiscent of the Citizen Preparedness Program in America undertaken by the Department of Homeland Security, the government announced in January 2003 a National Security Awareness Programme. This included the dissemination of an emergency handbook as well as a mobile exhibition by the Internal Security Department.[22] These measures are aimed at mobilizing community assistance in detecting and disrupting terrorist attacks, while at the same time spreading the awareness that would raise psychological resilience in the event of an attack.

The threat to aviation, maritime and land transport has been recognized, with the government moving swiftly to implement various security measures, including improved baggage screening as well as enhanced airport security. In January 2003, the government also announced that it would deploy air marshals on board Singapore Airlines and its regional subsidiary, Silkair. A year later, it announced it would work with other countries to develop effective countermeasures against portable surface-to-air missiles aimed at civilian airliners.[23]

Maritime security has been accorded increasing priority, given the fears of a maritime-version of 11 September 2001 on account of the maritime industry's poor state of security, the lack of proper vetting of crew, the inability to track ships in real time, the vulnerability of ships on the high seas to piracy and terrorism, and the presence of high risk, high value targets such as cruise ships and chemical tankers. Ships, and particularly containers, could also be used to smuggle terrorists as well as weapons of mass destruction. One scenario that worried security agencies has been the possibility of a chemical tanker being used as a floating bomb to devastate ports. Given Al-Qaeda's proven ability to carry out maritime attacks, demonstrated by its successful strikes against the USS Cole in October 2000 in Yemen, for instance, as well as the vast increase in piracy and the continuing threat of terrorism in the environs of the busy and strategic Straits of Malacca, it was clear that comprehensive measures to secure the entire logistics chain within the currently poorly regulated and poorly secured maritime industry are needed.

Singapore therefore moved swiftly to implement the requirements of the International Ship and Port Security (ISPS) Code, and the amendments to the Safety of Life at Sea (SOLAS) Convention, which came into effect on 1 July 2004. Under the code, adopted by the International Maritime Organization (IMO) in December 2002, governments, ships and ports are required to have enhanced security measures to ensure better control and monitoring of the movement of people and cargo, and to promulgate the appropriate security levels according to the prevailing threat assessments. The amendments include the installation of automatic identification systems on ships, a ship-to-shore alert system to signal emergencies, and other security measures.[24] Singapore went a step further with a series of measures to coincide with the implementation of the ISPS code, such as requiring all ships of 500 tonnes and above to comply with the Pre-Arrival Notification of Security (PANS) procedures 24 hours in advance. PANS includes information on whether the vessel is in possession of a valid International Ship Security Certificate (ISSC), the current security level of the ship, the last 10 ports of call and whether any additional security measures were taken during any ship-to-port or ship-to-ship interface. Ships which arrived from non-ISPS compliant ports would also be subject to an IMO checklist on additional security measures.[25] Singapore also moved quickly to implement a satellite-based ship tracking system as well as ship-to-shore alert systems.[26]

Singapore also became the first Asian port to join the U.S. Customs-led Container Security Initiative (CSI). It agreed to do so in 2002 and launched a programme in March 2003 to screen U.S.-bound containers and inspect suspicious cargo.[27] Navy patrol craft escort high-risk merchant vessels, such as oil and gas containers and cruise ships, through the Singapore Strait. Restrictions have also been placed barring all unauthorized sea traffic from waters around sensitive areas such as petrochemical installations, as well as the movement of ships and boats at night.[28] In 2004, Singapore also joined the U.S. Coast Guard-led International Port Security Program (IPSP), which will allow the U.S. Coast Guard to inspect Singapore's port facilities and verify their implementation of the ISPS code.[29] Singapore also welcomed the U.S. Pacific Command's Regional Maritime Security Initiative (RMSI), which was floated in March 2004 as a plan to deal with transnational maritime threats in the Asia-Pacific, although the plan encountered reservations from Malaysia and Indonesia.[30] On land, the authorities have promulgated a continuing series of measures to improve security and deter terrorist attacks. Parking restrictions have been introduced in areas frequented by Western expatriates, such as the Holland Village, Newton Circus, Boat Quay and Mohamed Sultan Road areas. A

S$30 million checkpoint has been built to screen vehicles entering Jurong Island, home to a number of petrochemical plants and a potential terrorist target. After the deadly Madrid train bombing in March 2004, the government removed rubbish bins from train station platforms and bus interchanges and stepped up patrols. Guards were also introduced to patrol subway trains, train stations and bus interchanges.[31]

Recognizing the transnational nature of the new terrorism, Singapore has actively collaborated with external partners on counter-terrorism. It has actively supported all regional and international counter-terrorism initiatives, such as at ASEAN, APEC and CSCAP, as well as supported the work of international bodies such as the IMO, particularly in implementing the ISPS code. Since 11 September 2001, Singapore has moved perceptibly closer towards the United States, given its awareness that it is a major target of the radical Islamists. Singapore has actively participated in all U.S.-led counter-terrorism initiatives, including the PSI, CSI and IPSP, and also welcomed the controversial RMSI. In October 2003, Singapore and the United States also agreed to begin negotiations for a comprehensive Framework Agreement for the Promotion of a Strategic Cooperation Partnership in Defence and Security, that would expand the scope of current bilateral security cooperation in areas such as counter-terrorism, counter-proliferation of weapons of mass destruction, joint military exercises and training, policy dialogues and defence technology.[32] Once implemented, such a Framework would in effect make Singapore a U.S. ally in all but formal terms. Yet, this has not come at the expense of bilateral cooperation with other countries. Singapore has moved to improve counter-terrorism cooperation with other states, such as with Australia, Japan, Philippines, Malaysia, Indonesia and Thailand. For instance, it carried out a maritime counter-terrorism training exercise with Japan in December 2003, and also signed an agreement with it in April 2004 to cooperate in controlling the spread of weapons of mass destruction and related materials.[33] In 2004, Singapore, Malaysia and Indonesia also agreed to carry out coordinated, year-round patrols in the Straits of Malacca and to explore further measures to counter the rise in piracy and possible terrorist threats.[34]

Aware of the ideological nature of the threat and the need for a hearts and minds approach to complement hard measures, the government also strongly supported the establishment of a terrorism centre headed by renowned Al-Qaeda expert, Rohan Gunaratna, that would maintain a terrorism database and develop an understanding of the complexities of the terrorist phenomenon. In opening the centre in February 2004, Minister of Home Affairs, Wong Kan Seng, noted that, "the greatest challenge is in the realm of the mind and the heart."[35]

Singapore's National Security Strategy

Singapore's response to the events of 11 September 2001 and after can best be described as comprehensive and vigorous. However, what was clearly still lacking was a well-articulated national homeland security doctrine. The government was also acutely aware of the seriousness of the terrorist threat. As Tony Tan noted, "Singapore is a prime target ... we are almost on top of the list of cities that terrorists would like to launch a successful attack in". Tan thus vacated the Defence portfolio to become Coordinating Minister for Security and Defence in August 2003 to concentrate on the task of developing a new, more flexible security framework, one that would help allocate scarce resources prudently as new or unexpected threats emerged.[36]

In July 2004, it was announced that a new National Security Coordination Secretariat (NSCS) would be established within the Prime Minister's Office, replacing the National Security Secretariat and overseen by a senior civil servant, the Permanent Secretary for National Security and Intelligence Coordination. The position reports to the Coordinating Minister for Security and Defence and through him, directly to the Prime Minister. The NSCS would incorporate two key agencies, the National Security Coordination Centre (NSCC) and the Joint Counter-Terrorism Centre (JCTC). The NSCC's tasks would include risk assessment, public awareness, training, monitoring CBRN developments and initiatives to enhance transportation security.[37] The JCTC would provide intelligence assessments on terrorist threats and integrate the work of existing intelligence agencies in Singapore. In addition, the existing Security Policy Review Committee, comprising the ministers for defence, home affairs and foreign affairs, and chaired by the Coordinating Minister, would continue to function, formulating both strategy and policy for security.[38] This reorganization was clearly necessary, given the plethora of agencies and ad hoc committees that had hitherto taken charge of various facets of security. While streamlining the evolving homeland security structure, the new set-up is still not the super-agency approach of the United States, with its massive, new bureaucracy. Instead, it echoed a key recommendation of the 9-11 Commission in America in the appointment of a key counter-terrorism official with access to the highest political authority in the country. It is also similar to the structure in Australia where policy coordination is carried out in the Department of the Prime Minister and the Cabinet, in order to ensure a whole-of-government approach to national security policy.

In August 2004, the new National Security Strategy was unveiled in a publication entitled "The Fight Against Terror". In his foreword, Tony Tan spoke of the need to have a "consensus on the definition and characteristics of transnational terrorism".

He described the new threat as strategic and long term in nature, with deep ideological roots, and that "the cornerstone of Singapore's strategy is a stronger and more robust inter-agency network ... we need to implement a suitable structure that will prevail over the traditional boundaries of various policy, intelligence and operations agencies". Furthermore, Tan added, "we need to strengthen our national resilience". The publication emphasized that "Singapore is high on the list of targets for terrorist action" and that "it is important that we recognize this stark reality". Singapore, it stated, "is part of this fight ... we cannot simply opt out". Home Affairs Minister Wong Kan Seng was quoted in his succinct summary of the objectives of Singapore's approach: "our approach must be to make it extremely difficult for terrorists to carry out their evil deeds while at the same time, be well prepared and ready to deal with the repercussions if such an attack does happen".[39] In other words, Singapore's strategy is to put into place structures that can detect and disrupt terrorist attacks, and if an attack did succeed, to mitigate the consequences and its impact. Indeed, the government's fears are clearly stated:

> Ultimately, the new transnational terrorism does not threaten Singapore's very existence as an independent, sovereign nation. Nonetheless, it has the capacity to inflict serious shocks on our economy and society, causing not only material and human damage, but also psychological injury. It has the potential to pit different communities against each other, weakening the multi-racial, multi-religious character of Singapore that is vital to our success.[40]

The rest of the publication dealt mainly with the new security architecture as announced by the government earlier in July 2004, as well as the government's strategy at prevention, protection and response. The government hoped that the public document would build national awareness and consensus regarding the nature of the terrorist threat, mobilize the community to help detect and disrupt terrorist attacks, and also raise psychological resilience in order to mitigate the political, economic and social impacts of any attack, in the deep awareness that the bedrock of Singapore's prosperity and viability lies in its stability.

Conclusion

The events of 11 September 2001 have resonated strongly in the region, following the discovery of Al-Qaeda-linked terrorist networks in Southeast Asia. Radical Islamists in the region have raised their effectiveness through the adoption of radical ideologies and new forms of terrorist organization and training. The Bali and the

Marriott Hotel bombings, as well as the audacious abortive bomb plots in Singapore, demonstrated a level of lethalness, technology, commitment and organization hitherto unseen among terrorists in the region. Yet, despite the "new" form of terrorism, there is growing recognition that its fundamental causes stem from political, economic and social conditions in the Middle East and within the region. But the problem is that such fundamental causes, be they corrupt and despotic regimes in the Middle East, the plight of Muslims in many parts of the world, the Isreali-Palestinian conflict, or closer to home, the grievances of the Moro Muslims and Acehnese, are not easy to resolve. There is also growing recognition that Osama bin Laden has pioneered a new form of terrorist organization suited to the age of globalization, and that this would lead to the emergence of much more lethal forms of terrorism that would outlive Al-Qaeda. Indeed, many recent terrorist attacks, in Istanbul, Casablanca, Madrid, Bali and Jakarta, have been carried out by local affiliates of Al-Qaeda, not by Al-Qaeda itself, indicating that the terrorist threat has become generalized, long term and ideological in nature.

These, in the context of Singapore's close identification with the United States and the West on security, political and economic issues, and its undoubted prominence on the radical Islamist target list, means that Singapore will face a continuing, even increasingly menacing, threat from international terrorism. Singapore has thus responded vigorously with a range of preventive and defensive measures, conscious that like the United States, it is a prime Al-Qaeda target. It is aware that it has to improve regional and international counter-terrorism cooperation in order to deal with the new terrorism. It is also aware that the long term, ideological nature of the war on global terrorism requires a strategy to win hearts and minds. But events in the Middle East and around the region, particularly in Indonesia and Malaysia, as well as recent U.S. strategic errors, will be beyond its control. The presence of interstate tensions within Southeast Asia has also constrained the depth and scope of security cooperation. The best Singapore can do is to put into place a rational, comprehensive national security structure that can manage and contain the threat. Outside its borders, the best that it can hope for is to try to assist moderates in the neighbouring countries in checking the appeal of radical Islamist ideology. Ultimately, Singapore's success in homeland security is dependent on progress in the global war on the new terrorism, and this progress can only take place if there is a global, multilateral consensus on the threat as well as a global commitment to combat it.

Notes

The assistance of the National Security Coordination Secretariat is gratefully acknowledged. All errors are the author's alone.

1   See *Total Defence Singapore*, http://www.totaldefence.org.sg.

2   See, for instance, *Straits Times*, 14 April 1987 and 7 August 1987.

3   *Pioneer* (Singapore Armed Forces News), no. 103, May 1986, pp. 12–13.

4   *Singapore Civil Defence Force Information Centre*, http://www.scdf.gov.sg/html/info/faq.htm.

5   *Defending Singapore in the 21st Century* (Singapore: Ministry of Defence, 2000), p. 5.

6   See *September 11 News.com*, http://www.september11news.com.

7   See, for instance, Joseph W. Foxell Jr., "The Debate on the Potential for Mass Casualty Terrorism: The Challenge to U.S. Security", *Terrorism and Political Violence* 11, no. 1 (Spring 1999).

8   Statement by Ambassador Kishore Mahbubani on 1 October 2001 to the UN General Assembly, at http://www.un.org.terrorism/statements/Singapore.htm.

9   *The Jemaah Islamiyah Arrests and the Threat of Terrorism* (Singapore: Ministry of Home Affairs, 2003), pp. 9–14, and "Malaysia Finds Explosive Cache", *BBC News*, http://news.bbc.co.uk/2/hi/asia-pacific/2867635.htm, 20 March 2003.

10   *Straits Times Interactive*, straitstimes.asia1.com, 15 October 2002.

11   "Carnage in Wake of Jakarta Blast", *CBS News*, http://www.cbsnews.com/stories/2003/08/06/attack/main566857.html, 5 August 2003.

12   "Bali, Marriott Attackers Still a Threat", Associated Press, 10 August 2003.

13   Speech by the Minister for Home Affairs, Mr Wong Kan Seng, in Reply to Members of Parliament in the Ministry of Home Affairs Committee of Supply Debate, 17 May 2002, http://www2.mha.gov.sg/mha/detailed.jsp?artid=192&type=4&root=0&parent=0&cat=0&mode=arc.

14   *Straits Times Interactive*, straitstimes.asia1.com, 5 November 2001.

15   "Challenges in National Security", speech by Dr Tony Tan, Deputy Prime Minister and Minister for Defence, at the National Security Seminar, 26 June 2003.

16   "About ICA", http://app.ica.gov.sg/about_ica/about_ica.asp. See also *Straits Times*, 15 March 2003.

17   "All Motorists Checked on Way into Singapore", *Straits Times*, 15 March 2003.

18   *Strategic Goods (Control) Bill*, http://www.parliament.gov.sg/ Legislation/Htdocs/Bills/020044.pdf.

19   "Singapore Builds up Capability Against Biological and Chemical Attacks", *Straits Times*, 17 January 2003. See also "Chemical Attack? Clean up at N-E Line", *Straits Times*, 14 February 2003, and *Fact Sheet on U.S.-Singapore Regional Emerging Disease (REDI) Center*, http://www.globalhealth.gov/Singapore_ REDI_MOU.shtml.

20   "Singapore Participates in U.S.-led Security Exercise in Arabian Sea", Channel NewsAsia, 11 January 2004 and Proliferation Security Initiative, http://www.state.gov/t/np/c10390.htm.

21   "Total Defence Campaign Takes on Anti-Terror Focus", *Straits Times*, 7 February 2003; "Civil Defence Beefs up Anti-Terror Skills", *Straits Times*, 19 December 2003; and "MRT Bomb Blast Drill Tests Response", *Straits Times*, 21 June 2004.

22 "Government to Launch Security Awarenes Programme to Raise Vigilance", *Straits Times*, 17 January 2003, and "First ISD Mobile Exhibit Educates Heartlanders on Security Threats", *Straits Times*, 20 July 2003.

23 "Singapore to Deploy Air Marshals on SIA, Silkair Flights", *Channel NewsAsia*, 20 January 2003, and "Singapore Lays out Plans to Beat Airline Terrorists", *Straits Times*, 5 January 2004.

24 "IMO Adopts Comprehensive Maritime Security Measures", Conference of Contracting Governments to the International Convention for the Safety of Life at Sea, 1974: 9–13 December 2002 in http://www.imo.org/Newsroom/ mainframe.asp?topic_id=583& doc_id=2689. See also "Keeping the Seas Safe", *Straits Times*, 22 January 2003.

25 "Singapore Issues 24-hour Security Rule for Ships", *Business Times*, 25 June 2004.

26 "Satellite-based Ship Tracking System Soon", *Channel NewsAsia*, 22 January 2003.

27 "Singapore Begins Screening U.S.-Bound Containers," *Straits Times*, 17 March 2003.

28 *Straits Times Interactive*, straitstimes.asia1.com, 5 November 2002, and "Singapore Steps up Port Security, Restricts Vessel Movements by Night", *Channel NewsAsia*, 20 March 2003.

29 "Singapore First to Take Part in U.S. Port Security Plan", *Business Times*, 1 June 2004.

30 "U.S. Plan to Secure Key Shipping Lane Upsets SE Asia", CNSNews.com, http:// www.cnsnews.com/ForeignBureaus/Archive/200404/FOR20040406a.html, 6 April 2004.

31 "High-Tech Checks to Deter Terrorists", *Straits Times*, 5 November 2003, "Singapore Beefs Up Anti-Terrorism Security Measures in 2003", *Straits Times*, 27 December 2003, "Uniformed Guards to be Deployed at MRT Stations, Bus Interchanges", *Straits Times*, 15 April 2004, and "Commuters are More Alert to Suspicious Items", *Straits Times*, 16 April 2004, "MRT Trains Too Will Have Marshals", *Straits Times*, 22 March 2004.

32 "Singapore and U.S. Team Up on Terror, Health Threats", *Straits Times*, 22 October 2003.

33 "Singapore, Japan Police Free 'Hijacked' Crew", *Straits Times*, 5 December 2003, and "Singapore-Japan Ink Deal to Curb Spread of WMD", *Straits Times*, 23 April 2004.

34 "3-Nation Patrols of Strait Launched", *Straits Times*, 21 July 2004, and "Malaysia, Singapore Agree to Find New Ways to Check Terror Threats", *Straits Times*, 27 July 2004.

35 "New Center to Probe into the Terrorist's Mind", *Straits Times*, 21 February 2004.

36 "Bombs or Bugs, New Defence Plan Will be Geared to Tackle Them", *Straits Times*, 31 July 2003 and "MRT Trains Too Will Have Marshals", *Straits Times*, 22 March 2004.

37 "Singapore to Set Up a New Security Coordination Secretariat", Interview with Tony Tan, *Radio Singapore International*, 20 July 2004.

38 *The Fight Against Terror: Singapore's National Security Strategy* (Singapore: National Security Coordination Centre, 2004), pp. 37–38.

39 Ibid., pp. 7–12.

40 Ibid., p. 59.

Thailand

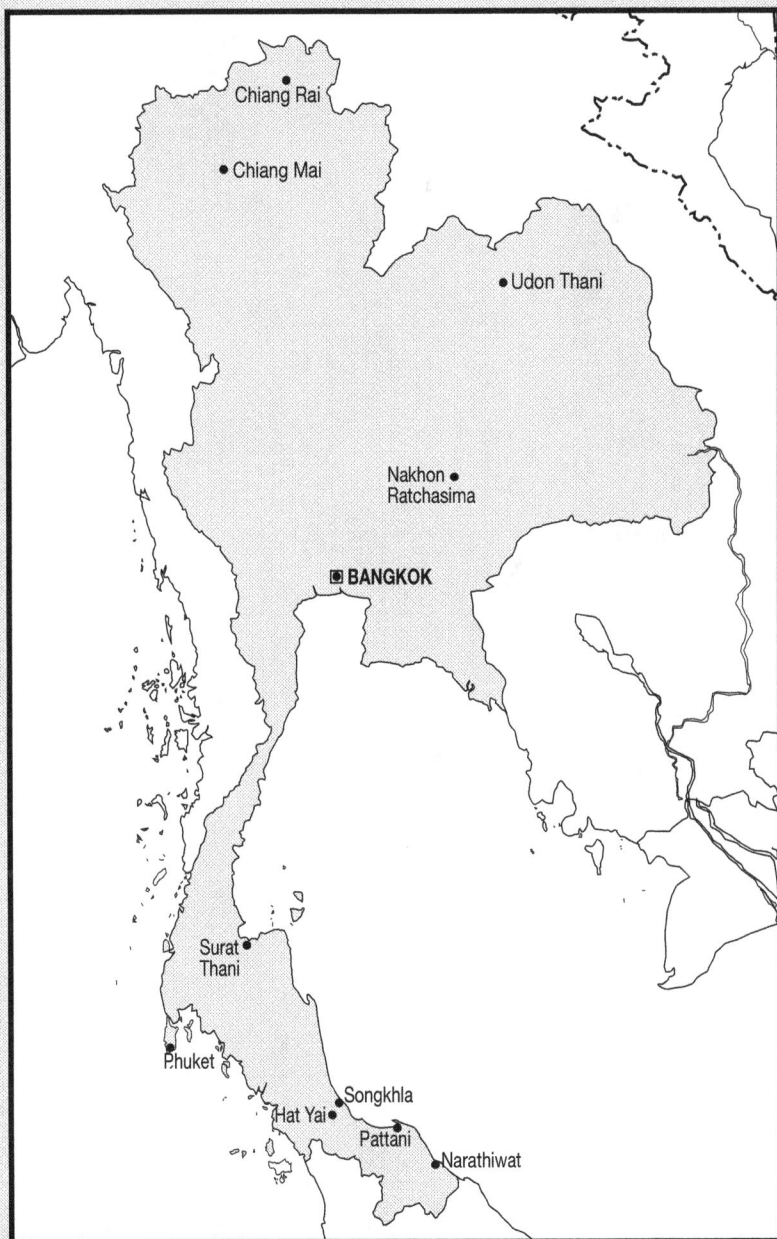

THAILAND
The Facts and F(r)ictions of Ruling

Michael Kelly Connors

Elected in January 2001, Thaksin Shinawatra went to the polls in early 2005 as the first elected Thai leader to serve a full term as prime minister. Although various crises in 2004 led to speculation of an early election, Thaksin's position was largely unassailable. This is not simply a story of individual triumph over circumstance; Thaksin's ascendancy and the possibility of a second-term consolidation illuminates much about post-reform Thailand. From the perspective of "democratic consolidation" a full term and succession by election demonstrates the habituation of democratic norms and conventions. Competing élites in Thailand now, seemingly, play by very minimal democratic rules of the game. Rumours of a *coup d'etat* have been rare, though not absent.[1] Paradoxically, all the milestones towards this achievement have involved diminishing the quality of Thailand's fledgling liberal democracy, underwritten by the 1997 constitution.[2] Previous chapters on Thailand in *Southeast Asian Affairs* have highlighted Thaksin's subversion of the institutions designed to check and balance the power of the political executive, deepening hostility and action against independent press, politicization of the nominally independent senate, and the normalization of extra-judicial killings.[3] 2004 witnessed an intensification of this democratic malaise, most notably in the deep South with the imposition of martial law in three southern provinces to quell a muddled mix of "separatist" and mafia-like violence. Thaksin's longevity under "democratic" rules has come at a time when shadowy state elements have exerted their presence in the south of Thailand and elsewhere, undermining the already tenuous constitutional nature of rule in Thailand. Despite this, Thaksin has gained praise from some observers for significant economic and diplomatic achievements in his first term in office.[4]

MICHAEL KELLY CONNORS teaches politics at La Trobe University, Melbourne, Australia.

The Thaksin Project Continues

Economically speaking, Thailand has rarely experienced such an ambitious government as Thaksin's. Its approach has been worthy of its own nomenclature: "Thaksinomics" is now a standard phrase, "CEOism" is not far behind. The former term captures the government's "dual track" policy orientation of simultaneously pursuing export-led industrialization, fuelled by foreign direct investment (into, for example, the auto-industry), and the building of a domestic "backbone" economy in urban and rural areas. The domestic, Thaksin says, needs to have a "considerable degree of immunity to the risks associated with globalization and increased integration into the global economic system".[5] "CEOism" captures the fact that Thaksin has embraced various management shibboleths and injected them into the bureaucracy and political realm. The basic component of Thaksin's Chief Executive Officer approach has been the importance of leadership, as if "voluntarist will" could shape economic, social, and political outcomes. The application of Thaksin's style of management in the context of the Thai bureaucracy has led to highly publicized ventures of social change, a rush of rhetoric, and then either embarrassed silence or a premature declaration of success, as in the "war on drugs". The complex task of organizing, adapting, and transforming the dynamic social formation of Thailand towards his business-driven ends has not been very susceptible to Thaksin's "leaderism". Thaksin, at least rhetorically, has waged a struggle against the bureaucratic-capitalist state and attendant predatory elements. However, his narrow managerial style has done little to uproot patterns of rule centred on clientelist networks. Consequently, he has fallen back on the forces and structures that he once declared he would transcend. In an important and persuasive analysis, McCargo and Ukrist detail how Thaksin has created a new political economy network linking military, bureaucratic, political and capitalist elements which rivals that of the former Prime Minister Prem Tinsulanonda. This network is seen as poorly institutionalized, being heavily centred on Thaksin.[6]

Thaksin's opportunity to ascend to the highest office emerged in the context of the 1997 Asian economic crisis, when dependency on international trade and investment demonstrated the fragile basis of Thailand's economy. Driven by the attempt of nationally based capitalist groupings to consolidate their position vis-à-vis transnational capitalism, the government has sought to mitigate the effect of the crisis, protect core sections of the economy and related capitalist groupings, and build a new political economy that is domestically robust. Contrary to earlier expectations of a heavily protectionist and anti-western government, it has enthusiastically embraced the opportunities offered by the international economy.[7] Its term in office has seen a return to stable levels of growth. In the years 2001, 2002 and 2003, GDP growth was 1.9 per cent, 5.3 per cent, and 6.6 per cent respectively. Despite the impact of rising oil prices in 2004, crisis in the South, and the re-emergence of the bird flu, growth for 2004 is expected to be only slightly below the previous year.[8] The return to growth has been premised on substantial efforts in the export sector, where growth has been 6.4 per cent, 4.6 per cent, 17.4 per cent for the years 2001, 2002, and 2003 respectively. Growth of over 20 per cent is expected in 2004.[9] Early in his term Thaksin declared the desire to shift Thailand from dependency on key markets, particularly the United States. The government launched trade fairs in Latin America and the Middle East to diversify export destinations. In the context of overall absolute export growth, exports to "Other Countries" (excluding the United States, members of the EU, Japan and ASEAN) have risen from 29 per cent of total exports in 2001 to over 34 per cent in 2004.[10] Thaksin has attempted to redress the imbalances created by structurally biased Bangkok-based growth, by dispersing growth to the regions through a series of measures involving capital injection into the provinces, support for small and medium enterprises, and by supporting the emergence of a locally based entrepreneur class that can forge linkages with the national and international economy. Thaksin has also launched significant poverty alleviation measures including debt moratoriums, poverty registration schemes, and asset realization schemes.[11]

Thirayuth Bunmi has suggested that Thaksin's domestic approach should be understood as a form of liberal-populism, given the efforts to create a dynamic layer of entrepreneurs.[12] Thaksin is not simply redistributing the cake of Thai national capitalism in some form of agrarian populism, he is attempting to lay the basis for a dynamic domestic economy, while also building his own network. Economic policies have been the cause of much controversy, with liberal economists claiming that little has been done to fundamentally improve the basic economy other than to shift state funds in and out of various projects as if in a game of musical chairs. Critics claim that when the music stops playing Thailand will awake to find unsustainable growth based on debt, consumption, and the lingering liability of stillborn schemes.[13] Thailand will face its second major crisis in less than a decade. The debate about Thaksinomics will no doubt continue into the government's second term, if it is returned. Critics have not dampened Thaksin's enthusiasm. During the TRT election campaign launch in October he announced further pledges to fund village development, lift the impoverished out of debt through a poverty registration scheme and provision of further microcredit. More broadly, he pledged easier access to education and health care, tax relief for middle-income earners, and to turn "paper into cash".[14]

Another key theme that Thaksin has pushed to the forefront in the second half of 2004 is the so-called "war on corruption". This was after a member of the Privy Council initiated a programme within the public service to stamp out corruption. It is notable that during Thaksin's first term in office little has been done to stamp out the prevalence of bribery, nepotism, and fraud that has long characterized elements of the Thai élite, including business, political, bureaucratic and military figures. The National Counter-Corruption Commission (NCCC) has reported an alarming rise in reported cases, which are the tip of the iceberg, of corruption in local government organizations (Table 1). Although the rise might simply reflect a greater willingness to report, the figures demonstrate an intractable problem.

However, with the Anti-Money Laundering Office and the NCCC now understood to be heavily influenced by the political executive, it is can be expected that the "war" will be highly selective.

Looking Outwards

Having won its major non-NATO ally status in 2003, the government has enjoyed relatively good relations with the United States. Although the 400-plus strong Thai contingent in Iraq, deployed in September 2003, returned in September 2004, Thai officials have hinted at offering further support in Iraq. The two governments continue to cooperate through the Counter Terrorism Intelligence Centre based in the south of Thailand, and through joint military exercises. The Thai government has paraded the mid-year commencement of free trade negotiations as indicative of

TABLE 1
Reported incidences of corruption by state officials
in local government bodies[15]

Year	Cases	Individuals
2000	501	813
2001	629	920
2002	918	1,661
2003	852	1,504
2004 (January–April)	285	529

Source: *Prachachart Thurakit*, 27 September 2004.

a healthy relationship. While Thaksin's motives primarily may be economic, the U.S. government has a wider perspective, as clearly spelt out in the following Congressional report:

> ... the Administration views the proposed FTA as strengthening cooperation with Thailand in bilateral, regional, and multilateral fora. Bilaterally, the FTA is seen as strengthening Thailand's position as a key military ally, particularly in the war on terrorism ... An FTA could encourage Thailand to actively cooperate with the United States in supporting multilateral trade negotiations ... .[16]

Economic Activism

Contemporary Thai foreign policy is driven by economic considerations. The lack of any significant conventional security threat beyond a hypothetical crisis involving China, the United States and Japan, Thailand's regional security environment is reasonably benign. In 2004 Thaksin led the government into negotiations with over half a dozen governments, including the United States and Japan, on the creation of Free Trade Areas (FTAs). While still supportive of multilateral liberalization within ASEAN, the World Trade Organization and APEC, Thaksin argues that FTAs allow Thailand to upgrade itself in the value chain in world trade:

> ... you see today there is a global business trend towards mergers and acquisitions among international firms. M&As enable them to achieve not only the economy of scale but also the economy of speed. Similarly, a state needs to foster closer economic ties with one another ... .[17]

In its own region, Thai diplomacy is marked by a similar activism. Thailand continues to court Cambodia, Myanmar and Laos, spearheading the so-called Economic Cooperation Strategy (ESC) aimed at reducing red-tape in trade and travel between the countries, and at harmonizing transport and communication linkages. With the provision of development aid by Thailand to its ESC partners, some observers suggest the revival of Thailand's vision of a subregional Thai dominance over its neighbours.[18] In 2004, the much-touted Asia Cooperation Dialogue, a Thai foreign policy initiative (launched in 2002) aimed at adding a loose institutional structure to a purported emergent regionalism, continued to wallow in obscure objectives. Nevertheless, the government uses it to push for the development of Asian bond markets that would have the potential to remove Asian dependency on Western finance markets.

Myanmar

As usual, the question of Myanmar has continued to exercise the Foreign Ministry and Thaksin. Following on from the February 2001 armed exchange between the Myanmar and Thai military, in May 2002 pro-Yangon forces encroached on Thai territory in pursuit of armed insurgents. The Thai military fired warning shots, indicating displeasure at the incursion. Forces swelled on both sides of the border. Thaksin intervened and ordered a Thai military retreat, claiming they had overreacted.[19] The accommodation to Myanmar has continued, while internationally the Thai government has sought to demonstrate its interests in supporting liberalization there. In late 2003 the Thai government launched the much lauded Bangkok Process, aimed at bringing Myanmar into dialogue on the question of political reform. The military junta stalled the process by refusing to attend the second meeting in April 2004. The Thai government has followed a pattern of soft diplomacy with the junta. Constructive engagement has meant continued trade. Indeed, the Export-Import Bank of Thailand has provided over 10 billion baht in loans to the junta for various projects, including support of a telecommunications broadband project, part of which was contracted to Shin Satellite Plc, controlled by the Shinawatra family.[20] While internal political developments in the latter half of 2004 in Myanmar indicated the further consolidation of hardliners, the Thaksin government continued its active engagement with the regime. In mid-December 2004, after meeting with Myanmar generals, Thaksin reported that, "General Than Shwe told me that there is trouble every time she [Aung San Suu Kyi] is released. Burma wants to arrange things and set things in order before freeing her". This very understanding statement was balanced by an obliging statement to the international community on the need for the country to accelerate democratization.[21] In contrast to the period of Democrat rule and the espousal of political liberalism, the government's regional foreign policy has been heavily influenced by a re-ignited "Asian values" position and the politics of non-interference in the affairs of members states of ASEAN.[22]

Internal Politics: Consolidation of Parliamentary Power, Elimination of Opposition

Of absolute majorities

In the January 2001 election Thaksin's party Thai Rak Thai (TRT) was a whisker short of an absolute majority, holding 248 seats in the 500 seat Parliament. In February 2001, 14 Seritham Party MPs applied to join TRT, giving Thaksin an absolute majority. Thaksin formed a coalition government with New Aspiration

Party (NAP) and Chart Thai. By early 2002 TRT had absorbed the NAP, pushing its majority close to 300 in a House of 500. Throughout 2003 and 2004, TRT continued to benefit from a steady flow of "grasshopper politicians" who sought a brighter future with the dominant party. Not all have rushed into the party however. On-again and off-again coalition partner Chart Pattana (CPP), with 30 MPs, failed to respond positively to an "ultimatum" to merge with TRT.[23] Consequently, Thaksin expelled it from the coalition in November 2003. Several pro-merger CPP MPs joined TRT. CPP subsequently unseated the TRT-supported Korat Mayor in March 2004 municipal elections.[24] Recognizing its electoral power in the Northeast, Thaksin moved to bring CPP back into the Coalition, and by August CPP initiated a merger with TRT.[25] Similar TRT overtures for a merger with coalition partner Chart Thai, led by former Prime Minister Banharn Silipahca failed, but key figures in Chart Thai, including Buri Ram faction boss Newin Chidchorp, led over a dozen MPs into TRT in mid 2004.[26] Several Democrat MPs have also left to join the government, especially in the South where the government has promised mega-projects to boost the economy. One Democrat MP explained his defection to TRT: "Before I decided to move parties I spoke to the *hua khanaen* (vote canvassers) and core people in local government. Everyone agreed ... if I am in opposition it is difficult to get the budget."[27] According to the official website of the Thai Parliament, by the end of 2004, of the 500 seats in the House of Representatives, TRT held 319 seats (up from 248 after the January 2001 election), coalition partner Chart Thai 27 (down from 41) and the opposition Democrats 110 (down from 128).[28]

The growth of TRT's parliamentary majority does not constitute evidence of stronger party cohesion; if anything it represents the internalization of coalition politics under the umbrella party that is TRT. The idea of smaller parties becoming "subsidiaries" of TRT was floated in April 2004. Supposedly modelled on the Malaysian ruling organization, UMNO, the idea was that minor parties maintain their own party organizations and identity, but would be more securely embedded in a coalition with TRT. While TRT had practiced a strategy of "merger and acquisition" throughout 2001–03, Nophakhun notes that having failed to lure CT and CPP by early 2004, TRT was willing to opt for the less optimal but politically expedient solution of becoming a holding company of the minor parties.[29] It would provide resources to the parties, but in return would gain guaranteed support. While it may well be the case that the entry of CPP into TRT disproves this analysis, TRT is indeed looking something like a holding company of large factions. The CT and CPP intake complicates an already difficult internal party factional structure: each faction, with its own source of funding and system of benefits to MPs, is increasingly expected to provide goods and largess to a demanding constituency.[30]

For TRT to thrive, Thaksin needs to tap into the networks that exist beyond his own. This explains his dependence on faction leaders and coalition partners. It also explains, in part, the two Cabinet reshuffles in 2004, bringing to a total of ten the times that Thaksin has initiated Cabinet changes. The changes in October 2004 were related to tensions between the Wang Bua Ban and Wang Nam Yen factions involving a turf war over the lucrative Ministry of Interior.[31] This dynamic of accommodation, contestation and precarious balancing within the party is evident in the March Provincial Administration Organization elections. The elections witnessed much infighting between factions and the coalition partners, past and present. TRT won 47 of the provinces, the Democrats won 13, with the rest being divided among Chart Thai, Chart Pattana and Independents.[32] While this would suggest TRT dominance, it must be noted that different factions within TRT fought heated campaigns against each other. In one documented case it appears that a provincial team distributed election material with four different party logos, depending on the site of electioneering.[33]

One reason Thaksin seeks to expand the basis of TRT through merger is to offset the influence of the Wang Nam Yen faction led by kingmaker Snoh Thiengthong. This objective has been a constant theme of TRT internal politics, from its merger with NAP in 2002. Not surprisingly, Snoh has been a constant critic of further mergers fearing the dilution of his factional influence. He reluctantly accepted the CPP merger in 2004. Thaksin has attempted both to accommodate and marginalize Snoh Thiengthong, depending on the relevant contingency. However, it is clear that TRT needs the support of Snoh's faction to maintain stability in government. Indeed, Thaksin's most obvious ambition is to gain as many seats as possible so as to neutralize the power of key factions in the party, and also to immunize TRT from scrutiny. Thus, throughout 2003 and into 2004 there was constant boasting that TRT would gain over 400 seats in the next election. As 2004 progressed this calculation underwent a recount, with the party declaring a target of around 350.

These targets should not be read as megalomania. It makes political sense for a leader who, despite appearances, is relatively vulnerable. TRT is a volatile political formation, born of crisis and subject to break-up pressures. In other words, despite Thaksin's dominance, the party may simply implode. If Thaksin reasonably assumes the possibility of TRT losing 50–100 MPs in a crisis, then having MPs in reserve is a logical insurance policy. Also, by declaring the objective of 400 seats, Thaksin was simply playing the old game of luring politicians to join TRT. A more sinister explanation of the 400 target, and one that is commonly accepted, is that Thaksin wants to ensure that a future government under his leadership would not be subject to any censure motions. During his tenure Thaksin has not had to face censure motions. The opposition does not have the required 200 votes to call for such a motion. However, Cabinet members can be subject to censure motion as only 100 votes are required. The overall effect of these censure debates is to make the government look sleazy. Going for outright control in the House of Representatives makes sense given the current close relationship between business and government and the possible exposure of conflicts of interest, concerns about policy corruption, and the continuing existence of patronage politics. Having 400 votes in the House of Representatives would provide a protective embrace around the entire government. While hopes of this have been dashed because of the problems encountered during 2004, should Thaksin return to office in 2005 he will pursue this objective, through merger, coalition, and luring defections from the opposition.

Opposition, subterfuge, and farce

Democrat leader Banyat Banyathan, who replaced Chuan Leekpai in 2003, has attempted to build the party's platform so that it could rival TRT in terms of concrete measures and policies. Imitating TRT policy boldness, the Democrats have declared policies aimed at the aspirant "poor", promising attention to debt eradication on a sustainable basis, as well as offering permanent organizational representation through the formation of a National Farmer's Council.[34] These developments should be seen in the context of the Democrats attempt to build a base in the Northeast, which holds 138 of the 400 constituency seats. Progressive organizations and farmers' groups campaigned against the Democrats in the 2001 because of their association with the IMF programme and because of their suppression of rural protests. The Democrats won only 5 seats in the Northeast. At a Democrat rally in April 2004 Banyat tried to out-do TRT promises, with promises of free health care, reduced university fees, and debt abolition for those who have acquired debts under the current government's various micro-credit schemes. The party has also attempted to project a liberal image, expressing concern for the independent functioning of a vibrant civil society.[35] The Democrats experienced some success in 2004. In the late February 2004 by-election in Songkhla a new Democrat candidate managed to hold the party's seat, against a forceful TRT campaign. The Democrats also won the Hat Yai municipal election, into which TRT was said to have expended considerable energy. Most significantly, in Bangkok — where TRT won 29 of the 37 parliamentary seats in 2001 — the Democrat candidate for governor of Bangkok won a decisive victory in late August. The TRT-associated candidate performed poorly, winning only 7 of the 50 districts in the poll.[36] This was Thaksin's biggest political upset, demonstrating a vulnerability to a Thai political cycle which involves "upcountry" voting in governments, and Bangkok bringing them down.[37]

However, 2004 held its share of losses for the Democrats. Election strategist and long-time party backer Sanan Kachornprasart, and deputy leader Anek Laothammathat left to establish Mahachon, in July. Early reports suggested that the new party was a beast of TRT, designed to further fragment the Democrats and give an opportunity for former Democrats to enter into coalition with TRT after the next election. Mahachon has enlisted some older-styled politicians as candidates and backers. Sanan's departure from the Democrats is said to have come from his failure to prevent a Democrat censure motion against TRT secretary general, Suriya Jungrungreangkit, said to be a close associate of Sanan.[38] Party leader Anek raised the possibility of working with TRT:

> If we were a coalition partner, we could monitor possible conflicts of interest ... Ideally, I want to lead a one party government. The next best thing is to join a Democrat led coalition. If that is not possible then under the circumstances, I believe the people want my party to act as a mechanism to provide checks and balances in the next coalition government.[39]

As Thaksin has continuously repeated his desire for a one-party government with an overwhelming number of seats after the next election, and TRT's Snoh has been reluctant to work with Sanan, Mahachon has moved to push its anti-government credentials. In mid-December Sanan explained that the establishment of Mahachon was required because of the inability of the Democrats to challenge TRT, particularly in the Northeast. Citing Kukrit Pramoj's minority coalition government in the 1970s, Sanan suggested that in the event that TRT gains less than 250 seats, Mahachon could possibly lead a coalition government as a minority party with the Democrats.[40] While this is an unlikely scenario, nothing should be ruled out, given the growing, but sporadic, opposition to TRT.

Opposition to Thaksin has surfaced in unlikely forms. Former national security chief and former foreign minister Prasong Sunsuri wrote an article in August 2001 ridiculing the Constitution Court decision of the same year that overturned the National Corruption Commission's finding that Thaksin had deliberately concealed assets.[41] The eight judges who overturned the Commission's decision sued Prasong for defamation. In October and November 2004 when the case was heard, the defence aired allegations that have long been made in private of Thaksin associates offering incentives to Constitution Court judges to make a judgment in Thaksin's favour. In December the Criminal Court dismissed the defamation case, finding

Prasong's article had been in the public interest, although finding his use of "abusive language" to be in contempt of court. The Criminal Court also criticized one of the plaintiffs for inconsistency in his "not guilty" verdict on Thaksin.[42] The defamation action resulted in the resurfacing of allegations of judicial interference, and further cast a shadow over the controversial 2001 decision, further undermining the legitimacy of the government.

The emergence of businessman Ekkayuth Anchanbutr is a more curious development. Ekkayuth announced in August that he and associates — mostly expatriate Thais — would provide the cash-strapped Democrats with substantial funds if they agreed to campaign against the Eleven Economic Laws forced on Thailand during the period of IMF tutelage.[43] The Democrats rejected the offer, with Banyat saying that the party was not a company that could be bought. Ekkayuth continued to cause waves claiming his own party, Prachatham would run candidates in the next election.[44] Thaksin antagonist and former Senate Speaker Manoonkrit Roopkachorn, connected to former prime minister Prem Tinsulanond, is also associated with Prachatham, as are associates of Prasong. This has led to speculation that certain highly connected military figures are behind Ekkayuth.[45] In September Ekkayuth accused 30 politicians in the ruling coalition of stock market manipulation, but failed to provide evidence. In exasperation to growing and unexpected opposition, Thaksin made an ill-considered remark: "Come on, overthrow my government. By all means, topple me. Otherwise, if you fail, I will beat you up."[46] Tapping into opposition to the government's privatization programme, Ekkayuth and other prominent nationalist businessmen helped organize an anti-government rally that drew in state enterprise workers, who have continuously and with reasonable success opposed the government's corporatization and privatization of state enterprises.[47] The Prasong and Ekkayuth episodes are suggestive of a familiar recurrence in Thai politics, the conspiratorial role of a "third force". In these cases, the term seems to capture nothing less than an emerging establishment opposition to Thaksin, which has been frustrated by Thaksin's capture of state apparatuses and his growing economic might.

Goodbye mediators

Thaksin's road to power in 2001 was not merely on the basis of policy or through the usual mechanisms of money politics. He tapped into various NGOs, and religious and intellectual networks, which rallied voters to his cause. For the most part these have now moved against Thaksin. Such groups include Thailand's liberal intelligentsia. The most dramatic expression of this opposition is the bestselling book titled *Seeing through Thaksin*, now into its second volume. These books provide popularly written essays critiquing various aspects of Thaksin's government, and have led to the formation of "Seeing through Thaksin" clubs, which involve a broad band of opponents who continuously critique the government, including some members of the elite Royal Bangkok Sports Club.

Thaksin also courted "senior citizens" and NGOs in his bid for power; few are now supportive of his government. Perhaps no individual supporter outside of political and business circles was as important as Dr Prawase Wasi. Prawase fronts several foundations and is seen as an intellectual leader of various moderate health, moral and cultural reform NGOs, with thousands of influential members across the nation. He has gradually moved away from Thaksin. The final break seems to have been catalysed when the Thaksin government moved against ThaiHealth, a publicly funded organization that oversees hundreds of projects and NGO initiatives, some of which have been critical of the government. The government removed a close associate of Prawase from the Directorship of ThaiHealth over unproven claims of financial and procedural irregularity. In an address in October Prawase, who rarely singles out individuals for blame, noted that,

> The Thai people should thank Khun Thaksin for having shown us that money has the power to exploit the political vacuum to seize control of state power and turn it into a dictatorship … *Thanatipathai* [Plutocracy] is a system in which money holds supreme power. Today, wherever you go you hear people talk about corruption, conflicts of interest and dictatorial rule in general. That's why I say we should thank Khun Thaksin for giving society these lessons. Let's extend our blessings to him.[48]

Thaksin has lost other supporters. Owing to disputes about the appointment of an acting Supreme Patriarch, influential monk Luangta Maha Bua, whose network is said to number in the hundreds of thousands, now opposes Thaksin. Luangta Maha Bua's network is said to have been responsible for mobilizing votes for Thaksin in the 2001 election, and in organizing support during the asset declaration case. The monk has now virulently criticized corruption in the government and its encouragement of consumerism.[49] State enterprise unions, who were formerly supportive of Thaksin, have passed a motion to oppose the government in the coming election.[50] Having cut his links with various networks of support, Thaksin clearly went into the 2005 election believing he no longer needed these mediators to continue winning the support of the masses. As Thailand buzzes with various schemes hatched by TRT, fuelled by cash injections, TRT seemingly needs few of the networks it used earlier. He also enjoys a degree of support within sections of the bureaucracy and the influential Ministry of Interior, that has long supported his heavily centralizing tendencies. This would suggest highly politicized state apparatuses that may, in some instances, be divided along partisan lines.

The South: When Fact Exceeds Fiction

The Malay Muslim-majority provinces in southern Thailand, Narathiwat, Yala, Pattani and, to a lesser extent, Satun have a long history of tense relations with the Thai Buddhist state. The southern region was once the centre of Islamic scholarship in Southeast Asia, and a Malay sultanate. Historical, cultural, political and economic grievances arising from the region's integration into the Thai nation-state early last century have been, and remain, breeding grounds for separatist or militant religious inspired politics among a minority of Muslims. Political liberalization in the 1980s opened a space for Muslim elites to enter the political sphere and by the early 1990s it was commonly believed that militant separatist groups were in terminal decline. However, during Thaksin's period in office, and climaxing in 2004, high levels of politicized violence returned.

During 2004, separatists are alleged to have executed over 500 local officials, police, teachers, monks and general citizens, mostly in surprise attacks. Some of the killings are similar to the extra-judicial killings of alleged drug traffickers during 2003, suggesting that at least in a number of cases private and vested interests may be using the scapegoat of "terrorism" to cover their tracks. Recent beheadings also suggest emulation or the presence of transnational militants. At the same time over 100 Muslims, seemingly targeted by state agencies, have gone missing.

The South has now become a playground of intelligence and counter-intelligence, making it hard to separate fact from fiction. For example, on 4 January armed separatists allegedly launched an assault on an army camp, seizing weapons and killing four soldiers. Within Thailand there were claims and counterclaims that military insiders had hatched the attack to cover their own arms sales to Achenese rebels. Thaksin, as well as scholars in the South, have often attributed current and past violence to bandits, criminal elements and corrupt elements, in the state apparatus, rather than to Islamic militants.[51]

General Sirichai Thanyasiri, Director of the Southern Border Province Peace-Building Command, summed up the prevalent befuddlement that surrounds events when he said that, "I admit that I don't know who the enemy are, but I will try my best to get them…".[52] In part this claimed ignorance is due to Thaksin's "perform or leave" mantra, which has led to an incapacitated state in the South: Thaksin has revamped structures and leaders so often that none have had time to deal with the problems. The government has failed to implement genuinely political, social, and economic measures that would alleviate the causes of grievance such as those proposed by Deputy Prime Minister Chaturon Chaisang, whose plan included amnesty measures, suspending the use of military and police from outside the region, and economic growth measures.[53] Forces in the government and military, threatened by the plan, rushed to marginalize Chaturon. Furthermore, subsequent events strengthened the hardliners around Thaksin.

On 28 April 2004 (the anniversary of a brutal crackdown on Muslim dissidents in 1948 that left hundreds dead) one hundred Muslims, mostly youth armed with machetes, apparently staged attacks on checkpoints, police stations and army bases. In one case they retreated into the sacred Krue Se Mosque, where over 30 were killed. In total 107 were killed during the crackdown. Some saw the "uprising" as evidence of a new but deeply entrenched network of Islamic militants. According to General Kitti Rattanachaya, a government security advisor and former Armed Commander in the south, the events were further evidence of a growing insurgency. From the beginning of the year Kitti repeated intelligence claims of having uncovered a seven-point insurgency plan, said to be linked to BERSATU (United Front for Patani Independence). The plan outlines attempts to create Islamic and Patani nationalist consciousness, demoralize the Thai state and launch an insurrection to establish an Islamic Patani state.[54] Reports on infiltration of Islamic schools by militant Islamic scholars escalated after this revelation.

Others, however, have treated these claims with caution. Fourth Army Commander General Pisarn Wattanawongkiri argued that the separatist sympathies of the youth had been exploited by criminal elements, including those that had been pushed from the North in the war on drugs, and by interests already established in the South, who sought to destabilize the government.[55] In subsequent commentary, various suspects (Islamic militants, older separatist networks, political-bureaucratic-military networks, the CIA, the mafia) were named as fanning the Southern fire, but none with any certainty. Consider some of the possibilities (arranged in no particular order of credibility): the January 4th raid and some assassinations may have been stage-managed; the threat of insurgency may have been exaggerated to bolster the security forces' position in the South, and thereby protect their varied interests involving control over resources and predatory extraction; exaggeration may serve the internal security perspectives of nationalist factions within the military; transnational militants may indeed be active in the region; the once Malay-ethnic nature of the separatist groups might now centre on militant Islamic politics; the

CIA (and other intelligence agencies) may have an interest in stirring up sectarian politics to further legitimate its "war on terror".[56]

Despite the uncertainty about who is behind the various events, the government has endorsed repressive measures against people in the South. The most dramatic example of this occurred on October 25 in Tak Bai, Narathiwat province, when thousands of protestors called for the release of villagers arrested for allegedly having handed border defence weapons, under their supervision, to "militants". Some protestors were shot during the peaceful demonstration. The military arrested and transported over 1,000 people to an army camp for questioning. En route, 78 people died of suffocation. Although Thaksin claimed that the military had adhered to his orders, in December a government inquiry found that he was not involved. The inquiry found that military officials were responsible for the events, but left it to the government to determine punishment.[57] During November and December, opposition Democrat MPs and political activists began to disseminate videos and VCDs of the Tak Bai incident. Police invoked internal security laws to suggest that distribution and exhibition were illegal. Indicative of a new generation of brave activists, the editors of *Faa Diaw Kan* (Under the Same Sky), issued their magazine with Tak Bai VCD inserts.[58]

As the year closed, Thaksin announced the capture of alleged masterminds of the unrest, and revealed the involvement of Malaysian and Indonesian Islamists, further deepening the rift between Malaysia and Thailand.[59] Thaksin appeared to now see the primary cause of the troubles in the South as a consequence of indoctrination of Muslim youth by Islamic scholars, and the influence of external militants. The Kitti line seems to have prevailed. To conclude that the events are primarily driven by separatist Islamic elements just as Thailand rolled into an election might have provided a convenient nationalist electoral windfall, but it downplayed the role of criminalized networks of state and private interests, and legitimated continuing repression under the cover of national security. Like the spectre of communism in earlier times, the spectre of "terror" serves to gloss over the inequalities and complex politics of identity and ethnicity that must be addressed if a genuine solution is to be found.

The South faced a challenge of a different nature after a massive tsunami, which hit Phuket, Phang Nga and Krabi on 26 December, and reportedly left in its wake over five thousand dead, and tens of thousands homeless and jobless. The government had, through the Tourist Authority of Thailand, done much to quarantine this region from the troubles further south, but the vital tourist industry is now struggling. The government has set in place a multi-billion baht reconstruction effort that encompasses relief, rebuilding homes, and aid to businesses and the fishing industry. At the time of writing, the tsunami appeared to strengthen a likely TRT win in the 2005 election, owing to the perceived strong response of the government.

Conclusion

While Thaksin has many critics, it must be said that he has expended enormous energy in advancing not only his own corporate interests, but what he sees as the interests of Thailand. There can be no doubt that creative and interesting measures have been applied to build the economy in Thailand. On its own terms, the government has had a measure of economic success. Thaksin has focused on policy measures that have long been neglected. However, coming to office on a wave of hope and with the trust of many progressive sectors in Thai society, Thaksin has delivered four years of tumult. He has hectored critics, asked for understanding, condoned crackdowns, and embraced stars. He has handled the top office in a manner that he likens to a cowboy's.[60] His supposed challenge to the global economic order, and his seemingly progressive domestic policies on health care and debt alleviation contrast with an unprecedented reign of extra-judicial murder and repression. The authoritarian tendencies that were evident in the first three years of rule intensified in 2004; carnage in the South has been the result. The elevation of the U.S.-Thai relationship under his watch has come at the cost of further alienating Muslims. In December military planes released millions of origami birds with messages of peace into the southern region. Thaksin declared: "This shows that the entire nation is united, regardless of religious beliefs. It's a signal that we love our land and nobody can divide it."[61] Dismissed by some as a gimmick, it is unlikely that such appeals to nationalism will contain the growing opposition to Thaksin.

Notes

Some parts of this paper are taken from "Thaksin's Thailand — to have and to hold", a paper presented to the Thai Update Conference, Macquarie University, 20–21 April 2004. Duncan McCargo provided characteristically penetrating criticism and corrections, for which I am grateful.

1   "Pluk krasae ratthaprahan" [Stirring up a coup d'etat] *Krungthep Thurakit* online, 1 October 2004.

2   See Ji Giles Ungpakorn, "From Tragedy to Comedy: Political Reform in Thailand", *Journal of Contemporary Asia* 32, no. 2 (2002): 191–205.

3   See especially, Thitinan Pongsudhirak, "Thailand: Democratic Authoritarianism", in *Southeast Asian Affairs 2003*, edited by Daljit Singh and Chin Kin Wah (Singapore: ISEAS, 2004). In 2004 Cabinet discussed the repeal of a Prime Ministerial Regulation

from 1996 requiring that public hearings be held into the impact of big projects. See *Matichon* online, 13 October 2004, http://www.matichon.co.th/.

4 Robert Looney, "Thailand's Thaksinomics: A New Asian Paradigm?", *Strategic Insights* 2, no. 12 (December 2003), http://www.ccc.nps.navy.mil/si/dec03/eastAsia.asp.

5 Cited in "Thailand Looks to a Global Strategy", *The Nation* online, 24 August 2001, http://www.nationmultimedia.com/.

6 Duncan McCargo and Ukrist Pathmanand, *The Thaksinization of Thailand* (Copenhagen: Nordic Institute of Asian Studies: 2005), pp. 209–47. On the repoliticization of the military, see pp. 121–65.

7 Jim Glassman, "Economic 'Nationalism' in a Post-nationalist Era", *Critical Asian Studies* 36, no. 1 (2004): 37–64.

8 Figures from NESDB website available at http://www.nesdb.go.th/econSocial/macro/NAD.htm#qgdp, accessed 14 December 2004 (in Thai).

9 Ministry of Commerce, "Talat song ok samkan khong thai pi 2535–2547" [Important Thai Export Markets, Years 1992–2004] available at http://www.ops2.moc.go.th/trade/trade_exp.html, accessed 14 December 2004.

10 This excludes the United States, members of the European Union, Japan and ASEAN each of which in 2003, accounted for 17 per cent, 14.7 per cent, 14.2 per cent and 20.6 per cent of Thai exports respectively. Ibid.

11 Pasuk Phongpaichit and Chris Baker, *Thaksin: The Business of Politics in Thailand* (Chiang Mai: Silkworm, 2004), pp. 116–17.

12 Thirayut Bunmi, "Wikro Sangkom Thai" [Analysing Thai Society] *Matichon* online, 6 January 2003.

13 These debates may be found in the yearly Economic Reviews issued by the *Bangkok Post*.

14 "Bid for Second Term", *The Nation* online, 18 October 2004.

15 These are figures for corruption in local government organizations only. The rise is most certainly related to increased budgets at the local level as a result of devolution and decentralization. These are reported cases only.

16 Raymond J. Ahearn and Wayne M. Morrison, "U.S.-Thailand Free Trade Agreement Negotiations", 1 April 2004, Congressional Research Reports RL 32314, p. 2.

17 Woranuj Maneerungsee, "Caught up in FTA Mania", in *Bangkok Post*, "Mid-Year Economic Review", 2004.

18 Anuraj Manibhandu, "Neighbours Turn to Mending Fences", *Bangkok Post* online, 14 October 2004.

19 "Thai Burmese Ties Back to the Usual Acrimony", *The Nation* online, 31 May 2004.

20 "Burma Power Play: Exim Loan Alarm", *The Nation* online, 21 October 2004.

21 "No Hint of Suu Kyi's Freedom: Thaksin", The *Nation* online, 10 December 2004.

22 Asda Chainam, "Kanthut yuk Thaksin (Thaksiplomacy)" [Diplomacy in the Thaksin Era], in *Ruthan Thaksin* [Seeing through Thaksin], Volume 2, edited by Chermsak Pinthong (Bangkok: Khokhit Duaykan, 2004), pp. 211–57.

23   *The Nation* online, 27 August 2003.

24   *The Nation* online, 8 March 2004.

25   "CPP Board Disbands, Agrees to Merge with Thai Rak Thai", *The Nation* online, 11 August 2004.

26   "Half of Chart Thai Party MPs to Defect to Thai Rak Thai", *The Nation* online, 23 July 2004.

27   "Pattani Darusalum", *Focus Pak Tai* online 347 (21–27 August 2004), http://www.focuspaktai.com.

28   It should be noted that the constant flow of MPs out of the opposition parties makes precise figures difficult to come by. The figures above come from the website of the Thai parliament (http://www.parliament.go.th:81/member/view-inf.php, accessed 12 December 2004) that provides the following information: TRT 319 seats, Democrats 110, Chart Thai 27, Mahachon 1, NAP 1, and 42 vacant seats (the site appears to have been updated after Newin's defection from Chart Thai and the merger of CPP with TRT).

29   Nophakhun Limsamarnphun, "Bringing the Holding Company Structure to Thai Politics", *The Nation* online, 18 April 2004; See also, Rangsan Thanaphornphan, "Thai rak Thai Kap amnat phukat thangkanmuang" *Phujatkan* online, 19 February 2003.

30   One report notes that TRT MPs receive an extra 200,000 baht a month to distribute in their respective electorates. MPs refer to this as *pasi sangkhom* or a social tax, used to help constituents: see *Thai Post* online, 20 September 2003, http://www.thaipost.net/.

31   See "Reshuffle Highlights Premiers Lack of Options, Confirms that Old-style Faction-Fighting is on its Way Back", *The Nation*, 7 October 2004; detailed analysis in *Matichon* online, 7 October 2004, "phinit pa mai kaey ang naiyok". Faction strength varies, but Wang Nam Yen is around 70–90 strong, while recent reports have Wang Bua Ban, associated with TRT party secretary-general Suriya Jungrungreangkit and Thaksin's sister Yaowapa Wongsawat, at around 100.

32   *The Nation* online, 17 March 2004.

33   For an extended discussion on the nature of TRT, see McCargo and Ukrist op. cit., pp. 70–120.

34   Democrat Party "Naiyobai" [Policy], available at http://www.democrat.or.th/aboutpolicy.asp, accessed 19 April 2004.

35   *The Nation* online, 26 April 2004; *Prachachart Thurakit* online, 3 July 2003, 7 July 2003.

36   "Apirak Wins in 42 out of 50 Districts", *The Nation* online, 31 August 2004.

37   See Anek Laothamatas, "A Tale of Two Democracies", in *The Politics of Elections in Southeast Asia,* edited by Robert H. Taylor (New York: Cambridge University Press, 1996), pp. 201–33.

38   "Political Warning: Untouchable Government?", *The Nation* online, 3 July 2004.

39   "A New Beginning" *The Nation* online, 8 July 2004.

40   "Sanan … yang juppak po.cho.po" [Sanan still kisses the Democrats] *Phujatkan* online,

15 August 2004. Sanan suggested significant wins in Bangkok and the Northeast for his party, and has hinted at winning between 60 and 100 seats. Independent analysts see Mahachon as getting no more than 30 seats.

41 Chamlong Srimuang removed Prasong and appointed Thaksin foreign minister in 1993.

42 "Prasong Libel Case: Ura Decides Not to Aid Defence as a Witness", *The Nation* online, 15 October, 2004; "Defamation case: Prasong Wins", *The Nation* online, 3 December 2004.

43 "Ekkayuth's Overture: Democrats Given Two Weeks", *The Nation* online, 14 August 2004. Ekkayuth had faced charges in the early 1980s of illegal business activities, and fled overseas. The statute of limitations has expired on this.

44 "Ekkayuth Bombshell: Data Support Manipulation Charge", *The Nation* online, 7 September 2004.

45 "Naew daan thai rak thai" [Opposing Thaksin], *Matichon Weekly* online, 10–16 September, p. 9.

46 Cited in Sutichai Yoon, "Thai Talk: Topple Me if You Can, but if You Cannot ...", *The Nation* online, 16 September, 2004.

47 "Anti Government Rally: Workers Vow to Oust PM", *The Nation* online, 26 September 2004.

48 Cited in Suthichai Yoon Thai Talk, "A Prescription from a Disillusioned Doctor", *The Nation* online, 28 October 2004.

49 "Luangta maha bua", *Phujatkan* online, 16 December 2004.

50 "Ruamphon khon (Ruthan) kliat Thaksin", [Assemble the People who (see through) hate Thaksin] *Matichon Weekly* online, 10–16 September 2004.

51 Pasuk and Baker, *Thaksin*, pp. 234–38. The idea that the military are often behind the events is a common theme in writings from the South. See Koi-lin Anwa and Suphalak Kanjonkhun *Fai tai krai jut* [Who is lighting the Southern Fire?] (Bangkok: Indochina Publishing, 2004), pp. 79–122.

52 Chang Noi (pseud.), "Knowing and Yet not Knowing the South", *The Nation* online, 8 November 2004.

53 "Chaturon's Peace Plan Faces Delay", *The Nation* online, 7 April 2004; Chiangsowlong (pseud.), "Naiyobai 66/2447 Yuthasat sang santiphap 3 jangwat pak tai" [Policy 66/2547: Strategy to build peace in the three provinces of the South], *Putjakan* online, 5 April 2004.

54 "Nuay khoa pluk pi phak tai tua mai paet 7 khandon" [Intelligence Agency Creates a New Southern Spectre: 7 Stages], *Thai Post* online, 20 January 2004. The Seven Point plan is occasionally alluded to in the Thai language press, but has mostly been ignored. Kitti persists in using it as a basis for claims of a planned and growing insurgency involving thousands of youths "indoctrinated" during attendance at Muslim schools. Kitti self-published a book carrying excerpts from various seized documents. PULO, BRN (Coordinate and Congress) Ulema, GMP, GMIP, BIPP are listed as members of

BERSATU. References, in the documents, to angelic rewards waiting in heaven for those killed while engaged in jihad appear to suggest an Islamist strain to the alleged insurgency — but some treat Kitti's claims and the authenticity of these documents with scepticism. See Kitti Rattanachaya *jut fai tai tang rat patani* [Igniting the South. Establishing the Patani State], (Bangkok, 2004).

55 "Jap dai loy kwaa sop" [More than a hundred deaths], *Focus pak tai* online, 1–7 May 2004.

56 On an alleged CIA extended presence in the South, beyond the joint US-Thai Counter Terrorism Intelligence Centre, see "CIA-palangngan-muslim-kankorai" [CIA-Power-Muslims=Terrorism], *Focus pak tai* online, 30 January–6 February 2004.

57 "Some Worrying Parallels with Krue Se", *The Nation* online, 3 November 2004; "Official Tak Bai inquiry: Report Stops Short of Blame", *The Nation* online, 18 December 2004.

58 "A Right to Know", *The Nation* online, 19 December 2004.

59 "PM Names Indonesia as Another Training Ground", *Bangkok Post* online, 19 December 2004.

60 "I'm a Cowboy too, Says Thaksin", *The Nation* online, 17 December 2004.

61 "Thais are United on the South", *The Nation* online, 3 December 2004.

Thailand's Paradoxical Recovery

Peter Warr

In Thailand's February 2005 parliamentary elections Prime Minister Thaksin Shinawatra's Thai Rak Thai (Thais Love Thais) Party achieved a sweeping victory. It had already formed the first elected government in Thai history to serve a full four-year term and was now the first individual party to be elected to a full parliamentary majority, and that a massive one.[1] The party's electoral success owes much to the Prime Minister's own political skills and much also to the economic recovery achieved under his government. In 2004, for the first time since the Asian crisis of 1997–98, real output per person exceeded its pre-crisis level of 1996 and in this respect Thailand had finally emerged from the economic after-effects of the crisis. In many dimensions, the economy was booming.

Despite setbacks from rural drought, panic-producing outbreaks of avian influenza and Severe Acute Respiratory Syndrome (SARS), combined with continued political violence in the Muslim southern provinces, estimated growth of real GDP reached a respectable 6.4 per cent in 2004, only marginally below the 2003 growth rate of 6.8 per cent. Growth for 2005 is expected to be slower, at a little over 5 per cent, reflecting a slowdown in export growth, diminished inflows of foreign direct investment (FDI) and the economic consequences of the tsunami of 26 December 2004.

The terrible human costs of the tsunami dominate its economic effects, but the latter are nevertheless significant. Thailand was less severely affected than some other countries with coastlines facing the Indian Ocean, especially Indonesia, Sri Lanka and possibly Myanmar (Burma), but many thousands lost their lives (perhaps between 8,000 and 9,000 out of a regional total approaching 300,000) and entire communities were destroyed.[2] Tourism was sharply affected in the short term and some long-term effect seems certain, but the long-term size of these effects remains

PETER WARR is the John Crawford Professor of Agricultural Economics and Director of the Poverty Research Centre, The Australian National University, Canberra.

unclear. Despite the inevitable problems arising from a disaster of this magnitude, the Thai response in assisting the victims was impressive, partly because of the good infrastructure already in place, partly because of a relatively effective government response, but also because of the kindness exhibited by ordinary Thai people towards those who suffered, both Thais and foreigners.

Thailand's economic recovery is significant and greatly welcome. This chapter examines its features at four levels. The first section describes the overall macroeconomic picture. The paradox is that the recovery is quite different from the economic outcome that Prime Minister Thaksin promised and seemingly planned, both in its rate and its composition. The second section reviews the record of the Thaksin government on poverty reduction relative to its stated goals. Third, we consider the economic origins of the ongoing political strife in the country's Muslim south. Do economic circumstances in this part of Thailand help in understanding the nature of this chronic conflict? The fourth section discusses the economic effects of the tsunami of December 2004. Finally, we review future prospects.

Macroeconomics[3]

Thailand's recovery from the crisis demonstrates the resilience of its market-oriented economy and, to a significant extent, the success of Thaksin Shinawatra's government in restoring economic confidence. The confidence-restoring feature of Thaksin's government lay not so much in the particular actions taken to promote economic recovery as in the fact that to many Thais the government seemed, unlike its immediate predecessors, to be doing *something*, to be capable of making clear decisions, and to be in control.

TABLE 1
Thailand: Rates of growth of GDP and GDP per capita, 1951–2004

Period	Real GDP growth	Real GDP growth per capita
1951 to 1986 (Phase I) Pre-boom	6.5	3.9
1987 to 1996 (Phase II) Boom	9.2	8.0
1997 to 1998 (Phase III) Crisis	−6.1	−7.1
1999 to 2004 (Phase IV) Post-crisis	4.4	3.7
Whole period 1951 to 2004	6.2	4.2

Sources: Bank of Thailand: data for 1951 to 1986; and National Economic and Social Development Board: data from 1987.

Economic output

We begin by placing Thailand's recent economic performance in a comparative East Asian perspective. Data on real GDP are presented for eight East Asian economies, including Thailand (heavy dashed lines in the figure). The pre-crisis period of 1986 to 1996 is covered in Figure 1, with each country's 1986 level of real GDP indexed to 100. The crisis and post-crisis periods of 1996 to 2004 are shown in Figure 2, this time with real GDP in 1996 indexed to 100. Figure 1 shows that Thailand's boom was the largest of the countries shown, but only marginally so. Singapore, Malaysia, Indonesia, Korea and Taiwan were not far behind.

In 1998 serious contractions occurred in Korea, Malaysia, and Indonesia, but Figure 2 shows that, relative to 1996, Thailand's initial contraction was the most severe (again the heavy dashed lines). Along with Indonesia, its contraction has also been the most long lasting. Thailand's crisis was initially more severe than Indonesia's, but Indonesia did not experience a comparable recovery in 1999. It is commonly

FIGURE 1
Real GDP in East Asia, 1986 to 1996

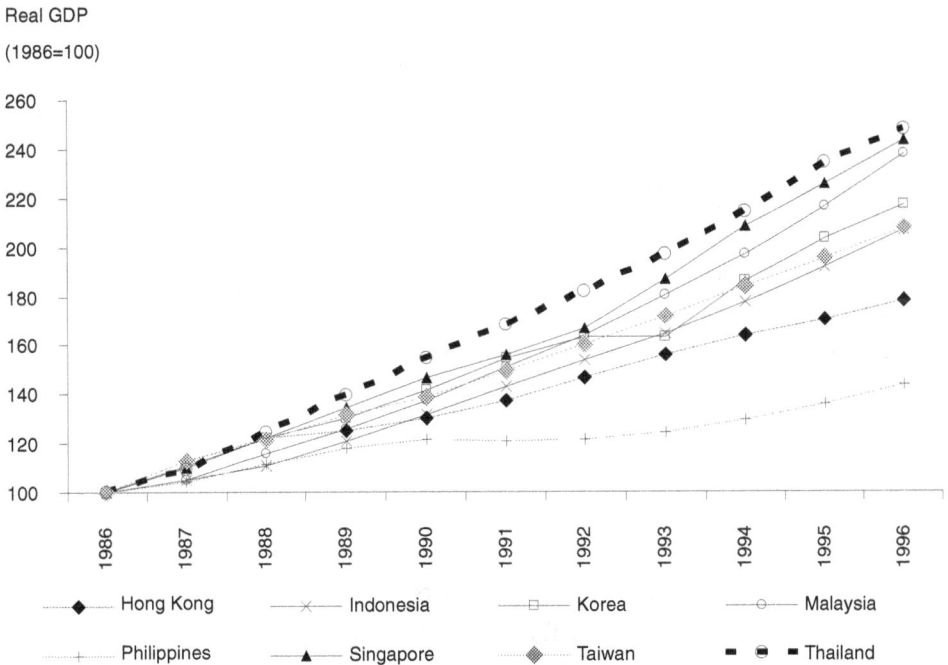

Real GDP
(1986=100)

Source: Asian Development Bank, *Key Indicators*, various issues.

FIGURE 2
Real GDP in East Asia, 1996 to 2004

Real GDP
(1996=100)

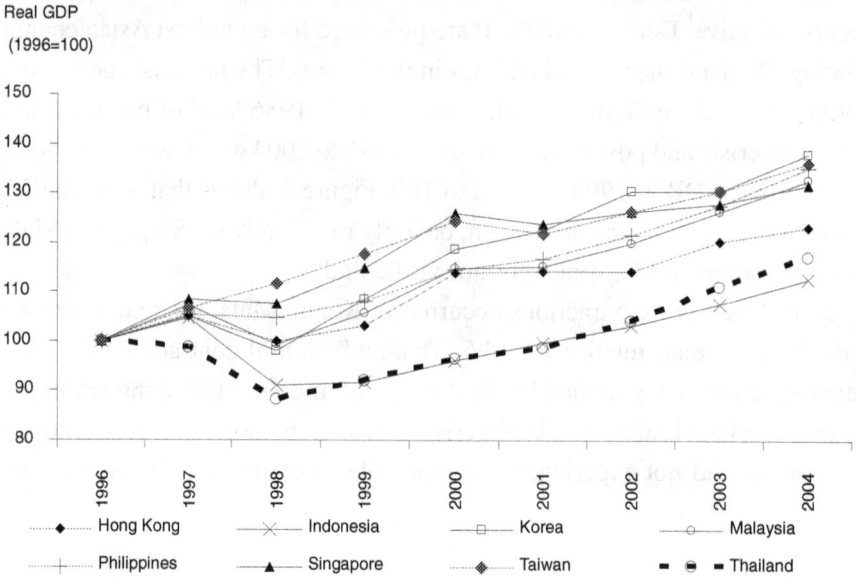

Source: Asian Development Bank, *Key Indicators*, various issues.

said that Indonesia's economic crisis was more severe than Thailand's, but these data show that as of 2002 the magnitude of their contractions of real GDP relative to their 1996 levels were almost identical. Indonesia's performance was inferior only after 2002.

Figure 3 tracks the path of Thailand's crisis and subsequent recovery more closely using data on quarterly real GDP and its growth rate covering 1994 to 2004 (third quarter). Following the severe contraction of 1998, during which the quarterly year-on-year real growth rate declined to –14 per cent per annum in the second and third quarters, there was an initial period of rapid growth, of over 8 per cent, in mid-1999. This rate then reverted to around 2 per cent in mid-2000, increasing steadily to over 6 per cent two years later, then tapering off in the third quarter of 2004 to 6 per cent.

To understand the changes that have occurred, it is helpful to look at the composition of Thailand's GDP. Table 2 summarizes the composition of aggregate demand for the years 1994 to 2003 (data for 2004 are not yet available). During the immediate crisis years of 1997 and 1998, the major macroeconomic change was the collapse of private investment demand — from 33 per cent of GDP to 10 per cent.

FIGURE 3
Thailand: Quarterly real GDP and its growth, 1995 (Q1) to 2004 (Q3)

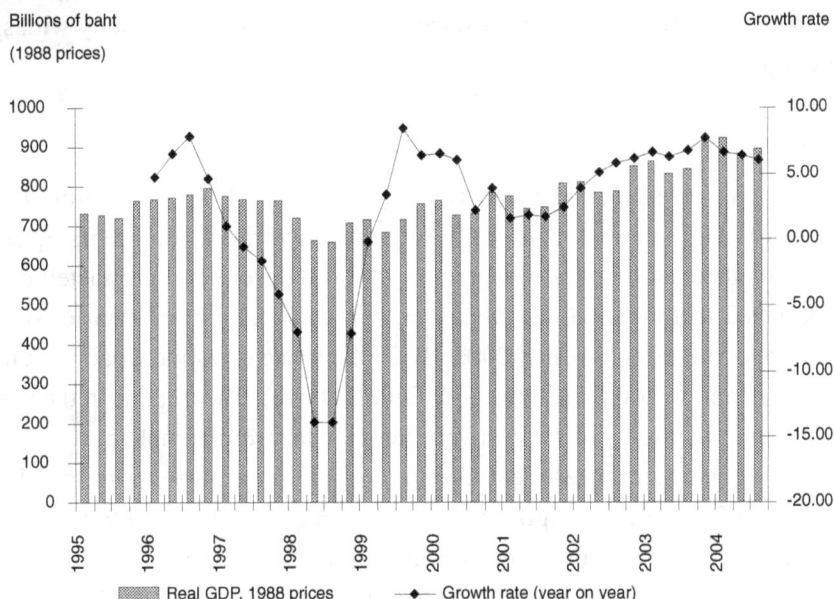

Source: National Economic and Social Development Board.

TABLE 2
Thailand: Composition of aggregate demand, 1994 to 2003
(per cent of GDP)

	1994	1995	1996	1997	1998	1999	2000	2001	2002	2003
Private consumption	55.2	54.4	54.4	54.4	53.8	53.7	53.8	54.8	54.5	54.7
Public consumption	8.2	7.9	8.4	8.2	9.6	9.4	9.3	9.3	8.9	8.3
Private investment	32.9	34.5	32.8	22.6	9.6	10.9	13.3	13.8	14.5	16.3
Public investment	8.7	8.9	10.4	11.6	9.2	8.5	7.4	6.8	6.1	5.0
Exports	44.6	47.1	42.0	45.7	55.3	57.7	64.8	61.0	64.3	62.2
Imports	−47.8	−52.5	−49.2	−44.3	−38.8	−41.0	−49.9	−46.3	−48.9	−47.8

Source: Author's calculations from NESDB tables, Quarterly Gross Domestic Product 2/2003, online at:
http://www.nesdb.go.th/Main_menu/Macro/GDP/menu.html tables 2 and 12.

The net outcome was a contraction in aggregate demand, especially in durables-producing industries like construction, which declined very severely.

The central problem of Thailand's economic recovery from the crisis has been the continued insufficiency of aggregate demand. The slowness of the recovery has not been due to a deficiency of productive capacity (aggregate supply) because excess capacity has been evident throughout the economy. Table 3 presents data on this matter for the manufacturing sector.[4] Relative to the pre-crisis period, the crisis and post-crisis years (1997 onwards) have been characterized by widespread excess capacity.

Investment

The decline in investment demand was not unique to Thailand. Figure 4 shows investment to GDP ratios for several East Asian countries from the first quarter of 1997 (ratios indexed to 1 for this period) to 2003. Severe and protracted declines have occurred in Indonesia and Malaysia, but Thailand's investment crisis is the most severe of all, extending into 2003. By 2002 private investment had risen to only 14.5 of GDP and in 2003 16.3 per cent (Table 2 above). The trend is in the required direction, but this aspect of the recovery remains far from complete.

Net foreign direct investment did not decline immediately with the 1997–98 crisis, but by 2003 it had contracted to around one-fifth of its 1998 level. This is indicated in Figure 5. Putting the decline of FDI together with the decline in domestic investment it is clear that the confidence of investors in the Thai economy has not yet fully recovered. Restoring investor confidence is an ongoing task of the Thaksin government in its second term. The sustainability of economic growth depends upon it. Maintaining the momentum of economic reform and upgrading Thailand's governance is necessarily the path forward.

The macroeconomic paradox is that upon taking government in 2001 Prime Minister Thaksin had "promised" double-digit rates of economic growth, fuelled

TABLE 3
Thailand: Industrial capacity utilization, 1995 to 2003
(per cent)

	1995	1996	1997	1998	1999	2000	2001	2002	2003
Total	77.5	72.5	64.8	52.8	61.2	55.8	53.5	59.9	66.2
Food	42.4	38.1	37.7	33.5	42.6	44.1	42.1	45.1	53.9
Beverage	82.3	83.0	79.1	77.2	101.9	32.6	36.4	50.5	56.6
Tobacco	75.2	84.2	75.8	60.4	54.4	53.7	52.1	53.8	55.8
Construction materials	97.3	78.7	72.9	44.6	49.8	50.1	52.3	56.9	57.6
Iron & steel products	64.2	65.2	50.6	35.9	39.6	47.0	50.0	60.6	62.7
Vehicles and equipments	81.4	67.6	48.5	23.4	35.6	40.1	44.5	54.6	69.6
Petroleum products	93.2	85.7	90.1	84.0	85.7	83.9	74.8	76.2	79.4
Electronic & electrical products	63.9	67.8	62.2	47.5	53.4	65.4	47.5	59.7	62.1
Others	80.0	77.7	66.1	68.9	72.9	75.4	77.0	71.5	73.9

Source: Bank of Thailand.
Note: The above categories account for 44.5 per cent of 1995 manufacturing sector value added.

FIGURE 4
East Asia: Investment to GDP ratios, 1997 to 2003

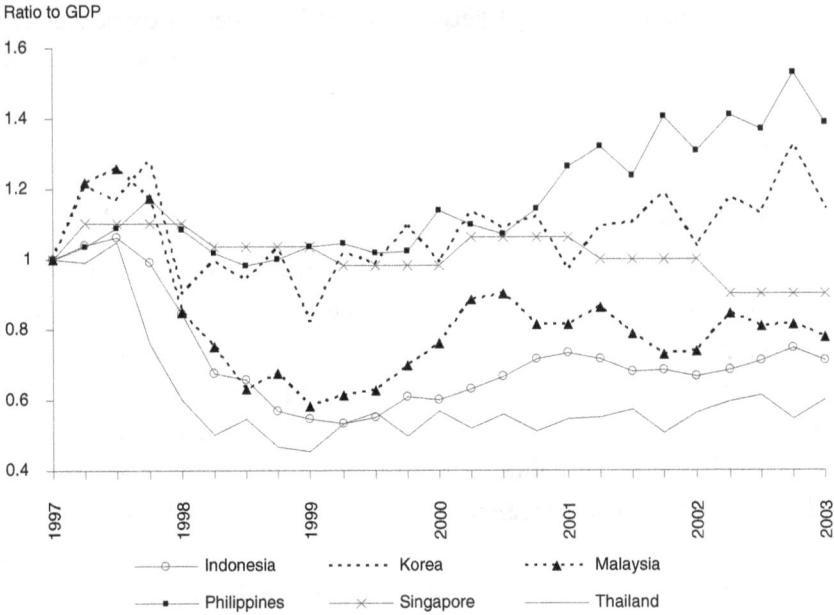

Source: Data from Roong et al. (2003), available at: http://www.bot.or.th/bothomepage/index/
index_e.asp

FIGURE 5
Thailand: FDI inflows and outflows, 1995 to 2003, US$

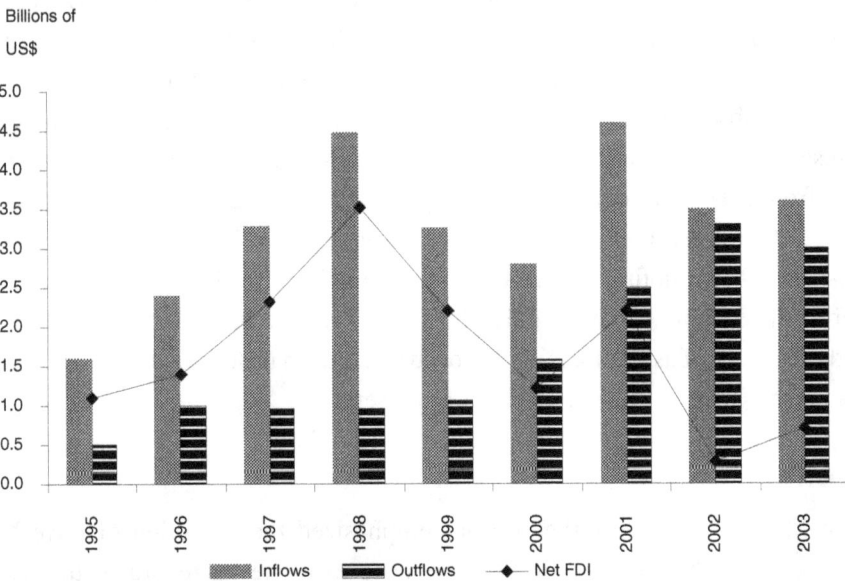

Source: Bank of Thailand.

not by export dependence as in the past, but by domestic demand. Growth has not reached those levels but has instead reverted to something close to Thailand's long-term pre-boom rate of growth, of between 6 and 7 per cent, experienced between 1950 and 1986 (see Table 1). More paradoxically, the importance of exports as a driver of growth increased rather than declined. Thailand is now more dependent on exports than ever before.

A New Growth Bubble?

Early in the Thaksin government, its populist rhetoric and seemingly exaggerated economic promises worried many observers that a bubble could result, similar to that producing the crisis of 1997–98. Thaksin had promised a return to double-digit growth rates, which, based on over-investment, had proven so unmanageable in the period leading up to the crisis. Moreover, it was feared that fiscal recklessness could produce crippling levels of public debt. Paradoxically, the outcome has been more sensible and more sustainable than it would have been had Thaksin's promises been achieved. Growth has reverted to rates similar to the long-term growth rate of between 6 and 7 per cent, experienced over the three and a half decades prior to the boom years of 1987 to 1996 (Table 1).

In addition, the fiscal expansion was smaller than was expected and the revenue-raising effects of economic recovery were larger than anticipated. Official public debt has actually declined, from 54 per cent of GDP at the beginning of Thaksin's period of office, to 39 per cent now.[5] Another paradox. But there is a worry in this. The Thaksin government has made extensive use of off-budget means of financing its favoured programmes. The implications of this for the true level of public debt are not yet well understood and require careful scrutiny.

Some observers still fear a bubble, noting increases in stock market indices and real estate prices. Figure 6 shows the Stock Exchange of Thailand's index of share prices from 1980 to the end of 2004. Although stock prices did indeed rise significantly during 2004 the level of the index is not similar to its level in the years preceding the crisis. It is worth noting that stock prices actually fell substantially over the year prior to the currency crisis of July 1997. The event to be feared is therefore not a steady recovery of asset prices, as has occurred, but an unsustainable boom, followed by a crash. There is no sign of either at present.

Poverty

Prime Minister Thaksin's rhetoric has emphasized the reduction of poverty as a policy goal. It therefore seems reasonable to examine its record in that respect.

FIGURE 6
Thailand: Stock exchange index, 1980 to 2004, monthly

SET index

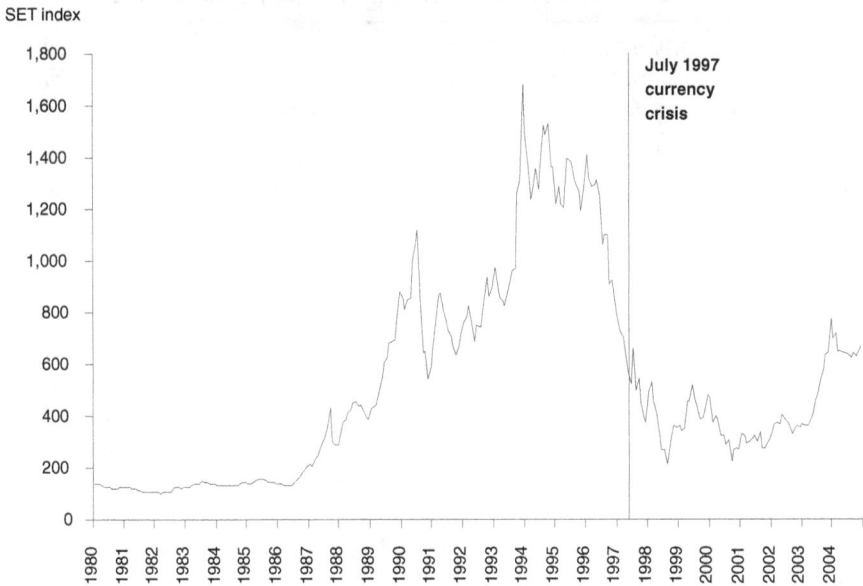

Source: Stock Exchange of Thailand.

Table 4 summarizes recently released data on poverty incidence in Thailand. The data are based on the Socio-economic Survey (SES) of Thai households, conducted every two years by the government's National Statistical Office. Estimates of poverty incidence, using these survey data, are then prepared by a sister agency, the National Economic and Social Development Board (NESDB). Preliminary results for 2004 have been posted on the NESDB's website and these data are used in the following discussion.

It is notable that the "2004" SES data are actually collected over a period that includes part of 2003, and the same applies to earlier years. The comparison of 2002 and 2004 may therefore more accurately be said to involve comparing the periods 2001–02 and 2003–04. Allowing for the lagged effects of policy on actual household incomes, the comparison of 2002 with 2004 SES-based data may therefore be considered to correspond roughly to changes within the first two years of the Thaksin government.

According to the NESDB's data, between 2002 and 2004 poverty incidence declined from 15.5 to 12.0, an average annual decline in poverty incidence of 1.75 per cent of the population. This is surely impressive. On average, the percentage of

TABLE 4
Thailand: Poverty incidence and Gini coefficient, 1988 to 2004
(headcount measure, per cent of total population)

	Poverty incidence (headcount measure, percent of population)			Inequality (Gini coefficient)
	Aggregate	Rural	Urban	Aggregate
1988	44.9	52.9	25.2	0.482
1990	38.2	45.2	21.4	0.520
1992	32.5	40.3	14.1	0.541
1994	25.0	30.7	11.7	0.522
1996	17.0	21.3	7.3	0.518
1998	18.8	23.7	7.5	0.515
2000	21.3	27.0	8.7	0.525
2002	15.5	19.7	6.7	0.501
2004	12.0	15.4	4.8	0.499

Source: National Economic and Social Development Board website: http://poverty.nesdb.go.th/
poverty_new/doc/NESDB/wanchat_20041220041907.ppt
Note: Data for 2004 are preliminary.
Higher values of the Gini coefficient indicate greater inequality.

the population deemed to be poor declined in *each year* from numbers like 15.5 per cent (the 2002 rate) to numbers like 13.75 per cent (an interpolated 2003 rate) and then in the following year to numbers like 12 per cent (the 2004 rate). If, hypothetically, poverty continued to decline at this annual rate, the 15.5 per cent poverty incidence recorded in 2002 would vanish in around nine years. This may not be quite the "eradication of poverty within six years" that Thaksin promised early in his premiership, but it would be marvelous, nevertheless.

How does the rate of poverty reduction indicated by these data compare with earlier periods? Not especially well. From Table 5, the average annual rate of poverty reduction over the pre-crisis boom period from 1988 to 1996 was a staggering 3.5 per cent of the population, double the rate of 2002–04. This was followed by four years of economic contraction and then stagnation from 1996 to 2000, during which poverty incidence *increased* at an average annual rate of 1.1 per cent. Then, during the moderate expansion of 2000 to 2002 the percentage of the population in poverty declined again at an average rate of 2.9 per cent, almost half as much again as the rate for 2002–04. Over the entire period from 1988 to 2002, including the crisis years, poverty incidence declined at an annual average rate of 2.1 per cent.[6] That is, the amount of poverty reduction achieved per year seems to have declined.

The comparison with the boom period from 1988 to 1996 may seem strained because the rate of growth of real output was much higher during the boom. It is

TABLE 5
Thailand: Poverty incidence and growth, 1996 to 2004

Period	Annual reduction poverty incidence (per cent of population per year)	Annual rate of real GDP growth (per cent per year)	Poverty reduction per unit of real GDP per growth
2002–2004	1.75	6.6	0.265
2000–2002	2.9	3.4	0.853
1996–2000	−1.1	−2.9	0.372
1988–1996	3.5	9.2	0.380
1988–2002	2.1	4.2	0.505

Source: Author's calculations based on Table 4 and growth data from National Economic and
Social Development Board, Bangkok.

hardly surprising that the rate of poverty reduction was also higher. The average rate of real GDP growth achieved in each of these periods is shown in the second column of the table. The third column divides the first column by the second, showing the annual rate of poverty reduction achieved per unit of economic growth in each period. During the 1988 to 1996 boom, poverty declined by an annual average of 0.38 per cent of the population per unit of real GDP growth. During the crisis years (1996 to 2000) the ratio of the *increase* of poverty incidence relative to the (negative) growth of output was almost the same as this. Then, immediately following the crisis (2000 to 2002) large numbers of temporarily underemployed and unemployed people emerged from poverty as output began to grow again and the ratio of poverty reduction to growth was temporarily 0.85. But data for the first two years of the Thaksin government (2002 to 2004) suggest, if anything, a decline in the poverty-reducing power of growth. There is certainly no sign that it has increased.

The explanation for these results is a good topic for future economic research. A simple hypothesis is as follows. When there is significant economic growth, many people find opportunities to raise their incomes above the poverty line. As this process continues, and the pool of poor people dwindles, those who have most difficulty in taking advantage of economic opportunity comprise an increasing proportion of those who remain poor. Examples include many of the aged, single mothers with young children, those with physical or intellectual disabilities, and groups living in socially excluded or physically isolated communities. Since economic growth has less effect on poverty among these groups than among others, the power of economic growth to reduce poverty declines as poverty incidence becomes lower. To reduce poverty among these groups, solutions that go beyond relying on economic growth become increasingly important. Unless effective steps are taken to reach these groups, the amount of poverty reduction that will occur each year will decline, even with steady economic growth.

The Thaksin government has indeed implemented policies for poverty reduction and these do go beyond simply relying on growth. But the policies that have been followed have consisted heavily of consumption-increasing loans and debt write-offs. There have been three main categories, announced in 2001, early in the Thaksin government: a loan programme for village groups known as the village fund; debt write-offs for indebted farmers; and subsidies to low-cost public health care. These policies have had some positive effects and are popular, but the above calculations suggest that they have not been sufficient to prevent the poverty-reducing effects of economic growth from declining.

More insight into the nature of poverty in Thailand is provided by Figure 7, showing measured poverty incidence in 2004 by region. The numbers appearing in the figure itself are the numbers of poor people in each region, measured in millions.

FIGURE 7
Thailand: Poverty Incidence by Region, 2004

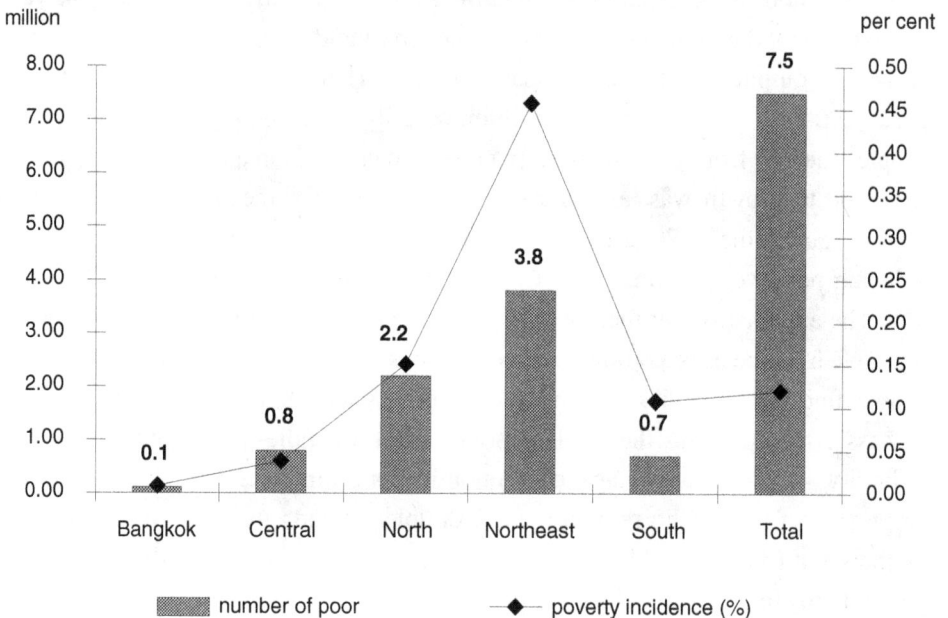

Source: Author's calculations from data provided on the National Economic and Social
        Development Board website: http://poverty.nesdb.go.th/poverty_new/doc/NESDB/
        wanchat_20041220041907.ppt
Note: Data are preliminary.

Poverty is highly regional. The incidence of poverty was lowest in Bangkok, at 0.9 per cent, followed by the Central region, 3.7 per cent, the South at 10.8 per cent, the North at 15.1 per cent and the Northeast, by far the highest at 45.7 per cent. In view of further discussion of the South below, it should be noted that this region accounts for 0.7 million poor people out of a national total of 7.5 million poor people and its poverty incidence, at 10.8 per cent is below the national average of 12 per cent. Nevertheless, we shall see below that this aggregate calculation for the South masks pockets of high poverty incidence within it, well above the national average and even above the regional average for the Northeast.

A more telling set of data relates poverty incidence to the educational attainment of the household head. These data, for 2004, are summarized in Figure 8. Poverty incidence is strongly related to education. For households headed by persons with no formal schooling, poverty incidence is double the national average, at almost 25 per cent. Poverty incidence declines steadily with educational attainment. Achieving lasting solutions to poverty involves going beyond distributing temporary grants or loans to poor people, popular though they are, and addressing the underlying causes

FIGURE 8
Thailand: Poverty incidence by education of household head, 2004

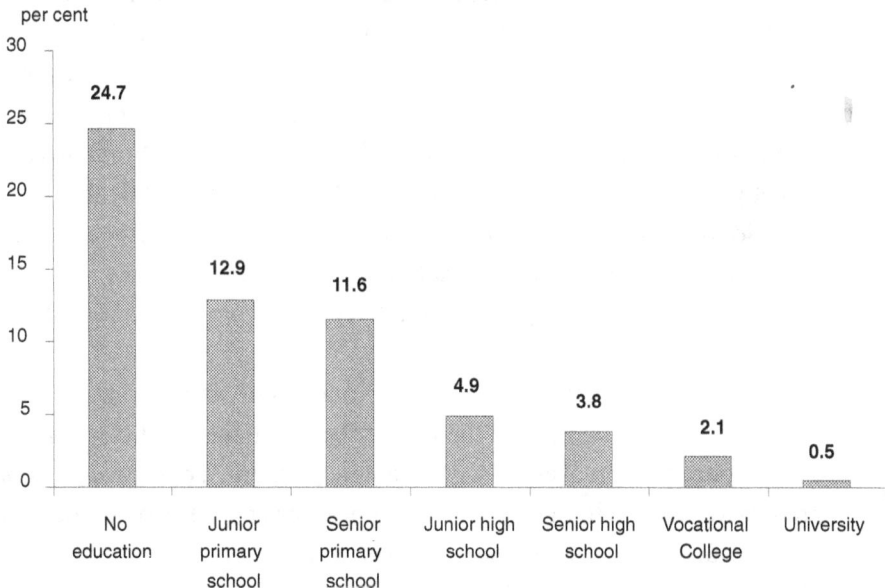

Source: Author's calculations from data provided on the National Economic and Social Development Board website: http://poverty.nesdb.go.th/poverty_new/doc/NESDB/ wanchat_20041220041907.ppt
Note: Data are preliminary.

of poverty. Temporary infusions of money do not necessarily raise the productivity of poor people on a sustained basis.

Improving the education system, especially for rural people, is an obvious starting point for a serious poverty reduction programme. Rural areas contain over 90 per cent of Thailand's poor people and educational standards there are low, both in quality and level of attainment. A recent survey by Sirilaksana Khoman[7] demonstrates the continued weakness of Thailand's education system, especially for rural people, and the importance of major reform in this area. Unfortunately, education reform proved one of the most difficult and least successful areas for the Thaksin government's first term. The entrenched power of the Ministry of Education's vast bureaucracy proved virtually immovable. Education reform should surely be a priority matter for the second term.

Economic Origins of Southern Violence

During 2004, politically inspired violence in Southern Thailand claimed the lives of over 500 Thais, including many civilians, but also policemen, soldiers and other government personnel. The three southernmost provinces of Narathiwat, Pattani and Yala, each with a large Muslim population, were the centre of these problems. Many factors contribute to these problems, but economics is one.

Table 6 shows gross regional product (GRP) in 2001 for each of Thailand's major regions and five of the 14 provinces of the Southern region. These are the three heavily Muslim provinces mentioned above and, for comparison, the two very different tourist provinces of Phuket and Songkhla. The data relate to 2001, the latest year for which provincial data of this kind are available. From these data it appears that while output per person in the Southern region is below the national average, the South is not poor compared with the North and Northeast regions. Many Thais are aware of these regional facts. "The South is not poor" is a commonly heard comment. But these broad regional comparisons mask large disparities within the South.

These data show that in the three Muslim provinces of Narathiwat, Pattani and Yala output per person is well below the rest of the South and well below most of the rest of the country. Moreover, this is not a new problem. These provinces have been unproductive relative to the rest of the country for at least two decades. Most telling of all, the disparity between these three provinces and every other part of the country shown in the table, especially other parts of the South, has been increasing steadily over time. The second column of the table shows that the three Muslim provinces are more agricultural than the rest of the country. They are also more agricultural than most other parts of the South.

TABLE 6
Thailand: GRP per capita and share of agriculture, 2001,
and household income per capita, 2002
(baht per person, current prices, and per cent [share of agriculture])

	GRP per capita, 2001	Share of Agriculture in GDP (%), 2001	Household income per capita, 2002
Bangkok Metropolitan	239,207	0.6	28,239
Central Region	78,588	10.7	14,128
North Region	40,352	20.1	9,530
Northeast Region	27,381	18.9	9,279
South Region	54,176	33.9	12,487
Narathiwat	31,412	37.1	7,603
Pattani	47,690	50.8	9,703
Yala	44,160	28.5	10,018
Phuket	225,060	10.5	26,363
Songkhla	62,544	35.1	14,192
Thailand	81,435	10.4	13,736

Sources: National Economic and Social Development Board, Bangkok, and *Thailand in Figures*, 8th ed., (Bangkok: Alpha Research Co., Ltd., 2005).

Data on household incomes per person, shown in the third column of the table, reinforce these conclusions. The three Muslim provinces of the South are poor, even by the standards of the Northeastern region, widely recognized as Thailand's poorest.

Table 7 uses data from the Labour Force Survey to compare measured unemployment rates in the three Muslim provinces with other parts of the country. In 2004 unemployment was higher in these provinces than any other area shown, but this was not true as recently as 1996. The economic deprivation of these provinces, relative to other areas at least, has apparently increased in recent years.

Finally, Table 8 uses the SES to compare poverty incidence in the three Muslim provinces with other parts of the country. In both 1990 and 2000 poverty incidence was higher in these three provinces than any other major region of the country, including the Northeast. Again, the disparity rose over this period. While poverty incidence declined significantly in these three provinces over this decade (from 46 to 21 per cent) it declined more slowly than in the rest of Thailand and more slowly than in the rest of the South.

The data reviewed above show that, contrary to popular opinion, there is indeed an economic basis for disaffection in the southern Muslim provinces of Narathiwat, Pattani and Yala. Economic factors are not the only problem fuelling the conflict, but they appear to be a contributor. These provinces are characterized by

TABLE 7
Thailand: Unemployment rate by location, 1996 and 2004

	Unemployment Rate (%)	
	1996	2004
Bangkok Metropolitan	1.11	1.50
Central Region	0.97	1.59
North Region	1.67	2.23
Northeast Region	2.11	2.27
South Region	1.06	2.03
Three Muslim Provinces	1.26	2.72
Phuket + Songkhla	0.74	2.04
Other	1.68	1.43
Thailand	1.10	1.50

Source: Author's calculations from National Statistical Office, Bangkok, *Labour Force Survey*, 1996 and 2004.

Note: "Three Muslim provinces" means the population weighted average of Narathiwat, Pattani and Yala. Similarly, "Phuket and Songkhla" means the population weighted average of those two provinces and "Other" means the population weighted average of the 9 remaining provinces of the Southern region.

TABLE 8
Thailand: Poverty incidence by location, 1990 and 2000

	1990			2000		
	Population Share	Poverty Incidence	Poverty Share	Population Share	Poverty Incidence	Poverty Share
Bangkok Metropolitan	10.13	2.41	0.83	6.66	0.18	0.15
Central Region	17.18	22.52	13.21	26.71	3.54	11.49
North Region	20.22	24.67	17.03	22.49	6.92	18.91
Northeast Region	35.82	44.47	54.39	27.18	16.46	54.37
South Region	13.78	30.03	14.13	16.96	7.31	15.08
Three Muslim Provinces	2.99	45.78	4.67	3.39	21.07	8.69
Phuket and Songkhla	2.36	16.85	1.36	0.04	1.28	0.49
Others	8.44	28.14	8.11	0.48	4.65	5.89
Thailand	100.00	29.29	100.00	100.00	8.23	100.00

Source: Author's calculations from National Statistical Office, *Socio-economic Survey* (SES), 1990 and 2000.

Note: See Table 7 for the definitions of "Three Muslim provinces", "Phuket and Songkhla" and "Other". "Population share" means the population of an area (province or district) as a percentage of the national population. "Poverty incidence" means the percentage of the total population of an area who are poor, meaning that they belong to households whose incomes per person fall below a poverty line held constant over time in real terms. "Poverty share" means the number of poor people in an area as a percentage of the total number of poor people in the nation.

low productivity, low incomes, high unemployment and high poverty incidence. Because the southern region as a whole is not poor, these features of the three provinces concerned are masked by the relative affluence of other parts of the southern region. The deprivation of the southernmost provinces has not been sufficiently recognized. The economic disparity between these three provinces and the remainder of the South has been increasing. Long-term resolution of the political and security problems in this region cannot rely on "policing" solutions alone. The economic deprivation of the area must also be addressed.

A matter of particular concern is that following the February 2005 elections, Prime Minister Thaksin announced a system of grading villages in these three provinces into three categories: "red", meaning those not cooperating with the government's security measures; "yellow", meaning those not cooperating sufficiently; and "green", meaning those who do cooperate. Red areas were to be denied some or even all development expenditures, without being exempted from the taxes which finance them.[8] Yellow areas were to receive partial reductions and green areas no reductions. Observers noted that this policy of collective punishment could only increase economic deprivation in the areas concerned and would be guaranteed to accentuate the feeling of exclusion from Thai society experienced by many of Thailand's Muslim people, especially those in the far South.

Economic Cost of the Tsunami

The government's National Economic and Social Development Board has assessed the economic impact of the tsunami.[9] According to its analysis, the net economic effect is actually *positive*, equivalent to 10.5 billion baht or 0.15 per cent of GDP. This conclusion was reached by dividing the net impact of the tsunami into two components — one negative effect and one positive, equivalent to 0.48 and 0.63 per cent of GDP, respectively. The negative effect is the economic value of the damage done to property and natural resources, which "will lead to a reduction in tourism earnings, especially in early 2005", together with the loss of output resulting from unemployment of people who would otherwise have been employed. Against this, the assessment says that the positive effect derives from the fact that "the restoration of the affected provinces will increase economic activities in 2005". This supposed positive effect is said to have three components: private sector investment to reconstruct enterprises; private spending to replace destroyed assets of households; and government spending for rehabilitation, including the government relief fund.

Unfortunately, the economic reasoning underlying the "positive" effect is erroneous. The assumption implicitly being made is that the resources used for reconstruction would otherwise have been unused. That is, the income generated from these expenditures is assumed to be income that would not otherwise have existed. In fact, the private and public funds that must now be used to repair the damage to assets and people resulting from the tsunami are not created from nothing, but must be diverted from other expenditures that now cannot occur. Consequently, these are not newly created expenditures, generating new income, but merely relocated expenditures. For example, the household whose house must now be repaired spends money that would otherwise have been spent on other goods and services by that household itself, or they are borrowed funds, which would otherwise have been spent by someone else. The "positive" effect is illusory.[10] Indeed, if it were valid, destruction of assets could literally be a source of economic growth.

The fact that the estimated "positive" effect exceeds the estimated negative effect means that expenditures on the replacement of assets damaged or destroyed (the supposed "positive" effect) will exceed the NESDB's estimate of their economic value (the negative effect). This presumably means that the assets will be upgraded in the course of being re-established. But any such upgrading has no bearing on the economic cost of the tsunami. The latter roughly corresponds to the "negative" effect mentioned by the NESDB's analysis. Despite the flaw in its overall analysis, the NESDB's accounting of the size of the negative effect is meaningful and interesting.

The estimated negative effects have the following components. First, there will be a loss of earnings from tourism. In the case of international tourists, this is estimated as a 40 per cent decline in the first quarter of 2005 and 30 per cent in the second quarter. The loss of income would be 34 billion baht, equivalent to 0.42 per cent of GDP. Reductions in domestic tourism and losses of private consumption amount to another 4.2 billion baht, corresponding to 0.06 per cent of GDP.

Damage to business enterprises is estimated at a further 35.6 billion baht, equivalent to 0.51 per cent of GDP. Much of this would occur in Phang Nga province. The NESDB analysis does not count this amount in its overall assessment because "damage of property assets [is] not counted in GDP since the assets were already invested". This argument is also invalid. It is true that destruction of assets is not counted in GDP. For example, depreciation of assets normally occurs in the process of production, and GDP (*gross* domestic product) does not allow for this destruction of assets that routinely occurs. This is widely understood as one of many deficiencies of GDP as a measure of true economic output. Many analysts prefer to use the measure of NDP (*net* domestic product) as a measure of true output because it does allow for depreciation of assets and other sources of asset loss.

The fact that GDP does not allow for something does not mean that it is not a true component of economic cost. It is obvious that destruction of business enterprises is a cost because it reduces productive capacity in the future. Investment in these assets must now occur at the expense of other forms of investment which would otherwise have been possible, but now are not. The destruction of assets should clearly be counted in an overall assessment of the economic impact of the tsunami.

The overall estimate of the economic impact of the tsunami that emerges from this, taking the NESDB's conservative facts at face value, is a cost almost exactly equivalent to 1 per cent of GDP. At a national level, this may not seem like much. But the cost is concentrated in the southern region, which accounts for a little under 9 per cent of national GDP. The cost of the tsunami, conservatively estimated, therefore amounts to about 11 per cent of gross regional product in the southern region. This is roughly the size of the GDP contraction that occurred, at a national level, in the case of the 1997–98 economic crisis. So far as the South is concerned, the tsunami is an event of similar magnitude. For the people of Phuket and Phang Nga, it is much larger.

Conclusions

Thailand has recovered well from the crisis in economic terms. This has occurred despite unexpected setbacks including rural drought, Asian influenza, SARS, political violence in the South and most recently, the terrible tsunami of 26 December 2004. The government of Thaksin Shinawatra has done much to restore economic confidence and was rewarded by a massive electoral victory in February 2005. The long-term future seems good in economic terms, provided issues of long-term reform are addressed. The country's archaic education system must be the most important of these and the promotion of competition within the domestic economy must be the second. Given its enormous parliamentary majority in its second term and the Prime Minister's own popularity, Thaksin's Thai Rak Thai government has a unique opportunity to address fundamental issues of reform. It remains to be seen whether the opportunity will be grasped.

Notes

[1]   At its election in 2001 Thai Rak Thai won just under half of the seats and was able to govern with a parliamentary majority only by absorbing minor parties.

[2]   On 15 February 2005 the website of the Phuket-based Tsunami Earthquake and Tsunami Relief Centre said that the number of confirmed dead, meaning those whose bodies had

been recovered) was 5,395, of whom 1,899 were known to have been Thais and 1,953 foreigners. The nationalities of the remaining 1,531 bodies had yet to be confirmed. Almost 3,000 other persons were missing, with bodies not yet recovered.

[3]   A fuller discussion of some of the issues discussed in this section is provided in Peter Warr, "Boom, Bust and Beyond", in *Thailand Beyond the Crisis*, edited by Peter Warr (London: Routledge, 2005), pp. 1–65.

[4]   These data are extracted from Roong Poshyananda Mallikamas, Yunyong Thaicharoen and Daungporn Rodpengsangkaha, "Investment Cycles, Economic Recovery and Monetary Policy", Monetary Policy Group, Bank of Thailand, August 2003. Available at: http://www.bot.or.th/bothomepage/index/index_e.asp.

[5]   Quoted in the *Economist*, 5 February 2005, p. 23.

[6]   Table 4 above shows that the 1988 to 2002 period coincided with increased inequality. In view of this, the reported (small) decline in the Gini coefficient between 2002 and 2004 is difficult to reconcile with the evidence cited here (Table 5) that the poverty-reducing power of growth in the later period was so much lower.

[7]   Sirilaksana Khoman, "Education: The Key to Long-term Recovery", in *Thailand Beyond the Crisis*, op. cit., pp. 251–84.

[8]   Some reports suggested that two-thirds of the villages in Narathirawat province could fall into this "red" category.

[9]   The document can be located on a website maintained by the Asian Development Bank: http://aric.adb.org/asiantsunami/tsunamiimpactassessment.asp#Thailand.
The link to the NESDB report is:
"Assessment of the Tsunami impact on the Thai Economy in 2005", National Economic and Social Development Board — Thailand, 18 January 2005.

[10] The argument presented here disregards funds which are now spent which would otherwise have been saved. Some increase in the proportion of income which is spent rather than saved is possible, giving rise to temporary net increases in income. But this short-run effect should be small and will be at least partially offset by increases in saving later.

Vietnam

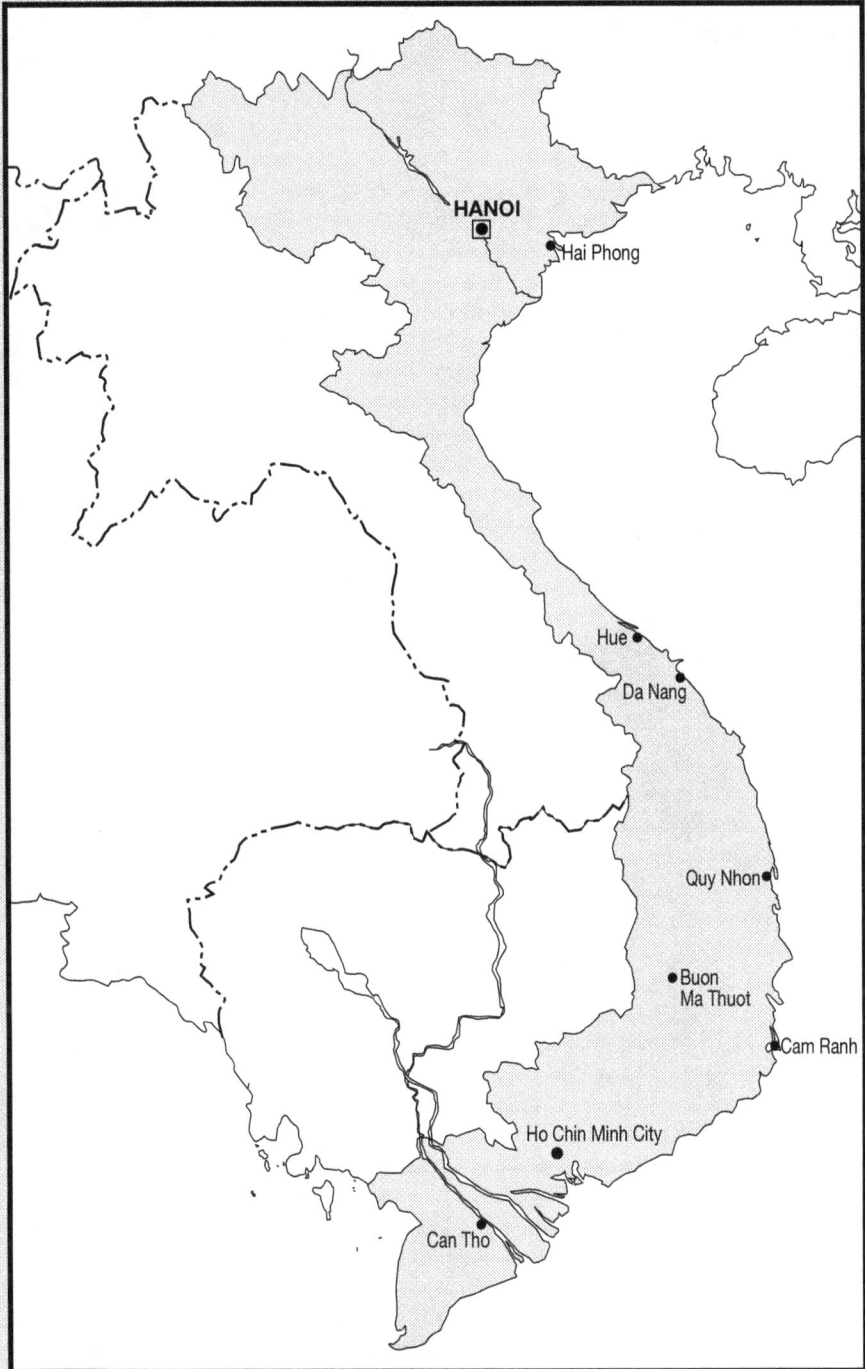

HANOI

Hai Phong

Hue

Da Nang

Quy Nhon

Buon
Ma Thuot

Cam Ranh

Ho Chin Minh City

Can Tho

Southeast Asian Affairs 2005

VIETNAM IN 2004
A Country Hanging in the Balance

Michael J Montesano

Introduction

In 2004 Vietnam continued on the path of political, social, and economic adjustment that has given direction to its affairs since the mid-1980s. The regional and global environments and a number of domestic realities defined the challenges and opportunities before the country. While indicators of progress proved impossible to overlook, close observation of events in Vietnam during the year also offered cause for concern. The period between the end of 2004 and the opening of the Tenth Party Congress of the Communist Party of Vietnam (CPV) during the first half of 2006 may well come to be seen as one in which the sustainability of Vietnam's remarkable economic and social progress of the recent past hung in the balance.

Endemic corruption and newly vigorous efforts to confront it, an increasingly active National Assembly, and serious disturbances among ethnic minorities in the Central Highlands counted among the highlights of Vietnam's politics during 2004. In the economic sphere, continued steady growth accompanied worries over the country's public investment strategy, its timetable for accession to the World Trade Organization (WTO), the pace of its equitization of state-owned enterprises (SOEs), and its long-term international competitiveness. The state of Vietnam's education and public health systems only added to these concerns. The year's developments in the area of international relations included Hanoi's success in hosting the Asia-Europe Meeting, continued albeit low-level tensions over the South China Sea and human rights, deepening of the Vietnam-United States military-to-military relationship, and the well publicized, somewhat embarrassing use of Ho Chi Minh City as a channel of escape for a large group of North Korean asylum-seekers on their way to South Korea.

MICHAEL J MONTESANO is Assistant Professor, Southeast Asian Studies Programme, National University of Singapore.

Vietnam's foreign affairs during 2004 thus mirrored Vietnamese affairs as a whole. Historical, ideological, political, and even demographic legacies framed the country's ongoing, almost inexorable integration into the post-Cold War international economic and political orders. The year raised not only the question of whether Vietnamese efforts at reform and adaptation have been "fast enough" but also the more basic one of whether these efforts have rested on viable foundations.

Facing up to Corruption

Official and public attention to Vietnam's serious corruption problem reached new levels in 2004. High-profile casualties of this attention included Minister of Agriculture and Rural Development Le Huy Ngo, forced out in June after the revelation of graft within his ministry, and Deputy Trade Minister Mai Van Dau, arrested in November along with his son for accepting bribes in the allocation of textile export quotas for the American market. Similarly, senior officials at Vietnam National Shipping Lines, the fuel-trading arm of Vietnam Airlines, and Vietnam Oil and Gas Corporation (PetroVietnam) suffered dismissal, arrest, or both because of corruption charges raised during the year.

In addition to individual sackings and arrests, the country's anti-corruption drive took a number of more general forms. First, the Vietnamese press devoted frequent, detailed coverage to cases of official malfeasance throughout the year. Second, Prime Minister Phan Van Khai took explicit notice of the problem in his opening address to the year-end session of the National Assembly in October. Chatter in Hanoi and Ho Chin Minh City attributed to Khai himself the estimates that corruption cost public investment projects some 20–30 per cent of allocated financing. The Voice of Vietnam reported somewhat euphemistically that that same session of the Assembly addressed "wastage" in capital expenditure.[1] Third, plans were made to create a new anti-corruption agency and to replace the 1998 Anti-Corruption Ordinance with a tougher, more effective anti-corruption law.

Officials of the Government Inspectorate announced that latter measure at a two-day gathering of foreign donors in early December in Hanoi.[2] Their audience was well chosen. A number of veterans of aid and development work in the region, now actively engaged with Vietnam, privately remarked in 2004 that levels of graft and greed in Hanoi had begun to recall the norms of Jakarta's New Order elite during Indonesia's booming 1980s.

Domestically, of course, public awareness of corruption had other, even more important, implications. Especially in the long, politically charged run-up to the CPV's Tenth Party Congress, the issue spoke directly to what the *Financial Times* aptly termed the party's "fears that public servants' increasingly visible opulence is eroding the legitimacy and effectiveness of its authoritarian, one-party rule".[3] At a time when international pressures to liberalize the Vietnamese economy made further widening of the country's income gap inevitable, such fears were unsurprising. At the same time, however, some observers considered anti-corruption moves during the year to be selective weapons in, and manifestations of, otherwise obscure intra-regime political contests.[4]

Reflective of both these domestic dimensions — legitimacy and politicking — of the worry during 2004 over abuse of official powers was a letter concerning the activities of the defence ministry's General Department No. 2 (GD2), apparently transmitted to CPV Secretary General Nong Duc Manh and the Politburo in June. Officially, GD2 takes responsibility for military intelligence. But this letter charged that it had long represented a dangerous and divisive political and financial rogue element in the Vietnamese state, essentially out of control. Suppressed, unreported but very widely discussed within Vietnam, this letter and its explosive charges allegedly came from a retired People's Army of Vietnam (PAVN) general and CPV Central Committee member.[5]

Energizing the National Assembly

Concern over corruption figured in the second of the signal developments in Vietnamese politics during 2004: the rising profile of the National Assembly. Early December brought the unprecedented spectacle of Prime Minister Phan Van Kiet facing direct parliamentary interpellation, in which he acknowledged responsibility for graft and malfeasance that occurred on his watch. The premier was not alone in explaining himself to the body at that time; five other members of the cabinet joined him in facing parliamentarians' questions during the closing days of the year's second session of the assembly. In May, during its first session, several of the Assembly's members tabled a request to hold votes of confidence in four ministers, including those of public health and education. This demonstration of legislators' assertiveness and apparent independence stunned many Vietnamese.

Much of the National Assembly's work is still prepared by its Standing Committee and thus scripted in advance. Its role in the initiation, as opposed to the consideration, of legislation remains minimal. Nevertheless, the higher calibre of its membership, the increased activity of its committees, its sometimes aggressive questioning of cabinet ministers, and its more active role in foreign affairs all point unmistakably to its ongoing emergence as a significant institutional player in Vietnam's politics.[6]

The role of Vietnam's media, not least television, in providing close coverage of the Assembly's proceedings only contributed to its growing significance. Public awareness of and even a public feeling of involvement with those proceedings have become unmistakable. The Assembly's engagement during the year with such matters of deep popular concern as education and health resonated with ordinary Vietnamese. During the Assembly's first 2004 session, the Minister of Public Health faced particularly tough questioning over the quality and cost of health care in Vietnam and the high prices that Vietnamese pay for their drugs. The Assembly's emergence as a forum for allegations that the local affiliate of Swiss drug importer and distributor Zuellig Pharma enjoyed monopoly power in the local market suggested its potential as a vehicle for popular sentiments in the future. Likewise, the National Assembly's coming role in the deliberation and passage of legislation necessary to Vietnam's eventual accession to the WTO[7] will keep it both closely engaged with the most important issues of the day and very much in the public eye.

Violence in the Central Highlands

If the National Assembly embodied the hopeful side of state–society relations in Vietnam during 2004, events in the Central Highlands highlighted a number of potentially serious threats to social harmony. Human Rights Watch estimated that the death toll resulting from the violent, frankly thuggish, suppression of demonstrations held by ethnic minority Montagnards at Easter totalled at least ten. An additional several hundred persons may have suffered injury. While the Montagnard Foundation in the United States claimed that substantially more people had lost their lives, the Vietnamese government put the death toll at only two.[8] If these demonstrations and the resultant violence proved less serious than those of February 2001, they nevertheless pointed to a series of persistent problems, with implications extending well beyond the Central Highlands.

First among these is land. Well-informed sources in Hanoi mention the possibility that a land seizure on the part of a local people's committee directly precipitated the Easter demonstrations. More broadly, however, ethnic tensions in the Central Highlands are fuelled, and ethnic differences exaggerated, by struggles over access to land. While die-hard anti-Communist observers outside Vietnam may see a deliberate state policy to turn Montagnards into a minority in the highlands, so called "unplanned" rather than officially sponsored migration accounts both for the shifting demographic balance and worsening competition for agricultural land there. The state's effort to slow and even check migration to the Central Highlands notwithstanding, more than 40 per cent of all interregional migrants within Vietnam during 2003 and the first eight months of 2004 moved to that region.[9] Commodity booms and busts, above all those for coffee, have only made more tense the resultant competition for resources in the Central Highlands.

Second are issues of internal security and international relations. Hanoi blamed the Montagnard Foundation for the Easter violence, and, while such outside agitation hardly suffices as an explanation, Vietnam watchers did report the Foundation's having alerted them in advance that something was due to happen. Also, reports of the flight of at least several hundred Montagnards across the Cambodian border in search of refuge and asylum provoked both angry denials in Hanoi and extreme reluctance on the part of the Phnom Penh regime to allow the Office of the United Nations High Commissioner for Refugees to extend assistance.

Third, issues of religious freedom also figured in the troubled Central Highlands. Montagnard Protestants and some of their foreign supporters allege official Vietnamese suppression of their faith. Just two months after the Easter disturbances the Standing Committee of the National Assembly approved an Ordinance on Beliefs and Religion. Official radio commentary on the new ordinance made specific note of "heresies", such as what it termed "the Degar Protestantism in the Central Highlands", from which putatively ignorant, isolated ethnic minorities required protection. The commentary cited similar heretical beliefs in the country's northern uplands.[10]

Like tensions over land and its cost and also like an enduring official obsession with internal security, the state's determination to regulate religious life extended beyond the Montagnard Christians of the Central Highlands. Elsewhere in southern Vietnam during the year, authorities demonstrated great sensitivity to activities of the banned United Buddhist Church of Vietnam.

In a fourth area, too, the Easter demonstrations pointed to a broader concern for Vietnam: poverty. While recent economic growth has brought Vietnam unquestionable success in poverty reduction, evidence has begun to suggest that upland minorities have shared remarkably little in this success. Especially in the Central Highlands,[11] but also in the uplands of northern Vietnam, ethnic minorities have emerged as Vietnam's "poorest of the poor". Foreign observers credit Hanoi with a clear understanding that it must do better, above all in the Central Highlands. Still, Montagnard exclusion from recent socioeconomic progress may present an ominous early indicator that, even beyond the uplands, the coincidence of economic growth and relative social stability that has characterized the recent past ought not be taken for granted.

Continued Healthy Growth, though with Inflation

Vietnam extended its recent record of healthy though unspectacular economic performance during 2004. GDP growth was expected to reach 7.3–7.5 per cent.[12] During the first ten months of the year exports exceeded US$21 billion, a year-on-year increase of almost 30 per cent. That January to October period saw exports of crude oil totalling US$4.66 billion, of garments totalling US$3.73 billion, of footwear totalling US$2.15 billion, of seafood totalling US$1.89 billion, and of electronics approaching US$900 million.[13] Further, the country's rice exports proved a sixth important pillar of the Vietnamese economy, valued at some US$860 million in the January to November period.[14] In those same eleven months, industrial production rose 15.8 per cent on a year-on-year basis. Decomposed, this figure resulted from increases of 12.3, 22.0, and 15.1 per cent for the SOE, private, and foreign-invested sectors, respectively.[15]

Foreign direct investment (FDI) during the year amounted to about US$3.3 billion.[16] All the same, Hanoi has never enjoyed the surge in FDI, particularly from the United States, that it had expected after the United States-Vietnam Bilateral Trade Agreement (BTA) of 2001. Official and press attention to widespread corruption during the year could hardly prove a lure to dramatically increased FDI levels. Neither can Vietnam's poor scores — relative, especially, to its Asian competitors for the FDI dollar — on a number of widely disseminated indices of corruption, competitiveness, transparency, and market freedom.

What the World Bank termed "the main macroeconomic development" in Vietnam during 2004 was a rise in inflation.[17] Estimates of likely inflation for the year as a whole ranged from the Bank's 3.0–5.0 per cent to the government's predicted 7.0 per cent.[18] Concern over this development led the government to attempt an across-the-board spending cut of 10 per cent. Remaining very generous to Vietnam, foreign donors pledged US$2.84 billion for 2004; for 2005, the figure was to rise to US$3.44 billion.[19] In addition, record levels of remittances from overseas were expected to exceed US$3.0 billion dollars.[20] At the same time, the country ran a trade deficit approaching US$4.0 billion.[21] While 2004 saw the United States apply basically arbitrary import tariffs on Vietnamese shrimp, as it had on Vietnamese catfish in 2003, final rates were less than initially feared. Still, American allegations that Vietnam's aquaculture benefits from being part of a "non-market economy" represent an irritant that Hanoi could easily do without.

While not yet a source of serious concern, the level and maturity structure of Vietnam's foreign debt struck some observers of the country's macroeconomy as worth watching; in this area, again, comparisons with Indonesia some years ago were, if somewhat overblown, at least cautionary. While the International Monetary Fund retained an advisory mission in Hanoi, Vietnam's unwillingness to reveal data on its holdings of foreign exchange and to permit auditors to scrutinize other central banking operations brought the Fund's three-year-old lending programme to a halt in April.[22]

Vietnam's real estate price bubble continued to swell during 2004. Its public investment strategy also continued to cause dismay in some circles.[23] Each of these problems had its roots at least in part in the serious inter-provincial and inter-regional disparities that remain an inescapable feature of the country's social, economic and political landscape. In addition, three further significant areas of potential trouble overshadowed Vietnam's economic performance during 2004. Shadows fell on the equitization of SOEs, on weaknesses in the provision of education and public health, and on what some saw as Vietnam's underperformance relative to its possibilities and to its competitors.

One can safely observe that, by any meaningful measure, Vietnam's progress in equitizing state-owned enterprises during 2004 proved slow. The state has touted equitization and enhanced transparency as among its most important goals for the economy. Yet the *Far Eastern Economic Review* reported the equitization between January and August of only 358 of the 1,000 firms scheduled for equitization in 2004.[24] Through July, a mere 12 out of 74 targeted SOEs had been equitized in the Vietnamese capital. Some critics also cite the de facto creation of new SOEs at the provincial level.

In addition to such unquestionably difficult technical matters as valuation and SOE debt, obstacles to timely equitization have included both bureaucratic inertia and potentially more serious political resistance. But the SOEs' drag on Vietnam's macroeconomy makes imperative progress in closing, equitizing, or otherwise modernizing firms in the sector. Such progress is also fundamental to the future health of the national banking system. Despite reports that the remarkable 50 per cent proportion of total bank credit still extended to SOEs has begun to fall,[25] SOE debt and probable additional bad loans impinge seriously on the condition of and future prospects for Vietnam's financial sector. While the real extent of the problem remains unclear, this debt, continued rapid extension of new bank credit, and worries over the possibility of a liquidity crisis in the banking system demand both attention to and reform of the sector.

Similarly, Vietnam's education system continued to represent a source of considerable dissatisfaction during the year. Problems included a shortage of teachers, the widely recognized lamentable state of the country's university system, and an effective consensus that education in Vietnam bore no relation to the country's human capital needs. Prime Minister Khai addressed the sector's problems in his appearance before the National Assembly in early December; earlier, the Minister of Education and Training urged commitment of 18 per cent of the government's budget to education in 2005 and 20 per cent within six years.[26] Public health presented further cause for concern. If in 2003 Vietnam emerged as an exemplary (and more than a bit lucky) case of success in combating SARS, bird flu accounted for some 20 deaths and did substantial damage to its poultry industry during 2004. International observers believed that this problem would be with Vietnam for a number of years and that it could well overwhelm the country's public health infrastructure. Concern about AIDS also mounted during the year, to the point that the People's Army of Vietnam announced and undertook a major effort to reduce incidence among its soldiers.

Slow progress in SOE equitization, manifest inadequacies in its banking system, serious weaknesses in the provision of education and health care are — like corruption — real drags on Vietnam's efforts to realize its ambitions for continued growth, further poverty reduction, and advantageous integration into the international economy. While the Enterprise Law of 2000 has in many ways transformed the day-to-day feel of commercial life in Vietnam, and particularly in its cities, the business boom has generated nothing approaching a critical mass of private firms of sufficient size to be drivers of growth and transformation in their own right. Likewise, economists willing and able to speak their minds on Vietnam and its prospects believe that a country favoured with the high aid levels, the oil revenues, and the remittance flows that Vietnam enjoys ought to be doing much better. They see in its underperformance relative to opportunity reason for serious worry over the country's long-term competitiveness and over the sustainability of its undeniable recent progress.

Toward the WTO?

Nothing brings such worries into such sharp focus as the success and timing of Vietnam's accession to the WTO. Its original target date for WTO accession by the end of 2004 having proved unrealistic, Vietnam was frequently described during the year as being in a "race against time" to enter the organization. Revised plans called for entry by the end of 2005.

October saw Vietnam complete negotiations with the European Union on the terms of its entry into the WTO. More demanding negotiations on "permanent normal trade relations" with the United States and similar talks with China remained unfinished at the end of the year. Analysts worried that China might drive a particularly hard bargain.

The delays in and consequences of Vietnamese accession to the WTO had both domestic and international dimensions.

Domestically, interests in such sectors as construction and telecommunications had the incentive and the opportunity to slow the process. Their resistance reflected more broadly held concerns over the impact of accession on Vietnam's political economy as a whole. Washington's unconcealed dissatisfaction with Hanoi's slowness in approving licences for a number of American insurance firms to operate in Vietnam almost certainly presaged future, even greater, battles over international access to the service sector. Further, the potential distributional effects of trade liberalization could vitiate the unthreatening model of healthy growth with social stability that the CPV regime has enjoyed in recent years.

In international terms, the textile sector stood at the centre of discussion over the pace of Vietnam's WTO accession. International textile quotas expired at the end of 2004, and while the United States extended import quotas for Vietnam's textiles for an additional year, this gesture was perceived, at best, as giving local firms borrowed time. Some observers argued that Vietnam's failure to accede to the WTO as soon as possible would dissuade new investments in the sector and leave jobless the many thousands of young workers whose families depended on their wages. But others, including not least former WTO Director-General Michael Moore, discouraged this sense of urgency. During a mid-November trip to Vietnam, he argued that it was far more important for Vietnam to take the time to negotiate favourable terms of entry into the organization with such economic powers as the United States, Japan, and China.[27]

Arguments like Moore's did not necessarily overlook the textile issue and the worries about expiration of quotas that it raised. They did, implicitly, stress that WTO accession was about far more than textiles. Washington's spate of measures against Vietnam's efficient catfish and shrimp sectors served in this context as an unmistakable reminder of American and Japanese tendencies toward agricultural protectionism and the need for Vietnam to win binding assurances of fair access for its products into the markets of rich trading partners. Similarly, whether under the quota system or after WTO accession, the ability of sectors like Vietnam's textile industry to compete with their Chinese rivals remained very much in doubt. As a follow-up to the United States-Vietnam BTA, then, WTO accession had both symbolic and practical importance to Vietnam's process of integration into the world economy. Realization of the benefits of accession would depend not only on the good faith of Vietnam's trading partners but also on the ability of Vietnam's rulers and producers to make many substantial adjustments in the way that they went about their respective business.

International Relations

Other symbols of Vietnam's progressive reintegration with the post-Cold War world marked the year. On 11 December, the arrival of a United Airlines flight at Ho Chi Minh City's Tan Son Nhat airport renewed direct flights between the United States and Vietnam for the first time in nearly three decades. Even more importantly, on 8–9 October Vietnam played successful host to the Fifth Asia-Europe Meeting (ASEM) in Hanoi. The meeting served as a forum for discussions among the leaders of the European Commission and the EU's 15 member-states and those of China, Brunei, Indonesia, Japan, South Korea, Malaysia, the Philippines, Singapore, Thailand, and Vietnam itself. It proved a firm step toward Vietnam's turn to play host to the Asia-Pacific Economic Cooperation (APEC) summit in 2006, before which Vietnam will chair APEC for a year. At the same time, neither the course of ASEM's informal colloquies nor press coverage of the event left little doubt that the chance to enhance linkages with a rising China accounted for much of its draw for European participants.

For all its success, ASEM also offered up a series of reminders of the distance that Vietnam must still travel as it seeks to assimilate the norms of the international stage on which it would now act. Fear of the disturbances that often accompany such multilateral gatherings led Hanoi to suspend issuance of standard tourist visas during the period around the meeting. Rather than concurrently with ASEM itself, the government allowed the Asia-Europe People's Forum of civil society organizations — another of the rituals that have become standard accompaniment to such gatherings — to take place during September. Even so, it rather awkwardly kept a number of Southeast Asian journalists in town for the Forum from actually attending it. Clearly, Hanoi will have to consider new approaches to such challenges in advance of the APEC summit in 2006.

On the other hand, ASEM did exemplify a trend in Vietnam's foreign relations on which the analysts from many countries who gathered in November in Singapore for the annual "Vietnam Update" conference agreed. The country has, that is, made remarkable progress in expanding the "quantity" — scope and number of interlocutors — of its foreign relations since the collapse of the Soviet bloc within which it previously conducted most of its diplomacy. The task ahead for Hanoi is to improve the "quality" of these relationships.

Four specific sets of relationships — and in some cases of entanglements — during 2004 illustrated both these conclusions. They underlined how far Vietnamese diplomacy has come and also how far it has to go.

First among these came the perennial matter of the South China Sea. In April, Vietnam sent a tourist cruise to contested islands in the Spratly chain as a means of asserting through means other than military its refusal to abandon territorial claims there. In September, the Philippine National Oil Company and the China National Offshore Oil Corporation announced an agreement for cooperation in the mapping of petroleum resources under contested sections of the South China Sea. Disingenuously or not, the Philippine press claimed that PetroVietnam had been invited to join the effort.[28] But Hanoi's critical reaction to the announcement made pretty clear that it viewed the project as provocative.

While it would be simplistic to see Vietnam's opening of a tender for offshore oil fields just the following month as a case of tit-for-tat, the fact is that for Vietnam and China the long-festering issue of the Spratlys has in the past several years taken on a new urgency. This urgency owes not to wanton sabre-rattling on either side but rather to the place of oil in the two nations' current growth trajectories. At a time when China's unprecedented demand for resources is bolstering local economies from the mines of Western Australia to the fields of the Brazilian interior, the importance that it may attach to access to South China Sea petroleum is no longer nearly so hypothetical as it long appeared. Likewise, and as was noted above, it is petroleum exports that, along with foreign aid and remittances, have played an unmistakable role in Vietnam's recent record of socioeconomic progress. If anything, then, Hanoi's determination to maintain its offshore claims will have intensified.

Second came human rights. In September the United States listed Vietnam — along with Saudi Arabia, Burma, China, Iran, North Korea, the Sudan, and Eritrea — as a "country of particular concern" in the area of religious freedom. Washington's report noted pressures on ethnic-minority Protestants, on the United Buddhist Church of Vietnam, on Catholics, and on the Cao Dai and Hoa Hao in southern Vietnam. Two months earlier, the U.S. House of Representatives passed a "Vietnam Human Rights Act", though the American Senate failed to ratify the measure. The American domestic political pressures that may affect the outcome of such exercises notwithstanding, repeated identification as a human rights violator is something that Vietnam does not need. The extreme heavy-handedness of its suppression of the Easter demonstrations in the Central Highlands, its nervousness about Buddhists operating independently of the Fatherland Front, and its decision in July to sentence to jail three aged dissident writers for "abusing democratic rights to jeopardize interests of the State, legitimate rights and interests of social organizations and citizens"[29] point to serious, ongoing constraints on the exercise of civil liberties in Vietnam. At the same time, ranking foreign diplomats posted to Hanoi comment that the Vietnamese government has been slow and unsuccessful in developing constituencies of official and non-official "friends" in foreign capitals. Vietnam's increased engagement with the world makes obsolete its earlier patterns of reliance on sympathetic foreign NGOs to prosecute its interests abroad. Among the concrete steps toward improving the quality of its international relationships to which the Ministry of Foreign Affairs can set its immensely talented corps of young diplomats is the development of such constituencies.

A third set of relationships, and one in which Vietnam has begun to develop an appreciative constituency overseas, fell in the area of military-to-military ties with the United States. Such ties remained in many ways sensitive. Veterans' groups in Vietnam ensured that they unfolded only so fast. The class action suit filed in New York by lawyers representing Vietnamese victims of the defoliant Agent Orange in August won the support of many NGOs abroad. It also served to caution those who would assume that the enmities of the period from the mid-1950s to the early 1990s had been totally forgotten. Nevertheless, and despite some Vietnamese reluctance and far less resultant publicity than the first American ship visit in 2003, a United States Navy destroyer called at Danang in July. In the context of the important evolving Vietnamese-American economic relationship, what the Pentagon at least views as a "security dialogue" with the PAVN has developed real breadth, with a mutually understood effort at relationship-building for the long term. Among other examples, contacts between Washington's National Defense University and Hanoi's National Defense Academy have allowed military-to-military relations to take on a relatively unstructured, almost informal, quality.

In Southeast Asia, Washington's most effective diplomacy has always, for better or worse, been military diplomacy. Its current ties with Hanoi offer grounds for believing that this truth retains at least some validity. Vietnam's increasingly sophisticated, increasingly well-funded cadre of security and international affairs specialists had clearly begun during 2004 to focus attention on the long-term implications of America's military posture toward, and presence in, Southeast Asia in the context of a rising, politically more ambitious and militarily more powerful China.

This focus pointed to a fourth series of international relationships worthy of note in any treatment of Vietnamese affairs in 2004 and of scrutiny in the years ahead. While Vietnam joined ASEAN in 1995 and subsequently emerged as a fully-fledged, active member of that Southeast Asian grouping, its historic "man in the middle" status between Southeast and Northeast Asia remains very much a feature of its place in contemporary international politics. During 2004, this feature figured not least in its almost unwilling engagement with Korean Peninsula affairs.

July saw nearly 500 North Korean asylum-seekers reach South Korea by way of Ho Chin Minh City, where many of them had taken refuge for months.[30] Quickly revealed in the international press, their temporary refuge in Vietnam was potentially embarrassing but in the end not terribly damaging for the country. Awareness of the ease with which such episodes could draw Vietnam into the international politics of Northeast Asia was further underlined by indications that Hanoi carefully monitored the progress of the Six Party Talks on North Korea's nuclear arsenal. In recognition of those talks' potential to become the basis for a new regional grouping focused on Northeast Asian security, a senior official in Vietnam's foreign ministry remarked casually — and perhaps half-jokingly — to a foreign interlocutor that Vietnam ought to be the seventh party to them. More than just bilateral ties with China will, then, demand the attention of Vietnam's diplomats in their efforts to bring quality and effectiveness to their country's foreign relations to the north and east. Rather, Hanoi seems bound to seek for itself a clearly defined place in the high-stakes multilateral politics of Northeast Asia as a whole.

Conclusion

Vietnam in 2004 presented a complex picture of ambition, potential, and concern. Many of the same issues that made 2004 a year during which Vietnam's prospects seemed to hang so uncertainly in the balance will only intensify during 2005. Whether the battle against corruption scores real successes or whether it proves just a stage in byzantine political manoeuvering in advance of the CPV's Tenth Party Congress can help serve as a test of those prospects. SOE equitization must finally begin in earnest; the troubles of the country's financial sector must be confronted. The timing and terms of Hanoi's accession to the WTO will, along with the success of its economy in deriving greater performance from the immense resources at its disposal, be a valuable indicator of the direction in which Vietnam is headed. Economic liberalization may result in increasing strains on ethnic minorities and the poor; it may exacerbate incipient struggles over human rights. The increasingly activist National Assembly and press can bring a measure of transparency to the trials ahead. Success in any, let alone all, of these areas is far from certain. But a domestically stronger, more prosperous Vietnam can surely play a more effective, more prominent role on the regional and international stage.

Notes

[1]   "Vietnamese Radio Praises Success of National Assembly Session", BBC Monitoring Asia Pacific, 6 December 2004.

[2]   "Vietnam to Map Out Anti-Corruption Strategy", Xinhua, 2 December 2004.

[3]   Amy Kazmin, "Hanoi Steps Up Drive to Weed Out Corruption as 'Greed Runs Amok'", *Financial Times*, 2 December 2004.

[4]   "Top Shipping Executive Sacked for Corruption in Vietnam", Agence France-Presse (AFP), 14 October 2004, and Carlyle A. Thayer, "Political Outlook for Vietnam, 2005–2006", paper prepared for Regional Outlook forum, Institute of Southeast Asian Studies, Singapore, 6 January 2005, p. 14.

[5]   "High Ranking Communist Party Veteran Denounces Excessive Powers of Hanoi's Military Intelligence and Reveals Schism within the Party Leadership", Vietnam Committee on Human Rights, Paris, 29 July 2004.

[6]   See further, Thayer, "Political Outlook for Vietnam, 2005–2006", pp. 5 ff.

[7]   Ibid., p. 13.

[8]   "Vietnam Jails Five Minority Christians for Anti-Government Activities", AFP, 21 September 2004.

[9]   "Vietnam Tackles Unplanned Migration to Central Highlands", BBC Monitoring International Reports, 17 September 2002.

[10] "Vietnamese Radio Commentary Says Heretical Beliefs 'Should be Eliminated'", BBC Monitoring International Reports, 16 August 2004.

[11] David Dapice, "The Situation: Vietnam Decides Its Future", working paper, Vietnam Program, Kennedy School of Government, Harvard University, July 2004, p. 6.

[12] "Vietnam's GDP Growth Likely to Exceed 7.2%, Says WB", Vietnam News Briefs, Toan Viet Limited Co, 26 November 2004.

[13] "Vietnam's Five Key Exports to Rake in over $1 bln Each in 2004", Vietnam News Briefs, Toan Viet Limited Co, 17 November 2004.

[14] "Vietnam Exports 3.7 mln tons of Rice in Jan–Nov", Vietnam News Briefs, Toan Viet Limited Co, 29 November 2004.

[15] "Intellasia November 2004 Economic Report", *Intellasia.com*, 7 December 2004, p. 1.

[16] David Dapice, "Celebration and Reflection: Vietnam's Economy Enters a New Era", working paper, Vietnam Program, Kennedy School of Government, Harvard University, November 2004, p. 2.

[17] The World Bank, "Press Release: Vietnam Development Report 2005: Governance", Hanoi, 25 November 2004.

[18] "World Bank Forecast Puts Vietnam's Inflation at 3–5 pct", Xinhua, 18 August 2004.

[19] "Int'l Donors Optimistic about Vietnam", Asia Pulse, 6 December 2004.

[20] "Overseas Remittance to Vietnam Expected to Hit Record in 2004", Vietnam News Briefs, Toan Viet Limited Co, 24 November 2004.

[21] "Vietnam Jan–Oct Trade Deficit Hits 3.78 bln USD", AFX-Asia, 28 October 2004.

22 Margot Cohen, "Not by the Book", *Far Eastern Economic Review* (*FEER*), 29 April 2004.

23 Dapice, "The Situation", op. cit., p. 20.

24 Margot Cohen, "Corporate Overhaul", *FEER*, 7 October 2004.

25 "Vietnam's Economy: The Good Pupil", *Economist*, 8 May 2004.

26 "Govt Makes First Report on Poor Education Quality", Vietnam News Briefs, Toan Viet Limited Co, 17 November 2004.

27 "Former WTO Director General Warns Vietnam of Tough Entry Negotiations", Vietnam News Briefs, Toan Viet Limited Co, 17 November 2004.

28 "RP-China Oil Study Rattles Vietnam", *Manila Standard*, 18 September 2004.

29 "Vietnam Jails Cyber Dissident", Reuters, 14 July 2004.

30 Onishi Norimitsu, "North Korea Denounces Seoul for Welcoming Defectors", *New York Times*, 30 July 2004.

www.ingramcontent.com/pod-product-compliance
Lightning Source LLC
Chambersburg PA
CBHW050227270326
41914CB00003BA/601